في ذكرى

مارك لينز

They All Made Peace – What Is Peace?

The 1923 Lausanne Treaty and the New Imperial Order

Edited by
Jonathan Conlin and Ozan Ozavci

GINGKO

First published in 2023 by
Gingko
4 Molasses Row
London SW11 3UX

The title of the book is taken from a poem by Ernest Hemingway who attended the first few weeks of the Lausanne Conference in his capacity as the Paris-based foreign correspondent of the *Toronto Star*.

A CIP catalogue record for this book is available from the British Library.

Hardback: ISBN 978-1-914983-05-4
Paperback: ISBN 978-1-914983-17-7
ebook: ISBN 978-1-914983-06-1

Typeset in Times by MacGuru Ltd
Printed in the United Kingdom by Clays Ltd, Elcograf S.p.A.

www.gingko.org.uk
@GingkoLibrary

MIX
Paper from responsible sources
FSC® C018072

Contents

Part 3: Making Concessions

Part 4: Moving the People

Part 5: Framing Lausanne

Introduction

Jonathan Conlin and Ozan Ozavci

They All Made Peace

Founded in 1961, the War of Independence and Republic Museum (*Kurtuluş Savaşı ve Cumhuriyet Müzesi*) in Ankara is housed in the building of the first Turkish National Assembly. An object lesson in patriotic commemoration, the museum tells the story of the nation's resistance to the Entente Powers' attempted partition of Anatolia after the First World War. In 1920 the defeated Ottoman Empire seemed doomed to be reduced to a small Anatolian rump under the terms of the Treaty of Sèvres (1920). Within two years that *diktat* had been rendered a dead letter, thanks not only to the defeat of Greek, Italian and French military forces by the nationalist army of Mustafa Kemal (hereafter Atatürk), but an equally significant (and equally violent) exercise in reorienting political, religious, ethnic and class loyalties towards a new, secular Republic of Turkey. And so the museum's medals and weapons jostle with prayer beads and identity cards. The prize exhibit is a table, displayed in the second room on the left, in the old Legal Commission room.

Measuring 360cm long and 76cm wide and covered with a dark red broadcloth, this was the table on which the Lausanne Treaty was signed in 1923.[1] It was brought to Ankara in 2008 as part of a state visit by the President of the Swiss Confederation, travelling in the luggage of the Swiss Army Orchestra. The Lausanne table was formally presented to then Turkish President Abdullah Gül on 11 November, at a concert given at Türk Ocağı Sahnesi (the Turkish Hearth Stage). As well as demonstrating that 'the Swiss Army can both carry a table and make

1 We would like to thank Fatma Hicret Un, the Director of the War of Independence and Republic Museum in Ankara, for this information.

[good] music,' for President Pascal Couchepin the sturdy table symbolised the strength of this bilateral relationship.[2]

Eighty-six years before, Couchepin's predecessor Robert Haab formally opened proceedings at the Near East Peace Conference summoned to the Swiss resort of Lausanne on 20 November 1922. For Haab, the battles of Sakarya and Dumlupınar were immediate and yet remote: even as he 'bowed' to those Greeks and Turks who had patriotically given their lives 'up to some weeks ago', their valour evoked heady tales of earlier 'innumerable and bitter fights, recounted to us in the legends of ancient times and the chronicles of the Middle Ages.' It had been war, and it had been ruinous. But now it was time to make peace. As a neutral country, helping conclude international agreements was 'an attitude and a policy which are for us [the Swiss] a holy tradition.'[3]

Lausanne had not been the first choice of venue. The Ankara government had proposed Izmir (Smyrna), a symbolic yet, as British Foreign Secretary George Nathaniel Curzon noted, somewhat impractical suggestion. Much of that great Ottoman entrepôt's core had recently been incinerated as the Turks drove the Greek Army into the sea. Beykoz (at the northern end of the Bosphorus), Rhodes, Istanbul, Venice and Paris were considered.[4] Experience of negotiating in Paris in 1919 had left many British diplomats disgusted with what they perceived as a venal French-language press. To this Curzon added a distaste for the 'Levantines' populating some of these cities. Venice emerged as an ideal option due to its location. But then, like Venice, Lausanne was on the route of the Simplon Orient Express, allowing easy access from Istanbul. Unlike Venice, which would give nominal leadership to Italian Prime Minister Luigi Facta (busy with Benito Mussolini's fascists), Lausanne would not favour any one delegation.

For all Haab's rhetoric of neutrality, Lausanne was hardly an Archimedean point. *Foyers Turcs* and their Armenian, Syrian and other equivalents not only served expat communities living and working inside Switzerland. They supplied a focus for continental diasporas. Switzerland's universities had provided education and networking opportunities to generations of Pan-Islamists, Young Ottomans, socialists and communists, from Lenin and Mussolini to the Young Turks and the Armenian revolutionaries. Swiss banks provided boltholes, too. During the war, Deutsche Bank stashed its Bagdadbahn and associated oil interests in the

---

2 'İsviçre'den Lozan masası jesti', *Milliyet*, 11 November 2008.

3 *Lausanne Conference on Near Eastern Affairs, 1922–1923: Records of Proceedings and Draft Terms of Peace*, 1923 (hereafter *Lausanne Conference*), 1–2.

4 Henderson to Balfour, 23 July 1922, *Documents on British Foreign Policy* (hereafter *DBFP*), Vol. 17, 890; Rumbold to Curzon, 13 and 14 August 1922, *DBFP*, Vol. 17, 923–924.

Zurich-based Bank für Orientalische Eisenbahnen.[5] To this day the funds (and archives) of the famed Committee of Union and Progress (CUP), the party which seized power in Istanbul in 1908 and led the Ottoman Empire into World War One, may well slumber in another of the city's many banks, silently earning interest for unknown (and probably unconscious) beneficiaries.[6]

As the history of Nestlé shows, however, Switzerland was not just a provider of education and financial services to Middle East elites: it was a source of consumer goods and, eventually, direct investment. Swiss neutrality certainly helped Nestlé escape pre-1914 Ottoman embargoes of other European manufacturers and win army contracts to supply Ottoman forces with condensed milk. In 1927 Nestlé opened a chocolate factory in Istanbul, which allowed it to exhibit its wares at trade fairs alongside signs urging visitors to 'Consume Local Goods!', parroting a mantra of Turkish economic nationalism.[7]

Though highly distasteful to career diplomats like Curzon, master of 'old diplomacy', one of the aims of this volume is to tear down the barriers between diplomatic history and other sub-disciplines: to view the press, faith groups and humanitarians, bankers and multi-national enterprises as more than interlopers. Our focus is trained here not only on the statesmen and diplomats that sat around the negotiation table: the Turkish, British, French, Greek, American (as 'observers'), Italian, Romanian, Yugoslavian and Japanese plenipotentiaries, joined on occasion by Belgian, Soviet, Ukrainian, Georgian, and Bulgarian delegates. What happened beyond and below the table, in the rooms next door, which teemed with a plethora of non-governmental actors, is also discussed in the following pages. We will highlight how economic and financial considerations informed political, legal, diplomatic and humanitarian decision-making processes, and vice versa.

In addition to highlighting these inter-sectoral diplomatic dynamics at Lausanne, we offer a contrapuntal reading of the episode, to expose the 'absent presences', the unheard as much as the heard, their manifold interests, expectations, frustrations and resentments.[8] Even though their delegations were not officially granted an audience, Lausanne was thronged with figures claiming to speak for Arabs, Armenians, Assyrians, Jews, Iraqis, Egyptians, Kurds, Nestorians, and

5 Werner Plumpe et al., *Deutsche Bank 1870–2020: The Global Hausbank,* 2020, 225–226.
6 Ozan Ozavci, 'Honour and Shame: The Diaries of a Unionist and the Armenian Question', *End of the Ottomans: The Genocide of 1915 and the Politics of Turkish Nationalism*, 2019, 219–220.
7 Yavuz Koese, 'Nestlé in the Ottoman Empire: Global Marketing with Local Flavor, 1870–1927', *Enterprise & Society* 9/4, 2008, 755.
8 Edward Said, *Culture and Imperialism*, 1993, 50.

other communities. As Laura Robson observes, surprisingly few of these aspired to their own Western-style nation-states ('national homes'), such as those promised to Armenians and Kurds under the Treaty of Sèvres.[9] Sarah Shields' contribution to this volume argues that some Kurds sought to resist inclusion in any nation-state or empire, content to remain within 'borderlands'. While all these communities looked to make peace, peace meant different things to different groups, and many communities were internally divided on what peace looked like to them.

The observations of the caricaturist Emery Kelen, who found himself in Lausanne in 1922 almost by accident, are particularly telling here. This Jewish 'boy from Györ' (Austro-Hungary) had been thoroughly worked over by history, then cast adrift with 'three and a half years of world war in my bones, and three revolutions, pink, red, and white' – as well as a salami, Kelen's principal means of support until an Egyptian journalist, Mahmud Azmi, spotted him sketching Mussolini in Lausanne's Beau Rivage. Buying the sketch for his satirical weekly *Al-Kashkul* (literally 'The Begging Bowl'), Azmi Bey started Kelen on a career as court jester to the *corps diplomatique*. As Julia Secklehner demonstrates in this volume, Kelen and his partner Alois Derso (also in attendance at Lausanne) proved adept at interpreting Lausanne diplomacy for audiences across the world.

Looking back forty years later, Kelen described an epiphany others shared, but failed to express so evocatively:

> It seems to me that I can spy the very spot where Britain's glory began to seep away into the dark; and I was there. It was in the third-rate hotels and crumbly family pensions of Lausanne, where the scent of insecticide and dust blended so happily with that of *poulet rôti, pommes rissolées*. There a penny-pinching caricaturist found his natural home among others of wobbly social status: Shi'ite mullahs from Persia, Sunnis from Iraq, Wahabis from the Hejaz, Zionists from Palestine, Kurds, Azerbaijanis, Macedonians, Gurkhas, Laks, and Lurs, who milled, swarmed, and plotted in an incessant rumbling, grumbling, undershudder to history. Each afternoon they would come to the surface and continue their sinister conspiracy to the tune of music at the *thé dansant* in the lobby of the Lausanne Palace Hotel.
>
> Like a viceroy reviewing native troops, Lord Curzon progressed through the lobby, staring with glassy eyes past the ragtag and bobtail that cluttered the plush-carpeted floor. Yet, in three decades, how many of these scrubby

9 Laura Robson, *States of Separation: Transfer, Partition, and the Making of the Modern Middle East,* 2017, 107.

> characters were to become sparkling ambassadors, or prime ministers of independent countries … holding appalling fate in their hands![10]

Kelen sketched those gathered around the famous Lausanne conference table, but also peeked below, spotting 'the little brother of the conference table': the green baize footstool provided for the chief British delegate Curzon's gout. A towering physical presence loomed above the table while, below, rebellious extremities were painfully propped up. Curzon really was a synecdoche for an empire then facing unrest in Egypt, Iraq, and India, thanks to the efforts of Saad Zaghloul, Simko Shikak and Mahatma Gandhi.

As Curzon noted to a colleague, 'hitherto we have dictated our peace treaties'. Yet at Lausanne he found himself 'negotiating one with the enemy who has an army in being while we have none, an unheard of position.'[11] Though all agreed that Lausanne witnessed a dramatic shift in the perceived balance of power, there was little consensus on who exactly the 'winners' and 'losers' were. For Kelen it marked the beginning of the end for Britain. For Basil Mathews of the London Missionary Society, it was 'the old authority of the white man' which had received its '*coup de grâce*' at Lausanne, as 'the Turkish people (totalling little more than the population of Greater London) … dictated terms to the world-powers', a process allegedly followed closely 'in every bazaar in India, by the night-fires of Arab sheiks, and in student debates from Cairo to Delhi, Peking and Tokyo.' Lausanne was a story of 'the clash of civilisations': 'white man' on one side, 'Young Islam' on the other.[12] The British historian A.J. Toynbee preferred 'contact' to 'clash' but was equally persuaded that Lausanne represented a turning point in the history of 'civilisations': the point where the 'Eastern Question' became *The Western Question,* where orientalist sifting of empires into nation states gave way to recognition of the barbarous occidentalism visited upon the 'East' in the name of this 'Westernisation'.[13]

---

10 Emery Kelen, *Peace in Their Time: Men Who Led Us In and Out of War, 1914–1945,* 1963, 98–99.

11 Curzon to Viscount d'Abernon, 20 December 1922, cited in David Gilmour, *Curzon: Imperial Statesman,* 1994, 556.

12 Basil Mathews, *The Clash of Colour: A Study in the Problem of Race,* 1924, 30–31. For 'Young Islam', see Basil Mathews, *Young Islam on Trek: A Study of the Clash of Civilizations*, 1926.

13 A.J. Toynbee, *The Western Question in Greece and Turkey: a study in the contact of civilisations,* 1922. See Georgios Giannakopoulos, 'A World Safe for Empires? A.J. Toynbee and the Internationalization of Self-Determination in the East (1912–1922)', *Global Intellectual History* 6/4, 2021, 484–505.

Within Turkey the legacy of Lausanne was immediate as well as enduring. From the moment the Turkish delegation signed the treaty on 24 July 1923, a Tuesday, at nine past three in the afternoon, it has been used as a trope to further political ends at the hands of Kemalist and (neo-)Ottomanist writers. As Hans-Lukas Kieser has noted in this volume (and in other publications), four members of the Turkish delegation later joined the *Türk Tarihi Tetkik Cemiyeti* (Turkish Historical Society) established in 1930.[14] '[Lausanne] not only contributed to rewriting contemporary history,' but laid the foundations of the Turkish History Thesis of the 1930s, that in turn presented the Turks as "proto-European" originators of human civilisation. Building on previous work by Fatma Müge Göçek, Gökhan Çetinsaya's discussion here ranges across historical as well as political discourse since 1923, showing how Turkish perceptions of Lausanne lurched from one extreme to the other, from a heroic victory marking the end of five hundred years of European meddling to 'Turkey's unconditional surrender to the West'.[15] When the Lausanne table arrived in Ankara, the conservative paper *Vakit* (Time) deplored it as an 'execution table' on which the Turks 'lost an empire!'[16] Here we trace the origins of today's conspiracy theories (espoused by 48% of Turks, according to a 2018 survey), which claim 2023 will see the revelation (and expiration) of Lausanne's 'secret clauses'. Though entirely without foundation, the authority enjoyed by analogous theories in many other nations makes the exploration of their origin and function especially urgent, a task in which social anthropologists and historians can usefully collaborate.[17]

Outside Turkey (and to a lesser extent Greece), Lausanne has received little scholarly attention from historians. This in contrast to anthropologists such as Renée Hirschon, whose study of Ottoman Greek refugees in Piraeus led to groundbreaking works such as *Heirs of the Greek Catastrophe* (1989) as well as an edited volume *Crossing the Aegean* (2003), which included important contributions

14 For a similar argument that traces the origins of the Turkish official historiography and the 'History Thesis' to Lausanne, also see Suavi Aydin, 'Resmi Tarihin Temeli: Ulusal Tarih Yazımı ve Resmi Tarihte Mitlerin Kaynağı', in *Resmi Tarih Tartışmaları* 1, F. Başkaya ed., 2008, 59.

15 Fatma Müge Göçek, 'The Politics of History and Memory: A Multidimensional Analysis of the Lausanne Peace Conference, 1922–1923', in Israel Gershoni et al., eds., *Histories of the Modern Middle East: New Directions*, 2002, 224.

16 *Vakit*, 'İşte İnfaz Masası', 12 November 2008.

17 Zeynep Oğuz, 'Matters of Conspiracy: oil prospects, geological knowledge, and temporality in Turkey', accepted paper, 2018 Conference of the Association of Social Anthropologists of the UK & Commonwealth.

from historians as well as anthropologists.[18] In 2011–2012 the Benaki Museum in Athens curated a series of exhibitions, films and other projects exploring the legacy of the exchange.[19] In his comparative analysis of modern international systems Eric Weitz nonetheless laments that 'it is barely known today except to specialists on the region.'[20] Though Zara Steiner echoes earlier British diplomatic historians in noting that Lausanne 'proved to be the most successful and durable of all the post-war settlements', her magisterial study of inter-war diplomacy only grants the conference two pages.[21] Other than Sevtap Demirci's 2005 monograph, itself focussing on the strategic calculations of Britain and Turkey, there is no scholarly volume dedicated to Lausanne in the English language.[22] Indeed, the much less significant 1922 Genoa Conference has received more attention from scholars.[23] Scholarship seeking to re-examine the familiar narratives of 1914–

18 Renée Hirschon, 'The Social Institutions of an Urban Locality of Refugee Origin in Piraeus', DPhil dissertation, University of Oxford, Oxford, 1976; idem, *Heirs of the Greek Catastrophe: The Social Life of Asia Minor Refugees in Piraeus*, 1989; idem, *The Creation of Community: Well-being without Wealth in an Urban Greek Refugee Locality*, 2000; idem, ed., *Crossing the Aegean: An Appraisal of the 1923 Compulsory Population Exchange between Greece and Turkey*, 2003; idem, 'History's Long Shadow: the Lausanne Treaty and Contemporary Greco-Turkish Relations' in O. Anastasakis, K. Nicolaidis and K. Oktem, eds., *In the Long Shadow of Europe: Greeks and Turks in the Era of Postnationalism*, 2009.
19 Anna Ballian, *Relics of the Past: Treasures of the Greek Orthodox Church and the Population Exchange*, 2011; Benaki Museum and the British Council, *Twice A Stranger,* temporary exhibition, 18 September to 25 November 2012.
20 Eric D. Weitz, 'From the Vienna to the Paris System: International Politics and the Entangled Histories of Human Rights, Forced Deportations, and Civilizing Missions', *The American Historical Review* 113/5, 2008, 1338.
21 Zara Steiner, *The Lights That Failed: European International History, 1919–1933,* 2005, 120, 122. For similar estimates of Lausanne see Michael L. Dockrill and J. Douglas Goold, *Peace Without Promise: Britain and the Peace Conferences, 1919–23,* 1981, 236; Alan Sharp, *The Versailles Settlement: Peacemaking in Paris, 1919,* 1991, 174. Lausanne receives similarly short shrift in Margaret MacMillan's *Peacemakers: The Paris Conference of 1919 and Its Attempt to End the War,* 2001, and Adam Tooze, *The Deluge: The Great War and the Remaking of the Global Order, 1916–1931,* 2014.
22 Sevtap Demirci, *Strategies and Struggles. British Rhetoric and Turkish Response: The Lausanne Peace Conference, 1922–1923*, 2005. See also Demirci, *The Lausanne Conference: the evolution of Turkish and British diplomatic strategies, 1922–1923,* 2014, a reprint of her 1997 LSE doctoral thesis. See also Salahi Ramsdan Sonyel, *Turkish Diplomacy, 1918–1923: Mustafa Kemal and the Turkish National Movement,* 1975; Mustafa Yılmaz, *British Opinion and the Lausanne Peace Conference and Treaty,* 1994.
23 Carole Fink, *The Genoa Conference: European Diplomacy, 1921–1922,* 1984; Stephen White, *The Origins of Detente: the Genoa Conference and Soviet-Western Relations, 1921–1922,* 1985; Carole Fink, Axel Frohn and Jürgen Heideking eds., *Genoa, Rapallo, and European Reconstruction in 1922,* 1991.

1918 by situating them within a 'greater war' that began in 1911 (with the Italian invasion of Ottoman Tripolitania) and 'failed to end' in 1918 – to cite Robert Gerwarth's landmark *The Vanquished* (2016) – has entirely passed Lausanne by. This is so despite the fact that, as Gerwarth notes in his book, Lausanne 'fatally undermined cultural, ethnic and religious plurality as an ideal to which to aspire and a reality with which – for all their contestations – most people in the European land empires had dealt with fairly well for centuries.'[24]

Accounts of the 'making' or 'creation' of 'the modern Middle East' usually devote only a few lines to the Lausanne Peace Conference: David Fromkin ignored it entirely.[25] As Elizabeth F. Thompson underlines in her chapter, it is equally commonplace to overlook Lausanne's part in ending 'the political moment towards popular democracy in Greater Syria and elsewhere in the former Arabic-speaking territories of the Ottoman Empire.' Frederick Anscombe and Michael Provence are notable exceptions to this cleavage between Arab and Ottoman history, emphasizing a shared legacy of what the latter refers to as 'Ottoman modernity'.[26] This volume seeks to provide an equivalent for the raft of volumes addressing Versailles, Trianon and other post-war settlements.[27] It also seeks to restore Lausanne to the historiography of the wider Middle East, that 'post-Ottoman' space that Einar Wigen has dubbed 'an area studies that never was'.[28]

---

24 Robert Gerwarth, *The Vanquished: Why the First World War Failed to End,* 2016, 246. See also Jörn Leonhard, *Der überforderte Frieden: Versailles und die Welt, 1918–1923*, 2018.

25 David Fromkin, *A Peace to End All Peace: The Fall of the Ottoman Empire and the Creation of the Modern Middle East,* 1989. See also D.K. Fieldhouse, *Western Imperialism in the Middle East, 1914–1958,* 2006; T.G. Fraser, *Contested Lands: A History of the Middle East since the First World War,* 2021; Peter Mansfield, *A History of the Middle East*, 2013.

26 Frederick F. Anscombe, *State, Faith, and Nation in Ottoman and Post-Ottoman Lands*, 2014; Michael Provence, 'Ottoman Modernity, Colonialism, and Insurgency in the Interwar Arab East', *International Journal of Middle East Studies* 43/2, 2011, 205–225; Michael Provence, 'Stateless Revolutionaries and the Aftermath of the Great War', *Journal of Modern European History* 13/3, 2015, 401–418; Michael Provence, *The Last Ottoman Generation and the Making of the Modern Middle East,* 2017. See also L. Carl Brown ed., *Imperial Legacy: The Ottoman Imprint on the Balkans and Middle East,* 1996.

27 Monographs on other post-war settlements include: Ann Byers, *The Treaty of Versailles and the League of Nations*, 2018; Michael S. Neiberg, *The Treaty of Versailles: A Concise History*, 2017; Istvan Bethlen, *The Treaty of Trianon and European Peace*, 1934; Arnold Suppan, *The Imperialism Peace Order in Central Europe: Saint-Germain and Trianon, 1919–1920*, 2019; C.A. Macartney, *Hungary and Her Successors: The Treaty of Trianon and Its Consequences, 1919–1937*, 1968; Georgi P. Genov, *Bulgaria and the Treaty of Neuilly,* 1935; Patrick J. Treanor, *Britain, Bulgaria and the Paris Peace Conference, 1918–1919: A Just and Lasting Peace?*, 2020.

28 Einar Wigen, 'Post-Ottoman studies: an area studies that never was', in Éva A. Cstató et al., *Building Bridges to Turkish: Essays in Honour of Bernt Brendemoen*, 2018, 313–324.

What is Peace?

A Paris-based correspondent of the *Toronto Star*, Ernest Hemingway spent three weeks (22 November–16 December 1922) in Lausanne covering the conference. He had already encountered many of the conference's protagonists earlier in the year, either at the Genoa Conference or in Istanbul, which he found 'packed with uniforms and rumors'.[29] Hemingway's despatches revelled in the incidental, seeking to capture the superficial detail that would, he hoped, reveal more profound truths. A poem he wrote at Lausanne, published in an American magazine *The Little Review* tested this 'iceberg method' to its limits.[30] Apparently assembled from snatches of conversation and snippets of copy, 'They All Made Peace – What is Peace?' affords a powerful if gnomic multi-sensory portrait of the seething press pack and *corps diplomatique* at Lausanne.

Hemingway's question, 'What is Peace?', is one many of our contributors have found themselves debating, with each other and (in the case of those with family ties to communities relocated under Lausanne's terms) with themselves as well. Did Lausanne end the 'Great War' of 1914–1918, the 'Greater War' of 1911–1923, or the Greek-Turkish War of 1919–1922? Was the peace of Lausanne merely the result of inter-state bargaining, or did it seek to reflect or resist internationalism – whether in the shape of the Bolshevik threat or the League of Nations, itself torn between legalism and technocracy? Did it involve settling past scores or trying to establish an order that would, at whatever cost to present and past, prevent future outbreaks of violent score-settling? To borrow from Martin Luther King Jr., was it merely the 'absence of tension', or the 'presence of justice'?

The head of the Turkish delegation at Lausanne, İsmet İnönü (hereafter İsmet) knew more of making war and signing ceasefires than making peace and signing treaties. A thirty-eight-year-old officer, İsmet had been at the battlefront, fighting the Turks' 'independence war' just sixty days before his arrival in the Swiss resort. As commander of the Western Anatolian Army, he had signed the Mudanya ceasefire on 11 October.[31] At Mudanya his taciturn manner and diminutive stature had 'not at all impressed' his opposite number in the Allied Occupation Army, General Charles Harrington. İsmet's appointment to lead the delegation surprised both the

29 David Roessel, 'New Information on Hemingway's "3 very fine weeks" in Constantinople in 1922', *Resources for American Literary Study* 34, 2009, 107–128. For his despatches see William White, ed., *Dateline: Toronto. Hemingway's Complete Dispatches for The Toronto Star, 1920–1924*, 1985, 211.

30 James Gifford, ed., *'In Our Time' and 'They All Made Peace – What is Peace?' by Ernest Hemingway*, 2015.

31 İsmet İnönü, *Defterler*, Vol. II, 2001, 40–42.

British and İsmet's own colleagues.[32] It reflected the importance Atatürk placed on having someone he knew would obey instructions, which consisted solely of a thirty-line brief and an expanded (fourteen-points, rather than six) version of the *Misâk-ı Millî* (National Pact), the set of guiding principles for peace-making hammered out by the last Ottoman parliament in February 1920.[33] Although the skill with which İsmet turned his lack of experience and *savoir-faire* to his and Turkey's advantage soon became evident, even in his memoirs (written much later) he played up his lack of *savoir-faire* amid the 'coquetry' of diplomacy.[34]

The head of the British delegation, George Nathaniel Curzon, Marquess of Kedleston, was twenty-five years older, a graduate of Eton and Oxford, a former Viceroy of India (1898–1905) and the proverbial embodiment of hauteur (though he could be charming in private). İsmet had only been to Europe once before 1922.[35] Curzon had set off around the world in 1887, exploring Central Asia and publishing two studies of Eastern 'problems'. In 1919 Curzon and David Lloyd George divided British peace-making between them: as Foreign Secretary Curzon (a Conservative) focused on Eastern questions while the Welsh Liberal prime minister focused on Europe. Unfortunately, Lloyd George's philhellenism had led him to push through plans for Greek occupation of Smyrna over Curzon's resistance. The resulting fiasco of Greek defeat and the Anglo-Turkish confrontation at Çanakkale (Chanak) in October 1922 had freed Curzon from Lloyd George (who was forced out of power by Conservative members of parliament), though leaving Curzon the resulting mess. Curzon was nonetheless confident of bringing negotiations to a quick and satisfactory conclusion (at least to Britain), realizing a grand vision of Mediterranean Empire that Erik Goldstein reconstructs in his chapter, complete with heady dreams of restoring Hagia Sophia to the Christian faith.[36] He felt he had got the measure of the Turks years before, in an 1889 tussle with Turkish customs officials during his circumnavigation of the globe.[37]

This was the new system he hoped Britain could establish in place of the

32 Rıza Nur, *Lozan Hatırları*, 1992, 21–24.

33 Abdi İpekçi ed., *İnönü Atatürk'ü Anlatıyor*, 1976, 32; cf. Metin Heper, *İsmet İnönü,* 1998, 68.

34 İnönü, *Hatıralar*, Vol II, 114–115; cf. Heper, *İnönü*, 68.

35 Heper, *İnönü,* 53.

36 See also Erik Goldstein, *Winning the Peace: British Diplomatic Strategy, Peace Planning and the Paris Peace Conference, 1916–1920,* 1991; Sean Kelly, 'How Far West?: Lord Curzon's Transcaucasian (Mis)Adventure and the Defence of British India, 1918–23', *International History Review* 35/2, 2013, 274–293; Daniel MacArthur-Seal, *Britain's Levantine Empire, 1914–1923*, 2021.

37 Harold Nicolson, 'Curzon,' *Foreign Affairs* 7/2, 1929, 9–10.

crumbling empire of the sultans. But that would happen not without making significant concessions, both strategic and economic, and not without cushioning the differences with the Turks and the rival powers first. The old imperial order in the wider Middle East and the Balkans had come to an end post-haste, after successive wars lasting nearly a decade. A new imperial order was unfolding in its place as a new arrangement was to be concluded between the winners (of the war of 1914–1918) and the winners (of the war of 1919–1922), i.e., the Allied Powers and the Turks. The rest could hardly make their voice heard. As Lerna Ekmekcioglu, Sarah Shields and Elizabeth F. Thompson have shown in their respective chapters, much of what the silenced voices (Arabs, Armenians, Kurds, etc.) said at the time still maintains its relevance today.

The conference at Lausanne opened on 20 November 1922, and was divided into two phases, separated by a short hiatus (4 February–23 April 1923) that resulted when İsmet refused to let Curzon bounce him into signing a draft treaty. Negotiations were held through three commissions: the first was for Territorial and Military Questions, the second on the Regime of Foreigners, and the third on Economic and Financial Questions. Several sub-commissions were tasked with researching the details and drafting the resultant treaty, conventions, protocols and declarations.

The First Commission (led by Curzon) saw the most heated discussions during the conference. Negotiations began with the territorial issues of Thrace and the Turkish Straits. Both regions had seen heavy fighting and remained a potential flashpoint, thanks to Greek and Turkish troops positioned either side of the Maritsa (Meriç) river, the pre-1914 border between Greek-controlled Western Thrace and Turkish-controlled Eastern Thrace. Thrace provided İsmet and his Greek counterparty Eleftherios Venizelos (1864–1936) with ample opportunity to accuse each other of precipitating the war and to trade population and refugee statistics, as Bulgarian premier Aleksandar Stamboliyski sought room for a port on the Aegean (Dedeağaç, recently renamed Alexandropouli, was offered), reclaiming some of the territory Bulgaria (another defeated ally of the Central Powers) had lost in the Treaty of Neuilly (1919). Curzon intervened, asking İsmet to 'justify their demands by historical, geographical, political and ethnographical arguments.'[38] But the Turkish delegation was unprepared for such a request. The Ankara government's two-sentence-long instructions (points 5 and 6) about Thrace were limited to maintaining the 1914 borders. In Western Thrace they would seek a plebiscite.[39]

The proceedings of the first session show that, as an experienced statesman,

38 *Lausanne Conference*, 21.

39 Bilal N. Şimşir, *Lozan Telgrafları* (hereafter *LT*), xiv.

Venizelos was better equipped for the opening of the conference. It was he who had developed a foreign policy on the premise of the irredentist Great Idea (*Megali Idea*), a vision of Hellenic expansionism in Asia Minor first propounded by Ioannis Kolettis some seventy-five years earlier.[40] Encouraged by Lloyd George as well as France and Italy, in May 1919, as Prime Minister, Venizelos put this plan into implementation by landing Greek troops in Izmir.[41] The following year, however, his position began to weaken.[42] Under Alexandre Millerand, France's policy shifted, pulling French occupying forces out of Cilicia in the wake of defeat at the Battle of Marash. Instead of grabbing the extensive 'Blue Zone' granted it under the 1916 Sykes-Picot Agreement, in October 1921 France signed a separate peace with Atatürk (the Ankara or Franklin-Bouillon Agreement), to the disgust of Ottoman Armenians who had looked to Paris as a protector, as well as to Curzon, who saw it as rank betrayal by an ally.[43]

After the Greek King Alexander died from a monkey bite in October 1920, the prospect of the return of his exiled father, Venizelos' old nemesis 'Tino' (Constantine I), led to Venizelos' election defeat in November.[44] Out of office, Venizelos opposed the subsequent purge of army officers as well as plans by his successor as Prime Minister, Dimitrios Gounaris, for a further offensive into the Anatolian heartland. Disregarding Venizelos' calls for peace, Gounaris and Constantine pressed on into Anatolia, where the tide turned against them at the 21-day Battle of the Sakarya in August-September 1921. The following flood of Greek soldiers and Ottoman Greeks pouring west went down in Greek history as the 'Catastrophe'. It cost Gounaris his life and Constantine the throne.

Venizelos' international stature notwithstanding, at Lausanne the Greeks found themselves in a weak position.[45] His wife Elena Venizelou wrote after Venizelos' departure for Lausanne that the seasoned Greek diplomat had little hope of a satisfactory peace.[46] Venizelos himself admitted that they had 'not only lost Northern Epirus, but also Western Asia Minor and Eastern Thrace, from the moment that

40 Michael Llewellyn Smith, 'Venizelos' Diplomacy, 1910–23: From Balkan Alliance to Greek-Turkish Settlement', in *Eleftherios Venizelos: The Trials of Statesmanship,* P.M. Kitromilides ed., 2008, 135.

41 Ibid., 161.

42 Andrew Dalby, *Eleftherios Venizelos*, 2010, 128–129.

43 Vahé Tachjian, *La France en Cilicie et en Haute-Mesopotamie: aux confins de la Turquie, de la Syrie et de l'Irak*, 2004; Vincent Duclert, *La France Face au Génocide des Arméniens: Une nation impériale et le devoir d'humanité,* 2015.

44 Dalby, *Venizelos,* 125.

45 Çağla Derya Tağmat, *Lozan Konferansı'nda Yunan Diplomasisi, 1922–1923*, 2018.

46 *Arheio Sofokli Venizelu, Fakelos 1,* 226.01.041.1; cf. Tağmat, *Lozan*, 99.

the three Great Powers, formerly our allies, decided to return them to Turkey.'[47] During the negotiations he justified Greek administration of Western Thrace on grounds of 'superior administrative capacity', even though the region held a Muslim majority. He quickly rallied, as he anticipated, the support of Curzon, as well as that of the other Balkan states and Romania, who all wanted the Turks kept to the other side of Maritsa.

The invocation of Wilson's mantra of 'self-determination' led a weary Curzon to question whether, 'though in many ways a great man' the US President had not 'dealt a considerable blow to the peace of the world' in 'inventing the phrase'.[48] If European troops had been powerless to stop bloodshed during the Silesian plebiscite of March 1921, what hopes for disputed borderlands like Thrace or Mosul, Curzon wondered? Seeing that a Balkan bloc was emerging before him, İsmet reported back to Ankara that he would not allow talks to break up over Thrace.[49] Thrace as well as the Aegean and Dodecanese Islands were the lesser concerns of the Ankara government. If sacrifices were to be made for further gain in other domains, they could be made on these issues. Yet, as Sevtap Demirci reminds us, this was an early breach of the National Pact at Lausanne.[50]

The Russian delegation were invited to Lausanne late, and hence the Turkish Straits were only brought on the *tapis* in December 1922.[51] This was only the second international conference the Soviets had attended. At Genoa 'The Unworldly Russians' (as Hemingway dubbed them) had fascinated and frustrated the press pack, and excited local Communists. At Lausanne they once again elected to maintain 'an air of mystery'.[52] The seventh point in İsmet's instructions was that no foreign armed forces were to be accepted in the Turkish Straits.[53] This sat well with the claims of the Russian delegation: the Turkish Straits had been a crucial route by which the Allies had supplied White (anti-Soviet) Russian forces, right down to 1921.[54] Under the 1841 London Straits Convention, the Turkish

47 Smith, 'Venizelos' Diplomacy', 170.

48 Lausanne, 1st Comm, 5th Meeting. For a broader discussion see Erez Manela, *The Wilsonian Moment, Self-Determination and the International Origins of Anticolonial Nationalism,* 2007.

49 İsmet to the Council of Ministers, 22 November 1922, in *LT,* 121.

50 Sevtap Demirci, *Strategies and Struggles,* 85.

51 A.V. Borkov and A.V. Loshkarev, 'Sovetskaya diplomatsiya i obcyzhdenie problem statusa chernomorskih prolivov na Lozanskoi Mezhdunarodnoi Konferensii, 1922–1923 gg.', 242.

52 White, ed., *Dateline Toronto*, 130, 153, 159.

53 Şimşir, *LT*, xiv.

54 L. N. Nezhinskiy and A.V. Ignatiev eds., *Rossiya I Cernomorksie prolivi (XVIII-XX stoletiya)*, 365; Maharramova, 183; Borkov, 243.

Straits had been closed to all warships, something Tsarist Russia viewed as guarantee of imperial security. Now the Allies sought free passage for all warships, only to find the Bolsheviks maintaining Tsarist-era policy. The People's Commissar for Foreign Affairs, Georgy Chicherin, cited the Kemalists' National Pact in support of closing the Turkish Straits entirely to all foreign armed vessels. Curzon replied that he felt he was listening to one of İsmet's *kalpaks* (generals), rather than the head of the Russian delegation. Chicherin was unperturbed: as he noted to a member of the American delegation, Joseph Grew: 'Every rebuke Lord Curzon addresses to me across the conference table strengthens me just so much with the Soviet Government, and strengthens the Soviet Government proportionately.'[55] As Samuel J. Hirst and Étienne Forestier-Peyrat note in their chapter, Soviet policy at Lausanne signalled a return to a Commissariat of Foreign Affairs' strategy of consolidating anti-colonialist partnerships with Middle East leaders, rather than the Comintern's preferred policy of fomenting revolution.[56]

Though Atatürk had ceded claims in Turkey's far east and accepted Russian financial and military aid under a convention signed on 16 March 1921, he was (contrary to rumour) far from being a communist stooge. The question of whether the Turkish Straits should be subject to tonnage restrictions (limiting the displacement of armed vessels allowed to transit) and the surrounding territory demilitarised was passed to a sub-commission. Even when packaged as a fillip towards wider naval disarmament (a cause popular with the French), neither the other Black Sea littoral states nor anyone else supported complete closure of the Turkish Straits to foreign warships.

The issue of 'the minorities' (used to refer to non-Muslim communities within Turkey) was next on the agenda, and one of the most sensitive issues addressed at the conference.[57] When it came to Ottoman Greek communities in Western Anatolia, Atatürk's instructions to İsmet were only two words: '*esas mübadeledir*' (the principal [course of action] is population exchange).[58] As Rıza Nur, one of İsmet's aides in the Turkish delegation, wrote in his memoirs, it was paramount to 'Turkify' Asia Minor and 'save' it from elements that had been 'a cause of its

55 Joseph Grew, 'The Lausanne Peace Conference of 1922–1923', *Proceedings of the American Philosophical Society* 98/1, 1954, 4.

56 On this subject, also see Alp Yenen, 'Internationalism, Diplomacy and the Revolutionary Origins of the Middle East's 'Northern Tier'', *Contemporary European History*, 2021, 8–10.

57 For context see Carole Fink, 'The Minorities Question at the Paris Peace Conference' in Manfred F. Boemeke, Gerald D. Feldman and Elisabeth Glaser, eds., *The Treaty of Versailles: a Reassessment After 75 Years*, 1998, 249–274.

58 Şimşir, *LT*, xiv.

frailty', elements that had revolted against Ottoman rule and served as 'an instrument of foreign powers' for centuries.[59]

Mathew Frank argues that Venizelos was the first to propose a Greek-Turkish population exchange, to Talât in 1913. Venizelos' international prestige purportedly played a key role in turning population exchange from a 'marginal idea propagated by a handful of political fantasists and extreme nationalists into an acceptable and a 'progressive' instrument of state policy, as amenable to bourgeois democracies and Nobel Peace Prize winners as it was to authoritarian regimes and Fascist dictators.'[60] Well aware that the Turks had insisted on a total, compulsory exchange in talks with him held earlier in Ankara, Rıza Nur found it both fortunate and bizarre (*tuhaf*) that a concrete plan for such an exchange was first mooted officially by the Norwegian Fridtjof Nansen, the League of Nations High Commissioner for Refugees.[61]

It was in Lausanne in November 1922 that Nansen first heard he had been awarded the Peace Prize for his refugee work. On 1 December 1922 he delivered a statement pleading for rapid Greek-Turkish action along the lines of the 1913 Ottoman-Bulgarian exchange, noting that 'the economic aspect of the matter' was a 'most important aspect'. A swift exchange would enable newly transferred communities to plant for harvest in 1923.[62] Convention or no, Venizelos had been urging Nansen to start the exchange since October.[63] Curzon reluctantly agreed to this plan, even as he warned that 'the world would pay a heavy penalty' for such a 'thoroughly bad and vicious solution'.[64] As Leonard V. Smith shows in his chapter, such statements were anything but 'rhetorical crocodile tears.' It seems prudent to conclude that the compulsory Greek-Turkish population exchange in fact had many fathers, few of whom were willing to avow paternity.

The idea of an autonomous zone for ethnic Armenians in Eastern Anatolia was of similar, if not older vintage. Denied a hearing at the conference, the Armenian delegation at Lausanne did have an interview with İsmet and did address a (unofficial) meeting of delegates, held in the absence of any members of the Turkish

59 Rıza Nur, *Lozan Hatırlaı*, 99.

60 Matthew Frank, *Making Minorities History: Population Transfers in Twentieth Century Europe*, 2017, 1 (quote), 32, 38. Article 143 of the Treaty of Sèvres refers to a separate 'arrangement relating to the reciprocal and voluntary emigration of the populations of Turkish and Greek race.'

61 Rıza Nur, *Lozan Hatırlaı*, 100.

62 *Lausanne Conference*, 115.

63 Smith, 'Venizelos' Diplomacy', 171.

64 *Lausanne Conference*, 212.

delegation. The Armenians also enjoyed strong American support founded on decades of Protestant missionary activity in the Empire. As Andrew Patrick notes in his chapter, this proved a hollow reed. The Armenian mission wanted a '*foyer arménien en Turquie*' (*Azkayin Dun*) for Ottoman Armenians who had escaped Turkey's wartime policy of extermination, a crime known since the 1940s as the Armenian Genocide. As an Armenian delegate put it to İsmet: 'Even a dog, after you've beaten him ten times over, goes back to his kennel'. This arresting (not to say devastating) quote is just one of the important records of the Armenian Mission's work at Lausanne revealed for the first time by Lerna Ekmekcioglu in her chapter.

For his part Curzon reminded İsmet of the call of the inviting Powers (Britain, France and Italy) issued on 23 September 1922, promising the return of Eastern Thrace to Turkey in return for Turkey putting in place measures for the protection of racial and religious minorities in Turkey. The Turks had accepted this call on 4 October. The Greek government had furthermore undertaken 'to leave alone' the 124,000 Turks in Western Thrace, Curzon noted, provided the Greek population of Istanbul was 'also left undisturbed'. He pointed to the 'deep interest' Britain, France and the United States took in 'the important group of Nestorian or Assyrian Christians' in Eastern Anatolia, and he hoped that the Turks would consider the question of an Armenian National Home 'in a humane spirit.'[65]

The first article of the instructions submitted to İsmet ruled out an Armenian National Home.[66] His speech in response to Curzon pinned the blame for the past 'sufferings of the minorities' on foreign interventionism, notably by Tsarist Russia and the British Premier William Gladstone. Foreign powers had exploited such minorities to advance their own interests, as well as encouraging the latter 'to liberate themselves in order to constitute independent States.'[67] İsmet repeatedly cited Ottoman Jews in support of his metanarrative of Ottoman toleration, one in which the Ottomans had 'invented minority rights': the Jews were a model 'minority' which had not dallied with foreign patrons, so the argument went, and so had been left alone to prosper.

Of course, İsmet was not alone in seeking to present his nation's record in a positive light at Lausanne. To give just one example, the French diplomat Camille Barrère claimed that French efforts 'to better the lot of all the peoples of the East have always been compatible with most friendly relations with the Ottoman

65 *Lausanne Conference*, 175–179, 183.
66 Şimşir, *LT*, xiv.
67 *Lausanne Conference*, 202.

government,' a remarkable statement that omitted French aggressions in Ottoman Egypt (1798–1801), Algiers (1830) and Tunis (1881).[68] Turkish newspapers such as *Tevhid-i Efkâr* knew enough of the Ku Klux Klan to remark on similar hypocrisy in American claims to the moral high ground: as İsmet put it to American diplomat Richard Washburn Child, would the United States government be willing to consider a plan to 'set aside Mississippi and Georgia as a national home for the Negro'?[69]

As Christmas 1922 approached, Curzon's patience grew thin. In addition to his partial (tactical?) deafness, İsmet's repeated invocation of 'independence and sovereignty' grated, as did his delegation's fondness for delaying strategies, whether they involved trying to recycle notes already circulated in text form as speeches, or suddenly circulating an entirely new Russo-Turkish text for a Turkish Straits convention, when all parties were still working on a joint text. Curzon seemed to be preparing to break off talks on the Armenian National Home question, making pointed references to how 'the feelings of justice and humanity of the civilised world' would view Turkey's decision to refuse such a modest proposal.

By late January 1923, Greek and Turkish delegations had drafted a separate bilateral agreement on population exchange, and a convention was finally signed on 30 January 1923. Disagreements over the Ottoman debt led to the break-up of the conference a few days later. Despite a flurry of eleventh-hour activity by the Americans and others to delay his train long enough to rescue talks, Curzon left for London on 4 February 1923. When negotiations resumed in April 1923, the chair of the First Commission was filled by Horace Rumbold, British High Commissioner at Istanbul (i.e., one of the administrators of the Allied Occupation of the Turkish Straits Zone, 1918–1923).

Compared to the twenty-three exhausting meetings racked up by the First Commission, the second ('Regime of Foreigners') and third ('Economic and Financial Questions') commissions had met only four and five times respectively, under the presidency of two diplomats-turned-senators, the Italian Camillo Garroni and the Frenchman Maurice Bompard. The Italians had convened an unofficial 'Ottoman Congress' in Rome back in January 1921 to canvass Turkish views on revising Sèvres. At Lausanne the Italian head of the sub-commission on Minority Rights, Giulio Cesare Montagna, proved a talented 'diplomatic fixer', repeatedly mediating between Greek and Turkish delegations in the prickliest questions.[70] Although

68 *Lausanne Conference*, 181.

69 For a discussion, see the chapters by Patrick and Ekmekcioglu.

70 Jay Winter, *The Day the Great War Ended. 24 July 1923: The Civilianization of War,*

Garroni and former Italian Prime Minister Luigi Facta were overshadowed by Mussolini (who succeeded the latter just before the conference opened), the latter departed after a couple days in Lausanne, and did not change Italian policy on the only other area of concern, the Italian claim to the Dodecanese Islands, which they had occupied since 1912.[71]

Garroni's commission sought to establish a replacement for the so-called 'Capitulations', that web of bilateral agreements which granted foreign citizens extra-territorial legal status. Prior to their abolition by the CUP in September 1914 many native Ottomans, especially members of the Ottoman Greek and Ottoman Armenian mercantile elite, had acquired foreign nationality as a means of protecting themselves from the vagaries of the Ottoman legal system, as well as for its tax benefits. Debate now centred on whether the Turkish legal system had developed far enough to reassure non-Turkish residents that they no longer needed to have recourse to special courts or *conseils mixtes*, courts of arbitration with the involvement of non-Ottoman judges.

Ever willing to draw on what he perceived as strong analogies between Japanese and Turkish history, Baron Hayashi Gonsuke noted that Japan had found that it took two decades to create a new legal system able to replace extraterritorial systems. İsmet could point to several decades of reform, including wholesale adoption of 'Western' codes. For Curzon, however, Turkish law was tainted at its root: its principles were 'the product of theological jurists' and it was 'based in last resort on Moslem religious law.' The Capitulations remained another red line for the Ankara government.[72]

Bompard's financial commission provided more opportunities for Venizelos and İsmet to trade figures for reparations, refugees and relative shares of the Ottoman debt. For the French, the subject was particularly sensitive. On 1 August 1914, the Ottoman debt stood at 158,045,327 Ltq.[73] But the war cost the Ottomans, as the Minister of Finance Mehmed Cavid announced in May 1918, an additional 250 million Ltq, around 210 million Ltq of which was borrowed from the Germans.[74] Ten months later, the French calculated the deficit as 209,944,588 Ltq, leaving aside the Ottoman Public Debt Administration's cash and reserves.

Oxford, 2022.

71 See Alan Cassels, *Mussolini's Early Diplomacy,* 1970, 21–45; Dilek Barlas, 'Friends or Foes? Diplomatic Relations Between Italy and Turkey, 1923–36', *International Journal of Middle Eastern Studies* 36, 2004, 231–252.

72 Simsir, *LT*, xiv.

73 Duparc to Pichon, 2 March 1919, AMAE 51CPCOM/346/8.

74 Defrance (French Minister in Egypt) to Pichon, 16 May 1918, AMAE 51CPCOM/342/24.

The Allies also demanded 20 million Ltq (reduced from 50 million Ltq) in occupation expenses. As at Genoa, so here the French position reflected their dominance among bondholders, combined with suspicions that those nations less exposed to sovereign debt might allow the French rentier to receive a heavy haircut, releasing capital for foreign direct investment in the 'New Turkey', an opportunity British and American enterprises were better placed to seize.

By late January 1923 the Turks' share of Ottoman debt had been reduced to 87 million Ltq: under any such settlement, Bompard noted, Turkey would become the only state to emerge from the general conflagration with less debt than she had at its start. Turkey's wartime debts to Germany and Austro-Hungary had been cancelled under the terms of the treaties of Versailles and St Germain. The commission also considered the status of concessions promised (but not quite awarded) in 1914: one for oil in the two Ottoman *vilayets* (provinces) of Mosul and Baghdad, promised to the Anglo-German condominium, Turkish Petroleum Company, in June 1914, the other a joint venture for naval shipyards negotiated with the British armaments giant Vickers.[75]

Whereas İsmet could cite the National Pact in support of the Turkish claim to the Ottoman *vilayet* of Mosul as an integral part of a Turkish National Home, Curzon was well aware of the risks of being seen to maroon negotiations in a grubby oil deal, even before the Turks raised the ante by reviving another, equally shaky pre-1914 claim, the vast Chester Concession, whose original concessionaire had been a retired American rear-admiral. Hand-dug oil 'wells' (actually shallow holes in the ground) had operated in this corner of northern Mesopotamia for generations. During the First World War, the German militarized oil survey (*Brennstoff Kommando Arabien*) had been the first to bring modern drilling equipment to the region, confirming there was oil to be found. In 1922 all American and European newspapers were filled with speculation surrounding an Anglo-American 'oil war' as well as reports of oil company executives roaming the halls of Lausanne hotels disguised as Turkish typists. Curzon's claim that Mosul belonged to Iraq on ethnographic as well as military grounds alone, as well as his insistence that oil executives' influence on British policy was 'NIL', failed to

75 Jonathan Conlin, 'Debt, Diplomacy and Dreadnoughts: the National Bank of Turkey, 1909–1919', *Middle Eastern Studies* 52/3, 2016, 525–545; Jonathan Conlin, '"Our Dear Resadiye": the Legend and the Loans behind Ottoman Naval Rearmament, 1908–14', *International History Review,* published online 22 June 2021.

persuade.[76] Turkish cartoons in *Karagöz* were not the only satires to tie Curzon to a kerosene can.[77]

Up until February 1923, commission meetings seemed to consist of delegates lining up to pummel İsmet. Curzon would begin by urging İsmet to be reasonable, warning against making a fetish of 'sovereignty' when future 'development' would necessitate foreign assistance. Barrère or Bompard would then express similar sentiments, with Hayashi or Child chipping in occasionally as *amici curiae*. Curzon would then quote their 'moving statements' in turn, and a fresh turn of the screw would begin. This routine could not continue forever, however. With the collapse of inter-Allied negotiations over German reparations (taking place in Paris) and the Franco-Belgian occupation of the Ruhr (11 January), French Premier Raymond Poincaré became determined to end the Lausanne talks at whatever price.

In Turkey news of the talks' collapse in early February 1923 was received cautiously. The conference was said to be on 'temporary holiday' so that the delegates could ponder the propositions at home. The Turkish delegates and Prime Minister feared that the word 'collapse' could provoke opposition groups in the parliament. Though the Turkish press blamed the situation on the Italians and particularly the French, the Turkish government struggled to secure the Great National Assembly in Ankara's approval of counterproposals to the draft treaty İsmet had rejected in early February. Prime Minister Hüseyin Rauf saw them as a 'softened version' of the Treaty of Sèvres.[78] Atatürk sent one of his bodyguards to murder the most obstreperous MP, Ali Şükrü of Trabzon, and even considered sending in the army to ram his proposals through the Assembly. The announcement of a snap election on 1 April achieved the same result without too much violence, delivering a new Assembly more amenable to Atatürk.[79] Talks in Lausanne resumed on 23 April and ran for another three months.

Under pressure from Athens to strike a separate, bilateral agreement with İsmet, Venizelos improvised (with Montagna's help), developing a face-saving solution on Thrace and reparations, under which the Turks would waive their demand

76 *Lausanne Conference*, 359. See also John A. DeNovo, *American Interests and Policies in the Middle East, 1900–1939*, 1963; Fiona Venn, 'Oil, Anglo-American Relations and the Lausanne Conference', *Diplomacy and Statecraft* 20, 2009, 414–433.

77 'Mosul Oil Stream', *Karagöz,* 3 January 1923. Our thanks to Ilkim Büke Okyar for this reference.

78 Taha Akyol and Sefa Kaplan, *Açık ve Gizli Oturumlarda Lozan Tartışmaları: TBMM'de Lozan Müzakereleri Tutanakları*, 2021, 341.

79 Sonyel, *Turkish Diplomacy*, 212–214.

for reparations from Greece in exchange for a small corner of territory around Karaağaç and (in lieu of any payment) a formal statement that Turkey had a moral right to receive compensation for the Greek army's invasion. A further Greek ultimatum threatening to leave Lausanne bounced Italy and France into dropping their own demands for reparations. Both İsmet and Venizelos were over-committed, having advanced ahead of what their respective governments and domestic public opinion were willing to swallow. Meanwhile international opinion would not, Rumbold and Curzon (in London) recognized, support any final stand by the British or French in support of 'rights of foreigners', or French rentiers' right to be reimbursed in gold rather than (inflating) francs. Poincaré's proposal to yoke Allied evacuation to the debt issue risked creating a second Ruhr crisis, this time on the Bosphorus. Even a delay over such matters increased the risk of the Turks and Greeks reaching a separate peace. As Patrick Schilling and Mustafa Aksakal explain in their chapter, the eventual partition and renegotiation of the Ottoman Debt left *rentiers* with little choice but to accept a significant haircut.

To the relief of the Americans and Turks, the Turkish Petroleum Company was jettisoned, and the Mosul dispute kicked down the road, the topic of separate, bilateral talks (which failed, sending the dispute to the League of Nations). After all the public speculation, neither the Chester Concession nor any of the other rumoured side-deals allegedly struck by İsmet and various American (or French, or British) concession hunters materialized. By 17 July all outstanding questions had been resolved. After a nervous week awaiting approval from Ankara, the treaty was signed on 24 July. It would subsequently be ratified by a freshly elected Turkish Grand National Assembly on 21 August. It is worth noting that this treaty, the Greek-Turkish Population Exchange Agreement and the Turkish Straits Convention were three separate conventions: all were negotiated at Lausanne, however. None was conceivable without the others, and hence this volume will follow custom in conflating them.

Syndromes and Histories: Settling the Eastern Question

The respect accorded to the aforementioned Lausanne table in Ankara contrasts jarringly with the display of similar artefacts in equivalent museums in other European capitals. In Budapest's Military Museum the flag flown at the Grand Trianon Palace during the Allies' negotiations with another defeated empire (the Austro-Hungarian) is certainly on show – but under a reinforced glass bridge, to allow visitors to perform their own ritual humiliation of 'trampling' it. The Treaty of Trianon awarded large parts of the Empire to a 'Greater Romania', as well as to Austria and Czechoslovakia. The Treaty was perceived as a national disgrace: throughout the Hungarian Republic the state flag was flown at half-mast until 1938, another ritual 'humiliation'.[80] Although German resentment at the *diktat* of the Treaty of Versailles would be cauterised by another world war, in Hungary 'Trianon Trauma' continues to this day.

The Ottomans formed the third of the First World War's defeated imperial Central Powers. Yet the story of Lausanne is represented as a victory in Ankara's War of Independence and Republic Museum. The Japanese delegate Baron Hayashi was arguably right when he observed that 'it seems to me that Turkey will be almost the only Power among our ex-enemies that has come out without loss of prestige and has emerged with a full promise of peaceful development.' The Treaty has been dubbed the 'birth certificate' of the Republic of Turkey.[81] The scope of the 'unmixing' ordained by Lausanne (as well as its perceived 'success') made it a point of reference in post-WW2 peace settlements, as well as the partition of India. This being said, over the past two decades this normalisation of 'unmixing' as a peace-making tool has been radically reinterpreted and is now viewed by many scholars as 'ethnic cleansing'.[82] For Michael Mann and Benjamin Lieberman, the victims of this 'Lausanne Trauma' are hiding in plain sight.[83]

Yet the 'traumas' and 'syndromes' of the interwar era and its aftermath did more than linger in diplomatic and political memory. Some of them continue to typify long-existing wounds from a deeper past, looking back to previous decades, or even centuries. They harness histories to political ends. In the Ankara museum, the Lausanne table is accompanied by an excerpt from Atatürk's 1927 'Great Speech', observing that the 1923 Treaty 'informs [us] that a great assassination

80 Gerwarth, *The Vanquished*, 207–208.
81 Fatma Müge Göçek, 'The Politics of History and Memory: A Multidimensional Analysis of the Lausanne Peace Conference, 1922–1923', in Israel Gershoni, Hakan Erdem, Ursula Wokock eds., *Histories of the Modern Middle East: New Directions*, 2002, 208.
82 Benjamin Lieberman, 'Ethnic Cleansing in the Greek-Turkish Conflicts from the Balkan Wars through the Treaty of Lausanne: Identifying and Defining Ethnic Cleansing', in Steven Bela Vardy and T. Hunt Tooley eds., *Ethnic Cleansing in Twentieth-Century Europe*, 2003; Benjamin Lieberman, '"Ethnic Cleansing" versus Genocide?', in Donald Bloxham and A. Dirk Moses eds., *Oxford Handbook of Genocide Studies*, 2010, 51; Matthew Frank, *Making Minorities History: Population Transfers in Twentieth Century Europe*, 2017.
83 Benjamin Lieberman, 'Ethnic Cleansing in the Greek-Turkish Conflicts from the Balkan Wars through the Treaty of Lausanne', in S.B. Vardy and T.H. Tooley eds., *Ethnic Cleansing in Twentieth-Century Europe*, 2003; Benjamin Lieberman, *Terrible Fate: Ethnic Cleansing and the Making of Modern Europe*, 2006; Michael Mann, *The Dark Side of Democracy: Explaining Ethnic Cleansing*, 2004.

[plot] on the Turkish nation, one which had been in preparation for centuries and which was supposed to succeed with the Treaty of Sèvres, remained in vain.' Such postulations have, on the one hand, enabled populist historiography in Turkey to frame Lausanne as 'a thousand year-long pay off' between the 'cross and the crescent,' during the 'march of the Turkish nation to the west.'[84] On the other, they exemplify the aforementioned syndrome-driven interpretations of history, drawing attention to the trans-imperial origins of calamities in the Ottoman world.

Despite all their nationalist, populist, and sometimes specious undertones, these readings embody a continuity in Ottoman and Turkish political thought. Since the turn of the nineteenth century, the Ottoman Empire had been caught in what we might describe as a syndrome or an ontological insecurity, an uncertainty as to the place of their Empire in the overall global imperial order of which it 'formed a part and upon which its fate depended.'[85] A series of wars with almost every major European power just before and during the Coalition Wars (1792–1815), as well as numerous proposals for partition of the Sultan's Empire, precipitated a defensive diplomacy in Istanbul that in turn led it to refuse the Great Powers' offer to guarantee the integrity of the Sultan's European dominions in the Final Act of the 1815 Congress of Vienna. This was one proposed solution to the Eastern Question – broadly speaking, how to deal with the alleged weakness of the Ottoman Empire. But it was accompanied by demands for further liberalization of trade and commercial privileges for the Great Powers' subjects. A project of minority protection (of Ottoman Serbians) under a multilateral code of international law was also propounded for the first time, hailed by Tsar Alexander I as 'the most valuable fruit of civilisation'.[86]

A few years later the Ottomans could not help but notice the contrast between the Concert of Europe's non-existent response to Greek slaughter of Muslims

---

84 Ali Güler, *Bin Yıllık Hesaplaşma: Lozan*, 2017.

85 Feroze A.K. Yasamee, 'European Equilibrium or Asiatic Balance of Power? The Ottoman Search for Security in the Aftermath of the Congress of Berlin', in *War and Diplomacy: The Russo-Turkish War of 1877–1878 and the Treaty of Berlin*, M. Hakan Yavuz and Peter Sluglett eds., 2011, 61. For a more detailed discussion of the notion of 'ontological security' in the Turkish context, see Ayşe Zarakol, 'States and Ontological Security: A Historical Rethinking', *Cooperation and Conflict* 52/1, 2017, 48–68.

86 'Soobrazheniya po povodu noty otnositel'no Serbii, s kotoroi pervomu upolnomochennomu Rossii nadlezhit obratit'sya k kongressu,' 3 (15) February 1815, *Vneshnyaya politika Rossii XIX i nachala XX veka. Dokumenty rossijskogo Ministerstva inostrannyx del*, 1972, 195–197. Also see, Ozan Ozavci, 'A Priceless Grace? The Congress of Vienna of 1815, the Ottoman Empire and Historicizing the Eastern Question', *The English Historical Review* 136/583, 2021, 1450–1476.

(and Jews) and pillaging of their property at the outbreak of Greece's war of independence and its response to ensuing Ottoman slaughter and pillaging of Greeks: armed intervention by Britain, France and Russia culminating in the catastrophic destruction of the Ottoman and Egyptian navies at Navarino in 1827. Greek and Serbian independence and the *de jure* autonomous status granted to Moldavia and Wallachia in the late 1820s and the 1830s led the Ottomans to reverse their diplomatic position.

From this point on, membership of the Concert of Europe became a paramount objective for the Sublime Porte, viewed as a means to guarantee the Empire's territorial integrity. It was then that the Ottoman ministers came to uphold the idea of 'civilisation' (however loosely defined) and to fashion themselves as the civilised face of the east. Despite its Islamic superstructure, an underlying motivation for the 1839 Gülhane Edict was to proclaim this Ottoman commitment to civilisation and humanity.[87] The Capitulations were placed on a new footing at about the same time, along with new agreements that further liberalized the Ottoman economy, especially with the 1861 Kanlıca Treaty and associated commercial agreements.[88]

In the aftermath of the Crimean War, the 1856 Treaty of Paris accorded the Ottoman Empire all the privileges of membership of the Concert of Europe, including commitments to non-intervention in the Sultan's domestic affairs and the territorial integrity of his Empire. Four years later, however, the Great Powers undertook another armed intervention in Ottoman Syria, when a civil war broke out in Mount Lebanon, which the Great Powers had partitioned back in 1842. Another *de jure* autonomous region was accordingly introduced in Mount Lebanon (1861), something proto-nationalist liberals of the Empire considered an infringement of Ottoman sovereignty.

All these developments down to the 1860s formed both the pedigree and blueprint of armed and legal interventionism of the Great Powers: of territorial partitions and autonomous zones in the Ottoman world. As Aimee M. Genell notes in her chapter, in lumping the diversely conceived territories administered by the Office of Privileged Provinces together as 'colonies', 'the meaning of sovereignty' was slowly hollowed out.

Forced population transfers may also have had their genesis in these fateful decades. Following the example of French colonial rule in Algiers, in the early 1860s Tsarist Russia's policy on Muslim 'disloyal aliens' resorted to ethnic

87 Ozan Ozavci, *Dangerous Gifts: Imperialism, Security, and Civil Wars in the Levant, 1798–1864*, 2021, Ch. 7.
88 Ozavci, *Dangerous Gifts*, 332–333.

cleansing in the Caucasus and 'compulsory removal of populations' to the Sultan's lands.[89] What the Ottomans made of this episode and to what extent it loomed over their diplomatic memory merit further investigation. The same applies to the reception of the Treaty of Berlin (1878), which recognized the independence of Romania, Serbia, Montenegro and (de facto) Bulgaria, only for hundreds of thousands of Muslim residents of these states to be forcibly evicted from their homes, a violent and unregulated exercise in ethnic cleansing.[90] This process was repeated at the end of the two Balkan Wars (1912–1913) before an equally violent deportation of the Greeks from Asia Minor began.[91]

By Articles 44 and 61, the Treaty of Berlin protected the civil rights of Romanian Jews, while the Ottoman government was obliged to guarantee the security of Armenians, implement reforms in Armenian-inhabited provinces and submit regular reports to the Great Powers. The minority protection regime in Ottoman dominions propounded by the Great Powers at Vienna in 1815 (but not realized) thus came into existence sixty-three years later. Yet this new attempt to settle the Eastern Question in the interests of Balkan communities as well as Ottoman Armenians proved disastrous.[92] The reform pledges stipulated in the Treaty of Berlin were never realised. Instead, the pogroms of the 1890s and 1900s saw the 'Eastern' become the 'Armenian Question'. In 1912–1914, the Armenian Question returned, in the aftermath of an Armeno-Kurdish civil war. An official reform plan was signed between Russia and the Ottoman Empire on 8 February 1914.[93] This was not implemented due to the outbreak of World War I, and arguably only contributed to the Committee of Union and Progress' upending of any concept of

89 V.O. Bobrovnikov, 'Ruskii Kavkaz i Frantsuzkii Alzhir: sluchainoe skhodstvo ili obmen opytom kolonial'nogo stroitel'stva', *Imperial inter pares: rol'transferov v istorii Rossiiskoi imperii (1700–1917)*, 2010; Peter Holquist, 'To Count, to Extract, and to Exterminate: population, statistics and population politics in late imperial and Soviet Russia', in Terry Martin and Ronald G. Suny, eds, *A State of Nations: Empire and Nation-making in the Age of Lenin and Stalin*, 2001, 116; Weitz, 'Vienna to Paris', 1322.

90 Umut Özsu, *Formalizing Displacement: International Law and Population Transfers*, 2015, 5; Weitz, 'Vienna to Paris', 1322; Isa Blumi, *Ottoman Refugees, 1878–1939: Migration in a Post-Imperial World*, 2013, 30.

91 Blumi, *Refugees*, 64–65. See also Justin McCarthy, *Death and Exile: the ethnic cleansing of Ottoman Muslims, 1821–1922*, 1995.

92 M. Hakan Yavuz and Peter Sluglett, 'Introduction: Laying the Foundations for Future Instability', in M. Hakan Yavuz and Peter Sluglett eds., *War and Diplomacy: The Russo-Turkish War of 1877–1878 and the Treaty of Berlin*, 2011, 3.

93 Hans-Lukas Kieser, Mehmet Polatel, and Thomas Schmutz, 'Reform or Cataclysm? The Agreement of 8 February 1914 Regarding the Ottoman Eastern Provinces', *Journal of Genocide Research* 17/3, 2015, 285–304.

a pluralist empire with ultra-nationalist propensities. What ensued was genocide of the Armenian and Assyrian populations in Asia Minor.

Unobserved by historians until recently, a diplomatic note penned in 1916 most possibly by Mehmed Münir (Ertegün), a member of the Ottoman Office of Legal Counsel who later advised İsmet at Lausanne, unilaterally announced that the Ottoman Empire 'definitely abandons her somewhat subordinate position under the collective guardianship of the Great Powers which some of the latter are interested in maintaining. She therefore enters the group of European Powers with all the rights and prerogatives of *an entirely independent government*.'[94] The note also declared that the Ottoman ministers no longer considered the provisions of the Treaty of Paris (1856) and the Treaty of Berlin (1878) as binding on their part, because, despite their stipulations on non-interventionism in the Ottoman Empire, these had not prevented interventions and occupations in the Levant, North Africa, Balkans, Yemen and the Persian Gulf. The Unionist government thus looked to vindicate its war-time policies, stripping itself from any legal responsibility towards the treaties.

The concept of sovereignty on which İsmet placed such emphasis at Lausanne seems to reflect Münir's insistence, in opinions drafted over the course of 1919, that sovereignty could not be divided. Genell's chapter points out that this was a novel idea in Ottoman jurisprudence. But what İsmet, Atatürk and many others appear not to heed in their historical reading is the fact that the Ottoman Empire was also an *empire*. It was a hierarchical system of inclusion, exclusion, exploitation, and domination with uneven cumulative benefits. Pax Ottomanica (just like Pax Romana or Pax Britannica) was a fantasy, as was the argument that the various *millets* under the Ottoman Empire lived in stability and, to cite İsmet, 'at full liberty'.

Only recently has the raft of literature on the Eastern Question taken the agency of Ottoman imperial actors and the subjects into account.[95] This has led to an oversight of Ottoman syndromes that preceded Sèvres, as well as incomplete interpretations of the manifold, yet predominantly domestic, origins of violence in the Ottoman Empire and consequent foreign interventionism since the late eighteenth century. Such oversight has also long helped to vindicate the paranoia-turned-myth of (Western) imperialism as the main cause of major political problems in

94 Emphasis ours. Hakki Pasha to M. Zimmerman, no date, BOA/HR.HMŞ.IŞO 65/14/4.
95 Christine Philliou, *Biography of an Empire: Governing Ottomans in an Age of Revolution*, 2011; Ozavci, *Dangerous Gifts*.

the Middle East (what Elie Kedourie dubbed 'the Chatham House Version' in 1970), overlooking their inter-sectoral nature.[96]

European and American observers could see 'the Islamic world' or even Mathews' 'Young Islam' as the 'self' seeking greater agency. Before the war the Young Turks had manipulated Pan-Islamist civil society groups such as the Ottoman Navy League, seeking to mobilize public opinion through subscription campaigns and boycotts.[97] Yet the Ottoman declaration of *jihad* in November 1914 had been a somewhat cynical exercise, pandering to German hopes of setting the widely-scattered Muslim subjects of the British and French Empires alight.[98] Similar fears surrounding the Pan-Islamist Khilafat Movement (1919–1924) so obsessed Edward Montagu, British Secretary of State for India, that he went public opposing plans to strip Turkey of Istanbul in March 1922 (and was immediately dismissed). Montagu as well as other Government of India officials feared that loss of the Caliphate's seat would deepen unrest, like a bad sequel to John Buchan's *Greenmantle* (1916).[99]

As Cemil Aydın has noted, if anything Montagu abetted the Khilafat Movement precisely because he overestimated the threat it posed, failing to understand the many ways in which Indian Muslims did not see loyalties to the Caliph and Britain as exclusive or conflicting.[100] Seen together, the 'Muslim world' served as a bogeyman, an atavistic throwback to that formative element of 'Britishness': anti-Roman Catholic sentiment.[101] Civil Commissioner of Iraq Arnold Wilson was not the only Indian Political Department officer to denigrate ulamas (in his case, the Shia mujtahids of Karbala and Najaf) as supposedly making 'the most corrupt and fanatical influences in the history of the Vatican' look tame.[102]

96 Elie Kedourie, *The Chatham House Version and other Middle Eastern studies,* 2004.
97 See Mehmet Beşikçi, *The Ottoman Mobilization of Manpower in the First World War*, 2012, Ch. 1; E. Ginio, 'War, Civic Mobilization and the Ottoman Home-Front during the Balkan Wars', in Dominik Geppert et al., eds, *The Wars Before the Great War: Conflict and International Politics before the Outbreak of the First World War*, 2015, 92–113; Jonathan Conlin and Filiz Yazıcıoğlu, 'The Libyan War and Student Pan-Islamism: The Edinburgh Declaration of 1911', *International Journal of Middle East Studies* 54/2, 2022, 1–7.
98 Erik-Jan Zürcher (ed.), *Jihad and Islam in World War I*, 2016.
99 S. Tanvir Wasti, 'Mushir Kidwai and the Ottoman Cause', *Middle Eastern Studies* 30/2, 1994, 259.
100 Cemil Aydın, *The Idea of the Muslim World: a Global Intellectual History*, 2017; Cemil Aydın, 'Muslim Asia after Versailles' in Urs Matthias Zachmann, ed., *Asia After Versailles: Asian Perspectives on the Paris Peace Conference and the Interwar Order, 1919–1933,* 2017.
101 Linda Colley, *Britons: Forging the Nation, 1707–1837,* 1992.
102 Sheffield, 'Interview with Lieut. Col. A. T. Wilson', 20 September 1920. NARA, RG59 890G.6363/8.

For many seasoned European and American diplomats, missionaries were busybodies who constantly stirred up trouble without actually converting anyone. Very likely owing to the professional gulf separating historians of Christian evangelism and historians of the Middle East, it has become commonplace to overlook how the Protestant ecumenical movement coloured debates surrounding the collapse of the Ottoman Empire, Islam and 'human rights'.[103] There is a 'Pan-Christianism' to be set alongside Pan-Islamism, which originated in the 1910 World Missionary Conference at Edinburgh convened by the American John R. Mott, developed into International Mission Council (1921) and World Council of Churches (1948) and culminated in the First International Congress on World Evangelization of 1974 – held in Lausanne, giving its name to the 'Lausanne Movement'.

If, as Michael Reimer argues, 'the triumphalism of Christian expansion was palpable in the early twentieth century, when many Protestants believed that the evangelization of the world was within reach', that belief surely coloured the developments addressed in this book, from the hopes of re-dedicating the Haghia Sophia noted by Erik Goldstein to the American humanitarianism discussed by Andrew Patrick and Laura Robson.[104] The latter proposes that the re-settlement of the displaced populations and humanitarian relief was intimately connected to 'a programme for the remaking of labour, capital, and agriculture on a global scale, and … the remaking of ethno-national landscapes under a specifically modern form of imperial rule.'

In a 2021 historiographical survey, Robert Gerwarth hailed the 'multiperspectivity and the simultaneous globalization and localization' of recent scholarship on the post-war settlements. At the same time, however, he remarked on the lack of scholarship 'in relation to the Ottoman Empire and its successor states'.[105] This volume and the wider Lausanne Project have certainly embraced a similar multi-perspectivity. We leave it to the reader to judge how far we have managed to fill the gap.

---

103 For exceptions see Heather J. Sharkey, *Missionary Encounters in an Age of Empire*, 2008, Ch. 5; John Stuart, 'Empire, Mission Ecumenism, and Human Rights: "Religious Liberty" in Egypt, 1919–1956', *Church History* 83/1, 2014, 110–134.

104 Michael Reimer, 'Converting the Missionaries' [review of Heather Sharkey, *Missionary Encounters*], *Diplomatic History* 35/1, 2011, 48–49. See also Nevzat Uyani, *Dismantling the Ottoman Empire: Britain, America, and the Armenian Question*, 2016.

105 Robert Gerwarth, 'The Sky Beyond Versailles: The Paris Peace Treaties in Recent Historiography', *Journal of Modern History* 93/4, 2021, 929.

1

From the Ottoman Empire to the Turkish Republic: International Law and Minority Rights before and after Lausanne

Aimee M. Genell

On 12 December 1922, İsmet İnönü (hereafter İsmet), the Ankara's government representative at the Lausanne peace proceedings, gave, by all accounts, an unexpected and lengthy speech on the history of minority rights protection in the Ottoman Empire. Supplemented with extensive quotes from Michelet's *History of France*, assorted European international law textbooks, British diplomatic documents, and memoires, İsmet argued that Islamic jurisprudence had dictated that 'the rights of minorities, which it is sought to assure in the twentieth century under the guarantee of the League of Nations, were spontaneously accorded to the non-Muslim elements of the Ottoman Empire.' Starting in the late eighteenth century, he continued, European states took advantage of these privileges and supported 'national communities ready for revolt' who were protected by the Great Powers 'not restrained by international law.'[1] The real problem with such 'privileges', he claimed, was that they eroded sovereignty and opened the door to foreign intervention leading to violence and international instability. The only way to guarantee the rights of minorities, he argued, was not for the emergent Turkey to sign on to the new minority rights treaties, which had been applied in the expanded

1 Great Britain, *Lausanne Conference on Near Eastern Affairs, 1922–1923: Records of Conference and Draft Terms of Peace*, 1923 (hereafter *Lausanne Conference*), 90.

and new Versailles states of Eastern Europe, but rather through a liberal domestic law code which would protect all communities equally without distinction. İsmet insisted that the emergent state did not need the sort of international oversight that new and expanded states in Eastern Europe were obliged to embrace at Paris because, quite simply, the Ottomans had invented minority rights.

At the Paris Peace Conference in 1919, European peacemakers justified the minority rights treaties as a reconfiguration of models worked out in Ottoman lands over the course of the nineteenth century.[2] International lawyers, bureaucrats and intellectuals in Istanbul agreed that the emergent discourse of new minority rights was rooted in their own imperial practices, but they understood this history rather differently from the diplomats gathered in France. In the last days of the war, before the idea of minority rights protection gripped Paris, and certainly before it became one of the three major issues debated at Lausanne – including the Capitulations and the status of Mosul – Istanbul intellectuals and elites across ethnic and religious lines fought bitterly over the status of pre-war 'privileges' accorded to non-Muslim subjects and Europeans residing in the Empire. International lawyers at the Ottoman Foreign Ministry churned out legal opinions on the problem of special legal privileges for religious and ethnic minorities. At the same time, Ottoman parliamentarians deliberated upon the history of special administrative and legal rights within the Empire. When the first Allied ships anchored in the Bosphorus in November 1918, initiating the unofficial occupation of the imperial capital (Ottoman Turkish, Greek, Karamanlidika, Ladino, Arabic, Kurdish and Armenian), the major newspapers in the capital engaged with each other in fierce debates over the status of non-Muslims.[3] The prevalence of the 'minority question' – as it would later come to be known – in Ottoman government documents, parliamentary debates and the press were tied to the debates on the future of the state which initially, for many subjects, was imagined as an imperial one. Arguments about minorities were entangled with an understanding of how Ottoman institutions and domestic legal structures had operated from the 1830s up to the

2 H.W.V. Temperley, *A History of the Peace Conference of Paris*, Vol. V, 'Economic Reconstruction and Protection of Minorities,' 1920–1924, Ch. 2; Umut Özsu, *Formalizing Displacement: International Law and Population Transfers,* 2015, 21–50. For the perhaps astonishing accuracy of these claims, see Laura Robson's excellent article 'Capitulation Redux: The Imperial Genealogy of the Post-WWI 'Minority' Regime,' *The American Historical Review* 126/3, 2021, 978–1000.

3 Mustafa Aksakal et al., 'The Ottoman Empire' in M. Demoor et al. eds.,' *The Edinburgh Companion to First World War Periodicals*, 2023; Erol A. F. Baykal, *The Ottoman Press, 1908–1923,* 2019; Orhan Koloğlu, *Osmanlı'da son Tartışmalar: Mondros'tan Mudanya'ya*, 2008.

First World War, especially those imposed by European states that had limited state sovereignty. Throughout the Armistice period (1918–1923), lawyers and publicists in Istanbul, and later in Ankara, generated policy papers, legal opinions, speeches and editorials on the place of 'exceptional' or autonomous provinces' (*eyâlet-i mümtaze*), non-Muslim 'privileges' (*imtiyazlar*) within the future state, and the function of the Capitulations (*kapitülasyonlar / imtiyazlar*).[4] While the postwar Ottoman state based in Istanbul initially committed itself to reorganizing the Empire as a series of autonomous provinces, and even considered reviving privileges for non-Muslims, after the Treaty of Sèvres (1920), there was broad resistance, especially among Muslims, to anything that looked like internationally imposed limitations on territorial sovereignty and domestic legal institutions.[5] Autonomy, non-Muslim privileges and the Capitulations were all lumped together as old tools of European imperialism used to eviscerate Ottoman sovereignty.[6] By the middle of 1920, Ottoman commentators understood legal privileges for particular groups, whether in the form of special administrative rights for the provinces, for non-Muslim Ottomans, or foreigners in the form of the Capitulations, as potentially lethal to the state sovereignty and an invitation to European intervention in the domestic order of the state. At Lausanne, these critiques were manifested in the rejection of minority rights treaties guaranteed by the League of Nations, and the refusal to accept Allied efforts to create autonomous provinces

4 The Capitulations were those unequal treaties that exempted European subjects from local law which were unilaterally abolished in 1914. Please see more below. I have dealt with the 'privileged provinces' at length in my current manuscript, entitled *Empire by Law: The Ottoman Origins of the Mandate System in the Middle East*, under contract, Columbia University Press. See too Lâle Can and Aimee M. Genell, 'On Empire and Exception: Genealogies of Sovereignty in the Ottoman World', *Comparative Studies in South Asia, Africa and the Middle East* 40/3, 2020, 468–473; Ayhan Ceylan, *Osmanlı Taşra İdarî Tarzı Olarak Eyâlet-i Mümtâze ve Mısır Uygulaması*, 2014; Nobuyoshi Fujinami, 'Between Sovereignty and Suzerainty: History of the Ottoman Privileged Provinces,' *A World History of Suzerainty: A Modern History of East and West Asia and Translated Concepts*, ed. Okamoto Takashi, 2019.

5 Genell, *Empire by Law*, Ch. 6.

6 Lerna Ekmekcioglu has shown how understandings of non-Muslim privileges during the Ottoman era fundamentally shaped constructions of citizenship during early the Turkish Republic. She argues, persuasively, that Republican formulations of citizenship excluded non-Muslims from full citizenship, while paradoxically assimilating them through compulsion into the new state. Lerna Ekmekcioglu 'Republic of Paradox: The League of Nations Minority Protection Regime and the New Turkey's Step-Citizens,' *International Journal of Middle East Studies* 46, 2014, 675–679. See too Yeşim Bayar, 'In Pursuit of Homogeneity: The Lausanne Conference, Minorities and the Turkish Nation', *Nationalities Papers* 42, 2014, 108–125.

for Armenians and Kurds in what would become Turkey.[7] İsmet and the Turkish Delegation at Lausanne flatly rejected Allied imposed limits on sovereignty that resembled older forms of European interference in Ottoman affairs. From the state's perspective, administrative autonomy, minority rights protections and legal privileges for foreigners were off the table.

This story reveals a deep shift in long-standing Ottoman approaches to negotiating with Europe that had been anchored in pragmatism and accommodation with international legal norms for much of the nineteenth and early twentieth centuries. The bundling and rejection of any form of legal privilege, and the abandonment of international law as a tool to ameliorate the international status of the Empire within Europe, was a striking reversal from past practices. In earlier disputes, the Empire negotiated and begrudgingly accommodated European demands for domestic reform, or the granting of administrative or legal rights to imperial subjects (almost always non-Muslim), as long as the agreement was agreed to by treaty and thus enshrined in the 'law and system of Europe.'[8] The Ottomans who forged the Republic gave up on international law as the saviour of empire and abandoned the old practice of preserving state sovereignty by treaty. Instead, sovereignty was a right claimed through force and violence. This episode matters because it explains the enduring resistance to special privileges and administrative rights in the Republic of Turkey, but it also reflects an important moment in the Ottoman history, where domestic legal institutions were divorced from international legal constraints and force was elevated over the burdens of law.

The Ottoman Empire

To draw out the implications of this argument, it is necessary to look at the ways in which international law structured relations between the Ottoman Empire and Europe over the course of the nineteenth century up to the outbreak of the First World War. While the nineteenth century began with the Ottoman Empire's leaders attempting to distance the state from the new international order of 1815 forged out of revolution and war, events in Ottoman Greece dragged the state into

7 For Armenian efforts to establish an autonomous province in the new Turkey, see Lerna Ekmekcioglu's chapter in this volume and Ercan Karakoç, 'Osmanlı Hariciyesinde Bir Ermeni Nazır: Gabriyel Noradunkyan Efendi', *Uluslararası İlişkiler Dergisi* 7, 2010, 157–177.

8 Mustafa Aksakal and Aimee M. Genell, 'Salvation through War? The Ottoman Search for Sovereignty in 1914,' *The Justification of War and International Order: From the Past to the Present*, eds. Lothar Brock and Hendrik Simon, 2021.

Europe's legal orbit.[9] In the aftermath, European empires increasingly imposed administrative, legal, and economic restrictions that not only limited Ottoman imperial sovereignty but also increasingly framed and governed relations between states, with powerful consequences for the Empire.

In the aftermath of the Napoleonic wars and the military and diplomatic reordering of Europe, the Ottoman Empire abruptly found itself on much less equal footing vis-à-vis its neighbours to the west. The emergent inequality between states was underlined most profoundly by two related episodes that undermined Ottoman sovereignty: a shift in the function and meaning of the Capitulations and new forms of European military intervention in Ottoman affairs, accompanied by demands for administrative reforms and reorganization – all products of the 1830s.

In the nineteenth century, the privileges known as the Capitulations, which exempted European merchants from local courts, were increasingly understood as unequal treaties governing the rights and status of foreign residents in the Empire.[10] European ambassadors and consuls insisted that the Capitulations not only released their subjects from the Sultan's jurisdiction, but also from taxation and conscription. This transformation of the Capitulations from a unilateral privilege granted by the Sultan, into a mark of sovereign difference between empires laid the foundation for domestic legal reform for the remainder of the Empire's history. One of the driving goals of Ottoman foreign policy from the mid-nineteenth century to their abolition in 1914 was to dismantle the system of

9 As Ozan Ozavci's recent work has shown, after an internal power struggle, the Ottomans opted not to participate in the Congress of Vienna concluding the Napoleonic Wars in 1815, casting European 'politics' as a space of intrigue and deception. Ozan Ozavci, *Dangerous Gifts: Imperialism, Security, and Civil Wars in the Levant, 1798–1864*, 2021. See too his 'A Priceless Grace? The Congress of Vienna of 1815, the Ottoman Empire and Historicising the Eastern Question', *The English Historical Review* 136/583, 2021, 1450–1476. See too Glenda Sluga, *The Invention of International Order: Remaking Europe after Napoleon*, 2021.

10 See especially Edhem Eldem, 'Capitulations and Western Trade: Western Trade in the Ottoman Empire,' ed. Suraiya N. Faroqhi, *The Cambridge History of Turkey*, 2006. For an examination of how the Capitulations functioned before the nineteenth century shift from privileges to unequal treaties see M. van den Boogert, *The Capitulations and the Ottoman Legal System: Qadis, Consuls and Beraths in the 18th Century*, 2005. Will Hanley has examined how consular courts functioned in Ottoman Alexandria during the late nineteenth and early twentieth century. Will Hanley, *Identifying with Nationality: Europeans, Ottomans, and Egyptians in Alexandria,* 2017. Much of the diplomatic energy and aims of Ottoman lawyers in the late Empire were directed towards abolition of the Capitulations. Umut Özsu, 'Ottoman Empire', eds. Bardo Fassbender and Anne Peters, *The Oxford Handbook of the History of International Law*, 2012, 429–448.

unequal treaties, and for much of the period in question Ottomans cast the Capitulations as *imtiyaz* or privileges that cut against imperial sovereignty.[11] As Ottoman lawyers regularly pointed out, the Capitulations sat uncomfortably alongside the Empire's long and continued history of treaty making with Europe.[12] It was not only the fact that in the Treaty of Paris (1856) to which the Ottoman Empire was a signatory European states had invited the Empire to join 'the public law and system (Concert) of Europe' that formed the basis of arguments for equality, but also Ottoman lawyers appealed to the positive international law arguments centred on state practice and insisted that the history of treaty making between the Ottoman Empire and its neighbouring empires formed the customary law of Europe.[13]

From the 1830s, the new iteration of the Capitulations as a mark of inequality was bound up with creeping European financial limitations on Ottoman sovereignty. The dismantling of monopolies and free trade, followed by the first European loans contracted during the Crimean War in 1855, had disastrous consequences for the Empire. Infrastructure and development were driven by concessionary capitalism. Throughout the Empire, railway lines, port infrastructure and shipping lines were owned by foreign companies. The Ottoman Public Debt Administration, formed in 1881 after the Empire defaulted on its loan repayments, collected debts on behalf of European creditors for the remainder of the life of the Empire.

The drive to destroy the Capitulations was intimately bound up with asserting economic sovereignty, and in both cases, facilitated the Empire's turn to international law as a tool to manage European imposed limitations on Ottoman authority.[14] This was manifested through both learning international law as a tool

11 Nobuyoshi Fujinami discusses the overlap between the Capitulations and privileges for non-Muslims in his 'Between Sovereignty and Suzerainty'.

12 Aimee M. Genell, 'Ottoman Autonomous Provinces and the Problem of "Semi-Sovereignty" in International Law', *Journal of Balkan and Near Eastern Studies,* 2016, 533–549.

13 Genell, 'Ottoman Autonomous Provinces,' 535–537. For the text of this treaty, T. E. Hall, *The European Concert in the Eastern Question: A Collection of Treaties and Other Public Acts*, 1885, 241–259.

14 See the recent edited volumes covering Ottoman approaches to international law in *The Subjects of Ottoman International Law,* eds. Lâle Can, Michael Christopher Low, et al., 2020, and the 2016 symposium in *Journal of the History of International Law*; Umut Özsu and Thomas Skouteris, 'International Legal Histories of the Ottoman Empire: An Introduction to a Symposium', *Journal of the History of International Law* 18, 2016, 1–4; Cemil Aydın, *The Politics of Anti-Westernism in Asia: Visions of World Order in Pan-Islamic and Pan-Asian Thought*, 2007; Mustafa Serdar Palabıyık, 'International Law for Survival: Teaching International Law in the Late Ottoman Empire (1859–1922)', *Bulletin of the School of*

of diplomacy and harmonizing domestic legal institutions to be intelligible to Europeans who claimed that the Ottoman state lacked the capacity to treat their subjects fairly in a court of law.[15] While domestic reasons were just as important in propelling imperial legal reform, the inequality of the Capitulations was a major incentive for reform. Between the 1860s and 1880s, new and reformed legal institutions and codification projects proliferated in Istanbul and the provinces, including the introduction of a three-tiered system of secular courts, codification of Islamic jurisprudence in the Ottoman Civil Code (*mecelle*), and the establishment of the Imperial Law School, which included international law as a required subject of study.[16]

Of equal importance to the Capitulations as a curb on the exercise of Ottoman sovereignty was the frequency with which European powers intervened militarily in the Ottoman Empire. Nineteenth century European interventions were framed in humanitarian terms and were often made on behalf of Christian subjects in the aftermath of rebellion or domestic disputes.[17] Concert diplomacy solved these crises, which more often than not rose to the level of international politics, by insisting upon administrative and legal reforms in exchange for the evacuation of foreign troops. While the Ottoman Empire introduced flexible administrative arrangements throughout its vast domains, starting in the 1830s, European intervention in Ottoman affairs resulted in the creation of a new type of province. Branded as 'privileged,' the new autonomous provinces (*eyâlet-i mümtaze*) emerged out of negotiations between the Ottoman and European empires.

The new category of privileged province was designed to respond to European critiques and to give local authorities more direct control over administration.

Oriental and African Languages 78, 2015, 271–291, as well as his 'The Emergence of the Idea of "International Law" in the Ottoman Empire before the Treaty of Paris (1856)', *Middle Eastern Studies* 50, 2014, 233–251; Turan Kayaoğlu, *Legal Imperialism: Sovereignty and Extraterritoriality in Japan, the Ottoman Empire, and China*, 2010; Will Hanley, 'When did Egyptians stop being Ottomans? An Imperial Citizenship Case Study', *Multilevel Citizenship*, ed. Willem Maas, 2013; Michael Christopher Low, 'Unfurling the Flag of Extraterritoriality: Autonomy, Foreign Muslims, and the Capitulations in the Ottoman Hejaz', *Journal of the Ottoman and Turkish Studies Association* 3/2, 2016, 299–323.

15 Avi Rubin, *Ottoman Nizamiye Courts: Law and Modernity*, 2011 and 'Modernity as Code: The Ottoman Empire and the Global Movement of Codification', *Journal of Economic and Social History of the Orient* 59, 2016, 828–856.

16 Ekmeleddin İhsanoğlu, *Darülfünun: Osmanlı 'da Kültürel Modernleşmenin Odağıi*, 2010.

17 Davide Rodogno's monograph on the origins of humanitarian intervention discusses the Ottoman position in Europe and international law. Davide Rodogno, *Against Massacre: Humanitarian Intervention in the Ottoman Empire 1815–1914*, 2012.

The provinces included imperial hotspots such as Serbia, Romania, Egypt, Mount Lebanon, Crete and Bulgaria. Autonomy in practice varied across the Empire. Each of the privileged provinces had individual agreements with Istanbul, and different local arrangements as far as law and taxation. Some of these provinces were exempted from empire wide polices such as the secular or *nizamiye* courts (1864) and others not. But they shared one important commonality: the status of these provinces was guaranteed in international law by treaty and in Ottoman administrative law.

Autonomous provinces were located in areas of strategic importance and arenas of intense imperial competition. The first such provinces were formalized out of regional disorders generated by the Greek War of Independence (1821–1832) – Serbia, the island of Samos and the Danubian Principalities. Egypt gained autonomy in 1841; Mount Lebanon in 1861. By the 1870s, European Great Powers, especially Britain, regularly threatened the Ottomans with more autonomous provinces whenever local imperial crises threatened to broaden – in Macedonia, Armenia, the Gulf and beyond. In the lead up to World War I, Britain and the European powers attempted to impose autonomous administrations in the *kaza* of Kuwait and in the six eastern provinces that European states designated as 'Armenia.' The Armenian Reform Agreement of February 1914 created two large autonomous provinces 'on the model of Mount Lebanon' with each overseen by a European inspector.

For our purposes, the significance of the autonomous provinces at Lausanne was two-fold. Like the Capitulations, administrative autonomy was yet another arena in which the Ottomans clashed with European powers. Whereas for European states autonomy was often understood as a way to limit the Sultan's reach and diminish Ottoman central control, for the state they became a means to satisfy locals in the provinces, and to shore up territorial claims, across the Empire – and nowhere more so than at the state's vulnerable fringes in North Africa and the Gulf. Secondly, like the legal reforms that emerged out of attempts to undo the Capitulations, the autonomous provinces posed yet another sovereignty problem for the Empire and pushed state bureaucrats to embrace international law as part of its diplomatic arsenal.

The autonomous provinces that arose out of the 1830s were at first managed by the state on an ad-hoc basis, but by the 1880s they were cast together as a type of administrative unit. They were distinct from the regular provinces like Kastamonu or Syria but were a fundamental part of the imperial legal order. Ottoman bureaucrats, as much as subjects, wrote about the provinces as a group, and they were recognized as a constituent category in the first Ottoman constitution of

1876. In the early 1880s, after territorial losses in the Balkans and a series of permanent military occupations in Bosnia-Herzegovina, Tunis, and Egypt, the new Office of Privileged Provinces (*vilayet-ı mümtaze kalemi*) was established within the Office of the Grand Vizier to maintain Ottoman sovereignty, and if possible extend central imperial control over them.[18] European diplomats and international lawyers commented upon Ottoman efforts to assert greater centralized control over the privileged provinces through this Office.[19] Provinces like Mount Lebanon and Samos did not cause much trouble for the new Office, but others, notably Egypt, Crete and Bulgaria, were among the most sensitive in terms of Ottoman relations with Europe and recurring hotspots.

The Capitulations, together with the autonomous provinces, helped to lay the groundwork for the Foreign Ministry's Office of Legal Counsel (*hukuk müşavirliği istişare odası*) which was staffed by international lawyers and which formalized international law as the main tool of argument in dealings with Europe from the Hamidian regime to the Balkan Wars. The Office of Legal Counsel played an outsized role policing the sovereign edges of the Empire in the age of high imperialism.[20] It was established as a result of the catastrophe of the 1877–1878 Russo-Ottoman War. Before that point, the Ottoman state relied upon international law and employed European lawyers as advisers on an occasional basis. It was only in the centralizing Hamidian era (1876–1909), which was marked by ambitious state building projects, that international law became central to Ottoman diplomatic practice and its engagement with Europe. From the 1880s, the Council of Ministers regularly called upon the Foreign Ministry's Office of Legal Counsel to draft legal opinions on European crises.[21]

Ottoman international lawyers developed expertise in both private and public international law.[22] The Capitulations demanded Ottoman engagement with

18 Eşref Eşrefoğlu, 'Mümtaze Kalemi ve Bulgaristan Belgeleri,' *Güneydoğu Avrupa Araştırmaları Dergisi*, June – July 1978, 189–203; Carter Findley, *Bureaucratic Reform in the Ottoman Empire: The Sublime Porte, 1789–1922*, 1980.

19 For example, the Russian international lawyer, Fedor Martens, noted that the new Office was designed to claim Ottoman sovereignty over such provinces against European encroachments. Fedor Martens, *Traité de droit international*, 1883–1887, 331.

20 Aimee M. Genell, 'The Well-defended Domains: Eurocentric International Law and the Making of the Ottoman Office of Legal Counsel', *Journal of Ottoman and Turkish Studies* 3, 2016, 255–275.

21 Carter V. Findley, *Ottoman Civil Officialdom: A Social History*, 1989, 197.

22 Private international law deals with questions of legal jurisdiction between private citizens and touches on issues of personal status, citizenship, nationality, and identity documentation. Public international law covers relations between states, such as war and peace, bilateral and multilateral treaties, agreements, acts, and conventions between powers, but also customary

questions of personal status, while the autonomous provinces compelled lawyers to regulate the line between domestic and international law.[23] After the 1830s, Ottoman diplomats, and later lawyers, pushed European empires to include guarantees in treaties that recognized the 'territorial integrity' of the imperial domains.[24] For Ottoman officials, these clauses did double duty – they served to further ensconce the Empire into the 'political system of Europe' and, because nineteenth century international lawyers cast treaties as one of the main sources of international law, these clauses demonstrated a shared legal culture in international law.[25]

Foreign Ministry lawyers did not just engage in high diplomacy and treaty making. They monitored Ottoman sovereign rights wherever they were in jeopardy, which often meant the autonomous provinces, as well as Ottoman territory in North Africa and the Gulf. Lawyers scrutinized relations between the autonomous provinces and European empires. Whenever a local governor exceeded his privileges, the lawyers drafted opinions to assert the Empire's rights. Legal opinions were transformed into policies carried by diplomatic cables into European foreign ministries. In several instances throughout the Hamidian era, this strategy worked surprisingly well. European states would begrudgingly acknowledge Ottoman sovereignty in the autonomous province in question. But the constant recourse to asserting Ottoman sovereign rights based on international treaty, also slowly hollowed out the meaning of sovereignty – a point that the Ankara government would later be quick to capitalize upon at Lausanne as well.

The international lawyers who directed the Foreign Ministry's Office of Legal Counsel and held the title of Chief Legal Adviser (a position shared by one Muslim and one non-Muslim subject) were few but played a major role in late Ottoman political affairs, even after leaving the Office.[26] Their expertise in public and private international law, and finance, meant that they often represented the Empire abroad at international conferences, like the Inter-Parliamentary Union,

---

practices such as trade. In the Ottoman case, it is not always possible to draw a clean line between these two bodies of law due to European imposed limitations on Ottoman sovereignty, particularly the Capitulations.

23 Lâle Can, *Spiritual Subjects: Central Asian Pilgrims and the Ottoman Hajj at the End of Empire,* 2020; Michael Christopher Low, *Imperial Mecca: Ottoman Arabia and the Indian Ocean Hajj,* 2020; Hanley, *Identifying with Nationality*.

24 The appearance and use of territorial guarantees by the European Great Powers and the Ottoman Empire is one of the leitmotifs of Ozan Ozavci's *Dangerous Gifts.*

25 Genell, 'Autonomous Provinces', 534.

26 Genell, 'Well-defended Domains.'

the Board of Health and the Permanent Court of Arbitration in The Hague.[27] The two most authoritative international law experts in the Empire during the Hamidian era, Gabriel Noradungian and İbrahim Hakkı, were assigned to important bureaucratic posts in the tumultuous years leading up to the First World War, and in İbrahim Hakkı's case, during the war itself. Both lawyers were the main architects of the Ottoman foreign policy that embraced international law as the protector of empire. Noradungian, who edited the definitive collection of Ottoman-European treaties and agreements in French translation, was the only Armenian Foreign Minister in the history of the Empire. He occupied the post during the Italian invasion of Libya and the First Balkan Wars. İbrahim Hakkı held the position of Grand Vizier, and later acted as the Ottoman Ambassador to Berlin during the First World War until his death in July 1918. Only one other Foreign Ministry lawyer, Mehmed Münir (Ertegün) who served as the chief adviser of the Turkish Delegation at Lausanne, would obtain a similarly important role in crafting state policy. Unlike his mentors, he would have a much less public position in doing so (a point which evidences the shift in international law's importance from imperial to early Republican foreign policy).

It was during the Young Turk era (1908–1918) that the Hamidian strategy of appealing to international law to manage European imperial encroachments started to fray. When Italy invaded and occupied Libya in 1911, the Office of Legal Counsel was responsible for crafting the legal case against Italy's illegal invasion. Ottoman lawyers made both *jus ad bellum* and *jus in bello* arguments and claimed that not only had Italy provoked war without legal grounds, but also the Italian methods of warfare including the use of exploding bullets and dropping bombs from airplanes were prohibited by the Hague Conventions (both Italy and the Ottomans were signatories). The lawyers requested mediation at The Hague, but these arguments were met with a shrug from Europe.

In an empire where every interaction with Europe was distorted through limitations on the exercise of sovereignty, the reading public was well versed in international law, and it was in the Istanbul press where international law was most harshly judged. Ottoman newspaper editors across the political spectrum, a stunning number of whom graduated from the Imperial Law School and were thus trained in international law and the treaty history between Europe and the Empire, saw Italy's brazen occupation as the death knell for international law as a policy to manage aggressive Europe. Newspaper editors from both the Committee of

27 Union interparlementaire, *Procès-verbaux de la Commission des détroits et des canaux maritimes*, 1913; Karakoç, 'Osmanlı Hariciyesinde Bir Ermeni', 159–160.

Union and Progress (hereafter CUP) and the ruling opposition party, the liberal Freedom and Accord Party (*Hürriyet ve İtilaf Fırkası*), argued that international law had spectacularly failed to stop the Italians, nor had it rallied the other European powers to protect the Ottoman domains. In the aftermath of the Italian war in Libya, Ottoman public opinion judged the merits of international law in harsh terms and increasingly viewed war as the only means to save the state and maintain sovereignty over imperial lands.[28] Europe's territorial grantees reflected Ottoman weakness and were nothing more than a con that prevented the Empire from asserting true equality with Europe.

The Libyan disaster was brought to a sudden close by the unexpected attack on Ottoman Macedonia in the Balkans, by former Ottoman principalities. On 23 January 1913, amid multiple internal and external crises, the CUP violently seized control of the government from the ruling opposition party. The CUP justified the coup d'état on the grounds that the opposition had recognized unacceptable territorial losses in the Balkans. The former Chief Legal Adviser, Gabriel Noradungian, serving as the Minister of Public Works, was present when the CUP raided the Grand Vizier's Office, which resulted in the assassination of the Minister of War and forced the resignation of the Grand Vizier, Kâmil Paşa.[29] Fearing for his life, Noradungian fled the capital to France, where he remained throughout the First World War. His expertise in international law, Ottoman governance, and managing non-Muslims and European powers would be put to the test throughout the Armistice period and especially at Lausanne.

Questions of legal privileges not the only concern for lawyers and high government officials. During the Second Constitutional period, the major debates among the Empire's subjects concerned imperial organization. While the CUP favoured administrative centralization, the liberal opposition (which included Noradungian) preferred administrative decentralization on the model of the autonomous provinces like Egypt and Mount Lebanon.[30] Even before the First World War

28 Mustafa Aksakal, 'Not "by those old books of international law, but only by war": Ottoman Intellectuals on the Eve of the Great War', *Diplomacy & Statecraft* 15, 2004, 507–554; Aksakal and Genell, 'Salvation through War?'; Stefan Hock, 'Waking us from this Endless Slumber: The Ottoman–Italian War and North Africa in the Ottoman Twentieth Century', *War in History* 26, 2017, 204–226.

29 Gabriel Noradungian, *Recueil d'actes internationaux de l'empire ottoman*, 1897–1903; Y. G. Çark, *Türk Devlet Hizmetinde Ermeniler, 1453–1953*, 1953; Karakoç, 'Osmanlı Hariciyesinde bir Ermeni', 164–167.

30 Hasan Kayalı provides one of the best and clearest assessments of this debate before the war. Hasan Kayalı, *Arabs and Young Turks: Ottomanism, Arabism, and Islamism in the Ottoman Empire, 1908–1918*, 1997, Ch. 4. Bedross Der Matossian examines the question of

broke out, there were massive debates in the Ottoman press across the Empire's linguistic, national, and religious communities about legal and administrative privileges and the role they should play in the domestic legal order of the Empire. When the CUP seized control of the government in 1913, those dreams of expanding autonomy were put on hold and centralization briefly won out, but they would return with a force as soon as the dust seemed to settle in 1918 and wartime press censorship was relaxed.[31]

Between 1913 and 1918, the CUP-controlled government shifted the position of international law in the state's diplomatic arsenal. It was still available, but now in a far more cynical and assertive register. The unilateral abrogation of the Capitulations on 9 September 1914 was the opening salvo in the new approach to international law, backed by a military alliance with Germany.[32] The letter sent to Foreign Ministries announcing the repeal of the Capitulations stated explicitly that the Capitulations damaged the Empire and were contrary to the principles of international law. 'Having thus freed itself from what was an intolerable obstacle to all progress in the Empire, the Imperial Government has adopted as the basis of its relations with the other powers the general principle of international law.'[33] The following month, Enver Paşa, the Minister of War, ordered the Ottoman fleet to attack Russian ships 'without a declaration of war' – a command that would have been unthinkable before the invasion and occupation of Libya.[34] In December, the government cancelled the Armenian Reform Agreement of February 1914, which

administrative decentralization and the 'extension of administrative responsibility' (*tevsi'-i mezuniyet*) in the Arabic, Armenian, Hebrew, Ladino and Ottoman press. Bedross Der Matossian, *Shattered Dreams of Revolution: From Liberty to Violence in the Late Ottoman Empire,* 2014, Ch. 2.

31 Throughout World War I, the CUP continued to pursue a policy of centralization. Indeed, incorporating the autonomous provinces into the regular administration of the Empire was an Ottoman war aim – the Unionists cancelled the contentious Armenian Reform Agreement in December 1914, and in July 1915 Mount Lebanon lost its privileged status. That August, Cemal Paşa, the wartime governor of Syria, publicly executed Syrian dissidents who had favoured decentralized administration before the war. See Ahmed Cemal (Ahmed Djemal), *Memoirs of a Turkish Statesman, 1913–1919*, 1922 and Yusuf Hikmet Bayur, *Türk İnkilabı Tarihi*, 1983, 12. For Cemal Paşa's wartime activities in Syria, see Talha Çicek, *War and State Formation in Syria: Cemal Pasha's Governorate during World War I, 1914–1917,* 2014.

32 Mustafa Aksakal, *The Ottoman Road to War in 1914: The Ottoman Empire and the First World War*, 2008; Feroz Ahmad, 'Ottoman Perceptions of the Capitulations, 1800–1914', *Journal of Islamic Studies* 11, 2000, 1–20.

33 *Foreign Relations of the United States: with the Address of the President to Congress December 8, 1914*, 1922, 1090. Quoted in Ahmad, 'Ottoman Perceptions', 19.

34 'Suchen Sie die russische Flotte auf und greifen sie sie ohne Kriegserklaerung an, so Sie sie finden.' Ali Kaşıyuğun, *Osmanlı Devleti'nin Birinci Dünya Savaşı'na Girişi,* 2015.

would have reorganized the six eastern provinces into two autonomous provinces with European inspectors.[35] The clearest statement that the old territorial guarantees were a dead letter was when İbrahim Hakkı - the former Chief Legal Adviser, now Ottoman Ambassador to Berlin – announced to the European powers that the Empire rejected all of the clauses in the Treaty of Paris (1856) and the Treaty of Berlin (1878) that had limited the Empire's sovereignty.[36] The occasion for this announcement was that the Empire had unilaterally revoked Mount Lebanon's autonomous status, the last of Great Power imposed *eyâlet-i mümtaze*.

The Foreign Ministry's international law reflex did not disappear overnight with war in Libya, or even the outbreak of the First World War. Ottoman international lawyers spent over thirty years crafting legal arguments, rooted in treaty law, to keep Europe at bay and to preserve the boundaries of the Empire. They accommodated European demands for reform but did so by doing everything possible to preserve imperial sovereignty. In an empire that was desperate to assert control at its frontiers, as much as to assert its sovereignty and to claim equality in the world of competing empires, Foreign Ministry lawyers were the authority on the problem of sovereignty in the age of empire. They were highly adept at dealing with the challenges posed by 'privileges,' whether personal, legal or special administrative. At Lausanne this legal expertise would be essential to block European attempts to revive the old limits on sovereignty.

International Law at Lausanne

From the start of the conference proceedings in November 1922, the Turkish Delegation attempted to preserve all that had been gained during the years of external and internal warfare. International law questions related to the Capitulations, the Ottoman debt, the status of Mosul, and the rights of ethnic and religious minorities in Turkey (secured through either minority rights treaties guaranteed by the League of Nations, or administrative autonomy) were subjects of intense debate and scrutiny. Many of these same questions had animated discussions in the aftermath of the Crimean War at Paris in 1856, at the Berlin Congress in 1878, at the Paris Peace Conference in 1919 and at the signing of the Treaty of Sèvres in 1920. In the earlier cases, the Ottoman Foreign Ministry embraced international law to

35 Hans-Lukas Kieser, *Talaat Pasha: Father of Modern Turkey, Architect of Genocide*, 2018, 191–192.

36 Başbakanlık Osmanlı Arşivleri (hereafter BOA), HR.HMŞ.İŞO/65/20, 30 November 1916; İbrahim Hakkı to Gottlieb von Jagow, 14 October 1916. See too Genell, 'The Well-defended Domains', 270–271; Ozavci, *Dangerous Gifts,* 359.

mitigate the sting of European interference. At Paris and Sèvres, the lessons of Libya were on full display. Ottoman attempts to negotiate with the Allies led to lost territory, further limitations on sovereignty, and demotion in the international arena, and they invited outside interference in the domestic administration and law. Like the wartime government, at Lausanne international law would be used as a battering ram to assert equality, rather than a tool of compromise.

İsmet's impromptu speech on the history of European intervention in Ottoman affairs and many others just like it delivered by him over the course of the Peace Conference which drew substantially on international legal questions were drafted by Mehmed Münir (Ertegün). Mehmed Münir arrived at Lausanne in late 1922 as the Chief Legal Adviser for the emergent Turkish state. Throughout the conference, he worked behind the scenes, assisting İsmet and the Turkish Delegation on the most contentious legal issues of the proceedings, including the Capitulations, the status of Mosul, and the legal position of non-Muslims in the future state. Between 1918 and the late 1920s, Mehmed Münir would lead or assist negotiations related to nearly every legal aspect of the dissolution of the Empire and the forging of the Republic – from the end of the Capitulations and the distribution of the Ottoman debt to the treatment of minorities in Turkey and the final borders of the state.[37]

Even though Mehmed Münir provided the legal substance to defend the state against Europe's efforts to restore pre-war limits on sovereignty, the lawyer does not figure prominently in stories about the Peace Conference. In the political caricatures from Lausanne drawn by Emery Kelen and Alois Derso, Mehmed Münir appeared to be the especially serious member among the Turkish Delegation. He looked anxious, gaunt, and was depicted clutching documents or hovering over maps.[38] But apart from these cartoons, and a handful of photographs that portrayed a correspondingly grave face and sombre demeanour, Mehmed Münir is a

37 Mehmed Münir served the Turkish state in several crucial roles and was perhaps one of the most important legal mediators between the Republic and post-war European states. He spent years in Europe as a Turkish observer at the League of Nations, where, among other things, he attempted to negotiate for the return of Mosul to Turkey, based on the armistice lines of 1918 and the National Pact (*Misak-i Milli*) of 1920. He defended the Republic's treatment of Greek minorities after the exchange of populations. In the early 1920s, he travelled between Geneva and Paris to settle the Ottoman debt. United Nations Archives Geneva/League of Nations (hereafter UNAG/LN), C.783.1925.I. 'Frontier between Turkey and Iraq'; UNAG/LN C.783.1925.I. 'The Greek Minority in Constantinople and the Turkish Minority in Western Thrace.'

38 Emery Kelen and Alois Derso, *Guignol à Lausanne,* 1923; Emery Kelen, *Peace in their Time: Men Who Led Us In and Out of War, 1914–1945*, 1964.

footnote in the drama despite the crushing volume of legal work he performed to dismantle the Empire and usher in the Republic.

Lausanne was far from Mehmed Münir's first experience dealing with fraught legal questions concerning European attempts to restrict Ottoman sovereignty. In fact, his early career was defined by these problems. During the war, he served as one of Chief Legal Advisers to the Office of Legal Counsel, a role to which he would return in Ankara in 1924, but for a radically reconfigured Foreign Ministry, one released from the spectacular and manifold pressures faced by the late Empire. Trained in international law at the Imperial Law School in Istanbul, he entered the Foreign Ministry as a legal assistant in 1909 and was promoted to Chief Legal Adviser in early 1913, amid the chaos surrounding the Balkan Wars and the Raid on the Sublime Porte (Bâb-ı Âlî Baskını). Mehmed Münir took charge of the legal work of the Empire at the precise moment that international law was most discredited in the eyes of Istanbul elites and certainly by the CUP.

During the war, Mehmed Münir wrote several legal opinions that justified the CUP's war aims. He authored, or commented upon, numerous legal opinions that defended episodes such as the abolition of the Capitulations in 1914, as well as the termination of Mount Lebanon's privileged status in 1915. Aiding İbrahim Hakkı, he acted as a legal adviser for negotiations at Brest-Litovsk in 1917 and early 1918. From an Ottoman perspective, this treaty was a success and fulfilled one of the Empire's war aims: restoration of lost lands. Russia ceded Kars, Batumi and Ardahan to the Empire, all of which had been under Russian occupation since the Russo-Ottoman War (1877–1878).[39] Mehmed Münir did not merely issue legal opinions that conformed to the CUP's vision of a post-war centralized empire. In the immediate aftermath of the war, he laboured on behalf of the old liberal opposition, who once again regained power in Istanbul.

The Ottoman Invention of Minority Rights

The Ottoman exit from the war in October 1918 ushered in a new round of legal uncertainty for the Empire. Almost immediately, pre-war debates between political factions (especially the CUP and the Ottoman liberals who had been forced out of office in 1913) were resumed. The Ottomans struggled with the difficult question of how to rebuild the Empire and remake the body politic in the aftermath of total war and, at the same time, wrestled with devising ways to limit European

39 Michael A. Reynolds, *Shattering Empires: The Clash and Collapse of the Ottoman and Russian Empires 1908–1918*, 2011.

interference in Ottoman affairs. As long as it was possible to imagine imperial continuity, many intellectuals anticipated a return to the ethnic and religious diversity of the pre-war Ottoman world. But as the Allied occupation became more entrenched, and as hopeful expectations for the Paris Peace Conference were crushed, Ottoman bureaucrats and intellectuals abandoned any commitment to special rights for non-Muslims, followed by the complete surrender of the imperial order in favour of a Muslim majority state.

These debates swirled in backroom conversations among high officials and unfolded publicly in the press and parliament during the early days of the Allied occupation of the capital. Ottoman newspaper editors continued to cast Europe as an existential threat as far as the Empire's external relations were concerned, but also in terms of its domestic politics. They argued that the long history of European military and legal intervention on behalf of Ottoman Christians had to end in order to build a strong post-war order. In the same way that the old pre-war political battle lines between partisans of centralized versus decentralized imperial administration reappeared in 1918, so too did Second Constitutional era debates on the problem of privileges and special legal protections for non-Muslims. Together with political analyses on the viability of a reorganized empire, editors debated the rights of non-Muslims as Ottoman citizens. It was in these particularly thorny disagreements that the question of minority rights arose and were later tied to that emergent rights discourse at the Paris Peace Conference which resurfaced at Lausanne.[40]

It was not just liberals committed to rebuilding the multi-ethnic empire who asserted that the Ottomans invented minority rights. Once the minority rights treaties hammered out in Paris were publicized in Istanbul, Ottoman editors and politicians argued that minority rights were already embedded in the 'constitutional' order of the Empire, and nothing further was required. Cemal Paşa's commentary was typical of this line of argumentation: 'I wonder if it is not the greatest model of the principle of 'rights of minorities' which today the American President Wilson has tried to get recognized by the civilized world – the privilege granted by the great Ottoman Sultan in the fifteenth century?'[41] Well before İsmet gave his Lausanne speech on the Ottoman minority rights protection, there was a persistent idea in the press that the new minority rights treaties were derived from Ottoman

40 Newspapers across the political spectrum weighed in on the question of minority rights during the early Armistice period, many of which argued that legal privileges tied to religion were inimical to modern ideas of citizenship. See, for example, Abdurrahman Şeref, 'İmtiyazat-i Mezhebiye', *Sabah*, 9 October 1918, 1.

41 Cemal Paşa, *Hâtırat: 1913–1919*, 1922, 237.

practices, but as İsmet later pointed out that meant they were at odds with new conceptions of state sovereignty. While the Ottomans celebrated Wilson early on as providing the blueprint for equality in international relations, and offering a way to save the Empire, by the summer of 1919 there was increasingly palpable disdain towards Wilson in government commentaries and newspapers, and never more so than in his attempt to take credit for inventing minority rights.

What is important here is that there was initially an open debate about how to solve the problem of European intervention in Ottoman affairs while maintaining the multi-confessional basis of the Empire. But these arguments morphed into a kind of stock repeated answer to reject minority rights in the Republic. İsmet's speech that opened this chapter was representative of an argument that would be made repeatedly at Lausanne and beyond – and used later to deny the Armenian Genocide. The Ottomans invented minority rights protection. As such, robust safeguards for minorities were embedded in the domestic legal order and did not require international oversight.

The Turkish Republic

Just as the first Allied ships anchored in the Bosphorus, Liberals were ascendent in the new political landscape. After the CUP dissolved itself, and the leadership fled Istanbul in the autumn of 1918, Mehmed Münir remained at his post and continued to issue legal opinions for the post-war liberal government. He wrote a particularly important one that served as the blueprint for reorganizing the Ottoman Empire as a series of autonomous provinces, without the privileges once attached to such provinces, in accordance with pre-war ideas shared by members of the Freedom and Accord Party. That legal opinion, which laid claim to all Arab lands currently under European military occupation, functioned as the basis for the Ottoman memoranda to the Paris Peace Conference in 1919.[42] Just like Brest-Litovsk, much of the legal work of diplomacy fell to Mehmed Münir to prepare for Paris.

The logic that connected Mehmed Münir's diverse legal opinions was the problem of sovereignty and the perpetual threat of European intervention in Ottoman affairs. In each of these opinions, Mehmed Münir disavowed an older Ottoman approach to diplomacy and international law that sought to increase Ottoman control over internal and external affairs, but ultimately accommodated European-imposed limitations on sovereignty such as the Capitulations, the Public

42 BOA/HR.HMŞ.İŞO/214/14, 21 October 1918.

Debt Administration, and the internationally guaranteed autonomous provinces (Egypt, Mount Lebanon, Eastern Rumelia, and Crete). Instead, he rejected any limitation on sovereignty. Sovereignty was singular and could not be divided, a radical departure from Ottoman views in the nineteenth century. He argued that the Ottoman state and now emergent Turkey should 'not fail to take advantage of the principles of international law in order to enforce its rights.'[43] While never explicit, the implications were clear. The only reason the Ottomans were back at the negotiating table at Lausanne was that force worked. It mattered more than the Foreign Ministry's old attachment to international law and empty European treaties that had promised to preserve the 'territorial integrity of the Ottoman Empire.'

Mehmed Münir was not alone in this view. During the Armistice period, Ottoman lawyers and intellectuals across a broad political spectrum – those favouring a revived Ottoman Empire composed of autonomous provinces, a Turko-Arab Federation, or a Turkish nation-state – argued that 'privileges' of any sort had to be replaced with a unitary form of citizenship and administration. In early 1920, Mehmed Münir joined İzzet's and Salih Paşa's mission to end the differences between the Ottoman governments in Istanbul and Ankara. Like so many other Ottomans that year, he abandoned the Empire and ditched the Sultan in favour of the nationalists, offering his legal services to the Ankara government.

İsmet's rejection of minority rights protection at Lausanne was matched by an equally vehement dismissal of Allied attempts to create autonomous Kurdish and Armenian zones within in a post-war state, arguments that Mehmed Münir helped craft. From an Ottoman legal perspective, both cases – minority rights treaties and nationally rooted autonomies – appeared indistinguishable from nineteenth-century European interventions.[44] The fight over autonomy was all the more dramatic because the stimulus for Armenian autonomy came from Gabriel Noradungian, the former Chief Legal Adviser to the Foreign Ministry. Noradungian arrived at Lausanne representing Armenian interests within the Republic.[45] In one of the more dramatic episodes at Lausanne, Noradungian requested a meeting with İsmet in order to discuss establishing an autonomous homeland for Armenians in the new Turkey.[46] İsmet unsurprisingly rejected the request.

Before arriving at Lausanne, Noradungian worked in exile, campaigning on behalf of an independent Armenia allotted by the Treaty of Sèvres. He held

43 BOA/HR.HMŞ.İŞO/214/14, 21 October 1918.

44 Ekmekcioglu, 'Republic of Paradox'.

45 See Lerna Ekmekcioglu in this volume.

46 Erkoç, 171–172; Bilal N. Şimşir, *Lozan Telgrafları,* 1990, 192.

meetings with other international lawyers and gave interviews to French newspapers, but also to the new internationalists congregating in Geneva. In September 1922, representing the United Armenian Delegation, Noradungian met with Erik Colban. Colban was a Norwegian international lawyer and the first director of the Minorities Section at the League of Nations.[47] Noradungian wanted to lay out a plan for minority rights protection, and insisted such protections could only work if the new Turkish state also gave Armenians autonomy within Turkey:

> As to the Armenian problem, M. Noradounghian said that minorities protection would, of course, be no real help unless a national home for the Armenians were created. The Armenians as a minority in the Ottoman Empire would have a much better standing if they had to support them the Government of an independent Armenian State.

Colban wrote in French that 'I think that to the contrary that would be a danger for the Armenians, because the Turks would see it as a sign and a threat of having their national territory divided again.'[48] Because the wartime 'massacres and deportations were a means of extermination' and had attracted the attention of the 'civilized world,' Noradungian provided Colban with a list of Kemalist tactics adopted to achieve the same ends. He noted that requisitioning continued against non-Muslims. He complained that they were overtaxed and compelled to repay loans in gold instead of paper currency. Unlawful arrests, the refusal to issue passports and general surveillance of non-Muslims were prevalent. The 'Kemalist tactics' achieved the same end as violence had in wartime: non-Muslims were 'terrorized' into leaving the country.

The second document Noradungian submitted to Colban, and the Minorites Section, was a piece entitled 'Examination of the Issue of Minority Rights.' The paper examined the new minority rights regimes in Bulgaria, Greece and Poland and specific laws created to protect minority rights, especially equality before the law. Noradungian noted protections for minority languages and their use, as well as those for religious, charitable, social, and educational institutions. He argued

47 UNAG/LN R1617/41/23457/807 '"Protection of Minorities in Turkey", Mr. Colban, Record of conversation with M.M. Gabriel Noradounghian and Mikael Papadjanian of the Armenian Delegation on the question of the protection of minorities in the Ottoman Empire, particularly Armenians,' 14 September 1922.

48 UNAG/LN R1617/41/23457/807 'Je crois au contraire que ce serait un danger pour les Armeniens parce que les Turcs y verraient le signe et la menace d'un nouveau partage de leur territoire national'.

that this bundle of rights was the precise set of rights that the Ankara government should provide to non-Muslims remaining in Turkey. He wondered what had happened to the existing 'Religious Privileges' of non-Muslim communities. Noradungian noted that 'European diplomacy never failed to insist on the Ottoman Government's need to grant and guarantee a special status to the (religious) Communities.' He then referred to the Imperial edicts of 1839 and 1856, as well as Article 62 of the Treaty of Berlin (1876), that had promised reform in the Eastern provinces of the Empire. Yet, he argued: 'Today, the Government of Ankara wants to eliminate all the special legislation of Privileges for which no commitment has been stipulated and replace it with the rights of Minorities inserted in the Treaties of the Entente. To European states, it appears that Ankara is making a concession by accepting minority rights, but in reality it was dismantling the ancient rights 'ab antique' that had protected Ottoman non-Muslims.'

We do not know if Mehmed Münir and Gabriel Noradungian met with each other, but they certainly knew that the other was at Lausanne. Mehmed Münir was the heir to the legal world Noradungian had created with İbrahim Hakkı. All of the accommodations with European states, and the arguments marshalled during the Hamidian era to preserve imperial sovereignty served as the foundation of Mehmed Münir's education in international law and his career as a Foreign Ministry lawyer. His legal opinions on the problems of the Capitulations, autonomous provinces and non-Muslim privileges were shaped by reading the legal archive, library, and treaty collections that Noradungian and İbrahim Hakkı had created.

Not only did the Allied powers demand international supervision beyond the terms of the Minority Treaties already hashed out at Paris, but they also demanded other privileges for non-Muslims including exemption from military service and taxation. Unsurprisingly, the Ankara delegation rejected these proposals as incompatible with territorial sovereignty. In an interview with Falih Rifki, Mustafa Kemal (hereafter Atatürk) expressed concern that Britain would establish an autonomous Kurdish region in Mosul, which would inevitably encourage Kurds in the emergent state of Turkey to demand their own autonomous province. While worried about the provisions for an autonomous Kurdistan in the Treaty of Sèvres, Atatürk was looking further back to how the privileged or autonomous provinces had functioned in the late Empire and argued that autonomy was merely a stepping-stone to independence.[49]

49 *Lozan Telegraf*. In the days leading to Lausanne, Refet Bele gave an interview to *The Manchester Guardian* just before Lausanne where he noted: 'Mosul is Turkish and we want it back. Here is England's opportunity. She could win our friendship with one strike if she gave

Europeans saw the same continuities, but simply tried to invent new words and colonial forms to describe them. In the days leading up to the opening of the Lausanne Conference, the Allied delegations agreed that the Capitulations must be retained but noted that the actual word 'Capitulations' should be used as little as possible and perhaps replaced though the substance of them would remain as they were before 1914. The British idea of creating new words for old legal forms that had disadvantaged the Ottoman state before the war was widespread during the Armistice years. For instance, in Egypt, several members of the Milner Mission, dispatched to Cairo 1919 to investigate the Revolution, noted that Egyptians bristled at the word 'protectorate' (*himaye* in Arabic) because the same word was used to 'indicate the protection accorded under traditional usage by Western Powers to subjects of the old Turkish Empire … (the word) thus implies a diminution of sovereignty to Egyptians and has an unwelcome suggestiveness for them, as implying foreign intervention.'[50] This idea was manifested further at Lausanne in discussions about creating autonomous provinces for Armenians and Kurds in the emergent Turkey, where 'autonomy' would now instead be a 'national home' along the lines of the Balfour Declaration. Lord Curzon argued that 'the suggestion of a national home implied no intention to attack the sovereignty of Turkey, to create an *imperium in imperio* or a state within a state, or to set up an autonomous regime.'[51] But of course everyone, especially the Ankara delegation, saw it that way.

Sovereignty without Restrictions

In 1935, Ahmed Reşid, a professor of comparative constitutional law at Istanbul University and a former legal adviser to the Ottoman Foreign Ministry, insisted that the minority rights treaties appended to the treaties concluding the First World War, including those enshrined in Lausanne (1923), had a clear Ottoman genealogy.[52] In the aftermath of the First World War, he retired from politics and dedicated

---

Mosul to us without bargaining. And if she were to give us Mesopotamia as well she would win not only our friendship but that of all Islam.'

50 Aimee M. Genell, 'The End of Egypt's Occupation: Ottoman Sovereignty and the British Declaration of Protection', *Beyond Versailles: Sovereignty, Legitimacy, and the Formation of New Politics after the Great War*, eds. Roberta Pergher and Marcus Payk, 2019.

51 *Lausanne Conference*, 299.

52 Ahmed Réchid [Ahmed Reşid], 'Les droits minoritaires en Turquie dans le passé et le présent', *Revue générale de droit international public*, 1935, 293–341; Ahmed Réchid [Ahmed Reşid], 'L'Islam et le droit des gens,' *Collected Courses of the Hague Academy of International Law / Recueil des Cours* 60, 1937, 371–506.

himself to teaching law, but never lost sight of those old Ottoman preoccupations with shoring up a fragile sovereignty against a rapacious Europe. During the interwar years, he wrote extensively for Turkish and European audiences on the Capitulations and minority rights.[53] In the gloom of the 1930s, when the minority rights treaties were on the brink of failure, he argued that they were not the spontaneous creation of Woodrow Wilson and the diplomats at Paris, designed to solve the problem of nation in place of empire. He noted that the 'international protection of minorities was not imagined, so to speak, from the outset; it was not developed all at once; it is not, finally, the invention of only the victorious Powers of the Great War, acting in this matter under the direction of Wilson.' Minority rights were Ottoman. He pointed out that though Turkey signed up to the minority rights regime dictated by Lausanne, the minority articles were qualitatively different from those in Europe because they protected religious minorities and not ethnic and linguistic minorities. Ultimately the Turkish state, he argued, was fortunate. So many of the new Versailles states failed to manage to assimilate their minorities into post-imperial states because they lacked robust domestic legal institutions to protect all citizens equally without distinction.

The Turkish State entered the negotiations at Lausanne on this basis: 'Whereas the Ottoman Empire has collapsed, the Government of the Grand National Assembly has been organized, and the new Government of Turkey has taken the place of the Ottoman Empire, and inherited its national boundaries.'[54] Despite the theory that the Ottoman Empire had been destroyed, the Ankara delegation had operated with many of the same goals that had animated the wartime government under the CUP: end the Capitulations and other privileges for foreigners, incorporate the remaining autonomous provinces into the regular system of administration, and achieve true equality (not paper equality) in international relations.

53 Ahmed Reşid, 'Kapitülasyonlar,' *Dârülfünûn Hukuk Fakültesi Mecmuası* 6/37, 1928, 1–38; *Hukuku Umumiyei Düvel*, 1928.
54 TBMMZC, XXIV:311, 30 October 1922, Raul Bey.

2

Britain's Plans for a New Eastern Mediterranean Empire, 1916–1923

Erik Goldstein

On 30 October 1918 the Ottoman Empire agreed an armistice with the Allies, ending the Great War in the Eastern Mediterranean. Signed aboard HMS *Agamemnon*, off the Turkish coast at Mudros, the seaborne venue served as a projection of British maritime power. British arms had played the major role in fighting the Ottomans, and Britain was now the dominant power throughout the region. On 13 November British forces landed in Constantinople, despite Admiral Calthorpe, who presided at the signing of the armistice, promising the Ottoman representative that no such action was contemplated.[1] This raises the question as to what were Britain's regional war aims, and its longer-term intentions. Between victory in 1918 and the Chanak crisis of 1922, Britain attempted to fill more of the footprint of the Ottoman Empire than it ultimately did. When the pieces of British policy at the time are assembled, there was something bigger going on than the final outcome indicates. Initially there were grand plans for a vast new British hegemony in the Eastern Mediterranean. Then as the reality of already overstretched imperial resources became evident the initial plans began to be scaled back. The entirely unanticipated vigour of Turkish nationalism which erupted during 1919

1 Nur Bilge Criss, *Istanbul under Allied Occupation 1918–1923*, 1999, 1. Article 7 of the Armistice allowed for the occupation of strategic points, and this was taken as the legal basis for deploying British forces in the city. Soon after other Allied forces also arrived. A full account of the occupation is in CAB 44/39, Brigadier-General Sir James E. Edmonds, 'The Occupation of Constantinople, 1918–1923 (provisional)', Historical Section, War Cabinet Secretariat, 27 September 1944, Cabinet Papers, The National Archives, Kew, London.

forced a further reconsideration of imperial ambitions. By late 1922 the tensions within the British government between the advocates of the earlier imperial ideas and those favouring a more modest regional presence would destroy the ruling coalition that had led Britain to victory in the First World War. The new government that succeeded the coalition would seek to bring this chapter of imperial aspirations to a close at the Lausanne Conference, the last of the post-war peace conferences. For British diplomacy this would be largely an effort to salvage what it could of the earlier grand vision, and to adjust for its failings.

Grand Strategy

Britain had great ambitions in the Eastern Mediterranean and towards the end of the war the Cabinet established an Eastern Committee to give shape to them.[2] As the Eastern Committee met and developed an ever longer list of territories to be added to British rule, Edwin Montagu, the Secretary of State for India, observed 'it would be very satisfactory if we could find some convincing argument for not annexing all the territories in the world.'[3] Nevertheless what evolved was a scheme, entirely in keeping with Britain's imperial traditions, to take control of as much of the region as possible, through a variety of mechanisms. Suitable regional allies were to be developed as proxies for British power. Greece was one such state, intended to become an Aegean power. Client rulers would be supported, such as the Hashemites to control the Arab lands, possibly with the Caliphate being transferred to them to bring wider Muslim support. The Egyptian Khedive, now elevated to be a King, would rule Egypt with the assistance of a British High Commissioner and a British army commander. Finally, groups dependent upon Britain for their existence could be utilized, for example the Jews to colonize and take control of Palestine, and thereby provide both a buffer for the Suez Canal as well as a geographical link between the parts of this new empire. Thus, a vast new region would fall to British control without the necessity of undue direct involvement or expense. This strategy would simultaneously block the ambitions of Britain's traditional rival, France; the increasingly irritating new regional player, Italy; and form a bulwark against any resurgence of Russian interest, in its new Bolshevik guise.

This grand scheme was based on taking advantage of the collapse of the

2 Erik Goldstein, 'British Peace Aims and the Eastern Question: The Political Intelligence Department and the Eastern Committee, 1918', *Middle Eastern Studies* 23/4, 1987, 419–436.
3 CAB 23/42/IWC44, Edwin Montagu, 20 December 1918.

Ottoman Empire, an event long anticipated. In September 1918 the historian C.H. Firth, writing to fellow historian H.A.L. Fisher about political predictions and their accuracy, commented:

> Premature predictions of the fall of the Turkish Empire are responsible for many political & military blunders & began a couple of centuries ago. Burnet quotes the prophecy of Dr Lloyd Bp [Bishop] of Winchester about the end of the Turkish power ... A recent writer has printed a vol. containing a hundred schemes for the partition of Turkey, put forth at different times, all based on similar beliefs (except that Lloyd's was based on studying the Revelations with amazing diligence & exactness).[4]

Ever since Nelson defeated Napoleon's forces at the Battle of the Nile in 1798, Britain had been a growing power in the Eastern Mediterranean, and for some the First World War provided a great opportunity for Britain. On the eve of the Gallipoli landings in 1915, Ronald Storrs, the Oriental Secretary of the British Residency at Cairo, was already speculating that 'a North African or Near Eastern Vice-Royalty including Egypt and the Sudan and across the way from Aden to Alexandretta would surely compare in interest and complexity, if not in actual size, with India itself.'[5] A British dominated Middle East was seen as the critical lynchpin of empire. Colonel Richard Meinertzhagen in preparing material for use at the peace conference recommended 'that the consolidation of our Middle East Empire should form the focus of all our African negotiations, as they protect our communications with India and the East.'[6]

With the end of the war Britain dominated much of the world, including the Middle East and much of the Near East. Britain was a maritime empire and 'since the seventeenth century it had been a principle of British strategy to control the great seaway which flanked the southern edge of Europe.'[7] British maritime strategy had led it to take control of many of the world's Sea Lines of Communication (hereafter SLOC). Such 'choke points' included the Straits of Gibraltar, the waters either side of Malta controlling the routes between the Western and Eastern Mediterranean, and the Bab-el Mandeb Strait between the Red Sea and the Gulf

4 MS. Fisher 63, Firth to Fisher, 17 September 1918, H.A.L. Fisher Papers, Bodleian Library, Oxford.
5 PRO 30/57/47/QQ18, Storrs (Cairo) to Oswald Fitzgerald (Kitchener's private secretary), for Curzon, 8 March 1915, Kitchener Papers, The National Archives, Kew, London.
6 Meinertzhagen Diary, 30 January 1919, Rhodes House Library, Oxford.
7 Piers Mackesy, *The War in the Mediterranean, 1803–1810,* 1957, 4.

of Aden. One of Britain's key strategic assets was the man-made SLOC, the Suez Canal. Britain's involvement in the region had been largely driven, initially, by the objective of securing in depth this critical link between Britain and its vast Indian empire. One of the few SLOCs not under British control were the Turkish Straits at Constantinople. Much of Britain's diplomacy for over a century had been concerned with preventing any other power, especially Russia, gaining control of the Turkish Straits. Now Russia was conveniently pre-occupied with revolution and civil war. The opportunity had arisen either to take control of the Turkish Straits or arrange their future control in a way harmonious to British interests.

Britain in 1918 was the world's one truly global maritime power, one of the coalition of victorious Powers in the First World War, and the largest land power in Asia. The weak spot in its imperial architecture was the region until now dominated by the Ottoman Empire, and with its now almost certain demise the British Empire, and its imperial visionaries, were presented with a tempting opportunity. In the immediate aftermath of victory there was a sense of euphoria and of British invincibility, or perhaps imperial hubris. Britain could now see itself possessing a vast empire stretching from the Middle East to South Asia, with a quasi-sovereign Persia in between. A protectorate was being established over Mesopotamia, the Caspian was in British hands, parts of the Caucasus were occupied by British army divisions, while Egypt, Palestine, and Syria were all under British control. At Constantinople British officials were well established, with the British commander, General Milne, commandeering as his residence the Krupp family villa, as well as the very nice automobile of the deposed Khedive of Egypt.[8] As the Australian prime minister, Billy Hughes, exclaimed at the 1921 Imperial Conference: 'What other worlds have we to conquer? We are like so many Alexanders.'[9] But what were British intentions when it found itself filling much of the footprint of what had once been the Ottoman Empire? British intentions changed over the period in which the Eastern Mediterranean settlement was evolved, from some initially grandiose ideas that when confronted with the reality of the region led to the final interwar settlement at the Lausanne Conference and created the general structure we see there today.

8 FO 371/5179/E2176/363/44, de Robeck (Constantinople) to Foreign Office, 24 March 1920, Foreign Office Papers, The National Archives, Kew, London.
9 CAB 32/2, Minutes of Imperial Conference, 2nd meeting, 21 June 1921.

Religion and Empire

In 1919 Britain was the largest empire the world has seen, before or since, and it was an empire of many identities. A key aspect of its identity, especially when considering this region, was religion. Britain was variously a Christian empire, the largest Muslim state, and since the Balfour Declaration had even become the protector of the Jews. A deep sense of mission played an important role in the thinking of key figures who helped shape British foreign and imperial policy. Many who served the British Empire were clear on the issue of imperial identity – it was a Christian empire. Sir Arthur Hirtzel of the India Office, in a pamphlet published in 1919, stated his belief that: 'The Empire … has been given to us as a means to that great end for which Christ came into the world, the redemption of the human race. That is to say, it has been given to us to make it Christian. This is to be Britain's contribution to the redemption of mankind.'[10] When news reached Britain that its forces had entered Jerusalem, church bells were rung spontaneously across the country, and *Punch* published an illustration of King Richard the Lionheart looking down upon the city, with the caption 'My dream comes true!'[11] The last public appearance in 1921 of the famous Liberal politician and diplomat Lord Bryce was at a meeting calling for the liberation of Christians from Turkish rule.[12]

In 1918, with the prospect looming of British control of Constantinople, a committee was established in London to lobby for the restoration to Christianity of the Hagia Sophia, once the greatest church in Christendom, but since 1453 a mosque. The St. Sophia Redemption Committee was formed 'for the purpose of taking any action that might be necessary to ensure that this Church be restored to Christendom.'[13] The committee was chaired by Bryce, with the future foreign secretary Sir Samuel Hoare as treasurer, and another future Foreign Secretary, Edward Wood MP (later Lord Halifax) as a member. This movement's supporters dreamt of the 'potentiality of Intercommunion between England and the Eastern Church, which would be the almost certain prelude to complete Christian reunion were a Pan-Orthodox Council summoned to meet in a St. Sophia redeemed by

10 Sir Arthur Hirtzel. *The Church, The Empire, and The World*, 1919. Sir Arthur Hirtzel (1870–1937). Entered the India Office, 1894; Secretary, Political Dept., 1909–1917; Assistant Under-Secretary, 1917–1921; Deputy Under-Secretary, 1921–1924; Permanent Under-Secretary, 1924–1930.

11 *Punch*, 19 December 1917, 415.

12 'A Million Christians Massacred', *The Times,* 13 December 1921, 5

13 Templewood Part I, File 8, 'S. Sophia Redemption Committee: Report', 3 January 1919, Templewood (Sir Samuel Hoare) Papers, Cambridge University Library.

British arms.'[14] The St. Sophia Redemption Committee enjoyed support from Foreign Office officials, the idea having been initially prompted by the Foreign Office Librarian, in effect the Office's chief researcher, Stephen Gaselee.[15] One of the supporters of the plan was the official responsible for preparing Britain's brief for the Paris Peace conference in respect of the Ottoman Empire, Arnold Toynbee, then of the Political Intelligence Department, who advised that, 'C'ple is not a Moslem Holy City, nor S. Sofia a Moslem Holy Place … it might savour of undue timidity to decide such a case as S. Sofia against the Orthodox Church, and might even lower our prestige with our Moslem subjects, who would attribute our policy to fear.'[16] Though Toynbee would later change his views on the region, at the time he was known as the author of the wartime agitprop book, *The Murderous Tyranny of the Turk*.[17]

Many figures in British government circles though were concerned about the impact that would result if Britain was seen as having destroyed the world's largest Muslim state, the ruler of which was not only the Sultan but also the Caliph ul-Islam. Lloyd George undoubtedly startled his colleagues at the Paris Peace Conference when he once announced that he sat there as the representative of 'the greatest Mohammedan power.'[18] The British Empire's Muslim population was estimated at 80 million, and by its acquisitions in the Middle East this position had been further enhanced, and Britain's relations with the world of Islam would prove to be a critical question in the shaping of its future role in this part of the world

Anything relating to the Muslim world was of concern to the British Empire, and especially the India Office, which ever since the Indian mutiny had feared a reawakening of anti-British Muslim sentiment. Sir Eyre Crowe, of the Foreign

---

14 J.A. Douglas, 'The Redemption of S. Sophia', *The Treasury*, 1919, 368. See Erik Goldstein, 'Holy Wisdom and British Foreign Policy, 1918–1922: the St. Sophia Redemption Agitation', *Byzantine and Modern Greek Studies* 15, 1991, 36–64; and Erik Goldstein, 'Redeeming Holy Wisdom: Britain and St. Sophia', ed. Melanie Hall, *Towards World Heritage: International Origins of the Preservation Movement, 1870–1930*, 2011, 45–62.

15 Stephen Gaselee (1882–1943), temporarily employed at the Foreign Office, 1916–1919, was himself an orientalist of note, having begun by teaching himself Coptic while still at school. A deeply religious individual, he had considered taking Anglican orders. In 1920 he was made Librarian and Keeper of the Records at the Foreign Office, serving until his death.

16 FO 371/3417/f192762/196919, Minute by Toynbee, 5 December 1918.

17 Arnold Toynbee, *The Murderous Tyranny of the Turks*, 1917, published with a preface by Lord Bryce. At the time of publication Toynbee was employed in the Department of Information's Intelligence Bureau.

18 Meeting of the Council of Four, 21 May 1919, *Foreign Relations of the United States: Paris Peace Conference*, Vol. 5, 1946, 756.

Office and soon to be its permanent under-secretary, noted with disdain in late 1918: 'The govt. of India see red when the word Moslem is mentioned.'[19] It was thought that the Sultan by combining in his person the office of Caliph made him a more potent force in the Muslim world. Indeed, in November 1914 the Sultan had proclaimed a holy war (*jihad*) against the Allies, and a Khilafat movement in India during the war had been seen as a threat to the *raj*. Although the power of Pan-Islamism proved to be greater in the minds of British officialdom than among the Muslims of the empire, the issue of the future of the office of Caliph attracted a great deal of British attention.[20] Although the issue was largely forgotten after the Caliphate's abolition in 1924, it would re-emerge as a force in the early twenty-first century, indicating that there was latent power in the title.

In discussions over the future of Constantinople, serious consideration was given to moving the Sultan's seat to Anatolia. If this were done it would have left the Ecumenical Patriarch as the leading religious figure in Constantinople, perhaps with Hagia Sophia once again a church. There was trepidation that Britain's Muslim subjects would be angered by what might be seen as Britain colluding in the mistreatment of the Caliph. Memories of the Indian mutiny were ever present. Therefore, having a Caliph who was congenial to Britain, with its vast Muslim population, was an important policy objective. Admiral Webb, the Assistant High Commissioner at Constantinople, observed in 1919 to Ronald Graham, head of the Foreign Office's Eastern Department: 'With the Caliph under our hand we have an enormous added control over the Moslem world, but with the Caliph estranged or actively hostile our task in Mesopotamia, Syria, & Arabia would be enormously increased.'[21]

One solution considered was moving the Caliphate to a suitable alternative candidate. This was not a new idea. As early as the 1870s, the idea was being suggested in Britain that the Caliphate should cease to be Ottoman and returned to Mecca, and placed in the hands of Sharif Hussein, the Emir of Mecca. The Emir was the head of the Hashemite family, one of the branches of the wider house to which the Prophet Mohammed belonged. It was also noted that his geographical location would place him 'as completely in our power as the Suez Canal.'[22]

19 FO 371/3417/192762/200096, Minute by Crowe, 7 December 1918.

20 On the failure of the effort at *jihad* see Erik-Jan Zürcher, ed. *Jihad and Islam in World War I: Studies on the Ottoman Jihad on the Centenary of Snouck Hurgronje's 'Holy War Made in Germany'*, 2016, and on its impact in India see Gail Minault, *The Khilafat Movement: Religious Symbolism and Political Mobilization in India*, 1982.

21 FO 371/4164/f707/19127, Adm. Webb to R. Graham, 19 January 1919.

22 George Birdwood, 'Indian and Turkish Mahomedans' (letter), *The Times*, 12 June 1877, 8.

Wilfrid Blunt, a pro-Arab and anti-Ottoman former diplomat and writer, in advocating such a development, made clear that such a Caliphate 'must be taken under British protection.'[23] These ideas, therefore, had been circulating for several decades when, during the war, Field Marshal Kitchener, the Secretary of State for War, recently returned from his post as Proconsul in Egypt, raised the transfer of the Caliphate to Sharif Hussein, who was now emerging as a British ally. Arthur Hirtzel, though, warned of combining the Islamic authority and Arab identity arguing that 'a strong Arab State might be more dangerous to Christendom than a strong Ottoman State, and Lord Kitchener's policy of destroying one Islamic State merely for the purpose of creating another, has always seemed to me disastrous, from the point of view no less of expediency than of civilization.'[24]

In support of the idea of a Hashemite Caliph were General Allenby, at the time the High Commissioner in Cairo and the regional military commander, and Robert Vansittart, a future Foreign Office permanent under-secretary and the diplomat most involved in the Eastern settlement. Vansittart commented that the head of the Hashemite clan 'Husein is not popular of course, partly because we made him. But as we made him we've got to stick to him. Strength is the only thing they appreciate in the East, and if we were weak enough to let our man go under we shd. lose more than by seeing him through in spite of his unpopularity. The whole of our prestige is at stake.'[25] The Hashemites themselves had been promoting just such a plan. British interest waned for a period during 1919, when relations briefly soured with Hussein and the Hashemites, but the utility of the idea kept appearing among the policy options.[26] In November 1920 Hubert Young, who had recently joined the Foreign Office's Eastern Department, after having served extensively with the army in the Middle East during the war, advised that 'the Sultan has become an insignificant person temporally and will soon lose any spiritual halo he may have acquired, especially if the temporal position of the Sheriff of Mecca is enhanced. This should be the first aim of our policy now, and I think, as I suggested at the last Palestine Committee meeting, that we have in a

23 Wilfrid Scawen Blunt, *The Future of Islam*, 1882, 204. On the British pre-war thinking on the Caliphate see Ş. Tufan Buzpinar, 'Opposition to the Ottoman Caliphate in the Early Years of Abdülhamid II: 1877–1882', *Die Welt des Islams* 36/1, 1996, 59–89.

24 L/P&S/586 P705, Minute by Hirtzel, 23 February 1916, India Office Records, British Library.

25 FO 608/80/342/2/8/13141, Minute by Vansittart, 19 June 1919.

26 In March 1924, two days after Turkey abolished the Caliphate, Hussein proclaimed himself Caliph, but not long after was driven into exile by Ibn Saud, though he continued to use the title.

possible Arab Caliph a most potent argument to set against French obstinacy on the boundary question.'[27] Regardless of the Hashemite gambit Lord Curzon and Lord Hardinge, both former Viceroys, were as Hardinge explained 'strongly of the opinion that it is very desirable to get the Turks out of Constantinople and thus to inflict a severe blow on the prestige of the Sultan which may in the long run lose him the Caliphate and will be a severe blow to Pan-Islamism, which those who know must realise is a most serious danger in India. Now is the time to grasp the nettle firmly.'[28]

The unanticipated rise of the Turkish Nationalist movement under Kemal (hereafter Atatürk) caused more moderate, and less avaricious, plans to be proposed. It took time for such options to emerge, as initially there was a widespread belief that Atatürk was a mere pawn of the Bolsheviks. There was a received view that the Turks could not be as capable as Atatürk's forces were proving unless they were receiving covert assistance.[29] The rise of the Turkish Nationalists meant that London now needed the Sultan at Constantinople as a legitimizing figurehead to provide an alternative to this new force. In 1921, in connection with the possibility of negotiating with the Nationalists, and seeing an end of the Ottoman dynasty, Sir Horace Rumbold, the British High Commissioner at Constantinople, reported his view that: 'In the Islamic world generally, we might easily be represented as having been parties to the overthrow of a Caliph, and the success of our present endeavours to conciliate Moslem opinion might be a good deal impaired.'[30] The India Office for its part argued for the need to keep Muslim opinion calm by retaining the Sultan in Constantinople. In the end it was the British who became the chief support for the weakened Sultan-Caliph, in the face of the rising Kemalist nationalist tide.

27 FO 371/5187/E13653/498/44, Minute by H.W. Young, 4 November 1920. Hubert Winthrop Young (1885–1950) was an Indian Army officer, who joined the Foreign Office in 1919 to work on Middle Eastern matters. He moved to the Colonial Office's new Middle Eastern Dept. as an Assistant Secretary, 1921–1926, and later served as Counsellor to the High Commissioner for Iraq, 1929–1932, and briefly as Envoy to Iraq, 1932.

28 Hardinge Vol. 41, Hardinge to Hohler, 15 December 1919, Hardinge of Penshurst Papers, University Library, Cambridge.

29 Alp Yenen, 'Elusive Forces in Illusive Eyes: British Officialdom's Perceptions of the Anatolian Resistance Movement', *Middle Eastern Studies* 54/5, 2018, 788–810.

30 MS. Rumbold dep. 29, Rumbold to Curzon, 10 December 1921, Sir Horace Rumbold Papers, Bodleian Library, Oxford.

Phobias

Francophobia was endemic in policymaking circles, and there was widespread agreement on the need to prevent France obtaining any presence in the region. Curzon's assessment of France was becoming increasingly acerbic, and is evident in his view of the post-Ottoman world:

> A good deal of my public life has been spent in connection with the political ambitions of France, which I have come across in Tunis, Siam, and in almost every distant region where the French have sway. We have been brought, for reasons of national safety, into an alliance with the French, which I hope will last, but their national character is different from ours, and their political interests collide with ours in many cases. I am seriously afraid that the great Power from whom we may have most to fear in the future is France, and I almost shudder at the possibility of putting France in such a position. She is powerful in almost all parts of the world, even around India … the French are born intriguers, as we have seen in the Lebanon and elsewhere. I can only say that I should be most reluctant to lend a hand to a scheme which would place France in a position of authority in this region.[31]

Sir Louis Mallet, the last British ambassador to the Porte, commented that if France received Syria and, as a result, controlled Alexandretta, 'she will be astride the land communications between Great Britain and the British Empire in the East.'[32] He advised that the objective should be to keep the region free of French intrigue.

In discussing the future plans for the still uncompleted Baghdad railway, during a very full discussion in the British delegation at Paris in February 1919, it was decided unanimously to oppose any non-British involvement as '[it] would be used by other nations to retain a political footing in our sphere … We might be forced, contrary to our political and strategic interests, to adopt alignments of which we did not approve.' It was concluded that:

> British interests cannot therefore be adequately safeguarded on the left flank of India unless the entire frontier of the territory under British control is pushed northward considerably beyond anything contemplated in the Sykes-Picot Agreement in order to afford adequate cover for the pipeline and lateral

31 CAB 27/24/EC 40.

32 FO 608/116/385/2/2/4605, Minute by Mallet, 17 January 1919.

> railway communication from Baghdad to the Mediterranean coast to connect with Egypt.[33]

There was little desire to be bound to France in any way in this part of the world, and this led to Britain seeking to exclude France from the region. Lloyd George's nimble diplomacy in seeking to avoid a French zone in Anatolia finally led Clemenceau to exclaim in exasperation that 'Lloyd George is a cheat.'[34] In a meeting of the Council of Four on 21 May 1919 Clemenceau, believing that Britain was going to renege on a commitment for a French zone in Anatolia, in what must be the nadir of Anglo-French relations, challenged the British prime minister to a duel.[35]

Anglo-French relations as to the future of the region continued to deteriorate. In February 1920 the French General Louis Franchet d'Espèrey, Commander of the Allied Army of the Orient, landed at Constantinople and commandeered Enver Pasha's palace at Ortaköy (Ortakeui), on the Bosphorus, as his residence. A false story has become current, probably starting in 1960 and since then oft repeated, that claims Franchet d'Espèrey entered Constantinople riding a white horse, emulating Mehmed the Conqueror's entry in 1453.[36] Franchet d'Espèrey's arrival certainly caused great consternation among the British, and uneasiness as to French intentions. The War Office cabled Cairo urgently requesting more troops for deployment at Constantinople, explaining that 'it is essential that General Milne should have under his command sufficient British troops to make him independent of Franchet D'Espèrey, who for months has been intriguing to oust us from the effective control of the situation in the city.'[37] Soon after the Royal Navy deployed eight battleships to the Turkish Straits and the Commander-in-Chief Mediterranean prepared to land 2,000 men.[38] This had the desired impact

33 FO 608/38/342/8/4/4393, Meeting of Middle East Section of the British Empire Delegation, Paris, 15 February 1919. The pipeline was of interest to the Royal Navy to help assure an oil supply.

34 Raymond Poincaré, *Au Service de la France*, Vol XI, À la récherche de la paix (Paris, 1974), 245. Entry for 14 March 1919.

35 Christopher M. Andrew and A.S. Kanya-Forstner, *France Overseas*: *The Great War and the Climax of French Imperial Expansion*, 1981, 197.

36 A full account of the story is given by Edhem Eldem, 'De quelle couleur était le cheval blanc de Franchet d'Espèrey? Petite enquête sur la vérité historique', *De Samarcande à Istanbul: étapes orientales. Hommages á Pierre Chuvin,* ed. Véronique Schiltz, 2015, 285–301.

37 FO 371/5043/E1531/3/44, War Office to G.H.Q. Egypt (repeated to G.H.Q. Constantinople), 10 March 1920.

38 FO 371/5043/E1549/3/44, Commander-in-Chief (Mediterranean), afloat, to Admiralty, 10 March 1920.

on Franchet d'Espèrey's plans as 'practically, he was excluded from command in Constantinople,' and left in March.[39]

In thinking about the settlement, to compound the presence of francophobia, there was a long tradition of anti-Turkish sentiment in Britain. Gladstone had campaigned against Turkish rule during the Bulgarian atrocities agitation of the 1870s, becoming associated with the phrase for the removal of Turkish rule 'bag and baggage'.[40] During the war the Earl of Cromer, the former British Proconsul in Egypt, stated that in his opinion: 'We are fighting in order that the Turkish hordes, who for five hundred years have camped in Europe, should be driven back into Asia', though adding that it had to be recalled that Britain was 'a great Mohammedan Power.'[41] The Foreign Office's historical adviser, G.W. Prothero, who was also editor of the influential *Quarterly Review*, publicly expressed the view that the Ottoman Empire was 'an anachronism and a monstrosity in Europe.'[42] In 1919 Hardinge, the permanent under-secretary at the Foreign Office, observed that 'here in this Office, we hold very strongly that the moment is opportune for turning the Turk out of Europe.'[43] Crowe was all for the Turks' total ouster from Europe, observing that 'the policy of allowing the Turk to remain in Europe is so contrary to our most important interests and so certain to involve the continuance of all the abomination associated with the Turks, that we cannot afford to treat this as a matter of just humouring Moslem feelings.'[44] Curzon, though sensitive to the needs of the Indian Empire, and of Britain's Muslim subjects was also unhappy with any continuance of Turkish rule in continental Europe. In December 1919 he advised the Cabinet that 'if it were necessary to make concessions to Moslem and Indian sentiment, he would transfer the capital of Turkey to Asia Minor and leave the Sultan in a 'Vatican on the Straits.''[45]

Churchill supported a similar plan, that would have made Constantinople a

39 CAB 44/39, 10.

40 William Gladstone, *Bulgarian Horrors and the Question of the East*, 1876, 62, had called for the Turks to be removed 'bag and baggage'. It is probable that in what was an ambiguous statement, Gladstone meant only the removal of the Turkish ruling population from Bulgaria, but it soon became understood to mean from Europe. On this question see John P. Rossi, 'The Transformation of the British Liberal Party: A Study of the Tactics of the Liberal Opposition, 1874–1880', *Transactions of the American Philosophical Society* 68/8, 1978, especially pp. 31–38; and Richard Shannon, *Gladstone and the Bulgarian Agitation, 1872*, 2nd ed., 1975.

41 Earl of Cromer, *Germania Contra Mundum*, 1915, 13.

42 G.W. Prothero, *A Lasting Peace*, London, 1917, 34.

43 Hardinge Vol. 41, Hardinge to Hohler, 15 December 1919.

44 FO 608/52/120/1/3/316, Minute by Crowe, 22 January 1919.

45 CAB 23/44B, Cabinet 12 (19) A, 10 December 1919.

League of Nations-run city. Churchill was becoming concerned with the logistical overstretch of British forces (as would later governments that opted to engage and deploy in this region) and, as long as a way could be found to keep Russia bottled up, Constantinople ceased to be a necessity for Britain to hold. As Churchill told his Cabinet colleagues, 'I know it will be found very hard to relinquish the satisfaction of those dreams of conquest and aggrandisement which are gratified by the retention of Palestine and Mesopotamia.'[46] This marks the first shift in thinking that Britain could not keep it all. Curzon was another early voice warning that the Ottoman Turkey might not be entirely down and out, arguing in April 1919 that plans for the partition of Anatolia were meant not only 'to decapitate the Turk, but to cut up and appropriate his corpse. It is more than likely that the body will decline to be treated as a corpse at all.'[47]

At an important meeting of British cabinet ministers at the Paris Peace Conference in May 1919, just as the Greeks were about to occupy Smyrna, the Prime Minister announced that the Council of Four had been forced to abandon provisional proposals to divide Anatolia into a number of areas which would be held as mandates by the Great Powers. Britain had mixed motives in supporting this decision. Partly it was the Curzon school of argument, but equally it was apprehension about allowing any expansion of French power or the enhancement of Italian power, which is what had prompted sending the Greek forces to Smyrna.

Constantinople and European Turkey were another matter. Balfour expressed the view that 'he would turn the Turk altogether out of Constantinople, and he was in favour of leaving the Greeks in Smyrna.' George Barnes, the Labour Party member of the British Peace Delegation at Paris, 'said that he was not an expert on the subject but he felt a bias in favour of turning the Turks out of Constantinople'. Curzon explained:

> … that he had no desire whatever to deal gently with the Turks. The Turks had voluntarily sided with Germany; they had treated our prisoners with unexampled barbarity; they had massacred hundreds of thousands of their own subjects. They therefore deserved any fate which was inflicted upon them. He thought that they should be deprived of all their outlying provinces, that is to say Arabia, Mesopotamia, Palestine, Syria and Armenia. He was further in favour of their being turned out of Constantinople … Above all

46 Churchill, Memorandum, 25 October 1919, in Martin Gilbert, *Winston S. Churchill*, Vol. 4, *Companion*, Part 2, 1978.
47 FO 608/83/342/8/4/7919, Memorandum by Curzon, 11 April 1919.

> unless we turned the Turks out of Constantinople the East would never believe that the Turks had been defeated in the war. The presence of the Turk in Constantinople was an outward and visible sign of his dominance.[48]

So who was going to replace the Turks in the areas where Britain did not want a direct role?

Proxies of Empire

One answer to the question of who could act as a proxy for Britain was to rely on the Greeks, or to be more accurate one Greek, Eleftherios Venizelos. The Greek Premier was seen as a figure of stability in a notoriously unstable region. During the war he had proven a reliable friend to the Allied cause, while also being an effective champion of Greece's territorial ambitions. Even before the war the British Prime Minister, H.H. Asquith, had considered Venizelos to be 'the most capable man in Eastern Europe.'[49] Lord Riddell, one of Lloyd George's closest confidants, rated him as one of the six greatest men in the world, ranking with Woodrow Wilson, Lloyd George, Clemenceau, Marshal Foch, and General Botha.[50] When Allen Leeper of the Foreign Office's Political Intelligence Department received an invitation to dine with Venizelos during the Paris Peace Conference, he wrote excitedly to his brother 'I've at last got Veniselos's autograph'.[51] Lloyd George dined often with Venizelos during the Paris Peace Conference and, after one such encounter, Lloyd George's secretary noted: 'The two have a great admiration for each other, & D [avid Lloyd George] is trying to get Smyrna for the Greeks.'[52] Greece had become one of Britain's most favoured allies, in part due to Venizelos' adroit diplomacy, but also based on strong philhellenic sentiments in London.[53] Beyond sentiment was the regional power reality, with Britain establishing its

48 CAB 23/44B, Meeting of ministers held at Rue Nitot, 19 May 1919, with papers from CAB 23/35 'S' Minutes.

49 Asquith to Venetia Stanley, 11 August 1914. *H.H. Asquith: Letters to Venetia Stanley*, eds. Michael and Eleanor Brock, 1982, 165.

50 Lord Riddell, *Lord Riddell's Diary of the Peace Conference and After, 1918–1923*, 1933, 6–7.

51 A.W.A. Leeper to R.W.A. Leeper, 19 May 1919. A.W.A. Leeper Papers, now at Churchill Archive Centre, Cambridge.

52 *Lloyd George: A diary, by Frances Stevenson*, ed. A.J.P. Taylor, 1971, 183, entry for 8 May 1919.

53 Erik Goldstein, 'Great Britain and Greater Greece, 1917–20', *Historical Journal* 32/3, 1989, 339–356.

networks behind the scenes. The British diplomat Harold Nicolson, who was negotiating for a British base at Suda Bay on Crete, informed General Groves 'that the Greek Ministry of Marine is very much under our control.'[54]

In May 1919 Lloyd George was able to persuade Clemenceau and Wilson to support Greece occupying Smyrna, in order to pre-empt a possible Italian seizure of this key port. The Royal Navy provided cover for the Greek landings in Anatolia, and the road seemed open to Greece controlling the shores of the Aegean. It was this action that sparked a Turkish nationalist revival led by Atatürk, who established his headquarters far from the reach of sea-power, in the middle of Anatolia, at Ankara. In the long running Anglo-French rivalry in the Eastern Mediterranean, it was not long before Paris had established relations with the Turkish Nationalists, while London remained loyal to Venizelist Greece. The British journalist Sisley Huddleston observed of this development that 'the British adopted the notion of making the Greeks their soldiers in the East.'[55]

Control of Palestine was among British ambitions, largely to add to the security buffer around the Suez Canal. The 1917 Balfour Declaration had, in its sixty-seven words, committed Britain to support for a Jewish home there.[56] Britain as a maritime empire sought direct control of a narrow coastal mandate, with indirect control of an Arab administered trans-Jordanian hinterland. The concept of a vaguely defined national 'home' for the Jewish people suited multiple British interests. Just as an enlarged Greek state was to act as a regional supporter of British interests in the Near East, many favoured in the Middle East a similar role for the Jews, though some looked more favourably on the newly emergent Arabs. This was the beginning of a tactical dilemma and debate that would bedevil British diplomacy in the region for decades to follow.

Lloyd George liked the idea of supporting smaller nationalities, at one point declaring: 'I am a believer in little nations. I have the honour to belong to one myself.'[57] The Welsh speaking British Prime Minister was not just being sentimental, but also pragmatic, as there was a place for Palestine in imperial defence.

54 Groves to Trenchard, 30 July 1919, P.R.C. Groves Papers, Liddell Hart Centre for Military Archives, King's College, London. At the time Groves was the Air Ministry representative at the Paris conference, and Trenchard was the Chief of the Air Staff.

55 Sisley Huddleston, 'France and Turkey', *Eastern Europe* 5/2, 1921, 103–108.

56 Jonathan Schneer, *The Balfour Declaration*, 2010.

57 Speech to the Inter-Allied Balkan Conference in 1917, quoted in Hugh and Christopher Seton-Watson, *The Making of a New Europe: R.W. Seton-Watson and the Last Years of Austria-Hungary*, 1981, 224.

Among British policymakers, there is a discernible school of strategical Zionists.[58] One of the most consistent of these was Winston Churchill, who in 1908 had stated: 'The establishment of a strong, free Jewish state astride the bridge between Europe and Africa, flanking the land roads to the East, would not only be an immense advantage to the British Empire, but a notable step towards the harmonious disposition of the world among its peoples.'[59] During the war there emerged a strong lobby in favour of a British-controlled Jewish colony in Palestine, for strategic reasons. It could be argued that the strategic imperative may have become infused with the exponents of Christian ideas of empire to support a return of the Jews to Palestine. Balfour told a friend: 'My personal hope is that the Jews will make good in Palestine and eventually found a Jewish State.'[60] Zionism was seen as in the interests of the British Empire. Amery noted in his diary in July 1917: 'Our ultimate end is clearly to make Palestine the centre of western influence, using the Jews as we have used the Scots, to carry the English ideal through the Middle East and not merely to make an artificial oriental Hebrew enclave in an oriental country.'[61] Such a colony would help to block France and simultaneously safeguard the Suez Canal. As he observed, 'I was keen on … establishing in Palestine a prosperous community bound to Britain by ties of gratitude and interest.'[62]

Some did voice concerns, among them Curzon who told a Cabinet committee in December 1918: 'They now talk about a Jewish State. The Arab portion of the population is well-nigh forgotten and is to be ignored. They not only claim the boundaries of the old Palestine, but they claim to spread across the Jordan into the rich countries lying to the east, and indeed, there seems to be very small limit to the aspirations which they now form.'[63] Curzon was uneasy that the scope of Zionist ambitions might jeopardize Britain's position. His view, which he imparted to Balfour in January 1919, was that Britain should preserve 'all we have won'. In this Curzon was supported by Allenby and Sir Alfred Money, chief

58 Wm. Roger Louis, *In the Name of God Go!: Leo Amery and the British Empire in the Age of Churchill*, 1992, 72–73. Amery later candidly admitted that his Zionism was strategical in origin.

59 Quoted in Roger Hyam, 'Churchill and the British Empire', eds. Robert Blake and Wm. Roger Louis, *Churchill*, 1983, 171.

60 Quoted in Howard Sachar, *A History of Israel from the Rise of Zionism to Our Time*, 1976, 110.

61 Amery Diary, 26 July 1917, quoted in Louis, *Amery*, 22.

62 Leo Amery, *My Political Life*, Vol. II, 1953, 15.

63 CAB 27/24/EC41, Curzon to the Eastern Committee, 5 December 1918.

administrator in Palestine, who both advised that Britain 'should go slow about Zionist aspirations and the Zionist state.'[64]

Britain in the immediate aftermath of the war retained its wider ambitions. It controlled Syria, and was at first reluctant to allow France its promised role there. Britain only evacuated Syria in the autumn of 1919 after it was clear that President Wilson was in deep political trouble domestically, and that the hoped-for closer working relationship with the United States could not be relied upon. It was then that it became more important not to estrange France over Syria. Keeping control of its prospective new empire was proving increasingly problematic. Britain had fought a difficult campaign to take control of Iraq, or as it was known to the biblically and classically minded officials 'Mesopotamia', or as it was referred to by the military, 'Mespot'.[65] British interests here were related to oil, a strategic resource essential for the Royal Navy. Control of post-Ottoman oilfields would avoid dependence for oil on the United States, which had embarked on building what was envisioned to be 'incomparably the greatest navy in the world.'[66] The borders of Mesopotamia were drawn to reflect these interests, and not the ethnic and sectarian realities on the ground.

The region, though, proved a hard area to govern, as the Ottomans had discovered, and concerns were expressed about the possible expense of maintaining control. Churchill proposed an experiment in high technology imperial control, by relying on the new Royal Air Force. Hardinge was a bit puzzled by this, writing in January 1920 to Curzon that Churchill's 'scheme for retaining control of Mosul by aeroplanes without any lines of communication, strikes me as unpracticable and frightfully expensive. I imagine the reason for retaining Mosul is on account of oil there. Is he going to carry the oil in aeroplanes? If not, there must either be tank-boats or pipelines, both of which are extremely vulnerable.'[67] It might be seen as a Churchillian flight of fancy, but Churchill was deeply involved with plans for the region as Secretary of State for War and Air, 1918–1921, and then as Colonial Secretary, 1921–1922. While his name is often associated with what proved to be the disastrous 1915–1916 Gallipoli campaign, conducted while he was First Lord of the Admiralty, it is worth recalling that his object in launching that operation

64 FO 800/215, f. 91, Curzon to Balfour, 16 January 1919.

65 On the British campaign see Charles Townshend, *Desert Hell: The British Invasion of Mesopotamia*, 2011.

66 President Wilson made this pledge in a public address at St. Louis, 3 February 1916, which was followed by the 1916 Navy Bill to fund a massive expansion of the US Navy, causing concern in London that a naval arms competition might ensue.

67 Hardinge Vol. 44, Hardinge to Curzon, 15 January 1921.

was to take Constantinople and to establish British control of the Turkish Straits. One of his first actions as Colonial Secretary was to summon the Cairo Conference to work out the framework of British control of the region.

The Allies presented a peace treaty to the representatives of the Sultan's government in the summer of 1920. On 10 August 1920 the Treaty of Sèvres was signed, intended as the last of the series of treaties officially ending the First World War. By its terms, Greece received significant territorial gains in Thrace and Asia Minor, and the Ottoman Empire's Arab provinces became League of Nations Mandates, ultimately to be controlled by Britain and France. The Nationalist government at Ankara denounced the Treaty, and the Constantinople government never dared to ratify the settlement. Events in the region were suddenly once again in flux and British ambitions were beginning to confront a dramatic reversal of fortune.[68]

End of the Imperial Vision

By late 1920 the grand vision of a new British Eastern Mediterranean empire was dissolving. In Greece the unexpected death in October 1920 of King Alexander, after being bitten by a pet monkey, initiated a totally unanticipated chain of events that culminated in the fall of Venizelos' government in November and the return of King Constantine. Venizelos had been key to British plans, although some had warned of the danger of pinning too much on one individual. Admiral de Roebuck at Constantinople observed: 'I cannot help wondering if the game is worth the candle. I should wonder, even if M. Veniselos were immortal; he is not immortal, but ephemeral, and he is not only ephemeral, but as regards Greece, a phenomenon.'[69] As events unfolded, as far as British plans were concerned, the Venizelist moment did prove ephemeral. Constantine was deeply distrusted by London which responded to his restoration by withdrawing vital British support for the Greek military effort in Anatolia, in the vain hope of forcing Venizelos' return to power. During the summer of 1921 the Greek advance into Anatolia was halted by the Turkish Nationalists, and what began as an orderly retreat soon became a rout. The events that followed came to be known in Greece simply as the 'Catastrophe'. At the end of September 1922, King Constantine abdicated and power passed to a military junta. Lloyd George to the very end of his government

68 The Foreign Office would later prepare a useful memorandum, 'Comparison of the Sèvres Treaty with last draft of Lausanne Treaty', 16 June 1923, FO 371/9083/E6330/1/44.
69 Admiral de Roebuck to Curzon, 9 March 1920, document no. 17, *Documents on British Foreign Policy, 1919–1939*, 1st series, Vol. 13, eds. Rohan Butler and J.P.T. Bury, 1962, 18.

hoped the original scheme could be saved, and when he heard of Constantine's downfall he thought 'it just possible God may now take a hand' and yet salvage British aspirations in the region.[70]

It was a last ditch effort to keep control of the Dardanelles that brought down the Lloyd George government. Britain now stood as the only power blocking the Nationalists from Constantinople and Turkish unification. In September most French and Italian forces had left Constantinople. As British plans began to collapse, France had moved rapidly to establish good relations with Atatürk, and so bolster its position in the region.[71] Italy, alienated ever since Britain had failed to support its territorial demands at the Paris Peace Conference, was in the midst of the political crisis that would see Mussolini become Premier at the end of October. Britain's comparatively small force at Chanak (Çanakkale) was now the key to maintaining its position at Constantinople and control of the Turkish Straits. It was soon confronted by the arrival of Nationalist forces.

Within the Cabinet there was a faction advocating using force, if necessary, to stop the loss of this strategic sea-lane, and to rescue what remained of Britain's wider regional aspirations. This group included Lloyd George and Churchill. The latter's view came as little surprise to Lord Hardinge, now ambassador at Paris, who commented: 'he always advocates expeditions and military operations which end in failure.'[72] The General Staff indeed was convinced that any such effort would result in defeat. Britain turned to the Dominions to bolster its military capacity, but found no support. In the end it was a test of empire unity, which failed, just as it was a test of the coalition government's unity, which likewise failed. Though for a brief moment war looked possible, diplomacy pre-empted military force with the successful agreement for an armistice, signed at Mudania on 11 October.

The Chanak incident, and the brinksmanship involved, precipitated the downfall of the Lloyd George coalition, and with it the end of any lingering thoughts of a vast new Eastern Mediterranean empire. The leading Conservative politician Andrew Bonar Law argued in a letter to *The Times* on 7 October: 'We cannot act as the policeman of the world' and that Britain should 'restrict our attention to the safe-guarding of the more immediate interests of the empire.'[73] On 19 October the

70 Lloyd George to Margaret Lloyd George, 28 September 1922, *Lloyd George Family Letters, 1885–1936*, ed. Kenneth O. Morgan, 1973, 196.

71 On 20 October 1921 the French diplomat Henri Franklin-Bouillon, a figure widely disliked by British officials, concluded an agreement with the Nationalists.

72 Hardinge Vol. 45, Hardinge to Curzon, 2 October 1922.

73 *The Times,* 7 October 1922, 11

governing coalition collapsed and Lloyd George resigned as Prime Minister. On 23 October a new Conservative government was formed under Bonar Law, with Lord Curzon retaining the Foreign Office. A week later in Constantinople, Sultan Mohammed VI was deposed, and the Sultanate abolished.[74] The last Sultan left the Yildiz Palace at dawn on 17 November 1922, escorted by the British commander General Harington, followed by a British ambulance carrying his luggage.[75] The Royal Navy took the last Sultan away aboard HMS *Malaya*, carefully chosen as the only Royal Navy vessel ever paid for by a predominantly Muslim colony. Some officials wondered if the deposed Sultan could be turned into a British asset and help vindicate Britain in Muslim eyes. The most senior Foreign Office official, Sir Eyre Crowe, thought serious consideration should be given to allowing him to live in India.[76] The Viceroy, Lord Reading, advised there was no way to make use of the deposed ruler and recommended standing aloof from his fate, and the idea faded.[77] While all this was transpiring, a peace conference was convening at Lausanne.

The formal end of the Ottoman Sultanate was probably precipitated by the Allied invitation to the Turkish Nationalists to participate in a peace conference. This had raised the possibility of there being two Turkish delegations, one representing the Sultan and one the Nationalists. Atatürk had no intention of allowing the Allies to play off two Turkish governments.[78] The expedient solution was to simply end the Sultanate, while retaining a member of the family in the office of Caliph. As the American observer at Lausanne noted of the Turkish delegation's arrival at Lausanne, the Turks 'are coming, not hat in hand, but with a victorious army behind them. That makes a lot of difference.'[79]

The Lausanne conference's first period was chaired by the Foreign Secretary, Lord Curzon, formerly one of the great proconsuls of the British Empire as Viceroy of India. He had aspired to be Prime Minister when Lloyd George was toppled, and was frustrated when Bonar Law was chosen instead, whose

74 The Nationalist Grand National Assembly, meeting at Ankara, voted for the abolition of the Sultanate on 1 November 1922. The country formally became a republic on 29 October 1923, after the last foreign forces had left its territory.

75 Bristol Diary, 17 November 1922. Admiral Mark Bristol Papers, Library of Congress, Washington, D.C.

76 FO 371/7910/E12293/27/44, 6 November 1922.

77 FO 371/7913/E12699/27/44, 10 November 1922.

78 On the end of the Sultanate see A.L. Macfie, *The End of the Ottoman Empire, 1908–1923*, 1998, 197–207.

79 Grew Box 20, Grew to M. Perry (sister), 13 November 1922. Joseph Grew Papers, Houghton Library, Harvard University.

ignorance of diplomacy he deplored.[80] His objective was to end the immediate crisis, though the detail of negotiation bored him. He told Crowe that 'I do not much care for the technical aspect of negotiation. But I think it is an obligation of honour.'[81] There was frustration at having British aspirations disrupted by the new Turkish regime. Rumbold, who had come from Constantinople to join the British delegation, complained that 'it is exasperating to think that a small country like Turkey, with only seven million inhabitants, should be giving so much trouble to the biggest countries in the world. The Turks ought to be seen and not heard!'[82]

The Turkish delegation did indeed prove more effective, and firm, than Britain had anticipated, and the conference moved towards collapse at the end of January. As it did so, the Army asked for permission to evacuate British forces from Constantinople to Gallipoli.[83] Curzon vehemently opposed any such move as detrimental to British interests and undermining the ability to ultimately make a peace with Turkey. Britain, though, was facing a plethora of problems with the crumbling of the wartime Entente, the danger to British forces at Mosul, the volatile situation in Egypt, combined with economic difficulties at home. The breakdown of the conference coincided with greater crises in international relations. On 11 January 1923 French forces occupied the Ruhr over the German default of its reparations payments. The Lausanne negotiators decided that the time had come when a respite would be beneficial for all sides and the conference was adjourned on 4 February. When it proved possible to restart the negotiations, Curzon was occupied with other matters and Rumbold took charge of the British delegation.

In the final settlement Turkey was able to overturn much of what had been intended by the Treaty of Sèvres, and a post-conference report observed that the Lausanne settlement 'leaves the Turks masters in their own house.'[84] Reporting to the King on the settlement, Rumbold was frank: 'We cannot nor do we pretend that the instrument we have just negotiated is a glorious one. It is anything but that. Still, given the circumstances in which we have had to negotiate with the Turks, I think that we have obtained the least unsatisfactory terms possible.'[85] The Treaty of Lausanne was signed on 24 July 1923, ratified on 24 August, with the last British troops departing Constantinople on 2 October.

80 Crewe Box C/12, Curzon (Lausanne) to Crewe, 5 January 1923, Marquess of Crewe Papers, University Library, Cambridge.
81 FO 800/ME/22/2, Curzon to Crowe, 17 December 1922.
82 MS. Rumbold dep. 30, Rumbold to Harington, 29 December 1922.
83 CAB 23/45, Cabinet meeting, 30 January 1923.
84 FO 371/9083/E6330/1/44, 'Treaty of Sèvres and Treaty of Lausanne', 16 June 1923.
85 MS. Rumbold dep. 31, Rumbold to George V, 16 July 1923.

Conclusion

In 1919 hopes for a new empire in the Eastern Mediterranean were great. There was a brief period between the World Wars when Britain became the predominant Eastern Mediterranean power, the successor of the Byzantine and Ottoman empires, but the original aspirations had been even greater, with hopes of perhaps having the great imperial city itself. There were plans for a great new Middle Eastern department, as important as the India Office. These aspirations had first flowered on the eve of Gallipoli and came to an end at Chanak, when the limits of British imperial power were glaringly illuminated. By late 1922 the initial grand strategy was much truncated. Britain's over-extended armed forces had been withdrawn from the Caucasus, and the Red Army soon reasserted Russia's control there. Greek power was crushed in what became known simply as the 'Catastrophe', and the country was economically and politically crippled by the need to accommodate the tidal wave of refugees from Asia Minor. Political reality had necessitated allowing France into the Middle East, with the mandates to govern Lebanon and Syria. Britain did manage to add Iraq, Palestine, and Jordan to its existing bag of territories under British imperial domination. All the acquisitions were in the form of mandates, which left open the possibility of subsequent withdrawal without loss of face if the situation became strained. This mechanism was indeed used in 1929 with Iraq. One success at Lausanne was to find a formula for the settlement of the Mosul issue which ultimately confirmed that region, and its oilfields, as part of Iraq and thereby available for the needs of the Royal Navy.

The idea of a new British imperium had never been a universal one in British policy making circles. Though there were several schools of thought as to the shape of the postwar order, they all shared an apprehension of any other Great Power, whether defeated enemy or wartime ally, intruding into any region with British interests. There was also a concern about the political power of Islam. After the grand, imperial scheme had failed and Lloyd George had left office, the Cabinet's Iraq Committee reported in 1923 that 'the Committee have been conscious from the start that there exists a powerful body of opinion, both in Parliament and the country, which favours, mainly for financial reasons, an early escape from the responsibilities which His Majesty's Government have been forced to assume in Iraq during and since the war; while in some quarters there has been a loud call for immediate evacuation.' The Committee advised against an early withdrawal as it feared the creation of, 'an aggressive Islamic State in a central site, where she would be in a position to control the fortunes of the Middle East, with results to British interests in those regions, and even in India, that might in the long run be disastrous.'[86] Such a concern would re-emerge from time to time among the makers of foreign policy.

The Lausanne Conference and resultant treaty marked the end of Britain's grandiose scheme for an Eastern Mediterranean empire as well as the end of Britain's centuries of imperial expansion. Imperial retrenchment would soon follow. Britain remained the predominant regional power for a few more decades, but not on the scale once envisaged. The modern map of the region has been much criticized, but the rationale for much of that map was because it was drawn with a much larger scheme in mind, one which soared briefly in 1919 and then ebbed away through 1922. For Britain the Lausanne settlement was an effort to smooth the ragged edges of its once grand imperial design. Britain's long imperial engagement with the fate of the Ottoman Empire was poignantly marked when, just prior to their final departure from Constantinople in October 1923, British forces conducted Farewell Services at the Haidar Pasha Cemetery, where the British soldiers who had died during the occupation lay buried alongside those of the Crimean War. On the final Sunday before sailing away from Constantinople, a memorial service was held in the Crimean Memorial Chapel. These events not only marked the coming into force of the Treaty of Lausanne, but also the end of the dreams of some in British government of a new Eastern Mediterranean empire.[87]

86 CAB 23/45, Cab 22 (23) 26 April 1923, considering 'Committee on Iraq: report', 23 March 1923.
87 CAB 44/38, Gen. Harington, 'Commander-in-Chief's Dispatch, Period, 1920–1923', October 1923.

3

On the Margins of the Lausanne Conference: The Soviet Union and the Exclusions of the Post-World War I International Order

Samuel J. Hirst and Étienne Forestier-Peyrat

Historians have rarely recognized how the Lausanne Conference shaped Soviet diplomacy. The Treaty of Brest-Litovsk (3 March 1918) and the Genoa Conference (April–May 1922) are the favoured case studies of early Bolshevik diplomatic engagement with the world abroad, each representing a different extreme. In Brest-Litovsk, Lev Trotsky, in his capacity as the first Commissar of Foreign Affairs, decried the capitalist order, stalled, and made territorial concessions to win time for the revolution and state-building at home. In Genoa, Georgy Chicherin – Trotsky's immediate successor – refused to accept the conditions tied to Western diplomatic recognition; instead, he circumvented Allied unity by negotiating a separate agreement with Germany in Rapallo.[1] Trotsky's cynical use of diplomacy in Brest-Litovsk and Chicherin's aborted détente in Genoa seem to capture the spectrum of an outsider's tactics for engaging with the Allies' post-World War I diplomacy: the radical desire to overthrow and the pragmatic attempt to exploit divisions among capitalist states.[2] Lausanne, where the Soviet delegation

1 N.N. Liubimov and A.N. Erlikh, *Genuezskaia konferentsiia. Vospominaniia uchastnikov*, 1963.
2 Stephen White, *The Origins of Detente: The Genoa Conference and Soviet-Western Relations, 1921–1922,* 2005.

supported other excluded groups' challenges to the international order, was something in between. It was, however, formative.

In contrast to the far-reaching lessons drawn from the diplomatic gatherings in Brest-Litovsk and Genoa, historians have treated Soviet involvement at the Lausanne Conference narrowly, in relation to the legal statutes that govern passage through the straits between the Mediterranean and the Black Sea (hereafter the Turkish Straits).[3] Despite clear connections to later events, most prominently to the Soviet support for decolonization that took off in the 1950s, historians have had less to say about the Bolsheviks' participation in the diplomatic events that shaped the post-Ottoman Middle East.[4] Yet archival records reveal that influential figures who shaped Soviet foreign policy recognized the Lausanne Conference as a critical juncture. Chicherin especially, who spent two months in Switzerland in late 1922 and early 1923, negotiated methods and attitudes that prefigured the Bolsheviks' challenges to the hierarchies of the international order in subsequent decades.

Lausanne encouraged the Bolsheviks to re-evaluate their strategies for diplomatic cooperation with opponents of Western imperialism. On 15 December 1922, Trotsky (by then Commissar of Military and Naval Affairs) articulated the broader significance of the Lausanne Conference in a letter to Vladimir Lenin and the Politburo. In response to Chicherin's reports on the Soviet delegation's struggles, Trotsky advocated abandonment of the conference: 'Concerning the signature of an agreement about the Near East, I am increasingly convinced that it would be unwise to sign such a treaty. This would be the first international pact where we – without physical duress (like we faced in Brest with regard to Ukraine or Finland) – would ratify imperialist violence with our own signature and thus give the social democrats a powerful weapon to use against us'.[5] Trotsky recognized that, for the first time, Soviet diplomats at Lausanne had the opportunity to contribute to the post-World War I international agreements from a position based on more than their defence of Soviet state interests. His invocation of the 'Near East' rather than the Turkish Straits was characteristic of the Bolsheviks' understanding of the broad scope of the conference, and his reference to social democrats

3 L.N. Nezhinskii, A.V. Ignat'ev, eds., *Rossiia i Chernomorskie prolivy (XVIII-XX stoletiia)*, 1999; I.A. Khormach, 'Sovetskaia Rossiia na Lozannskoi konferentsii po uregulirovaniiu polozheniia na blizhnem vostoke (1922–1923)', *Novaia i noveishaia istoriia* 2, 2019.

4 An exception is T.L. Musatova, 'G.V. Chicherin i arabskii vostok', *Vestnik Ministerstva inostrannykh del* 21, 15 November 1990.

5 Rossiiskii gosudarstvennyi arkhiv sotsial'no-politicheskoi istorii (RGASPI) fond 5, opis' 2, delo 304, list 1, Trotsky to Lenin, 15 December 1922.

points to the ideological considerations that shaped Soviet diplomacy. In one of the clearest statements of the Bolsheviks' overarching rationale, the Berlin-based diplomat Pavel Lapinskii was even clearer than Trotsky that Lausanne was about more than the Turkish Straits. Lapinskii argued that the conference was only partly about Soviet Russia's 'real' and 'concrete' needs for security in the Black Sea, and he urged defence of oppressed peoples against 'the imperialist world'.[6] Trotsky's reference to social democrats illustrated the challenge the Bolsheviks faced. They had to avoid the impression that their diplomatic engagement with the Allies was a pragmatic manoeuvre and a violation of their ideological principles. Lapinskii's words illustrate their bid to make mediation between capitalist West and oppressed East a strategy of revolutionary diplomacy.

Turkish nationalists were among the Bolsheviks' earliest and most important anti-imperialist partners, and Lausanne assumed such significance because the Ankara government's reconciliation with the Allies forced the Bolsheviks to reconfigure anti-imperialism for the ebbing of the post-war revolutionary wave. The Soviet government had initially offered support to Mustafa Kemal (hereafter Atatürk) as part of a transnational anti-imperialist alliance and in the name of world revolution. The Bolsheviks simultaneously supported a range of Turkish revolutionary groups and encouraged connections between Anatolia, Afghanistan, and anti-colonial movements across Asia.[7] But, in the months before Lausanne, Atatürk's government had appealed to the Allies to transfer disagreement from the battlefield to the negotiating table. The Bolsheviks, in turn, began to establish that anti-imperialism need not be militant and might instead take the form of interstate diplomatic and economic cooperation. As the Bolsheviks recalibrated their expectations from Kemalists who were giving up revolutionary radicalism, they sought to expand their list of diplomatic partners. In Lausanne, the Soviet delegation met extensively with Arab nationalists and were impressed by the latter's opposition to British and French imperialism. As the Soviet delegation sought to coordinate Turkish and Arab protests against the League of Nations' mandate system, they were drawn further into a broad international response to the hierarchies and exclusions of the Allies' post-war arrangements.[8]

6 RGASPI f. 159, op. 2, d. 18, l. 58, Lapinskii to Chicherin, 23 October 1922.

7 Samuel J. Hirst, 'Transnational Anti-Imperialism and the National Forces: Soviet Diplomacy and Turkey, 1920–1923', *Comparative Studies of South Asia, Africa and the Middle East* 33/2, 2013; Alp Yenen, 'The Other Jihad: Enver Pasha, Bolsheviks, and Politics of Anticolonial Muslim Nationalism during the Baku Congress', *The First World War and its Aftermath: The Shaping of the Middle East,* ed. T.G. Fraser, 2015.

8 Antony Anghie, *Imperialism, Sovereignty, and the Making of International Law,* 2004,

Lausanne proved an ideological test for the Bolsheviks because at home they were in the midst of reworking concepts such as state, sovereignty, and law in response to the legacy of the Tsarist Empire.[9] At first, the Bolsheviks had constituted a Soviet political space by creating multiple nominally independent republics. In 1922, on the same day that Chicherin delivered his most wide-ranging remarks on international affairs in Lausanne, leaders of four Soviet republics signed the international agreement that created the Soviet Union. The international role and the existence of entities such as Soviet Ukraine and the Caucasian republics were at stake, and Lausanne raised questions about the ideological and legal principles that determined nations' international representation. At Lausanne and in the conference's aftermath, the Bolsheviks combined their revolutionary commitment to national self-determination with the older tools of Russia's great power diplomacy. They found that the two could be mobilized in combination to obstruct the Allies' attempts to define the post-Ottoman Middle East, and they tied revolutionary diplomacy to Soviet state interests to minimize the ideological risk of cooperation with partners they did not trust.

Bolshevik Diplomacy and the post-Ottoman Middle East

Walter Duranty, Moscow correspondent for the *New York Times* in 1922, reported that he overheard revolutionaries celebrating the Lausanne Conference as 'a chance for a Russian Bismarck'.[10] He explained that, with the Russian Civil War over and the Kemalists pitted against the Allies, the Soviet delegation expected that growing domestic strength and international neutrality might allow them to be kingmakers. Yet in Lausanne, Chicherin and his comrades found themselves outsiders. Just a few months earlier in Genoa, they had had their triumphant moment of entrance into the circles of Allied diplomacy, but the situation in Switzerland was different. The Allies now had little hope of obtaining payment of Tsarist debts and begrudgingly accepted a Soviet delegation as unequal and unwanted guests. Shortly after he arrived, Chicherin reported to Moscow that 'no

115–195; Adom Getachew, *Worldmaking After Empire: The Rise and Fall of Self-Determination,* 2019, 37–70.

9 Sabine Dullin and Étienne Forestier-Peyrat, 'Flexible Sovereignties of the Revolutionary State: Soviet Republics Enter World Politics', *Journal of the History of International Law/ Revue d'histoire du droit international* 19/2, 2017; Leonard V. Smith, *Sovereignty at the Paris Peace Conference of 1919,* 2018.

10 Walter Duranty, 'Soviet Sees Russia as Europe's Savior', *New York Times*, 23 November 1922.

Wises or Keyneses come to see us' (he had met with the British economists Frank Wise and John Maynard Keynes in Italy), and that the Bolsheviks' 'isolation was incomparably greater than in Genoa'.[11] But the note of optimism and confidence that Duranty sensed in Moscow carried over into the Soviet delegation's insistent internationalism. Soviet and Turkish representatives disagreed first and foremost on a new regime for the Turkish Straits, but that disagreement was part of a larger tension. Gradually, the Bolsheviks embraced an ideologically-driven and global projection of diplomatic and economic influence. In their role as a former great power at odds with but present at the building of a new system, the Bolsheviks searched for new allies in Lausanne.

The Bolsheviks' internationalism was visible in the composition of the Soviet delegation itself. In theory, the Unified Soviet Delegation at the Lausanne Conference included representatives from the three Soviet republics that bordered the Black Sea: Georgia, Russia, and Ukraine.[12] In practice, Chicherin, who was both Soviet Russia's Commissar of Foreign Affairs and head of the unified delegation, corresponded only with Moscow and nevertheless spoke on behalf of all three states. Despite the apparent hypocrisy, the Bolsheviks' insistence on Georgian and Ukrainian inclusion was more than token consolation to the non-Russian nations that Moscow represented internationally, as it entailed *de facto* recognition of the two republics, a step the French were less willing to agree to than the British.[13]

The Bolsheviks' position was based on a professed commitment to inclusiveness, and they had begun building the case for diversified representation early. Soviet Ukraine had clear interests in the Black Sea, and had already been allotted a semi-autonomous role in the region, demonstrated by Mikhail Frunze's visit to Ankara to sign a Ukrainian treaty of friendship with the Kemalist government (21 January 1922).[14] Georgia, too, had an extensive Black Sea coastline, and the port of Batumi had been a focal point of tensions with Turkey during the Bolshevik-Kemalist rapprochement in 1921.[15] A Georgian delegation headed by Budu

---

11 RGASPI f. 159, op. 2, d. 19, l. 55, Chicherin to Litvinov, 5 December 1922; RGASPI f. 159, op. 2, d. 19, l. 58, Chicherin to Litvinov, 9 December 1922.

12 V.M. Korets'kyi, ed. *Ukraïns'ka RSR na mizhnarodnii areni. Zbirnyk dokumentiv (1917–1923 rr.),* 1966, 520–522, RSFSR to the governments of England, France and Italy, 2 November 1922.

13 Archives du Ministère des Affaires étrangères (AMAE, Paris), Correspondance politique et commerciale (1918–1940), Série E – Levant, Turquie, 280, ff. 46–47, Poincaré to the French ambassador in London, 24 October 1922; Dennis Odgen, 'Britain and Soviet Georgia, 1921–22', *Journal of Contemporary History* 23/2, 1988.

14 Ihor Datskiv, *Ukraïns'ka diplomatiia (1917–1923 rr.) u konteksti svitovoï istoriï,* 2013, 502.

15 L.N. Kalandarishvili, T.I. Nefedova, S.F. Tabakua, eds. *Bor'ba za pobedu sovetskoi vlasti v Adzharii. Dokumenty i materialy (1917–1921 gg.),* 1961, 365–372.

Mdivani, a leading Caucasian statesman, had arrived in Ankara in late October 1922 with a commercial and political agenda for Soviet-Turkish relations.[16] Conspicuously absent in the delegation, however, were Soviet Armenia and Azerbaijan, two republics whose relations with Turkey could be the source of tensions, as was the case at the Kars conference (September–October 1921).[17] For Lausanne, the local authorities and newspapers in all three South Caucasian republics were asked to insist on the importance of achieving a deal on the Turkish Straits and consolidating friendship with Turkey, but their presence was part of the Bolsheviks' claim to have broken with the notions of empire.[18]

From Atatürk's first appeal in the spring of 1920, Moscow's involvement in the Turkish War of Independence had included an internationalist rationale that stretched beyond a narrow definition of the Soviet state's military security. Following the occupation of Istanbul, the landings of British and French armies on the northern shores of the Black Sea certainly impressed upon the Bolsheviks the interconnected nature of the Soviet and Turkish struggles against Allied intervention. And, in the build-up to Lausanne, when the Bolsheviks doubted whether Britain would evacuate positions near the town of Çanakkale on the Dardanelles, Chicherin interpreted troop deployments for his colleagues in nearly apocalyptic terms. Pointing to the precedents set in Gibraltar and Singapore, Chicherin argued: 'We cannot develop, we cannot breathe if there is to be a British Chanak [Çanakkale]'.[19] The Turkish Straits were important enough to be part of the First Soviet-Turkish Treaty, even though the document was negotiated when the Allies still controlled the waterway. Signed in March 1921, the Soviet-Turkish Treaty stipulated that regulations for passage would be worked out by Black Sea littoral states at a later date. Yet Bolshevik-Kemalist 'solidarity in the fight against imperialism', formalized in that treaty, was more than a pragmatic military alliance to safeguard the Black Sea and its environs.[20] The Soviet government committed to the Kemalists and backed them even after Mustafa Suphi, head of the

---

16 AMAE (Paris), Correspondance politique et commerciale (1918–1940), Série E – Levant, Turquie, 280, ff. 52–53, General Mougin to the Ministry of Foreign Affairs, 25 October 1922.
17 N.I. Chernichenkina, ed. *Rus Arşivlerine Göre Moskova ve Kars Konferansları. Tutanaklar ve Belgeler*, 2014.
18 Sakartvelos Shinagan sakmeta Saminist'ros Arkivi – P'olitik'uri Arkivi (SSShA PA, Tbilisi), f. 13, op. 1, d. 46, l. 80, Orakhelashvili to the newspapers Pravda Gruzii, Kommunist and Zaria Vostoka, 21 October 1922; see also a Caucasian publication insisting on the need for friendly relations with Turkey: N. Sokol'skii, *Ocherki sovremennoi Turtsii*, 1923.
19 RGASPI f. 159, op. 2, d. 19, 1. 1, Chicherin to Radek and Mikhailovskii, 14 October 1922.
20 *Dokumenty vneshnei politiki SSSR,* Vol. 3, 1959, 597–604, Treaty between Russia and Turkey, 16 March 1921.

Soviet-backed Turkish Communist Party, was killed entering North-Eastern Anatolia in early 1921. The Communist International (hereafter the Comintern) was largely side-lined in Soviet relations with Turkey over the course of the interwar period, and it fell to the Commissariat of Foreign Affairs to fit cooperation with the Kemalists into a revolutionary vision.[21] Chicherin and the diplomats around him were convinced that Turkish society had not developed enough to be ready for communism, and they appreciated the revolutionary role the Kemalists played in international relations.[22] Even after the disappointments of Lausanne, the Bolsheviks continued to coordinate diplomatic, economic, and military cooperation with the Turkish Republic.

The Soviet position on a new regime for the Turkish Straits was itself part of their systematic objection to the Allies' control of the post-World War I international system. At the Paris Peace Conference, the Allies had internationalized control of the Turkish Straits and broken with the European tradition of affirming Ottoman sovereignty in principle. What is more, the Allies made their decisions without representatives from the Ottoman Empire or Soviet Russia present. During the preparations for Lausanne, the Soviet government protested that, before Paris, 'Russia' had been included in every previous international agreement on the Turkish Straits, and, along with Georgia, Ukraine, and Turkey, would not accept any arrangement arrived at without the Black Sea states' participation.[23] The Bolshevik leadership – Chicherin and Maxim Litvinov from the Commissariat of Foreign Affairs, Karl Radek from the Comintern, Trotsky, Lenin, and Stalin – all participated in the drafting of a Soviet position that combined Soviet security interests and a call for the equal participation of all nations in international affairs.

For pragmatic reasons, the Politburo sought a return to the nineteenth century practice that closed the Turkish Straits to warships, and a special commission composed of Chicherin, Radek, and Trotsky came to the unanimous decision to frame this in ideological terms as a defence of Turkey's independence and sovereignty.[24] But divisions among this small group indicate that these positions were hardly

21 Bülent Gökay, *Soviet Eastern Policy and Turkey, 1920–1991: Soviet Foreign Policy, Turkey and Communism,* 2006, 36–47.

22 RGASPI f. 159, op. 2, d. 57, l. 1, Chicherin to Lenin, 16 May 1920; RGASPI f. 5, op. 1, d. 2068, ll. 1–3, Chicherin to Radek, 9 July 1921; for similar sentiments about Iran, see Kayhan A. Nejad, 'To break the feudal bonds: the Soviets, Reza Khan, and the Iranian left, 1921–1925', *Middle Eastern Studies* 57/5, 2021.

23 *Dokumenty vneshnei politiki SSSR,* Vol. 5, 1961, 574–576, Karakhan to Curzon, 12 September 1922.

24 RGASPI f. 5, op. 2, d. 1982, ll. 4–5, Chicherin to Stalin, 17 October 1922; RGASPI f. 17, op. 3, d. 317, l. 2, Politburo decisions, 12 October 1922.

predetermined. Litvinov and Chicherin differed on the best tactical outcome. They sparred over whether control of the Turkish Straits should be given to Turkey or to the League of Nations, with Litvinov objecting that the 'Pan-Islamist' Kemalists could not be trusted and Chicherin arguing that to give control to the League of Nations would mean 'to let a goat into the vegetable garden, Britain into the Straits'.[25] Even as the Bolsheviks came to a consensus that they should push to close the Turkish Straits to warships in the name of Turkish sovereignty, they were well aware that they risked appearing 'more Turkish than the Turks' and might well not get what they wanted.[26] The Soviet delegation arrived in Lausanne with a set of concrete goals related to the Turkish Straits, but recognized their limits and sought equally to push a broader revolutionary agenda.

The Bolsheviks' politicization of representation at the conference produced the first significant strains with the Kemalists. When the Allies had announced that the conference would be dedicated to negotiating peace between themselves, Greece, and Turkey, the Bolsheviks immediately feared exclusion. At the Genoa Conference a few months earlier, Chicherin had already made the exclusivity of the international system a central element of the Soviet platform. There, he had lobbied both for the inclusion of non-Russian republics and for an invitation to the Kemalists.[27] The Bolsheviks' outreach to the Iranian government during the preparations for Lausanne was an early sign that they intended to do the same again: in October, the Soviet government encouraged Tehran to apply for representation; in Switzerland, Chicherin met personally with Zaka od-Dowleh, the Iranian ambassador to the country; and in January 1923, Chicherin supported Iran's call for representation.[28] The Bolsheviks requested that the Kemalists return the favour of Genoa and advocate that Soviet Russia be invited to Lausanne. The Kemalists, however, feared that the Bolsheviks' desire to expand the conference would inhibit their ability to achieve much-needed peace with the Allies. The Ankara government insisted to the Allies that a Soviet delegation be present for discussions of

25 RGASPI f. 159, op. 2, d. 19, l. 11, Chicherin to Stalin, 18 October 1922; Khormach, 'Sovetskaia Rossiia na Lozannskoi konferentsii'.

26 Lord Curzon would later mock Chicherin for being more Turkish than Ankara's delegation, but it was a charge for which the Bolsheviks had prepared. RGASPI f. 159, op. 2, d. 18, l. 58, Lapinskii to Chicherin, 23 October 1922.

27 Carole Fink, *The Genoa Conference: European Diplomacy, 1921–1922*, 1984, 68.

28 M.I. Volodarsky, *The Soviet Union and its Southern Neighbours: Iran and Afghanistan, 1917–1933*, 2013; 71; RGASPI f. 159, op. 2, d. 19, ll. 271–2, Chicherin to Litvinov, 19 January 1923; *Dokumenty vneshnei politiki SSSR,* Vol. 6, 1962, 153, Chicherin to the commissioners of the Lausanne Conference, 13 January 1923.

the Turkish Straits, but not as a fully-fledged participant of the conference.[29] The lead Turkish delegate, İsmet İnönü (hereafter İsmet), later explained that Soviet Russia's presence would have created a sense of continuity with the nineteenth century, when the European great powers had collectively decided the Ottoman Empire's fate.[30] At the last moment, the Allies agreed to accept the participation of Ukraine and Georgia, in the same limited capacity in which Soviet Russia was invited, and Chicherin continued to challenge the assumptions on which representation was based after he arrived.

The Bolsheviks' and the Kemalists' conflict over the Turkish Straits, despite the fact that this issue would fester and become one of the primary factors that drove the post-World War II Soviet and Turkish governments into opposing camps in the Cold War, was confined to the first weeks of the meetings in Lausanne.[31] A full month before the conference began, Chicherin had heard from his representative in Ankara that Soviet Russia's position was more than Turkey would ask for at the conference.[32] Both Chicherin and Stalin insisted to the Central Committee that any signs of tension between Turkey and Soviet Russia should be hidden – neither side stood to gain if the Allies learned of their differences.[33] In Lausanne, İsmet's position was similar. The Turkish delegation stood alone against a united Allied front and he wanted Soviet support, but İsmet worried that the Bolsheviks would disrupt the conference.[34] When Chicherin and İsmet first met on 1 December 1922, the latter repeated that the Turkish delegation could not hope that the Allies would agree to close the Turkish Straits to military vessels and Chicherin responded in anger that the Turkish delegation's politics were 'the politics of Damat Ferid', i.e. the politics of capitulation to the Allies.[35] By 8 December, just a week after Chicherin's arrival, the Soviet commissar and İsmet acknowledged the impossibility of a common position on the Turkish Straits. And yet, Chicherin

29 The National Archives, Foreign Office (FO) Confidential Print 424/255, no. 72, Rumbold to Curzon, 5 October 1922.

30 İsmet İnönü, *Hatıralar*, 2009, 318.

31 On the unravelling of the post-World War I Soviet-Turkish diplomatic partnership, see Onur İşçi, *Turkey and the Soviet Union during World War II: Diplomacy, Discord, and International Relations*, London, 2019.

32 RGASPI f. 159, op. 2, d. 58, l. 99, Aralov to Chicherin, 31 October 1922; RGASPI f. 159, op. 2, d. 19, l. 23, Chicherin to Stalin, 31 October 1922.

33 RGASPI f. 159, op. 2, d. 57, l. 103, Chicherin to Lenin, 24 October 1922.

34 Bilâl N. Şimşir, *Lozan Telgrafları: Türk Diplomatik Belgelerinde Lozan Barış Konferansı*, Vol. 1, 1990, 149–150, İsmet to Hüseyin Rauf, 29 November 1922; Sevtap Demirci, *Strategies and Struggles: British Rhetoric and Turkish Response: The Lausanne Conference, 1922–1923*, 2005, 91–92.

35 Şimşir, *Lozan Telgrafları*, Vol. 1, 157–160, İsmet to Hüseyin Rauf, 2 December 1922.

asked İsmet not to speak of their disagreement in public and the two continued to meet on the side lines of the conference for more than a month.[36] The Turkish Straits was certainly the most important issue for the Bolsheviks at the Lausanne Conference, but the Soviet delegation was aware early that there was little chance of achieving the Bolsheviks' desired solution.

Chicherin and 'the East'

The Soviet delegation's conflict with the Politburo reveals the way that core tenets of Soviet diplomacy were questioned on account of events in Switzerland. Trotsky's call to abandon the conference came on 15 December, when it had become clear that the Turkish Straits would be left open to military ships, but Chicherin stayed until early February. When Trotsky arrived at his pessimistic conclusion, the Soviet leadership was as yet divided. Litvinov argued that staying at the conference, perhaps even signing the Turkish Straits convention, was imperative; otherwise, Soviet Russia might not be invited to other major international conferences in the future.[37] Litvinov and many of his comrades held that Genoa had been an economic conference, and that Lausanne was the first time that the Bolsheviks were party to one of the political conferences that were establishing the new international order. Hence Trotsky referred to the Near East rather than the Turkish Straits, and hence the Politburo ordered Chicherin to justify rejecting the convention with a programmatic speech on 'the Near Eastern question in its entirety'.[38]

Chicherin delivered the Soviet position two weeks after the Politburo had asked him to, and he said little about the Turkish Straits. Chicherin insisted that the conference's discussion of minority rights could not be separated from a broader revision of minority rights across the globe, a proposal that he had confirmed with Stalin before leaving Moscow.[39] Chicherin argued that the conference was focused too narrowly on Turkey, especially because the Kemalists' victory had benefited from Soviet aid and from Arab resistance in Syria, the latter of which had forced France to seek peace with Ankara.[40] In the following month that Chicherin stayed in Lausanne, under pressure to return home, he protested to the Politburo that the

36 Şimşir, *Lozan Telgrafları*, Vol. 1, 184–187, İsmet to Hüseyin Rauf, 8 December 1922.
37 Khormach, 'Sovetskaia Rossiia na Lozannskaia konferentsii'.
38 RGASPI f. 17, op. 3, d. 327, l. 2, Politburo decisions, 15 December 1922.
39 RGASPI f. 159, op. 2, d. 19, l. 17, Chicherin to Stalin, 29 October 1922.
40 *Dokumenty vneshnei politiki SSSR*, Vol. 6, 123–133, Memorandum of the Russian-Ukrainian-Georgian delegation, 30 December 1922.

Soviet stance was creating vital connections with Arab nationalists.[41] The Politburo tolerated his absence up to a point, until 'categorically' ordering him to return to Moscow on 2 February 1923.[42] Before the Soviet delegation left for Lausanne, in October and November of the previous year, Chicherin and the Politburo had hoped to use the conference to spread a revolutionary message with little sense of specific targets, and it was this strategy that Chicherin developed on the ground. His meetings with Arab nationalists from across the former Ottoman Empire were unexpected and critical in the development of Soviet diplomatic relations with the Middle East.

The Soviet delegation was a natural ally for political activists excluded from the Lausanne Conference, and Chicherin's reports describe a remarkably varied agenda. Within three days of his arrival in Switzerland, Chicherin had received visits from the former Khedive of Egypt Abbas Hilmi, the Assyrian military leader Agha Petros, and the Lebanese-born activist Shakib Arslan.[43] In the first weeks of the conference, as Chicherin was preoccupied with negotiations over the Turkish Straits, other members of the delegation stood in for him. Sergei Pastukhov, an emerging Soviet orientologist, was among them, as were the senior diplomats Ivan Arens and Vatslav Vorovsky.[44] Chicherin calculated that Vorovsky, the top Soviet representative in Italy, would go on to play the role of intermediary with anti-British Arabs who found sanctuary in Benito Mussolini's Rome.[45] The Soviet delegation's contacts on the margins of the Lausanne Conference grew in importance as the official meetings became mired in the technicalities of borders and finances.

The primary tie between the Soviet delegation and many of their interlocutors was an immediate opposition to the expansion of British and French power in former Ottoman lands. Many of Chicherin's conversations focused on sharing information and practical coordination against the British. To Naji al-Asil, the Baghdad-born plenipotentiary of King Hussein of the Hejaz, he passed on rumours that the British would transfer Mehmet VI, the last Ottoman Sultan, to Mecca,

41 RGASPI f. 159, op. 2, d. 19, l. 303, Chicherin to Stalin, 26 January 1923.

42 RGASPI f. 17, op. 3, d. 331, l. 1, Politburo decisions, 25 January 1923; RGASPI f. 17, op. 3, d. 333, l. 1, Politburo decisions, 2 February 1923.

43 RGASPI f. 159, op. 2, d. 19, l. 51, Chicherin to Litvinov, 5 December 1922.

44 RGASPI f. 159, op. 2, d. 19, ll. 115–116, Chicherin to Litvinov, 21 December 1922. On Pastukhov and the transformation of Tsarist Russia's Oriental Studies in the Soviet period, see Denis V. Volkov, *Russia's Turn to Persia: Orientalism in Diplomacy and Intelligence,* 2018, esp. 240.

45 RGASPI f. 159, op. 2, d. 19, l. 92, Chicherin to Litvinov, 17 December 1922; RGASPI f. 159, op. 2, d. 19, l. 321, Chicherin to Litvinov, 30 January 1923.

only to be corrected by the better informed al-Asil.[46] Chicherin interpreted both his successes and his failures in the context of competition with the British. When he was slow to establish contact with Jafar Pasha al-Askari, representative of King Faisal of Iraq, and the Egyptian politician Ahmed Lutfi al-Sayed, he surmised that these men's governments were particularly dependent on the British.[47] Whereas Chicherin frequently referred to the progressive aspects of Turkish politics and to a basis for Soviet-Turkish cooperation, he rarely found such positive words for the Arabs with whom he met in Lausanne.[48] The convergence with Arab nationalists was almost entirely based on opposition to the British.

Chicherin (and, indeed, the Bolshevik leadership) referred to 'the East' loosely and expansively, and he entertained individuals of whose politics he had only a vague understanding.[49] In his first description of the meetings he was having alongside those with the Turkish delegation, Chicherin referred to 'representatives of Muslim and non-Muslim Eastern peoples and groups … [Saad] Zaghlul's followers, Mesopotamians, Arab Palestinians, and others'.[50] His list employed political affiliation, ethnic and religious identities, and, although he repeatedly invoked 'the Arab nationalist movement', he held a deep scepticism about the strength of Arabs' national identity. On several occasions, Chicherin repeated for Moscow condescending words that he had heard from the Turkish delegation, and in particular from Rıza Nur. Although he refrained from commenting upon the assessment, Chicherin relayed Rıza Nur's claim that 'only the intelligentsia dream of independence for Syria, and the common folk want to return to Turkey's fold'.[51] In his own analysis of the Arab elites with whom he met, Chicherin ascribed the activists' disconnectedness in terms that suggested a lesser stage of historical development. 'The majority of the Arab princes', he argued, possessed less authority among Arabs than Scottish chieftains did within their clans or than Mongolian khans did among their tribes. It was impossible, he continued, to hope for a 'republican movement' in most of the Arab lands, and the Bolsheviks

46 RGASPI f. 159, op. 2, d. 19, l. 185, Chicherin to Litvinov, 1 January 1923.

47 RGASPI f. 159, op. 2, d. 19, ll. 163–166, Chicherin to Litvinov, 29 December 1922.

48 RGASPI f. 159, op. 2, d. 49, l. 3, Chicherin to Trotsky, 14 October 1921; RGASPI f. 159, op. 2, d. 57, l. 112, Chicherin to Aralov, 3 April 1923.

49 Masha Kirasirova, 'The "East" as a Category of Bolshevik Ideology and Comintern Administration: The Arab Section of the Communist University of the Toilers of the East', *Kritika* 18/1, 2017.

50 RGASPI f. 159, op. 2, d. 19, l. 51, Chicherin to Litvinov, 5 December 1922.

51 RGASPI f. 159, op. 2, d. 19, ll. 115–116, Chicherin to Litvinov, 21 December 1922; RGASPI f. 159, op. 2, d. 19, l. 126, Chicherin to Litvinov, 21 December 1922; RGASPI f. 159, op. 2, d. 19, l. 185, Chicherin to Litvinov, 1 January 1923.

could only hope 'that good princes replace bad ones'.[52] In general, Chicherin was interested in class divisions. On the basis of his conversations with Rıza Nur, he reported that the Turkish nationalists' economic policies were driven by the fact that the Ottoman bourgeoisie was Greek and Armenian, but he saw little relevance for class analysis in his meetings with men like Shakib Arslan.[53] Even with men who were theoretically sympathetic to socialism, Chicherin was uninterested in ideological union. After meeting with someone whom he described as from the left wing of Zaghlul's party, Chicherin wrote that the man was both a mason and a member of the French communist party. 'I do not know how he will resolve this dilemma'. Chicherin concluded: 'I have little trust for him, as I do for all Eastern people'.[54] These condescending remarks came in the same letters in which Chicherin advocated support for Arab activists, and he was forced to reconcile a partnership that he saw as insurrectionary in diplomatic terms with the absence of revolutionary or ideological sympathy.

In many of his meetings with Arab nationalists, Chicherin paid most attention to the ways that Soviet Russia could support their requests within the existing framework of international law. When Shakib Arslan asked Chicherin to protest against the mandate system, and in particular against the French mandate in Lebanon, the logic of the protest was similar to the Soviet delegation's objection to the Allies' revision of regulations for passage through the Turkish Straits. Arslan pointed out that the Russian Empire, along with France and Great Britain, had signed agreements about Lebanon in 1861 and 1864, and that these agreements had now been violated without Russia's consent.[55] When an Egyptian delegation visited him, they provided him with extensive materials documenting British violations of the Convention of Constantinople regarding the Suez Canal, of which Tsarist Russia had been a signatory in 1888.[56] Chicherin's adoption of this legalistic approach to endorsing Arab protests against British and French actions was perhaps most visible in the warmth with which he greeted representatives of Hussein, King of the Hejaz. In addition to Naji al-Asil, Chicherin met on several occasions with Habib Lotfallah, and he advised Moscow to confer diplomatic recognition on the Hejaz. Chicherin listened to Lotfallah's description of plans to create an Arab confederation and his claims to have Mussolini's support for an anti-British coalition, but the Soviet commissar was most interested in humbler steps – establishing a

52 RGASPI f. 159, op. 2, d. 19, ll. 163–166, Chicherin to Litvinov, 29 December 1922.
53 RGASPI f. 159, op. 2, d. 19, l. 100, Chicherin to Litvinov, 19 December 1922.
54 RGASPI f. 159, op. 2, d. 19, l. 296, Chicherin to Litvinov, 23 January 1923.
55 RGASPI f. 159, op. 2, d. 19, l. 51, Chicherin to Litvinov, 9 December 1922.
56 RGASPI f. 159, op. 2, d. 19, l. 321, Chicherin to Litvinov, 30 January 1923.

consulate in Jeddah, developing trade relations, and gradually working to develop relations with a diplomatic ally on the Arabian Peninsula.[57] Although the rationale was often left unarticulated, Chicherin inclined towards support for the platforms of the men he met without endorsing any of them politically.

In two letters from near the end of Chicherin's stay in Switzerland, he was frank about his caution in relations with individual Arab nationalists. He penned the first on 17 January 1923, just after Ahmet Lutfi al-Sayed, a man that Chicherin had believed firmly pro-British, finally visited the Soviet delegation. Chicherin advised Moscow that al-Sayed was part of one of two different Egyptian delegations in Lausanne and that it was unwise to support either. Much as Trotsky feared the condemnation of Europe's social democrats if the Bolsheviks signed the Lausanne Treaty, Chicherin worried that endorsing one of two imperfect options would be held against the Bolsheviks. Chicherin advocated invoking British violations of international law and finding a way to support al-Sayed while 'referring to our own self-interest'.[58] Chicherin demonstrated a similar reluctance to adjudicate among competing political claims after his last conversation with Naji al-Asil. Al-Asil explained that the title 'King of the Hejaz' was limiting and imposed by the British, and that Hussein wanted to be recognized as King of the Hashemites. Chicherin apologized to Moscow that he was in the process of leaving Lausanne and that he would not have time to learn from his Syrian and Palestinian colleagues what was at stake with this title, but he urged caution in any case. Under no circumstances, Chicherin argued, could the Soviet Union recognize a contested state, as that would be to interfere in Arab domestic affairs.[59] Each of these two letters reflects reluctance to endorse political actors who could not safely be identified with a nation-state.

Despite the conflict over the Turkish Straits with the Turkish delegation, the Kemalists' seat at the negotiating table encouraged Chicherin to push Arab interests in revolutionary terms with İsmet. On multiple occasions, Chicherin implored İsmet and Rıza Nur to join him in taking up the Arabs' cause with the Allies. At a minimum, Chicherin advocated tactical solutions. He tried, for example, to achieve a compromise between Agha Petros and İsmet, whereby Assyrians would be granted autonomy within Turkey in exchange for Agha Petros's support for Turkish control of the disputed province of Mosul.[60] He considered a request from Shakib

57 RGASPI f. 159, op. 2, d. 19, l. 92, Chicherin to Litvinov, 17 December 1922.
58 RGASPI f. 159, op. 2, d. 19, l. 266, Chicherin to Litvinov, 17 January 1923.
59 RGASPI f. 159, op. 2, d. 19, l. 321, Chicherin to Litvinov, 30 January 1923.
60 RGASPI f. 159, op. 2, d. 19, l. 51, Chicherin to Litvinov, 9 December 1922.

Arslan and Ihsan al-Jabiri to pressure İsmet to allow resources and people across the Turkish border to aid the Syrian independence movement.[61] Most frequently, however, he urged İsmet to use the Lausanne Conference as an opportunity to carry out ideological propaganda against the Allies, much as the Soviet delegation itself did. İsmet promised Chicherin to denounce the mandate system if Turkey joined the League of Nations and half-heartedly endorsed Egyptian demands for independence, but İsmet worried that a stronger stance would hinder his delegation's ability to make claims in its own interest.[62] And, on this issue, the Soviet and the Turkish delegations clashed. Chicherin lamented that the Turks had 'no idea how to use the beneficial conditions created by the Arab nationalist movement'; Riza Nur responded that the Arabs had betrayed the Ottoman Empire.[63] Towards the end of the conference, Chicherin increasingly saw the Kemalists' failure to take a revolutionary stand in the name of Arab independence as an opportunity to bolster the Bolsheviks' own reputation as staunch defenders of Eastern nations.

Revolutionary ideology consistently shaped the Soviet delegation's diplomacy at Lausanne, but the diplomacy depended heavily on context. The Bolsheviks' most consistent position was the commitment to a more inclusive international system, visible in Chicherin's programmatic statement on the Near Eastern question and many of the delegation's other public remarks. With the Turkish delegation, despite needing their cooperation to make headway on the key issue of the Turkish Straits and despite resistance to his overtures, Chicherin insistently advocated a revolutionary defence of the Arab cause. With stateless Arab activists themselves, he was more reserved. Confronted by competing Egyptian delegations, Chicherin felt he had to make a decision that he did not have to with the Turkish delegation. After one argument with İsmet, Chicherin wrote to Litvinov: 'The Turkish nation … is only going to come into its own slowly, and to aid it we cannot break with the Kemalist government abruptly'.[64] The Kemalists' claim to speak for the Turkish nation allowed Soviet diplomats to imagine a more revolutionary partnership with them than with any individual Arab activist, for the Bolsheviks needed no ideological justification to collaborate with an Eastern nation whose role was determined by its position in the international system rather than by domestic politics.

61 RGASPI f. 159, op. 2, d. 19, ll. 271–2, Chicherin to Litvinov, 19 January 1923.

62 RGASPI f. 159, op. 2, d. 19, l. 126, Chicherin to Litvinov, 21 December 1922; Şimşir, *Lozan Telgrafları*, Vol. 1, 297–298, 30 December 1922; Şimşir, *Lozan Telgrafları*, Vol. 2, 315, 16 May 1923.

63 RGASPI f. 159, op. 2, d. 19, l. 185, Chicherin to Litvinov, 1 January 1923.

64 RGASPI f. 159, op. 2, d. 19, l. 51, Chicherin to Litvinov, 5 December 1922.

Soviet Diplomacy and the Legacy of Lausanne

The Kyiv-born writer Mikhail Bulgakov described 'an electricity in the air' on the streets of Moscow shortly after Vatslav Vorovsky's assassination.[65] Vorovsky had returned to Lausanne despite the Allies' refusal to invite the unified Soviet delegation for the second session of the Lausanne Conference, and he was shot in the restaurant of the Hotel Cecil by a White Russian émigré on 10 May 1923.[66] Vorovsky's death came just two days after the British emissary in Moscow had presented the Soviet government with a set of demands that came to be known as 'the Curzon ultimatum', amidst a major crisis in Anglo-Soviet relations. According to Bulgakov, Soviet citizens marched down Tverskaia Street in protest with an effigy of Lord Curzon holding a whip over manacled Asian subjects. The crowds also carried signs denouncing Vorovsky's murder and proclaiming 'the Soviet Union is not the Ruhr'.[67] The conflation of these various issues signalled a general protest against the inequity of the international order. The lack of protection for Soviet diplomats abroad took its place alongside an ultimatum that threatened the Soviet Union's sovereignty, the occupation of the Ruhr and the violation of Germany's sovereignty, and the British Empire's denial of colonial sovereignty. The Soviet government's response, however, was diplomatic. The Bolsheviks faced down what they considered to be the most humiliating of Curzon's demands – the recall of plenipotentiaries from Kabul and Tehran, but they agreed to restrict anti-British propaganda in Asia. Like Chicherin's politics at Lausanne, the Soviet government's approach to the May crisis indicated that Soviet diplomacy was shifting towards challenging the international order based on Westphalian ideals of sovereignty on its own terms rather than through revolutionary struggle.

Even before the Curzon ultimatum, the position Chicherin formulated in Lausanne had begun to directly shape Soviet foreign policy in the Middle East. On 3 January 1923, Lev Karakhan, Deputy Commissar of Foreign Affairs, drew a set of preliminary conclusions from Chicherin's Lausanne reports for the Politburo. He observed that, while Soviet Russia's attention 'in the Near East' had thus far been focused on Turkey, British and French imperialism had strengthened nationalist movements in the Arab lands. He cited Chicherin's conversations with İsmet to show that the Kemalists would not support these movements. İsmet's failure to speak for Arabs in Lausanne had created an opportunity that, Karakhan insisted,

65 M.A. Bulgakov, 'Benefis lorda Kerzona', *Nakanune*, 19 May 1923.

66 Antoine Fleury, Gabriel Imboden, eds., *Documents diplomatiques suisses*, Vol. 8, 1988, document 271, Swiss Federal Political Department to the Swiss Legation in Italy, 8 May 1923.

67 O.R. Airapetov, *Vneshniaia politika Sovetskoi Rossii i SSSR v 1920–1939 godakh i istoki Vtoroi mirovoi voiny*, 2020, 125.

Soviet Russia must capitalize upon. Concretely, he advocated that Moscow confer diplomatic recognition upon Hussein and the 'Kingdom of Hejaz'.[68] In the context of the requests Chicherin was receiving, Karakhan's proposal was a conservative step. Indeed, Karakhan emphasized to the Politburo the low costs of recognizing Hussein: not only was the Kingdom a member of the League of Nations but it also had diplomatic relations with Britain, France, and several other states. The day after receiving Karakhan's proposal, the Politburo voted to establish relations with the Hejaz, but it was not until late summer 1924 that the Bashkir revolutionary Karim Khakimov arrived in Mecca and became the first official Soviet representative to an Arab state.[69] 1923 was a year of crises for Soviet foreign policy, and Vorovsky's death and the delayed inauguration of Soviet relations with the Hejaz reflected the tenuous nature of the connections that Chicherin had established.[70]

For the rest of the interwar period, the Soviet Commissariat of Foreign Affairs continued to challenge the principles of the international system as applied in the Middle East while prioritizing relations with governments that had already received international recognition. The policy was visible in contrast with the Comintern, which, free from these rules, invited Egyptian and Syrian students to Moscow.[71] Shakib Arslan was their guest in 1927, for the tenth anniversary of the October Revolution.[72] For the entirety of the interwar period, however, the only Arab nations with whom Soviet diplomats established representation were the Hejaz – and they then adopted a position of strict neutrality during the conflict between Hussein and Ibn Saud – and Yemen.[73] During the Rif War in Morocco, the Commissariat employed the strategy that Chicherin had favoured in Lausanne and protested against the Soviet Union's exclusion when Spain requested changes to the Algeciras agreement of 1906, of which Tsarist Russia had been a signatory.[74]

---

68 RGASPI f. 5, op. 2, d. 210, ll. 1–2, Karakhan to the Politburo, 3 January 1923. A translation of Karakhan's letter to the Politburo is available in Eileen Kane, Masha Kirasirova, and Margaret Litvin, eds., *Russian-Arab Worlds: A Documentary History,* 2023.

69 RGASPI f. 17, op. 3, d. 328, l. 1, Politburo decision of 4 January 1923; A.N. Kheifets, *Sovetskaia diplomatiia i narody Vostoka, 1921–1927*, 1968, 312–313. See also Norihiro Naganawa's forthcoming work on Karim Khakimov.

70 Airapetov, *Vneshniaia politika Sovetskoi Rossii i SSSR*, 121–127.

71 G.G. Kosach, *Kommunisty Blizhnego Vostoka v SSSR v 1920–1930-e gody*, 2009; Kirasirova, 'The "East" as a Category of Bolshevik Ideology and Comintern Administration'.

72 William Cleveland, *Islam against the West: Shakib Arslan and the Campaign for Islamic Nationalism,* 1985, 76.

73 John Baldry, 'Soviet Relations with Saudi Arabia and the Yemen, 1917–1938', *Middle Eastern Studies* 20/1, 1984.

74 N.A. Zherlitsyna, '"Zashchitnik ugnetennogo Marokko': Osveshchenie rifskoi voiny v Sovetskom Soiuze v 1920-x gg.', *Vestnik Tomskogo gosudarstvennogo universiteta* 6, 2016, 16.

This diplomacy, however cautious it may seem in contrast with the Comintern, had a distinct revolutionary element.[75] At the League-sponsored economic conference in Geneva in 1927, the Soviet delegation took the opportunity to again denounce the mandate system.[76] And in 1933, during preparations for the Soviet Union's entrance into the League of Nations, the Commissariat of Foreign Affairs demanded that the covenant be changed to exclude any mention of mandate rule.[77] In Lausanne, the Bolsheviks found themselves party to negotiations of the international order and yet nonetheless excluded. Their response focused on expanding representation, whether for Georgia and Ukraine or Iran and Arab nations, and it was shaped by the fear of legitimizing great power intervention and associating too closely with non-communist political movements.

Post-Lausanne developments in Soviet-Turkish relations also reflected this transition to an anti-imperialist collaboration that was conservative in its approach to international law. As the Turkish consul in Batumi noted in his diary in May 1923, events in Switzerland had a profound effect on the broader space that stretched between Moscow and Ankara.[78] In February 1923, İbrahim Abilov, the Transcaucasian Socialist Republic's Azerbaijani representative in Ankara, died shortly after making a speech at the Izmir Economic Congress, in which he had spoken of the promise of economic cooperation rather than world revolution. With Abilov's death, the heyday of direct representation of multiple Soviet republics in Ankara came to an end.[79] In the Caucasus, too, where the Kemalists had maintained diplomatic missions since 1920, the signature of the Lausanne Convention on 24 July 1923 provided Soviet authorities with an opportunity to ask for the closure of those representations, a step Soviet Armenia was particularly swift to implement.[80] The months of negotiations in Lausanne, which encompassed both

75 Trotsky feared social democrats, but scholars have judged Soviet diplomacy in similar terms. See, for example, Jon Jacobson, *When the Soviet Union entered World Politics,* 1994, 179–180.

76 I.A. Khormach, *Vozvrashchenie v mirovoe soobshchestvo: bor'ba i sotrudnichestvo Sovetskogo gosudarstva s Ligoi natsii v 1919–1934 gg.*, 2011, 122.

77 Khormach, *Vozvrashchenie v mirovoe soobshchestvo,* 528.

78 Erdal Aydoğan, Şaban Ortak, eds. *Dr. İbrahim Talî Bey'in (*Öngören*) Günlüğü,* 2000, 177, 17 May 1923.

79 On Abilov and his close connection to Turkish leaders, despite his limited diplomatic leeway, see Jalə Qurbanova, Musa Piriyev, eds. *Azərbaycan-Türkiyə münasibətləri (1920–1922). Sənədlər və materiallar*, 2002.

80 Hajastani Azgajin Arkhiv (HAA, Yerevan), f. 113, op. 3, d. 103, l. 207, Armenian Council of People's Commissars to the Kemalist representative in Yerevan, 28 July 1923; Étienne Forestier-Peyrat, 'Maisons étroitement surveillées. Consuls et maisons consulaires dans le Caucase soviétique de l'entre-deux-guerres', *La maison consulaire. Espaces, fonctions et usagers XVIe-XXIe siècle*, ed. M. Grenet, 2021, 254–255.

international recognition of the Turkish Republic and the establishment of the Soviet Union, reshaped the Bolshevik-Kemalist partnership into a more traditional interstate relationship.

The Bolsheviks' reluctance to engage in contested domestic politics at Lausanne carried over into a retreat on the issue of ethnic minorities in Turkey. After a history of Tsarist engagement with Kurdish populations in the Ottoman Empire, the Bolsheviks' silence on Kurdish issues for the length of the interwar period was striking.[81] Armenian issues were harder to ignore, and Chicherin found himself confronted by representatives of Armenian organizations in Lausanne. He wrote in a letter to Litvinov, in December 1922, that he had responded to members of the International Philarmenian League: 'Russia has been excluded from discussions about everything except for the Straits, so let those who made the porridge eat it. Armenians suffer because the Entente used them, so let the Entente eat that porridge'.[82] The Lausanne Conference became a key example for the Bolsheviks to contrast their approach with what they claimed was the exclusively instrumental use of minorities by Western powers. In 1926, in the foreword to a translation of Lausanne Conference minutes related to the Armenian issue, a Georgian publication criticized Western approaches to the right of self-determination: 'The difference is that we implement our principles, whereas European and US diplomats use them [minorities] as bargaining chips. This is exactly what happened at the Lausanne conference'.[83] This Soviet interpretation of anti-imperialism sparked domestic criticism already in the 1920s, as, for example, in a 1929 work by the Armenian Bolshevik Bagrat Bor'ian, who referred to the 'satisfaction of the imperialist-annexationist instincts of Turkish proto-capitalism at the expense of the Armenian nation and in the name of destroying the colonial powers rule in the East'.[84] After the Second World War, and especially beginning in the 1960s, the sacrifices required to support anti-imperialist Turkish nationalism were to become an open source of dissent and grievances against the regime in Soviet Armenia.[85]

The Lausanne Conference thus formed part of the Bolsheviks' broader negotiation of relations with nationalist movements in the Middle East and Asia. Lausanne coincided with the Fourth Comintern Congress (November–December

81 Michael A. Reynolds, 'Abdürrezzak Bedirhan: Ottoman Kurd and Russophile in the Twilight of Empire', *Kritika* 12/2, 2011.

82 RGASPI f. 159, op. 2, d. 19, l. 141, Chicherin to Litvinov, 24 December 1922.

83 *Armianskii vopros na Lozannskoi konferentsii*, 1926, iv.

84 Bagrat Bor'ian, *Armenia. Mezhdunarodnaia diplomatiia i SSSR,* Vol. 2, 1929, 299–300.

85 Maike Lehmann, *Eine sowjetische Nation. Nationale Sozialismusinterpretationen in Armenien seit 1945,* 2012.

1922) which officially formulated the strategy of a 'united anti-imperialist front' with nationalist movements against imperialist powers. The debate continued into the 1920s and vexed Soviet Orientalists, who expressed their views in journals such as *Revoliutsionnyi Vostok* (The Revolutionary East) and institutions such as the Communist University for the Toilers of the East (KUTV) about the possibility of collaboration with non-communist nationalists.[86] The rise of Reza Khan in Iran, and in particular the uneasy relationship with the Kuomintang in China, complicated the narrative of 'anti-imperialist' interstate cooperation worked out in the Soviet-Turkish partnership. The significance of the Turkish model, however, re-emerged after the Second World War, when decolonization opened a venue for Soviet cooperation with newly independent states and gave birth to Khrushchev's proclamation of 'non-capitalist paths of development' that Third World countries could follow to avoid dependence on their former colonial patrons. Khrushchev reactivated the idea current at Lausanne, that the Soviet Union could occupy an intermediary role between capitalist West and oppressed East. The patterns of diplomatic engagement and economic cooperation established in the interwar period influenced experts and engineers who would play a key role in the expansion of Soviet technical cooperation in developing countries.[87]

86 Taline Ter Minassian, *Colporteurs du Komintern. L'Union soviétique et les minorités au Moyen-Orient*, 1997.
87 Samuel J. Hirst and Onur İşçi, 'Smokestacks and Pipelines: Russian-Turkish Relations and the Persistence of Economic Development', *Diplomatic History* 44/5, 2020; Étienne Forestier-Peyrat, 'Fighting Locusts Together: Pest Control and the Birth of Soviet Development Aid, 1920–1939', *Global Environment* 7/2, 2014.

4

The Lausanne Treaty in the Contested Narratives of World Politics

Cemil Aydın

About two and a half years before the signing of Lausanne Treaty, the Turkish Parliament in Ankara adopted a patriotic poem penned by Mehmet Akif Ersoy (1873–1936, hereafter Ersoy) as the new government's national anthem. Ersoy had been a prolific intellectual of the late Ottoman era well-versed in Pan-Islamic ideas and currents from India and Egypt, and his poem reflected the arguments and emotions of late Ottoman Muslim modernism. The last line of the second quatrain of the national anthem, still known by heart by millions of Turkish citizens today, proclaims the right to the self-determination of an imagined Muslim-majority nation: 'Independence is the absolute right of my God-worshipping nation' (*Hakkıdır Hakka Tapan Milletimin İstiklal*). The poem was composed in the context of the Greek invasion of Western Anatolia, sanctioned in the Sèvres Treaty through a caricature of Muslim Turks as a semi-civilized people holding no right to sovereignty in either Europe or post-WWI Ottoman territories in Anatolia. Thus, to substantiate Turkey's claim to self-determination, Ersoy had to challenge the Eurocentric vision of civilization which formed the basis of the Western imperial world order. As phrased in another line of the poem, one which did not make it into the national anthem, Western civilization was 'a single-fanged monster (*Tek Dişi Kalmış Canavar*).[1]

1 Eric Goldstein's chapter in this volume illustrates how the arguments of Ottoman Turks not belonging to Europe (and needing to be expelled from it) had been a crucial part of British Islamophobia and imperial visions, and peaked during and in the aftermath of WWI. For a

This Pan-Islamic critique of Western imperial Islamophobia and vision of civilization paved the way to the Lausanne Treaty, yet within just ten years the Treaty became the basis of a new universalist paradigm rejecting the clash of civilizations narrative and asserting an alternative narrative of world politics based on westernization's inevitability and the rise of majoritarian nationalism.

The Lausanne Treaty of July 1923, the abolition of the Caliphate in March 1924 and subsequent radical reforms within the Turkish government refashioned the narrative, symbolizing Turkey's shifting allegiance from an imagined Muslim world to membership in the regional European imperial order of the interwar period and, along with it, Western civilization. The Turkish government may not have changed the national anthem, which, to this day, evokes the victimhood of the Anatolian Muslims at the hands of sinister Western imperialism. Yet Mustafa Kemal (hereafter Atatürk) left Ersoy out of his 1927 Nutuk speech in which he presented his official historical thesis. By that point, Ersoy had already left the new Republic for a life of exile in Egypt. On account of the secular credentials of post-Lausanne Turkey, it became difficult to make sense of not only Ersoy's Pan-Islamic poem, but also the extraordinary Pan-Islamic mobilization in India in support of the Turkish War of Independence. In fact, India's Hindu nationalists of today now praise Atatürk's secularism which they perceive as a dose of much-needed shock therapy for the Islamic internationalism of Indian Muslims.

Recent scholarship on the global history of empire, transnational Muslim identity and international law can help us make sense of the links between competing yet entangled narratives about Lausanne. Why does the Lausanne Treaty appear so significant for both the Pan-Islamic internationalist as well as the liberal Eurocentric theories of nationalism and secularism? Theories of nationalism, secularism, and modernization propagated by the Turkish Republic represented a paradigm shift in the perception of international relations, from one focusing on and framed by a clash between races and civilizations to a Eurocentric notion of the universality of nation states.

This paradigm shift did not involve the complete abandonment of earlier narratives based on imperial, racial and religious identities. Nation state theory co-existed with ideas of competing multiple civilizations in the writings of both European and non-European intellectuals globally. But the reorientation of contested narratives of the global order after the Lausanne Treaty deserves closer

discussion of the Turkish national anthem as an intellectual history text, İsmail Kara, *Bir Düşünce Tarihi Metni Olarak İstiklâl Marşı*, 2021.

attention as this issue still provokes controversy, and there exist conflicting historical memories of Lausanne in broader public opinion in Turkey and abroad.

On Narratives of the World Order

Historians approach grand narratives, such as the post-Cold War vision of the end of history celebrating the triumph of Western liberalism, or the clash of civilizations theory, with suspicion.[2] Almost three decades after the end of the Cold War, proponents of both the civilizational narrative of the world order, as well as advocates of the liberal internationalism, claim vindication.[3] The first half of the twentieth century witnessed similar rivalry between master narratives of world politics. One was a Eurocentric narrative of progress, civilization and security. There were also civilizational and racial narratives of the world order co-existing with this Western-centred universalism. One leading journal of international relations, *Foreign Affairs,* first appeared as the *Journal of Race Development* in 1910, and 'yellow peril', 'terrible Turks', and the conflict between Cross and Crescent were perfectly respectable explanations of world affairs on the eve of WWI.[4]

Despite challenges from alternate narratives, including Cold War-era socialism and capitalism, the civilizational narrative is one of the most enduring frameworks, employed by individuals from the mid-nineteenth century to the present to perceive and interpret world events. It was only after WWII that master narratives built around race and civilization came to be considered obsolete (if not extremist), and that there emerged calls for new narratives of the self-determination of nations, or Cold War ideological conflicts.[5] Yet civilizational narratives never disappeared and bounced back to win new credibility in the 1990s after the end of the Cold War. It behoves us to ask how civilizational narratives, whether in their

---

2 Samuel P. Huntington, 'The Clash of Civilizations?' *Foreign Affairs* 72/3, 1993, 22–49; Francis Fukuyama. *The End of History and the Last Man*, 1992.

3 Some scholars see a move away from a Euro-American centred liberal order to a multi-centred system based on diverse civilizational values in the assertiveness of China, India and Russia in international affairs. Charles Kupchan, *No One's World: The West, the Rising Rest, and the Coming Global Turn*, 2012.

4 Weale B.L. Putnam, *The Conflict of Colour: Being a Detailed Examination of Racial Problems*, 1910.

5 For an influential book by a Young Turk on the intellectual interpretation of the Ottoman Empire's relationship with European empires through clash of civilization theories, see Halil Halit, *The Crescent Versus the Cross*, 1907. For the Terrible Turk literature, see Roni Margulies, *The Terrible Turk: Batı'nın Gördüğü 'Türk,'* 2016; John M. VanderLippe, 'Racism and The Making of American Foreign Policy: the "Terrible Turk" as Icon and Metaphor,' *Research in Politics and Society* 6, 1999, 47–63.

European/Western, Pan-Asian, Pan-African, or Pan-Islamic forms, persisted from the age of empires to that of nation states in new forms, and have indeed become more assertive in conjunction with the rising power of non-European states such as China and India.

Master narratives of world politics in the early twentieth century were not necessarily political ideologies, as in the case of Marxism, liberalism or late Cold War-era Islamism. When Ottoman intellectuals blamed contemporary European powers for behaving like anti-Muslim crusaders, or when Atatürk appealed to Indian Muslims to mobilize their support for Turkey against British hegemony, this was not backed by an ideological project to create a theocratic Islamic state and impose Islamic law on all citizens. Lausanne's Turkish delegation members were not conservative Islamists, but they were familiar with and benefited from the power of the Pan-Islamic narrative of world politics. Turkish leaders were also not responsible for originating the narrative of a clash of civilizations between Islam and the Christian West. These narrative frameworks emerged in the second half of nineteenth-century Europe, both in the Eastern Question diplomacy and colonial discourses on the white man's civilizing mission in Muslim-populated Asia and Africa. Thus, when Lloyd George or Venizelos justified the Greek invasion of Anatolia by invoking the superiority of Hellenic and Christian civilization to Muslim civilization and the Turkish race, they were mobilizing a master narrative of both past and future without mobilizing a modern political ideology. Similarly, Ahmed Riza, leading Young Turk intellectual and former speaker of the Ottoman parliament, couched his challenge to the 'immoral crusader policies' of the Western powers toward the Orient in terms of encounter and peace between civilizations during his public tour on behalf of Turkish nationalist demands in Paris after the Sèvres Treaty.[6] This is also true of the pro-Turkish pamphlets penned around the same time by Abul A'la Maududi.

The end of the Ottoman Empire and emergence of the Turkish Republic were subjected to competing interpretations, and Turkish nationalists owned and disowned multiple narratives over subsequent periods, combining Pan-Islamism, Bolshevism and nationalism at different points, but eventually settling on a master narrative built around the inevitability of the secular Westernized nation state by the late 1920s. Given how discourse surrounding contemporary events is riven by

6 Ahmed Riza, *The Moral Bankruptcy of Western Policy Towards the East*, Ankara, 1988. For another civilizationist defence of Ottoman Turkey's right to self-determination and sovereignty during the Paris Peace Conference, see Carolin Liebisch-Gümüş, 'Defending Turkey on Global Stages: The Young Turk Reşit Saffet's Internationalist Strategy in 1919,' *New Global Studies* 10/3, 2016, 217–251.

competing narratives of world politics, it is no coincidence that new battles are being fought over the meaning and legacy of Lausanne in its centennial, unleashing a cacophony of conflicting stories.[7]

Utilizing Pan-Islamic Narratives for Equality in the European Club of Empires

The Lausanne Treaty of 1923 is celebrated in the official Turkish historical narrative as the foundational document of the modern Republic. It is similarly recalled as the basis of the post-1923 radical Westernizing and secularizing reforms, including the abolition of the Caliphate, changing the alphabet, and the adoption of Swiss civil codes, acts which together created a rupture with Turkey's imperial and Islamic past to pave the way for the emergence of a modern European nation.[8] The interpretation of Lausanne as a triumph of Turkish modernism and Westernism makes the assumption that, until Lausanne, Ottoman rulers could not figure out how to move away from their Islamic outlook and embrace civilized European norms. [9] Only after Turkey became less Muslim, this interpretation implies, could Europeans overcome their anti-Turkish prejudice and accept Turkey as a civilized modern nation and potential member of Europe's comity of nations, thus recognizing Turkey's security and sovereignty.[10] The intellectual father of European unity, Richard von Coudenhove-Kalergi, was persuaded during a visit to Ankara and Athens in the early 1930s that Turkey too could be included within European civilization.[11] 'We came to speak of racial questions,' Coudenhove-Kalergi later recalled. 'Venizelos held that there were no racial differences between Greeks and

7 Gökhan Çetinsaya's chapter in this volume discusses the current conservative and Islamist critics of the Lausanne Treaty.

8 Mustafa Aksakal, 'Not "by those old books of international law, but only by war": Ottoman Intellectuals on the Eve of the Great War,' *Diplomacy and Statecraft* 15/3, 2004, 507–544; Mostafa Minawi, 'International law and the precarity of Ottoman sovereignty in Africa at the end of the nineteenth century', *The International History Review* 43/5, 2021, 1098–1121.

9 Bernard Lewis, *The Emergence of Modern Turkey*, 1961, 1–39; Jacob. C. Hurewitz, 'The Europeanization of Ottoman Diplomacy: The Conversion from Unilateralism to Reciprocity in the Nineteenth Century', *Belleten* 25, 1961, 455–466.

10 Arnold. J. Toynbee, *The Western Question in Greece and Turkey; A Study in the Contact of Civilisations*, 1923.

11 Dina Gusejnova, 'Europe tomorrow: the shifting frontiers of European civilization in the political thought of Richard Coudenhove-Kalergi', *Istanbul University Journal of Sociology* 38/2, 2019, 227–253.

Turks,' adding that 'Venizelos convinced me of the need to include Turkey in the Pan-European project.'[12]

There are, however, many contradictions in this thesis of Lausanne as rupture with both Pan-Islamism and the Eastern Question. The leaders of the Turkish War of Independence, including Atatürk and İsmet İnönü (hereafter İsmet), were comfortable utilizing Pan-Islamic anti-imperialism in the ten years preceding Lausanne. They combined their Pan-Islamic rhetoric with espousal of an international law free from Christian bias towards Muslims, and with calls for recognition of Turkish sovereignty. The Lausanne delegation was not very different from their Ottoman predecessors.[13] It is therefore necessary to see the Pan-Islamic thought and identity that emerged among Ottoman elites in the quarter century after the Paris Treaty of 1856 not as a rejection of European diplomacy and legal internationalism in favour of a revival of the Islamic character of the Empire, but as a strategy complementing Ottoman legal internationalism.[14] Ottoman elites could and did uphold multiple narratives of the world order, viewing them as complementary rather than contradictory.

The caliphate titles of the Ottoman Sultans and Pan-Islamic support for the Ottoman Empire may give the impression that the Ottoman Empire belonged to an Islamic world outside of Europe. Yet, attachment to the Ottoman Caliph outside of Ottoman sovereign territories became important for colonized Muslim societies as well as for Ottoman diplomacy only from the 1870s onwards. This relationship was not intended to signify rejection of Ottoman membership of the European club of empires, but to solidify European orientation. Muslims living under the rule of European empires in Asia and Africa highlighted their ties to the Ottoman Sultan as their spiritual Caliph partly because the Ottoman Sultans were seen as modern European monarchs ruling over diverse populations with civilized values of equality and tolerance. Geopolitically, the Ottoman Sultan's spiritual leadership over Muslims outside of his sovereign domains was seen as the basis for Ottoman-British cooperation, not as a challenge to European imperialism.

---

12 Count Coudenhove-Kalergi, *An Idea Conquers the World*, 1954, 131–132.

13 Aimee M. Genell's chapter notes the continuity in service of the international lawyers trained in the Ottoman era and representing Ankara at Lausanne.

14 For Tanzimat reforms, see Roderic Davison, *Reform in the Ottoman Empire, 1856–1876*, 1973. For one of the first positive assessments of Abdulhamid-era Ottoman diplomacy in English language literature, see F.A.K. Yasamee, *Ottoman Diplomacy: Abdülhamid II and the Great Powers, 1878–1888*, 1996. Also see Azmi Özcan, *Pan-Islamism: Indian Muslims, the Ottomans and Britain, 1877–1924*, 1997; Selim Deringil, *The Well-Protected Domains: Ideology and the Legitimation of Powers in the Ottoman Empire 1876–1909*, 1998.

Pan-Islamic references to the Ottoman Caliphate in support of radical and revolutionary diplomacy in Asia and Africa appear only after the 1911 Italian invasion of the Ottoman North African territories in Libya. The Italian occupation of Ottoman lands was a clear violation of international law, yet European powers did not intervene to censure Italians and defend the international legal rights of the Ottomans. Indian Muslims mobilized to pressure London to intervene on the Ottomans' behalf against the Italian violation of international norms, arguing that Britain, as the biggest Muslim empire in the world, had a moral responsibility to help the Ottomans. A manifesto issued by Muslim students in Edinburgh quoted a Turkish newspaper article stating 'treaties are concocted by European powers to mislead and cheat, to be torn up and jettisoned whenever necessary' before beseeching Muslims to collect donations to strengthen the Ottoman navy.[15] It was during this period that Ottoman military forces were identified as 'the last army of Islam', a slogan that would be repeated many times in later generations.[16] It is worth noting here that the idea of Muslim solidarity takes shape only in response to the violation of the universal norms of international law by European imperial powers.

The Balkan Wars of 1912–1913 further confirmed the Ottoman elite's conviction that the policy of utilizing international law to defend their Empire was not working. Following two years of fighting and the subsequent displacement of a large Muslim population from the Balkans to the Ottoman interior, as well as a series of massacres, the Ottoman Empire was forced to cede almost all of its European territories to a coalition of Balkan states.[17] This event was perceived within European conservative circles as a necessary expulsion of barbaric Muslim Turks from civilized Europe, with the Bulgarian military assault on Istanbul leading the broader European public to develop heady visions of restoring the city's former Christian identity. Despite the European powers' initial promises that they would not accept any changes resulting from the war, the expansion of the Christian Balkan states was internationally recognized at the London Conference of 1913.[18]

15 Jonathan Conlin and Filiz Yazıcıoğlu, 'The Libyan War and Student Pan-Islamism: The Edinburgh Declaration of 1911', *International Journal of Middle East Studies* 54/2, 2022, 387–393.

16 Yahya Kemal Beyatlı, a celebrated Turkish poet, described the armies of Turkish War of Independence as 'the Last Army of Islam' in a poem published on 26 August 1922.

17 For the ethnic cleansing of the Muslims in the Balkans, see the sections on the Balkans Wars in Justin McCarthy, *Death and Exile: The Ethnic Cleansing of Ottoman Muslims, 1821–1922,* 1995, 135–164.

18 After about six months of negotiation, during which a second Balkan War occurred, the Treaty of London signed on 30 May 1913 ended the Balkan Wars. With this treaty, Turkey ceded most of its territory in Europe.

European condoning of massacres perpetrated by Christians against Balkan Muslims, as well as the inability of European international law and the European nation-state system to prevent these incidents, supported a general perception among the Ottomans that there was a new 'Christian crusade' launched by Europe against the Muslim world, and that Ottoman Turkey had to consider new policies.

The sense of disappointment at the failure of Ottoman elites to successfully appeal to European international law to defend their sovereignty in the Balkans was articulated by Young Turk intellectual Celal Nuri who addressed the racial politics of international law in his book *International Law from Our Perspective* (1911): 'There is not one, but two, kinds of international law. One for us, and one for them, the Europeans. Europe's morality and consciousness is also not one but two. One never feels empathy with our suffering and catastrophe … If you scratch the skin of any European today, you would discover a crusader under it.'[19] Despite its disillusionment with European international law, the Ottoman government refrained from promoting an anti-imperialist and anti-European notion of the Caliphate and Pan-Islamism until 1914. Even then, the Ottoman Holy War, declared in November 1914 against the British, French and Russian Empires, was announced in the context of a formal alliance with the German Empire, an act seen as a sign of the Ottoman Empire's membership of a European club of empires.

This background should help us understand why the Turkish delegation at Lausanne could espouse two different narratives of imperial order. One narrative sought a renewal of European international law and notions of sovereignty and nationhood, with the goal of making post-Ottoman Turkey a member of the club of European states. The other was Pan-Islamic in outlook, appealing to the collective power of the Muslim world and the East for the leverage necessary to achieve the goal of sovereign equality within Europe. Ottoman elites saw commitment to Europe and the discourse of representing an awakening Muslim world as complementary, not contradictory. Turkey's Lausanne delegation thus continued to utilize a hybrid mix of Ottoman elite narratives in interpreting and solving their problems: twentieth-century Ottoman claims to leadership of the Muslim world were an extension of investment in Eurocentric global governance and laws, and, ironically, so-called Pan-Islamism aimed to tame and reform the rules of the European law of nations, correcting their Christian bias.

This continuity makes the post-Lausanne paradigm shift less surprising: Turkish nationalists at Lausanne simultaneously synthesized two master narratives. Upon

19 Celal Nuri, *Kendi Noktai Nazarimizdan Hukuk-i Düvel* (International Law from Our Point of View), 1911, 5.

the conclusion of the Treaty, they found the first narrative, namely reform of the European imperial system with full equality for Turkey, more convenient. Turkish nationalists turned the power of the Pan-Islamic narrative to their geopolitical advantage from 1919 to 1923, but that narrative imposed burdens that risked Turkey's place within the European imperial system after Lausanne. The Turkish elite presented their achievement at Lausanne as a re-inclusion of their state into Europe following more than a half century of struggle against racist international law.[20] According to the new Turkish national narrative, the world order that excluded the Ottomans from 1856 to 1914, and eventually included the Republic in 1923 with recognition of legal equality (sovereignty without Capitulations), was the same European imperial world order. But the 1923 Lausanne Treaty was not a return to the 1856 Paris Treaty. Nor was it a precedent for the decolonization of Asian and African states that took place in the 1950s and 1960s. Turkey was a post-imperial state, not a post-colonial nation state. The interwar Turkish Republic resembled Austria, Greece, Poland or Hungary more than 1960s Indonesia, Ghana or Algeria.

Founders of the Turkish Republic may have presented their achievement as the fulfilment of their right to self-determination as Muslim Turks in Anatolia in 1923, but that was not the same as imagining a decolonized world without civilizational hierarchies or empires. After all, the Arab populations of the Ottoman Empire were subjected to a mandate regime justified by claims about their civilizational inferiority, and racialized empires persisted in Asia and Africa. Despite obtaining sovereignty without extraterritoriality or unequal treaties, the leaders of the Turkish Republic still felt they could face exclusion due to religious or racial difference. At that point, instead of continuing earlier Ottoman attempts to prove that Muslims deserved respect, rights, and equality, the Turkish government changed its cultural diplomacy approach completely by abandoning Pan-Islamic civilizational discourse.

Pan-Islamic Narratives of the Imperial World Order: Myth and Reality

As we have seen, a persistent myth has Turkish leaders betraying the same Muslim world that helped them to get to the negotiating table. It is certainly true that the Turkish fight for independence between 1919 and 1923 had the widespread support of Asian and Muslim public opinion, but where was the Muslim world

20 Mehmed Cemil Bilsel, *Cemiyet-i Akvam* (League of Nations), 1924; idem, *Lozan* (Lausanne Treaty), 1933.

political order accompanying that support? The late nineteenth-century Ottoman government's appeal to Muslim world solidarity was not a return to the medieval juridical concept of the *Darül Islam*. On the contrary, the Ottoman claim to leadership of the Islamic world sought to further internationalize the diplomatic crisis between the Ottoman Empire and other European empires. In this sense, Pan-Islamic caliphate diplomacy from the 1880s to the 1920s complemented the official Ottoman preference for, and participation in, multilateral European diplomacy and international law.

Some voices in immediate post-WWI America and the British Empire argued that the Muslim world should be rewarded for taking the side of the Allied powers. American scholar Albert Ten Eyck Olmstead wrote in December 1918, as preparations for the Paris Peace Conference were underway, that:

> Two hundred and fifty million Muslims of the world, a bare five percent was ever on the side of our opponents, that nearly the entire remainder was definitely pledged to the cause of liberty, that many were fighting side by side with our boys in France. By their action in this way, as well as by the weight of their numbers and their unrivalled position at the very heart of the old world, they demand and will secure adequate treatment at the peace table. [21]

Olmstead emphasized that the peace conference should endorse a great Arab Kingdom and treat Palestinian Muslims with fairness in regard to Zionism. As it happened, developments during and after the peace conference failed to support the political demands of Muslims who cooperated with the Allied powers.

After 1917, everything that the Allied powers did in the former Arab provinces of the Ottoman Empire, from Iraq and Syria to Palestine and the Hejaz, and especially the betrayal of Arab political demands and the colonial mandate regime, confirmed the perception among colonized Muslim populations that there was a true clash of civilizations. It is in the context of this rejection of a Wilsonian deal for Arab-majority lands in the Middle East and Turkish-majority Anatolia at the Paris Peace Conference, and of ambiguity concerning the future of the Ottoman Caliphate, that the Pan-Islamic Khilafat movement emerged in India, with activism reaching its peak between 1920 and 1923.[22] This movement emphasized the

21 A.T.E. Olmstead, 'The New Arab Kingdom and the Fate of the Muslim World', *University of Illinois Bulletin* XVI/17, 1918.

22 Mushirul Hasan and Margrit Pernau, ed., *Regionalizing Pan-Islamism: Documents of the Khilafat Movement*, 2005.

implicit obligations of the British Empire following Muslim sacrifice during WWI, namely that the British Empire must respect Muslim religious sensibilities and demands once British victory over the Ottoman Empire had been won. When not only Jerusalem but also Istanbul were occupied by British forces, when Greek armies invaded Western Anatolian cities and towns, the British Empire's credibility among Indian Muslims was compromised. Once the betrayal of British promises to Muslims was exposed, the Indian Khilafat Congress mobilized large masses behind anti-British slogans in support of the Turkish War of Independence.[23]

On 17 May 1919, three Indian Muslim leaders met United States President Woodrow Wilson and British Prime Minister Lloyd George in Paris to make a case for the preservation of the Ottoman Caliphate in Istanbul, and for the national self-determination of Anatolia as a homeland for Turkish Muslims.[24] The delegation included prominent loyalists to the British Empire such as Abdullah Yusuf Ali, Agha Khan and Sahibzade Aftab Ahmad Khan. The delegation articulated that the rights and dignity of Muslims all over the world were linked to the destiny and demands of Ottoman Muslims.[25] Loyalty to the British Empire, Pan-Islamism, internationalism, and Wilsonianism were all present in the eclectic argument of support for Turkey.[26] In this context, many who wrote about world events, such as the white supremacist Lothrop Stoddard, interpreted the post-WWI revival of Muslim world unity, and turn from fragmentation to nationalism, as a sign of the rising tide of colour against worldwide white supremacy.[27] In the early 1920s, journalist and Pan-Asianist Japanese intellectual Okawa Shumei depicted the formation and military success of the Turkish government in Ankara as a sign of the awakening of the Islamic world, not of the growth of secular nationalism.[28]

Between 1918 and 1923, Turkish-Muslim nationalists in Anatolia tried to leverage their geopolitical alliance with the revolutionary Bolshevik government while

23 Abul Kalam Azad, *'Khilafat and Jaziratul-Arab': Address delivered at the Bengal Provincial Khilafat Conference*, 1920; Syed Mahmud, *The Khilafat and England*, 1920.

24 Perin Gürel, *Wild Westernization: Figuring America in Twentieth Century Turkey*, 2017.

25 Foreign Relations of the United States, Paris Peace Conference, 'Stenographic Notes of a Meeting Held at President Wilson's House in the Place des État-Unis, Paris, on Saturday, May 17, 1919, at 4.30 pm'.

26 John Willis, 'Debating the Caliphate: Islam and Nation in the Work of Rashid Rida and Abul Kalam Azad', *The International History Review* 32/4, 2010, 711–732; S. Mushir Hosain Kidwai, *The Future of the Muslim Empire: Turkey*, 1919; idem, *The Sword Against Islam; or, A Defence of Islam's Standard-Bearers*, 1919.

27 Lothrop Stoddard, *The New World of Islam*, 1921; idem, *The Rising Tide of Color against White World-Supremacy. with an Introduction by Madison Grant*, 1921.

28 Okawa Shumei, *Fukkô Ajia no Shomondai* (Various Problems of a Resurgent Asia), 1922.

also invoking Muslim world solidarity in their struggles against Allied plans to divide Ottoman territories. The arguments produced in the context of the alliance between Bolsheviks and an imaginary Islamic world employed a combination of a secular socialist language of the resistance of the oppressed Muslims against their imperialist oppressors with the clash of civilization language common among publics in both Europe and Asia. It was in the context of what Alp Yenen terms 'the Young Turk international of the 1918–1922 period' that former Ottoman leaders such as Enver, Talât and Cemal established links with Moscow and Berlin, as well as between Tehran, Ankara and Kabul, to remake Asia along the principles of Muslim awakening and liberation, and the notion of self-determination.[29]

Despite losing the imperial war that they had joined in WWI, Young Turk intellectuals could console themselves by noting that the post-WWI debate on Asian self-determination inspired by both the Bolshevik Revolution and Wilsonian promises resembled their own pre-WWI calls for revolt against European empires. The Bolshevik government in Moscow supported this interpretation, welcoming Enver as an anti-imperial hero of the oppressed Islamic Orient, rather than as the former leader of a rival empire. It was in this context that Turkish nationalists under the leadership of Atatürk could receive support from Pan-Islamists in India, a newly independent Afghan government, and the Bolshevik government in Moscow.[30]

Pan-Islamism in India was criticized by both Hindu nationalists and later Muslim nationalists as an unnecessary emotional and irrational attachment to the declining Ottoman Empire, born of a nostalgia for the lost imperial glory of the Mughal Empire. Yet as Faridah Zaman has argued, this Indian Muslim nostalgia was primarily concerned with rights and equality, and with the future of colonized Muslims, and was not a reactionary project aimed at reviving old polities. Indian Muslim support for the Ottoman and Turkish nationalist causes relied on the perception of a shared mistreatment and destiny of Muslims across empires in the Eurocentric world order. Indian Muslims' humanitarian aid for Turkish war victims and orphans boosted the confidence of the Ottoman elite and provided leverage against the British Empire. Pan-Islamic campaigns equated justice for Turkey with justice for Islam and the entire Muslim race.[31] Atatürk himself was in

29 Alp Yenen, 'The Other Jihad. Enver Pasha, Bolsheviks, and Politics of Anticolonial Muslim Nationalism during the Baku Congress 1920', in T.G. Fraser, ed., *The First World War and its Aftermath: The Shaping of the Middle East*, 2015, 273–293.

30 For Pan-Islamic, Pan-Asian and Pan-African mobilization after WWI, see Cemil Aydın, *Politics of Anti-Westernism in Asia*, 2007.

31 Faridah Zaman, 'Pan-Islamism in Post-War Europe', unpublished paper presented at Cold War Islamism Symposium, Free University, Berlin, March 2019, 4–5.

touch with the Indian Pan-Islamic Khilafat movement, and Khilafat leaders such as Oxford-educated Muhammad Ali Jauhar (1878–1931, hereafter Jauhar) assured Turkish leaders that Indian soldiers would not join a British war against Turkey, and would indeed respond to such a call with non-cooperation.[32] Thus, when the terms of the Sèvres Treaty were publicized Indian Muslim leaders quickly condemned it as a violation of the moral principles of world order and the promises made to them by the British Empire at the beginning of WWI. Jauhar was in France when the Sèvres Treaty was announced. When asked about his opinion of the Treaty, he said:

> Is there any shameless Turk in this assembly or at Versailles or in Constantinople or even in the camp of Mustafa Kemal who is prepared to sign this treaty, then tell him as we have told Lloyd George and the Viceroy of India – we at least will not accept this treaty … If you look at this question from our religious point of view this treaty is unacceptable to us, and remember there are more than 300 million Musulmans in the world, in India, Turkey, Algeria, Morocco, Asia Minor, Egypt and Central Asia, whose religious obligations are being disregarded in this treaty. Again there are distinct pledges which had been given to us and which have got to be respected by you and by England. If they are disregarded today remember you who are a banking nation … that a dishonoured cheque is not accepted twice. We ask for no gratitude for anything that we may have done for France or England but I say this to you that if the Indian soldiers knew that after their defence of France and of England and after victories of Mesopotamia (Iraq) and Palestine, not British victories but Indian victories, if they had known that this would be the kind of treaty that would result from their victories, they would not have come to your aid in those dark hours of October 1914.[33]

Turkish victories against Greek armies in Anatolia, as well as their diplomatic achievements in relations with the Bolshevik government and with France, were already hailed by Indian Muslims as blazing a path to victory for the Muslim world. On 1 November 1922, just before the negotiations at Lausanne, the Ankara

32 Hadiye Yılmaz. *Kurtuluş Savaşımız ve Asya, Afrika'nın uyanışı: Hâkimiyeti Milliye yazılarıyla*, 2007.

33 Noor Mohammed Khalid, 'The Treaty of Lausanne: Role of Indian Muslims,' quoted from A.C. Niemeijer, *The Khilafat Movement In India: 1919–1924*, 101, at: https://turkvehint.org/2019/12/mohammed-ali/the-treaty-of-lausanne-role-of-indian-muslims/#_edn7 (Accessed on 15 March 2022)

government abolished the Ottoman dynasty. However, they kept a member of the Ottoman royal family as Caliph of all Muslims. Sultan Vahdettin, the last monarch of the Ottoman Empire, used the spiritual title of Caliph for seventeen days after being stripped of his sovereign title of Sultan. When he left the country, his cousin Abdulmecid was elected Caliph by majority vote of the Turkish Parliament in Ankara. Prominent Indian leaders including Dr. A.M. Ansari endorsed this decision as a return to authentic democratic Islamic political values. In fact, the Khilafat Conference at Gaya on 27 December 1922 bestowed upon Atatürk the titles Seyfu'l Islam [The Sword of Islam] and Mujahid-i Khilafat [Protector of the Caliphate].[34]

The same Khilafat Conference passed the following resolution in support of Turkey during the Lausanne negotiations, emphasizing that Muslims:

> will oppose all those terms of the Allies at the Lausanne Conference which either impair the power and the prestige of the Khilafat or in any way interfere with the Khalifah's complete independence or do not safeguard the sanctity of the Holy Places and do not free them from non-Muslim influence or help to place other Muslim states under non-Muslim control … This meeting warns that in the event of war with Turkey due to the unjust attitude of the Allies, particularly Britain, the Muslims of India would immediately launch civil disobedience with a programme which would include spreading their propaganda among the police and the army, stopping of fresh recruitment, refusal to subscribe to war loans, recruitment to the Ankara Legion, picketing of foreign cloth and liquor, and preventing the exports of food grains.[35]

What is important in this process is the direct identification of the Turkish War of Independence with the destiny and freedom of the Muslim world and indeed Islam itself. This was a risky association for Indian Muslims in that they were linking their own struggle for rights within the British Empire with the political crisis of Ottoman Muslims. In the climate of that era, however, it was not unusual to link a racial or transnational identity to a particular country, empire or cause. Using the same logic, Ethiopia was associated with the 'black race' and Japan or China associated with the 'yellow race'. The head of the Lausanne delegation,

---

34 Mohammad Sadiq, *The Turkish Revolution and the Indian Freedom Movement*, 1983, 104–130.

35 M. Naeem Qureshi, *Pan-Islam in British Indian Politics: The Politics of the Khilafat Movement, 1918–1924*, 2009, 341–342. The Ankara Legion was a proposal for Indian Muslim volunteers to travel to Ankara to support the Turkish War of Independence.

İsmet, made a point of meeting Indian Muslim leaders in Paris and Switzerland before the start of the Lausanne meetings, and he publicly stated that Turks and Muslims were civilized people deserving of equality, self-determination, and sovereignty throughout the period from 1919 to 1923.

Indian Muslims saw Lausanne as an incomplete success because it did not resolve the legitimate demands of the Arab populations of the former Ottoman Empire. After the signing of the treaty, they continued to make demands on behalf of the Muslim world. As Elizabeth F. Thompson's contribution to this volume illustrates, the Turkish delegation renounced all rights of sovereignty over Ottoman Arab provinces and abandoned those regions to British and French colonialism under the League's mandate regime established after the Lausanne Treaty.[36] Indian Muslims articulated a set of claims on behalf of the populations of former Arab provinces of the Ottoman empire in discussions on the *Jazirat-ul-Arab* (Arabian Peninsula) question, arguing that Lausanne left the dignity and liberation of Arab populations from Syria and Iraq to Palestine and the Hejaz unresolved. Indian Muslims emphasized the Muslim duty to ensure that sacred Arab lands were never ruled by non-Muslims, but they also clearly had secular concerns about the rights and freedom of colonized Muslims in mind when they articulated these norms.

In March 1922 the President of the Bombay Khilafat Committee sent a telegram to Lloyd George with demands for the independence of the former Arab provinces of the Ottoman Empire. He demanded:

> Specific restoration of legal rights of Khalifa of Muslims over Holy Places as pledged by England to Muslims … Religious obligations compel Muslims to insist on this point … Freedom of *Jazirat-ul-Arab* namely Syria Irak (Mesopotamia) Palestine and Arabia from non-Muslim domination and control is likewise not provided for in accordance with England's pledges to Islamic world. This is religious obligation on which there can be no compromise.'[37]

Lausanne can be seen as a bargain struck between the Ankara government and the British Empire over Turkey's role in the governance of the post-Ottoman Arab provinces and the Indian Ocean region. What resulted was a sovereign Turkish nation state that preserved a spiritual Caliphate in Istanbul but would leave the

36 Elizabeth F. Thompson's chapter.

37 Qureshi, *Pan-Islam in British Indian Politics*, 439–440.

Arab provinces of the former Ottoman Empire to European mandatory powers. In October 1923, just three months after the conclusion of the Lausanne Treaty, Turkey was declared a republic with its capital in Ankara. The Caliph in Istanbul continued to have immense prestige and respect among Muslims in Africa, Asia, and Central Asia, including among Shia and Ismaili Muslims, thanks to the power of the transnational Muslim identity. By electing a new Caliph from an Ottoman lineage in Istanbul under the protection of a Republican parliament, the Turkish government was creating a system akin to a papal institution for Muslims. The declaration of the Republic meant that a Caliph was fully detached from the political system and government in Ankara, and it is in this context that Indian Muslim leaders Agha Khan and Syed Ameer Ali wrote a letter to the Ankara government pleading with them to retain the political function of the Caliphate, and not to make any significant decisions without consulting Muslims outside Turkey. The publication of this letter in the Istanbul press even before it officially reached its address in Ankara gave the Turkish leaders a pretext to criticize Pan-Islamic intervention by Indian Muslim leaders as a British imperial plot. Turkish leaders also insulted both Agha Khan and Syed Ameer Ali by implying that, as Shia Muslims, they were not supposed to believe in the legitimacy of a Sunni Caliphate.

The abolition of the Ottoman Caliphate by the Turkish Grand National Assembly on 3 March 1924 came as a shock to many Pan-Islamic supporters of Turkey. The success of the Pan-Islamic narrative in empowering Turkey at Lausanne became its undoing, precisely because it fulfilled the goal of securing Turkey's membership in the European nation-state system.[38] It may seem paradoxical that even after the abolition of the Caliphate in Istanbul the Republic of Turkey continued to play a key role in the political imagination of other Muslim societies, thus embodying the persistence of a Pan-Islamic network of ideas and international visions.[39] Many Muslims and non-Muslim Asians celebrated the signing of the Lausanne Treaty as the much-deserved and belated triumph of the colonized Muslim world (or 'East') against the modern crusading armies of the West. Sun Yat-Sen, leader of Republican Revolution of China and its first President, referred to Turkey's achievement at Lausanne in his Pan-Asianism speech of 1924 as inspirational for all Asians, in terms of demonstrating both how an Asian nation could fulfill their moral rights and use military might and force to gain these rights,

38 Nurullah Ardıç, *Islam and the Politics of Secularism: The Caliphate and Middle Eastern Modernization in the Early 20th Century*, 2012.

39 Chiara Formichi, 'Mustafa Kemal's Abrogation of the Ottoman Caliphate and Its Impact on the Indonesian National Movement,' *Demystifying the Caliphate: Historical Memory and Contemporary Contexts*, ed. Madawi al-Rasheed et al., 2013, 95–115.

stating: 'To rely on benevolence alone to influence the Europeans in Asia to relinquish the privileges they have acquired in China would be an impossible dream. If we want to regain our rights, we must resort to force.'[40] Indonesian Muslim elites also followed developments in Turkey closely, with leaders such as Sukarno advocating for a secular Muslim nation modeled on post-1924 Turkey. In India, both Muhammad Iqbal and Muhammad Ali Jinnah followed the radical reforms of the Turkish Republic, admiring Atatürk's achievements. King Amanullah of Afghanistan continued to look up to Atatürk and the Turkish model as an inspiration for his reforms. Chinese Muslim intellectuals debated whether the Turkish Republic model provided a much-needed reform of their religious tradition.[41]

Creating a New Universal Narrative through Secularization and Westernization

The attempt to build a new narrative for Muslim-majority Turkey began during the War of Independence, when Wilsonianism and nationalism were used to highlight the legitimacy of Turkish political demands. On 26 April 1920, Atatürk gave an interview to Paul Williams of the *Chicago Daily Tribune* in which he stressed the basic goal of the nationalists, which was to 'keep the Turkish land for the Turks, maintaining the integrity of Turkey as it stood when the armistice was signed.' Moreover, Atatürk expressed his disenchantment with the idea of Wilsonian self-determination. For him, the application of self-determination to Armenians and Greeks in Turkey, but not to Turks, was an injustice on the part of civilized Europe. Although Atatürk echoed nationalistic rhetoric, the *Chicago Daily Tribune* described him as 'militant leader of the Moslem world' busy 'organizing the Moslem millions in Asia Minor to fight the Allied partition of his country.'[42]

---

40 For the text of Sun Yat-Sen's Great Asianism Speech in Kobe, see Marius Jansen, *The Japanese and Sun Yat-sen*, 1954. During the speech, Sun Yat-Sen praised the Turkish War of Independence: 'There is another country in Asia who joined with the Central Powers during the European War and was partitioned after her final defeat. After the war, however, she was not only able to regain her territory, but to expel all Europeans from that territory. Thus she attained her status of complete independence. This is Turkey. At present Asia has only two independent countries, Japan in the East and Turkey in the West. In other words, Japan and Turkey are the Eastern and Western barricades of Asia.'

41 Qureshi, *Ottoman Turkey, Atatürk and Muslim South Asia: Perspectives, Perceptions and Responses*, 2014; Hale Eroğlu Sager, 'Islam in Translation: Muslim Reform and Transnational Networks in Modern China, 1908–1957', PhD dissertation, Harvard University, 2016.

42 Heath Lowry ed., *Clarence K. Streit's The Unknown Turks*, 2011, 189–192; Paul Williams, 'Wilson's 14 Points or War – Kemal Pasha,' *Chicago Daily Tribune*, 4 May 1920.

References to Atatürk as a Pan-Islamist and anti-Western Muslim nationalist persisted in European and American newspapers until 1924. In a later interview by the *Philadelphia Public Ledger*, Atatürk promoted a positive image of Muslims by hinting that he might appoint a female ambassador, Halide Edip (Adıvar), to Washington if the United States recognized Turkey[43]. In doing so, Atatürk attempted to demonstrate the progressive nature of the new Turkey with regard to the status of women. Halide Edip, who acted as interpreter for this interview, wore a headscarf to the meeting, and the idea of appointing her as an ambassador to the US was in keeping with modernist Muslim visions of new Muslim women. Yet for European and American observers, the Turkish War of Independence was a Muslim revolt against the West, supported by a Pan-Islamic public in India and other European colonies.

When the Turkish Republic tried to change the clash of civilizations narrative after abolishing the Caliphate and initiating radical westernization reforms in 1926, *Young Islam on Trek: A Study in the Clash of Civilizations,* a book by erstwhile Christian missionary Basil Mathews, insisted on promulgating the old framework of the Muslim world versus the West.[44] From 1924 onward Mathews worked at the Geneva headquarters of the World Alliance of Young Men's Christian Associations. Mathews argues that the abolition of the Caliphate presented Indian Muslims with a dilemma, in that they could neither be Pan-Islamic nor support Indian Home Rule by a Hindu majority. While Mathews observes the revolutionary turmoil in 'the Muslim world' resulting from nationalism, Bolshevism, and the abolition of the Caliphate, he also confirms the continued existence of a global Muslim public opinion engaged in discussing the reforms of Atatürk, Said Zaghlul, Ibn Saud, and Riza Shah. He views the secularizing reforms of Republican Turkey with some misgiving, however, arguing that 'Islam really liberalized is simply a non-Christian Unitarianism. It ceases to be essential Islam.'[45] Other interwar-era European and American accounts shared the same commitment to equating 'Muslim world' with an unchanging framework of a civilization, history, and faith. Thus, Turkish secularism was represented as a new experiment in the

43 From Mark L. Bristol to the Secretary of State, Desp. 162, 25 April 1921, quoted in Turgay Akbaba, 'Reimagining Turkey as an American Ally, 1919–1960', PhD dissertation, University of North Carolina at Chapel Hill, 2020, 39.

44 Basil Mathews, *Young Islam on Trek: A Study in the Clash of Civilizations*, 1926; Lothrop Stoddard, *The New World of Islam*.

45 Mathews, *Young Islam on Trek*, 196.

Muslim world, as was Soviet policy towards Muslims inside the Soviet Union and out.[46]

A new narrative of a secular and westernized Turkey emerged gradually, with firm footing by the early 1930s, as a challenge to this ideal of unchanging Islam and Muslim unity. Sensational reforms such as the 'hat revolution' that made wearing European hats compulsory, or the abolition of madrasas and changing the alphabet to Latin script persuaded Western observers that their former enemy was trying to emulate them. The unveiling of Turkish women was also noted as a positive secularizing reform.[47]

Among the many Western promoters of Turkish reform, American diplomats such as Charles Sherrill and Joseph Grew were influential in helping the Turkish government build a new narrative. Sherrill, for example, wrote an authorized biography of Atatürk while serving as US Ambassador to Turkey between 1932 and 1933. Sherrill's comparison of Atatürk with George Washington in a draft of this book led to an invitation to meet with Atatürk in Ankara on 30 June 1932. Sherrill published his admiring biography of Atatürk, *A Year's Embassy to Mustafa Kemal*, upon leaving his post and continued to eulogize Atatürk and the new Turkey throughout his life.[48] Sherrill's predecessor, Joseph Grew shared his convictions and facilitated the preparation of American documentary films praising Turkey's modernization and westernization.

In his 1932 address at Brown University, Wallace Murray, Chief of the Division of Near Eastern Affairs at the US State Department, argued that the idea of 'the unchanging East' was only applicable to Near Eastern countries before the First World War. Emphasizing the world-historical significance of Turkey's westernization, which, for him, rendered the traditional idea of the Orient meaningless, Murray explained how a theocratic Ottoman Empire was transformed into 'a modern secular state, modelled after the nationalist states of Europe.' The new Turkey not only severed the ties binding it to the East; it also embraced Western civilization. Although Murray mentioned other reforms, he focused on

---

46 Samuel Zwemer, *Across the World of Islam*, 1925; Hamilton Gibb, *Whither Islam: A Survey of Modern Movements in the Moslem World*, 1932; Charles Adams, *Islam and Modernism in Egypt: A Study of the Modern Reform Movement Inaugurated by Mohammad Abduh*, 1933.

47 For the Turkish government's political utilization of the 1932 crowning of Keriman Halis as Miss University Beauty Contest, see Ansev Demirhan, '"We Can Defend Our Rights by Our Own Efforts": Turkish Women and the Global Muslim Question, 1870–1935', unpublished PhD dissertation, University of North Carolina at Chapel Hill, 2020.

48 Charles H. Sherrill, *A Year's Embassy to Mustafa Kemal*, 1934.

the alphabet reform as the key development separating Turkey from the Muslim East.[49]

This grand narrative of a secularizing Turkish nation leaving the Muslim world and joining Western civilization bolstered Turkish elites' legitimacy in the Eurocentric imperial world order. When the young Turkish Republic was unable to form an alliance with any Western power during the turbulent interwar period, westernization and secularization became two master narratives used to shift public opinion in Europe and America from anti-Turkish to pro-Turkish. For the Turkish republican elite, persuading European and American elites that Turkey had become less Muslim and more secular through westernization was necessary for the future survival of their Republic in an insecure international order. In this geopolitical vision, secularism serves as an invitation for citizens of European nation states to overcome their white racial and Christian biases and embrace a universal interpretation of Eurocentric modernity by accepting that non-Europeans can join the West if the latter meet certain standards of westernization and secularization. The resulting international legitimacy of the Republic of Turkey was later appropriated by US and Turkish elites in the first two decades of the Cold War to justify their alliance and Turkey's joining NATO in 1952. When Cold War modernization theory presented Turkey as a successful case of modernization in a Muslim majority country, it incorporated elements from earlier interwar-era narratives, including the theory of secularism.[50]

Conclusion

Given Turkey's position as one of the few sovereign non-European states of the interwar period, the Turkish nationalist strategy of gaining security and legitimacy

---

49 Wallace Murray, 'Westernization in Turkey and Persia', 5 March 1932.

50 Cemil Aydın and Burhanettin Duran, 'Arnold Toynbee in Cold War Era Islamism: Sezai Karakoç's Civilizational Cosmopolitanism', *Comparative Studies of South Asia, Africa and the Middle East* 35/2, 2015, 310–323. For books adopting the paradigm of the 'new Turkey' vs. 'old Turkey': Henry Elisha Allen, *The Turkish Transformation: a study in social and religious development*, 1935; Eliot Grinnell Mears, *Modern Turkey: a politico-economic interpretation, 1908–1923,* 1924; Clair Price, *The Rebirth of Turkey*, 1923; Lilo Linke, *Allah Dethroned: a journey through modern Turkey*, 1937; Hanss Froembgen, *Kemal Ataturk: a Biography*, 1937; Donald Everett Webster, *The Turkey of Ataturk: social process in the Turkish reformation*, 1939. For examples of canonical Cold War modernization literature extolling Turkey as a model for non-Western – and particularly Muslim societies, see: Daniel Lerner, *The Passing of Traditional Society: Modernizing the Middle East*, 1958; George C. McGhee, 'Turkey Joins the West,' *Foreign Affairs* 32/4, 1954, 617–630.

through a discourse of westernization and secularism had a large impact on the new language of international affairs. The debate on Turkey after Lausanne merits close examination if we are to make sense of the gradual changes and theoretical reformulations it encouraged during the transition from the era of empires to the era of nation states. It would, however, be a mistake to make a direct link between the Lausanne Treaty of 1923 and the Bandung moment of 1955 or the 1960 UN Resolution 1514 on self-determination. Turkish leaders were not seeking a third world or Afro-Asian alliance to create a world without empires. Instead, the early Republic focused on its precarious position as a post-Ottoman Muslim-majority nation state in a world still dominated by European empires.

Post–World War II modernization and nationalism scholarship promoted by American social scientists was full of praise for the Turkish experience of nation-building. Given that American and European depictions of 'the terrible Turk' in the early 1920s relied on the clash of civilizations theory, this transformation signifies a significant change in the leading narratives about world order.[51] Early Cold War American and Western European praise for Turkish modernization was partly the achievement of Turkish leaders and intellectuals who used the theories of nationalism, secularism, and westernization to erase the negative connotations of their Muslim identity. The nationalism and secularism associated with Lausanne confirmed the Treaty's status as a turning point in modern Turkey's relationship with the West, and provided useful new universalist narratives that Americans, Western Europeans, and Turks could invoke to strengthen their geopolitical alliance in the early Cold War.[52]

Given Lausanne's place in altering master narratives of world politics in the interwar period, it is no coincidence that, once the 'Clash of Civilizations' theory returned in Samuel Huntington's much discussed 1993 *Foreign Affairs* essay, the author had to discuss Turkey as a 'torn country,' because of the supposed contradiction between its Westernized orientation and its Muslim identity. Disturbed and puzzled by the return of clash of civilization narratives after the Cold War,

51 Roger Trask, 'The "Terrible Turk" and Turkish-American Relations in the Interwar Period', *The Historian* 33/1, 1970, 40–53.

52 For scholarly writings on Turkish nationalism and modernization, Roger Trask, *The United States Response to Turkish Nationalism and Reform, 1914–1939*, 1971; Dankwart Rustow, 'Politics and Islam in Turkey 1920–1955,' in *Islam and the West*, ed. Richard N. Frye, 1957, 69–107; Robert E. Ward and Dankwart Rustow, eds., *Political Modernization in Japan and Turkey*, 1964; Niyazi Berkes, *The Development of Secularism in Turkey*, 1998. In 1958, American television station CBS aired a documentary on Atatürk full of praise for Turkey's nation-building experience. See *The Twentieth Century Documentary Series*, 'The Incredible Turk,' produced by Burton Benjamin and narrated by Walter Cronkite.

Turkey's secular elites and foreign ministry were quick to respond to the implications of this 'torn country' narrative after the events of 11 September 2001 by organizing and hosting big international conferences on inter-civilization dialogue, inviting leaders of the EU and the Organisation of Islamic Cooperation to Istanbul for dialogue. Yet, only by examining the key role of Lausanne in the formation of contemporary conflicting narratives of the world order can we make sense of the historical roots of the contemporary appeal of the clash of civilizations theory in a world of sovereign nation states.[53]

53 For the United Nations Alliance of Civilization initative co-sponsored by Turkey and Spain, see https://www.unaoc.org/who-we-are/history/.

5

Debates over an Armenian National Home at the Lausanne Conference and the Limits of Post-Genocide Co-Existence

Lerna Ekmekcioglu[1]

At the 1922–1923 Lausanne Conference, Armenians asked for the establishment of an 'Armenian National Home' *(Foyer Arménien en Turquie* in French, *Azkayin Dun* in Armenian, *Ermeni Yurdu* in Turkish). This 'home' was going to be a place of refuge where the survivors of the 1915 Armenian Genocide would return in order to congregate, sustain their culture, and feel safe and secure. The proposed place and the political structure of an Armenian National Home (hereafter ANH) evolved during the conference deliberations. The demand for the ANH changed from an independent statelet in either Eastern Anatolia or Northern Syria to an autonomous and demilitarized zone anywhere *within* Turkey. Armenian representatives vowed that an ANH could turn resentful and vengeful Armenian refugees into grateful and loyal Turkish citizens.

1 Thank you: Hayarpi Papikyan for translating materials from French to English; Sinan Çetin, Houry Pilibbossian, and Shogher Maria Doughramajian for research assistance; Melissa Bilal, Ohannes Kılıçdağı, Michelle Tusan, Elyse Semerdjian, Lerna Yanık, and Seda Altuğ for reading different versions of this chapter, and Ahmet Demirel and the National Association for Armenian Studies and Research (NAASR) for sending me relevant primary source materials when needed. Thank you, Jonathan Conlin and Ozan Ozavci for the Lausanne Project and for all the valuable feedback.

The ANH had supporters among the Allied representatives, but they all knew that it would be very hard to convince the Turks to accept it and had communicated this point to the Armenians before the conference. Indeed, the Turkish delegation opposed it vehemently. The Turks argued that 'home' for Armenians was the Armenian Soviet Socialist Republic which was established in December 1920. They claimed that all Armenians belonged to that republic or at least they should. Moreover, Turkish statesmen and the Turkish press perceived the Allies' support of Armenian demands for a national home as yet another example of Great Power meddling in the internal affairs of the Turkish state. In the same vein, they associated the 'humanitarian crusade' on behalf of Armenians as a hypocritical exercise that willfully ignored the violence caused by the colonialism and racism of the Great Powers.

In hindsight, we can argue that the ANH was a stillborn project. Why would a victorious, unrepentant government allow the survivors of genocide claim an autonomous zone within its newly recognized international borders? If we look at the process from the perspective of the Armenian leadership, however, their mobilization for ANH was neither naïveté nor idealism. Their memoirs show that they knew how extremely difficult the realization of their demands would be.[2] They simply had no other option but to try for some sort of self-determination because not doing so would amount to accepting the consequences of the genocide: the Armenians' total elimination from their native lands. It was one last effort to salvage something meaningful out of the post-WWI shuffling of power and territory in the Middle East. This is why, despite their history of loss – the genocide, the Allied withdrawal from Anatolia, the annulling of the Sevrès Treaty (which had in 1920 marked out a space in Anatolia for an Armenia), and loss of the 1920 Turkish-Armenian War in the Caucasus – Armenians tried to convince everyone at Lausanne that an ANH was one of the requirements for achieving political stability in the region. One can hardly exaggerate the degree of pro-Armenian sentiment in Western public opinion from at least 1915 onwards (in this regard Armenians are comparable to Ukrainians in Western imagery in 2022). Quite a number of NGOs and church groups from different Western countries were at Lausanne for the sole purpose of supporting the Armenian cause. But the Armenians faced an insurmountable hurdle in realizing the demand for an ANH – nonc

2 Alexander Khatissian, *Hayastani Hanrabedutyan Dzakumn u Zarkatsume*, 1930, 318. Khatissian's memoirs were first serialized in the Armenian Revolutionary Federation's *Hairenik* periodical (published in Boston) in its original Eastern Armenian. For a French translation, see Alexandre Khatissian, *Éclosion et développement de la République arménienne*, 1989.

of the Allies had any incentive to resume military conflict with the Turks on behalf of the Armenians who had no armed force of their own sufficient to back up their demand.

The story of the non-establishment of an autonomous Armenian zone within Turkey has not been integrated into the general histories of the Lausanne Conference and remains understudied. One exception is Turkish nationalist historians' treatment of this 'territorial demand' as proof of treasonous, separatist activities by Armenians, which, according to this logic, retrospectively justifies their elimination.[3] Armenian historiography has viewed the topic as peripheral, as just another example of the Allied failure to support the Armenians. This chapter is the first in-depth treatment of the topic to use both Armenian and Turkish primary sources alongside conference proceedings and diplomatic correspondence.[4]

In the literature on Lausanne the topic of autonomy usually receives scant attention, while other population policies such as plebiscites and population exchanges are relatively well studied. The contemporary scholarship on population movements, especially the Greek-Turkish Population Exchange, tends to see the goal of 'unmixing of populations'[5] as ethnic cleansing.[6] While I agree

3 Another exception is Hans-Lukas Kieser, *When Democracy Died: The Middle East's Enduring Peace of Lausanne*, 2023, which has a chapter dedicated to the Armenian National Home.

4 Even though he does not use Turkish or Armenian newspapers or periodicals, Levon Marashlian's 1992 dissertation is an exception in that he consults English, French, Armenian, and Turkish conference proceedings and memoirs. This extensive work unfortunately remains unpublished. Levon Marashlian, 'The Armenian Question from Sevrès to Lausanne: Economics and Morality in American and British Politics, 1920–1923', PhD dissertation, UCLA, 1992, 647–825.

5 The term 'unmixing of populations' which is usually (and wrongly) attributed to Lord Curzon refers to the goal of segregating groups from each other within a general population so that peace is achieved and sustained. This widely used term entered the literature in 1995 with Roger Brubaker's article 'Aftermaths of Empire and the Unmixing of Peoples: Historical and Comparative Perspectives', *Ethnic and Racial Studies* 18/2, 1995, 189–218. Brubaker references another book when attributing the term to Curzon. This book (Michael R. Marrus, *The Unwanted – European Refugees in the Twentieth Century*, 1985), however, does not provide any citations as to when Curzon specifically used the term. According to the proceedings of the Lausanne Conference in English, the term 'unmixing' was used only once, by Fridtjof Nansen, the League of Nation's High Commissioner for Refugees, when he proposed the Greek-Turkish Population Exchange to the conference – *Lausanne Conference on Near Eastern Affairs, 1922–1923: Records of Proceedings and Draft Terms of Peace*, 1923 (hereafter *Lausanne Conference*), 114.

6 The literature on the Exchange of Populations is too large to cite here. For some recent samples, see the works of Renée Hirschon, Onur Yıldırım, Umut Özsu, Aslı Iğsız, and Sarah Shields.

with this designation given the compulsory character of the 'home(land) swap', I remain ambivalent about condemning it as such in this context which is what the term 'ethnic cleansing' commands. This is because the Armenians based their desire for an ANH on the need to segregate themselves from people, their former neighbours, who killed, raped, or kidnapped their families. One of the aims of this chapter, therefore, is to question the assumed merits of continued and unsupervised cohabitation for groups who have recently experienced severe inter-ethnic violence. In other words, in the absence of legally binding and enforceable guarantees for the protection of survivors in the land of unapologetic perpetrators it is wishful thinking to expect a peaceful coexistence for decades to come.

Critical scholarship in the field of the post-WWI Arab Middle East, on the other hand, usually associates unmixing measures with colonial(ist) policies (such as 'divide and rule') involving different communities in a region sharing commonalities (rather than different political imaginations) which are then exploited by a colonial power. While I do not necessarily reject such conclusions, here I bring an example that complicates this picture. By delving into the demands of the Armenian delegation at Lausanne, I demonstrate how the (primarily colonial) discourse of unmixing may have been justified by local subaltern groups within novel political forms. Armenians, for example, demanded segregation not because a colonialist power was behind the project but in order to sustain a decent future for the displaced Armenians. Being an initial attempt at understanding the contours of the ANH, this chapter only scratches the surface. More studies are needed to provide its diplomatic genealogy and evolution as well as to put it in a comparative lens, especially with the Irish Home Rule movement and the 'Jewish National Home' of the Balfour Declaration.

The Armenian Mission at Lausanne

The Armenian Mission to the Lausanne conference was made up of five individuals who called themselves the United Armenian Delegation (*Miatsyal Badviragutyun*) and claimed that they represented all Armenians, both the Western (or Ottoman/Turkish) and Eastern (former Russian) Armenians,[7] though Soviet Armenia did not recognize this delegation, and some factions of Armenians in

7 The names of these individuals are Latinized differently in different publications and languages. Alternatives to the ones used in this chapter are: Kapriel Noradounghian (or Gabriel Noradunkyan), Leon Pachalian (or Levon Paşalyan), Avedis Aharounian (or Aharonyan), Alexandre Khatissian (Alexander Khatisian or Khadisyan), Krikor Snabian (or Sınapyan).

Constantinople tried to distance their group from the Mission.[8] The Armenian Mission acted as the continuation of the delegations that went to the Paris, San Remo, and London Conferences to push for the Armenian cause. At these conferences there were two delegations, one representing the 'diaspora Armenians and Ottoman Armenians' and the other representing the Republic of Armenia (or 'First Republic') which had existed from May 1918 to December 1920 (after which it became part of the Soviet Union as a result of being attacked by the Kemalist armies).

In the immediate post-war years, the 'Armenian cause' entailed the demand for full statehood in Eastern Anatolia and/or Cilicia either independently or under the protection of a Western mandate. The Sèvres Treaty of August 1920 approved a 'free and independent Armenia' whose borders were going to be demarcated by the US president but was certainly going to be in Eastern Anatolia. But in time, and in response to Turkish military victories and Allied loss of interest in the region, the Armenians had to scale down their demands. The idea of a 'National Home' for Armenians was first broached at the 1921 London Conference which the Allies convened to revise the Sèvres Treaty. It was discussed in the League of Nations Assembly discussions up to the very opening of the Lausanne Conference. A few days before the opening of the Conference, the Armenian Delegation sent a note to Lord Curzon in which they proposed three areas for an ANH: Eastern Anatolia, expansion of Soviet Armenia, or a part of Cilicia.[9] The Turkish refusal to even discuss the topic of an ANH would lead the sympathetic Allies increasingly to more modest versions of the proposal. By the end of the Lausanne Conference, when the topic was discussed, it became, in the words of Lord Curzon, 'just a place to be set apart under Turkish rule and with a Turkish Governor-General, where the Armenians could congregate for the purpose of maintaining their race, language and culture.'[10]

At Lausanne, the Armenian Mission had two co-chairs: Gabriel Noradungian on behalf of the Ottoman/Turkish Armenians and Avedis Aharonian on behalf of the Russian Armenians and the former independent Republic of Armenia. Born

8 See Lerna Ekmekcioglu, 'Kalanlar: Savaş Sonrasında ve Tek Parti Döneminde İstanbul Ermeni Cemmati', *1915: Siyaset, Tehcir, Soykırım,* eds. Fikret Adanır and Oktay Özel, 2015, 537–553.

9 British Foreign Office FO371–7875. 'Formation of National Home for Armenians.' Copy of letter of 16 November 1922 addressed to Lord Curzon in Paris by United Armenian Delegation. (I thank Daniel MacArthur for helping me locate this document).

10 *Lausanne Conference*, 299. At this stage of the proceedings, Lord Curzon said that it was not even an autonomous regime that the Armenians were asking for.

and raised in Istanbul, Noradungian (1852–1936) had been an Ottoman statesman all his life. He was the Minister of Foreign Affairs of the Ottoman Empire until 1913 when he left the country after the coup d'état in January. Aharonian (1866–1948) was the former head of the Armenian National Council during the Republic of Armenia's brief existence as a sovereign state, when it was ruled by his party, the Armenian Revolutionary Federation (*Tashnaktsutyun*, hereafter ARF). Aharonian had signed the Treaty of Sèvres as the Armenian representative. He had been pushed into exile after Sovietization, along with all ARF members. It is important to note that differences of opinion existed within the Armenian Mission regarding the ANH. While Noradungian was more modest in his demands (a dominion within Turkey would suffice), Aharonian was more maximalist in that he sometimes replaced autonomy with independence in the way he talked about the ANH.[11] In general Armenians wanted self-government of any sort, and the Allies translated this demand into the Lausanne negotiations as autonomy. To obtain Turkish acquiescence, they kept emphasizing that the ANH would be an integral part of Turkey.

In mid-October 1922, the United Armenian Delegation applied to the Allies to ask for Armenian participation in the Lausanne Conference.[12] The Allies refused to invite the Armenians on the grounds that Armenia was now a Soviet Republic, and the Soviets were already invited to the conference, albeit only for the sessions pertaining to the Turkish Straits. If the conference needed to hear the Armenian viewpoint, they would invite the United Armenian Delegation based in Paris.[13] In early November, the Armenian Mission nonetheless arrived at Lausanne where they would stay for three months, lobbying, networking and propagandizing for the ANH.

'We Can No Longer Live Side-by-Side': Armenians and Turks Meet after the Opening of the Conference

Even though the Turkish Delegation objected to hearing the Armenian Mission in any official session of the conference, in private the two groups met and discussed various topics, chiefly the ANH. The first meeting between İsmet İnönü

11 Their differences went back as early as December 1921. See Avedis Aharonian, 'Hay Bedutyun te *Home*?', *Saradarabadits Minchev Sevr yev Lozan*, 1943, 184–185.

12 They based their claims, among other things, on the idea that (Ottoman) Turkey recognized Armenia as a 'free and independent state' in Article 88 of the Sèvres Treaty which was true.

13 The texts of the Armenians' application to the Allies and the latter's rejection are provided in Khatissian's memoirs as historical documents. Khatissian, *Hayastani*, 312–316.

(hereafter İsmet) and the Armenians took place on 25 November, the fifth day of the conference. İsmet received the vice-chair Krikor Sinapian and secretary Levon Pashalian in his hotel room. Noradungian had not yet arrived and İsmet avoided meeting with the Russian Armenian Aharonian in order not to upset the Soviets. Before entering the room, Atıf Esenbel, a military commander and one of İsmet's ten bodyguards, greeted the two Armenians and patted them down for weapons.[14]

These bodyguards were there for a reason: despite the tiny size of the (unofficial) Armenian Mission, the Turkish Delegation feared Armenians, not so much for their demands but more for their 'terrorism.' Armenians had demonstrated their capability in putting together well-planned, precise assassinations. Beginning with the March 1921 assassination in Berlin of Talât (the Ottoman Minister of Interior Affairs at the time of the Armenian Genocide), by the summer of 1922 the ARF's clandestine Operation Nemesis had killed the main orchestrators of the Armenian Genocide. This is why İsmet had brought to Lausanne ten bodyguards, some of them also acting as his aides. He also demanded and received from the Swiss government two police officers for his personal protection.[15] Rıza Nur, the Turkish representative to the Minorities' Sub-commission, would write in his memoirs that during the conference four people from the International Philarmenian League implied that the Turkish delegates would be targeted if an ANH was rejected. He replied to them that 'the Turkish society had vowed that if [Armenians] kill one more Turk, they would massacre ten thousand Armenians in response.'[16]

When Vorovsky (the Soviet Ambassador to Rome) was assassinated later during the conference, it made headlines in Turkish newspapers with special reports mentioning that an assassination plot against İsmet by Armenians was also possibly in the making.[17] The Swiss police issued a statement that they had successfully foiled an attempted assassination of İsmet three months ago by an

14 Levon Pashalian, 'Lozani khaghahgutyan khorkhurtaghove', *Aysor* 1/5, 12 January 1951. The Lausanne chronicles of Pashalian (1868–1943) were serialized in the Armenian daily *Aysor* [Today] (published in Paris) from 9 January 1951 (year 1, no. 2) to 8 March 1951 (year 1, no. 52). This 50-part chronicle of the conference which also includes multiple letters between Noradungian and Pashalian was published as a book in 1983 in Beirut. Levon Pashalian, *Lozani Khaghaghutyan Khorkhrtazhoghove*, 1983.

15 Şerafettin Turan, *İsmet İnönü, Yaşamı, Dönemi ve Kişiliği*, 2000, 55.

16 Dr. Rıza Nur, *Lozan Hatıraları, İlaveli Üçüncü Baskı*, 1992, 125.

17 *Vatan* [Homeland], 11 May 1923; İleri [Forward] 12 May 1923. It was also reported by the Armenian papers. For example, *Jagadamard* [Battle] on 13 May 1923. On 14 November 1922, İsmet noted in his diary that he had learned that Armenians were preparing an assassination attempt against him. *İsmet İnönü, Defterler 1919–1973*, 2001, 45.

Armenian who managed to enter Lausanne.[18] The *New York Times* reported that the Swiss frontier was now closed to all Greeks and Armenians unable to give satisfactory reasons for entering Switzerland.[19] The Swiss government asked İsmet to discontinue eating in the public dining room of the hotel so that they could protect him better. İsmet was, therefore, 'practically a prisoner in his room,' which upset him because it made him look like 'a coward[ly] Turk.'[20] To compensate, he told Western reporters that Armenians could not scare a Turkish general and that he was going to spend all his spare time in a chair facing the door waiting for the assassins at the ready.[21] Since İsmet embodied the new Turkey, he did not want to present an image of a weak and vulnerable leadership terrorized by a few Armenian radicals. He must have seen these Armenians as a reincarnated '*komitadji*', the type of 'revolutionary' separatist Armenian that had rebelled against Ottoman rule. At Lausanne no Turkish diplomat was hurt by Armenians. Armenian diplomats' memoirs note that it was Turks who produced these lies to present Armenians as terrorists and that there was never any real assassination plan or attempt.[22]

Despite all these anxieties, Levon Pashalian's later account of the meeting describes how the secretary of the Armenian Mission encountered a fatherly İsmet who welcomed them warmly, putting his hand over Sinapian's shoulder, asking him to speak louder (İsmet was hard of hearing) and acting pleased when he learned that Sinapian was the former Ottoman Minister of Forestry and Mining (in 1911) and later Minister of Public Works (in 1912).[23] Sinapian explained their demands: an enclave inside Turkey for the 700,000 to 800,000 Ottoman Armenian refugees. İsmet asked why these people could not 'return' to the Yerevan Republic. Sinapian replied that there was no space for them, as the 9,000 km^2 of inhabitable land was barely enough for the Soviet Republic's 1.3m inhabitants. Observing İsmet's hesitation, Sinapian noted that the places around Van where Armenians would ideally settle had been laid waste. Meanwhile, Turkey had a vast area of land: its 800,000 km^2 was more than enough for its 8 million Turks and the Armenians. To convince İsmet that it would be better to assign Armenians to a

18 'Swiss order Ahrens to leave', *New York Times*, 12 May 1923; 'Ismet Pasha's Safety', *The Manchester Guardian*, 12 May 1923.

19 'Ismet warned of murder plot; Swiss give him a Bodyguard', *New York Times*, 22 May 1923.

20 'Swiss isolate Ismet, shadow Venizelos. Guard Conference delegates against Vorovsky's Fate – Turk leader no longer eats in public', *New York Times*, 21 May 1923.

21 'Ismet in rage. Plot to assassinate. Lausanne Turks alarmed', *The Times of India*, taken from *The Times* (London), 23 May 1923, 9.

22 Khatissian, *Hayastani,* 326.

23 *Aysor* 1/6, 13 January 1951. Sinapian was one of the many Armenians who spoke Turkish.

designated region, Sinapian acknowledged that 'the Turks do not want to live side by side with Armenians.' Armenians did not want to live side by side with Turks anymore either. His proposal was the best solution for a majority who had to deal with an unwanted minority and a survivor population who would rather remain separated from hostile neighbours. His argument is worth quoting at length:

> When, tomorrow, Hagop or Garabed [classic Armenian names] goes back to Turkey and sees that his house is in Mehmed's hands, that his field is in Hasan's hands [classic Turkish names], and that his wife or daughter or son is in this or that harem, how can you expect anything other than occasions for endless strife? If you want peace, satisfy the Armenians' rightful demand, which is to have a place for themselves in which they can live freely. Otherwise, wherever you go, whatever you may do, you will find us standing against you; or, if not us, then our friends, of course. Those hundreds of thousands of refugees survive today thanks to America's and Europe's humanitarianism and, to keep that humanitarianism burning bright, an intense propaganda campaign is being waged: every day, everywhere, it is being said over and over again that the Armenians must be helped, because they have no place they can call their own, because the Turks do not want to give them a place of their own.
>
> You made beggars of this hard-working, industrious people. After the Great War, the principle of *réparation*, *restitution*, and *sanctions* [in French in Armenian letters] found acceptance everywhere, and you, too, invoke those principles. We do not ask you for anything at all because of the past; we do not demand any kind of retribution at all. The only retribution we want from you is a place in which we can live, and that is something that we shall always, and rightfully, demand from you. Even a dog, after you have beaten him ten times over, goes back to his kennel. We want to go back to those lands on which we have lived for three thousand years. If we have our Home [*Dun*] we will be good neighbours for you, because, as one of you has said, if we are good enemies, we are also good friends, and we can be of more use to you in the future than the Europeans who will, perforce, come to take our place tomorrow. If we have a Home of our own, all the issues dividing us will be settled. That is the only possible resolution of our question, because circumstances are now such that we can no longer live side-by-side.[24]

24 *Aysor* 1/7, 14–15 January 1951. Translation from Armenian by G.M. Goshgarian.

According to Pashalian's account, İsmet looked frustrated, confused, and slightly overwhelmed. After Sinapian's last words he murmured a half sentence, '*Vous vous découragez. Je pensais que …*' ('It is not that bad. I think that …') but did not finish his sentence.[25] The next day İsmet wired Ankara that 'it is clear that they [Armenians] will cause storms in the conference.'[26] Otherwise İsmet relayed nothing of Sinapian's passionate remarks, in which he invoked indigeneity, reparations, and the Armenians' dispossession of their land and of their women and children as grounds for an ANH. None of it mattered.[27] Ankara's main goal for the Armenians was the opposite: full removal by an exchange of populations.

Even though this did not form part of the discussions at the time, the demand for an ANH can be seen as an extension of the Armenian Reform Agreement of 8 February 1914. This agreement between the CUP government and the Russians allowed for an internationally monitored and comparatively democratic local government in the mainly Armenian- and Kurdish-populated provinces in Eastern Anatolia. Since it restricted their sovereignty, the CUP feared that it was an imperialist design to divide the Ottoman Empire, and as such this agreement became one of the major factors motivating the Ottomans to enter the war in alliance with Germany in October 1914.[28] The war aborted the reform package. The de-Christianization of Anatolia ensued. Ankara was bent on continuing the process at the negotiation table at Lausanne.

The 14-point protocol (a 'to-do list') that Ankara handed to the delegation before their departure for Lausanne included the statement that the ideal solution to the minority question was an exchange of populations.[29] Five days after the opening of the conference and after conversations with the British and the Americans, İsmet informed Ankara that it would be difficult to push for the extraction

---

25 *Aysor* 1/7, 14–15 January 1951.

26 Telegram no. 31, from İsmet to Prime Minister's Office (26 November 1922) in *Lozan Telgrafları: Türk Diplomatik Belgelerinde Lozan Barış Konferansı, Cilt 1 (Kasım 1922- Şubat 1923)*, 1990.

27 In his memoirs İsmet did not mention this meeting, instead noting the one that he had with Noradungian on 9 December 1922 which, according to him, went quite tense as Noradungian asked for territory and İsmet resisted it using forceful language. *İsmet İnönü Hatıralaları Kitap II*, haz. Sabahattin Selek, 2006, 80–81. Pashalian's description of the meeting differs from İsmet's as he pays more attention to the words of Noradungian rather than İsmet's answers. *Aysor* 1/13, 22 January 1951.

28 Hans-Lukas Kieser, Mehmet Polatel, and Thomas Schmutz, 'Reform or Cataclysm? The Agreement of 8 February 1914 regarding the Ottoman Eastern Provinces', *Journal of Genocide Research* 14/3, 2015, 285–304.

29 Mustafa Budak, *99 Soruda Lozan*, 2018, 54–55.

of the Armenians out of the country, though it would be possible for the Greeks.[30] At first Ankara rejected İsmet's proposal to keep the Armenians. Prime Minister Rauf Orbay told İsmet that the Armenians in Turkey should be exchanged with the Turks in [Soviet] Armenia (i.e., Tatars and Azeri Turks).[31] İsmet resisted the idea, giving as explanation the lack of an interlocutor. He did not want to engage Soviet Russia in any discussions other than those about the Turkish Straits lest it led to discussion of the 1921 Moscow Treaty which the Turks upheld as finalized. Worse, it could lead to Soviet Russia wanting to discuss the expansion of Soviet Armenia's borders at Turkey's expense. 'Under these conditions,' İsmet noted, 'we do not have any other option but to accept that Armenians will stay in our land.' He added that all 'American missionaries and all Armenian communities are here. My idea is to make them look like [normal, ordinary] citizens' (*benim fikrim onlara vatandaş yüzü göstermektedir*). I intend to refuse the ANH and if possible, the minority protections.'[32] Ankara approved İsmet's strategy.[33] The question of the exchange of Armenians was therefore never discussed in the conference.

Une Zone Autonome vs. *Imperium in Imperio*: The Conference Listens to the Armenians

Beginning on 12 December 1922, the Territorial and Military Commission discussed the question of minorities for three days, after which they created a Minorities Sub-commission for in-depth conversations. The Sub-commission met a total of seventeen times between 15 December 1922 and 11 January 1923.[34] The ANH stood as the tenth and last item in the agenda of the Sub-commission chaired by the Italian delegate Sig. Montagna. Rıza Nur rejected bringing it up for discussion, but Montagna begged him to be more understanding.

The only area where the Turkish delegation did not show any flexibility was on

30 Telegram no. 23, from İsmet to Prime Minister's Office (25 November 1922), *Lozan Telgrafları*, 124.

31 Telegram no. 50, from Hüseyin Rauf to İsmet (28 November 1922), *Lozan Telgrafları*, 143. Rauf repeated this point in Telegram no.73, from Hüseyin Rauf to İsmet (4 December 1922), *Lozan Telgrafları*, 162–163.

32 Telegram no. 86, İsmet to Prime Minister's Office (6 December 1922), *Lozan Telgrafları*, 172.

33 Telegram no. 93, Hüseyin Rauf to İsmet (7 December 1922), *Lozan Telgrafları*, 176.

34 Minorities Sub-commission's minutes are not included in the Lausanne Conference's English or French version of the proceedings but they are included in the Turkish version (141 pages total). 'B. Azınlıklar Alt-Komisyonu', *Lozan Barış Konferansı: Tutanaklar Belgeler* Takım 1, Cilt 1, Kitap 2, 1970, 151–292.

the ANH, even though the Allies and the Americans brought it up repeatedly. For Turks, autonomy amounted to *imperium in imperio*, a state within a state. Turkey, İsmet noted, 'now reduced to essentially Turkish provinces, no longer contains any minority which can form within it an independent State,' adding that asking for an ANH was like the Greeks of Marseilles asking to have an independent Greek State or annexing it to their mother-country. İsmet's words that talk about both independence and being a state within a state (self-rule, local government) are revealing of the overall (partially purposeful) confusion regarding what an ANH and autonomy meant. Regardless, İsmet underlined in no uncertain terms that Turks would be willing to resume military operations if the Allies imposed this on Turkey.[35] He also asked why the Allies could not find a place for the Armenians 'in the regions quite recently detached from Turkey,' implying that mandates in the Near East could be a refuge for dispersed Armenians. From Ankara's perspective, Turkey was 'inhabited by a Turkish majority and each part of it formed an indivisible whole.'[36] The Turks always referred to the fact that Turkey had already recognized an Armenia (Soviet) with whom it had signed a treaty and with whom it had 'friendly relations and neighbourly feelings.' They would not agree to another Armenia.[37]

On 26 December 1922, three members of the Armenian Mission presented their case for an ANH. Despite the protests of the Turkish delegates, Sub-commission members listened to the Armenians even though they were not an official delegation. They were thus allocated seventy minutes of time in which to make their representations. The Turkish Delegation boycotted the meeting and declared that it could not be considered an official session on that very account. In his protest to Curzon, İsmet noted that the Armenian Delegation did not represent Armenia since Soviet Armenia did not recognize this delegation and did not themselves participate in the conference (which was true).[38] If the Armenian Mission was meant to represent Armenians inside Turkey, he argued, then it meant that the Allies were intervening in the domestic affairs of the country. If so, he continued, 'we should listen to the minorities in Romania, Bulgaria, Greece and others as well as Muslim countries' delegates.' Rıza Nur added that Egypt, Palestine, Syria, India, Tunisia and Libya should be granted a hearing as well as Ireland.[39]

35 *Lausanne Conference,* 203.
36 *Lausanne Conference*, 219.
37 *Lausanne Conference*, 203.
38 Hüseyin Câhid, 'Lozan Konferansı'nda Noel günleri kopan fırtına (Lozan Mektupları: 45)', *Tanîn* 79, 31 December 1922.
39 Hüseyin Câhid, 'Lozan Konferansı'nda'.

While the Turkish Delegation could not prevent Armenians, Bulgarians, and Assyrians from lobbying the British, French, and Italian delegates, their request not to consider the session as official and not to record it in the proceedings of the conference was granted. It remains difficult to find the minutes of the session at which the Armenians spoke.[40] The Armenian Mission made a point of giving a copy of their speech to all parties in the conference, including the Turks. *Tanin*'s Lausanne correspondent Hüseyin Câhid published the text along with İsmet's and Rıza's protest notes.[41] It appears that the Armenians did not share copies of Aharonian's speech which was less measured and diplomatic than Noradungian's.

Gabriel Noradungian, Alexander Khatissian and Avedis Aharonian, along with the delegation secretary Levon Pashalian, entered the Sub-commission room at 4:30 pm. Pashalian distributed the French text of their speeches as well as English translations and maps.[42] Each co-chair spoke for about fifteen minutes. After mentioning that their demands were modest and that they wanted peace, Noradungian said that 'the 1915 catastrophe opened a wide gap between the Turks and the Armenians.' But he quickly added that they preferred to focus on the present and the future. He could not but make a direct connection between territory and history, however. 'Only the establishment of an Armenian homeland can draw a curtain on the catastrophes of the past, eliminate the accumulated feelings of vengeance, and reconstitute mutual trust.'

On 13 December 1922, İsmet had declared that 'Armenians who desired to remain in Turkey would be able to live in brotherhood with their Turkish compatriots, who would be full of solicitude for them and would willingly forget the events of the past.'[43] Yet this did not include those Armenians returning to Turkey. As the Turkish government put it in their note to İsmet on 17 December: 'We cannot accept the return of Armenian refugees who departed our country because

40 Armenian National Archives (Hay Azkayin Badviragutyun Archives) fond 430 include both Noradungian's and Aharonian's speeches as well as questions posed to them. To my knowledge, other than Levon Marashlian's unpublished 1992 dissertation, no other study consulted these minutes. The Q&A session of the meeting is included in the Appendix section of Vahan Papazian's memoir: Vahan Papazian, *Im Hushere, Yerrort Hador*, 1957, 418–424. The texts of the speeches are included in Khatissian's memoir *Hayastani*, 335–342.

41 Hüseyin Câhid, 'Lozan Konferansı'nda'.

42 Alexander Khatissian, 'Lozani Khorhrtazhoghove yev mer yergu badviragutyunneru chankere,' *Im Hushere*, 237–306. These are Khatissian's chronicles of the Lausanne Conference which were published in the third volume of Vahan Papazian's memoirs. They were translated into English and serialized in the *Armenian Review* starting from year 14, no. 3–55, September 1961.

43 *Lausanne Conference*, 208.

of various events.'[44] Throughout the negotiations İsmet somehow managed to fudge the issue, giving the impression that Turkey would in fact allow them to return. In their speeches to the Sub-commission, the Armenian delegates took exception to what they understood to be İsmet's proposal. They argued that refugees could not be convinced to return to their original homes where they would only find 'sad memories and innumerable unsolvable problems.' Only an autonomous zone would persuade them to return (even though any such return had already been ruled out by the Turks).

In his presentation to the Allies, Noradungian openly asked that an ANH become a 'dominion' for Turks much like British dominions. As an Ottoman diplomat, he knew the vulnerabilities and sensitivities of the Turkish government. To further incentivize the Turks, therefore, he said that it would be prestigious for them to have a dominion. He also emphasized that world public opinion recognized the fairness of Armenian demands, including 'many Muslims in India, Iran, Azerbaijan, and even inside Turkey.'[45]

The Eastern Armenians' representative, Aharonian, did not mince his words. He accused the Kemalist armies of having attacked the independent Armenian state 'without any grounds or provocations,' seizing territory and aggravating the situation of Armenians in the Caucasus. He also denied İsmet's argument that Tsarist Russia and Great Britain had instigated Armenian liberation movements. Instead, he noted proudly that 'this Armenian movement was the result of the same profound reasons which led to the emancipation of the peoples in the Balkans.' 'Yes, we wanted the liberation of our fatherland, and the unified Armenia remains the ideal of our entire nation.' Given the facts on the ground, however, Aharonian joined Noradungian in settling for a national home 'in the ancient Armenian fatherland' of northern Cilicia. 'In the regions that we claim as our national heritage,' he noted, 'the Turkish race has never been a majority.'[46]

The details of the autonomous zone, its borders and who would be allowed to live there were left ambiguous, likely because the Armenians wanted the freedom to adjust their demands in response to Turkish counter-proposals. During the Q&A

---

44 Telegram no. 157, Hüseyin Rauf to İsmet, *Lozan Telgrafları*, 132. This telegram is in response to İsmet's summary of the 15 December discussion in Telegram no. 143, *Lozan Telgrafları*, 220.

45 'Exposé du M. Noradoughian devant la Sous-Commission de la Conférence de Lausanne le 26 décembre 1922,' Hay Azkayin Badviragutyun Archives, fond 430, section 3, file 1371, documents 9–15.

46 'Discours de Monsieur Aharonian,' Hay Azkayin Badviragutyun Archives, fond 430, section 3, file 1371, documents 16–27.

session, when asked if Eastern Anatolia was a viable option for a national home, Aharonian answered in the affirmative. 'Armenians got on well with Kurds,' Aharonian claimed, 'who are from the same Aryan race and barely Islamised.' Unconvinced about this rosy depiction of Kurds, the French delegate asked Noradungian if he agreed. The latter responded that there were 200 different types of Kurdish tribes and that while Yezidis and Kizilbashes were friends of Armenians ('the latter sheltered more than 20,000 Armenians during the deportations of 1915'), Djelalis and Hayderanlis were hostile.

Both Aharonian and Noradungian emphasized that previous undertakings of the Allies bound them to seek the realization of the ANH. They insisted that the Armenian Mission's views represented those of the Armenian nation as a whole, regardless of party or origin. The Sub-commission delegates assured the Armenians that their concerns would be taken into account.

On 7 January 1923, the chairman of the Minorities Sub-commission tried to broach the subject one more time. Montagna tried to set the Armenian position in context by explaining to the Turks that treaties with some other European states included similar provisions for minorities. He gave the example of the Carpathian Ruthenians in Czechoslovakia who were granted much more expansive rights than those proposed for the ANH. The ANH, which could be established anywhere in Turkey that the Turks deemed appropriate, would have neither a judiciary power nor an autonomous parliament, as the Ruthenians did. The ANH would not be closed to others living in Turkey nor would it act outside of Turkish governance. Minutiae could be discussed at the League of Nations, as long as the Sub-commission came to an agreement about the basic conditions of local governance. This, he added, would also solve the question of refugees.[47]

The British delegate, Horace Rumbold, stated that 'the Turkish State will prove its progress and broadmindedness by accepting the ANH on behalf of the smartest and most hardworking subjects of Turkey.'[48] In this way the ANH would prove to the outside world that the new Turkey was different from the previous regime that had massacred Armenians, and that the Turks were civilized and rule-following new members of the family of nations.

This was just too much to bear for Rıza Nur. He warned that he would leave if the conversation continued. Montagna warned him that he had to listen. But Rıza Nur *knew* that he did not have to. Other than the Capitulations, the Armenian question was the only issue over which the Turkish government had granted

47 *Lausanne Conference*, 308.
48 *Lozan Barış Konferansı,* 277.

authority to the Turkish Delegation at Lausanne to break up negotiations without having to seek Ankara's approval. In fact, it was the first point noted in the protocol given by Ankara to the delegation leaving for Lausanne. 'Eastern Border: An Armenian National Home cannot become a reality; it cannot even become a point of discussion. If it becomes a point of discussion, leave the conference.'[49] Like the Capitulations, it touched the most sensitive spot in the Turkish body politic: sovereignty. Rıza Nur took the initiative and walked out. On the way he managed to squeeze in some words that Rumbold considered 'serious accusations'. Rıza Nur said that they were making these pro-Armenian statements because they had made pledges to the Armenians and the Assyrians. 'In fact, it was the Allies who used these groups as political tools to attack Turkey. The Allies, therefore, are the reason for the catastrophes that they have faced.'[50]

The Sub-commission came to a close. Unresolved topics, mainly the ANH, were referred back to the Territorial and Military Commission which convened again on 9 January 1923. Montagna was disappointed by the Turkish delegation's rejection of his proposal as an ANH 'would have had the advantage of solving once and for all the old racial and religious problems which up to now have occasioned so much suffering and have been one of the causes of the decay of Ottoman power.'[51] The topic was bounced, somewhat vaguely, to the League of Nations.

Armenians left the conference on 5 February 1923. After the signing of the Treaty which did not mention the name 'Armenian' even once, they wrote a letter to the League of Nations asking for their cause to be picked up by the League.[52] The representative of the Eastern Armenians, Avedis Aharonian, wrote a strongly worded protest letter to the representatives of the Allies. He noted that 'this treaty disregards Armenians totally as if they do not exist. The Treaty of Lausanne, by leaving an Oriental society in such ambiguous conditions, cannot serve either peace or justice.'[53]

As for the representative of the Western Armenians, Gabriel Noradungian, he thought it would be wise not to fully sever relations with the Allies as they had assured Armenians that when the League convened to accept Turkey as a member, the ANH would be brought up again. Representatives of the British Labour Party told Khatissian that settling the ANH would be 'a strong proof of the League's

49 Budak, *99 Soruda Lozan*, 54–55.

50 *Lozan Barış Konferansı,* 278.

51 *Lausanne Conference*, 307.

52 Khatissian, *Hayastani,* 355.

53 Khatissian, *Hayastani,* 357.

ability.'[54] To my knowledge the League never took up the subject.[55] 'The poor Armenian Home,' wrote Vahan Papazian, 'remained under ruins.'[56]

Turkish vs. Western Colonialism: Clean, Cleaner, Cleanest Hands

The Lausanne conversations about minorities in general, and Armenians in particular, are an insight into the unstated sub-texts of negotiations between the Turks and the Great Powers. One such sub-text was the assumed moral supremacy of the 'Western world' in managing ethno-diversity which in the nineteenth century had become the standard by which the 'civilizational level' of any non-Western country could be measured. In other words, the treatment of Armenians was a measure used to assess the Turks' 'civilizational level.' The Turks grasped this equation all too well. This is why on the day that the Territorial and Military Commission began discussing the question of minorities (12 December 1922) İsmet delivered a 90-minute history lecture with the goal of rejecting the proposed minority protections. He listed proof after proof of how tolerant Turks had been, contrary to the stereotype of them as 'cruel Asiatic tyrants.'[57] In the following days, the Turkish statesman and the Turkish press would use the same argument (of 'tolerant Turks') to attack British and French imperialism as well as American racism.

The French delegate, Camille Barrère, set the tone on the first day of minority discussions. 'In the vast and diverse regions over which her political activities have spread,' Barrère intoned, 'France has always taken scrupulous care to respect all forms of thought, religion and civilization, however various and however different from her own tradition, and to permit their full development.'[58]

Lord Curzon moved this self-righteousness up a gear on the next day. The British and French Empires, he began:

> … include countless minorities, numbering not thousands, nor hundreds of thousands, but millions of people. Both France and the British Empire

54 Khatissian memoirs in Papazian, *Im Hushere*, p. 288.

55 The League's role regarding Armenians remained in the sphere of humanitarianism and refugee care as well as the confiscated properties of Armenians. See esp. Chapter 6 of Keith David Watenpaugh, *Bread from Stones: The Middle East and the Making of Modern Humanitarianism*, 2015; Carolin Liebisch-Gümüş, 'Embedded Turkification: nation building and violence within the framework of the League of Nations, 1919–1937', *International Journal of Middle East Studies* 52/2, 2020, 229–244.

56 Papazian, *Im Hushere*, 235

57 *Lausanne Conference*, 190–204.

58 *Lausanne Conference*, 181.

> are members of the League; they are not afraid of their minorities making mischief and stirring up trouble within the League, because *their hands are clean*.[59]

This was too much for the Turkish Delegation as they recognized the implication that Turkish hands were bloody from massacring minorities, specifically Armenians. İsmet responded the next day:

> The hands of the Turks now at work in their own country, which had been devastated and ruined by foreign invasion, are quite peculiarly clean. Those hands had never violated, invaded or devastated any foreign country, and could without fear sustain comparison with any other hands.[60]

As the head of an 'oriental' power, İsmet thus exposed the colonialists' double standards in disciplining the Ottomans. This comeback also illustrates how the Turks wanted to (mis)remember their own imperial past. The ideologues of Turkish nationalism, who produced the intellectual foundations upon which İsmet drew in Lausanne, agreed that Central Asia was the Turks' main ancestral homeland. Moreover, they were *proud* that from the eleventh century onwards Turks settled in Anatolia and *conquered* lands belonging to others, especially Constantinople (hence 'the Conqueror' title for Mehmed II). It is fair to say that Armenians would diverge from the opinion of İsmet that 'Turks never violated, invaded or devastated any foreign country.' Even though the Allies did not make indigeneity the main platform for their arguments for an ANH, they noted more than a few times that 'Armenians had lived in Anatolia for centuries.'[61]

İsmet's response above was part and parcel of the discourse that Turkish statesmen and nationalist intellectuals had been developing since the 1876 Bulgarian massacres, in response to Western accusations of Christians being massacred by the Ottomans. Especially after the Balkan Wars and in collaboration with the Indian Muslims, Turks developed their own propaganda machinery in order to 'talk back.' They denied accusations of the use of unrestrained force against civilians by arguing either that they were lies or exaggerations, or that the Western powers had been doing the same thing anyway.

Whereas the Turkish press had previously refrained from using anti-British

59 Italics mine. *Lausanne Conference*, 213.

60 *Lausanne Conference*, 219.

61 *Lausanne Conference*, 221.

rhetoric, Curzon's speech and İsmet's reply were published in full by the official organ of the Ankara government.[62] On the next day, the same publication proudly translated İsmet's 'cleaner hands' passage adding that İsmet taught Curzon a lesson and the latter had to soften afterwards.[63] The Armenian press in Istanbul also translated the passages though usually without much commentary.[64]

The ensuing debates in the Turkish press regarding hand 'sanitation' reveal how the Turkish public saw humanitarianism and imperialism as linked. The phrase 'under the cloak of humanism/humanitarianism' (*insâniyet perdesi arkasında*) was used as shorthand to refer to the imperialists' pretexts to violate Turkish sovereignty by making a cause out of the suffering of minorities in Ottoman lands.[65]

The well-known journalist Ahmed Emin (Yalman) wrote a long essay about the cleanliness of hands and its connection to colonialism.[66] He was of the opinion that the Allies wanted to poke holes in the final peace so as to leave room for future exploitation. He too used the phrase 'under the cloak of humanitarianism' to summarize the past attempts at partitioning the Empire via its minorities.[67] Furthermore, he cited British mistreatment of Indians, namely, the Amritsar Massacre of April 1919 when the British killed at least 379 unarmed civilians and injured more than a thousand people in Punjab. The suffering of the Irish under the British was also brought up.[68]

The main Turkish criticism of Americans was of a different kind. The United States had not shown any territorial ambitions towards the Ottoman lands and was not seen as imperialist. But Americans had long been committed to extending help to Ottoman non-Muslims, especially Armenians. At Lausanne, Americans supported Armenians' demands for autonomy though everyone knew that they would not risk war for this cause.

On the very first day of the Minorities Sub-commission's deliberations, the

62 Rıf'at, 'İstanbul Rumları, Ermeni Yurdu münâkaşası- Lord Kurzon ma'nâsız bir hiddet ve 'asabiyet İle müzâkerâtın inkıtâ'a uğrayacağı tehdîdinde bulunmuştur'. *Hakimiyet-i Milliye* 689, 18 December 1922.

63 'Lozan Konferansı – husûsî muhâbirlerimizin telgrafları, bizim de ellerimiz temizdir ve mukâyeseye hâzırız! 'Ismet Paşa Kurzon'a hakîkaten bir ders teşkîl eden bir cevâb vermiş ve hadîd re'îs çok yumuşamışdır!', *Hâkimiyet-i Milliye* 690, 19 December 1922.

64 It is telling that *Jagadamard* used the phrase 'Our Hands are Clean' as a subtitle and in quoting Curzon's words italicized 'because our hands are clean': 'Hay Azkayin Dun yev pokramasnutyants khorkhurtagtsutyunnerun manramasnutyunnere; Mer tserkere makur en', *Jagadamard* 3070, 19 December 1922.

65 For example, 'Lozan Konferansı', *Hâkimiyet-i Milliye* 690. 19 December 1922.

66 Ahmed Emin, 'Çivili sulh', *Vakit* 1804, 20 December 1922.

67 Ibid.

68 Ibid.

first delegate of the American Mission Richard Washburn Child framed the whole issue as one of humanitarianism and continued to do so in the coming days. He explained American interest in the topic: 'The comfort and safety and settlement of the hundreds of thousands of human beings, most of them non-belligerents, many of them women and children, many dislodged forever from their homes by the disturbances in the Near East, is a matter which has for the people of the United States a vital interest.'[69] After listing seven instances in which the Allies pledged to establish an autonomous zone for Armenians[70], he urged the conference to create '*safe territorial refuges* for special populations if it be determined that they require separation from other nationalities, religions or races' (meaning, requiring unmixing).[71] These preventative measures, Child argued, were better than mere relief. Both the Federal Council of the Protestant Churches of America at Lausanne and the Armenia America Society submitted memoranda to the Sub-commission detailing the necessity of an ANH.[72]

The Turkish public interpreted American support for minorities in general and for Armenians in particular as moral posturing intended to reassure a domestic audience of religious humanitarians. Ahmet Şükrü, *Vakit*'s correspondent in Lausanne reported that Washington instructed the American Mission to support the ANH but refrain from committing itself to anything .[73] Şükrü wrote that Mr. Montgomery, the head of the Armenia America Society, pretended to be a friend of the Turks while in his bag he 'carried the numbers of Armenians whose nose had bled recently.'[74] Şükrü asked one American delegate why America did not give land to

---

69 *Lausanne Conference,* 185.

70 These were: The text of the Treaty of Sèvres; the statement of the Secretary of State for Foreign Affairs of Great Britain in the House of Commons on 11 March 1920; the statement of the Prime Minister in the House of Commons on 29 April 1920; the letter of M. Poincaré, President of the French Republic, to the Armenian Archbishop of Cilicia, dated 16 February 1919; the resolutions of the Supreme Allied Council on 8 March 1921; the resolutions of the Allied Ministers for Foreign Affairs on 26 March 1922; and the resolutions of the League of Nations on 22 September 1922. *Lausanne Conference*, 186.

71 Italics mine. *Lausanne Conference*, 186

72 This included securing a $20 million loan from the US government which they claimed that the Congress had approved on 16 December 1922. This information is from the memorandum of the Armenia America Society (signed by its director George Montgomery) which was submitted to the Minorities Sub-commission and discussed on 30 December 1922. *Lozan Barış Konferansı,* 245.

73 Ahmet Şükrü, 'Ermenilerin konferans etrafındaki mesâ'isi', *Vakit* 1789, 5 December 1922.

74 Şükrü was likely referring to George R. Montgomery, 'The Massacres of Armenians in 1915' *Current History* (*New York Times* supplement) (1916–1940) 17/1, October 1922, 25–28.

Armenians instead of forcing Turks to do it.[75] His interlocutor responded that their laws would not allow it. 'Same for us,' Şükrü replied.[76]

The Turkish press also used the 'racism card' against the Americans in order to expose American humanitarianism's double standards. *Tevhid-i Efkâr* published a report about the Ku Klux Klan (hereafter KKK) from the *Le Matin*.[77] The point of the piece was to suggest that Americans lacked the moral authority to act as the sponsors of minorities while they harboured organizations like the KKK, who sought to eliminate blacks, Catholics, and Jews. A drawing of two KKK members on horseback holding the US flag accompanied the article, which concluded: 'Here is a sample of the mentality of American civilization which does not require any more explanation!'

Conclusion: Unmixing as Survival?

At Lausanne, the Armenians presented their demand for autonomy within Turkey as a plausible way to co-exist with Turks without cohabiting. They saw co-existence as inevitable, but cohabitation was dangerous given recent violence. They needed outsiders' guarantees that their own government would not try to eliminate them as it had in the past. In an ideal world, Armenians would want unmixing (a separate state) but they had to abide by winners' rules, so they asked for an autonomous zone.

The Turkish government also preferred unmixing, namely, exchanging the remaining Armenians with Muslim Turks from neighbouring Soviet Armenia. But it required extensive diplomatic acrobatics that they deemed not worth the risk. Meanwhile, autonomy was out of the question, but granting Armenians minority status inside Turkey was acceptable as long as the Armenian numbers did not grow to form any meaningful presence. This is the reason why Turkey did not allow Armenian refugees to return to Turkey even when they held Turkish citizenship.[78] The granting of minority status to Armenians was seen by the Turkish

75 When the topic was discussed in the Turkish parliament, MPs sarcastically suggested that Wilson (whom, as they knew, was no longer President) find space for Armenians in America since they had vast lands. 'Lozan Konferansı müzâkerâtı hakkında Ra'ûf Bey'in nutkunun metni', *Vakit* 64, 19 December 1922; 'İcrâ Vekîlleri Re'îs Ra'ûf Bey Efendi'nin mühim beyânâtı', *Tanîn* 67, 19 December 1922.

76 Şükrü, 'Ermenilerin konferans etrafındaki mesâ'isi'.

77 'Amerikalıların ekalliyetleri himayeye hakkı var mı? Şarkdaki Hristiyanlardan evvel kendi memleketlerindeki zencileri, Katolik ve Musevileri kurtarsalar daha iyi olur!', *Tevhid-i Efkâr* 3587–559, 28 December 1922.

78 This the Ankara government managed to do without denaturalizing Armenian refugees in

political elite as a viable option because the total number of Armenians had dwindled to the point that they could easily be neutralized if the need arose.[79]

Post-WWI population policies, and in particular population exchanges, are viewed today as akin to ethnic cleansing. The involuntary nature of the Greek-Turkish Population Exchange warrants this depiction. However, our (implicit) condemnation of population exchanges and the human suffering that they brought about should not blind us to the very possibility that for some victim groups separation and segregation could have been the best option. The survivors of the Armenian Genocide first sought external self-determination (a separate state of their own) and then internal self-determination (an autonomous zone within Turkey) because they did not trust that they would be safe amongst the Turks in a world in which the perpetrators of the recent crimes were not brought to justice and victims were not getting reparations of any sort. In the end, they achieved neither.

The Treaty of Lausanne rendered the Armenian Genocide politically inconsequential. If one of the reasons for the Allies' failure to bring justice to the cause of Armenians was *realpolitik*, the other was that their assumed moral authority rested on shaky ground. Their carving up of the world into colonies or settlements had disqualified Europeans and Americans from setting meaningful and widely accepted international norms for the protection of civilians or minorities. In other words, as they competed for moral supremacy, the hands of neither the conquerors (the Turks) nor the colonizers (the imperial powers) were clean.

The Turks did not necessarily see humanitarianism and politics as mutually exclusive. Based on their interpretation of the Ottoman past and the contemporary political (and racist) situation in the United States and in the British and French colonies, the Ankara government and the broader Turkish public interpreted humanitarianism as a pretext legitimizing intervention, or even partition, by external forces.[80]

---

order to be able to confiscate their property. Taner Akçam and Ümit Kurt, *Kanunların Ruhu: Emval-i Metruke Kanunlarında Soykırımın İzini Sürmek*, 2012.

79 For more on the conditions of Armenians who remained in Turkey after the Treaty of Lausanne and the Turkish government's treatment of them, see the second half of Lerna Ekmekcioglu, *Recovering Armenia: The Limits of Belonging in Post-Genocide Turkey*, 2016. For the debates about the Armenian refugee question in post-Ottoman Syria under the French mandate see Seda Altuğ, 'From refugees to decent Syrian citizens: Armenians in Syria under the French Mandate (1921–1939)', *Armenians in Syria*, ed. Antranik Dakessian, 2018, 163–178.

80 Michelle Tusan, '"Crimes against humanity": human rights, the British Empire, and the origins of the response to the Armenian Genocide', *The American Historical Review* 119/1, 2014, 47–77; idem, *The British Empire and the Armenian Genocide: Humanitarianism and Imperial Politics from Gladstone to Churchill*, 2017.

Last but not least, this story of an unmet demand for a 'national home' finds an echo today in contemporary Kurdish demands in the Middle East. Since 2007, the Kurdistan Workers' Party (Partiya Karkarên Kurdistan, PKK) has changed its goal from an independent socialist state to democratic autonomy within Turkey. While a thorough comparison cannot be undertaken here, it is important to note that the precedents afforded by Armenian visions of autonomy have been forgotten. The Republic of Turkey has suppressed its own past to such an extent that even those challenging its foundational myths have remained blind to their ideological forebears.

6

Iranian Attempts to Participate in the Lausanne Conference

Leila Koochakzadeh

> We must never forget the speech that İsmet Pasha made during the second session of the [negotiations for the] Treaty of Lausanne, in which he declared: 'We, the Turks, have achieved recognition for our civilization on the part of all the civilised nations and states of the world by the force of the sword […].'[1]

> O thou, the elite of Iran, keep in mind that the right of a nation will never be preserved except by the force of its army […]. We [the Iranians] must, like Turkey, without taking into consideration the opinion of others, abolish Capitulations and reform our courts.[2]

These passionate pleas both appeared in the pages of *Habl ol-Matīn* (Strong Cord), a Persian newspaper published in Calcutta but widely read in Iran, especially by members of the country's political elite. Writing in the summer 1924, a time of considerable political upheaval in Iran, the author of these lines presents the new Republic of Turkey as a role-model for Iran in terms of both domestic reform and foreign policy. When it comes to the latter, the article is full of admiration for Turkey's achievements at Lausanne. If Iranians admired, or rather envied, Turkey's negotiators at Lausanne for their diplomatic nous, Iran's reactions to the Conference were far from enthusiastic.

1 *Habl ol-Matin* 1, 23 June 1924, 15.
2 *Habl ol-Matin* 4, 14 July 1924, 3.

During the war the belligerent powers had ridden roughshod over Iran's neutrality. At Sèvres in 1920, however, Iran managed to secure some recognition of their place in the post-war order.[3] Iran's foreign policy makers, therefore, deeply resented being left out of the Lausanne settlement. Their claim to participate in the conference was based on their status as Turkey's immediate neighbour, and their interest in the resolution of the border between the two countries and with Mesopotamia, of the related issue of the Kurds, who were numerous in Iran, and the question of the Armenian and Assyrian minorities. The repeated refusal of the Allies to include Iran in the discussions seemed unfair.

The context in 1922 was quite different from that of two years earlier. Russia, with Bolshevik power now firmly entrenched, had once again become a key player in international relations, so much so that the Western powers had to concede her the right to participate in negotiations. The rise of Mustafa Kemal (hereafter Atatürk) and his victory over the Allies had erased the affront of Sèvres. The French and British expected the Iranians to join the Turks and the Russians in a hostile front at Lausanne. Part of the Iranian political elite, including the powerful Minister of War Reza Khan (the future Reza Shah), did not hide their sympathy for the new regime established in Turkey while clearly displaying a certain proximity to the Soviets.[4]

The Lausanne Conference was closely related to the very volatile situation in which Iran found herself during that period, in terms of both her international relations and her domestic politics, marked on the one hand by the pressure of the imperial powers on Iranian independence, and on the other by the aftermath of the 1906 Constitutional Revolution and the 1921 coup d'état led by Reza Khan and Seyyed Zia. This chapter thus aims to highlight how Iran's repeated efforts to participate in the Lausanne Conference were part of a global attempt to assert her sovereignty on the international scene. The failures of these efforts reflected the Allied fears engendered by the joint rise of the Soviets and Kemalist Turkey, and in the erroneous perception the latter had of the Iranian position relative to the former.

Iranian attempts to join the Lausanne Conference

On 1 November 1914, immediately following the outbreak of war between the

3 Oliver Bast, 'Les "buts de guerre" de la Perse neutre pendant la première Guerre mondiale', *Relations internationales* 160/4, 2014, 106.

4 On Reza Khan's sympathy towards the Soviets, see Kahyan A. Nejad, 'To break the feudal bonds: Reza Khan, the Soviets and the Iranian left, 1921–25', *Middle Eastern Studies* 57/5, 2021, 758–776.

Ottoman Empire and Russia (who were joined shortly by their respective allies), Iran declared her neutrality. The conflict nevertheless transgressed the borders of the country, which endured 'multiple interventions of Russian, Ottoman, and British troops as well as the activities of German agents.'[5] Having been drawn into a devastating war against her will, Iran was determined not to be deprived of a part in making peace. An Iranian delegation was sent to Paris on 17 December 1918 to participate in the Peace Conference which was to draw up a new world order. This participation was aimed as much at asserting Iranian rights to material reparations, as it was at having symbolic recognition of Iran's voice in the concert of nations, as a sovereign and independent state. The efforts of the Iranian diplomatic mission to participate in the Peace Conference were met with a refusal, however, despite the initial support of President Wilson and the French: the Iranian delegates were initially told that Iran, having been neutral during the war, had no place at the table of the victors, and then, after the Iranian-British agreement of 1919, that Iran was no longer a sovereign state.[6] On the other hand, Iran was allowed to join the League of Nations, which enabled her to 'secure her independence' and offered her a new legitimacy by which to defend her interests.[7] In the 1907 agreement and the clandestine agreement of 1915 the United Kingdom and Russia had agreed things among themselves, deciding the fate of Iran without consulting the Iranian government or parliament. New international bodies now allowed Iran to sit at the table and make herself heard.

In 1920 Iran had obtained assurances from the signatories of the Treaty of San Remo that an Iranian representative would participate in negotiating what became the Treaty of Sèvres, 'in particular for the establishment of the borders of the territory planned for the Kurds to the north of Mosul'.[8] The Treaty of Sèvres was never implemented, of course, but Iran used it as an argument to legitimize her participation in the negotiations leading to the treaty that was to replace it. The Lausanne Conference took place at a time when Iran's western borders were shaken by the revolt of the Kurdish leader Simko Shikak, also called Simitqu, and Iran was deeply concerned that the issue of Kurdish, Armenian and Assyrian minorities

5 Bast, 'Les "buts de guerre"', 95.

6 Oliver Bast, 'La mission persane à la Conférence de la Paix en 1919 : Une nouvelle interprétation', *La Perse et la Grande Guerre*, ed. Oliver Bast, 2002, 375–425.

7 French Minister Plenipotentiary in Persia to the Minister of Foreign Affairs Édouard Herriot, P11838, Asie 1918–1940, Perse-Iran, Archives du ministère des Affaires Étrangères, La Courneuve.

8 Bast, 'Les "buts de guerre"', 16.

be addressed.[9] At the same time, the Iranian authorities closely monitored British activities in Suleymaniyeh and feared the formation of an independent Kurdistan supported by the United Kingdom.[10]

Iran's position as 'the only representative of the Muslim world in the League of Nations entitled to defend the interests of Muslims' was supposed to strengthen her claim to take part in the discussions concerning Anatolia and Mesopotamia.[11] Confident of their rights, the Iranian authorities applied for admission to the Conference immediately after its opening in November 1922.

They were informed that the programme of the Conference would be limited to resolving disputes between Greece and the Ottoman Empire (*sic*) and the Turkish Straits issue, in which Iran had no direct interest. Her participation was, therefore, not appropriate.[12] This first refusal did not discourage the Iranian government, which persisted in its request and sent a 'special envoy' to Lausanne in order to monitor the progress of the negotiations.[13] A new request for admission was sent by Iran through her diplomats posted in Europe and Istanbul, at the same time as dispatches were sent to the Allied legations in Tehran. The reports sent to the Ministry of Foreign Affairs by Fernand Prévost, minister plenipotentiary of the French legation in Iran, are enlightening in this regard:

> I have just received an official communication from the President of the Council [Qavam os-Saltaneh, the Iranian Prime Minister] asking me to inform Your Excellency of 'the legitimate request of the Persian government and to support it favourably so that the government of the Republic may lend its effective assistance to Persia, in order that this power may transmit a (passing word) [sic][14] to the (Lausanne) conference.' This communication ends as follows: 'It is well understood that before the arrival of the Persian

9 On Simko Shikak/Simitqu, see Hashem Ahmadzadeh & Gareth Stanfield, 'The Political, Cultural, and Military Re-Awakening of the Kurdish Nationalist Movement in Iran', *The Middle East Journal* 64/1, 2010, 13; Michael M. Gunter, 'Iran's Forgotten Kurds', *Journal of South Asian and Middle Eastern Studies* 43/2, 2020, 56–57. Whether Simitqu's revolt was fuelled by a Kurdish nationalist sentiment or was rather motivated by local political concerns is a matter of debate.

10 Hassan Farahani & Hedāyatollāh Behbūdī, *Rūz-shomār-e tārikh-e moaser-e Iran* (Chronology of Iran's Contemporary History), 1388/2010, Vol. III, 143–145.

11 *Setareh Iran* (Iran's Star) 129, 11 January 1923, 1. Turkey did not join the League of Nations until 1932.

12 Hossein Makī, *Tārīkh-e bīst sāleh-ye Īrān* (Twenty Years of Iran's History), Vol. II, 1359/1980, 196.

13 Makī, *Tārīkh-e*, 196.

14 '(mot passé)' in French.

> (delegate) at the conference, all the rights of Persia, of whatever nature, shall be preserved.'[15]

In another telegram dated 20 December 1922, Prévost partially acknowledged the legitimacy of the Iranian claims, while seeking to find an alternative to actual participation by an Iranian delegate:

> In the event that the Allied Powers wish to give satisfaction to the Persian Government, they may be led to do so in another form (than that of) the admission of a Persian representative to the Lausanne Conference. The rights which the latter (invokes) concern, in fact, the delimitation of the frontiers of Kurdistan, and Article 62 of the Treaty of Sèvres provides precisely for the creation of a Commission, including, among others, a Persian delegate, and which should visit the places in view of the possible ratifications to be made to the frontier of Turkey 'where this frontier coincides with that of Persia'. If the Allied Powers also envisage in the new treaty (the) existence of such a commission, Persia would be called upon to benefit from the (provisions) of the aforementioned Article 62.[16]

The British position was much less conciliatory. On 24 December 1922, Curzon wrote to Eric Phipps (British Minister Plenipotentiary to France) and Sir Ronald Graham (British Ambassador to Italy):

> Since French and Italian plenipotentiaries are away for 25th December holiday, please ask Government to which you are accredited to instruct their representatives at Tehran to join their British colleague at once in explaining to Persian Government that Allied Powers regret that they cannot invite any Persian representative to come to Lausanne.[17]

Finally, on 25 December 1922, the French legations in Tehran, London, Rome and Lausanne were asked to consult with their British and Italian counterparts

15 P11838, Asie 1918–1940, Perse-Iran, Archives du ministère des Affaires Étrangères, La Courneuve.

16 P11838, Asie 1918–1940, Perse-Iran, Archives du ministère des Affaires Étrangères, La Courneuve.

17 The Marquess Curzon of Kedleston to Mr. Phipps (also to Sir R. Graham, Rome), Lausanne, 24 December 1922, FO 424/255, Turkey. Further Correspondence Part II, Confidential Print: Middle East, October–December 1922, 745, The National Archives, London.

in order to give an identical answer to the Iranian government.[18] It is important to note here the joint effort of the three Allies to provide a unanimous response to the request of the Iranian government. In 1919, when the Iranian government was negotiating with the Allies to participate in the Peace Conference, the former had skilfully played on the divergent replies offered by each of the latter, causing much discomfort among British diplomats in particular.[19] It seems that this time the Allies agreed to speak with one voice and to leave no room for Iranian manoeuvres. The reply came once again that since Persia was neither a belligerent State nor one with a Black Sea littoral there was no reason for her to be heard at Lausanne, where, in any case, the question of the Iraqi-Persian boundary would not come up.[20] The Iranian government received the decision with very ill-grace, and appealed against it, albeit in vain.[21]

The reasons given by the British, French and Italians might have come as somewhat of a surprise. On the one hand, the Conference was attended by states which, measured by these same criteria, had no more or no less interest than Iran in the issues raised, as Chicherin, the head of the Soviet delegation, pointed out publicly: 'The Japanese and Scandinavian states, which have no interest in this region, have been invited to the Conference, while Iran, which is one of the nearby countries, was prevented from participating.'[22] On the other hand, the Turkish Straits issue and the delimitation of Turkey's western borders were in fact far from being the only problems on the agenda: they included the question of Mosul and its allocation to Iraq under the British mandate or to Turkey, and that of the minorities in eastern Anatolia, which greatly worried the Iranian authorities.[23]

At the beginning of January 1923, the Iranian government sent the three Allied representatives a further note reiterating its demand for admission to Lausanne.

18 French Ministry of Foreign Affairs to the French Legation in Tehran and to the French Delegations in Lausanne, London and Rome, 25 December 1922, P11838, Asie 1918–1940, Perse-Iran, Archives du Ministère des Affaires Étrangères, La Courneuve.

19 In Oliver Bast's words, the then Iranian Prime Minister Vothugh od-Dowleh (incidentally the brother of Qavam os-Saltaneh) sought to take advantage of the 'lack of a single policy' among the Allies as to the role of Iran; Bast, 'La mission persane', 420.

20 Mr. Phipps to The Marquess Curzon of Kedleston, Paris, 25 December 1922, FO 424/255, Turkey. Further Correspondence Part II, Confidential Print: Middle East, October–December 1922, 748, The National Archives, London.

21 FO 416/112, Annual Reports on Persia, 1922–1923, Confidential Print: Middle East, 3, The National Archives, London.

22 Quoted in *Now Bahar* (New Spring) 17, 17 January 1923.

23 Kaveh Bayāt, *Ravābet-e Īrān va Torkiyeh az soghūt-e dowlat-e os̱mānī tā bar āmadan-e nezām-e jomhūrī* (Relations between Iran and Turkey from the Fall of the Ottoman Government to the Rise of the Republic), 1394/ 2014, 122–123.

On 3 January 1923, the three Allied representatives sent an 'identic note to the Persian Government in the required sense', i.e., still a refusal.[24] Three rejections did not discourage the Iranians, however, who renewed their request to the French, British and Italian representatives in Iran, pointing out the bad faith of the Allies. Zaka od-Dowleh, the Iranian ambassador to Switzerland, and most likely the special envoy to Lausanne mentioned above, highlighted the fact that 'neutral' countries had been invited to participate in the negotiations, in which 'some discussions have taken place about Kurdistan, where Persian and Ottoman Governments [had] common interests'. The Conference had also 'listened to remarks of Chaldean representatives, which were contrary to proprietary rights of Persia'.[25]

The last remark was a reference to the hearing given to the Assyrian-Chaldean military chief Agha Petros, who had come to plead on behalf of his community. The Iranian government was much alarmed by this and feared a revival of the proposal to create an autonomous Assyrian-Chaldean State in Upper Mesopotamia, on the North-West frontier of Iran, and the inclusion therein of the Christian populations inhabiting Orumiyeh, in western Iranian Azerbaijan.[26] Their greatest concern was that a territorial loss for Iran would be decided in her absence, but they also recognized that any discussion of a Christian state on her borders might give rise to secessionist impulses among the Chaldean, Nestorian and Armenian populations of western Iran.[27] Curzon regretted the stormy departure of İsmet İnönü (hereafter İsmet) during Agha Petros' speech, explaining that when people had been waiting for a long time to express their demands, the least that could be done was to listen to them.[28]

This did not prevent the Allies from responding on 24 January 1923 'in identic terms' that they regarded their reply of 3 January 1923 as definitive, and were unable, without fresh arguments, to support a request for reopening a question on which 'inviting Powers' had already pronounced themselves.[29] This kind of double standard could only inflame Iranian resentment towards the Allies and, on

24 FO 424/256, Turkey. Further Correspondence Part III, Confidential Print: Middle East, January–March 1923, n° 27, 52, The National Archives, London.

25 *Chehreh Nama* (The Portraitist) 107–108, 1923, 24.

26 Bayāt, *Ravābet*, 125; Farahani & Behbūdī, *Rūz-shomār*, Vol. II, 620–621.

27 Correspondence from the Iranian Legation in Paris to the Iranian Ministry of Foreign Affairs, dated 2 January 1923, quoted in Nezām 'Alī Dehnavī, *Asnādi az ravabet-e siyāsī-e Torkiyeh va Erāq* (Documents on Relations between Iran and Turkey),1386/2007, 31; Anonymous, *Conférence de Lausanne*, 1923, Vol. I, 247.

28 *Conférence de Lausanne*, Vol. I, 246.

29 FO 424/256, Turkey. Further Correspondence Part III, Confidential Print: Middle East, January–March 1923, 132, 222, The National Archives, London.

the contrary, strengthen their sympathy for the government of the Turkish Grand National Assembly.

Iran, Kemalism and Pan-Islamism

One of the interesting points in the Zaka od-Dowleh letter cited above is the repeated mention of joint Iranian and 'Ottoman' interests. The Iranian ambassador objected to the hearing of the Assyrian-Chaldean delegation during the Conference, the participants 'having heard baseless representations of Chaldeans, many of whom are Persian subjects'.[30] He warned that 'any intervention or support for the Assyrian-Chaldeans, whether in Iran or in the Ottoman Empire, would be of no benefit [to the Allies]'.[31]

It was on the basis of these common interests on the Assyrian-Chaldean issue that Zaka od-Dowleh met with the 'Ottoman' delegation in Switzerland, from which, according to the report of the Iranian ambassador, a constructive exchange with Farid Beg and İsmet resulted. During this meeting, the latter had 'assured that the government of Ankara [would] resist at all costs the independence of the Armenians [*sic*] in Mesopotamia'.[32] According to İsmet, 'since on all issues Iran [had] common interests with the Turks, it would [have been] beneficial for the Iranians to align their policy with that of the Turks'.[33] İsmet expressed surprise at Iran's exclusion from the Conference, and it was he who advised Zaka od-Dowleh to include in his letter of protest the argument that neutral countries had been invited.[34] In fact, İsmet was probably partly responsible for the much firmer tone this letter displayed, compared to previous ones sent by Iran.

Such Turkish-Iranian collaboration was not without precedent. Arfa' od-Dowleh, Iran's first delegate to the League of Nations, had received in September 1922 a letter from the representative of the Turkish Grand National Assembly in Rome, asking him to report to the League 'the cruelty of the Greeks' towards Turkish prisoners. In addition to sending a letter to the President of the League of Nations assembly requesting the organisation of 'an impartial enquiry on the atrocities committed during the present war in the Near East', Arfa' took the

30 FO 424/256, Turkey. Further Correspondence Part III, Confidential Print: Middle East, January–March 1923, 56, 119, The National Archives, London.

31 *Chehreh Nama* 107–108, 1923, 24.

32 Correspondence from the Iranian Legation in Paris to the Iranian Ministry of Foreign Affairs, quoted in: Dehnavi, *Asnādi*, 31.

33 Dehnavi, *Asnādi*, 43.

34 Dehnavi, *Asnādi*, 44.

podium to address the issue on the very same day he received 'the request of Mustafa Kemal'.[35]

Such cooperation was based on the attraction of Iran and other neighbouring states to Atatürk, Kemalism and its successes.[36] War Minister Reza Khan, the real strongman of the Iranian government since his 1921 coup, was a fervent admirer of Atatürk, whose anti-elite rhetoric and opposition to the old corrupt dynasties, Ottoman or Qajar, he shared. He too aspired to establish a modernising republic. Many army officers and members of the Iranian political and intellectual elites were publicly sympathetic to the Kemalist movement, including those who opposed Reza Khan.[37]

This solidarity was also tinged with strong Pan-Islamic overtones, characteristic of both the early Kemalist movement[38] and Iranian foreign policy of the time, and which infused the public discourse of both countries. The editor of the Iranian newspaper *Setareh Iran* (Iran's Star) attributed the refusal to admit Iran to the negotiating table to the fact that Iran was 'officially recognised as the representative of the Islamic world', and hence argued that the manoeuvre was intended by the Allies to cut ties between Islamic states and 'isolate the victorious Ottoman government' in order to increase the 'share of votes of the greedy, imperialist Christian governments'. In order to thwart these plans, it continued, the Iranian government had to persist in its demand on the one hand, and on the other remind the 'Ottoman' authorities, and in particular the 'brave and zealous leader of this Islamic government', Atatürk, that an increase in the number of Muslim countries represented at Lausanne would further Turkish objectives. The analysis concluded that Iran's participation in Lausanne was as necessary as that of the Soviets.[39] In the same way, the hearing of the Assyrian-Chaldeans, for whom Curzon did not have only a 'purely platonic interest', since the British government had financed Agha Petros to the tune of 4 million pounds since the Armistice, appeared to the Iranian press as a British 'plot against the three Muslim countries of Iran, Turkey and Iraq'.[40]

35 Ali Dehbashi, ed. *Khāterāt-e perans Arfa'* (The Memoirs of Prince Arfa'), 1378/1999, 553; FO 371/8019, 1919–1929, 238.

36 Nathalie Clayer, Fabio Giomi & Emmanuel Szurek, 'Introduction', *Kemalism. Transnational Politics in Post-Ottoman World*, ed. Nathalie Clayer, Fabio Giomi & Emmanuel Szurek, 2018, 1–37.

37 Stephanie Cronin, *The Making of Modern Iran. State and Society under Riza Shah, 1921–1941*, 2003, 54.

38 Clayer, Giomi & Szurek, 'Introduction', 9–10.

39 *Setareh Iran* (Iran's Star) 129, 11 January 1923, 1.

40 Anonymous, *Conférence*, I, 247; Farahani & Behbudi, *Rūz-shomār*, Vol. II, 622.

For their part, Turkish newspapers also nurtured the idea of a regional alliance with Iran. For example, the Harput-based newspaper *Satvet-i-Hilie* (Assault of Sweetness) wrote that Iran was seeking to 'form a nationalist government similar to that of Ankara' and that for this purpose Iran was preparing agreements and treaties with the Soviets, the Afghans and the Caucasus countries. 'At the end of these negotiations a formidable bloc will be created in the East. A glance at the map will show the value and importance of this bloc, which will include Turkey, Persia, Afghanistan, Azerbaijan, Dagestan, Bukhara, Khiva and Turkistan, which contain a homogeneous mass of twenty million men with whom the world will have to reckon.'[41]

This did not go unremarked by Western observers. Arfa' od-Dowleh's speech to the League of Nations in favour of Turkish prisoners was described by the French journalist Maurice Muret as a 'plea for Islam'.[42] More importantly, British representatives in Iran reported the existence in Tehran of 'a group of political agitators working under the guidance of the authorities at Ankara to promote sympathy for the Turks, to assist the anti-British movement in Iraq and to spread Pan-Islamic and anti-British propaganda.'[43] This group calling itself the 'Tehran Kemalist Society' collaborated with the Khilafat movement in India which supported the Ankara government politically and financially.[44] Well aware of the Pan-Islamist and pro-Kemalist tendencies in Iran, the Allies, especially the British, must have feared that an Iranian presence in Lausanne would add weight to Turkish claims. This is probably one of the reasons why the British, French and Italians refused to invite Iran to the negotiations.

If this was indeed the case, however, the Allies' analysis was only partial. On the one hand, it overlooked the real scepticism towards Atatürk that existed among the highest Iranian authorities, starting with the Shah himself, who did not recognise the government of the Turkish Grand National Assembly until three months after Atatürk's proclamation of the Turkish Republic.[45] Pan-Islamism had an essentially rhetorical dimension. As much as Kemalism had used it as a lever

41 *Correspondance d'Orient: revue économique, politique & littéraire*, 15–30 July 1922, 289–290, 413. It is interesting that at the same time, on the Western side, Toynbee too saw the same potential for a block including Turkey, Iran and Afghanistan; Arnold Toynbee, 'The New Status of Turkey', *Contemporary Review* 123, 1923, 281–289. I would like to express my deepest thanks to Jonathan Conlin for this reference.

42 *Journal des débats politiques et littéraires* 255, 14 September 1922, 2.

43 IOR/L/PS/18/C211, 9, British Library: India Office Records and Private Papers, London.

44 Farahani & Behbudi, *Rūz-shomār*, Vol. II, 3.

45 Bayat, *Ravābet*, 143.

for mobilisation in its struggle against the Allies, the Iranian leaders used it essentially to assert Iran's weight, particularly within major international settings, with the primary aim of consolidating national sovereignty.

The defence of a Caliphate, *a fortiori* a Sunni one, behind which the unity of the Muslim world would be achieved, was hardly a concern of the Iranians. Besides the admiration for Atatürk, the article published in *Setareh Iran* insists above all on Iran's own role as representative of the Islamic world on the international scene. As Cemil Aydın puts it, 'where the term 'Pan-Islamism' continued to be used in the post-war period in the vocabulary of international affairs, it referred more to the general activism of the nationalist movements in specific Muslim nations and their moral and material solidarity, rather than expressing concern about the emergence of a united Islamic state.'[46] While it was adorned with the vocabulary of Pan-Islamism and the struggle against the Christian West, the rapprochement of Turkey and Iran during this period was mostly circumstantial and responded to the needs of both sides to find support in the face of adversaries with whom they were both struggling.

Iran between the British and the Soviets

Another reason for the Allies' refusal to allow Iran to participate in the Lausanne Conference might lie in the presence of another protagonist that has so far appeared only in the background in this discussion, namely the Soviets. Indeed, the Allies were overly concerned 'by Russian attempts to draw Persia into an Islamic alliance with Turkey and Afghanistan under [their] own aegis'.[47] Since their victory, the Soviets had counted on spreading their anti-Western ideology in the countries of the region. As the Allies prepared for the Lausanne negotiations, Iranian newspapers reproduced a report published by Moscow radio dated 11 November 1922 that 'the Great National Assembly of Ankara had addressed a proclamation to the civilised world in which it exposed the hypocrisy and cunning of the English and French diplomats who forced Turkey to sign the armistice with Greece.'[48]

Both the British and the French kept a close eye on these developments and

46 Cemil Aydın, *The Politics of Anti-Westernism in Asia*, 2007, 140.
47 FO 416/112, Annual Reports on Persia, 1922–1923, Confidential Print: Middle East, 3, The National Archives, London. In an annual report of Sir P. Loraine (Tehran) written to Mr. MacDonald on 4 March 1924.
48 P11838, Asie 1918–1940, Perse-Iran, Archives du ministère des Affaires Étrangères, La Courneuve.

saw Soviet activities in Iran as 'an endeavour to deal the final blow to British position and influence in this country or to blackmail His Majesty's Government into recognising [the Soviet Union].' Iran and her unstable political situation seemed to them to be a particularly fertile ground for Soviet designs: 'Weakness of Persian Government, corruption of the press, influence of anti-British party in Medjliss [the Majles, the Iranian parliament] and credulity of pseudo-demagogues and extreme Nationalists are playing into Russia's hands'.[49]

These fears are directly related to the Allied position on Iran's repeated requests to join the Conference. In a confidential communication sent on 20 December 1922, Prévost advised the French Minister of Foreign Affairs:

> At a time when the Allied Governments are called upon to consider Persia's application for admission to the Lausanne Conference, I think I should recall the pressure which the Soviet Government had put on the Persian Government three months ago to bring it to support the Russian memorandum sent to London on September 12 regarding the issue of the Straits. My British colleague and I succeeded in making Shawam-es-Saltaneh [Qavam os-Saltaneh] understand the dangers of such a step and in dissuading him from following it. But the presence of a Persian delegate in Lausanne might perhaps offer the Soviet delegation an opportunity to (seek) again to secure the support of the Persian delegate, possibly by using the means of pressure which Russia may have in respect of a weak neighbour.[50]

It is very clear here that the Allied refusal was in fact motivated by the fear that an Iranian presence at the Conference would be nothing more than a pawn in the service of the Soviets in the arm-wrestling match between them and the West over the Turkish Straits. The issue of the Turkish Straits was indeed discussed on several occasions in Iranian newspapers and in the memoirs of politicians of the

49 FO 424/255, Turkey. Further Correspondence Part II, Confidential Print: Middle East, October–December 1922, 59, The National Archives, London. A telegram sent on 29 January 1923, by the French Legation in Tehran to the French Foreign Office, illustrates British concerns: 'The French Consul in Baghdad informs me of the arrival of Russian forces in Astara and Lankoran [sic] (Caspian). He also informs me that the British authorities do not believe the official assurances of neutrality of the Persian government. Several reports indicate the presence of Persian officers at Ravandous and large quantities of ammunition appear to have been supplied to the Turks by the authorities of [Iranian] Azerbaijan.' P11838, Asie 1918–1940, Perse-Iran, Archives du ministère des Affaires Étrangères, La Courneuve.
50 P11838, Asie 1918–1940, Perse-Iran, Archives du ministère des Affaires Étrangères, La Courneuve.

time. In its 11 December 1922 edition, *Setareh Iran* warned the 'nations of the Orient' that British domination of the Turkish Straits and Istanbul would 'put an end to the political existence of the Eastern states'. The newspaper stated that 'for the time being' the Soviets were 'the only hope' of the Oriental nations, 'unless they change their colour'.[51] As we shall see, the suggestion that there was an Iranian-Soviet rapprochement is questionable.

It is true that the fall of the Tsarist regime and the rise to power of the Bolsheviks had raised many hopes in Iran, not least that it would reset Iranian-Russian relations, which until then had been marked by imperialist pressure exerted by the great northern neighbour together with the United Kingdom. The anti-capitalist and pacifist slogans of the Bolsheviks had profoundly changed the Iranian view of Russia, from a constant threat to Iranian sovereignty and a hindrance to the country's development to a potential ally that could help emancipate Iran from the clutches of the imperial powers, especially Britain. This resulted in the cancellation of the 1907 and 1915 treaties that divided Iran into Russian and British zones of influence, increasing the Russians' newfound credibility among the Iranians and raising the wrath of the British. More importantly, the Bolshevik government promised the Iranian state to withdraw the Russian army from northern Iran: for the Iranian state, this action meant not only the liberation of a part of its territory drawn into the First World War against its will, but also the recognition, at last, of its territorial sovereignty by its powerful neighbour.

The first agreement signed between Bolshevik Russia and an Asian state was the Iranian-Russian friendship agreement of 26 February 1921.[52] This agreement 'formalized and extended the abrogation of Russian concessions in Iran, but also prohibited Iran from entering into any anti-Soviet alliances, and even reserved the right of intervention should hostile forces threaten the Soviets from Iranian territory', which was more in keeping with the Russian policy of the Tsar's time.[53] The signing coincided with the seizure of power by Seyyed Ziya and Reza Khan, both notoriously pro-Bolshevik (but certainly not communist), five days earlier, and with the abrogation of the 1919 British-Iranian treaty, which had never been ratified by the Majles.[54]

This was indeed a cause of concern for the British. In particular, Article 6 of the new Iran-Russia treaty could be seen as a threat to Iran's neighbours, that

51 *Setareh Iran* 105, 11 December 1922, 1.

52 Mikhail Volodarsky, *The Soviet Union and Its Southern Neighbours*, 2016, 49.

53 Nejad, 'To break the feudal bonds', 760.

54 Volodarsky, *The Soviet Union*, 55.

is, British India and the Iraqi mandate. According to this Article, if a third party attempted to invade Iranian territory by force of arms or to turn Iranian territory into an armed base to be used against Russia, and if the Iranian government were unable to prevent it, the Russian government would have the right to send its forces into Iranian territory for its own defence. 'This posed the threat of Turkish-Russian armed cooperation in the event of a conflict between Turkey and the British Empire.'[55] In the event of the Turks and Russians declaring war on the United Kingdom, free passage of Russian troops through Iran was granted.

This possibility was taken extremely seriously by Saunders, the British military attaché at Tehran, who reported to his government that the Bolsheviks would cross Iranian territory into Iraq to support the Turks if the Lausanne Conference failed to reach a peaceful solution, and that 'if, however, Russians fail to prevent a settlement at Lausanne, the Azerbaijani Communist party [would] forthwith organise new revolutionary movement in Gilan [northern Iran]'.[56] Saunders thus arranged meetings with several senior Iranian military officers and Reza Khan to remind them that 'though undoubtedly great difficulties were being experienced' during the negotiations at the Conference, 'there [was] every reason to hope that a solution may be found resulting in a satisfactory peace', and 'that the British authorities were, nevertheless, taking proper naval and military precautions so as to be ready to act, should war be forced on us'.[57]

A Soviet-led revival of the Socialist Republic of Gilan, however, was nonetheless unlikely[58]. Although they had initially supported the Jangali movement

---

55 FO 416/112, Annual Reports on Persia, 1922–1923, Confidential Print: Middle East, 3, The National Archives, London.

56 Most Secret Telegram of Sir P. Loraine to the Marquess Curzon of Kedleston, Tehran, 1 January 1923, FO 416/72, Persia. Further Correspondence Part XIV, January–June 1923, Confidential Print: Middle East, 10 and 40, The National Archives, London. The newspaper *Correspondance d'Orient* also published on 15 November 1922 a telegram received from London which reported the conclusion of an Iranian-Russian treaty according to which Iran would allow Soviet troops to cross her territory in order to attack Mesopotamia in case of an Anglo-Russian war; *Correspondance d'Orient*, 15 November 1922, 693; Farahani, *Rūz-shomār*, Vol. II, 578.

57 Lieutenant-Colonel Saunders to Sir P. Loraine, Tehran, 22 January 1923, FO 416/72, Persia. Further Correspondence Part XIV, January–June 1923, Confidential Print: Middle East, 82, The National Archives, London.

58 In June 1920 the revolutionary movement of the Jangalis ('Forest Men'), born in 1915 under the leadership of Mirza Koochak Khan, proclaimed the Soviet Socialist Republic of Gilan (Northern Iran) with the support of the Bolsheviks. However, dissensions soon appeared and the Republic was liquidated by Reza Khan in November 1921. See Pezhmann Dailami, 'Jangali Movement', in *Encyclopaedia Iranica*, Vol. XIV, 2008, 534–544, https://www.iranicaonline.org/articles/jangali-movement.

in 1920, the Soviets had abandoned Mirza Koochak Khan by 1921 in favour of relations with the Iranian government, more likely to serve their political and economic interests. By early 1923 it was clear that the Soviets intended to support the formation of a strong central state in Iran under the leadership of Reza Khan, who was paving the way for his ultimate goal, the overthrow of the Qajar dynasty.[59] There were good reasons, therefore, for the Allies' repeated refusal to invite Iran to Lausanne. Nevertheless, it seems that when it came to Iran's stance towards the Russians, the Allies had been clear-sighted with one eye but blind with the other. Indeed, both the Bolsheviks' initial support for the Jangali movement and the onerous clauses of the Iranian-Russian Friendship Treaty of 1921 had clearly dampened Iranian enthusiasm for the Russian Revolution. In particular, Article 6 of the Treaty was seen as a potential threat to Iran's sovereignty and integrity. The year 1922 saw major tensions between the Iranian and Russian governments over the signing of a trade treaty, to the point that 'during the summer of 1922 Iranian business circles started an energetic campaign to boycott trade with Soviet Russia'.[60] Thus, the newspaper *Shafagh-e Sorkh* (Red Twilight), in two long articles dated 7 and 15 September 1922, criticised Soviet trade policy in Iran. The paper emphasised that the Iranians 'will not put up with a trade treaty that is many times as unbearable as British capitalism' and that 'Iran for the Iranians' was their 'sacred principle' and that their 'daily strategy' was resistance to 'aggressors, whether British, Russians, Ottomans or Afghans'.[61] As we have seen, even the article from *Setareh Iran* calling for a common front with the Soviets was nonetheless tinged with caution, if not distrust. In fact, the central axis of Iranian policy seems to have been above all the defence of national independence.

A good example of this was the Iranian government's position on the Iraqi issue. In January 1923, the British Minister Plenipotentiary to Iran, Sir Percy Loraine, sent Curzon a dispatch about telegrams written by High Representatives of Mesopotamia in Tehran against British Rule in Mesopotamia, and addressed to 'to the foreign Legations and to the Lausanne Conference through the intermediary of

59 Nejad, 'To break the feudal bonds'. Many other aspects also come into play and considerably complicate the issue of the relationship between Iran, the Allies and Russia after the First World War and in the early 1920s. These included the vexed question of oil and of the Semnan/Khoshtaria concession in northern Iran that was granted in 1916 to the Russian Akaki Khoshtaria by the Iranian government. In 1920, Khoshtaria sold this concession to the Anglo-Iranian Oil Company, but the Iranian government rejected the validity of this arrangement.

60 Volodarsky, *The Soviet Union*, 69.

61 *Shafagh-e sorkh* (Red Twilight) 97, 7 September 1922, 2 and 100, 15 September 1922, 1.

the Turkish representatives', while copies were given to Russian representatives in Lausanne.[62] These telegrams stated that 'the whole people of Mesopotamia despise steps taken by British Government in Mesopotamia against their integrity, protest against the illegal interference of the British, and do not recognise or submit themselves to the convention of the 10th Teshrin [October] 1922 [which established the British protectorate over Iraq]'.[63]

In the parliamentary session of 19 January 1923, the Iranian government was questioned about its efforts to join the Lausanne Conference and its position on the British mandate in Mesopotamia. The Prime Minister replied that the question of Mesopotamia did not concern Iran, but that the Iranian government, while appealing to the League of Nations for the fate of Mesopotamia to be settled in accordance with the wishes of her people, did not recognise the new pro-British government in Iraq. This response did not seem to satisfy the deputies, and it was decided that the aforementioned telegrams should be published in booklet form to be 'distributed throughout the world'.[64] They were published in the Iranian press on 21 January, which led Loraine to issue an official protest to the Iranian government.

The latter, however, stuck to its policy of neutrality. Ayatollah Al-Khalesi, exiled from Iraq to Iran by the British, writes in his memoirs that his letters to the Foreign and War Ministries, warning them against 'Assyrian-English' intrigues, 'had no effect whatsoever'.[65] Moreover, even though he was helped by Iranian ulamas to form an association called the Supreme Association of Iraqi Representatives and even though they managed to mobilize the people of Tehran to take to the streets, his memoirs indicate that in the end neither the deputies nor even the ulamas were going to support Iraq at the cost of being attacked by Britain or letting the Soviets cross the country to get to Iraq. Al-Khalesi says that the ulamas feared that 'if they fought the British, the Bolsheviks would take advantage of it'.[66] Iran simply did not want to experience foreign intervention again. The Iranians would not support the independence of their co-religionists at the cost of seeing their territory and independence violated.

Finally, as proof of the tensions between Iranians and Soviets about the trade

62 IOR/L/PS/18/C210, 53, British Library: India Office Records and Private Papers, London.
63 Sir P. Loraine to the Marquess Curzon of Kedleston, Tehran, 11 February 1923, FO 416/72, Persia. Further Correspondence Part XIV, January–June 1923, Confidential Print: Middle East, 94, The National Archives, London.
64 *Setareh Iran* 136, 19 January 1923, 1.
65 Pierre-Jean Luizard, ed. *La vie de l'ayatollah Mahdî al-Khâlesî*, 2004, 291.
66 Luizard, *La vie*, 318.

agreement, the latter used the issue of joining the Lausanne Conference, which had become embarrassing for the Iranian authorities, to destabilise the government of Qavam os-Saltaneh. Well aware of the sensitivity of the Majles, and the National Party in particular, to the Lausanne issue, the Soviets made public Qavam os-Saltaneh's response to the Russian recommendation to insist on attending the Conference. Qavam's response had stated that 'his government did not intend to participate because the question of the Black Sea Straits did not infringe on Iranian interests'.[67] We have seen that this was not in fact the case, and we can only interpret the Prime Minister's response as a desire not to be manipulated by the Soviets, which shows how mistaken the Allies' analysis of the relationship between Iran and Russia was. Nevertheless, Qavam os-Saltaneh was accused by members of the Iranian parliament 'of indifference to the national problems of Iran and to the international authority of the country'.[68] The affair degenerated into a political crisis and on 23 January, shortly before the end of the first round of negotiations at the Lausanne Conference, Qavam os-Saltaneh was forced to resign.

Conclusion: Iranian-Turkish Relations after the Lausanne Treaty

Ironically, instead of taking 'constructive steps to limit Soviet influence', the Allies' refusal to allow Iran to participate in Lausanne for fear of a Russian-Turkish-Iranian axis led to a rapprochement between Turkey and Iran on the one hand, and the fall of an Iranian government on the other. That government had been distrustful of the Soviets, whereas its replacement was, ironically enough, far more conciliatory to them.[69] The incoming Prime Minister Mostowfi ol-Mamalek struggled to form a government, with 'uncertainty as to the result of the Lausanne Conference adding to his difficulties.'[70] He asked one last time, on 31 January, for Iran to participate in the Conference. Curzon replied that 'the conference has practically ended without touching on any Persian interests.'[71]

67 Volodarsky, *The Soviet Union*, 71.
68 Volodarsky, *The Soviet Union*, 71.
69 Volodarsky, *The Soviet Union*, 74.
70 Sir P. Loraine to the Marquess Curzon of Kedleston, Tehran, 12 February 1923, FO 416/72, Persia. Further Correspondence Part XIV, January–June 1923, Confidential Print: Middle East, 107, The National Archives, London.
71 FO 424/256, Turkey. Further Correspondence Part III, Confidential Print: Middle East, January–March 1923, The National Archives, London, 132 (The Marquess Curzon of Kedleston to Sir P. Loraine), 31 January 1923, 280.

Iranian interests were, however, directly affected by the Lausanne Conference. Iran's insistence on being accepted at the negotiating table illustrates how crucial this was in asserting its sovereignty on the international scene. The equally insistent refusal of the Allies shows how the issue went beyond the mere participation of a minor power like Iran, but was intertwined in the complex knot of relations between Turkey, Soviet Russia, the United Kingdom, France, and Italy. Finally, far from being a mere peripheral episode, the Lausanne Conference was decisive in Iranian internal politics and, despite Iran's non-participation, was a critical national issue.

For both Iranian rulers and public, Lausanne elicited both admiration for Kemalist Turkey, which had managed to wrest sovereignty from the West, and resentment at being excluded. However, many disputes resulted from this. Far from the rapprochement feared by the Allies, the period following the signing of the Treaty of Lausanne was one of extreme tension between Turkey and Iran, which was exacerbated by Iran's exclusion from the negotiations. For example, the Turkish ambassador in Tehran (Muhyeddin Pasha) continued to claim Capitulatory privileges for his nationals in Iran, without success. Each time he was told that these no longer existed in Turkey, and that the Turks could hardly claim a reciprocity denied Iranians in Turkey.

Another dispute concerned the nationality of nomadic groups whose transhumance routes overlapped Iran and Turkey, and over which the Turkish state claimed exclusive protection. This was based on the stipulations of the Treaty of Lausanne concerning the nationality of individuals originating from the territories taken from Turkey and residing outside these territories (notably the Turks originating from Mosul). To this Iran replied that she did not recognise these terms, as she had not been consulted in their elaboration, and Iranians continued to refer to the old protocol on migration across the Turkish-Iranian border which stipulated that nomadic groups were considered Turkish while in Turkey and Iranian the rest of the time.[72]

Another issue was the new Republic of Turkey's denunciation, under the terms of the Lausanne Treaty, of all old treaties signed with other states, including Iran, during the time of the Ottoman Empire. To this the Iranian authorities retorted that since Iran was not one of the belligerents in the First World War and had not been invited to the Lausanne Conference, the resulting decisions were not binding

72 Report of the French legation in Iran to the Ministry of Foreign Affairs, 1925, P11838, Asie 18–40, Perse-Iran, Archives diplomatiques, La Courneuve.

on her.[73] They added that, according to international law, the change of regime of a country could not lead to the nullification of previous treaties, for which the consent of all signatory parties was required.[74] Tensions reached such a point that there was speculation that the Turkish embassy in Iran would be transformed into a mere legation.[75]

Finally, there was the question of Pan-Turkism. The Pan-Turkists considered Iranian Azerbaijan to be Turkish, which caused concern among both the Iranian authorities and the Iranian public. An Iranian newspaper such as *Mihran* saw the shift from Pan-Islamism to Pan-Turkism in Turkey's foreign policy as an effect of the Lausanne Conference: Curzon and İsmet were said to have signed a clandestine agreement giving the Turks a free hand in Azerbaijan and the Caucasus in exchange for Mosul and Mesopotamia.[76] Tensions were also provoked by political personnel and the situation within Iran. The Iranian ruling elites, mostly of aristocratic origin, were wary of the upheavals in neighbouring Turkey and were very concerned that the ambitious Reza Khan would take advantage of the political chaos in Iran to emulate Atatürk. For them, in this regard, the Turkish model was not one to emulate.

In April 1926, when Reza Shah came to power, a five-year treaty of friendship was signed between Turkey and Iran. This treaty did not, however, resolve the stumbling blocks between the two countries, especially concerning the Kurds (the Iranian Kurds gave refuge to the Turkish Kurds without the Iranian state intervening) and it was only with the Treaty of Sa'dabad, a non-aggression pact signed in July 1937 between Turkey, Iran and Afghanistan, that tensions finally eased somewhat[77].

---

73 Dehnavī, *Asnādī*, 1386/2007, 20–22; Report of the French legation in Iran to the Ministry of Foreign Affairs, 1925, P11838, Asie 18–40, Perse-Iran, Archives diplomatiques, La Courneuve.

74 Report of the Iranian Ministry of Foreign Affairs, 17 February 1925; Dehnavī, *Asnādī*, 16.

75 Report of the French legation in Iran to the Ministry of Foreign Affairs, 1925, P11838, Asie 18–40, Perse-Iran, Archives diplomatiques, La Courneuve.

76 Kaveh Bayāt, *Pāntorkism va Īrān*, 1395/2015, 37.

77 On the Treaty of Sa'dabad, see Donald Cameron Watt, 'The Saadabad Pact of 8 July 1937' *The Great Powers in the Middle East, 1919–1939*, ed. Uriel Dann, 1988, 333–352.

7

Arab Exclusion at Lausanne: A Critical Historical Juncture

Elizabeth F. Thompson

On 24 July 1920, the French Army of the Levant invaded the Syrian Arab Kingdom to assert France's *de facto* claim to rule it under a mandate tentatively assigned by the Paris Peace Conference.

Exactly two years later, on 24 July 1922, the League of Nations Council voted to ratify the French mandate in Syria and Lebanon and the British mandate in Palestine.

And on 24 July 1923, the Allies signed the Lausanne Treaty with Turkey, completing the work of the Peace Conference begun in 1919. Within weeks, the mandates over Syria, Lebanon, and Palestine formally entered international law and finally took *de jure* force.

The symmetry of dating between France's occupation of Syria and the award of its mandate suggests the unfolding of a linear process. Indeed, textbooks on Middle Eastern history do not dwell upon political details in the years following the 1920 San Remo conference, where Allied leaders, in the absence of Arab representation, assigned mandates in the Arabic-speaking lands of the Eastern Mediterranean. While historians have focused on armed revolts against the mandates in Iraq (1920), Syria (1925) and Palestine (1936), they have ignored Arabs' legal and diplomatic protests that the mandates were imposed in violation of the League of Nations covenant. Scholars of the Lausanne Conference have likewise neglected Arab efforts to join the treaty negotiations.

The devil is, in fact, in the details. Lausanne was not simply the culmination of a process that had begun with the October 1918 fall of the Ottoman Empire and

European occupation of Greater Syria (including today's Syria, Lebanon, Jordan, Palestine, and Israel). Nor was the French mandate in Syria the 'climax of French imperial expansion' since 1914, as a classic in colonial history termed it.[1] Historians of the post-war period have relied almost exclusively upon European archives, thereby suppressing Arabs' voices in the peace process. This silencing has deep roots in European imperial historiography.

Arabic-language sources cast Lausanne in an utterly different light, revealing it to be a critical juncture in the region's political history. Social scientists define critical juncture as a moment that launches 'trajectories of political change in which major episodes of innovation are followed by the emergence of enduring institutions.'[2] Lausanne represented the sudden and final defeat of Ottoman Arabs' effort to realise their place in a liberal world order. Their exclusion and defeat at Lausanne fundamentally altered the course of Arab politics for decades afterwards. Appreciation of Lausanne's importance as a critical juncture compels a rethinking of Arab politics in the remainder of the twentieth century. This chapter focuses mainly on the Arabs of Greater Syria, with some reference to other Arabic-speaking politicians from formerly Ottoman territories, including the newly created Iraq, the Hejaz region of the Arabian Peninsula, and Egypt.

At stake in the post-war years of 1919–1923 was the long-held claim by Arabic-speaking politicians to their liberal rights as citizens of the Ottoman Empire. By the late nineteenth century, a preponderant portion of the Arab political elite had come to support the efforts to establish a constitutional monarchy. Constitutionalists intended not only to establish equal rights under representative government at home, but also to assure the Empire's place in the European family of (so-called) civilized nations. The sovereign rights of such nations would thereby be protected under international law from colonization. Amid setbacks caused by Ottoman reactionaries and foreign powers, Ottoman liberals briefly realised their aims in the constitutional moments of 1877–1878 and 1908–1912. In both periods, Arabs had elected representatives to parliament in Istanbul. However, under the Young Turks' brutal military rule in World War I, a significant segment of the Syrian-Arab political elite decided to withdraw their support of the Ottomans. They viewed the 1916 Arab Revolt, in alliance with the Entente Powers, as a more auspicious avenue toward independence and just government. After the war, politicians in

1 Christopher M. Andrew and A.S. Kanya-Forstner, *The Climax of French Imperial Expansion, 1914–1924*, 1981.

2 David Collier and Gerardo L. Munck, 'Building blocks and methodological challenges: A framework for studying critical junctures,' *Qualitative and Multi-Method Research* 15/1, 2017, 2.

Damascus drafted a constitution for the Syrian Arab Kingdom that was more democratic than the Ottomans' version. As they had before 1914, they expected the establishment of a modern constitutional regime to assure their sovereignty in the new world order heralded by the American President, Woodrow Wilson.

The peace process of 1919–1923 first ignited, then encouraged and finally extinguished the political momentum towards popular democracy in Greater Syria. By then, the Allies had already replaced the constitutional regime at Damascus with hand-picked, unelected, colonial-style administrations based in Beirut, Damascus, Jerusalem, and Amman. Political leaders of 1920 were in jail or exile. Failure at Lausanne further undermined the leadership of liberals, who had rallied Syrian Arabs around their legal-diplomatic project and who had opposed the resort to armed resistance. The Allies discredited the post-war world order by invoking the authority of the new League of Nations to impose mandates that transformed Syrian Arabs from rights-bearing citizens into colonial subjects. Arab liberals regarded Lausanne as a last chance to redeem liberal constitutionalism and to claim their rights under international law. The effect of their defeat on Arab politics was revolutionary and long lasting.[3]

The peace process ending at Lausanne cannot therefore be characterised, as suggested in Erez Manela's *The Wilsonian Moment,* as an inspiration for non-European peoples to seek sovereign rights a quarter-century later, after the Second World War.[4] Reliance on European documents has distorted historiography of the interwar period, wherein discussion of a 'crisis of liberalism' omits the ways in which Arab politicians had in fact sought to revive and popularise the democratic politics of the late Ottoman, pre-war era.[5] This study of Arabs' response to Lausanne offers a corrective by locating the origins of anti-liberal and militant movements in the post-Ottoman peace process.[6]

---

3 Elizabeth F. Thompson, *How the West Stole Democracy from the Arabs: The Syrian Congress of 1920 and the Destruction of Its Historic Islamic-Liberal Alliance*, 2021. Because many Syrian Arabs sought exile in Egypt, and because Egyptians too suffered exclusion and the suppression of popular democracy in 1919, this chapter includes Egypt in its concluding section.

4 Erez Manela, *The Wilsonian Moment: Self-Determination and the International Origins of Anticolonial Nationalism*, 2007, xi–xii, 12–13, 60–62.

5 Albert Hourani, *Arabic Thought in the Liberal Age, 1798–1939,* 1962.

6 Elizabeth F. Thompson, *Justice Interrupted: The Struggle for Constitutional Government in the Middle East*, 2013. By contrast, James L. Gelvin, *Divided Loyalties: Nationalism and Mass Politics in Syria at the Close of Empire*, 1998, ignores the liberal revival in Syria. Michael Provence, in *The Last Ottoman Generation and the Making of the Modern Middle East,* 2017, characterises the response to the mandates primarily in terms of military revolt.

In sum, this chapter demonstrates that the post-war moment in the Middle East cannot be understood simply in terms of borders and national independence. As crucial was the struggle of Syrian-Arab politicians to revive liberal constitutionalism and to expand its popular base after the 1918 armistice, an effort integrally linked to their effort to obtain sovereignty in the Wilsonian world order. Syrian Arabs' ultimate failure to secure their rights in 1923 therefore represented a critical juncture, after which the movement for popular democracy died. It was in the wake of Lausanne that anti-systemic, anti-European movements arose in the Middle East as a response to the violent rejection by the Supreme Council of the Peace Conference of the universal application of liberal principles in the new world order. In the conclusion, I suggest that post-war Arab movements are better viewed alongside other anti-systemic movements of the 1920s in Europe and South Asia that rejected the neo-liberal, neo-colonial world order. This critical juncture must become a new starting point for understanding the roots of anti-Westernism and the weakness of democratic movements in Arab politics over the last century.

Exclusion at the Paris Peace Conference, 1919–1920

Since Napoleon's invasion of Egypt in 1798, Ottoman politicians, including Arabs, had resisted European imperial encroachment. Syrian Arabs supported the Ottomans' entry into World War I against the Entente as a struggle against colonization. But in the second year of the war, some Arab leaders lost faith in the Ottoman government's ability to defend their sovereignty. Syrians, in consultation with Sharif Hussein of Mecca, determined that Arab sovereignty could be better assured by striking a wartime deal with the Entente. In 1915, Hussein opened correspondence with the British High Commissioner in Egypt, Lt. Col. Sir Henry McMahon. Based on the understanding that Britain had promised an independent Arab state including Greater Syria, Hussein launched the Arab Revolt in alliance with the Entente Powers in 1916. In October 1918, the northern Arab army occupied Damascus; its leader, Hussein's son Prince Faisal, proclaimed an Arab constitutional state in the Syrian lands north of his father's Hejaz-based kingdom in the Arabian Peninsula. At the same time, several of Faisal's top generals joined a movement to establish an independent state of Iraq, in federation with Syria and Arabia. Egyptian leaders meanwhile formed the Wafd Party to claim their independence against British plans to prolong their wartime protectorate. (Egypt had remained legally part of the Ottoman Empire even following the British occupation of 1882.)

The first move to block Ottoman Arabs' claim to sovereignty came in Damascus where British General Allenby informed Faisal that Britain would not withdraw its troops from Greater Syria until the end of the Peace Conference. However, because Britain formally recognised the Arabs as fellow combatants, they were granted a seat at the Peace Conference. Hussein chose Faisal to represent him in Paris. A second attempt to exclude Arabs came at the port of Marseille, where French officials sought to block Faisal's entry into France, for fear that he would make claims to Syria. Britain intervened and in February 1919 Faisal made a formal presentation to the conference, asserting Arabs' claim to a sovereign state, based on support of the Allied war effort, Britain's explicit promises, and Woodrow Wilson's principle of national self-determination. As erstwhile citizens of the Ottoman Empire, Faisal argued, Arabs were as politically developed as the former citizens of the Austro-Hungarian Empire who had won recognition of their own nation-states at Paris.

However, the Big Four at the Peace Conference (the Prime Ministers of Britain, France, and Italy and the President of the United States) instead agreed to impose a temporary period of provisional independence, under cover of a League of Nations mandate. Article 22 of the League covenant consequently cast Greater Syria and Iraq as among 'those colonies and territories which as a consequence of the late war have ceased to be under the sovereignty of the States which formerly governed them and which are inhabited by peoples not yet able to stand by themselves under the strenuous conditions of the modern world.' Such immature peoples, including colonial subjects of the German Empire in Africa and Asia, would be placed under mandates. The Article assured Arabs that their mandates would be minimal, temporary and governed with their consent: 'Certain communities formerly belonging to the Turkish Empire have reached a stage of development where their existence as independent nations can be provisionally recognised subject to the rendering of administrative advice and assistance by a Mandatory [power] until such time as they are able to stand alone. The wishes of these communities must be a principal consideration in the selection of the Mandatory [power].'[7]

Faisal's assistants in Paris, Rustum Haidar and Awni Abd al-Hadi, had both attended law school in Paris before the war. They were sceptical about the vague guarantee of provisional independence under Article 22, but with American

7 Article 22, The Covenant of the League of Nations. Accessed 15 June 2021 at The Avalon Project: Documents in Law, History and Diplomacy, https://avalon.law.yale.edu/20th_century/leagcov.asp#art22.

assurances they reluctantly signed the Treaty of Versailles on 28 June 1919 as representatives of the Sharif of Mecca.[8] As events unfolded, Sharif Hussein would ultimately refuse to ratify the Versailles Treaty.

Meanwhile, back in Damascus, Faisal hurried to fulfill the conditions for obtaining full independence. He had convinced US President Woodrow Wilson to send a commission of inquiry to poll Arabs on their preferred Mandatory power. Elections were held for a Syrian Congress to prepare a joint statement to Wilson's envoys. In the eyes of the deputies elected, the Syrian Congress was no mere *ad hoc* body, but rather an expression of past Ottoman political practice. On 3 July 1919, the deputies submitted their proposal for 'complete political independence' and a 'democratic, civil, constitutional monarchy' to Wilson's commission of inquiry, led by Henry King and Charles Crane.[9] The commission toured all of Greater Syria, including Palestine and Lebanon. Popular support for the Congress' proposal was demonstrated in more than 1,000 interviews conducted by the King-Crane commission in Greater Syria. The overwhelming majority rejected British and French mandates and rejected British aims to partition Palestine into a separate Jewish homeland.

The King-Crane report was quickly buried at Paris. American restraints on European imperialism disappeared that autumn, when Wilson suffered a stroke and the American Senate opted out of the League and Treaty of Versailles. Remaining leaders of the Paris Peace Conference proceeded to impose mandates by force, not, as Article 22 stipulated, in accordance with the wishes of the communities. France insisted on the mandate for the northern portion of Greater Syria, while Britain continued to support a Jewish home in a mandate on the southern portion. When the British withdrew their troops from Damascus in deference to the French military occupation, popular demonstrations exploded in the streets. Prince Faisal travelled to Europe in a vain effort to reverse plans for a French occupation.

In March 1920, the Congress voted to declare independence unilaterally. It established a constitutional monarchy with Faisal elected as king. The declaration made clear that Syrian Arabs' motive was to join the Allies in the family of nations, not to reject the liberal world order. It also made clear that Syrian

---

8 Official text accessed 15 June 2021 at the Library of Congress: https://www.loc.gov/law/help/us-treaties/bevans/m-ust000002–0043.pdf.

9 Mari Almaz Shahrastan, *al-Mu`tamar al-Suri al`Amm 1919–1920,* 2000, 62; English translation is found in the King-Crane Commission Digital Collection at Oberlin College (hereafter *KCCDC*): 'Statement of Syrian Conference, Damascus, July 3, 1919,' accessed 27 August 2022 at *http://dcollections.oberlin.edu/digital/collection/kingcrane/id/2525.*

Arabs saw their kingdom as the fulfillment of democratic aspirations that had been thwarted by the war:

> During Ottoman times the political associations and political parties of the Arabs, who are the heirs of ancient glory and brilliant civilization, waged a difficult political struggle culminating in a bloody revolt against the central [Ottoman] government, because they wanted complete independence … and the right of self-rule enjoyed by other peoples who are not superior to us in civilization and progress … They also relied on President Wilson's lofty principles espousing the freedom and independence of great and small peoples, equality of rights, the termination of the policy of conquest and imperialism … In the name of the Syrian Arabs who have chosen us to represent them we shall preserve the friendship of the noble Allies and fully respect their interests and those of all other nations as well.[10]

But their British and French allies refused to recognise the independent regime. The following month they gathered at San Remo to assign the mandates as planned. Sharif Hussein's delegates were left waiting outside of the meeting room door and refused admission.

At San Remo, Arabs were definitively expelled from the Peace Conference and from the family of civilized nations. France sent its colonial army to occupy Damascus in July 1920 without protest from the League of Nations, which still had to ratify the San Remo agreement. The French confiscated and destroyed all documents pertaining to the Syrian Arab Kingdom, including Congress records and any copies of the constitution they could find. They aimed to erase all trace of Syrian democracy or Syrians' ability for self-rule.

At least one copy of the 1920 Syrian constitution survived in the suitcase of a minister who fled to Transjordan and later published it.[11] The text, ratified *in toto* two weeks before the French invasion, established a more democratic regime than the Ottoman constitution of 1909. It granted greater power to the legislature than to the monarch and, in light of Syria's diverse population, it removed Islam as a state religion and source of legislation. This was done under a Congress whose president was a leading Muslim cleric, Rashid Rida. Against French pretensions

10 Reprinted in Yusuf Suyufi, *Dhikra Istiqlal Suriya: 17 jumada al-thania 1338 al-muwafiq 8 maris sanat 1920*, 1920.

11 Hasan al-Hakim, *al-Watha'iq al-tarikhiyya al-muta'alliqa bi al-qadiya al-Suriya* (Historical Documents Relating to the Syrian Question), 1974, 194–213. Translated into English in Thompson, *How the West Stole Democracy from the Arabs*, 353–370.

to protect Christians from Muslim tyranny through the establishment of a separate Christian enclave in Lebanon, Rida and the Congress (which included more than a dozen representatives from the Lebanese coast) insisted on equality and coexistence. 'This newborn Arab government was closer to justice, freedom, equality, and reform' than the British and French regimes were, Rida wrote. 'Zionist Jews were favoured in Palestine over Muslims. Likewise, Christians and Catholics were favoured on the [Lebanese] coast. But Muslims were not favoured in the government of Damascus over Christians or Jews.'[12]

Political and Legal Challenges to the Mandate System, 1920–1922

Exiled politicians dispersed across the Arab East after July 1920 expressed bitter disappointment with the liberal world order being constructed at Paris. But they did not yet reject it in principle. They defended their strategy of playing according to Paris rules rather than launching armed revolt against European occupation, as the Turks and Iraqis did.

Despite their defeat at Damascus, these civilian statesmen and lawyers still believed (as their parents and grandparents had) that liberalism was the basis for the universal rights of nations. The Allies might still be proved wrong through an appeal to the institution imagined by Woodrow Wilson to adjudicate international law. Rashid Rida and a group of Syrian exiles in Cairo therefore formed the Syrian-Palestinian Congress (hereafter SPC). It included a Christian prince from Lebanon, Michel Lutfallah, and a secularist from Damascus, Abd al-Rahman Shahbandar. They were later joined by Shakib Arslan, a Druze prince from Lebanon who took up residence in Geneva, headquarters of the League of Nations.

In August 1921, members of the SPC travelled to Geneva before the inaugural opening of the League of Nations Assembly. Rida took the trip in the belief that Europe's liberals would uphold Wilsonian principles. 'I would like Arab nations to know that mandates are not inevitable and that the League of Nations will not be a puppet in the hands of colonialists,' he wrote in his widely read magazine, *Al-Manar*.[13]

Rida and the SPC met with the sympathetic administrator of the Permanent Mandates Commission (hereafter PMC) and several members of the League

12 Muhammad Rashid Rida, 'Al-rihla al-Suriya al-thaniya (10)' (The Second Syrian Trip, Part 10), *Al-Manar* 23, May 1922, 390–391.

13 Rashid Rida,' al-Haqa'iq al-jalia fi al-mas'ala al`Arabiya' (Clear facts about the Arab question), *Al-Manar* 22, June 1921, 478–479.

Assembly. They demanded the repeal of the French and British mandates in Greater Syria on the basis that their violent imposition against the people's will had violated Article 22. The SPC also argued that the Syrian Arab Kingdom had demonstrated their political maturity and capacity for self-rule.

The Geneva encounter was pivotal in the transformation of Arab political aims and strategy. The SPC discovered that the League Council, to which the PMC reported, consisted of colonial officials. The League's first secretary general, Eric Drummond, was a close associate of Arthur Balfour, known for his note promising a Jewish homeland in Palestine. Members of both the Council and the PMC declined to meet with the SPC. After filing a written report with the PMC's administrator, members departed from Geneva in late September.

When Rida learned that the League Council had scheduled a meeting to vote on ratification of the mandates, he published an ultimatum. 'It does not befit the honour of the League, which President Wilson proposed to include all civilized nations … to be used as a tool by the two colonial states,' he wrote in *Al-Manar*. 'If the Balkans were the spark of war in the West, then Syria, Palestine, and other Arab countries will ignite the fires of war in both the West and the East.'[14]

His warning went unheeded. In July 1922, Balfour chaired a meeting of the League Council that ratified the British and French mandates in a resounding rejection of the SPC appeal. Shakib Arslan, who had travelled to London to witness the vote, was shut out of the room just as Arab delegates had been at San Remo.

And yet, in the eyes of the SPC, the game was not over in July 1922. They had perceived a loophole in international law that might yet serve their cause: The text of the mandate charters pretended that the Ottoman Empire had already renounced its rights to Syria, Lebanon, and Palestine in the Treaty of Sèvres. But Sèvres had never been ratified. In support of the Arabs, the Turkish nationalist government in Ankara had protested that the mandates must not be assigned before the signing of a peace treaty. And in September 1922, the Turkish army won a decisive victory in Western Anatolia against the Allied-backed Greek army, enabling them to demand a revised treaty.[15] Arabs looked to the Turkish national leader, Mustafa Kemal (hereafter Atatürk), for support.

The world press also raised questions about the legality of the mandates. In June 1922, front pages of British newspapers had reported that the House of Lords

14 Rashid Rida, 'Al-Rihla al-Urubiya (5)' (The European Trip Part 5), *Al-Manar* 23, July 1922, 559–560.

15 'The Turkish Diplomatic Mission to the Department of State, May 18, 1922,' *Foreign Relations of the United States*, 1922, Vol. 2, *Great Britain,* 281.

rejected the Palestine mandate on a vote of 60 to 29, despite a personal appeal from Arthur Balfour, on grounds that it violated official promises and the will of the majority in Palestine.[16] Winston Churchill, as Colonial Secretary, managed to override that rejection in the House of Commons, but doubts remained among the British public. In October 1922, an editorial in *The Times* of London cast the upcoming Lausanne Peace Conference as a reckoning for British policy in the region:

> The struggle and the victories of [Mustafa] Kemal Pasha have stimulated throughout the East a movement that must be regarded as an incipient revolt against the West. It is significant that among the Arab peoples who welcomed our aid in effecting their deliverance from Turkish rule, admiration for Kemal's achievements has been widespread, while the sympathy they once felt for us has been chilled by our confused and unintelligible policy.[17]

New controversy also swirled around the French mandate in Syria. In April 1922, Syrians had petitioned Charles Crane, a leader of Wilson's 1919 commission of inquiry, to publish the long-suppressed King-Crane report when he visited the Syrian Arab Kingdom's former foreign minister, Abd al-Rahman Shahbandar. From his jail cell, Shahbandar sent a note to Woodrow Wilson. 'Your well-known pledges,' he wrote, 'are now an inspiration to all people in the East. But alas! What we tried to avoid most fell as a crushing stone on the head of our people.'[18]

Following reports in the *New York Times* and other papers, Crane won Wilson's permission to publish the King-Crane report in the summer of 1922, despite efforts of the Harding administration to suppress it. A sympathetic *New York Times* editorial compared Syrians' complaints about French rule to grievances listed in the American Declaration of Independence. The *New York Times* even summarised the report's warning that the 'erection of a Jewish state … could not be accomplished without the gravest trespass upon the civil and religious rights of existing non-Jewish communities in Palestine.'[19]

---

16 'Palestine mandate defeated in Lords,' *New York Times,* 21 June 1922, 1; 'Palestine' and 'The Palestine mandate: Government defeat in the Lords,' *The Times* (London), 21 June 1922, 6, 10.

17 'The approach to peace,' *The Times* (London), 23 October 1922, 11.

18 *KCCDC*, Shahbandar to Wilson, 6 April 1922. In apparent error, the archive dated the letter 6 May 1922. Accessed 23 September 2018, at http://dcollections.oberlin.edu/cdm/compoundobject/collection/kingcrane/id/1466/rec/1.

19 'The Crane-King report,' *New York Times,* 20 August 1922, 44; Dept. of State memo to Mr.

Arab 'Present Absentees' at Lausanne

In autumn 1922, the Syrians and Palestinians perceived new openings among the European Allies that led them to believe they might yet overturn the mandates. In October, the British attempt to intervene against Turkey at Chanak brought down the government of David Lloyd George and, with him, Winston Churchill. The new Bonar Law government might relinquish Britain's interest in the mandates. In November, French General Gouraud appeared ready to resign as High Commissioner of Syria and Lebanon, after Paris cut the mandate budget.

There were also signs that Italy, long critical of the mandates, might support the Arabs at Lausanne. Some Italian diplomats favoured supporting the Arabs as a wedge against British and French influence.[20] A prominent Italian scholar of international law published a blistering article that questioned the legality of the mandates. Amadeo Giannini concluded that if members of the League of Nations raised objections, the mandates issue might be referred to the Permanent Court of Justice at The Hague.[21] More auspicious, in late October Benito Mussolini took over as Prime Minister from the government that had voted to ratify the mandates during the previous July.

Syrian Arabs therefore approached the Turks, reminding them that they were still legally citizens of the Ottoman Empire and that the 1920 National Pact included a demand for Arab self-determination.[22] Atatürk favoured the establishment of an independent, united Arab state, according to a Cairo newspaper.[23] Even Rashid Rida expressed guarded optimism that his friend Shakib Arslan might

Harrison, 6 April 1922, and Dept. of State Undersecretary Memo to Mr. Turlington, 7 April 1922, National Archives and Record Administration, College Park, RG 59.763.72119/7156–7210, Microfilm M367 Roll 439, Images 0067–69; 'The Secretary of State to the Ambassador in Great Britain (Harvey)', 3 April 1922, in *Foreign Relations of the United States,* 1922, Vol. 2.0012, *Great Britain*, 271–275; 'The Secretary of State to the Ambassador in France (Herrick)', 19 May 1922 in *FRUS*, 1922, Vol. 2.0010, *France*, 117.

20 Vincenzo Strika, 'L'Italia e il nazionalismo arabo del vicino oriente tra le due guerre mondiali,' *Quaderni di Studi Arabi* 5/6, 1987–1988, 726–746.

21 Amadeo Giannini, 'I mandati typo A e la loro natura Giuridica' (The type A mandates and their legal nature), *Oriente Moderno* 2/3, 15 August 1922, 139.

22 Awad Halabi, 'Liminal loyalties: Ottomanism and Palestinian responses to the Turkish war of independence, 1919–22,' *Journal of Palestine Studies* 41/3, 2012, 21–22; Mutaz Qafisheh, 'Genesis of citizenship in Palestine and Israel: Palestinian nationality during the period 1917–1925,' *Journal of the History of International Law* 11/1, 2009, 1–36.

23 'A Turco-Arab alliance: Kemalist proposal,' *The Times* (London), 4 November 1922, quoting *Al-Mokattam* newspaper of Cairo. Also quoted in Eliot Grinnell Mears, *Modern Turkey*, 1924, 549.

persuade the Turks to insist on Arab independence, in defiance of what he saw as Lord Curzon's plot against the Islamic world.[24]

Some Syrians and Palestinians also looked to Sharif Hussein of Mecca, who had resisted British pressure to sign both the Versailles or Sèvres Treaties and who, in 1922, refused to sign a separate bilateral treaty endorsing the mandates. After the July 1922 League ratification, a Palestinian delegation had travelled to Mecca. In response, Lord Curzon threatened Sharif Hussein with support for his arch-enemy, Ibn Saud, and with exclusion from the Lausanne conference. Hussein, reportedly 'outraged,' sent his representative Naji al-Asil to Lausanne anyway.[25]

But hope dimmed again in late November, upon the opening of the Lausanne Conference. Delegates chose Lord Curzon as conference president and defeated a Turkish proposal to make the proceedings public. 'At all costs, public passions must not be brought into the debates of the conference,' warned the leading French delegate, Camille Barrère.[26] Worse, the Allies dismissed Arab demands for inclusion as 'ridiculous,' because they were a people defined by Article 22 as 'not yet able to stand by themselves under the strenuous conditions of the modern world.'

Arabs were also handicapped because they could not speak with the same unified voice with which they had addressed the Paris Peace Conference and the King-Crane commission at Damascus. Since 1920, they had been exiled and divided into distinct polities, subjected to intense surveillance, and split by British and French techniques of buying collaboration. Faisal had accepted Churchill's offer to rule Iraq under a separate treaty with the British. His brother Abdullah signed the treaty that his father, Sharif Hussein, refused. The once unified SPC that had travelled to Geneva in 1921 now split. A Palestinian congress designated Musa Kazim al-Husseini, former mayor of Jerusalem, as leader of their delegation. Syrian exiles in Cairo sent a separate delegation.

The various Arab delegations pitched their appeals to different and rival powers. Before arriving in Lausanne, Syrians and Palestinians met with representatives of Egypt's ex-Khedive Abbas Hilmi about his proposal to rule them under a united state. They also met with the new Italian leader, Mussolini, who

24 'Mu'tamar Luzan: Ahwal al-`alam al-islami, mu'tamar al-sulh' (The Lausanne conference: The condition of the Islamic world at the peace conference), *Al-Manar* 24, February 1923, 145–152.

25 Suleiman Mousa, 'A matter of principle: King Hussein of the Hijaz and the Arabs of Palestine,' *International Journal of Middle East Studies* 9/2, 1978, 183–194; Timothy J. Paris, *Britain, the Hashemites and Arab Rule, 1920–1925*, 2003, 277–298, 341–353.

26 *Lausanne Conference on Near Eastern Affairs, 1922–1923: Records of Proceedings and Draft Terms of Peace*, 1923 (hereafter *Lausanne Conference*), 4.

expressed support for an independent state.[27] But once in Lausanne, Palestinians perceived an opportunity to negotiate bilaterally with Churchill's successor as Colonial Secretary. They departed for London, leaving the Syrians behind.[28] And while Egyptian nationalists shared similar concerns with the Syrians and Palestinians, they chose not to combine forces. Instead, rival Egyptian parties sent separate delegations to Ankara.[29] Egyptian officials also sent official letters directly to Lausanne, demanding participation in the negotiations.[30] Meanwhile, Lebanese exiles in Cairo sent a petition directly to the French, British, Italian and Turkish delegates in Lausanne. On behalf of the Lebanese people, it declared: 'We demand that the peace treaty recognize the independence of the Lebanese state within its current boundaries.'[31]

Arab leaders were painfully aware that European methods of divide-and-rule weakened them. The Palestinian newspaper *Al-Karmil* newspaper deplored the fractured Arab effort:

> In preparation for the Lausanne conference, the Arab presence is limited to the joint Palestinian-Syrian delegation which is led by Kazim Pasha al-Husseini. The Iraqi delegation, led by Jaafar Pasha al-Askari and Tawfiq al-Suwaidi, went to London to discuss preparations for Lausanne. The recognised [independent] Hejaz did not send a delegate to Lausanne, and Transjordan sent their prince [Abdullah] but we do not know what he has in store for the Arabs in his briefcase.[32]

The paper warned Arab diplomats to defy Britain's divide-and-rule tactics or face subordination to European rule. Likewise, *Al-Ahram* of Cairo urged Egyptian

27 'Akhbar al-akhira: malik Suriya wa Filastin' (Latest Report: The King of Syria and Palestine), *Filastin*, 24 November 1922, 2.

28 'The Palestinian Arabs' case,' *The Times* (London), 23 December 1922, 7.

29 'Tasrihat rijal al-hizb al-watani li-mandub al-Ahram bi-Luzan' (Statement of National Party Leaders to Al-Ahram's correspondent in Lausanne), *Al-Ahram,* 8 January 1923; 'Rival Egyptian missions seeking favours at Angora [Ankara],' *The Times* (London), 28 December 1922, 8.

30 'Misr fi Luzan' (Egypt in Lausanne), *Al-Ahram,* 4 January 1923, and 'Illa mu'tamar Luzan' (To the Lausanne Conference), *Al-Ahram,* 22 February 1923.

31 Untitled article, *Al-Ahram,* 29 January 1923.

32 'Mawqif al-Arab,' *Al-Karmil,* 15 November 1922. The Hejaz actually did send a delegate later.

envoys to unite with Syrian Arabs at Lausanne in protesting their exclusion from the negotiations.[33]

The British deployed multiple additional strategies to block Arab participation. The first was to refuse personal meetings and presentations to the conference. Lord Curzon's advisers suggested that 'permission to address the Conference should be formally laid before the Conference in order that it may be refused, and that Lord Curzon should decline to receive them on the ground that they have already been given ample opportunity of bringing their views before the [Secretary of State] for the Colonies, who is the minister primarily concerned.'[34] Accordingly, the High Commissioner of Palestine, Herbert Samuel, warned Musa Kazim that his trip to Lausanne would be 'a waste of time.'

In fact, as the Palestinians argued, the mandates had not yet entered international law, so the Arabs did have standing to challenge their expulsion from rights-bearing nations into the category of colonial peoples without rights. 'Now that the Treaty of Sèvres in which Palestine was intimatly [sic] involved has been abolished,' wrote the Palestine Arab Delegation in Lausanne on 28 November 1922, a revised peace treaty may now be 'based on the most noble considerations.' The Palestinians insisted that because they are citizens of 'the Turkish Empire', they adhere to the Turkish National Pact, adopted at Ankara, which demands that 'the destiny of Arab countries should be determined by their inhabitants.' They also argued that the Balfour Declaration on a Jewish home in Palestine violated Article 3 of the Hague Convention, which required that an occupying power was not to introduce essential changes to a country. 'We appeal to your conference to remove this injustice from Palestine.'[35]

However, legal cases like these, carefully crafted by Arab lawyers who had studied in Europe, were ignored at Lausanne, as they had been in London, Paris, and Geneva. The British made it clear that international law intended justice for Europeans only. Lord Curzon regarded such appeals as 'insolent.' He even snubbed Sharif Hussein, ruler of an independent state who had aided the Allied war effort. On 8 December 1922, Hussein's envoy, Naji al-Asil, requested a meeting with Curzon to present a note from the Sharif. Curzon refused to meet him.[36]

33 'Misr fi Luzan' (Egypt at Lausanne) and 'Ill mu'tamar Luzan' (To the Lausanne Conference), *Al-Ahram*, 4 January and 22 February 1923.
34 FO 839/25, File 3, memo from Forbes Adam and memo from R.V. Vernon, 24 November 1922.
35 FO 839/31, memo from Palestine Arab delegation, 28 November 1922, Lausanne, 225.
36 FO 839/37, memo by Forbes Adam, 8 December 1922. Curzon's remark on insolence is found in FO 839/9 telegram Curzon to Sir Eyre Crowe, London, 10 December 1922.

The British also discouraged Turkish-Arab cooperation. *The Times* of London, mouthpiece of the British ruling establishment, dismissed the Turks' contention that Britain had no right to represent Egyptians at Lausanne. An article titled 'Turkish Pretension' nonetheless gave the public a hint of the legal controversy by quoting Atatürk's statement to an Egyptian delegation to Ankara: 'It is only the Turkish delegation that can defend Egypt's cause at Lausanne, because Turkey's rights over Egypt remain the same as in the past.'[37]

The second British strategy was to insist that the conference would not address any issues of relevance to Arabs. On 27 December 1922, Lord Curzon warned fellow British delegates to avoid any mention of the Hejaz railroad, in response to queries from Sharif Hussein.[38] On 5 January 1923, he cabled Sharif Hussein to assure him that neither the status of Islamic holy relics, nor the religious foundations in the holy cities of Mecca and Medina or the Arab-built Hejaz railway would be discussed at Lausanne. Indeed, he promised, the Kingdom of the Hejaz would not be mentioned in the treaty, its 'independent status having been in any case admitted by the Allies when her representative [Prince Faisal] took a seat at the Peace Conference in 1919.' Curzon reminded Hussein that the Hejaz is 'at liberty' to join the League of Nations by ratifying the Treaty of Versailles (and so accept the mandates).[39] Hussein responded by insisting on his claim to the Hejaz railway which he intended to repair. He correctly feared that the Turks would try to claim it.[40]

Two days later, on 29 January 1923, the conference held a meeting on the status of Mosul, a city claimed by both Arabs and Turks. Naji al-Asil objected to discussing Mosul and the borders of Syria and Iraq in the absence of Sharif Hussein: 'No arrangement that harms Arab interests must be given definitive shape in a conference only between Turks and Allies.'[41]

Arabs were painfully present at the conference albeit as 'present absentees'.[42] Snubbed by Lord Curzon and without the clout of the Sharif, the only sovereign Arab ruler, they met privately with İsmet İnönü (hereafter İsmet), the leader of

---

37 'Turkish Pretension', *The Times* (London), 17 January 1923, 9.

38 FO 141/589, 27 December 1922.

39 FO 141/589, memo no. 21, 5 January 1923, Curzon to Sir Eyre Crowe, enclosing text of telegram sent to Major Marshall, Jeddah, and 27 January 1923 memo to Curzon.

40 FO 141/589, Colonial Office to FO, 27 January 1923, based on a report from Herbert Samuel.

41 FO 836/16, Naji El Assil [al-Asil] to Curzon, 29 January 1923.

42 This term was later commonly used to refer to the ambiguous legal status of Palestinians who returned to their homes in territory claimed by Israel during the 1948 war.

the Turkish delegation. While İsmet affirmed full Turkish support to the Arabs, in negotiations with the British he wielded a double-edged rhetorical sword. In a 23 January 1923 meeting, for example, İsmet had rejected attaching Mosul to the British mandate in Iraq by claiming that 'the Arab element is insignificant' in the province and that it legally still belonged to the Ottoman Empire. İsmet scolded the British for not respecting Article 22, which required them to solicit an independent opinion of the population. Citing Wilson, he declared that 'the people of a country may not be transferred against their will from the sovereignty of one state to another.' But Curzon responded that the Turks were contradictory on mandates: while they were willing to saddle them with the Ottoman debt, they refused to recognise them. İsmet insisted that assigning debt to Syria and Iraq was not a form of recognition of mandates. In the end, İsmet agreed not to insist on Arab rights to self-determination at Lausanne. 'We restrict our claims at Lausanne to regions that ought to be returned to Turkey [meaning Mosul].'[43]

İsmet's opening remarks to the conference on 20 November 1922 had stated the bald truth. The Lausanne conference was not the fulfillment of the Wilsonian vision of a post-war order, based on international law and self-determination. Rather, İsmet acidly remarked, the Turks were forced to achieve their self-determination by war. 'The Turkish nation has conquered its place in civilized mankind with all those rights to existence and independence which are inherent in nations capable of a vigorous vitality …'[44] By implication, İsmet's remarks cemented the Arabs' new colonial status, as a people without an army, and therefore without rights.

In a similar rhetorical affirmation, the British title of the Lausanne Treaty omitted any reference to the Near East or the Arabs: 'Treaty of Peace with Turkey Signed at Lausanne July 24, 1923.'

And yet more than twenty of the final Treaty's 143 Articles addressed issues of direct concern to inhabitants of the Ottoman Empire's former Arabic-speaking provinces. Without Arab consultation, the Lausanne conference had detached their provinces from the Empire, drawn boundaries of their states (Art. 3, 16–17), established conditions for claiming nationality (Art. 30–36), burdened them with

43 *Lausanne Conference*, 339–353, 370, 388–389, 395. On page 444, İsmet reiterated Turkish support for the self-determination of Syria, Mesopotamia, Egypt, and the Hejaz on 27 January. His demand that these same territories share in repaying the Ottoman debt is found on pp. 538, 543, 555 and 567. While Arabs were not present, Greek and Albanian representatives were permitted to contest these claims in person. The line drawn between European and non-European rights was clear.

44 *Lausanne Conference*, 11.

payments for the outstanding Ottoman debt (Art. 46–55), deprived them of the Ottoman civil and military pensions they had earned (Art. 61), and excluded them from the right to return of moveable property that had been granted to inhabitants of formerly Ottoman territories in the Balkans (Art. 67).

The silences of the treaty were loud. While assuring the Allies' return of prisoners of war and right to maintain military cemeteries, the Treaty gave no such assurances for the Arabs who had fought alongside them. (The Arab presence at Gallipoli remains barely documented today.) Likewise, despite Lord Curzon's promises, the Treaty made no provisions for the return of religious relics to the Hejaz or Jerusalem, or for compensation for war crimes committed by the Turks. Turks and Egyptians, but not Syrians, were granted representation on a sanitary commission overseeing the pilgrimage to Mecca (Art. 117). Article 139's provision requiring the return of documentary archives and deeds to 'detached' territories was evidently never carried out, given the difficulty Palestinians encounter today in obtaining them.

The most resounding silence concerned the mandates. While the mandates had been mentioned in the Treaty of Sèvres, they were omitted in the Lausanne text. The silence served the interests of the British and the French, who claimed at Lausanne to represent Palestine, Transjordan, Iraq, Lebanon, and Syria under stipulations of mandate charters that granted them full control of foreign affairs. However, as noted above, the mandates had not yet come into legal force. As contemporary legal scholars and the Ankara government protested, the mandates could not be assigned until a peace treaty governing the Ottoman territories was signed. In the debate on Mosul, Lord Curzon went so far as to argue that the Iraq mandate had been confirmed at Sèvres and that Britain could not legally surrender it.[45]

Within weeks of the Lausanne Treaty's signing, the mandates entered into legal force. The inhabitants of predominantly Arab territories detached from the Ottoman Empire in Asia and Egypt became virtual 'present absentees' in international law, long before the term would be coined by the state of Israel for internally displaced Palestinians.

Decolonizing the Historical Narrative: Lausanne as Critical Juncture

The narrative constructed at Lausanne stuck. While Turks had won a sovereign country, Arabs were discursively consigned to the colonial or 'developing' world.

45 'Lord Curzon on Mosul,' *The Times* (London), 24 January 1923, 9.

The official texts produced at Lausanne epitomised European legal practice which, according to legal historian Antony Anghie, aimed to obscure the colonial origins of international law.[46]

But Arab scholars and politicians were not duped. They understood that Lausanne had shredded the universal principles of liberalism that should have united Muslims and Christians and Asians and Europeans; instead, Lausanne made the League of Nations, which Wilson had promised would uphold the rights of even small nations, an instrument to enforce Arabs' expulsion from the civilized world.

Following Anghie, we must regard Lausanne as a critical historical juncture that established the colonial origins of international law and the new world order created at Paris. The final closure of the legal door to Arab sovereignty in 1923 transformed the institutional basis of political action for Arab liberals. In Anghie's terms, this juncture established a distinctly 'Third World' form of truncated sovereignty, permitting unequal intervention by foreign powers. Consequently, the once hegemonic principles of liberal constitutionalism gave way to anti-systemic political movements in the Arab world that reshaped Arab politics for the rest of the twentieth century.

Recognizing this critical juncture disrupts the prevailing, neo-colonialist historiography of Arab politics after World War I. The colonialist narrative was taken up most saliently by Quincy Wright, a prominent American legal scholar who in 1930 published the definitive volume, *Mandates Under the League of Nations*. Even though Wright had visited the Middle East shortly after the demise of the Ottoman Empire, he wrongly assumed Arabs and Armenians had been colonial subjects of the Turks, not fellow citizens. He consequently regarded Arabs as having the same status as former subjects of the German Empire now placed under British and French mandates. For example, Wright described how the Allies at the Peace Conference aimed to block 'the restoration of the colonies to Germany and Turkey.' He likewise quoted a Peace Conference resolution to the effect that 'because of the historical misgovernment by the Turks of subject peoples … the Allied and associated powers are agreed that Armenia, Syria, Mesopotamia, Palestine, and Arabia must be completely severed from the Turkish Empire.'[47]

The durability of the Allies' legal fiction – that Arabs had been colonial subjects, not Ottoman citizens – is demonstrated in that Antony Anghie himself repeated it. The mandate system, Anghie wrote, 'applied only to the territories

46 Antony Anghie, *Imperialism, Sovereignty and the Making of International Law*, 2004.
47 Quincy Wright, *Mandates Under the League of Nations*, 1930, 28–29.

formerly annexed to Germany and the Ottoman Empire.'[48] Relying on this historical fiction, Anghie and others have regarded mandates as a step toward sovereignty, rather than a stripping of Arab rights. The most recent major book on the mandate system, by Susan Pedersen, follows Wright and Anghie in neglecting Lausanne, which is mentioned just once in the book's 571 pages.[49] David Fromkin's seminal *A Peace to End All Peace* likewise ignores the efforts of Arab liberals at Lausanne. In a new Afterword, Fromkin explains today's lack of Arab democracies in the following terms: 'while it may have been chauvinist of British officials in the 1920s and 1930s to say that Arab countries were not ready for self-government – which is to say, liberal democratic constitutional regimes with rule of law – evidence as of our own late date does not seem to prove them wrong.'[50] In 1923, Lord Curzon would have no doubt agreed with Fromkin's contention that the lack of liberal constitutional regimes in the Middle East was due to Arabs' cultural immaturity rather than the destructive effects of violent European intervention in 1920.

Middle East specialists have also perpetuated Allied fictions about Lausanne. Standard English-language history textbooks continue to frame the Lausanne conference as concerning only the Turks. Albert Hourani, the grandfather of modern Arab history, mentions Lausanne only as the prelude to the establishment of the Turkish Republic in his *A History of the Arab Peoples*. He too replicated colonial language about Arabs as politically immature, lacking the Turks' experience and their 'remarkable leader, Mustafa Kemal'.[51] More recent textbooks barely mention Lausanne or omit it completely, in favour of arguments that military might set peace terms, not diplomacy.[52]

In the fictitious world created by the Allies and these scholars, there is no room to explore Lausanne's profound political impact. In their view, Arab liberals either

48 Anghie, *Imperialism*, 172–186.

49 Susan Pedersen, *The Guardians: The League of Nations and the Crisis of Empire*, 2015, 264.

50 David Fromkin, *A Peace to End All Peace: The Fall of the Ottoman Empire and the Creation of the Modern Middle East*, 2009 (originally published 1989), 559, 573, 575.

51 Albert Hourani, *A History of the Arab Peoples*, 2002 (originally published 1991), 315–319. Ottoman historians also neglect the importance of Lausanne for the Arabs. See Caroline Finkel, *Osman's Dream: The History of the Ottoman Empire*, 2005, 545–546; Erik Zürcher *Turkey: A Modern History*, 2004, 160–166.

52 William L. Cleveland and Martin Bunton, *A History of the Modern Middle East*, 2019, 169; James L. Gelvin, *The Modern Middle East: A History*, 2020, 197–205; Eugene Rogan, 'Divide and Rule: World War I and the Postwar Settlement', *The Arabs: A History*, 2009, 147–174; Rashid Khalidi, 'A Failure of Leadership', *The Iron Cage: The Story of the Palestinian Struggle for Statehood*, 2006, 65–104.

did not exist or did not understand political realities. Rather, historians of the interwar era depict militant soldiers as the sole realists in the Arab world. Liberal constitutionalists who negotiated with Europeans were, by default, dupes. And yet, there is ample evidence that civilian Arab leaders were quite astute in the analysis of their political predicament in 1923. They clearly understood that their weakness at Lausanne owed more to Allied maneuvering than to political immaturity or cultural backwardness. Such legal and political expertise enabled the SPC to argue in September 1922 that the mandates were illegal colonies that stripped Arabs of rights they had enjoyed before the war, when they elected representatives to the Ottoman parliament.[53]

The colonialist narrative ignores the evidence, readily available in contemporary newspapers, that Arab civilians saw themselves as waging a higher battle than soldiers, to save liberalism from military rule. They certainly were not unaware of the trade-off between democracy and military dictatorship. In December 1922, Musa Kazim spoke in realistic terms in his interview with *The Times* of London: 'There is a very strong feeling that all Arab peoples must unite as the Turks have done, if they want to get anything from the Powers. The lesson they have learned from the Turks is that the latter won their power by the sword'.[54]

Delegates from Palestine, Syria, Iraq, the Hejaz, Yemen, Nejd, and Muscat met in April 1923 to discuss creating a federation to 'establish a common centre abroad to defend the cause of the Arabs,' according to *Oriente Moderno*. The Italian journal also published a declaration by Faris al-Khoury, former minister in the Syrian Arab Kingdom, that 'all negotiations conducted in Lausanne on Syria's borders of Syria and on the dissolution of relations with the Turkish government, in which the country did not participate, will not be recognised by Syria.'[55]

A July 1923 editorial in *Lisan al-Arab* of Jerusalem demonstrates how Arab political elites clearly understood the rules of the game, that only sovereign states carried rights and standing in the Paris world order. The editorial concerned Sharif Hussein's widely publicised telegram reassuring Palestinians that he would never recognise the British mandate. While the editorial praised Sharif Hussein's steadfast opposition to the mandates, it also warned 'fanatics' that they should not allow themselves to be split by appeals to allow the Turks to represent them in

53 *Oriente Moderno,* 15 October 1922, quoting a 5 September 1922 petition to the League of Nations by the SPC.

54 'Palestinian Arabs' case,' *The Times*, 23 December 1922, 7.

55 'Confederazione Araba', *Oriente Moderno*, 15 April 1923, 642–643 and 'For Syria in Lausanne,' *Oriente Moderno*, 15 June 1923, 51, quoting an article in *Lisan al-Arab* of Jerusalem.

the international arena. Unity behind Sharif Hussein was a key to success. In June 1923, when the Third Palestinian Arab Congress heaped 'rude' criticism on the Sharif, it weakened the only sovereign pillar that Arabs enjoyed.[56] Palestinians and other Arabs should be gathering in the Hejaz, not sending separate delegations to London or Ankara.

After their defeat at Lausanne, Arab liberals remained integral to shaping the new Arab politics. They spread awareness of the unjust and illegal measures taken by the Arabs' former Allies between 1919 and 1923. Arabs had entered World War I and attended the 1919 Peace Conference as citizens of a sovereign state, expecting to share rights accorded to white citizens of the defeated European empires. However, unlike Europeans, Arabs exited the peace process under foreign military occupation. Instead, they were subjected to the same mandate regime as African peoples who had not been sovereign before 1914. For decades after the Lausanne Treaty was signed, Arabs regretted it as a historic betrayal and injustice.[57]

The influence of disenchanted Syrian Arabs spread when they fled Damascus in 1920 to take up positions of influence in Egypt, Iraq, Jordan, the Hejaz, Saudi Arabia and ultimately even after their return in Palestine, Lebanon, and Syria. They became ministers and teachers, newspaper editors and leaders of anti-European political movements. Contrary to assumptions of mainstream historical narratives, they did so not out of a cultural hostility to the West, nor out of ignorance about liberal democracy. Among them were men educated in Paris and other Western schools of law, and particularly in European scholarship on international law: Faris al-Khoury, foreign minister of the Syrian Arab Kingdom in 1920 and a future prime minister of the Syrian Republic; Ihsan al-Jabiri, King Faisal's chief of staff in 1920 and a leading member of the SPC afterwards; Riad al-Solh, SPC member and future Lebanese prime minister; and Awni Abd al-Hadi, legal adviser to King Faisal in 1919–1920 and future president of the Palestinians' first political party, the Istiqlal (Independence) party. Other leading opponents of the mandates included Abd al-Rahman Shahbandar, a medical doctor fluent in English and trained at the Syrian Protestant College in Beirut, who founded the Syrian People's Party, was the former foreign minister of the Syrian Arab Kingdom and played a leading role in the 1925 Syrian revolt against France.

These European and American-educated men associated closely with Arab

56 'Palestine, the Treaty, and the Sharif,' *Lisan al-Arab,* translated in *Oriente Moderno,* 15 July 1923, 87.

57 Fadil Husayn, *Muhaddirat `an mu'tamar Luzan wa Atharuh fi al-bilad al-`Arabiya* (Lectures on the Lausanne Conference and its Influence in Arab Countries), 1958.

politicians who had been educated at the highest schools of law and administration in the Ottoman capital, like Hashim al-Atassi and Shukri al-Quwwatli, future Syrian presidents. The bitterness that would fuel new anti-Western movements rested not solely on emotion, but mainly on their intimate knowledge and engagement in law and politics. Interwar political opposition movements expressed far more than anger at Britain's broken promises of independence. They were motivated to redeem the subversion of law and their rights by the very world powers that proclaimed the victory of democracy in the war.

No leader expressed the post-Lausanne political mood more prominently than Rashid Rida, the president of the Syrian Congress. At the opening of the critical juncture, he had devoted most of the December 1918 issue of his widely read magazine, *Al-Manar,* to the praise of President Woodrow Wilson as an instrument of God's peace who promised equal rights for even small nations. In 1921, he told his readers that he travelled to Geneva to meet with 'independent-thinking liberals of Europe' who might pressure the Powers to respect Arab sovereignty. 'God's rules apply to all nations.' But these liberals were too weak to challenge the colonial parties in their countries, Rida reported. He correctly predicted years of violent revolt should Europe insist upon denying Arabs' sovereign rights.[58]

Rida's rejection of liberalism as a Western ruse was evident in his article on Arab failure at the Lausanne conference. He scorned the pursuit of justice through international law, instead praising the Turks for sacrificing their lives to resist colonization. In a phrase that anticipated one made famous by Frantz Fanon decades later in *The Wretched of the Earth*, Rida wrote: 'The greatest merit for the new Turkish renaissance goes to its leaders who vomited the poison of despair that European policy had inflicted on them'. The Turks understood European wiles, in contrast to the Arab leaders who trusted them and sold their peoples into 'slavery.'[59] Rida now expressed solidarity with the East. Arabs of Iraq, Syria, Palestine and the Hejaz would join a general revolt against the West.

---

58 Rashid Rida, 'Al-Rihla al-Urubiya (7)' (The European Trip, Part 7), *Al-Manar* 23, November 1922, 696.

59 Rashid Rida, 'Mu`tamar Luzan' (The Lausanne Conference), *Al-Manar* 23, December 1922, 794–796. The reference is to Fanon's famous call to colonial subjects to 'vomit up' European civilization that has dehumanised them: 'in the period of decolonization the colonized masses thumb their noses at these very [Western] values, shower them with insults and vomit them up.' Frantz Fanon, *The Wretched of the Earth*, trans. Richard Wilcox, 2004, 8.

'India has included the independence of Palestine and other Arab countries in its programme,' he reported in February 1923.[60]

Arab exclusion from the rights-bearing family of nations at Lausanne was a critical juncture that ended the hegemony of liberal constitutionalism in Arab politics. Rida would rarely write again about his role as president of the Syrian Congress and of the Syrian constitution. After 1923, his lectures drew the attention of Muslim activists in Cairo, including the young Hasan al-Banna, who would found the Muslim Brotherhood in 1928. Like similar Islamist groups that emerged across Greater Syria, the Brotherhood called for the rule of Islamic law against liberal secularism. Post-1923 Islamic populists broke sharply with the Islamic liberalism of Rida's youth and earlier generations of religious leaders. Syrian cleric Kamil al-Qassab had built a popular movement in support of the Syrian Congress in 1919–1920. However, upon his return to Syria after years of exile, he joined local opposition leaders to build the nascent Brotherhood there.

At the same time, communist parties attracted followers especially among peoples who were not granted states by the Paris Peace Conference, including Kurds and Armenians as well as Arabs and among groups marginalised under the sectarian policies of the mandates, like Shi`ites in Lebanon and Iraq.[61] Militant right-wing groups organised against the weak, unrepresentative governments set up by Britain and France, demanding a strong populist state like Atatürk's Turkey, which promoted economic development and built schools for its citizens. By the 1930s, groups like the Syrian Iron Shirts and Young Egypt drew inspiration from Mussolini and Hitler as well. While these groups may have retained language on constitutional goals, they shunned participation in what they regarded as a false liberalism of constitutions imposed under European rule.[62]

From this perspective, interwar Arab politics may be compared with the anti-systemic movements that emerged in defeated European countries after World War I. Such a comparison would reveal, for example, that the moralism of post-war Islamic movements was a response to Arabs' dehumanization in the Paris peace process.[63] As Adam Tooze remarked, the world order that took shape after World War I 'threatened nothing less than historical oblivion' to those who decided to

60 Rashid Rida, 'Ahwal al-`alam al-Islami: Mu'tamar al-Sulh' (Conditions of the Islamic World: The Peace Conference), *Al-Manar* 24, February 1923, 148.

61 Rula Jurdi Abisaab and Malek Abisaab, *The Shi`ites of Lebanon: Modernism, Communism and Hizbullah's Islamists*, 2014, 51–60; Hanna Batatu, *The Old Social Classes and the Revolutionary Movements of Iraq*, 1978, 367–432.

62 Thompson, *Justice Interrupted,* 8–10.

63 Thompson, *How the West Stole Democracy from the Arabs,* 324–333.

join Communist and Fascist movements. Instead of granting rights to nations, the treaties imposed by Paris 'hollowed out' the sovereignty of defeated peoples and exposed them to exploitation by European and American capital. This was the origin of political violence that flared in the interwar era both in Europe and the Middle East, Tooze argues.[64]

The Lausanne Treaty represents the tragic closure to an exceptional liberal opening in 1918–1923. It effectively legitimized France's military occupation of Damascus in 1920, and so foreclosed the flowering of an indigenous democracy in Syria and elsewhere. The imposition of the British mandate in Iraq had a similar effect, as Tooze also noted: 'The humiliation of the Arab political class reached its finale in March 1924 when the elected members of Iraq's constituent assembly were dragged into parliament by armed British guards to ratify the Anglo-Iraq Treaty that established Iraq's independence, but gave Britain control of its army and finances. A new order had been created in the Middle East … based on a wilful disregard for political legitimacy.'[65] As Caroline Elkins has recently shown, Palestinian Arabs suffered most from a convergence of British colonial violence enabled by the imposition of the mandate. Debt and police terror drove educated young men into radical nationalist movements that launched armed revolt in 1936.[66] The Arabs' popular heroes became armed militants, not liberal statesmen.

The mandates were an inherently violent project that made a mockery of rule of law in their effort to impose rule over unwilling populations. Mandatory governments, as Anghie and others have shown, became laboratories of surveillance repression. While historians have discerned the roots of today's Arab dictatorships in the mandate regimes, they have ignored the seminal act of violence that undercut liberal democrats and erased the valiant effort by Syrian Arabs to uphold democratic governance.[67] The result is often to assume a continuity of undemocratic leadership between the pre-war and post-war eras.[68]

As this chapter has demonstrated, Arab liberals' aspiration to seek sovereignty among the family of nations predated Woodrow Wilson's call for self-determination. It was the Paris Peace Conference that disrupted that aspiration.

---

64 Adam Tooze, *The Deluge: The Great War, America and the Remaking of the Global Order, 1916–1931,* 2014, 4–7.

65 Tooze, *The Deluge*, 381.

66 Caroline Elkins, *Legacy of Violence: A History of the British Empire*, 2022, 193–208.

67 See, for example, Daniel Neep, *Occupying Syria under the French Mandate: Insurgency, Space and State Formation,* 2012.

68 See, for example, Philip S. Khoury's classic *Syria and the French Mandate: The Politics of Arab Nationalism, 1920–1945*, 1987.

After 1923, the bitterness of exclusion overwhelmed, but did not defeat, faith in liberal principles in Syria and other Arabic-speaking lands of the former Ottoman Empire. By recovering this critical juncture, historians can decolonize subsequent accounts of Islamism, violence, and authoritarian militarism in the Middle East. Future research must re-examine the ways that the fundamental claims to human dignity and liberal rights lay behind the turn to violence and remained a driving force in Arab politics long before the Arab Spring of 2011.

8

Oil over Armenians: The 1920s 'Lausanne Shift' in US Relations with the Middle East

Andrew Patrick

The United States is perhaps the Lausanne Conference's least appreciated contributor, with historians often dismissing the American delegates as 'observers.' While this term was technically correct, their presence was consequential particularly because American economic power meant that the other participants could not ignore the US delegation. Rather than focus on every aspect of American involvement at the conference, this chapter will be necessarily parsimonious and argue that two main issues determined the path and outcome of the American negotiations at Lausanne. The first issue was oil. Although the US delegation sought a more general 'open door' for American businesses in the new political formations of Turkey and the mandates, it was clear that access to the region's potential petroleum reserves was the biggest source of economic conflict between the parties involved. The second issue was the Armenians. The wartime Armenian Genocide had been widely publicized in the United States and American advocates for the Armenian cause, who were often aligned with missionaries, believed that the United States was ethically bound to help secure an Armenian state or autonomous region in Anatolia.

Analysing American involvement at Lausanne as being the heart of an 'economic versus ethical' foreign policy debate demonstrates that Lausanne was much more central to the evolution of American Middle East policy than historians have generally noted.[1] If Lausanne was a battle for the direction of American

1 Several major works on American involvement in the Middle East entirely ignore Lausanne.

policy in the region, Warren Harding's administration quietly declared that the result was no contest. Their aim was to defend American business interests in the post-Ottoman states and mandates, and the most pressing battle was for regional oil rights. This manifested itself in clashes with Turkey, Britain, and France over Mosul oil and the Chester Concession. With the Turkish refusal to sacrifice land or sovereignty at Lausanne, the Harding administration showed itself unwilling to insist on the establishment of an Armenian state or autonomous region because doing so could harm American commercial opportunities, and the administration did this despite knowing that such a policy left them open to domestic political attacks. This moment illustrates the precipitous decline of missionary influence over American policy in the Ottoman lands that had been so prominent throughout the nineteenth century. With Turkey unwilling to be coerced and missionary-aligned pro-Christian regional policy side-lined, a narrower, business-focused US foreign policy in the Middle East emerged during the interwar years. Thus, American policy towards the Middle East dramatically changed in the 1920s and Lausanne was at the heart of this change.

Pre-Lausanne US-Ottoman Relations

In the century that preceded Lausanne, the United States and the Ottomans had developed several specific ties that would colour the conference's proceedings. Missionaries, more than merchants or diplomats, formed the foundation of the American presence in the region. They began arriving in the 1820s and established scores of educational and medical facilities in the Empire.[2] Despite Ottoman officials increasingly viewing American missionaries as agitators as their presence

---

See Rashid Khalidi, *Resurrecting Empire: Western Footprints and America's Perilous Path in the Middle East*, 2004; Michael Oren, *Power, Faith, and Fantasy: America in the Middle East, 1776 to the Present,* 2007. Ussama Makdisi does recognize the major policy shift of the 1920s in his *Faith Misplaced: The Broken Promise of U.S.-Arab Relations: 1820–2001*, 2010, but does not discuss the centrality of the American debate over Lausanne. Charlie Laderman also acknowledges this shift, but his argument focuses on the era before the 1920s. Laderman astutely contends that the 'Armenian question encapsulated the nation's internal conflict over its world role' but glances over the role of business in the policy that emerged during the decade. See Charlie Laderman, *Sharing the Burden: The Armenian Question, Humanitarian Intervention, and Anglo-American Visions of Global Order*, 2019. Quote on 207.

2 Benjamin Fortna, *Imperial Classroom: Islam, the State, and Education in the Late Ottoman Empire*, 2002, esp. 50–60, 85–87; Selim Deringil, *The Well-Protected Domains: Ideology and the Legitimation of Power in the Ottoman Empire 1876–1909*, 1999, 125–134; Emrah Şahin, *Faithful Encounters: Authorities and American Missionaries in the Ottoman Empire*, 2018, esp. 14–37, 72–98.

grew, the United States enjoyed a comparatively strong reputation in the Ottoman lands largely because their lack of regional aggression contrasted with that of the European powers.[3] The First World War had made the existence of these missionary institutions tenuous because their mostly Christian clientele had either fled, died, or been massacred. Arguably the most germane American missionary contribution to the Lausanne proceedings was their long history of publicizing the plight of the Armenians. Following the Armenian Genocide during the war, numerous missionaries, along with influential supporters and vocal Armenian-Americans, believed that it was time for the United States to support an Armenian national home diplomatically, financially, and, perhaps, militarily.[4]

Trade and diplomatic relations, though slower to develop than the missionary projects, had been growing in the pre-war years. The number of salaried US diplomatic staff in Istanbul had gone from a mere one in 1872 to eleven in 1911.[5] Trade between the countries was increasing as well, with around 23 per cent of Ottoman exports going to the United States in 1913.[6] Importantly, Standard Oil had been selling petroleum products in the region since 1864 and had purchased the exploration rights to plots in the Empire shortly before the war, thus placing them in competition for the region's potential resources with their European competitors.[7] Another American player had inserted itself into the Ottoman political picture in the pre-war years as well: a syndicate led by retired Admiral Colby M. Chester, a well-connected socialite who had dabbled in the region for years, had been attempting to obtain railway and adjacent mineral development concessions between 1909 and 1914.[8]

Woodrow Wilson's wartime decisions and rhetoric were also consequential to the post-war Middle East. Wilson chose not to declare war on the Ottomans, despite his detractors noting that without such a declaration, the United States

3 Andrew Patrick, '"These People Know about Us": A Reconsideration of Attitudes towards the United States in World War I-Era Greater Syria,' *Middle Eastern Studies* 50/3, 2014, 397–411; James Field, *America and the Mediterranean World 1776–1882*, 1969.

4 Joseph Grabill, *Protestant Diplomacy in the Near East: Missionary Influence on American Policy, 1810–1927*, 1971, esp. 46–53, 155–185, 247–268; Karine Walther, *Sacred Interests: The United States and the Islamic World, 1821–1921,* 2015, 1–23, 241–318.

5 United States Department of State, *Register of the Department of State*, 1872, 11 and United States Department of State, *Register of the Department of State*, 1911, 23.

6 Leland James Gordon, *American Relations with Turkey, 1830–1930: An Economic Interpretation*, 1932, 163–164.

7 Andrew Patrick, 'Standard Oil and the Battle for the Ottoman Market, 1864–1914,' *Diplomacy & Statecraft*, 2023 (forthcoming).

8 John DeNovo, *American Interests and Policies in the Middle East, 1900–1939*, 1963, 58–87.

technically would have no say in the future of the Ottoman lands.[9] Furthermore, Wilson's anti-imperialist pronouncements gave the seemingly vanquished Ottomans and their devolving millets the tools to argue that they should become (or remain) independent.[10] Despite having little leverage on Ottoman matters at the Paris Peace Conference, Wilson supported the ultimately disastrous Greek invasion of Anatolia and two ineffectual American fact-finding commissions to the Ottoman lands.[11] The Americans were not invited to the London Conference to discuss Ottoman affairs (February to April 1920) and had a minimal presence at the subsequent San Remo Conference (April 1920), where the lead American delegate believed himself to be a 'glorified reporter.'[12]

Americans with missionary ties, many of whom supported the Armenian cause, looked on in dismay as the impotent US peace conference delegations did little to shape the region. Those who believed that the United States should back a new Armenian state grew frustrated when no serious international support for a state beyond the diminutive Yerevan Republic emerged. They were, however, somewhat heartened when the Europeans at San Remo requested that Wilson draw up new borders for this grander Armenia, which he eventually did in November 1920.[13] Their hopes for American involvement in Armenia diminished again as the US Senate overwhelmingly rejected a proposed US mandate over the new country in June 1920, while the Turks regrouped in central Anatolia to fend off the Greeks and, in December, Soviet troops overran Yerevan. Advocacy for American involvement in Armenia, however, was not yet over.[14]

---

9 See Andrew Patrick, 'Woodrow Wilson, the Ottomans, and World War I,' *Diplomatic History* 42/5, 2018, 886–910.

10 See Andrew Patrick, *America's Forgotten Middle East Initiative: The King-Crane Commission of 1919*, 2015, 130–164; Erez Manela, *The Wilsonian Moment: Self-Determination and the International Origins of Anti-Colonial Nationalism*, 2007; Elizabeth F. Thompson, *How the West Stole Democracy from the Arabs: The Syrian Arab Congress of 1920 and the Destruction of its Historic Liberal-Islamic Alliance*, 2020.

11 See Patrick, *America's Forgotten*; Grabill, *Protestant Diplomacy*, 227–235.

12 Bainbridge Colby to French Ambassador Jusserand, 24 March 1920, *Papers Relating to the Foreign Relations of the United States* (hereafter *FRUS*), 1920, Vol. III, 750–753; Robert Underwood Johnson, *Remembered Yesterdays*, 1923, 517–530.

13 Paul C. Helmreich, *From Paris to Sèvres: The Partition of the Ottoman Empire at the Peace Conference of 1919–1920*, 1974, 298–299.

14 Fifty-two voted for a resolution rejecting a mandate (thirty-nine Republicans, thirteen Democrats), twenty-three voted against this (all Democrats). Levon Marashlian, 'The Armenian Question from Sèvres to Lausanne: Economics and Morality in American and British Policies, 1920–1923,' PhD dissertation, UCLA, 1992, 126–132; Charlie Laderman, 'Sharing the Burden? The American Solution to the Armenian Question, 1918–1920,' *Diplomatic History* 40/4, 2016, 664–694; John Milton Cooper, *Breaking the Heart of the*

Concurrently, the fight for international oil sources, with the Ottoman lands being one such potential source, had become a major issue. Standard Oil and other American oil companies were furious when the British and French kept them out of the deal dividing up these potential resources signed at San Remo. This agreement, which the United States protested, raised the larger question of business rights in the new successor states and mandates. Would, American businessmen wondered, the metaphorical economic 'door' of the region be 'closed' to narrow national interests and secretive concessionary negotiations, or 'open' to competition among international corporations?[15] Furthermore, reports from American geologists caused a stir in 1919 predicting that the American oil supply was insufficient to meet rising US demand, though oil men at the time knew this to be overstated.[16] Based on this and the fact that European oil companies seemed to be capturing most of the world's new oil fields, the Department of the Interior recommended that government 'encouragement of and effective assistance to our nationals in developing foreign fields is essential,' singling out the fight for 'equal rights' in the 'countries newly organized as mandatories.'[17] In August 1919, the State Department duly instructed its foreign officers to do this.[18] This statement came out at the time when the British were allowing Royal Dutch Shell geologists to prospect in Mesopotamia while barring Standard Oil geologists from doing the same, as well as denying Standard Oil access to their pre-war concession in Palestine.[19] It seemed that, despite the pre-war détente between the major oil interests

World: Woodrow Wilson and the Fight for the League of Nations, 2001, 379–380.

15 John A. DeNovo, *American Interests*, 167–184, Michael Hogan, *Informal Entente: The Private Structure of Cooperation in Anglo-American Economic Diplomacy, 1918–1928*, 1977, 159–185; Gregory P. Nowell, *Mercantile States and the World Oil Cartel, 1900–1939*, 1994, 59–61.

16 Roger J. Stern, 'Oil Scarcity Ideology in US Foreign Policy, 1908–97,' *Security Studies* 25/2, 2016, 214–257. See also Robert Vitalis, *Oilcraft: The Myths of Scarcity and Security that Haunt U.S Energy Policy,* 2020.

17 'Wanted – A Foreign Supply,' *Reports of the Secretary of the Interior for the Fiscal Year Ended June 30 1919*, Vol. I, 1919, 22–24.

18 'The Secretary of State to Diplomatic and Consular Officers,' 16 August 1919, *FRUS*, 1919, Vol. I, 167.

19 John A. DeNovo, 'The Movement for an Aggressive Oil Policy Abroad, 1918–1920,' *The American Historical Review* 61/4, 1956, 854–876; Andrew Patrick, 'Standard Oil in the Ottoman Lands, 1909–1927' (working paper); George Sweet Gibb and Evelyn H. Knowlton, *History of Standard Oil Company (New Jersey): The Resurgent Years 1911–1927*, 1956, 284–289; E.S. Sheffield to Oscar Heizer, 14 January 1920, 'Correspondence American Consulate Bagdad 1920 Vol. II,' RG84, Vol. 41, Series 300, and Bristol to Hughes, 16 August 1920, RG353, Roll 67, both in United States National Archives (hereafter *NA-State*).

of the world, a new era of international competition for oil resources and markets might be dawning.[20]

As these controversies simmered, Warren Harding was inaugurated as President in March 1921. Harding, a senator from Ohio, immediately announced that the United States would not join the League of Nations but that the United States would seek to become more actively engaged in global commerce. During the war, he had voiced sympathy for the plight of Armenia, yet he voted against the American mandate for Armenia in the Senate.[21] Harding chose Charles Evans Hughes, the New York senator and wartime Armenian advocate, as his Secretary of State and gave him broad autonomy over his pro-business foreign policy. Thus, both Harding and Hughes sought to support American commerce abroad without the idealistic accompaniments of Wilson's grander world vision, yet both had a history of Armenian advocacy as well.[22]

Events in the Middle East immediately tested the Harding administration. When the resurgent Turkish nationalist forces halted both the French and Greek advances into Anatolia in 1920 and 1921, it became increasingly clear that the Treaty of Sèvres would not stand. In the summer and autumn of 1921, the US sent an informal representative (Robert H. McDowell) to the Turkish nationalist government to begin the initial discussions about re-establishing relations and American rights in the country.[23] Standard Oil sent a representative to Ankara the following summer but failed to get definite assurances from the nationalist government on any issue.[24] American diplomats constantly rehashed the one principle that constituted their main policy: all new political formations in the Middle

20 On the pre-war détente, see Nowell, *Mercantile States*, 59–61 (quotes on 59, 61); Ralph W. Hidy and Muriel E. Hidy, *Pioneering in Big Business 1882–1911*, 1955, 567; Jonathan Conlin, *Mr. Five Per Cent: The Many Lives of Calouste Gulbenkian, the World's Richest Man*, 2019. 67–75; A.A. Fursenko, *The Battle for Oil: The Economics and Politics of International Corporate Conflict over Petroleum, 1860–1930*, trans. Gregory L. Freeze, 1990, 107–116; Frederik Gerretson, *History of the Royal Dutch*, Vol. 3, 1957, 101–106.

21 John Milton Cooper, 'A Friend in Power? Woodrow Wilson and Armenia,' *America and the Armenian Genocide of 1915,* ed. Jay Winter, 2003, 103–112.

22 Betty Glad, *Charles Evans Hughes and the Illusions of Innocence: A Study in American Diplomacy*, 1966, 133–136; Eugene P. Trani and Daniel L. Wilson, *The Presidency of Warren G. Harding*, 1977, 141–149; Donald A. Ritchie, 'Congress confronts the Armenian Genocide,' *America and the Armenian Genocide of 1915*, ed. Jay Winter, 2003, 276–293; Adam Tooze, *The Deluge: The Great War, America, and the Remaking of the Global Order, 1916–1931*, 2014, 347–349, 372; Cooper, *Breaking the Heart*, 387–398.

23 Mark Bristol to Charles Evans Hughes, 28 September 1921; Robert H. McDowell, 'Notes on Ankara Trip,' undated; Bristol to Hughes, 28 October 1921, *NA-State*, M365, Reel 2.

24 Bristol to Hughes, 23 August 1922, *NA-State*, M353, Reel 67.

East, be they independent states or mandates, should allow equal opportunity for American businesses.[25]

The British saw nefarious machinations in all of these moves, partly because they were happening in the context of Standard Oil's successful attacks on Royal Dutch Shell and the San Remo agreement on multiple fronts.[26] They also believed that, despite its denials, Standard Oil might be linked to the Chester Concession, particularly with a concession representative renewing negotiations with the Turkish nationalist government (the same Robert H. McDowell) in February 1922.[27] The British saw the oil of Mosul and Persia as the way to end their reliance on the oil of the United States and asserted the legitimacy of the Turkish Petroleum Company's (hereafter TPC) pre-war concession for Mosul. The concession, though never officially conferred by the Ottomans, was funded by Deutsche Bank, Royal Dutch Shell, and British financiers, and it excluded Standard Oil. After protracted discussions, British oil interests finally softened their stance on American involvement in Mosul mainly because prolonged battles with Standard Oil and other American companies would harm profits. They tentatively invited a consortium led by Standard Oil of New Jersey, who had now joined together with six other American oil companies, to buy into the TPC in April 1922. Despite the wartime and post-war competitive posturing by these companies, they had decided to once again move back towards cartelization as they had in 1907.[28] These negotiations were put on hold, however, as the coming of a new peace conference introduced further political uncertainty.

In the summer of 1922, Turkish nationalist forces were in the ascendancy and pressure increased on the Harding administration to escalate the American presence in the region. In May 1922, there had been a British proposal for an ultimately stillborn international inquiry into 'the atrocities against the Armenians' partly pushed by Americans. President Harding was hesitant to join such an undertaking despite its political popularity because he believed that the United

---

25 Annie Tracy Samuel, 'The Open Door and U.S. Policy in Iraq between the World Wars,' *Diplomatic History* 38/5, 2014, 926–952.

26 Nowell, *Mercantile States*, 133–144.

27 'American Commercial Interests in Anatolia' (British intelligence report somehow acquired by State Department in Prague around 18 September 1922), *NA-State*, M353, Reel 67. See also Anand Toprani, 'An Anglo-American "Petroleum Entente"?: The First Attempt to Reach an Anglo-American Oil Agreement, 1921,' *Historian* 79/1, 2017, 56–79.

28 Nowell, *Mercantile States*, 80–147; Jonathan Conlin, 'An Oily Entente: France, Britain, and the Mosul Question, 1916–1925,' *Diplomacy & Statecraft* 31/2, 2020, 231–256; William Stivers, *Supremacy and Oil: Iraq, Turkey, and the Anglo-American World Order, 1918–1930*, 1982, 88–91.

States would 'be utterly helpless to do anything effective in case an investigation proves statements concerning atrocities are substantiated.'[29] Hughes and Harding were already aware of the pitfalls of their advocacy for American access to oil in the region, with Hughes arguing that if they did not send a representative to this committee, their adversaries could argue that they had been 'far more solicitous about American interest in oil than about Christian lives.'[30] As the Greek forces crumbled, American religious leaders called on the United States to intervene militarily on behalf of the Greeks and the Christian minorities in Anatolia, which Hughes and Harding were reluctant to do. Harding privately expressed his annoyance at these leaders, stating 'it is difficult for me to be consistently patient with our good friends of the Church who are properly and earnestly zealous in promoting peace until it comes to making warfare on someone of a contending religion.'[31] Following the Armistice of Mudanya on 11 October 1922, another peace conference approached.

Lausanne: Phase One

The nature of American participation in the coming peace conference remained uncertain throughout October, with the fact that the United States had not declared war on the Ottomans still looming large. On 18 October, Hughes appointed Joseph C. Grew, the ambassador to Switzerland, to represent the United States at Lausanne. Grew was a career diplomat who had been the secretary of the American delegation at the Paris Peace Conference. Hughes also appointed Richard Washburn Child, a confidant of Harding and the ambassador to Italy, to be the head of the delegation.[32] Hughes articulated the American position in a statement sent to their diplomats and to the British, French, and Italians on 20 October. The United States wanted the pre-war Capitulations maintained as well as protection for American educational, philanthropic, and religious institutions. It wanted equal commercial treatment with all business rivals and a general 'open door' policy. It wanted restitution for American entities which had lost property during the war and guarantees for the protection of minorities in Turkey. The statement

29 Harding to Hughes, 20 May 1922, *FRUS*, 1922, Vol. II, 922.
30 Hughes to Harding, 25 May 1922, *FRUS*, 1922, Vol. II, 924.
31 Harding to Hughes, 24 July 1922, *FRUS*, 1922, Vol. II, 931. See Hughes' summary of an appeal by the General Conference of the Methodist Episcopal Church, South, in Hughes to Harding, 24 July 1922, *FRUS*, 1922, Vol. II, 931.
32 Grabill, *Protestant*, 270; Francis Russell, *The Shadow of Blooming Grove: Warren G. Harding in his Times*, 1968, 405, 439.

mentioned Armenia, but in a tellingly indeterminant way: 'The question of the homeland of the Armenians may be raised. It is possible that upon the return of more settled conditions in Russia, the Russian Caucasus may offer the best refuge for Armenians from Turkey.' Overall, the Americans simply wanted their interests protected and equality with the other powers in commercial terms.[33]

The conference commenced on 20 November with a public ceremony. İsmet İnönü (hereafter İsmet) began his speech with a reference to Wilson's wartime pronouncements, arguing that the Armistice of Mudros in 1918 was concluded 'on the basis of, and in the belief in, the principles of President Wilson,' yet he inferred that these principles had been violated by outside powers, particularly by allowing the Greeks to land at Smyrna.[34] Child had a conversation with Celalettin Arif Bey of the Turkish delegation on 22 November and they discussed the Turkish position on issues of import to the Americans. Arif Bey stated that they would protect American institutions in the region but that they would not countenance a 'territorial home' for the Armenians to be carved out of the land they occupied. Minorities, he argued, 'were no longer wanted' because they were like an 'open wound not only painful in itself but inviting infection from foreign countries.' He also noted that they had not signed any secret treaties with the other powers and wanted American participation in the development of the Mosul oil fields 'equal to and exceeding participation by other nations.'[35]

The first major American contribution to the conference came towards the end of the morning session on 25 November, when Child gave the first public pronouncement of American aims. In this, he chose not to comment on many of the specific issues articulated in the longer discussion of American interests which Hughes had sent on 30 October but instead focused primarily on economic equality. Child argued that 'the equality of economic opportunity' in 'Turkish territory,' rather than national rivalries over 'the establishment of zones of special commercial and economic influence,' would be a 'powerful element in the establishment of any stable peace.'[36] In his rationale for making this speech, Child saw himself as a key advocate of the idea that free trade brings peace. The 'Open Door policy in Turkey,' Child contended, would help by 'breaking the vicious connection between commercial expansion of the greater powers and their diplomacy of

33 Hughes to Ambassador in France (Herrick), 27 October 1922, *FRUS*, 1922, Vol. II, 886–888.

34 *Lausanne Conference on Near Eastern Affairs, 1922–1923: Records of Proceedings and Draft Terms of Peace*, 1923 (hereafter *Lausanne Conference*), 4. Accessed on archive.org.

35 Grew, *Turbulent*, 492–493.

36 *Lausanne Conference*, 92–93.

political intrigue within smaller nations.'[37] Child had conveniently crafted a justification for the increased American business presence in the region: the region's people could overcome their belligerent tendencies if dealt with in a fair manner by stronger outside powers. Americans would play a calming role on all other participants who were more inclined to war. Mandatory powers, according to this line of argument, had to eschew not just colonial modes of political domination but also colonial protectionism. Hence, American magnanimity and the soothing competition of capitalism would solve the region's problems. This was a point that the Europeans viewed with suspicion, particularly with Standard Oil and the Chester Concession looming in the background.

The speech turned out to have a larger impact than Child had intended it to. Seeing that the negotiations had thus far concerned the status of Thrace, it appeared to disrupt the tone and direction of the conference. The problem was that although Child saw himself as simply protecting American interests, others saw it differently. The French Foreign Office was reportedly confused by the speech and circulated a query, asking 'Does it refer to Mesopotamian oil?'[38] A *New York Tribune* reporter noted that the 'undercurrent opinion' at the conference amounted to indignation that the United States was not willing to participate in the risky endeavour of reshaping the post-Ottoman lands, yet wanted to 'share in the pot.'[39] Child was indignant that his statement was seen as having anything to do with oil, noting in his diary that 'we have seen no representative of oil interests,' nor had he any 'instruction from the Government concerning oil.' He did, however, call for further instruction on 26 November, realizing that 'questions relating to Mesopotamia are imminent and urgent.'[40] Regardless of Child's intent, Mosul quickly became the topic of many backroom discussions and continued rumours at, and about, the conference.

Although direct contact between American oil companies and State Department officials during the conference appears to have been minimal, accusations of directly pandering to these companies were rehashed by anyone who did not like what they perceived to be happening at Lausanne. Such perceptions abounded amongst the influential Armenia lobby in the United States, which was the group most keenly following the proceedings. One pro-Armenian lobbyist in the United States, for example, asserted on 29 November that 'there is an awakening thought

37 Richard Washburn Child, *A Diplomat Looks at Europe*, 1925, 91–92.

38 'U.S. Ukase on Turk Open Door Puzzles France,' *New York Tribune*, 27 November 1922, 2.

39 'U.S. Opposes Secret Pacts at Lausanne,' *New York Tribune*, 26 November 1922, 1.

40 Child, *Diplomat*, 93–94; Child and Grew to Hughes, 26 November 1922, *FRUS*, 1922, Vol. II, 345.

that oil receives more consideration than humanity.'[41] Another activist noted in early December his 'shock' that the United States was 'coming forward so majestically for a share of the oil fields of Mesopotamia,' yet 'will not say a word for the Armenians.'[42]

The Armenia lobby in the United States was split between those advocating for a large Armenian mandate (the Armenia America Society) and those who wanted US aid for an independent or autonomous Armenia (the American Committee for the Independence of Armenia, hereafter ACIA).[43] The Armenia America Society had sent George R. Montgomery to lobby for their cause at Lausanne. Montgomery had been born in Marash in 1870 to missionary parents and had an itinerant career as a journalist, minister, and academic with lengthy experience in the Ottoman lands.[44] In speaking about the establishment of an Armenian state several years before Lausanne, Montgomery had argued that the Armenians were 'a brave and valiant race' who were 'progressive,' 'trustworthy,' and 'dependable.' He stated that they were Christians being 'slaughtered by anti-Christian soldiery,' and the creation of a country for them would establish a 'neutral Christian nation' in the region that would help to create a lasting peace.[45] Also advocating for the Armenians at the conference were James Barton and William W. Peet, two prominent American missionaries with extensive experience in the region. Barton was the Foreign Secretary of the American Board of Commissioners for Foreign Missions (hereafter ABCFM) and had been a missionary in Harput from 1885–1892. He had been a tireless advocate for Armenian and Syrian relief during the war and was the Chairman of Near East Relief. Peet was an elder statesman of Americans in the Middle East, having lived in Istanbul since 1881 serving as the treasurer of the ABCFM Near East Mission at Bible House. Barton and Peet, who were officially in Lausanne as representatives of the Federal Council of Protestant Churches but also reported back to the ACIA, privately understood that an Armenian national home might be unfeasible in the realities of 1922. In public, however, they pushed for 'a specific territory into which refugee populations, including orphans, could be conducted.'[46]

41 Walter George Smith to George R. Montgomery, 29 November 1922, Box 22, Fol. '1922, Sept.-Nov.', Montgomery Family Papers, Manuscript Division, Library of Congress, Washington D.C. (hereafter *Montgomery Papers*).

42 M. Vartan Malcolm to George R. Montgomery, 8 December 1922, Box 22, Fol. '1922 December and Undated,' *Montgomery Papers*.

43 Grabill, *Protestant Diplomacy*, 242, 248–249.

44 Patrick, *America's Forgotten*, 56.

45 'Armistice Day Mass Meeting' Cathedral of St. John the Divine, New York City, 11 November 1920, Box 21, Fol. '1921, Jan.-Mar.,' *Montgomery Papers*.

46 Grabill, *Protestant Diplomacy*, 269–275; Peet and Barton to Special Mission at Lausanne,

On 12 December, the issue of protecting minorities in the region became the focus of negotiations. As these began, Hughes reiterated to his delegation how sensitive this issue was with influential Americans, stating 'there is no question in which the people of the United States have more immediate concern than that of minorities.'[47] In the opening discussions, Lord Curzon proposed seeking protections and assurances that might involve foreign intervention and mentioned the possibility of an Armenian national home in Cilicia. The Turks countered that foreign protection of minorities had historically been an excuse for foreign treachery in the Ottoman Empire and that any such assurances would come from the internal laws of the land. Any foreign intervention would violate sovereignty and hence not be allowed. İsmet also addressed other proposals for national homes floating around in Lausanne, arguing 'it was inadmissible and inconceivable that each minority should claim to dismember Turkey in order to have a separate territory granted to itself.' Child's contribution to the discussion somewhat belied the seeming importance of Armenia in the United States but reflected his initial instructions, amounting to little more than a vague speech about how minority rights needed to be guaranteed in some way and that the Allies had promised this many times.[48]

In mid-December, the American delegation petitioned Montgomery, Barton, and Peet for their specific proposals on Armenia. In response, Montgomery argued for a League of Nations-guaranteed Cilician Armenia not attached to the Yerevan Republic, which was firmly controlled by the Bolsheviks in 1922. He stated that his group would defer to the conference on the actual borders of the Armenian state, but he suggested that it would be advantageous to have the new territory as a 'neutral zone between Turkey and Syria.' He also hoped that American loans would help finance the new state.[49] Barton and Peet sent a letter to the American delegation similarly arguing that the 'best solution of the Armenian minority question would be the designation of a specific territory into which refugee populations' could go.[50] The American delegation was still officially advocating for an Armenian national home and did so at the Minorities Sub-commission on

14 December 1922, *FRUS*, 1922, Vol. II, 943–944.

47 Hughes to the Special Mission at Lausanne, 14 December 1922, *FRUS*, 1922, Vol. II, 922.

48 *Lausanne Conference*, 173–215. Quote on 189.

49 'Supplementary Memorandum on the Armenian National Home presented on behalf of the Armenia America Society,' 16 December 1922, Box 22, Fol. '1922 December and Undated,' *Montgomery Papers*.

50 James L. Barton and W. W. Peet to Child, 14 December 1922, *FRUS*, 1922, Vol. II, 943–944.

20 December.[51] In private, however, Child began to denigrate the pro-Armenia missionaries who, he noted, were constantly 'on my neck' at Lausanne. 'Agitation by me for a National Armenian Home,' Child argued, 'would not only cause resentment but would be useless,' partly because he believed that the British, French, and Italians were merely using such a demand as a 'trading point.'[52] On 29 December, Child had a junior American delegate present the appeals of Montgomery, Barton, and Peet to the Minorities Sub-commission and asked that they be 'given full consideration.'[53] The Armenian delegation finally received a hearing before the British, French, and Italians on the Minorities Sub-commission (which the Turks boycotted) on 26 December and they requested an autonomous national home in Turkey.[54] The Americans were not invited to the hearing.[55]

Secretary of State Hughes was trying, and failing, to thread a difficult diplomatic needle. Word that the US delegation was not advocating for the Armenian cause spread amongst supporters in the United States and animosity between these people and the State Department grew. Barton, Peet, and Montgomery directly telegrammed Hughes in late December that 'several hundred thousand Armenian refugees' had no place to go and needed an 'officially designated territory' as a destination. Demands for such a territory were, they correctly noted, 'meeting great opposition' at Lausanne. They requested that the State Department needed to give the American delegation 'decisive instructions' on this matter.[56] In early January 1923, Hughes instructed the American delegation that they were to support 'measures of assistance' for the Armenians and to 'informally' discuss a potential autonomous home in Cilicia, possibly backed by 'charitable funds' raised in the United States.[57] To the Turks, the American position was too pro-Armenian, and they broke off negotiations with the representatives of the Chester group because of this.[58] To Child, the policy was nonsensical. He continued to express displeasure at the constant pressure placed on him by the 'Church element' and had mostly closed the Armenian issue in his mind. In his diary, Child approvingly recounted a conver-

51 Marashlian, 'Armenian Question,' 709.

52 Child, *Diplomat*, 103–106. Quotes on 103 and 106.

53 Child to State, 30 December 1922, *FRUS*, 1922, Vol. II, 940; Marashlian, 'Armenian Question,' 723–727.

54 Child, *Diplomat*, 112; Marashlian, 'Armenian Question,' 712–720.

55 'Report from Dr. Montgomery, dated Lausanne, 26 December 1922,' Box 22, Fol. '1922 December and Undated,' *Montgomery Papers*; 'Turks Turn Back on Armenia's Plea,' *New York Herald,* 27 December 1922, 5.

56 Barton, Peet, and Montgomery to Hughes, 26 December 1922, *FRUS*, 1922, Vol. II, 934.

57 Hughes to the Special Mission at Lausanne, 6 January 1923, *FRUS*, 1923, Vol. II, 946–947.

58 Marashlian, 'Armenian Question,' 726–729; DeNovo, *American Interests*, 224–225.

sation in which İsmet argued that the United States had 'as much right to demand that Turkey set aside a piece of her territory for Armenians as Turkey would have to demand that the United States set aside Mississippi and Georgia as a national home for the Negro.'[59] Child further contended that there were only three ways that the Allies could influence Turkey. The first was counsel, which the Turks were disregarding. The second was force, which the Allies were not 'willing to employ.' The third was economic pressure, but with the Allies squabbling over concessions and financial gain from the region, no unified front on that matter was possible.[60] Child had come to believe that the demand for an Armenian national home was futile because there was no commitment from the United States to provide funding for the new country, to take a mandate for it, or to dedicate troops to defend it. Officially, Child told the conference that the United States had 'no intention to take any initiative at this time or to make any commitments' on the Armenian issue unless a 'definite program' was put forth by the Allies, which he believed was 'entirely unlikely.'[61] He was correct on this last point: the Turks refused to address the issue in the Minorities Sub-commission at Lausanne and it was not specifically taken up at the second session.[62]

This lack of vigorous backing for an Armenian national home infuriated many supporters in the United States, but Americans at Lausanne no longer saw this as a possibility. Some, like the ACIA, angrily doubled down on their advocacy. At a meeting on 7 January 1923, James Gerard (former Ambassador to Germany) and Henry W. Jessup (minister and son of famed missionary Henry H. Jessup) accused both Presidents Wilson and Harding of promising to help the Armenians but 'doing nothing.' They passed a resolution reiterating that Cilicia should be set aside as a national home for the Armenians and sent this to Harding, Hughes, and the Senate Foreign Relations Committee.[63] By 23 January, however, Montgomery had given up, telling the Armenia America Society that 'there is nothing to be expected from this conference for the Armenians.'[64] Child did not mention the Armenians or any sort of national home in his closing summary of the American position.[65] Barton, for his part, was resigned to failure and acknowledged that the numerous

59 Child, *Diplomat*, 115–116.

60 Child to Hughes, 9 January 1923, *FRUS*, 1923, Vol. II, 948–949.

61 Child to Hughes, 1 January 1923, *FRUS*, 1923, Vol. II, 941–942.

62 Marashlian, 'Armenian Question,' 730–762.

63 '[ACIA] Wants Cilicia Given to the Armenians,' *New York Times*, 7 January 1923, 3.

64 Montgomery to Armenia America Society, 23 January 1923, Box 22, Fol. '1923 Jan.-Mar.,' *Montgomery Papers*.

65 Child to Hughes, 31 January 1923, *FRUS*, 1923, Vol. II, 962–964.

interests he represented needed to 'recognize that Turkey has been invited to enter the sisterhood of nations.' 'Physical force,' he added, 'has failed in dealing with Turkey.' All that they had left to make the new country of Turkey 'worthy' of its place in the world was the use of 'moral force.' While Barton remained angry at the Harding administration's unwillingness to support the Armenian cause, he also knew that his organizations (ABCFM and Near East Relief) would need to have positive relations with the new Turkey.[66] It was a grudging surrender to this new reality, but the domestic rebukes for this lack of American diplomatic pressure on Turkey had only just begun.

As the Armenian advocates floundered throughout December, discussions about economic matters grew in importance. Curzon and İsmet had started discussing Mosul in private on 26 November 1922, and it was immediately clear that this was going to be a contentious issue, with both sides insisting that the oil lands of Mosul were theirs.[67] A month later, İsmet probed Child on the matter of the border near Mosul. Child parried this, arguing that Americans had no interest in border questions but simply wanted the region open to American businesses.[68] As the Mosul debate became more contentious in late January, Child submitted an American statement reiterating that the United States still did not recognize 'the validity of the claims of the Turkish Petroleum Company,' which Curzon had cited during a debate.[69]

On 31 January 1923, the Allies handed the Turkish delegation a unilaterally drawn treaty after they had become frustrated with the delegation's tenacity. The Americans knew that the draft was impossible for the Turks to accept, and it even contained a validation of the TPC claim and other economic clauses that Child stated were 'inimical to our interests and vicious in principle.'[70] Child sent another note protesting the validity of the TPC claim on 1 February, and then tried to mediate between İsmet and the Allies over the next few days. This failed, and the Turkish delegation left on 4 February without signing anything. Grew blamed İsmet's inexperience as a diplomat, Curzon's arrogance, and the lack of a unified Allied front.[71] Child employed a more common American trope in his assessment

66 '[Barton] Recommends New Policy,' *New York Times*, 8 February 1923.
67 Sevtap Demirci, 'Turco-British Manoeuvres on the Mosul Question in the Lausanne Conference, 1922–1923,' *British Journal of Middle Eastern Studies* 37/1, 2010, 57–71.
68 Child to Hughes, 18 January 1923, *FRUS*, 1923, Vol. II, 951–952.
69 *Lausanne Conference*, 23 January 1923, 405.
70 Child, *Diplomat*, 119.
71 Joseph C. Grew, *Turbulent Era: A Diplomatic Record of Forty Years 1904–1945: Volume I*, 1952, 553–554.

of the conference, blaming the 'old' ways of Europe (as intrinsically opposed to the 'new' ways of America) and the character of the negotiators for the failure: 'Suspicion and fear. Old complications, old Europe's tangles! Not wicked men, but weak.'[72]

One telling (if somewhat opaque) moment of backroom negotiations involving Americans at Lausanne also occurred on 4 February. When Grew and Child were attempting to mediate proceedings at the very end of the conference, they ran into one of their own aides, Julian Gillespie, in Turkish delegate Hüseyin Bey's room. 'What he was doing on his own initiative,' Grew exclaimed, 'heaven only knows.'[73] Before the conference, Gillespie had been in Istanbul as the Assistant Trade Commissioner and also had served as a liaison to the Turkish nationalist government in 1922, yet, like Robert McDowell, he seemed able to slide from public to private business with ease.[74] The delegation brought him to Lausanne to help with economic matters but Gillespie seemed to be looking towards a post-government career that might include having a stake in future concessions or oil deals. On the side at the conference, he was discussing oil matters with Deutsche Bank, who were in Lausanne trying to defend their stake in the TPC. Gillespie, claiming to have close friendships with L.I. Thomas of Standard Oil as well as Sinclair Oil and Refining Corporation-linked William Boyce Thompson (a mining magnate), was posing as a fixer of the Calouste Gulbenkian ilk. He reportedly attempted to broker a deal to sell Deutsche Bank's TPC shares to Standard Oil, but he was rebuffed, and Deutsche Bank went on to lose their shares in the TPC.[75] He appears not to have been such a fixer but more resembled the often-reviled 'concession hunter' who had no established standing with any important player but hoped to cultivate such connections. Though the historical record remains unclear on what exactly Gillespie did at Lausanne, it shows that much was happening beyond official channels. Commercial interests were moving forward on their own, though they were keeping a close eye on political developments.

72 Child, *Diplomat*, 124.

73 Grew, *Turbulent,* 551–552.

74 Laurence Evans, *United States Policy and the Partition of Turkey, 1914–1924*, 1965, 332–337.

75 Various correspondence, Franz Günther (the bank's representative at Lausanne) to Deutsche Bank (esp. 4, 7, 10, 13, 14 & 20 December 1922 and 5 January 1923), fol. OR1315 Türkische Friedensverh. in Lausanne, 1922–1923, Historisches Institut der Deutschen Bank, Frankfurt, Germany. Notes and advice on this paragraph provided to me by Dr. Jonathan Conlin.

Lausanne: Interim and Phase Two

As negotiations broke down, events unfolded that would influence future proceedings. The British, knowing that the Mosul issue had not been decided, sent troops to secure the region. Turkey had considered an invasion of its own, but the Turkish Grand National Assembly realized that the country was in no financial or material position to wage yet another war.[76] The US government continued monitoring Turkish attitudes, with an American in Ankara reporting that the Turks 'greatly resented' American advocacy for the Armenians and the minorities at Lausanne which they believed had been 'dictated' by the 'churches and the missionary element.' This view was tempered, the diplomat reported, by 'moderate' American stances on other issues and the push for the 'Open Door.'[77] American Armenian advocates were also vocal between the two phases of the conference. James Gerard of the ACIA, for example, wrote a letter to Hughes arguing that his organization would oppose any treaty with Turkey that did not include 'a provision of justice for Armenia.' Anything less, according to Gerard, would prove that the administration cared only to 'promote American material interests.'[78] A summary of Gerard's letter wound up in the *New York Times* and this clearly worried the State Department: Allen Dulles, the head of the Near East Division, sent the clipping to Hughes, noting that he had seen 'no other notice of Gerard's statement nor any editorial comment.'[79] Noticing the difficult position that the State Department was in, Cornelius Van H. Engert, an experienced Middle East diplomat and intelligence-gatherer, wrote to Dulles that their policy of re-establishing diplomatic relations with Turkey without holding them to account for the atrocities against Armenians would likely 'lay ourselves open to criticism which it would be difficult to answer.' The State Department needed to show, according to Engert, that it was 'not above manifesting righteous indignation even at the risk of prejudicing purely commercial interests.' 'No oil-field in the world,' he continued, 'could ever compensate us for the loss of our self-respect.'[80]

Commercial interests were indeed an ongoing concern of the Harding administration. The Americans continued to believe that the Allies were crafting secret

76 Demirci, 'Turco-British,' 67–68; Salahi Ramsdan Sonyel, *Turkish Diplomacy, 1918–1923: Mustafa Kemal and the Turkish National Movement*, 1975, 206; Conlin, *Mr Five Per Cent*, 137.

77 Robert W. Imbrie to Hughes, 15 February 1923, *FRUS*, 1923, Vol. II, 970–971.

78 Gerard quotes in 'Friends of Armenia protest on treaty,' *New York Times*, 26 February 1923.

79 Dulles to Hughes, 28 February 1923, *NA-State*, M365, Reel 3.

80 Cornelius Van H. Engert to Dulles, 14 March 1923, *NA-State*, M365, Reel 3.

concessionary deals with the Turks.[81] The Allies, for their part, had the same distrust of the Americans. This was particularly true after the Turks announced the approval of the Chester Concession on 10 April 1923, with the investment group reconfigured as the Ottoman American Development Company. This came in the wake of a campaign in Hearst newspapers claiming that the British were on the verge of dominating global oil sources.[82] Admiral Chester did his part later in 1922 by publishing a sycophantic pro-Turkish article in the popular periodical *Current History*. In this, he made the appalling claim that the Armenians had merely been moved from 'the inhospitable regions where they were not welcome' to 'the most delightful and fertile parts of Syria' where, after the war, they were found 'entirely unmassacred and fat and prosperous.'[83] The resurrection of the Chester Concession, which was now largely Canadian-backed, infuriated both the British and the French as it could infringe upon the pre-war claims of the TPC. Curzon considered not inviting the United States back to Lausanne, though he was convinced otherwise by advisers.[84]

As the negotiations reopened on 23 April 1923, the American position had changed little. Joseph Grew was now the lead American delegate. In his instructions, Hughes noted that Grew's primary aim was to protect American economic and legal interests in any negotiations over the Capitulations or pre-war concessions. The 'protection of minorities,' Hughes contended, was a 'settled' issue, though he believed that the 'problem of refugees' was bound to emerge as part of the discussion.[85] Despite being sceptical of the Chester group's finances and competence, Hughes instructed Grew to support the Chester group in principle because it was not 'monopolistic,' unlike the TPC. Hughes knew that negotiations on American inclusion in the TPC were 'pending' and believed that the 'arrangement contemplated might mitigate the monopolistic nature of the enterprise if it admits adequate American participation in such a way as to be considered consistent with the open door.'[86] The metaphorical door, it seemed, could be closed as long as the American companies were on the inside.

81 See Dulles to Hughes, 4 April 1923, *FRUS*, 1923, Vol. II, 974–980; DeNovo, *American Interests*, 145–146.
82 See, for example, Henry Woodhouse, 'Great Britain Grabbing the World's Oil; Bars U.S. from its Legal Rights Abroad,' *Washington Times*, 30 October 1921; Gibb and Knowlton, *Resurgent*, 262–264.
83 Admiral Colby M. Chester, 'Turkey Reinterpreted,' *Current History* XVI/6, 1922, 939–946.
84 Sonyel, *Turkish Diplomacy*, 214–215; DeNovo, *American Interests*, 217.
85 Hughes to Grew, 19 April 1923, *FRUS*, 1923, Vol. II, 981–986.
86 Hughes to Grew, 10 July 1923, *FRUS*, 1923, Vol. II, 1030–1034.

A subsidiary American aim was to agree upon a new bilateral treaty with the Turks, though Hughes had instructed Grew not to embark upon this until the direction that the conference was taking became apparent. It was immediately clear to Grew that the Turks wanted to use the Chester Concession 'as a means of barter,' with İsmet stating that if the United States remained unyielding on the Capitulations (a position Grew maintained as a bluff), the concession would 'be looked upon with a cold eye at Ankara.'[87] The first unofficial negotiation took place on 16 May, with Grew being taken aback by the hard-line Turkish stance on just about every issue. Conversations continued sporadically in May and more formal negotiations got underway on 31 May.[88]

Grew's second phase of Lausanne became truly eventful when oil re-emerged as an item of controversy. On 6 June, İsmet informed Grew that the Allies wanted to retain the provision in the treaty 'confirming pre-war concessions,' including those that had not been made 'legally valid' like the TPC. İsmet reported that 'the Chester Concession was the specific object of this move' and that Turkey might be compelled to accept. Grew immediately went on an offensive against this provision.[89] After about ten days of fruitless lobbying, the State Department protested formally to the governments of Britain, France, and Italy. Grew also convinced İsmet that the TPC clause violated Turkish sovereignty, and hence the United States and Turkey became allied on the matter. After more wrangling in July, British representative Horace Rumbold accused Grew of having 'specific companies in mind' with his objections, but eventually the British relented. Grew and İsmet had won and the door to oil exploration in Turkey and Iraq remained technically open.[90]

Though commercial and legal conversations dominated the discussions, the minority issue continued as an occasional point of contention. On 5 June, Grew informed Hughes that the Allies were planning to make 'forcible representations' in support of Armenian rights at the last meeting of the conference. Grew suggested that the United States should join in this but that trying to 'coerce the Turks' into giving the Armenians rights of return or compensation might actually harm these rights.[91] Hughes agreed but requested, in light of domestic political realities, that Grew inform the Turks that the 'protection of minorities in Turkey'

87 Grew to Hughes, 27 April 1923, *FRUS*, 1923, Vol. II, 990–991.
88 Waldo H. Heinrichs, *American Ambassador: Joseph C. Grew and the Development of the United States Diplomatic Tradition*, 1986, 83–85.
89 Grew to Hughes, 6 June 1923, *FRUS*, 1923, Vol. II, 1016–1017.
90 Heinrichs, *Grew*, 85–91; Demirci, 'Turco-British,' 68–69.
91 Grew to Hughes, 6 June 1923, *FRUS*, 1923, Vol. II, 1015–1016.

was of 'great interest to a large body of Americans' and that any treaty 'which did not deal with this subject would not be understood' in the United States.[92] On 20 June, Grew tried to get İsmet to make a 'voluntary declaration' to the United States embodying the 'Protection of Minorities' clauses in the draft peace treaty but İsmet refused, stating that the clauses in the draft treaty should be enough to assuage the people of the United States.[93] Grew then relented, believing that the United States should not 'link our treaty obligations directly to this statement.'[94] Showing the pressure he was under, Hughes prompted Grew to continue pushing for some sort of note to the United States confirming Turkish guarantees to minorities and stating that the United States had been partly 'responsible for the attainment of the results achieved in this matter.'[95]

Immediately after the Allies and the Turks signed their treaty on 24 July 1923, Turkey turned more intently towards its treaty with the United States. Grew hoped that the strong relationship he had developed with İsmet would lead to easier negotiations, but it did not. He was now on the receiving end of Ismet's unyielding diplomacy. İsmet essentially wanted a copy of the Allied treaty with minor modifications, but Grew had orders to pursue several other matters. Negotiations were tedious, with İsmet willing only to give the United States exactly what the Allies received in terms of clauses to replace the Capitulations. They spent much time debating clauses concerning a Turkish law denying naturalized American citizens of Ottoman origin the right to return to Turkey, as well as claims made by American citizens about property lost during the war. Turkey allowed no 'open door' wording in the treaty, though this mattered less in terms of oil because of the firm British grip on Mosul. The United States did receive 'most favoured nation' wording in the treaty, meaning that treatment of American companies on matters such as taxation would be no worse than businesses from any other country. Grew considered this a victory.[96]

İsmet would not budge on the question of minorities either, having already done as much as he was going to do in the Allied treaty. The pledge that the Turks made in that treaty, he argued, was that the League of Nations could investigate grievances of minorities in Turkey, so Turkey was not going to grant this same power to a country not in the League. Grew made a final appeal to obtain a letter from Turkey confirming the American role in obtaining the minority clauses in

92 Hughes to Grew, 11 June 1923, *NA-State*, M365, Reel 3.

93 Grew, *Turbulent*, 588–589.

94 Grew to Hughes, 21 June 1923, *FRUS*, 1923, Vol. II, 1092–1093.

95 Hughes to Grew, 26 June 1923, *FRUS*, 1923, Vol. II, 1097.

96 Grew, *Turbulent*, 586–605.

the Allied treaty. İsmet again refused.[97] When informed of this, Hughes relented on the issue, stating that it was not 'necessary to break off negotiations' because of this.[98] Even though the State Department was not happy with the final wording of the treaty, Hughes told Grew to sign it because without it, Turkey could 'take measures injurious or at least vexatious to American interests' and put the United States 'in a position of disadvantage as compared with the European powers.'[99] Both parties signed the treaty on 6 August 1923. Grew made no statement on minorities at the signing.[100]

The Aftermath

In the autumn of 1923, debates about the Lausanne Treaty continued in the United States, with oil and Armenia remaining the main flashpoints for dispute. Some of the winners of the Harding Administration's commerce-first policy were, as expected, the American oil companies, though not the hapless Chester group. The Turkish Grand National Assembly cancelled its concession on 18 December 1923 because of the group's lack of finances. With the TPC concession also in limbo, the American oil consortium resumed negotiations with their competitors to finalize their stake in Middle East oil. Although this took until 1928 partly because of the unsettled matter of Russian oil under the Bolsheviks, the new regional cartel of Western oil companies began developing and dominating the region's oil resources.[101]

The Armenian advocates in the United States were not finished. Angered that the treaty had not included advocacy for the Armenian cause, they began to campaign against its ratification. After Harding died on 2 August 1923, new President Calvin Coolidge decided not to send the treaty to the Senate for approval until further support could be solidified. The Democrats in the Senate presented the biggest obstacle, with opposition to the treaty making it into the 1924 Democratic Party Platform, which stated that the treaty 'barters legitimate American rights and betrays Armenia, for the Chester oil concessions,' apparently unaware that these had been cancelled.[102] The Republicans, though controlling the Senate, doubted

97 Grew to Hughes, 22 July 1923, *FRUS*, 1923, Vol. II, 1107–1113.
98 Hughes to Grew, 22 July 1923, *FRUS*, 1923, Vol. II, 1113–1116.
99 Grew to Hughes, 31 July 1923, *FRUS*, 1923, Vol. II, 1133–1134.
100 'Minutes of the Meeting Held at Lausanne,' 6 August 1923, *FRUS*, 1923, Vol. II, 1144–1147.
101 Conlin, 'Oily Entente.'
102 '1924 Democratic Party Platform,' *The American Presidency Project*, https://www.presidency.ucsb.edu/node/273208.

that the treaty could get the necessary two-thirds majority necessary for approval, so they continually delayed putting it up for a vote.[103]

The matter came to a head in late 1926, when Senator William Borah, Chair of the Senate Foreign Relations Committee, finally brought the treaty to the floor for debate. Those vocally against ratification included the still-active ACIA and the newly formed 'American Committee Opposed to the Lausanne Treaty' (with the prolific spokesperson Vahan Cardashian). Those for ratification included the US Chamber of Commerce, American businesses with a presence in Turkey (including Standard Oil), and Near East Relief. People like James Barton and Caleb Gates (President of Robert College, Istanbul), though disappointed with elements of the treaty, were now lobbying for its ratification in order to protect their institutions in the region.[104] Senator William H. King led the Senate opposition to the treaty, arguing that Armenia's 'political and territorial rights were sacrificed, apparently, to secure for the special interests a share in Mosul oil.'[105] When the Senate finally voted on the treaty in 1927, it received 50 votes for and 34 against, which was six votes short of what was needed for approval.[106] The treaty was essentially finished, though Armenian activists continued to appeal to President Coolidge with some going so far as to call for an investigation into the American negotiators of the Lausanne Treaty.[107] Shortly after this, the United States and Turkey exchanged diplomatic notes and Joseph Grew became the first American ambassador to Turkey. He negotiated a new treaty with 'less favourable' terms for the United States and the Senate approved it without debate in 1930.[108]

Conclusion

What does this treaty fight show about the evolution of American Middle East policy? It is important to note that American policy in the region was partly crafted

---

103 DeNovo, *American Interests*, 153–166.

104 See various correspondence in William Edgar Borah Papers, Manuscript Division, Library of Congress, Washington D.C., esp. Box 252, Folder Lausanne Treaty, Fol. 1–4 (hereafter *Borah Papers*).

105 Congressional Record, 69th Congress, 2nd Sess., Vol. LXVIII, Part 2, 13 January 1927, 1573.

106 DeNovo, *American Interests*, 165. If one (perhaps speciously) equates the votes against this treaty with votes for the 1920 American mandate for Armenia, support for the Armenian cause had indeed improved.

107 Vahan Cardashian to President Coolidge, 7 May 1928, *Borah Papers*, Box 252, Folder Lausanne Treaty, Fol. 4.

108 Grew, *Turbulent* Era, 678–679; DeNovo, *American Interests*, 153–166, 236–240.

by the new post-war realities. Turkey put itself into a strong bargaining position through sheer force of will. Despite the fragility of their new state, they negotiated uncompromisingly in ways that often belied their position of relative weakness, but which displayed continuity from the pre-war CUP years. The Turkish nationalists believed that attacks on Ottoman sovereignty were one of the elements that led to the Empire's demise. They were not going to let this happen again.

In American domestic politics, oil and Armenia were the main issues that dominated the American debate about the Lausanne Conference. The American delegation at Lausanne did care about American oil companies gaining access to regional oil supplies, but not in the insidious way that Armenian advocates accused them of. Standard Oil cared about Lausanne's outcome but did not actively seek to influence the American delegation. The Armenian advocates exaggerated the influence of American oil companies, but the claim had rhetorical power because of the poor reputation of the oil industry and pre-existing debates over the future of the United States in the world.[109] The American Armenian advocates argued that the Christians in the Ottoman lands at least deserved autonomy and protection, and the United States was an ethical, non-imperial power which should ensure that this happened in some form. The Harding administration could have taken a stand on this issue, but it knew that American commercial interests would have been harmed if it did, partly because the British and French were not, in the end, willing to take such a stand. American companies, Harding believed, required equal status in every global market if the United States was going to take its rightful place at the head of the world economy. This was not a retreat into isolationism but the beginning of a new kind of commerce-driven global engagement. In this new formulation, potentially perilous support of an Armenian national home was not on par with commerce in terms of American foreign policy goals.

The battle over the Lausanne Conference represented a moment of acrimony between economic and ethical forces in American politics. By 1922, American economic might had grown, and its companies had turned their sights on the Middle East. Harding's anti-imperialism was more economic than Wilson's in that he opposed imperialism primarily because American companies had limited access to European colonial holdings.[110] Furthermore, Harding had promised to keep the United States from becoming too entwined in international affairs and he was probably correct that, short of a military intervention that was unpalatable to most Americans, the United States was in no position to help the Armenians. The

109 See Laderman, *Sharing the Burden*.

110 Tooze, *The Deluge*, esp. 12–16.

activist, imperial policies that the United States had used in its own hemisphere and the Philippines were deemed inappropriate for the Middle East. The missionaries and their advocates knew the region well and attempted to get their many well-placed friends to sway the government to aid the Armenians. They could not convince enough senators to support an Armenian mandate in 1920, but they managed to gain the consolation prize of defeating the Lausanne Treaty in 1927. Though the United States occasionally did (and still does) wield the co-religionist, or now the 'Judeo-Christian,' cudgel in defence of various policies, the defeat of the treaty can be seen as a last gasp of missionary strength in determining US policy towards the Middle East. It must be said, however, that missionaries who were more familiar with the post-Ottoman realities of the region had supported the treaty, whereas their stateside missionary colleagues and supporters largely had not. Those in the region realized the situation had changed. With their institutions closed, forced to secularize, or co-opted by the Turkish state, some of these missionaries and their children moved into the US State Department, aid work, the Office of Strategic Services (later the CIA), academia, or oil corporations.[111] A century after its inception, the American missionary moment in the Middle East came to an end in the 1920s, and Lausanne was its death knell.

111 David A. Hollinger, *Protestants Abroad: How Missionaries Tried to Change the World but Changed America*, 2017, 117–138.

9

The Mosul Question: Lausanne and After

Sarah Shields

The dispute over Mosul province threatened to derail the entire Lausanne Conference. Despite British Foreign Minister Curzon's apparent belief that he could buy off Turkey's chief negotiator İsmet İnönü (hereafter İsmet) with the promise to share oil resources, the Turks rebuffed every offer that would have turned the disputed province over to Britain. Nearly all of the big issues of the conference came into play over the Mosul dispute: Turkey offered to support Britain on the Turkish Straits, end ties with the Soviet Union, and sign a treaty on British terms if Curzon agreed to restore Mosul to Turkey.[1]

Both the new Turkish Republic and the British government responsible for the Iraq mandate recognized the strategic importance of the Mosul province. Nonetheless, by the time the Mosul Question came to Lausanne, the dispute was framed not in terms of military strategy, but according to Wilsonian principles. The world had moved on from the old Vienna System, 'centred on dynastic legitimacy and state sovereignty within clearly defined borders', to the new Paris System, 'focused on populations and an ideal of state sovereignty rooted in national homogeneity.'[2] Government was to be based on the consent of the governed. For the conferees in Lausanne, the members of the League of Nations, and the governments of

1 Sevtap Demirci, 'Turco-British Diplomatic Manoeuvres on the Mosul Question in the Lausanne Conference, 1922–1923,' *British Journal of Middle Eastern Studies* 37/1, 2010, 62.
2 Eric D. Weitz, 'From the Vienna to the Paris System: International Politics and the Entangled Histories of Human Rights, Forced Deportations, and Civilizing Missions,' *The American Historical Review* 113/5, 2008, 1314.

Turkey, Iraq, and Britain, consent required a decision about who would govern 'the governed.' For the Kurds who formed the majority in the contested province, however, 'consent' for the nation-state project was hardly the goal.

Mosul at Lausanne

A part of the Ottoman Empire for centuries, Mosul remained in Ottoman hands until after the Armistice of Mudros in 1918. The warfare in the years following redefined Mosul's importance. As British-sponsored Greek forces invaded Anatolia from the west in 1919, Turkish nationalist forces logically feared British invasion from Iraq to the east. At the same time, the new Bolshevik government's support for the Turkish nationalists beginning in 1920, along with Turkey's growing prowess against the Greeks, loomed as a threat over British colonial interests. Mosul seemed to be the missing piece that would either allow Turkey to defend against British invasion or stop any Turkish attacks on Iraq. Britain was so nervous about Turkish claims on Mosul that much of the immediate post-war years saw a series of ever-changing strategies on using Mosul as a buffer area. Having tried unsuccessfully for years to find a compliant local leader to carry out their programme in an autonomous 'Southern Kurdish' zone, London left the possibility for local autonomy open in the final Sèvres Treaty.[3]

Economic, political, and nationalist concerns came into play as well. For Turkey's nationalists, Mosul was an intrinsic part of their territory. It had been included in the 1920 Turkish National Pact, the consensus definition of the new Republic's goals and territory. Mustafa Kemal (hereafter Atatürk) emphasized Mosul's importance to the new Turkey, telling the Grand National Assembly on 1 May 1920 that 'Turkey would never compromise over the issue of the Mosul Vilayet. Let it be clear to everybody that our eastern national frontier goes as far as Arbil, Suleymaniyeh, and the city of Kirkuk [in the Vilayet of Mosul]. Yes there are Kurds there. But we do not differentiate between them and Turks.'[4] The new Turkish leadership had no doubt that Mosul's Kurds would willingly become part of the Turkish Republic. After all, they had been active participants in the national war of liberation against the Greek invasion and European domination.

That 1919 invasion had demonstrated the necessity of secure borders. The

3 'Treaty of Peace with Turkey' (Treaty Series No. 11, 1920), Articles 62–64 https://treaties.fcdo.gov.uk/awweb/pdfopener?md=1&did=63986.

4 Othman Ali, 'The Career of Ozdemir: A Turkish Bid for Northern Iraq, 1921–1923,' *Middle Eastern Studies* 53/6, 2017, 968.

Turkish government understood the role Britain had played in encouraging the Greeks. Even after a brutal war to push Greek forces out of Anatolia, Britain would remain perched on Turkey's eastern border as mandatory power over Iraq. If Mosul, its resources, and its mountains were to become part of Iraq, then Britain would have all of the necessary elements required to launch another invasion of Turkish territory, this time over land with no natural boundaries. By 1923, the victorious Turkish nationalists knew that the British had encouraged Armenian aspirations in Eastern Anatolia, and had supported Kurdish resistance as the British tried to divert Turkish attention from the Greek invaders. For the Turkish government, having Mosul went well beyond a matter of national 'pride,' as British officials alleged. Their vulnerability was much too clear after the hard-fought victories of the previous four years, and Mosul seemed a matter of survival.[5]

Britain likewise considered Mosul essential for their programme as mandatory power over Iraq. Turkey had just demonstrated its military prowess, not only defeating Britain's Greek protégés, but in the process also overturning the post-war treaty signed at Sèvres. Having just begun the process of converting their ships from coal, Britain also coveted Mosul's oil resources.[6] Despite their interest in Mosul's strategic location, its place on their route to India had ceased being so significant during the decades since the Suez Canal had begun

---

5 Peter J. Beck, '"Tedious and Perilous Controversy": Britain and the Settlement of the Mosul Dispute, 1918–1926,' *Middle Eastern Studies* 17/2, 1981, 257. Beck listed six reasons for Mosul's importance to the new Turkish republic: Nationalist sentiment, inclusion in the national pact, oil, strategic value, pressing the victory over Britain, and assimilationist policy (making an example of assimilating the Kurds).

6 Beck, 'Tedious and Perilous Controversy,' 258. The *New York Times* report on 25 April 1925 when the League Commission returned to Geneva, ended with serious questions about oil: 'Some persons on the Commission are not overly impressed by the prospects of Mosul becoming a great oil centre. The natives have a few wells from which they take oil for cooking, but the cost of a railroad, a pipeline, villages, &c., make the concessions doubtful propositions.' 'Mosul Commission Starts Report Today', https://timesmachine.nytimes.com/timesmachine/1925/04/25/98824308.pdf?pdf_redirect=true&ip=0. Nonetheless, as both Conlin and Venn have pointed out, the negotiations over oil were an important part of ongoing back-room negotiations during the conference (and before and after). In Paris, London, and Washington, these negotiations offered an opportunity for important economic elites to influence foreign policy, sometimes in ways that remained invisible to high-ranking foreign policy officials. See Jonathan Conlin, 'An Oily Entente: France, Britain, and the Mosul Question, 1916–1925,' *Diplomacy & Statecraft* 31/2, 2020, 231–256; Fiona Venn, 'Oleaginous Diplomacy: Oil, Anglo–American Relations and the Lausanne Conference, 1922–23', *Diplomacy & Statecraft* 20/3, 2009, 414–433.

to facilitate shipping.[7] Perhaps most important of all, however, was Britain's need to cut expenses in the Iraq mandate. The First World War had depleted Britain's coffers, and the uprisings in 1920 had demonstrated that expenses in Palestine and Iraq were likely to remain prohibitive unless some sort of solution was found.

The solution to the overwhelming expense of controlling Iraq would be the creation of a façade of local Arab government. Britain's collaborator government would be headed by Emir Faisal, for whom Mosul was an essential part of Iraq. To keep Faisal on board, and to avoid losing the limited support he already had among Iraqis, the British could not afford to lose Mosul. Faisal insisted that it was not possible for a government in Baghdad to survive without Mosul. Without Mosul, Iraq would need a permanent military station at the Turkish border. Even then, the risks of continuing insecurity and possible invasion would keep foreign investors out of Iraq. In Faisal's estimation:

> Therefore I consider that Mosul is to Iraq as the head is to the rest of the body; and it is my unshakeable conviction that, though the question is only one of fixing a boundary between Iraq and Turkey, it is nevertheless and in fact the question of Iraq as a whole. Accordingly, the happiness or misery of four millions of human beings is placed in the hands of the members of your honourable Commission. If for any reason the Commission may consider that it should recommend to the League of Nations any alteration or modification of the present frontiers of Iraq, it should at the same time recommend to the League the choice of a new status for Iraq in its entirety, and it shall be responsible for the destinies of this mass of human beings.[8]

---

7 Curzon summarized his discussion with French Ambassador Cambon on 3 December 1919. 'Our interest in Mosul arose, not from any *a priori* desire to possess or control that region (for two years ago no one dreamt that such a denouement was likely), but solely from the fact that Mosul was united, physically, politically, and administratively with Mesopotamia; that the inhabitants of the Mosul Vilayet declined to be severed from the populations of Middle and Lower Mesopotamia; and that if, as seemed likely, Great Britain was to be entrusted with the future control of Mesopotamia, Mosul, whether we liked it or not, must inevitably form a part of the charge.' Curzon to Stanley, 12 March 1919, The National Archives of the UK, Public Record Office, Foreign Office (hereafter *National Archives*), FO 371.4179.

8 League of Nations, 'Question of the Frontier between Turkey and Iraq (Report by the Commission)', 20 August 1925 (hereafter *Report*), 7, https://biblio-archive.unog.ch/Dateien/CouncilMSD/C-400-M-147–1925-VII_BI.pdf. This was the speech with which Faisal greeted the Commission.

Britain needed to extricate itself from the demands of its mandate, but their newly-installed King Faisal insisted that Mosul was the price.

It was no surprise, then, that the Lausanne Conference foundered as the members considered the disposition of the province of Mosul. The stakes were existential: only Mosul would provide the military security and resources that would allow either Turkey or Iraq to become secure, viable states in the immediate future. Neither was willing to defer to the other, and it was only when the rest of the treaty was threatened that Curzon suggested the decision over Mosul be deferred. Representatives of Japan and France immediately acclaimed his suggestion to turn the question over to the League of Nations. İsmet refused, reminding the group that Britain had a seat at the League and Turkey did not, and that Turkey had never been consulted and never agreed to the whole system of mandates on which Britain was basing its own standing as mandatory power over Iraq. By the end of the Lausanne Conference, they had agreed to a six-month window to try to resolve the Mosul Question before bringing it to the League for arbitration.[9]

Track of Diplomacy

From the time British forces occupied Mosul in November 1918 (*after* the Armistice of Mudros), Turkey continued to insist that it had never relinquished the territory. Since the Ottomans remained in legal possession of the area, the Allied Supreme Council did not include Mosul in the Iraq mandate assigned at San Remo in April 1920.[10] Nonetheless, at the end of that summer, the region became part of the British zone in the Sèvres Treaty, despite having been assigned to France in the infamous Sykes-Picot agreement. By the start of negotiations at Lausanne, therefore, the Mosul region was legally still part of Turkey, but had been allotted to British administration during the intervening pivotal five years.

That five years turned out to be decisive for the future of the region. By September 1921, Turkey had begun to turn the tables on the invading Greeks. The Turkish nationalists' victories on the battlefield reframed their situation in negotiations. Instead of a vanquished adversary without any alternative to accepting the dismemberment envisioned in the Sèvres Treaty, the Allies now had to

9 *Lausanne Conference on Near Eastern Affairs, 1922–1923: Records of Proceedings and Draft Terms of Peace*, 1923 (hereafter *Lausanne Conference*), 403.

10 Quincy Wright, 'The Mosul Dispute', *The American Journal of International Law* 20/3, 1926, 455. As legal scholar Quincy Wright pointed out, the League of Nations commission agreed with this assessment. 'The disputed territory must be regarded as an integral part of Turkey until that Power renounces her rights …'

face a successful Turkish nationalist government already making their intentions clear. France saw the writing on the wall and signed the Accord of Ankara (aka Franklin-Bouillon Agreement) one month later (20 October 1921). The Soviet Union recognized Turkey even earlier and continued to provide support.[11] By the time the Lausanne Conference began in November 1922, almost all of the major Allied powers had come to terms with the new Turkish nationalist successor to the Ottoman Empire. The exceptions were Great Britain, under its first Labour government apparently more ready to deal with Turkey, and her Greek protégé, now in ignominious retreat. As Coşar and Demirci explained, this was the first of the post-war treaty negotiations in which the parties came to the table as anything like equals.[12]

When they met at Lausanne, negotiations over Mosul were framed in Wilsonian terms from the start: both the Turkish and British representatives agreed that Mosul would be governed by its people's choice. Britain referred repeatedly to Wilson's Fourteen Points, especially number 12: 'The Turkish portions of the present Ottoman Empire should be assured a secure sovereignty, but the other nationalities which are now under Turkish rule should be assured an undoubted security of life and an absolutely unmolested opportunity of an autonomous development.'[13] Both agreed with the need for Turkey to have its own secure sovereignty, and İsmet insisted that Ankara had already relinquished all of the Ottoman Empire's Arab zones. Curzon maintained that the people of Mosul were not Turkish, and thus deserved that 'autonomous development.' The question had become a demographic issue: if the Mosul population was Turkish, it belonged in Turkey. If it was Arab (or not Turkish, as the British would have it), it belonged in Iraq.

On 23 January 1923, İsmet began by outlining his argument. Mosul had always been part of Turkey, and its economy had long been connected with Anatolia. The British occupation was illegal, having occurred after the armistice had been signed, and Turkey had not participated in assigning or accepting mandates over any former Ottoman area. The people had demonstrated their rejection of British rule by rising against them in 1920, by refusing to take part in the recent British-sponsored plebiscites, and by joining with Turkey whenever they could. Despite what the British were suggesting, Kurds had long cooperated with the Turks as

11 See the chapter by Hirst and Forestier-Peyrat in this volume.

12 Nevin Coşar and Sevtap Demirci, 'The Mosul Question and the Turkish Republic: Before and after the Frontier Treaty, 1926', *Middle Eastern Studies* 42/1, 2006, 125.

13 'Avalon Project – President Woodrow Wilson's Fourteen Points, http://avalon.law.yale.edu/20th_century/wilson14.asp.

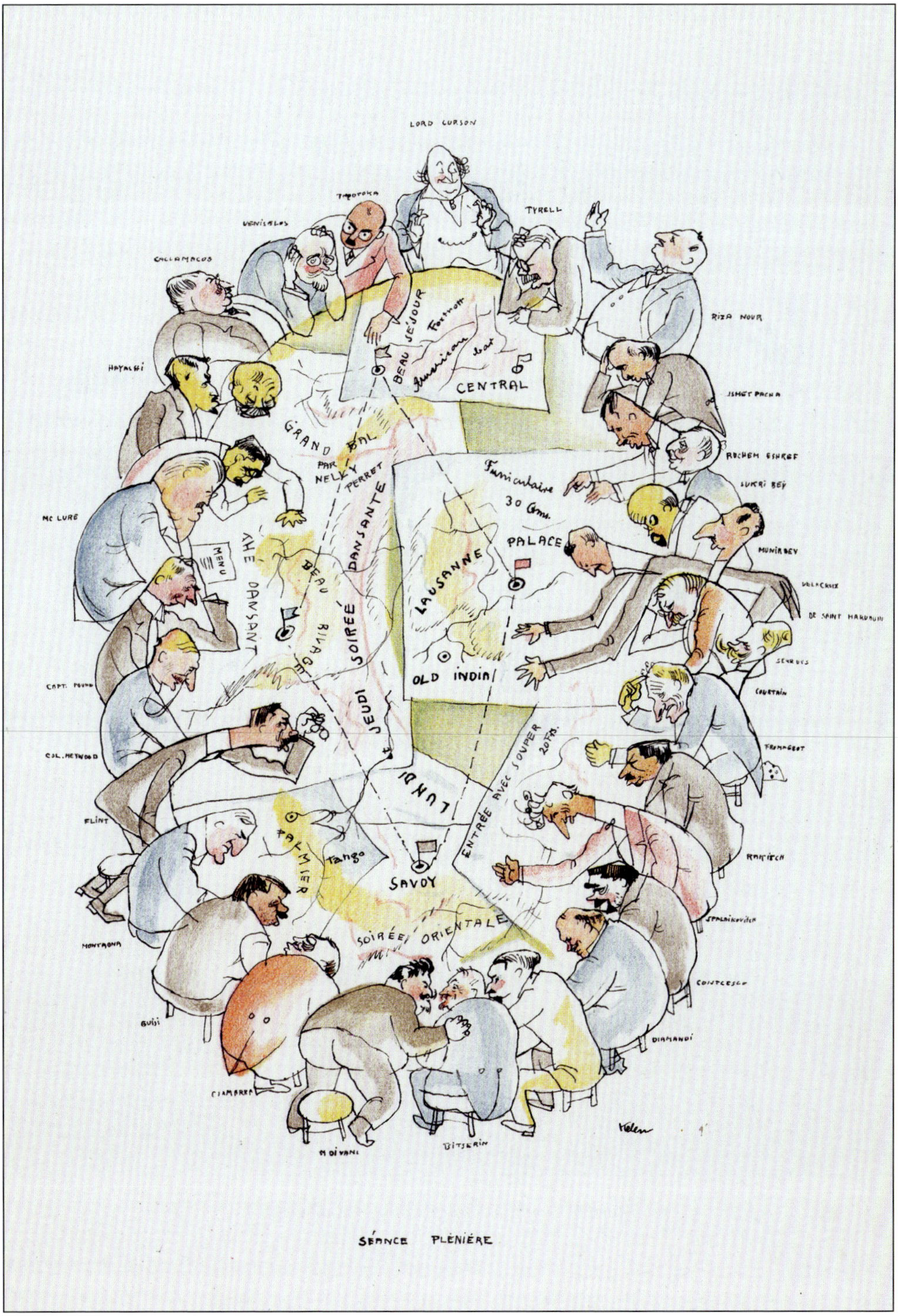

Figure 1: 'Plenary Session'

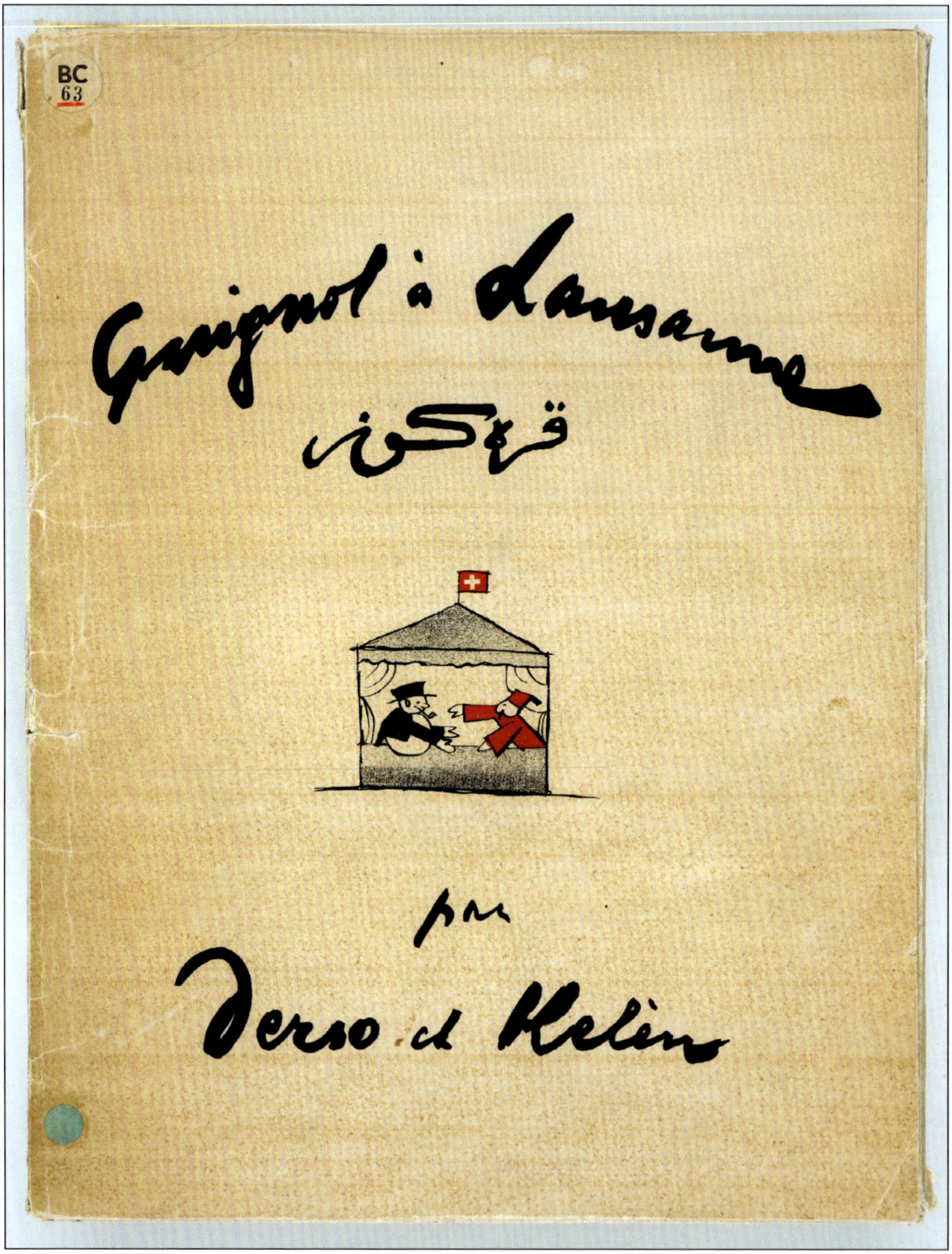

Figure 6: *'Guignol à Lausanne'* (book cover)

Figure 7: Delegates attending the Conference

Figure 8: Journalists attending the Conference

Bal masqué au Lausanne-Palace

11

Figure 9: 'Masked Ball'

Figure 10: ‘The Latest Discovery of Lord Carnarvon’

Figure 11: 'Cercle de la Presse'

Figure 12: 'The Apotheosis of Peace'

partners, even in the war of independence that had just concluded. Kurds were at that moment well-represented in the Turkish Grand National Assembly. Turkey demanded a plebiscite like those in many other disputed regions so that the local population could determine their own political future.

Curzon looked on these arguments with disdain, insisting that Mosul had been part of the Iraq mandate and Britain was unwilling to 'give it up,' something that all of the treaties so far would prohibit. In any case, there were no Turks in the disputed zone: even the so-called Turkish population was not really Turkish ('Osmanli Turks'), but instead had been living there long before even the Seljuk conquests. Like İsmet, he agreed that the Kurds were the largest group by far, but Curzon claimed that the Kurds were not Turks. With a tone that was remarkably condescending, Curzon schooled the Turkish representative by insisting that everyone recognized that Kurds were Iranians. 'I have been in the Kurdish country myself; I have stayed with the Kurds, and though I do not pretend to be an authority I would undertake to pick out a Kurd from a Turk any day of the week, and I could not unless I were blind possibly confuse the two.'

İsmet disputed the rejection of a plebiscite, a method 'commonly employed when it was necessary to decide by whom and how the population of a country should be governed.' Direct consultation, after all, had already been 'agreed unanimously' to be the 'most rational and equitable procedure with a view to settling the destinies of a nation or population … leaving it free to express its opinion on the subject in full independence.' The British had clearly recognized this in the past, he reminded them, even choosing to consult the people of Iraq in this very way about the choice of Emir Faisal to be their king.[14] Curzon's derision was clear as he persisted in rejecting the plebiscite. The Kurds had their own 'history, customs, manners and character … Why should these people in this condition be taken and handed over to Angora [Ankara], why should there be a plebiscite of this people? … Poor fellows, they do not know what it means.'[15] The question, the British kept insisting, must be defined not as the fate of the territory, but instead as the demarcation of the border, 'an entirely different question, and of all questions the least suitable for decision by a plebiscite. I venture to think that I have had far more experience of plebiscites than İsmet. Since the war I have had a great deal to do with plebiscites concerning frontiers, and I am determined never to deal with another. The plebiscite is a fatal and pernicious system of endeavouring to settle a

14 Summaries of the testimony and proceedings that follow are taken from *Lausanne Conference*, 337–403.
15 *Lausanne Conference,* 355–357.

frontier.' It would take too much work to decide who could vote (age, residence, etc.) and locate an army that was unrelated to either contending party willing to suppress the inevitable violence.

Without any representatives of the stateless Kurds present, both parties tried to prove the Kurds' preference for living in either a Turkish- or a British-controlled state. Despite the discussions about oil, economies, history, and strategy, most of the discussion alternated between the identities and the political preferences of the inhabitants. Curzon argued that the local Kurds were never successfully controlled from the Ottoman capital, and recent experience illustrated the local population's strong preference for British rule. Kurds had made their loyalties known by assisting the British instead of the Turks in the recent war. As far as the anti-British uprising of 1920 was concerned, Curzon suggested that it did not represent anti-British sentiment but had been the result of outside agitators. (He knew 'a good many stories about the Turkish propaganda which brought it about,' and the British, he said, even knew who was responsible.) In any case, the resistance had been the natural outcome of a people not used to orderly administration, including collection of taxes for the general good, 'quite a novel experience, and I can well believe unpopular with a good many.' By contrast, Curzon tried to illustrate the distance between Turks and Kurds by citing recent Turkish repression of Kurds in Bitlis and Dersim. Indeed, he argued, Kurds were continually 'bombarding' the British with demands for Kurdish autonomy or independence – for which the British, of course, 'felt much sympathy.' The Assyrians were pleading with the British not to turn them over to the Turks.

İsmet tried to debunk Curzon's argument that the local people would choose Iraq (and Britain). 'The Arabs, even if they are coupled with the non-Moslems, form … as the British delegation themselves admit, a minority in the Mosul Vilayet.' Using Wilsonian language, İsmet continued: 'It would therefore be unjust and contrary to the right of self-determination to demand the union of the Mosul Province with Iraq on this ground.' He rejected the argument that Kurds did not want to live with Turks. 'Centuries have passed during which these two peoples, united by community of race, religion, aspirations, manners, usage and customs, have lived together in perfect understanding; history shows that the Kurds came under Turkish administration and associated their destinies with those of Turkey most willingly.'[16] According to İsmet, the current government represented in the Turkish Grand National Assembly is:

16 *Lausanne Conference*, 344, from the session held on 23 January 1923.

> … the Government of the Kurds just as much as the Government of the Turks. The Kurdish people and their above-mentioned representatives do not agree that their brethren who live in the Mosul Vilayet should be separated from the mother-country, and are ready to endure any sacrifice in order to prevent such a separation. It is undeniable that the Kurds and the Turks, who form the vast majority of the population of the Mosul Vilayet, have never ceased and never will cease for a single instant to fight with all their strength to ensure that their province shall continue to form an integral part of Turkey.

Just as the British claimed that the 1920 uprising had been the result of outside agitators, the Turkish delegate insisted that the Turkish government had been forced to suppress Kurdish resistance in Bitlis and Dersim that had been the result of foreign consular agitation. In any case, he insisted, the British could make no claim to Kurdish support: 'The Kurds enrolled by the Iraq Government have seized every favourable opportunity for passing to the Turkish side … British air squadrons have often had to bombard Turkish and Kurdish villages in order to prevent them by terrorization from displaying their devotion to Turkey; and finally … at the time of the so-called plebiscite organized in regard to the Emir Faisal, despite all the pressure exercised upon the population of the Vilayet, it was only the minorities in the town of Mosul who took part in the vote.' Turks and Kurds, he insisted, had no loyalty to the government of Iraq.

Finally, Curzon insisted that Mosul's commercial ties were with Syria and Baghdad, the latter dependent on Mosul's grain. Turkey's control over the contested region would bring it only 60 miles from Baghdad, allowing Turkey to cut off essential food supplies to the rest of Iraq. Curzon also insisted that the British demand had nothing to do with oil. 'The question of the oil of the Mosul Vilayet has nothing to do with my argument. I have presented the British case on its own merits quite independently of any natural resources there may be in the country. I do not know how much oil there may be in the neighbourhood of Mosul, or whether it can be worked at a profit, or whether it may turn out after all to be a fraud.'[17]

17 *Lausanne Conference*, 360. Curzon, claiming never to have discussed concessions for oil anywhere, insisted that Turkish representatives went to London to offer oil concessions in the Mosul area to British concessionaires without his knowledge. They returned to Turkey unsuccessful, but Curzon invited them to return. He promised to call on them when they returned to London, 'and I will have the greatest satisfaction in taking them personally to the British Museum.' Richard Washburn Child, *A Diplomat Looks at Europe,* 1925, 117. Child wrote about his conversation with Curzon: 'Mosul has oil but more than that it is the military

When İsmet remained unmoved by the British arguments, Curzon recommended that, since Britain was in Iraq by virtue of a League of Nations mandate that it could neither surrender nor modify without permission, this issue be turned over to the League. Turkey's representative was opposed, claiming the situation would hardly be fair as 'Turkey would be staking a portion of her national inheritance, while the British Government would at the most be in the position of submitting to discussion the control exercised by them over a territory which was not their own.' In turn, Curzon tried to extol the League as a fair and equitable arbitrator. Finally, he resorted to threats: the British feared war if Turkey did not agree to this arbitration. They already had reports of troop movements toward Mosul, and Article 11 of the League of Nations Convention stated that any war or threat of war affecting a member would be a matter of concern to the League as a whole. So while posing as a peacemaker trying to avoid war, Curzon insisted that 'if the Turkish delegation refuse my proposal I shall act on that article.'[18]

The League of Nations Commission

Unable to reach agreement in Lausanne or during the follow-up efforts in Istanbul in the following year, Britain and Turkey agreed to submit the dispute over Mosul to the League of Nations. The League created a commission with three neutral representatives from European countries to decide the disposition of the Mosul Province.[19] The three commissioners, though of diverse background, shared a lack of knowledge of the region and a dearth of experience in this sort of project.[20] Carl Einar Thure af Wirsén, the Minister Plenipotentiary of Sweden to Romania chaired the commission. Count Paul Teleki, former Prime Minister of Hungary,

---

key to Mesopotamia and Persia. Curzon says that public opinion in England and honor of obligations will not permit him to give up territory under a mandate – especially when that loss of territory would menace the Arab State!'

18 *Lausanne Conference*, 398–402.

19 Lori Allen argues that these international commissions, under the guise of assessing disputed situations to gather information necessary to achieve an outcome consistent with emerging international consensus, were, instead, part of the scaffolding that reinforced existing structures of power. Her conclusions on investigative commissions in Palestine is borne out also in the League of Nations commissions to Mosul and to the disputed Sanjak of Alexandretta (1936). Lori Allen, *A History of False Hope: Investigative Commissions in Palestine*, 2020.

20 As Ozan Ozavci has noted, even the first European 'commissioners' to the region, there to address the 1860 Lebanon riots, had some diplomatic experience even if they had no expertise in the region. Ozan Ozavci, *Dangerous Gifts: Imperialism, Security, and Civil Wars in the Levant, 1798–1864*, 2021, 322–323.

purported to be an expert on the Turkish language but seemed unable to carry out basic conversations. Colonel Albert Paulis, of the Belgian Army Reserve, was the only one with extensive experience outside Europe. He had been so important as a colonial official in the Belgian Congo and in the creation of the local train system that one of the important railway stations was named after him.[21] The Commission sent out dozens of questions to the Turkish and British governments. The responses marshalled the best scientific evidence of the era, producing competing demographic tables, historical racial narratives, and brightly-coloured ethnographic maps. They set to work examining all of this information before deciding what to do next.

While they were determining their next steps, violence in the border area escalated. From the armistice on, Turkey and Britain had tried to gain the loyalty of the people living in the borderland. They distributed wealth, promised political autonomy, provided weaponry, and encouraged attacks on supporters of the other power. Cross-border conflicts had become so frequent by the time the League began work that the League of Nations Rapporteur for the Mosul dispute recommended creating a tentative border. The League Council accepted the recommendation proposed by Hjalmar Branting that a temporary boundary follow a natural line somewhere between the borders that Turkey and Britain demanded. That boundary, agreed at Brussels on 29 October 1924, became known as the Brussels (or Branting) line, and would ultimately serve as the formal border.[22]

The Mosul Commission decided against a plebiscite, planning instead to travel to the region, assess the situation, and interview as many people as they could. They were joined by assessors from Turkey and Britain, and numerous staff. After a visit to Ankara, the group toured Baghdad, finally arriving in Mosul on 27

21 Mai Taha, 'Nation and Class Subjectivity in International Law and Its Institutions in the Middle East (1919–1939)', Law thesis, University of Toronto, 2015, 102.

22 John Rogers, 'The Foreign Policy of Small States: Sweden and the Mosul Crisis, 1924–1925', *Contemporary European History* 16/3, 2007, 360–361; H. I. Lloyd, 'The Geography of the Mosul Boundary', *The Geographical Journal* 68/2, 1926, 104–113. The editors of the *Journal of the Royal Central Asian Society* were dismayed with the Brussels line, summarizing its conclusions: '(a) It does not fulfil the object of British policy completely in that it surrenders to Turkey the control of Assyrian destinies. It does, however, provide for the establishment and security of an Iraq state sufficient to assure our own security. (b) The frontier does not, and cannot, satisfy the linguistic, racial, and religious requirements of a good frontier owing to the chaotic intermixture of these elements in its vicinity. (c) It is not strategically the best frontier for Iraq, but it is sufficiently defensible to guarantee the security of the Iraq state. It is economically sound. (d) It satisfies the political desires of the minorities concerned, except those of the Kurd and Assyrian.' 'Reflections on the Mosul Problem', *Journal of The Royal Central Asian Society* 13/4, 1926, 362–363.

January 1925. To see as much of the province as possible and speak with as many different people as they could, the Commissioners separated, each of the three men taking his own staff.[23] Each group visited warehouses and markets and made their own maps and observations on topography, resources, and communications. They wanted to observe the physical surroundings and gather information about the economies and societies of the province.

In small rooms throughout the province, the Commissioners and translators asked selected groups of local men about the current economic and political situation, about each man's work, and about what needed to be done in the area. The men included religious leaders, landed property holders, tribal leaders, local notables, farmers, merchants, and craftsmen. Representatives of each district were interviewed collectively; then the local interviewees left the room and filed back in one by one for the 'secret question,' called 'votes' by some of the members of the League party. Then a few remained behind for longer interviews.[24] Altogether, the commission interviewed some 800 people.[25]

The most important project, in an era when people and territory were supposed to complement each other, was to find out who the people were. Were they Arabs or were they Turks? From shortly after their arrival in Mosul, the Commissioners realized that these choices might be too limited. While they were asking people to identify themselves as either a Turk or an Arab, some of the people they talked with insisted not on discussing their identity, but on the myriad other issues that determined their political desires. They wanted to talk about trade, the treaty, the role of religion, the new administration in Turkey, and the British role in Iraq.[26] Even people of similar linguistic backgrounds and occupations framed their preferences differently. For example, many of the Kurdish farmers that Count Teleki interviewed in the area around Amadia wanted to stay with Iraq, insisting that the current government had been better for them, bringing irrigation and security. The majority of his Kurdish farmers, however, preferred Turkey or no one at all. One of these Kurds sold his farm products in Mosul city and in the mountains, and bought his supplies in Van, Aleppo or towns in Iran. He claimed that the Turks were more just; another farmer in the same city claimed that it would

23 *Report*, 12.

24 Diary of Liaison Officer, Edmonds to Cox, 7 March 1925, St. Antony's College Middle East Centre Archive, Oxford; 'Pronouncement by De Wirsén,' League of Nations Secretariat, S15 Files D22 & D23.

25 *Report*, 75.

26 *Report*, 10.

be impossible to live in peace under the current government in Baghdad.[27] The people wanted to ask complex questions and bring up thorny problems, not just respond to a choice between one identity and another, between domination by one neighbour or the other. For a population who had lived so long in a multi-lingual, religiously diverse empire, the Arab/Turk question made little sense.

The League of Nations had begun with a presumption that people's identities would determine their political goals. As a result, in the new global context of self-determination, the League of Nations Commission needed to know *who* lived in Mosul. Those were the people who would get to decide their own future. The assumption of the era was that different peoples wanted different futures, simply because they were different. Of course, Poles would want a different kind of government from Germans, and Germans from Czechs, and Serbs from Bulgarians. Nationalism was the order of the day, and nationalism assumed that only like groups living in independent states could reach the fulfillment of their dreams. And only that fulfillment would prevent another horrific catastrophe like the one so recently over, one begun (in the minds of some leaders) because of frustrated nationalism.

The Mosul Commission worked hard to count the groups within the population, sifting through information provided by a variety of sources, counting households themselves, estimating numbers. Their report is replete with extensive descriptions of each of the population groups they encountered, hundreds of words for each that traced their origins back to the earliest mists of pre-recorded time. Classical literature and archaeology, linguistics and physical observations were marshalled to define a Turk, an Arab, a Chaldean, a Kurd. Nonetheless, their efforts were often frustrated by centuries of intermarriage that made 'pure strains' difficult to find.[28]

The Mosul Commission agreed that Kurds formed by far the greatest numbers in the Mosul province. Once outside Arab-dominated Mosul city, the rest of the towns and the countryside, though mixed, were overwhelmingly Kurdish. The Commission report spilled a great deal of ink identifying the Kurds, largely because of Turkey's claim that Kurds were actually brother Turks. According to the British, Kurds were Iranians, 'not of the same blood as the Turks; that they are, in fact, as little related to the Turks as are the Chinese; that they speak an Iranian language which is closely connected with, or is even a dialect of, Persian.' The British claim echoed Curzon's at Lausanne: 'The Kurds of the disputed territory have greater leaning

27 League of Nations Secretariat, S14 Files D16 & D18.
28 *Report*, 78.

towards their co-nationals in Persia than towards those living in Turkish territory.' They were dissimilar to the Turks in customs and habits, especially regarding women, and the physical difference between the two is so great according to the British 'that any traveller can distinguish one from the other at first sight.'[29] Turkey disputed these Iranian origins, claiming that Kurds were instead Turanian, quoting the Encyclopaedia Britannica which claimed that same origin for the Gudu, who had lived from ancient times in the same area. According to Ankara, 'there are no differences of race, religion or customs between Turks and Kurds' and despite their different languages, the two peoples 'form a single unit.'[30]

The Mosul Commissioners were unwilling to come to a definitive conclusion on the origin of the Kurds. They attempted a scientific historical analysis, looking to cuneiform tablets that mentioned mountain tribes. They referred to various scholars who had tried to connect the Kurds with various ancient peoples, and tried to trace their language through those scientific taxonomic trees by which people were now identified. Those scholars had identified Kurds variously with Medes, Chaldeans, a branch of the Arab tribes, even Armenians. The Commission concluded, though, that 'the ethnical composition of the Kurdish nation is as obscure as its history.' Some claimed that the Kurds were an amalgam of many peoples; others that there were significant variations between the shepherd Kurds and the warrior Kurds who came from different 'stock' and even looked different. Thus, despite the effort to trace a prehistoric origin, to define the Kurds within a linguistic ethnic group, to discover a pure 'race,' the Commissioners in the end concluded that Kurds were the descendants of migrating and interrelated peoples.[31] Nonetheless, despite their unknown origins, the Commissioners concluded that Kurds had been 'aryanised.' 'However small the infiltration of Aryan blood may have been, it has been strong enough to make them wholly adopt an Iranian language … The Kurds are neither Arabs, Turks, nor Persians, though they are most nearly related to the Persians. They are different and clearly distinguishable from the Turks, and still more different and remote from the Arabs.'[32]

---

29 *Report*, 43.

30 *Report*, 43.

31 *Report*, 44–45. The Commission Report agreed with the 'Turkey in Asia' section of the British Foreign Office *Handbook* as preferring Kurds to Arabs: 'Where Kurds and Bedawi [Arabs] have taken to the land, the Kurd has shown himself so far to be the better man. If, therefore, the economic development of the country proceeds gradually, and if the local population is not swamped by reservoirs of manpower from abroad, Northern Mesopotamia seems destined to become Kurdish land,' 45.

32 *Report*, 46.

The Report also questioned the assumptions about Kurdish political sympathies. While some in the east around Suleymaniyeh might feel themselves more connected to Iran, those in the north had no connections with that country. Instead, the Kurdish nomads regularly crossed the new Brussels line and were much more connected to those on the other side of that line in Turkey. Despite those ties, the Commissioners were surprised that Mosul's Kurds seemed to know little about the Sheikh Said revolt just across the border.[33]

The revolt by Sheikh Said and an estimated 15,000 followers began in early February 1925 in the city now known as Dicle. Within two months they had successfully defeated local military units, taking territory as far as Diyarbakır. Turkey used fighter planes against the rebels, who were very close to the Brussels line, even as the Mosul Commission was travelling in the area. The Turkish government declared martial law in the eastern provinces and cracked down on any displays of Kurdish nationalism. According to British military sources, the fighting continued well into the summer, with Turkey brutally repressing the uprising, executing the leaders, and displacing thousands.[34] In the face of their military subjugation, the Turkish government changed their rhetoric to extol the brotherhood of Sunnis instead of the Kurdish-Turkish connection. Britain also engaged in brutal air and infantry attacks against Turkish-supporting Kurds who had dared to demonstrate their affinity during the Commission visit, despite the ban on political events. The British Foreign Office explained that they were punishing tribes who 'threatened the region's stability.'[35] While both Turkey and Britain insisted that they already had the loyalty, affinity, and support of the Kurds, each violently suppressed those who dissented.

Borderlanders

Turkey's demand for Mosul continued to rest on demographic and nationalist claims, the only ones that were valid for League of Nations analysis. Nonetheless,

---

33 *Report*, 46.

34 Hakan Özoğlu, 'Exaggerating and Exploiting the Sheikh Said Rebellion of 1925 for Political Gains', *New Perspectives on Turkey* 41, 2009, 181–210, argues that the revolt provided an opportunity for the new government to consolidate their hold over Turkey. Robert Olson, *The Emergence of Kurdish Nationalism and the Sheikh Said Rebellion, 1880–1925*, 1989, 107, 125; *National Archives*, AIR 23/280.

35 Aryo Makko, 'Arbitrator in a World of Wars: The League of Nations and the Mosul Dispute, 1924–1925', *Diplomacy & Statecraft* 21/4, 2010, 639–640; Jordi Tejel, 'Making Borders from Below: The Emergence of the Turkish–Iraqi Frontier, 1918–1925', *Middle Eastern Studies* 54/5, 2018, 10.

while insisting that Kurds and Turks were so similar as to be equivalent, they feared that Kurds left under British rule could make common cause with Turkey's Kurds to undermine the new state. The nascent Turkish nationalist government had moved quickly to rein in Kurdish demands. After Kurds helped Turkish forces against invading Greeks from March 1919 to December 1920, Atatürk had shut down their nationalist organization and arrested their leaders, accusing them of collaborating with the British. The Dersim uprising soon followed, and after that the Koçgiri revolt. Turkey's Grand National Assembly sent a commission of inquiry, which claimed Britain had instigated the unrest.[36] Since so much of Turkey's forces were still tied down fighting the invasion that Britain had set in play, these risings reinforced the new Turkish government's fear that the British had not given up its designs on eastern Turkey.

While Turkey had never wavered over its claim to Mosul, British officials argued over Mosul policy, and changed those arguments as conditions on the ground evolved. They had initially advocated a Kurdish and an Armenian state, which they expected would function as a buffer against the Turks. Mosul began to seem indispensable as the terms of the Sèvres Treaty became increasingly anachronistic, with Turkey prevailing against the Greek invasion, the US refusing a mandate for Armenia, and Britain unable to locate a compliant and popular Kurdish puppet. Without a buffer, its Iraq mandate would be open to the Turks; Mosul must be retained to provide that essential protection.

The British government identified Sheikh Mahmud as early as 1919 as their man in Kurdistan, convinced that he would carry out their plans and provide that buffer between the Iraq mandate and its neighbours. Instead of carrying out their interests, Sheikh Mahmud intermittently seemed to ally with anti-British leaders in Turkey, Iran, and neighbouring Kurdish areas. He saw his own leadership going well beyond the boundaries with which the British insisted on circumscribing him. By 1925, British reports described Sheikh Mahmud with confusion, derision, disappointment, or anger. How could he be so ignorant as to betray them and lose his power? His loyalty had forfeited their trust, and, in the process, the possibility of a Kurdish state.[37]

---

36 Robert Olson, 'Kurds and Turks: Two Documents Concerning Kurdish Autonomy in 1922 and 1923', *Journal of South Asian and Middle Eastern Studies* 15/2, 1991, 25. For more on the Koçgiri rebellion, see Elise Massicard, 'The Repression of the Koçgiri Rebellion, 1920–1921', *Online Encyclopaedia of Mass Violence*, n.d.

37 David McDowall, *A Modern History of the Kurds,* 1996, Ch. 8; Tejel, 'Making Borders from Below'; Ali, 'The Career of Ozdemir'; League of Nations Secretariat, S14 File D18; Zeynep Arıkanlı, 'British Legacy and Evolution of Kurdish Nationalism in Iraq (1918–1926)', *Alternatives: Turkish Journal of International Relations* 9/4, 2010, 7–9.

While the meeting was ongoing at Lausanne, Iraq High Commissioner Percy Cox asked the Secretary of State for the Colonies to demonstrate Britain's support for Kurdish 'aspirations.' Cox claimed to detect a 'wave of Kurdish national feeling which has arisen,' urging that he be allowed to encourage it. But the 'enlightened Kurds' were reluctant to offer a 'definite programme' because British intentions were not clear. In the meantime:

> … [the] more ignorant and fanatical elements as typified by Sheikh Mahmud and his party are indulging in more or less fantastic demands which according to them represent wishes of all true Kurds. It would greatly assist to stabilize situation and encourage more moderates to come forward with reasonable proposals if I could announce that both His Majesty's Government and the Government of Iraq recognise right of Kurds within the frontiers of Iraq to set up for themselves a national Government within their frontiers. Such an announcement would have [the] effect of consolidating Kurds and rallying them to us and would thus provide us with a most valuable weapon for countering Turkish activities from which we are now suffering and for resisting any serious attack which might be made.[38]

The British High Commissioner in Baghdad was convinced that 'fanatics' would cease their agitation and 'moderates' would begin the civilized process of state-building if the British would tip their hand. The Colonial Office refused.

Turkey claimed that the British had fomented disorder to compromise their claims to be able to govern Kurds. But as Hakan Özoğlu has argued, the Sheikh Said revolt offered a convenient opportunity for the new and vulnerable regime in Ankara to impose a draconian new law restricting political rights.[39] If one instead traces the path of the borderlanders' own actions, it seems clear that the goal was not to aid either Britain or Turkey, but instead to maintain borderlands as borderlands.

Lausanne, Kurds, Borders, and Statelessness

The Kurds frustrated both British and Turkish officials who somehow expected

---

38 Telegram HC Iraq Cox to Secretary of State for the Colonies Milner, 19 November 1922, FO 371/7782.

39 Özoğlu, 'Exaggerating and Exploiting', 181–210; Coşar and Demirci, 'The Mosul Question and the Turkish Republic', 128.

that their loyalty, once acquired, would persist. Historians have tried to trace the labyrinthine politics of intermittent Kurdish alliances, explaining them with limited success as either nationalist or proto-nationalist or autonomist. Nonetheless, it seems clear that their loyalty remained quite consistent: Kurds sought to stymie the imposition of alien forms of government by disrupting the efforts to impose settled spaces and centralized power. The stories of Kurdish 'treachery' that the British tell make it appear that the Kurds did not 'receive' their state at the end of the war because there were no sufficiently civilized protégé 'leaders' they could count on. The Turkish nationalists, though grateful for the assistance of Sunni Kurds in the national liberation war, feared the loss of territory in their eastern provinces. London, Baghdad, Istanbul, and Ankara used some Kurds to destabilize their adversaries, and all they gained was continued disruption of their imperial projects.

Although European geographers and statesmen were intent on establishing borders and safely organizing statelets, the land and its people had no interest in the project. League of Nations Special Commissioner General Johan Laidoner visited frontier zones and insisted that tribal and village raids crossing the Brussels line in both directions 'cannot be regarded as exceptional occurrences.' The Brussels line was 'not a natural frontier; certain parts of it, indeed, are purely fictitious ...'[40]

Historians, like politicians, tend to assume the importance and desirability of the establishment of recognized borders. But for many local populations, the Lausanne project stepped beyond acceptable as it tried to allocate territory. Kurds, generally acknowledged to be the predominant group in the disputed territory, had a variety of political preferences. Some rejected Turkey, when the League Commissioners queried them, because Atatürk had turned away from the Caliphate. Others preferred connection to Turkey, with which they had most of their trade ties. Anti-imperialist Kurds might prefer Ankara to Baghdad/London. All had a variety of considerations beyond identity group that determined their choices. In retrospect, their actions suggest that these political choices were based on astute analyses of how to accomplish their broader goals.

Even while both Turkey and Britain claimed affection for (and from) the Kurds, the activity of the people Jordi Tejel calls 'borderlanders' clearly demonstrated their own demands. While some preferred the political independence of a state, and some sought a more amorphous autonomy, most seemed intent on

40 Peter Sluglett, *Britain in Iraq: Contriving King and Country, 1914–1932,* 2007, 78–79; H.I. Lloyd, 'The Geography of the Mosul Boundary', *The Geographical Journal* 68, 1926, 109.

maintaining their livelihoods and connections which were inconsistent with the European border-making project. As he pointed out, their activism influenced the post-war settlements in myriad ways.[41]

In the end, it seemed that many of Mosul's Kurdish majority preferred the status quo of no effective central government. If that was the goal, disruption would be an obvious method to achieve it. Accepting payments from Turkish and British governments wanting to control them, or for disrupting the 'other side', was simply an added benefit. As Wendelmoet Hamelink and Hanifi Bariş wrote: 'Instead of defining the fragmented structure of Kurdish politics as primitive and primordialist, one could also explain this feature as an important mechanism to deliberately avoid being incorporated into a central state structure.' They relied on recited songs (*kilamên dengbêjan*) to analyze Kurdish political activism, concluding:

> We suggest that the fact that the Kurds have no nation-state of their own cannot be explained by sheer failure on the part of Kurdish nobility, but that the element of deliberate choice to avoid and evade the state is also involved. Although this is not a mainstream understanding of freedom and independence in the era of nationalism, it is clearly a no less valuable line of thought. The Kurds did not only resist incorporation in state-structures when they were pressured to do so, they also prevented 'states from springing up among them' until the early twentieth century.[42]

The Kurds were hardly unique in this desire to avoid being incorporated into the new nation-state structures of the post-war period. Exploring the history of the mountain peoples over a large swathe of mountainous Asia, James Scott described 'shatter zones or zones of refuge':

> Virtually everything about these people's livelihoods, social organization, ideologies, and (more controversially) even their largely oral cultures, can be read as strategic positionings designed to keep the state at arm's length. Their physical dispersion in rugged terrain, their mobility, their cropping practices, their kinship structure, their pliable ethnic identities, and their devotion to

41 Tejel, 'Making Borders from Below', 1–16.

42 Wendelmoet Hamelink and Hanifi Barış, 'Dengbêjs on Borderlands: Borders and the State as Seen through the Eyes of Kurdish Singer-Poets', *Kurdish Studies* 2/1, 2014, 36. Their framework relies on James C. Scott's work (see footnote 43 *infra*).

> prophetic, millenarian leaders effectively serve to avoid incorporation into states and to prevent states from springing up among them.[43]

This was clearly not only an Asian phenomenon. As Kate Brown argued about European borderlands: 'Nation itself worked in a colonial pattern as a formula to replaced localized identities and cultural complexities, which made modern governance so difficult in places like the borderlands … The gift of marginality lies in the amorphous, hybrid flexibility of a place where cultures and historical periods have accumulated in sedimentary layers, the latest innovations unheeded, the long arm of authority distant and weak.'[44]

Conclusion

The Lausanne Conference set out to complete the final treaty from World War I but was unsuccessful in resolving one of the most important issues. It would take another conference in Istanbul, a series of meetings in Geneva, and a League of Nations Commission to decide which state would get the contested Mosul region. In the end, the League of Nations awarded Mosul to Iraq, on the condition that the British mandate be extended for 25 years.[45] As consideration shifted from demographics ('who were the governed?') to the state, the Commission focused on economic and political issues. The five years of British occupation proved pivotal, as Mosul's economy and transportation infrastructure had been successfully redirected to the south and integrated into Iraq.

Nonetheless, both Turkey and Britain claimed Mosul not only because it was

43 James C. Scott, *The Art of Not Being Governed : An Anarchist History of Upland Southeast Asia*, 2009, x. Scott turns arguments about civilizing mountain people on their head. 'The huge literature on state-making, contemporary and historic, pays virtually no attention to its obverse: the history of deliberate and reactive statelessness. This is the history of those who got away, and state-making cannot be understood apart from it.'

44 Kate Brown, *A Biography of No Place: From Ethnic Borderland to Soviet Heartland,* 2004, 2, 11–13. Writing about the Ukranian-Polish-Jewish-German borderlands, Brown could be describing the inter-tribal rivalries and disputes that condemned the Kurds to a lack of state organization: 'Yet it was not the sheer desire for annihilation alone, but visions of progress and a better future, that dictated the shape of destruction of the borderlands. The *kresy* was considered backward, in dire need of cultural and economic elevation. Improvements conceived for the borderlands led to the death or exile of large segments of the population and the isolation and regression of the region.'

45 The Commission had been concerned about the treatment of minorities should Iraq become independent sooner. The League revisited these issues when they decided in 1932 to admit Iraq as a member.

sitting on a sea of oil. In 1923, both Turkey and Britain viewed it as even more important because it formed an area that both Britain and Turkey considered essential for the safety of their new states, even for their survival. The government of Turkey feared that Kurds living in Mosul under a hostile foreign Iraq mandate would encourage Kurds within Turkey to resist Turkish authority. At the same time, King Faisal and the British were worried that Kurds living in Mosul under a hostile foreign Turkish state would encourage Kurds to resist Iraq's government.

But the Lausanne Conference was to focus not on defence, but instead on the Wilsonian framework, in which territories were to be assigned based on the taxonomic characteristics of their population. The League of Nations had overseen a variety of these deliberations, in which they sought to forestall border wars (still ongoing in Central and Eastern Europe in the years following World War I) by asking people to 'elect' their affiliation in disputed regions. The system assumed that each person had one predominant identity, and that this identity necessarily determined their political preference.

In Mosul, it seems that everyone agreed that the Kurds were the predominant group. Both Turkish and British/Iraqi leaders tried to convince the Lausanne Conference, and then the League of Nations, that the Kurds were 'their' people, similar and loyal to them. The Kurds seemed to accept neither affiliation. Some supported the British, others supported the Turks, and many appeared to change their 'loyalty' at will. As one Kurdish farmer explained to the Commission, he wanted no government in principle, but he would accept the one currently existing.[46]

Perhaps it will help to remember that Kurds' loyalty remained tied to their status as borderlanders, and the whole Paris/Lausanne project of self-government paradoxically threatened their own continuing survival. As Hamelink and Barış have argued, it is important to recognize their actions in the Mosul dispute as neither treacherous nor nationalist. Each country participating in the Lausanne Conference represented a state, and the contestants insisted on interpreting Kurds and their behaviour as 'belonging' in their state. The only way that the Kurds could introduce their own political agenda was to disrupt the allocation of their lands to one state or the other. In this, they had much in common with diverse global communities who used a variety of strategies to actively assert their agency as opponents to the nation-state.

Nonetheless, in the end the 'Mosul Question' was not resolved based on the new Paris System. All agreed in the end that 'the governed' were overwhelmingly

46 League of Nations Secretariat, S14 File D18.

Kurdish. None of the contestants for Mosul trusted that the Kurdish majority could fit into the new system. The struggle at Lausanne, the last of the World War I treaties, gave way to the League of Nations' Mosul Commission, which recommended that the decision would be based not on identity but on economics, politics, and protection – the needs of a non-majority state. Despite their efforts to disrupt the march of the centralized nation-state, the borderlanders found themselves divided and dominated, an outcome inconsistent with the assumptions underlying the Lausanne process.

10

Turkey and the Division of the Ottoman Debt at Lausanne

Patrick Schilling and Mustafa Aksakal

In March 1923, during the break in the Lausanne Conference talks, Ankara's chief negotiator and the future successor to Mustafa Kemal (hereafter Atatürk), İsmet İnönü (hereafter İsmet), likened the Allies' refusal to make concessions with regard to the Ottoman debt to an open invitation to resume war.[1] İsmet's comment underscores the critical importance which the question of what should happen to the debt owed by the Ottoman state occupied in the eyes of the Ankara government. This chapter examines the negotiations over the fate of the debt at Lausanne from the perspective of Ankara, drawing on the conference proceedings, diplomatic correspondence, parliamentary minutes, memoirs and diaries, newspaper articles, and the few relevant secondary publications on this issue.

The chapter consists of three parts, each of which focuses on a key aspect of the debt negotiations at Lausanne: the first part analyses the Ankara government's decision, at the outset of the negotiations, to take on a share of the Ottoman debt. The second examines the very different interpretations held by the Turkish and Allied delegations as to the relationship between the Ankara government and the Ottoman state, with important implications for how to handle the debt. The third part focuses on the negotiations over the currency in which the Turkish state would pay its share of the Ottoman debt, which dominated the proceedings during the second half of the Lausanne Conference.

1 İsmet to Paris Embassy, telegram, 26 March 1923, in *Lozan Telgrafları II (Şubat-Ağustos 1923)*, ed. Bilal N. Şimşir, 1994, 178.

The Turkish delegation's approach to the debt negotiations, this chapter suggests, was informed by conflicting considerations. The Ankara government was adamant that Turkey needed to be fully independent and sovereign, an aim which had informed the armed struggle led by Atatürk between 1919 and 1922, was enshrined in the National Pact of 1920, and was repeated again and again by the Turkish negotiators at Lausanne. Independence meant freedom from European political and financial control, but it also meant freedom from the legacy of the defunct Ottoman Empire, and from any obligations which this legacy might impose on the nascent Turkish state. Yet this insistence on Turkish sovereignty and independence was tempered by the desire to come to an agreement with the Allies which – the Ankara government hoped – would grant Turkey full membership in the post-war international order and, with it, access to international credit and trade. The tension between these conflicting aims is evident throughout the debt negotiations at Lausanne.

During the final decades of its existence, the Ottoman Empire contracted a large amount of foreign debt. The settlement of this debt was now to be regulated by the Treaty of Lausanne. The Empire took out its first foreign loan in 1854 to finance its participation in the Crimean War. Over the following two decades, the Empire contracted further foreign loans at increasingly unfavourable interest rates until, in 1876, the Istanbul government found itself forced to declare a total default on interest payments on foreign loans. Political pressure from European governments whose subjects had invested heavily in Ottoman bonds (particularly France), and the Ottoman government's own desire to maintain access to foreign credit markets, pushed the Ottoman government to renegotiate terms with foreign bondholders. These negotiations culminated in the Decree of Muharrem, promulgated by Sultan Abdülhamid II on 20 December 1881. The decree provided for the establishment of the Ottoman Public Debt Administration (hereafter OPDA), an organization charged with the collection and administration of certain Ottoman revenues for the service of the foreign loans contracted by the Empire.[2] On paper the OPDA was a private institution, headquartered in Istanbul and presided over by a council consisting of representatives of French, German, British,

2 The revenues ceded to the Ottoman Public Debt Administration were the revenues from the Ottoman salt and tobacco monopolies, the stamps and spirits tax, the fish tax, the silk tithe of a number of Ottoman districts, the Bulgarian tribute payments to the Ottoman Empire, the revenue of Eastern Rumelia, and the surplus of the Cyprus revenue. Murat Birdal, *The Political Economy of Ottoman Public Debt: Insolvency and European Financial Control in the Late Nineteenth Century*, 2010, 7.

Austro-Hungarian, Italian, Dutch, and Ottoman holders of Ottoman bonds.[3] Yet despite the council's ostensibly private nature, council members maintained close ties with their home governments. It is thus not surprising that, in the eyes of many Ottomans, the OPDA appeared as a tool for European interference in the internal affairs of the Empire.[4]

The establishment of the OPDA improved the Ottoman Empire's international credit standing and permitted the Empire to contract further foreign loans over the subsequent decades, to the extent that 'in the years leading up to World War I, the Ottoman government […] used external borrowing as the basic method of financing its budget deficits.'[5] By the time of the outbreak of the First World War in 1914, the Ottoman foreign debt stood at 140 million British pounds (or about 155 million Turkish gold lira, at an exchange rate of 1.1 Turkish lira to the pound),[6] and external debt repayments made up more than one-third of the Ottoman budget.[7] Around sixty per cent of the Ottoman debt was held by French investors, with the share held by German investors a distant second at twenty per cent, and British investors holding less than fifteen per cent.[8]

To finance its participation in the First World War, the Ottoman government contracted further loans from its German and Austro-Hungarian wartime allies.[9] It also sold a small number of war bonds to its own citizens. Yet the most important means by which the Ottoman government financed its war effort was the issue of paper bills, or *kaime*. These bills were endorsed by the council of the OPDA, which during the war was composed of only Ottoman, German, and Austro-Hungarian members (the French, British and Italian members having left the council at the outbreak of the war). They were backed by a combination of gold deposited in banks in Berlin and Vienna by the governments of Germany and Austria-Hungary (later confiscated by the Allies) and of German treasury bonds. In 1918, the total

3 For a detailed account of the history of Ottoman foreign borrowing from 1854–1875 and of the events culminating in the establishment of the OPDA, see Birdal, *The Political Economy of Ottoman Public Debt*, 17–54.
4 Donald Blaisdell, *European Financial Control in the Ottoman Empire: A Study of the Establishment, Activities and Significance of the Administration of the Ottoman Public Debt*, 1966 (originally published 1929), 181–182.
5 Şevket Pamuk, 'The Ottoman Economy in World War I', *The Economics of World War I*, eds. Stephen Broadberry and Mark Harrison, 2005, 126.
6 Pamuk, 'The Ottoman Economy', 114.
7 Z.Y. Hershlag, *Turkey: The Challenge of Growth*, 1968, 21.
8 Pamuk, 'The Ottoman Economy', 114.
9 Pamuk, 'The Ottoman Economy', 128.

amount of paper money in circulation reached 161 million Ottoman lira.[10] By the time the Armistice of Mudros was signed on 30 October 1918, therefore, the Ottoman Empire had accumulated a significant amount of debt, as a result of both its pre-war and its wartime borrowing. What to do about the Ottoman debt emerged as one of the key issues to be resolved at Lausanne.

Turkey Takes on a Share of the Ottoman Debt

As the Frenchman Hervé Alphand pointed out in an early study of the division of the Ottoman debt at Lausanne, there existed numerous historical precedents on which the participants in the conference could draw as they debated how to resolve this question.[11] The division of a state's public debt among its successors was an internationally accepted principle (even though European Continental and British jurists disagreed over whether this was a binding rule of international law or merely a moral obligation),[12] and most international treaties regulating cases of state succession included provisions for the division of the public debt of the dismembered or cessionary state.[13] These included the peace treaties signed between the Ottoman Empire's war-time allies – Germany and Austria-Hungary – and the victorious Allied Powers following the end of the First World War. The Treaty of Versailles contained provisions for states assuming control of formerly German territory to take on a share of the German pre-war debt;[14] the Treaty of St. Germain provided for the division of the Austro-Hungarian public debt among that empire's successor states.[15]

Delegates at the Lausanne Conference could also look back to specifically Ottoman precedents.[16] The 1878 Treaty of Berlin, the 1881 Ottoman-Greek Con-

10 By the end of the war, the value of this paper currency, as compared to that of gold, had declined five-fold. Pamuk, 'The Ottoman Economy', 128–129; Blaisdell, *European Financial Control*, 184–187; William H. Wynne, *State Insolvency and Foreign Bondholders, Volume II: Selected Case Histories of Governmental Foreign Bond Defaults and Debt Readjustments*, 1951, 482–483.

11 Hervé Alphand, *Le Partage de la Dette Ottomane et Son Règlement*, 1928, 7.

12 M.H. Hoeflich, 'Through a Glass Darkly: Reflections upon the History of the International Law of Public Debt in Connection with State Succession', *University of Illinois Law Review* 1, 1982, 65–66.

13 For a useful overview of various historical cases, see Gaston Jèze, *Le Partage des Dettes Publiques au Cas de Démembrement du Territoire*, 1921, 22–28.

14 Articles 254–257 of the Treaty of Versailles.

15 Article 203 of the Treaty of St. Germain.

16 On these earlier divisions of the Ottoman debt, see İbrahim Sıtkı, *La Répartition de la Dette Publique Ottomane par les Traités de Paix*, 1935, 62–106.

vention, and the 1912 Treaty of Ouchy between Italy and the Ottoman Empire all contained provisions for the various states which had gained control of a piece of Ottoman territory as a result of these treaties to also take on a share of the Ottoman debt.[17] The Treaty of London, signed on 30 May 1913 to settle the outcome of the First Balkan War, similarly adopted the principle that the Ottoman debt should be divided between the Ottoman Empire and those Balkan states which had acquired Ottoman territory as a result of the war; it also established a commission to determine how the Ottoman debt should be divided in this case. It was on the basis of the conclusions reached by this commission that the 1920 Treaty of Sèvres, forced on the defeated Ottoman Empire by the Allies, sought to divide the Ottoman debt in the aftermath of the First World War.[18]

Yet there existed another kind of precedent as well: cases in which a successor state had refused to take on the debt of its predecessor. After the Franco-Prussian War of 1870–1871, the German Empire had refused to take on any part of the French public debt for which it might have become liable as a result of its occupation of Alsace-Lorraine (in return, the Treaty of Versailles exempted France from taking on a share of the German public debt following its recapture of Alsace-Lorraine after the First World War).[19] In a similar vein, the United States had refused to accept liability for the share of the Spanish public debt attributable to Cuba following its de facto annexation of this Spanish colony in 1898.[20]

A more recent and – from the perspective of the Ankara government – potentially more relevant example was the Bolshevik government's repudiation, in February 1918, of the entirety of the public debt accrued by its Tsarist predecessor. Writing a few years after the event, the Soviet jurist Evgeny Korovin justified this decision by arguing that in the case of a state's political transformation, the new regime was not liable for the debt of its predecessor; this debt should be seen as the personal debt of the old regime, and the new regime was thus in no way responsible for its repayment.[21] While the Bolshevik repudiation of the Tsarist debt was met by repeated and strident protest on the part of a number of European

17 Articles 9, 33, and 42 of the Treaty of Berlin; Article 10 of the Convention of Constantinople; Article 10 of the Treaty of Ouchy.

18 Articles 241–243 of the Treaty of Sèvres.

19 Jèze, *Le Partage des Dettes Publiques*, 26.

20 Hoeflich, 'Through a Glass Darkly', 51–56.

21 Cited in Alexander Nahum Sack, *Les Effets des Transformations des États sur leurs Dettes Publiques*, 1927, 68. In this regard, the Bolsheviks broke with the precedent set by the French revolutionary government, which after the revolution of 1789 had committed to honouring the debts of the French monarchy. See Hoeflich, 'Through a Glass Darkly', 62.

governments (notably France, whose citizens had invested heavily also in Russian bonds), these protests had not succeeded in convincing the Bolshevik government to reverse its decision.[22]

The situation in which the Turkish nationalist government in Ankara found itself on the eve of the Lausanne Conference bore certain similarities to that of the Bolshevik government in 1918: on 1 November 1922, just weeks before the conference was to commence at Lausanne, the Turkish Grand National Assembly had voted to abolish the Ottoman Sultanate, leaving the Ankara government solely in charge of what remained of the former Ottoman state. It is therefore perhaps not surprising that during the parliamentary debates on 3 November, over the line to be followed by the Turkish delegation to Lausanne, several deputies suggested that the Ankara government should entirely repudiate the Ottoman debt. Articulating a line of reasoning which foreshadowed that of Korovin a few years later, Mehmed Vehbi Efendi, the Minister of Religious Affairs and Pious Endowments and a representative for the Central Anatolian province of Konya, argued that:

> … this Government [*Hükümet*] has no debt. This is a new Government, and it has no contract or agreement with Europe regarding any debt. Yes, in the time of the old Istanbul Government, some loans from Europe occurred, some agreements and contracts happened [were made]. Let them find the Government which signed those contracts; let them ask for [the debt repayment] from [that government] […] Did this Government take shape on the ruins of the old Government? Was it newly created [*Yeniden mi meydana gelmiştir*]? It was newly created. Its account books, its records, everything was newly created, and therefore this Government is not and cannot be indebted to Europe in any way.[23]

This was not the position taken by the Ankara government, however. The 1920 National Pact, which the Turkish nationalist government regarded as its founding charter and which provided the general framework for the positions taken by the Turkish representatives at Lausanne, did not call for the repudiation of the Ottoman debt, but merely stated that 'the payment conditions of our debt whose amount is still to be determined [*tahakkuk edecek düyunatımızın şerait-i*

22 John Landon-Lane and Kim Oosterlinck, 'Hope Springs Eternal … French Bondholders and the Soviet Repudiation', Working Paper CEB 05–013.RS, Université Libre de Bruxelles, 2005, 5–7.

23 T.B.M.M. Zabıt Ceridesi, Devre 1, Cilt 24, İctima Senesi 3, 3 November 1922, 348.

tesviyesi]' should not in any way hinder the country's ability to develop economically.[24] Accordingly, point 10 on the list of instructions handed by the Turkish cabinet to İsmet prior to the Turkish delegation's departure for Lausanne stated that the Ottoman debt should be divided between Turkey and 'the countries that have separated from us [*bizden ayrılan ülkelere*].'[25]

In line with these instructions – and contrary to rumours circulating in the early days of the conference that Ankara might renege on its share of the Ottoman debt[26] – İsmet proposed during the opening session of the Third Commission of the Lausanne Conference (which was tasked with the resolution of economic and financial questions) on 27 November 1922 that the Ottoman debt should be divided among all those states which had acquired formerly Ottoman territory as a result of the First World War, as well as states which had acquired Ottoman territory at an earlier date but had not yet taken on a corresponding share of the Ottoman debt. He went on to announce that 'the Government of the Grand National Assembly of Turkey recognized its due share in the debt of the former Ottoman Empire.'[27] The chief Allied negotiators – Camille Barrère for France and Lord Curzon for Britain – accepted this basic principle.[28]

The Turkish readiness to take on a share of the Ottoman debt stood in sharp contrast to the reluctance of other Ottoman successor states to do the same. While he would eventually sign off on the Lausanne settlement of the Ottoman debt, the Greek chief delegate, Eleftherios Venizelos, initially offered a variety of reasons why his country should not be held liable for its share of the debt. These included the claim that the division of a state's debt among its successors was not a settled principle of international law;[29] the dire economic straits in which Greece found

---

24 Images of the original document can be found at 'Misak-ı Milli Kararları', in *Hukuk Ansiklopedisi*, https://hukukbook.com/misak-i-milli/.

25 Bilal N. Şimşir, *Lozan Telgrafları: Türk Diplomatik Belgelerinde Lozan Barış Konferansı. Cilt I: Kasım 1922-Şubat 1923*, 1990, xiv.

26 Hüseyin Cahid, 'Siyasiyat: Düyun-ı umumiye müessesesinin namusuyla oynamamalı', *Tanin*, 4 December 1922; 'Lozan sulh konferansı muhabir-i mahsusumuzun işaratı: Pazartesi 27 Teşrin-i sani: Maliye komisyonu', *İkdam*, 3 December 1922.

27 *Lozan Barış Konferansı Tutanaklar – Belgeler, Birinci Takım Cilt III: Üçüncü Komisyonun Tutanakları ile Raporları*, ed. Seha L. Meray, 1993, 3; *Lausanne Conference on Near Eastern Affairs, 1922–1923: Records of Proceedings and Draft Terms of Peace*, 1923 (hereafter *Lausanne Conference*), 539.

28 *Lozan Barış Konferansı Tutanaklar – Belgeler, Birinci Takım Cilt III*, 3–4; *Lausanne Conference*, 539–540.

29 This assertion was consistent with the consensus developed by British and American jurists over the course of the nineteenth century, according to which there existed a moral obligation for successor states to share in the debt of their predecessor, but no legal obligation. This was

itself at present; the fact that none of the loans taken out by the Ottoman Empire had supposedly been used to benefit the inhabitants of that part of the Ottoman Empire which Greece had seized during the Balkan Wars; and, most intriguingly perhaps, the argument that the loss of that territory had not in any way diminished the overall revenues of the Empire (and therefore the Empire's ability to pay its debt) as any revenue derived from it was more than offset by the military expenditures necessary for the Empire to maintain control of these provinces.[30] The chief Albanian delegate Mehdi Frashëri – who had served the Ottoman Empire as a high-ranking civil servant until the Albanian declaration of independence in 1912 – followed a similar line of reasoning, arguing that the devastation which the Balkan and World Wars had wrought on Albania made it impossible for the country to pay a share of the debt. He also stated that it would be unjust to ask Albania to participate in the Ottoman debt, as the Ottoman state had not made any kind of productive investments in Albania.[31] The Yugoslav delegation took a different approach, arguing that the division of the Ottoman debt among the Balkan states had already been settled in the aftermath of the Balkan Wars, and that there was therefore no need to include any provisions on this matter in the Lausanne Treaty.[32] The fact that the final text of the Lausanne Treaty did include the Balkan states among those Ottoman successors liable for a share of the Ottoman debt eventually led the Yugoslav delegation to refrain from signing the treaty.[33]

Why, in contrast, did the Ankara government prove willing to take on a share of the Ottoman debt? In their analysis of the contrasting attitudes of the Austrian, Soviet, and Turkish governments to the debts of their predecessor states in the aftermath of the First World War, Moore and Kaluzny have argued that each government's decision about whether or not to repudiate the debt of its predecessor was determined by the value which it placed on continuing access to international credit. They suggest that, for the embattled Bolshevik government, the immediate financial benefit of cancelling debt repayments outweighed the longer-term damage which the repudiation of the Russian debt would do to the international

---

in opposition to the Continental European consensus, which held that a legal obligation in this regard *did* exist. Hoeflich, 'Through a Glass Darkly', 65–66; Jèze, *Le Partage des Dettes Publiques*, 6.

30 *Lozan Barış Konferansı Tutanaklar – Belgeler, Birinci Takım Cilt III*, 8–10, 59, 163, 243.

31 *Lozan Barış Konferansı Tutanaklar – Belgeler, Birinci Takım Cilt III*, 223–224.

32 *Lozan Barış Konferansı Tutanaklar – Belgeler, Birinci Takım Cilt III*, 13.

33 *Conférence de Lausanne sur les Affaires du Proche-Orient (1922–1923). Recueil des Actes de la Conférence. Deuxième Série, Tome I: Procès-Verbaux et Documents Relatifs à la Seconde Partie de la Conférence (23 Avril-24 Juillet 1923)*, 1923, 503–505; Alphand, *Le Partage de la Dette Ottomane*, 28–29.

credit standing of the Soviet state. By contrast, the Turkish and Austrian governments regarded access to international credit as critical to their future economic development. They therefore agreed to honour the commitments contracted by their predecessors, in the hope that this would demonstrate their creditworthiness in the eyes of international lenders.[34]

The Turkish delegation was certainly aware that their country's continued access to international credit depended on a satisfactory resolution of the question of the debt at Lausanne.[35] Yet there were arguably also broader considerations at play. Elaborating at Lausanne on the Ankara government's position on economic and financial matters, İsmet stated that, while 'the economic and financial development of Turkey depended on its full and complete independence,' the country also 'fervently desired to maintain economic relations with other countries on the basis of reciprocity and international law.'[36] İsmet's comments demonstrate Ankara's basic commitment to the existing international order, in contrast to the Bolsheviks. Ankara was therefore keen to show that – as Baskın Oran has put it – it was not 'anti-system.'[37] From this perspective, taking on a share of the Ottoman debt can be seen as a price which the Ankara government felt it had to pay to be admitted into the capitalist international order.

This was a significant concession for the Turkish government to make, both in terms of principle and in terms of its impact on the Turkish economy. The formula which the Lausanne negotiators eventually agreed on for the division of the Ottoman debt was based on the so-called 'principle of the proportion of

34 Lyndon Moore and Jakub Kaluzny, 'Regime change and debt default: the case of Russia, Austro-Hungary, and the Ottoman Empire following World War One', *Explorations in Economic History* 42, 2005, 237–258.

35 In his memoirs, İsmet recounted a private conversation with Lord Curzon during the conference, in which the latter complained about the Ankara delegation's intransigence and threatened that the British government would not authorize any loans to Turkey in the future if Turkey refused now to accede to the Allies' demands. İsmet İnönü, *İsmet İnönü'nün Hatıraları: Büyük Zaferden Sonra Mudanya Mütarekesi ve Lozan Antlaşması*, 1998, 130.

36 *Lozan Barış Konferansı Tutanaklar – Belgeler, Birinci Takım Cilt III*, 3; *Lausanne Conference*, 539. These comments foreshadowed Atatürk's opening address to the Izmir Economic Congress, which was held between 17 February and 4 March 1923 and played an important role in establishing the principles according to which the economy of the Turkish state would be organized. In his address, Atatürk emphasized that, despite his government's insistence on Turkey's complete political and economic independence, Ankara would welcome foreign investment in the Turkish economy. Vedat Eldem, *Harp ve Mütareke Yıllarında Osmanlı İmparatorluğu'nun Ekonomisi*, 1994, 159.

37 Baskın Oran, 'Lausanne Barış Antlaşması', *Türk Dış Politikası: Kurtuluş Savaşından Bugüne Olgular, Belgeler, Yorumlar. Cilt I: 1919–1980*, ed. Baskın Oran, 2001, 218.

revenues:'[38] as framed in Article 51 of the Lausanne Treaty, the share of the Ottoman debt which each of the Ottoman successor states would assume was to be proportionally equal to the contribution which the formerly Ottoman territory acquired by that state had made to the overall Ottoman state revenue during the financial years 1910–1911 and 1911–1912. This division of the Ottoman debt was almost exactly the same as that provided for in the 1920 Treaty of Sèvres – a treaty whose signature by the now-defunct Ottoman government in Istanbul the Ankara government had refused to recognize.[39] According to the post-Lausanne calculations of the OPDA, this division left Turkey responsible for well over 60% of the total Ottoman debt, which amounted to roughly 107 million gold lira.[40] As we shall see below, the Turkish government was able to repeatedly negotiate reductions of its debt with holders of Ottoman bonds in the years after the signing of the Lausanne Treaty, but debt repayments would nevertheless continue to form a not insignificant drain on the Turkish budget.

The Ottoman Debt and the Question of State Succession

While the Allied and Turkish negotiators at Lausanne agreed quickly on the principle of the division of the debt, other issues proved much more controversial. One major disagreement between the two sides emerged over the division of the debt accrued by the Ottoman Empire during the First World War. This disagreement was rooted in different conceptions of the relationship between the Ankara government and the Ottoman state: the Turkish delegation argued that the state which they represented was but one of many successor states of the Ottoman Empire to have emerged in the aftermath of the First World War, and that the Ottoman war debt should be divided between all these states. The Allies, on the other hand, maintained that Turkey was not merely a successor but rather the continuation of the Ottoman state, and should therefore be solely responsible for the repayment of the Ottoman war debt.[41]

The question of the Empire's war debt was raised by Hasan Bey, the chief

38 *Lozan Barış Konferansı Tutanaklar – Belgeler, Birinci Takım Cilt III*, 42; *Lausanne Conference*, 576.

39 Article 243 of the Treaty of Sèvres.

40 Şükrü Saraçoğlu, 'Borçlar Meselesinin Halli', *Ülkü Halkevleri Mecmuası* 1/5, 1933, 338.

41 For a survey of the debates over whether Turkey should be considered the continuing or successor state of the Ottoman Empire in international law, see Emre Öktem, 'Turkey: Successor or continuing state of the Ottoman Empire?', *Leiden Journal of International Law* 24, 2011, 573–577.

Turkish negotiator on economic questions, during the first session of the finance sub-commission, on 30 November 1922. In his opening comments to the commission, Hasan Bey proposed a modification to the way in which the Ottoman public debt had been divided in the Treaty of Sèvres. Article 242 of that treaty had foreseen a twofold division of the Ottoman debt. The annuities on loans which the Ottoman Empire had contracted prior to the outbreak of the First Balkan War on 17 October 1912 would be divided between the Ottoman Empire and those Balkan states (including Albania) which had annexed territories from the Ottoman Empire as a result of the Balkan Wars; the remainder of the annuities for the payment of which the Ottoman Empire remained liable after this initial division, as well as the annuities on further loans which the Ottoman Empire had contracted between 17 October 1912 and 1 November 1914 (the day after the Empire's entry into the First World War on 31 October 1914), were to be divided between the Ottoman state and those states in whose favour territory was detached from the Ottoman Empire as a result of the Treaty of Sèvres.[42] In this provision, in other words, the Ottoman state remained solely responsible for the repayment of any debt which it had contracted after its entry into the First World War. If the Treaty of Lausanne did not modify these dates, Turkey would find itself solely responsible for the repayment of the Ottoman war debt.

Hasan Bey therefore proposed that the sub-commission should set a new date for the second division of the Ottoman debt: instead of 1 November 1914, the cut-off point should be 30 October 1918, the date of the Armistice of Mudros which, he argued, marked the point when the Ottoman Empire had ceased to exist. This way, the debt which the Ottoman Empire had contracted over the course of the First World War would be divided among all the states, including Turkey, which had succeeded to the Empire in the aftermath of the First World War.[43]

The Turkish delegation justified its position by arguing that the Ottoman Empire had come to an end, and had left behind a number of successor states. The state led by the Ankara government was but one of these successor states, no different from any of the others. As Hasan Bey explained to the Turkish parliament during the break in the Lausanne negotiations in March 1923: 'Turkey is not the continuation [*mabaadı*] of the Ottoman Empire … [The Ottoman Empire] is our father, but we are not the only son. There are other offspring besides us. Therefore, we are faced with the settling of debts contracted on the property of a father who

42 Article 242 of the Treaty of Sèvres

43 *Lozan Barış Konferansı Tutanaklar – Belgeler, Birinci Takım Cilt III*, 165–166.

has died and left many children.'[44] From this perspective, he insisted, it was only just that the Ottoman war-time debt should be included in the total of the Ottoman debt to be divided. This argument can be seen as an early articulation of what would become a key element of the Turkish Republic's ideological underpinnings: that the events between the ceasefire of Mudros and the signing of the Lausanne Treaty marked a profound historical rupture separating the Ottoman past and the Turkish Republican present.[45]

The Turkish position on the Ottoman war debt also reflected a particular understanding of the nature of the Ottoman polity during its final years. In his speech to the fourth general meeting of the Third Commission on 13 January 1923, İsmet made the point that the Ottoman Empire had, since the revolution of 1908, been a constitutional, unitary state. The inhabitants of all those territories which had been a part of the Empire during the First World War had, until the armistice of 1918, continued 'to take part in the Government of the Empire through constitutional organs.' Based on the principle 'which had constantly been brought forward in recent years' that peoples should be held responsible for the actions of their governments, he argued that all territories which had formed part of the Ottoman Empire during the First World War should therefore be held equally liable for the Ottoman wartime debt.[46] Hasan Bey, in his presentation to the Turkish Grand National Assembly on 3 March 1923, made a similar point:

> … we want to set aside a part of [the Ottoman war debt] for the territories that fought with us and next to us. Even if this is a war debt, this cannot be a reason to forgive the share [of the debt] of these parts of the country which were as responsible for the war as us.[47]

---

44 T.B.M.M. Gizli Celse Zabıtları, Devre 1, Cilt 28, İctima Senesi 3, 3 March 1923, 42.

45 As a Turkish history textbook published in the early 1930s put it: '… with the ceasefire of Mudros and the Sèvres Treaty, the Ottoman Empire accepted its own disappearance; with the ceasefire of Mudanya and the Lausanne Treaty a new Turkish State gave notice of its own existence.' Türk Tarihi Tetkik Cemiyeti, *Tarih IV: Türkiye Cümhuriyeti*, 1931, 131.

46 *Lozan Barış Konferansı Tutanaklar – Belgeler, Birinci Takım Cilt III*, 28–29; *Lausanne Conference*, 565–566.

47 T.B.M.M. Gizli Celse Zabıtları, Devre 1, Cilt 28, İctima Senesi 3, 3 March 1923, 44. These arguments had some basis in reality: the Ottoman parliament which sat – with interruptions – from May 1914 until its dissolution in December 1918 did indeed include elected representatives from all parts of the Empire. Yet it should also be noted that the 1914 elections had been neither particularly free nor particularly fair, and that the parliament which resulted from them had relatively limited influence on Ottoman wartime policy. See Hasan Kayalı, 'Elections and the electoral process in the Ottoman Empire, 1876–1919', *International Journal of Middle East Studies* 27/3, 1995, 279–281.

The Allies rejected the Turkish arguments. In their eyes, the state headed by the Ankara government was the direct continuation of the Ottoman state; neither the abolition of the Ottoman sultanate nor the loss of the majority of the Ottoman pre-war territories changed this state of affairs. The Ankara government could not reject the responsibilities which it had taken on in its earlier, Ottoman, incarnation. In the words of Maurice Bompard, any given political regime was 'the continuation of the regime which precedes it; a country cannot, by changing its name and its regime, escape the obligation which it has previously incurred.' The Ottoman government had entered the war in 1914 of its own accord; the Ankara government, as its continuation, should take on the entirety of the debt which had financed the Ottoman war effort. The final date for the division of the Ottoman debt fixed in the Treaty of Sèvres should therefore remain unchanged.[48]

The Allied negotiators also rejected the Turkish argument that – given the constitutional nature of the Ottoman Empire during its final years – all former Ottoman subjects bore equal responsibility for the Ottoman participation in the First World War, and could therefore reasonably be expected to take on a share of the war debt. They argued instead that the inhabitants of those formerly Ottoman territories other than that controlled by the Ankara government (i.e., the inhabitants of the Ottoman Arab provinces) had taken part in the war unwillingly, and should not be asked to shoulder a share of the debt burden. In the words of Lord Curzon, the former Ottoman subjects outside Anatolia 'had little sympathy' for the Ottoman involvement in the First World War, and 'had not taken a notable part' in it.[49] Curzon's French colleague, Maurice Bompard, made a similar point, arguing that these former Ottoman subjects had taken part in the war 'against their will.' Bompard also cited the recent precedent of the peace treaty of St. Germain, concluded between Austria and the Allies in September 1919: that treaty had, he pointed out, exempted the new states of Croatia and Slovenia from paying any part of the Habsburg Empire's wartime debt, on the grounds that the inhabitants of these formerly Habsburg territories had – like the inhabitants of the Ottoman Arab territories – been dragged into the war against their will.[50]

48 *Lozan Barış Konferansı Tutanaklar – Belgeler, Birinci Takım Cilt III*, 170.
49 *Lozan Barış Konferansı Tutanaklar – Belgeler, Birinci Takım Cilt III*, 30; *Lausanne Conference*, 567.
50 *Lozan Barış Konferansı Tutanaklar – Belgeler, Birinci Takım Cilt III*, 29; *Lausanne Conference*, 566. This was only a partial reading of the terms of the Treaty of St. Germain. That treaty indeed held Austria solely liable for the repayment of war bonds held by individuals and institutions outside the borders of the former Habsburg Empire. Yet the treaty exempted Austria from responsibility for the repayment of war bonds that were held by the

Despite the strenuous objections of the Turkish delegation, the Allied position on the Ottoman war debt prevailed. Article 50 of the Lausanne treaty enshrined 1 November 1914 as the final date for the division of the Ottoman public debt. This left the Turkish state solely liable for all of the debt the Ottoman Empire had accumulated during the First World War.[51]

A second major point of discussion during the first half of the debt negotiations also hinged on whether Ankara was the continuation or merely a successor of the Ottoman state. This was the division of the nominal capital of the Ottoman debt: should the Lausanne Treaty provide for the division of the debt's capital, or only for the division of the annuities payable on that debt? The division of the debt's nominal capital was initially proposed by Hamid Bey, speaking for the Turkish delegation, at the third session of the finance sub-commission on 5 December 1922. He argued that the division of the capital of the Ottoman debt was a matter both of practical consideration and of principle. In practical terms, the Turkish government was concerned that – if the capital of the Ottoman debt was maintained intact – Turkey might in future be held responsible for the potential failure of the Empire's other successor states to pay their share of the annuities on the debt.[52] As a matter of principle, he repeated the now familiar argument about the lack of continuity between the Ottoman Empire and the Turkish state. The Ottoman Empire had come to an end, and there could therefore be no question of maintaining the Ottoman debt intact; rather it would be appropriate to create in

other successor states of the Habsburg Empire or their citizens. *Cf.* Article 205 of the Treaty of St. Germain.

51 Article 50 of the Treaty of Lausanne. Article 62 of the Treaty of Lausanne freed Turkey from the obligation to repay the war-time loans made to the Ottoman Empire by Germany and Austria-Hungary; Article 58 of the Treaty permitted the Allies to confiscate the gold which Germany and Austria-Hungary had deposited in German and Austrian banks to back the first war-time issue of Ottoman paper bills. The Ottoman war debt for which Turkey therefore remained solely liable as a result of the Lausanne settlement were the internal loan contracted by the Ottoman government in 1918 and the 161 million lira in paper currency issued over the course of the war.

52 This was not, as İbrahim Sıtkı pointed out, an unreasonable concern. Earlier divisions of the Ottoman debt had maintained the capital of the debt intact, only enjoining the Empire's successor states to pay a share of the annuities on the debt. When the successor states failed to meet their obligations in this regard – as they almost invariably did – the Ottoman Empire was forced to continue paying the entirety of the annuities by itself. This was a situation which the Turkish government was keen to avoid. Sıtkı, *La Répartition de la Dette Publique Ottomane*, 138.

place of the Ottoman debt as many separate debts as there were Ottoman successor states: a Turkish debt, a Greek debt, a Syrian debt, etc.[53]

The Allied negotiators expressed sympathy for the Turkish government's concerns regarding the potential non-payment of the Ottoman debt by other Ottoman successor states, but initially rejected Hamid Bey's proposal. Maurice Bompard argued that, in practical terms, it would be too complicated to replace all extant Ottoman bonds with bonds issued by the Ottoman successors; also dividing the capital of the Ottoman debt would result in the Ottoman Empire's creditors making a loss on their investment, as the market value of any bonds issued in place of the existing Ottoman bonds would be much lower than that of the original bonds.[54] Bompard also, once again, rejected the Ankara delegation's argument that Turkey was merely one Ottoman successor state among many. The Allied governments would never accept, he declared, that 'the Turkish Government was not responsible for the transactions carried out by the Ottoman Empire or that it was not tied to the Ottoman Empire by any bond of solidarity.'[55]

Over the following weeks, the division of the debt's capital became a major source of conflict between various members of the Turkish delegation. Mehmed Cavid, the former Ottoman finance minister and prominent Unionist whom İsmet had privately invited to Lausanne to advise the Turkish delegation on financial matters, agreed with Bompard's assessment that dividing the capital was logistically difficult, if not impossible. Hasan Bey shared Cavid's viewpoint. Yet other members of the Turkish delegation – notably Rıza Nur, the second delegate – believed that it was critically important that the capital of the debt be divided, and that Turkey thereby be able to disassociate itself completely from the share of the debt held by other Ottoman successor states. They were eventually able to convince İsmet of both the necessity and the feasibility of dividing the debt's capital. In a private conversation with Bompard in early January 1923, İsmet once again broached the division of the capital of the Ottoman debt.[56]

The Allied delegates expressed considerable frustration at the Turkish attempt to revisit a matter which they believed had already been settled. Yet ultimately, they agreed to accept the Turkish demands. Article 46 of the Draft Treaty of Peace which the Allies presented to the Turkish delegation on 25 January 1923 provided for the division of the nominal capital of the Ottoman Public Debt

53 *Lozan Barış Konferansı Tutanaklar – Belgeler, Birinci Takım Cilt III*, 181.
54 *Lozan Barış Konferansı Tutanaklar – Belgeler, Birinci Takım Cilt III*, 181.
55 *Lozan Barış Konferansı Tutanaklar – Belgeler, Birinci Takım Cilt III*, 277.
56 Cavid, *Meşrutiyet Ruznamesi, IV. Cilt*, trans. Hasan Babacan and Servet Avşar, 2015, 439–444; Rıza Nur, *Hayat ve Hatıratım, III. Cilt*, 1967, 1121–1126.

between the Ottoman successor states 'if one of the States so requests within a period of three months from the date of the coming into force of the present Treaty,' and 'with the consent of the bondholders.'[57] In a further concession to the Turkish delegation in the final days of the first round of negotiations at Lausanne, the Allies agreed to omit the words 'with the consent of the bondholders' from the Article.[58] The provisions outlined in Article 46 of the draft terms of peace would ultimately be enshrined in Article 49 of the Treaty of Lausanne.[59] Despite the initial position of the Allies that the Ottoman public debt needed to be maintained indivisible and whole, the negotiations at Lausanne thus ultimately resulted in the division of the nominal capital of the Ottoman debt among all Ottoman successor states.[60]

From the point of view of state succession, the Lausanne Treaty's provisions regarding the Ottoman war debt and the division of the nominal capital of the Ottoman debt are difficult to reconcile. While the Treaty's holding Turkey solely liable for the Ottoman war debt reflects the Allied argument that Turkey was the continuing state of the Ottoman Empire, the division of the Ottoman debt's nominal capital is in line with the Ankara government's contention that Turkey was but one Ottoman successor state among many. Hervé Alphand noted this contradiction in his study. Arguing that the Lausanne Treaty as a whole reflected the premise that Turkey was the continuation of the Ottoman Empire,[61] he nevertheless acknowledged that

> … the division of the capital [of the Ottoman public debt] cannot be justified legally if one accepts that … Turkey continues the personality of the Ottoman

57 *Lausanne Conference*, 704.

58 *Lausanne Conference*, 832.

59 Article 49 of the Treaty of Lausanne. This Article also provided for the establishment of a separate commission consisting of representatives of all Ottoman successor states and of representatives of the council of the OPDA to work out the details of the division of the capital of the debt. This commission met eleven times between July and October 1925, and settled most of the technicalities relating to the division of the capital. Alphand, *Le Partage de la Dette Ottomane*, 95–109.

60 Rıza Nur described this outcome as 'a major victory.' Cavid was less impressed, noting that the substantial efforts of the Turkish delegation in this largely symbolic matter might have been more usefully expended on other issues. Rıza Nur, *Hayat ve Hatıratım, III*, 1126; Cavid, *Meşrutiyet, IV*, 468.

61 This was also the interpretation of the League of Nations arbiter Eugene Borel, in his 1925 ruling on the Treaty's provisions regarding the division of the Ottoman Public Debt. 'Affaire de la dette publique ottomane (Bulgarie, Irak, Palestine, Transjordanie, Grèce, Italie et Turquie), 18 Avril 1925,' *Recueil des Sentences Arbitrales*, Vol. I, United Nations, 2006, 573.

> Empire. In providing for the division of the nominal capital of the Debt, the treaty is in contradiction with itself.[62]

We can explain this seeming contradiction with reference to what the legal scholar Michael Hoeflich has termed the 'principle of expediency.' Hoeflich argues that the degree to which successor states have agreed to take on the debt obligations of their predecessors has historically been determined not by this or that principle of international law, but by the solution the states involved in the division of the debt regarded to be expedient in the particular historical circumstances they found themselves in.[63] This insight can help to explain the Lausanne Treaty's seemingly contradictory provisions regarding the division of the Ottoman war debt and of the debt's capital. Both sides were keen to make peace and found themselves forced to make concessions to achieve that aim. Just as the Turkish delegation was eventually forced to accept responsibility for the Ottoman war debt, so the Allied negotiators found it expedient to accede to Turkish demands for the division of the capital of the Ottoman debt – even if these concessions ran counter to their respective positions on the relationship between Turkey and the Ottoman Empire.

The *Kuponlar Meselesi*

Whereas the division of the Ottoman war debt and of the nominal capital of the debt dominated negotiations over the Ottoman public debt during the first half of the Lausanne conference, the main issue during the second round of negotiations was what the Turkish press termed the *kuponlar meselesi*, or the 'matter of the [debt] coupons.' This issue – which for a time threatened to derail the peace negotiations entirely – concerned the currency in which the Turkish government would repay its share of the Ottoman debt to the bondholders.

In accordance with the Decree of Muharrem of 1881 and subsequent loan contracts, holders of Ottoman bonds could choose to redeem their debt coupons either in return for Turkish gold lira, or in return for an equivalent sum in British pounds or French francs. Between 1913 and 1923, the lira had suffered a sevenfold decrease in value compared to gold, largely as a result of the multiple issues of paper currency to finance Ottoman participation in the First World War. This meant that debt repayments would become ruinously expensive for the Turkish

62 Alphand, *Le Partage de la Dette Ottomane*, 36–37.
63 Hoeflich, 'Through a Glass Darkly,' 65–69.

state if the bondholders were able to demand repayment in gold lira. Repayment of the debt in British pounds would be equally expensive, as the lira's loss of value relative to the pound closely mirrored its loss of value relative to gold.[64] As the Turkish prime minister Hüseyin Rauf explained in a speech to the Turkish parliament during the break in the Lausanne negotiations in March 1923, the Ankara government was therefore determined to avoid any provisions in the Treaty that could be interpreted to commit it to repaying its share of the Ottoman debt in either gold lira or British pounds.[65]

The currency in which the Ottoman debts would be repaid had been discussed repeatedly within the Turkish delegation during the first half of the Lausanne negotiations. In the course of these discussions, Cavid suggested to İsmet that Ankara should negotiate directly with the bondholders' representatives on this matter, with a view to coming to an agreement separate from the prospective Lausanne Treaty. İsmet considered Cavid's proposal, but ultimately did not take any action.[66] The matter was thus left to be resolved during the second half of the conference.

The Ankara government considered this issue to be of primary importance for Turkey's future economic independence, and not one that they could afford to compromise on. This position was in line with the stipulation in the Turkish National Pact, cited above, that the payment conditions of the Turkish share of the Ottoman debt should not prejudice Turkey's economic development in any way. The importance which the Ankara government attached to this issue emerges clearly from the telegram sent by İsmet to the Turkish ambassador in Paris on 26 March 1923 – cited in the introduction to this chapter – in which he stated that Allied demands that Turkey repay its debt in either gold or British pounds were akin to a declaration of war.[67] Once the negotiations resumed, the Ankara government reminded the Turkish delegation of the importance of this issue: concessions could be made on other questions, but 'an acceptable peace is tied to the issue of the coupons [...] being resolved in accordance with our point of view.'[68] Turkish intransigence in the 'matter of the coupons' is also reflected in a

64 For a table showing the changes in the lira's value compared to a variety of currencies between 1913 and 1923, see Eldem, *Harp ve Mütareke Yıllarında*, 144.
65 T.B.M.M. Gizli Celse Zabıtları, Devre 1, Cilt 28, İctima Senesi 3, 4 March 1923, 85. See also the comments to parliament of Ali Cenani Bey two days later: T.B.M.M. Gizli Celse Zabıtları, Devre 1, Cilt 28, İctima Senesi 3, 6 March 1923, 167.
66 Cavid, *Meşrutiyet Ruznamesi, IV*, 423, 472, 479.
67 İsmet to Paris Embassy, telegram, 26 March 1923, in *Lozan Telgrafları II*, 178.
68 Hüseyin Rauf to İsmet, telegram, 7 June 1923, in *Lozan Telgrafları II*, 407.

number of telegrams from Sir Horace Rumbold – who headed the British delegation during the second half of the Lausanne negotiations – to Lord Curzon, where he highlighted the 'fanaticism' of the Turks in this regard.[69]

The Allied negotiators, for their part, were equally adamant that the final version of the Treaty should in no way prejudice the rights of the bondholders, a large majority of whom were their own citizens, and who stood to make a significant loss on their investments if Turkey failed to repay its share of the debt in gold lira or the foreign-currency equivalent. They therefore insisted that the Treaty needed to include some form of commitment by the Ankara government to honour the debt repayment conditions agreed to by the Ottoman government. General Maurice Pellé, who headed the French delegation during the second round of negotiations, made this very clear in his statement to the committee on financial and economic matters on 2 May 1923. He stated that the Ankara government needed to respect the engagements made between the Ottoman state and the bondholders regarding the currency of payment, and went on to point out that 'the Powers incontestably had the right to protect the interests of their nationals' in this regard.[70] Pellé's declaration was supported by both the British and the Italian delegations.

Over the course of the following two and a half months of negotiations, the two sides made various attempts to bridge the gap between their respective positions. During the third session of the financial committee on 9 May, the Turkish delegation proposed the suppression of Article 56 of the draft terms of peace, which had confirmed the terms of the Decree of Muharrem and of later loan contracts between the Ottoman state and its debtors. Any confirmation of these decrees by the Treaty of Lausanne, the Ankara government feared, could be read as a confirmation of the bondholders' right to be repaid in gold lira or the foreign-currency equivalent. They therefore proposed to replace Article 56 by a declaration to the bondholders, issued separately from the Treaty, in which they committed to honouring the contracts between the Ottoman state and the bondholders while reserving the right to revisit the question of the currency of payment at a future time. The Allies agreed to the replacement of Article 56 by a Turkish declaration, but

69 Rumbold to Lord Curzon, telegram, 14 June 1923, in *Documents on British Foreign Policy 1919–1939. First Series, Volume XVIII: Greece and Turkey, September 3, 1922–July 24, 1923*, eds. W.N. Medlicott, Douglas Dakin and M.E. Lambert, 1972 (hereafter *DBFP*), 870; Rumbold to Curzon, telegram, 16 June 1923, *DBFP*, 873; Rumbold to Curzon, telegram, 18 June 1923, *DBFP*, 877.

70 *Conférence de Lausanne. Deuxième Série, Tome I*, 191.

objected to any reservation on the question of currency of payment. The meeting was adjourned without any resolution of the matter.[71]

A few days later, at a private meeting with General Pellé, İsmet suggested a different resolution to the issue. He proposed that his government would repay the bondholders in French francs, at that currency's current valuation.[72] This was a compromise that the Turkish cabinet had previously agreed would be acceptable: the value of the franc had also decreased over the war years, and the lira's loss of value compared to the franc had therefore been less severe than its loss of value against gold and the pound.[73] Paying the debt in francs would thus only increase the Turkish debt burden by a factor of 2.5 (as compared to payment in Turkish paper lira).[74] The French government, however, rejected this proposal.[75] A Turkish delegation headed by Hasan Bey made a similar proposal at a meeting with the bondholders' representatives in Paris in late May. The bondholders also rejected the Turkish proposal, agreeing only to revisit the issue once the peace negotiations between Turkey and the Allies had been concluded.[76]

In a third attempt to break the deadlock, the Allied negotiators, in a private meeting with İsmet on 10 June, proposed to revisit the initial Turkish proposal to make a declaration to the bondholders, subject to a reservation on the currency of payment.[77] While İsmet accepted this proposal in principle, this attempt at compromise foundered on disagreement between the two sides on the precise wording of the Turkish declaration, and on the increasing intransigence of the

71 *Conférence de Lausanne. Deuxième Série, Tome I*, 203–206.

72 Ebuzziya-zade, 'Altın Faiz Meselesi', *Tevhid-i Efkar*, 17 May 1923, in Ahmet Temiz, 'Velid Ebuzziya'nın Mektuplarına Göre Lozan', MA thesis, Marmara University, 2005, 162.

73 Eldem, *Harp ve Mütareke Yıllarında*, 144.

74 T.B.M.M. Gizli Celse Zabıtları, Devre 1, Cilt 28, İctima Senesi 3, 4 March 1923, 85.

75 Ebuzziya-zade, 'Akd-ı Sulhdaki Müşkülat', *Tevhid-i Efkar*, 20 May 1923, in Temiz, 'Velid Ebuzziya', 166; 'Le payement des coupons', *Le Temps*, 16 May 1923. Not all bondholders were happy about the Allied negotiators' refusal to consider the Turkish proposal. In a reader's letter to *The Economist* printed after the peace negotiations had concluded, a British holder of Ottoman bonds argued that the Turkish proposal had constituted his best chance of recouping at least part of his investment, as the Turkish government was clearly not willing or able to repay its debt in gold or British pounds. He also pointed out, not unreasonably, that the French government paid its pre-war debt in paper francs, and so could not rightly insist that Turkey pay its debt in gold. 'Lausanne and the Ottoman Debt', *The Economist*, 28 July 1923, 151.

76 Ebuzziya-zade, 'Hasan ve Şefik Beyler eli boş döndüler!', *Tevhid-i Efkar*, 30 May 1923, in Temiz, 'Velid Ebuzziya', 235–236; Alphand, *Le Partage de la Dette Ottomane*, 111.

77 Ebuzziya-zade, 'Faizler Meselesinde Fransızların Attıkları Hatve!', *Tevhid-i Efkar*, 15 June 1923, in Temiz, 'Velid Ebuzziya', 332; Rumbold to Curzon, telegram, 10 June 1923, *DBFP*, 848.

French delegation.[78] By 20 June, negotiations had ground to a halt. The conference, Rumbold admitted in a personal telegram to Lord Curzon, had sunk into a 'slough of despond,'[79] and there were growing concerns that the negotiations would break down over this issue.[80]

The Turkish press took a keen interest in the ins-and-outs of the negotiations over the *kuponlar meselesi*. In his detailed, near-daily dispatches from the conference, published in the newspaper *Tevhid-i Efkar*, the journalist and prominent supporter of the Turkish nationalist government, Velid Ebuzziya, commented frequently on the negotiations over the Ottoman debt. Ebuzziya framed the *kuponlar meselesi* as a matter of crucial importance to Turkey's economic independence. If the Allies were permitted to insist on the repayment of the Ottoman debt in gold or British pounds, he wrote, Turkey would 'be economically enslaved to [European] capitalists.' He went on to list the consequences of such an economic enslavement: 'no school will be opened, no scientific progress will be made, no road or railroad will be constructed, no factory will be founded, no branch of industry will be created, no bank will be opened, in short our country will be deprived of all the kinds of material and spiritual development which it needs and is capable of.' The resolution of the *kuponlar meselesi* in line with the position of the Ankara delegation was therefore key for Turkey's future economic development.[81]

The *kuponlar meselesi* was finally resolved during what was, by all accounts, an exhausting and bad-tempered series of meetings between the Turkish and Allied delegations which lasted from 7 July until the early hours of 9 July. In return for Turkish agreement to maintain the pre-war concessions of several European companies operating in Turkey, the Allies agreed that the final draft of the

78 Ebuzziya-zade, 'Konferansta formül meselesi maskaraliği', *Tevhid-i Efkar*, 24 June 1923, in Temiz, 'Velid Ebuzziya', 373–374; Rumbold to Curzon, telegram, 18 June 1923, *DBFP*, 879.
79 Rumbold to Curzon, telegram, 21 June 1923, *DBFP*, 883.
80 The French government appears to have seriously considered abandoning the negotiations over Turkish intransigence in the *kuponlar meselesi*. In a note which he submitted to the Turkish president Celal Bayar in 1950, Fuat Baban – a former high-ranking Ottoman bureaucrat – recounted a conversation which he had in Paris with Georges Clinchant, the head of the office of Eastern and Asian affairs at the French foreign ministry, during the final days of the Lausanne conference. Clinchant told Baban that the French government would break off negotiations within three days due to Turkish obstinacy on the currency of debt repayment. Baban rushed to Lausanne to inform İsmet about this conversation. İsmet professed to be unaware of any French plans to abandon the conference. Soon after this, the peace treaty was signed. Celal Bayar Archive, Folder 38, Document 21. Our thanks to Ozan Ozavci for bringing this document to our attention.
81 Ebuzziya-zade, 'Esaret-i İktisadiyeye Razı Olamayız', *Tevhid-i Efkar*, 12 July 1923, in Temiz, 'Velid Ebuzziya', 452.

peace treaty should contain no article confirming the Decree of Muharrem or decrees relating to later Ottoman loans. They also agreed to free the Turkish delegation from the obligation to address a note to the bondholders confirming these decrees. The Allies insisted only that they would make a declaration during the final meeting of the second committee to the effect that they reserved the right of future intervention in order to safeguard the rights and interests of the Ottoman bondholders; the Turkish delegation would be able to make a counter-declaration during the same meeting insisting on their own point of view.[82] This compromise effectively left the question of the currency in which the debt would be repaid as a matter for the Ankara government to settle directly with the bondholders after the peace negotiations had concluded.

This resolution of the *kuponlar meselesi* owed much to the obstinacy of the Turkish delegation. Yet it owed also to the growing disunity among the Allies during the final weeks of the conference. The British held that 'this matter [was] predominantly a French interest' – as the great majority of bondholders were French citizens – and that only 'relatively unimportant British interests [were] involved.' They were therefore reluctant to see the peace negotiations break down over this issue,[83] a position which appears to have been shared by the Italian delegation.[84] Other delegations at the conference also became increasingly impatient with the Allies' failure to come to an agreement with Ankara. Venizelos approached Rumbold on 28 June 1923 to urge that the Allies conclude peace with Turkey as soon as possible.[85] In a meeting with Rumbold a few days later, the Romanian and Serbian delegates similarly expressed their desire for a swift conclusion of the negotiations, and stated that 'they considered that a rupture of conference for sake of bondholders [was] difficult to justify.' The French delegation, Rumbold concluded in a telegram to Curzon from 3 July, was increasingly 'isolated' in its insistence that the matter of the coupons be resolved in favour of the European bondholders.[86] They were therefore ultimately unable to resist British pressure to agree to the compromise which resolved this issue.[87]

82 Ebuzziya-zade, 'Nihayet sulha doğru son hatveyi atabildik!', *Tevhid-i Efkar*, 13 July 1923, in Temiz, 'Velid Ebuzziya', 455–461; Rumbold to Curzon, telegram, 7 July 1923, *DBFP*, 929–934; Rumbold to Curzon, telegram, 10 July 1923, *DBFP*, 937–944.
83 Curzon to Rumbold, telegram, 13 June 1923, *DBFP*, 858.
84 *DBFP*, 911, fn.3.
85 *DBFP*, 907, fn.1.
86 Rumbold to Curzon, telegram, 3 July 1923, *DBFP*, 919–920.
87 The Marquess of Crewe to Curzon, telegram, 6 July 1923, *DBFP*, 927–928; Rumbold to Curzon, telegram, 7 July 1923, *DBFP*, 928–929.

Velid Ebuzziya regarded the agreement reached in the final days of the Lausanne negotiations as a success for the Turkish delegation. He particularly singled out the resolution of the *kuponlar meselesi* for praise. By resolving this issue in line with their own point of view, he wrote, the Turkish delegation had guaranteed their country's future economic independence.[88] Cavid – who was not invited to the second round of the negotiations and whose assessment of the negotiating tactics of the Turkish delegation became increasingly critical as the conference wore on – nevertheless agreed that the Lausanne Treaty was a great victory which had 'delivered [Turkey] from servitude.' Yet he also cautioned that İsmet's obstinacy in the negotiations over the *kuponlar meselesi* had undermined the country's standing in the eyes of international investors, and would make it more difficult for Turkey to contract international loans in the future. Without such loans, he wrote, 'the country [was] condemned to remain in its current devastated state for a long while.'[89]

There is little doubt that the Turkish government was able, in the drawn-out negotiations with its creditors which began in August 1925, to use the terms of the Lausanne Treaty to its advantage. Having long insisted that it would only be able to pay its debt in paper lira, the Turkish government eventually accepted – as part of the contract signed with its creditors on 13 June 1928 – to pay its debt in gold lira (or rather in the equivalent amount in British pounds).[90] Yet in return, it was able to extract significant concessions from the bondholders. These included a major reduction in the annual debt repayments to be made by the Turkish state and, even more importantly, a fundamental reduction in the status of the OPDA. Whereas the OPDA had previously been directly in charge of collecting and administering a part of the Ottoman revenues to pay the Empire's debt,[91] the 1928 contract placed the Turkish state in charge of collecting that part of its revenues pledged to the service of the debt. The status of the OPDA was reduced to that of an observer, a fact underscored by the removal of the organization's headquarters from Istanbul to Paris.[92]

Having escaped the tutelage of the OPDA, the Turkish government was able to negotiate a further reduction of its debt with the bondholders following the outbreak of the economic crisis of 1929. According to this new agreement with

88 Ebuzziya-zade, 'Nihayet'.

89 Cavid, *Meşrutiyet Ruznamesi, IV*, 559.

90 Alphand, *Le Partage de la Dette*, 116–117.

91 Although from 1920 onwards, the Turkish nationalist government had seized control of the revenues collected by the OPDA. Eldem, *Harp ve Mütareke Yıllarında*, 201–202.

92 Alphand, *Le Partage de la Dette*, 125–128.

the bondholders, signed on 23 April 1933, the total amount of the Turkish debt was reduced from roughly 107 million gold lira to about 8.5 million gold lira,[93] with annual payments fixed at 700,000 gold lira.[94] Even under this agreement, Hershlag pointed out, debt repayments accounted for between 13 and 18 per cent of the Turkish budget in the early 1930s. Yet this compared favourably to the more than one-third of the Ottoman budget of 1914–1915 which had been allocated to debt repayments.[95]

In his speech to the Turkish parliament on the eve of the ratification of the Lausanne Treaty on 23 August 1923, İsmet hailed the Treaty as a success for Turkish diplomacy.[96] With regards to the Treaty's provisions on the Ottoman debt, this seems like a fair assessment. While the Turkish delegation had not been able to get the Allies to agree to all of their demands – most notably on the division of the Ottoman war debt – the division of the capital of the Ottoman debt and, more significantly, the Turkish delegation's successful objection to the inclusion of any provisions on the currency of payment in the Treaty can be seen as diplomatic victories which permitted the Ankara government to eventually negotiate a significant lightening of its debt burden. As Cavid had warned, however, this victory came at the cost of temporarily reduced access to international capital markets. During the 1920s, as the Ankara government began to rebuild a country devastated by a decade of war, it was unable to contract any foreign loans for this purpose.[97]

93 This was the equivalent of about 80 million Turkish paper lira at the contemporary rate of exchange. Eldem, *Harp ve Mütareke Yıllarında*, 228.

94 Saraçoğlu, 'Borçlar', 340–341. Under this agreement, the Turkish government was able to finally liquidate its share of the Ottoman debt in 1954. Eldem, *Harp ve Mütareke Yıllarında*, 228.

95 Hershlag, *Turkey*, 21. *The Economist* commented that this final agreement had reduced Turkey's annual repayments of the Ottoman debt to 'manageable figures', thereby greatly improving the credit of the Turkish state. 'Turkey: Trade Agreements – Budget Balanced – Interest Rates', *The Economist*, 3 June 1933, 1191.

96 T.B.M.M. Zabıt Ceridesi, Devre 2, Cilt 1, İctima Senesi 4, 23 August 1923, 266.

97 Hershlag, *Turkey*, 88.

11

International Law and the Greek-Bulgarian and Greek-Turkish Population Exchanges

Leonard V. Smith

Population exchanges in South-Eastern Europe and Anatolia after the First World War marked the last stage of a protracted international project matching borders and peoples in ethno-national successor states to the multinational empires.[1] A term usually attributed to Lord Curzon became current as peace-making began, the 'unmixing' of peoples.[2] Essentially, the peacemakers had two broad choices – tailoring borders to peoples, or peoples to borders. Given that all the successor states sought to maximize borders they considered legitimized by both ethnicity and history, drawing actual borders proved a daunting task, the results of which pleased almost no one. Minority treaties and plebiscites sought to tailor peoples to boundaries, likewise with highly controversial results. Population exchanges took place on the fringes of the effective authority of the peacemakers, where drawing 'national' borders did not suit thousands of people and where neither plebiscites nor minority treaties proved feasible. Exchanges proved a simple if ultimately brutal means of 'unmixing.'

As Eric Weitz has argued, contemporary participants as well as historians

1 For a broader context see Leonard V. Smith, *Sovereignty at the Paris Peace Conference of 1919*, 2018, Ch. 3–4.

2 Opinions differ as to whether Lord Curzon ever actually used this expression or not. See the chapter by Lerna Ekmekcioglu in this volume, footnote 5.

regarded the exchanges as an embarrassing exception to the liberal principles motivating the Paris Peace Conference, principles underpinning both minority treaties and plebiscites. As he put it, population exchange as a policy was 'an intrinsic element of the principles enunciated at Paris.'[3] Liberalism extended its benefits not so much to human beings in general so much as to members of national communities, increasingly ethnic in nature. In an international system in which one nation inhabited one state, and in which 'ethnicity' and 'nation' became increasingly the same thing, exchanges provided the simplest way to determine the ethnic 'self' eligible for 'national self-determination.' Individuals of a certain ethnicity, the logic went, would want to live in their own self-determined, ethno-national state. Those who did not could legitimately be coerced into relocating anyway, in the name of peace and stability between and within the new states. Where nationalism conflicted with liberalism in Paris, nationalism usually won.

Population exchanges had a unique relationship to the international system as changes begun in Paris continued in Lausanne. Not all transfers of large numbers of people were considered equal in that system. The Great Powers could simply 'expel' rather than 'exchange.' The French, for example, removed some 150,000 persons deemed 'German' from reconquered Alsace and Lorraine.[4] Successor states, not the Great Powers who ostensibly directed peace-making after the First World War, initiated population exchanges. But the Great Powers accepted and legitimized exchanges as part of the international system, through agreements accepted as constituting international law.

Traditionally, the history of international law has tended toward exegesis, that is, largely decontextualized history not dissimilar to the history of theology. More recently, Marcus Payk has argued that 'the endeavour should be less about the history of international law and more about international law in history.'[5] If

3 Eric D. Weitz, 'From the Vienna to the Paris System: International Politics, and the Entangled Histories of Human Rights, Forced Deportations, and Civilizing Missions', *The American Historical Review* 113/5, 2008, 1313–1343.

4 Philipp Ther, *The Dark Side of Nation States: Ethnic Cleansing in Modern Europe*, trans. Charlotte Kreutzmüller, 2014, 68–70.

5 Marcus M. Payk, 'The History of International Law – or International Law in History? A Reply to Alexandra Kemmerer and Jochen von Bernstorff,' https://www.ejiltalk.org/the-history-of-international-law-or-international-law-in-history-a-reply-to-alexandra-kemmerer-and-jochen-von-bernstorff/. See also his *Frieden durch Recht? Der Aufsteig des modernen Vökerrechts und der Friedensschluss nach dem Ersten Weltkrieg*, 2018, and a précis in English, '"What We Seek Is the Reign of Law": The Legalism of the Paris Peace Settlement after the Great War', *European Journal of International Law* 29/3, 2018, 809–824.

international law can benefit from a more meaningful engagement of historical context, history can benefit from taking international law as something that shapes history, as well as being shaped by it. Previous historians have explored the population exchanges in the context of international law, such as through the 'human rights' perspective taken by Christa Meindersma.[6] Umut Özsu has considered the exchanges through the lens of World-Systems Theory, situating them in the history of global capitalism and the imperatives of the global division of labour.[7] This chapter considers the exchanges in the context of how international law underpinned the international system.

The Greek-Bulgarian and Greek-Turkish population exchanges became matters of international law through two bilateral conventions attached respectively to the Treaty of Neuilly (with Bulgaria, November 1919) and the Treaty of Lausanne (with Turkey, July 1923).[8] There has never been a clear distinction between the treaty and the convention as instruments of international law. Traditionally, treaties tended to define state relations, often between individual states.[9] According to British jurist Arnold McNair, the term 'treaty' tended to be reserved for the most consequential international agreements, such as those making alliances and ending wars. Conventions tended to cover multilateral activities, such as the Hague Conventions governing rules of warfare, or such matters as international transit or postage. For example, the signatories would seek to resolve the long-vexed question of navigation along the Turkish Straits through the Montreux Convention of 1936.[10]

Given the lack of a strict distinction between 'treaty' and 'convention,' and given that both had standing under international law, it would be a mistake to make too much of the distinction between the two terms. In fact, Bulgaria and the Ottoman Empire signed a bilateral convention in September 1913 to facilitate a 'voluntary' exchange, and discussions were underway for a similar convention between Greece and the Ottoman Empire when the First World War began.[11]

6 Christa Meindersma, 'Population Exchanges: International Law and State Practice,' *International Journal of Refugee Law* 9, 1997: Part I, 9/3, 335–363; Part II, 9/4, 613–653.
7 Umut Özsu, *Formalizing Displacement: International Law and Population Transfers*, 2015, esp. 70–98.
8 'Convention Between Greece and Bulgaria Respecting Reciprocal Emigration, 27 November 1919', *American Journal of International Law* (hereafter *AJIL*) 14/4, 1920, Supplement: Official Documents, 356–360; 'Convention Concerning the Exchange of Greek and Turkish Populations, 30 January 1923', *AJIL* 18/2, 1924, Supplement: Official Documents, 84–90.
9 Lord Arnold McNair, *The Law of Treaties*, 1961 (originally published 1938), 22–23.
10 Nihan Ünlü, *The Legal Regime of the Turkish Straits*, 2002.
11 Stephen P. Ladas, *The Exchange of Minorities: Bulgaria, Greece and Turkey*, 1932, 18–20.

As we will see, both post-war conventions on population exchange evolved as annexes to the treaties to which they were appended, the emphasis being more on the bilateral rather than multilateral nature of the conventions. They afforded the Great Powers both implication in and plausible deniability of the grim business of population exchange. This became particularly important in the Greek-Turkish exchange.

This chapter considers the Greek-Bulgarian and Greek-Turkish population exchanges at the intersection of the history of international law and the history of state sovereignty. The exchanges proved a critical episode in the construction of the ethno-national state itself. The complexities and dilemmas of ethnic difference that had so bedevilled drawing boundaries, minority treaties, and plebiscites in Central and Eastern Europe were reduced by the time of the Greek-Turkish exchange to a single criterion – religion as the sole determinant of ethnic identity. International law legitimized both exchanges, though the transfers themselves largely had already taken place. The conventions helped to create a largely fictional distinction between a 'voluntary' exchange between Greece and Bulgaria and an 'involuntary' exchange between Greece and Turkey. The legalism underpinning the exchanges also supported a mistaken impression that the Great Powers who still largely controlled the making of international law actually played the determining role in the movement of peoples along these two former fronts of the First World War. Through the exchanges, international law after the First World War served to articulate the purposes both of successor state nationalism and Great Power politics.

Both conventions on population exchange, and the treaties to which they were appended, served the same basic political purpose – the creation or affirmation of ethno-national states recognizable as such in the international system. But the differences in the two documents, in their origin, their content, and their application, speak to considerable changes that took place in that system in a relatively short period of time. I will begin each section with a discussion of the convention as written. I will then examine the evolving international system which produced the conventions and then proceeded to implement them as matters of international law.

The Greek-Bulgarian Exchange and the Individual Plebiscite

The 'voluntary' nature of the Greek-Bulgarian exchange was written into the language of the convention. The 'unmixing' of the two peoples would happen through personal decisions. Group particulars would be worked out between the two states. The preamble referred to Article 56, paragraph 2 of the Treaty of

Neuilly, which stated that the Principal Allied and Associated Powers 'consider it opportune' that such a convention exist, but that only plenipotentiaries from Greece and Bulgaria would actually sign it. The preamble demarcated the calculated distance between the Great Powers and the population exchanges, as well as a reliance on new international institutions, notably the League of Nations. The League, in helping to administer the transfers, would facilitate the incorporation of the exchanges into international law. Thus, individuals, states, Great Powers, and the League would all collaborate in relocating peoples along ethnic lines where they 'belonged,' in law as in fact.

The convention as written presumed a strong desire on the part of populations to self-designate and migrate to respective ethno-national states – a plebiscite at the level of the individual. The convention held that members of 'racial, religious or linguistic minorities' henceforth had a recognized right 'to emigrate freely to their respective territories' (Article 1). Bulgaria and Greece agreed 'not to place directly or indirectly any restriction on the right of emigration,' to the point of annulling existing domestic law (Article 2). But the convention remained silent on whether Greece or Bulgaria could actually facilitate emigration through encouragement, pressure, or outright coercion. The 'voluntary' act would consist of a declaration of the intent to emigrate before a mixed commission or its representative (Article 4). As was the custom at that time in the Balkans, adult men could make a declaration on behalf of wives and minor children. The mixed commission would comprise a Greek member, a Bulgarian member, and two members of neither nationality named by the Council of the League of Nations, one of whom the League Council would choose as president. In the case of a tie-vote, the president could vote twice (Article 8).

In addition to certifying the 'voluntary' nature of emigration, the mixed commission had the task of lowering financial barriers. Emigrants maintained unrestricted rights over moveable property (Article 10). Immoveable property (most commonly land and houses) would be assigned a value by the mixed commission, and that sum would be forwarded to the emigrant as an advance, 'according to the funds available' (Articles 11–12) – a dubious prospect given the penury prevailing in both Greece and Bulgaria after the war. Title to the transferred property would revert to the relevant states (Article 10), which, in theory, would supply the funds to compensate the former owner. The mixed commission had broad if unspecified powers to facilitate the liquidation of properties belonging to churches, schools, convents, hospitals, etc (Article 6). In short, the mixed commission would serve as an honest broker of persons and goods.

How had the machinery of making peace after the First World War produced such a convention? Defeated Bulgaria lost Western Thrace to victorious Greece through the Treaty of Neuilly. But having 'unmixed' the lands, how now to 'unmix' the peoples? Many Christians and Muslims spoke both Greek and Bulgarian, as well as Turkish.[12] Religious division within Christian Orthodoxy further complicated matters. Greek speakers recognized the Greek Patriarchate based in Constantinople. Most but not all Christian speakers of Bulgarian recognized the Bulgarian Exarchate, also based in Constantinople but separated from the Greek Patriarchate since the mid-nineteenth century. Bulgarian nationalists tended to make language the primary marker of Bulgarian ethnic identity. Greeks, on the other hand, generally emphasized religious adherence to the Patriarchate, at least in Western Thrace.[13]

On 25 July 1919, the New States Committee of the Paris Peace Conference received a proposal from the Greek delegation, to add clauses to a Greek treaty for minority protections.[14] The clauses would establish a mixed commission 'to superintend and facilitate emigration of Greeks resident in Bulgaria to Greece, and of Bulgarians resident in Greece to Bulgaria.'[15] Three days later, the committee sent a favourable report on the Greek proposal to the Supreme Council.[16] Indeed, the committee posited that facilitated migration 'might with advantage be extended to all Balkan countries,' and that such migration could 'do much to help a permanent settlement of the troubles which have so long affected the Balkans, and might be a valuable supplement to the clauses dealing with the protection of minorities.' At least on paper, the committee gave every indication of believing in genuinely 'voluntary' migration and annexed to its report a draft minority treaty with Bulgaria to protect those who wished to remain where they were.

The Supreme Council of the peace conference and its members still needed to articulate their precise relationship to any population exchange before they

12 A.A. Pallis endeavoured to categorize the various populations of Western Thrace using pre-war Ottoman and post-war censuses in 'Racial Migrations in the Balkans during the Years 1912–1924', *Geographical Journal* 66/4, 1925, 315–331, esp. 326–327.
13 Theodora Dragostinova, 'Speaking National: Nationalizing the Greeks of Bulgaria', *Slavic Review* 67/1, 2008, 154–181, esp. 162–164.
14 The Bulgarians would have preferred a bilateral convention to a multilateral treaty because the convention could have handled Greek-Bulgarian issues separately from those of the much larger Bulgarian communities in the new Serb-Slovene-Croat state.
15 Thirty-Seventh Meeting, New States Committee, 25 July 1919, in David Hunter Miller, *My Diary at the Conference of Paris* (hereafter *Miller Diary*), 21 Vols., 1924, Vol. 13, 306.
16 'Letter to the Council of Five on the Special Clauses Proposed by M. Veniselos', Thirty-Eighth Meeting, New States Committee, 28 July 1919, *Miller Diary*, Vol. 13, 309–321.

could finalize the treaty with Bulgaria.[17] On 19 November 1919, Frank Polk of the American delegation raised the issue of whether signing the treaty meant endorsing the exchange.[18] With President Woodrow Wilson seriously ill and with ratification prospects of the Treaty of Versailles withering in the Senate, Polk hesitated to agree to anything that might even hint at increased American involvement in European affairs should the exchange not go smoothly. Matsui Keishiro of Japan opined that all the Great Powers should sign, though he added that his government was unlikely to do so if the Americans declined.[19] Giacomo de Martino of the Italian delegation countered that signing the treaty with the exchange included constituted a 'moral obligation' on the part of the Great Powers to take 'an effective part in the execution of these clauses with Bulgaria by affixing their signatures thereto.' Allen Dulles of the American delegation suggested that as the exchange and minority provisions would come into effect 'under the aegis of the League of Nations,' perhaps it was not necessary for all the Great Powers to sign.

On 25 November, just two days before the signing of the Treaty of Neuilly, the Supreme Council formally established its distance from the population exchange.[20] The Council endorsed the conclusion of the Drafting Committee 'that the Treaty between Bulgaria and Greece relative to reciprocal immigration was in no way dependent upon the signature of the Bulgarian Treaty by the Principal Allied and Associated Powers.' De Martino renewed his protest, on the basis that 'the decisions already taken by the Council relative to affairs in the Balkans seemed to him to have created many opportunities for trouble in the future. As a general matter, he felt that the signatory Powers, ultimately responsible for maintaining the peace in the Balkans, should participate more actively in Balkan affairs.' Nevertheless, given the pressing need to conclude the treaty with Bulgaria, de Martino left the matter there. The exchange would come into effect through a convention signed by Greece and Bulgaria alone, signed the same day as the treaty. This distancing of the Great Powers from the population exchange set the pattern for the later convention between Greece and Turkey.

---

17 Ladas, *Exchange of Minorities*, 31–48.

18 'Notes of a Meeting of the Heads of Delegations of the Five Great Powers Held in M. Pichon's Room, Quai d'Orsay, Paris, on Wednesday, November 19, 1919, at 11:00 a.m.', *Papers Relating to the Foreign Relations of the United States, 1919: The Paris Peace Conference,* 13 Vols., 1942–1947 (hereafter *FRUS: PPC*), Vol. 9, 222.

19 Neither the United States nor Japan had declared war on Bulgaria, though both would sign the Treaty of Neuilly.

20 'Notes of a Meeting of the Heads of Delegations of the Five Great Powers Held in M. Pichon's Room, Quai d'Orsay, Paris, on Tuesday, November 29, 1919, at 10:30 a.m.', *FRUS: PPC*, Vol. 9, 332–333.

As Theodora Dragostinova has shown, 'voluntary' emigration presented Greek-speaking Bulgarians and Bulgarian-speaking Greeks with an unappealing choice.[21] They could choose to self-identify as minorities in states that had expressed a public preference that they leave, or they could become refugees, strangers in new lands, often with resentful neighbours with whom they happened to share a common language and/or religion. Moreover, Greeks and Bulgarians had asymmetrical responses to the convention. Greeks generally encouraged the 'return' of Greek Bulgarians, to bolster the presence of Greek speakers in newly acquired territories in Macedonia and Thrace. Bulgarians, on the other hand, generally wanted Bulgarians to remain in place as minorities, to support claims for border revision later.[22] Individually as well as collectively, people did not always want to 'unmix' according to state preferences. As late as the signing of the Treaty of Lausanne in July 1923, only 197 Greek families and 166 Bulgarian families had registered their desire to emigrate.[23]

Much more substantial population exchanges in Thrace occurred thereafter. Terrified Greeks fled Anatolia after the burning of Smyrna in September 1922. Their flight conflated categories of 'migrants' and 'refugees.' The Greek government, eager to settle the new arrivals, forcibly removed large numbers of Bulgarians in Western Thrace to other parts of Greece to make room.[24] Eventually, Bulgaria responded in kind toward its Greek minority. Many migrants made formal declarations to the mixed commission to try to protect as much of their property as possible, calling into question the 'voluntary' nature of such declarations. By the end of 1925, 154,691 people submitted declarations to the commission – 101,800 Bulgarians and 52,891 Greeks.[25] About 80,000 others migrated without making use of the commission, many of them Bulgarians who hoped eventually to return. But substantial numbers of people resisted 'unmixing' – indeed in roughly the same numbers as those who left. Some 140,000 Bulgarians chose to remain in Greece, and 12,000 Greeks chose to remain in Bulgaria.[26] The peacemakers, and

21 Theodora Dragostinova, *Between Two Motherlands: Nationality and Emigration among the Greeks of Bulgaria, 1900–1949*, 2011, 117–156.

22 Theodora Dragostinova, 'Navigating Nationality in the Emigration of Minorities between Bulgaria and Greece, 1919–1941', *East European Politics and Societies* 23/2, 2009, 185–212.

23 Dragostinova, 'Navigating Nationality', 194.

24 The population of Western Thrace previously classified as 'Muslim' combined mostly speakers of Bulgarian, Turkish, and Roma. Further precision remains at best problematic, as Greece stopped including religion in its census figures in 1913, and Bulgaria in 1912. Pallis, 'Racial Migrations in the Balkans', 320.

25 Dragostinova, 'Navigating Nationality', 186.

26 Dragostinova, 'Navigating Nationality', 186.

for that matter anyone else, could draw the conclusion that a 'voluntary' exchange was a confused and incomplete exchange.

The Greek-Turkish Exchange: Religion as Ethnicity

The Treaty of Lausanne, signed on 24 July 1923, replaced the stillborn Treaty of Sèvres, signed on 10 August 1920.[27] The Treaty of Sèvres, made with the regime of the Sultan in a partly occupied Anatolia, called for protections for minorities similar to those in minority treaties with the other successor states (Articles 140–151). These protections would cover a vestigial Turkey, following the de facto partition of Anatolia envisaged by the Treaty of Sèvres. Unlike the other minority treaties, however, protections would be supervised not by the League of Nations, but by the Allies themselves in association with the League Council.[28] No provisions were made for a population exchange, either in the Treaty of Sèvres itself or in any adjacent convention.

The convention on Greek and Turkish population exchange, signed along with the Treaty of Lausanne on 24 July 1923, opened a new chapter in the history of international population policy.[29] Parallel to the Greek-Bulgarian exchange, only Greek and Turkish representatives signed the convention. But the convention constituted an inseparable part of peace-making with the greatly transformed Turkish national state that succeeded the Ottoman Empire. According to the Lausanne convention, the Greek and Turkish states became the exclusive identifiers of peoples within their borders. Article 1 called for:

> … a compulsory exchange of Turkish nationals of the Greek Orthodox religion established in Turkish territory, and of Greek nationals of the Moslem religion established in Greek territory.

Gone was the inclusive reference to 'racial, religious or linguistic minorities' in the Greek-Bulgarian convention. 'Greek' and 'Turk' had ceased to be a matter of national spirit, culture, language, or even political loyalty. Least of all could ethnic identity remain a matter of personal choice. Religion became the exclusive

---

27 'Treaty of Peace Between the Allied Powers and Turkey, 10 August 1920', *AJIL* 15/3, 1921, Supplement, Official Documents, 179–295.

28 Turkey did not actually join the League of Nations until 1932.

29 'Convention Concerning the Exchange of Greek and Turkish Populations, 30 January 1923', *AJIL* 18/2, 1924, Supplement, Official Documents, 84–90.

marker of ethnicity, by state decree. Even convicted criminals and prisoners were to be expelled to their countries of religious origin (Article 6). Emigrants lost nationality upon departure and acquired a new nationality upon arrival (Article 7). Sovereignty in the ethno-national state required ethnic clarity. However, also for reasons of state, Christians in Constantinople and Muslims in Western Thrace were excluded from the exchange.[30] Other Greeks, notably the substantial community of Pontic Greeks in Eastern Anatolia, were not.[31]

The mixed commission, the linchpin of the 'voluntary' exchange between Greece and Bulgaria, became the instrument for classifying and dividing people and property between Greece and Turkey. The commission would comprise four members named by Greece, four by Turkey, and three named by the League, from countries that had not participated in the First World War (Article 11). As with Bulgaria and Greece, the commission would assess the value of properties that expelled individuals and communities could not take with them (such as churches and mosques). But transfers based on the liquidation of this property would occur only between states (Article 14). Displaced individuals and communities could collect compensation only from their new states of residence.

The mixed commission also had the vast but vaguely defined power 'to take the measures necessitated by the execution of the present convention and to decide all questions to which this convention may arise' (Article 12). This included the delicate issue of just how to determine who was subject to the exchange. Greek and Ottoman authorities had required a statement of religion in civil registers. But most Albanian speakers in Greece were Muslim, and followers of the 'Greek Orthodox' religion in Turkey could consider themselves Serbs, Romanians, Russians, or Arabs.[32] Greek speakers in Turkey could likewise adhere to Protestant, Catholic, or Jewish faiths. No religious conversion that could not be demonstrated to have taken place before 1 January 1922 could exempt an individual from the exchange. Through the mixed commissions, the very souls of the expelled population became indicators of successor state sovereignty.

30 Ladas estimates some 300,000 Christians in Constantinople and some 130,000 Muslims in Western Thrace. *Exchange of Minorities*, 400. Alexis Alexandris, on the other hand, estimates 110,000 Christians in Constantinople and 100,000 Muslims in Western Thrace. 'Religion or Ethnicity: The Identity Issue of the Minorities in Greece and Turkey', *Crossing the Aegean: An Appraisal of the 1923 Compulsory Population Exchange between Greece and Turkey,* ed. Renée Hirschon, 2003, 118, 122.

31 Volker Prott, *The Politics of Self-Determination: Remaking Territories and National Identities in Europe, 1917–1923*, 2016, 197–206.

32 See Ladas, *Exchange of Minorities*, 377–398.

What does the content of the convention say about what had changed in the international system and in international law under that system? The defeat of Greece by Turkey in 1922 also constituted a proxy defeat of the European empires on the winning side of the First World War. In treating successor Turkey as a negotiating partner rather than a defeated enemy, the Conference of Lausanne differentiated from the Paris Peace Conference. Lausanne served to demarcate the limits of Allied influence in Anatolia, and to incorporate Turkey into the new international system. As part of that settlement, it was for the Greek and Turkish successor states to decide on populations within their new borders, with the once-removed approval of the Great Powers. At the behest of the Allies, the Conference of Lausanne would implicate the League of Nations in the resulting brutal tailoring of populations to suit borders. The Great Powers would go to a good deal of trouble to keep the population exchange at arm's length, both as a matter of law and politically.

Until recently, the Conference of Lausanne and the Greek-Turkish population exchange maintained surprisingly distinct historiographies. Some of the most informative English accounts of the conference either scarcely mention the exchange or leave it aside altogether.[33] Historiography on the exchange has focused more on the human cost and on the experience of exchanged individuals.[34] Onur Yildirim has provided a much-needed addition to our understanding of the relationship between the conference and the exchange.[35]

Yildirim's central claim – that both the Greek and Turkish delegations arrived at Lausanne preferring compulsory exchange – puts state interests at centre stage. The Greeks saw compulsory exchange as a means of stabilizing domestic politics. Three kings reigned between 1920 and 1922, each with his own political friends and enemies. Prime Minister Eleftherios Venizelos had survived an assassination attempt, the ongoing threat of paramilitary violence, and electoral defeat in December 1920, only to return to lead the Greek delegation at Lausanne. Defeat against successor Turkey in 1922 exacerbated an existing, grave

33 Roderic H. Davison, 'Turkish Diplomacy from Mudros to Lausanne', *The Diplomats, 1919–1939*, eds. Gordon A. Craig and Felix Gilbert, 1953, 172–209; Briton Cooper Busch, *Mudros to Lausanne: Britain's Frontier in West Asia, 1918–1923*, 1976, 359–392; Erik Goldstein, 'The British Official Mind and the Lausanne Conference, 1922–1923', *Power and Stability: British Foreign Policy, 1865–1945*, eds. Erik Goldstein and B.J.C. McKercher, 2003, 185–206.

34 See, for example, Hirschon, ed., *Crossing the Aegean*; Bruce Clark, *Twice a Stranger: The Mass Expulsions that Forged Modern Greece and Turkey*, 2006.

35 Onur Yildirim, *Diplomacy and Displacement: Reconsidering the Turko-Greek Exchange of Populations, 1922–1934*, 2006.

refugee crisis. Compulsory population exchange, according to Yildirim, provided a way to address this crisis and to lay the demographic foundation for a more 'Greek' ethno-national state. The Turks, for their part, had broken with Allied peace-making and had waged war with Greece in the name of a more 'Turkish' post-Ottoman Turkey. Yet early republican Turkey still wanted recognition from an international system still led by the European imperial powers. Compulsory population exchange offered common ground to all of these parties.

As Yildirim has shown, Greeks, Turks, and the Allies also generally agreed on making ethnicity a function of religion. Christians became 'Greek' and Muslims 'Turkish.' No serious discussion of any other criteria took place, either within the Greek and Turkish delegations or at the conference itself. To be sure, the Turkish delegation in late November 1922 proposed a plebiscite in Western Thrace.[36] But given the dismal record of the plebiscite in Upper Silesia, not to mention the failed or partly failed plebiscites in Teschen, Wilna, and elsewhere, there was no reason to expect the Great Powers to accept the idea, let alone contribute the military resources necessary actually to carry out a plebiscite. The Allies, in short, and having just lost their proxy war through their Greek ally, needed the war in Anatolia to end by the simplest means available.

By 1922, the war between Greece and Turkey had effectively split the Allies. The French cared most about a stable border for their new mandate in Syria, and toward that end had ceded Cilicia to Turkey in the Treaty of Ankara of October 1921.[37] The French also held enormous amounts of Ottoman debt, the regularizing of which required an overall settlement with the new regime in Turkey. The Chanak Affair of 1922 fractured the coherence of the British Empire itself, as the self-governing Dominions declined to send assistance. As Erik Goldstein has shown, the British 'official mind' at Lausanne had plenty of reasons to settle with the new regime – the Turkish Straits, the disposition of Thrace and Mosul, as well as the Kurdish and Armenian lands, the fate of the Capitulations, and the future of the Caliphate. The imperial powers had compelling incentives to get population issues off the table.

As a result, most of the drama at the Conference of Lausanne about the compulsory population exchange revolved around avoiding responsibility for it. The protagonists sought to distance themselves from the exchange, even more overtly than the Paris Peace Conference had from the Greek-Bulgarian exchange. The

36 See Busch, *Mudros to Lausanne*, 366.

37 Yücel Güçlü, 'The Struggle for Mastery in Cilicia: Turkey, France, and the Ankara Agreement of 1921', *International History Review* 23/3, 2001, 580–603.

public sessions of Lausanne, published with remarkable speed as the official record, recorded elaborate performances of evasion and self-contradiction toward that end.[38]

At Lausanne, a First Commission on Territorial and Military Questions considered refugees, minorities, and population exchange mostly as interchangeable topics. On 1 December 1922, the commission heard a report from League of Nations High Commissioner for Refugees, Fridtjof Nansen. His report employed the circumspect language of the international civil servant, dispassionately laying out the issues handed to him by his political superiors. The League had asked Nansen, in his words, 'to bring some small relief with the funds placed at my disposal by the members of the League to the starving refugees of both nationalities' (113). The four Great Powers represented in Constantinople (Britain, France, Italy, and Japan) then charged him 'to initiate negotiations between the Turkish and Greek Governments with a view to the conclusion of a treaty for the exchange of minority populations' (114). He thereby became simultaneously the representative of the Great Powers and the League. Nansen followed the direction received as he understood it: 'I based my action upon a knowledge that all the Governments here represented are in favour of what I proposed' (114). The international system led by the Great Powers had decided the matter:

> I know that the Great Powers are in favour of this proposal because they believe that to unmix the populations of the Near East will serve to secure the true pacification of the Near East and because they [the Great Powers] believe an exchange of populations is the quickest and most efficacious way of dealing with the grave economic results which must result from the great movement of populations which has already occurred (114).

Nansen spoke very positively of the record of the Greek-Bulgarian Mixed Commission in practice, and generally considered the Greek-Bulgarian convention as the model for any Greek-Turkish exchange. The conference took his lead in considering the Greek-Bulgarian exchange as the ideal. But a sense of urgency

38 Ministère des Affaires Étrangers, Documents Diplomatiques, *Conférence de Lausanne*, 2 Vols.; and *Lausanne Conference on Near Eastern Affairs, 1922–1923: Records of Proceedings and Draft Terms of Peace*, 1923 (hereafter *Lausanne Conference*). The French and British publications are essentially identical in content. French was the official language of the conference, though the British, American, and Japanese delegates spoke in English. The British version (quoted here) provides translations of the French texts. Citations of quotes from this source will appear in parentheses in the body of the text.

in a very different situation underpinned Nansen's report. Time was not on the side of gradualism. To begin rebuilding the Greek and the Turkish economies, the exchange needed to take place as soon as possible, ideally in time for the massive displaced rural populations to take to the fields in their new countries in time for spring planting. Most of the exchange had already occurred by the time of Nansen's report, transforming a 'minority' problem into a 'refugee' problem. Of those peoples who remained where they did not 'belong,' speedy migration seemed inconsistent with voluntary migration. For most migrants, the real issue was preventing them from returning whence they came.[39] From the need to preclude any right of return came the need to make the exchange compulsory.

İsmet İnönü (hereafter İsmet) spoke immediately after Nansen's report to try to change the subject. While he had listened 'with interest' to the report, 'he could only attach a personal character [to the report] as no official relations existed between Turkey and the League of Nations; he regarded it as emanating from a private person.'[40] İsmet thus sought to make an issue not of the exchange, but of Turkey's relationship to the League. If the League was responsible for the involuntary nature of the exchange, the new regime in Turkey was not. The discussion quickly moved on to a testy debate about other populations affected, notably prisoners of war, civilian prisoners, and residents of Thrace and Constantinople.

Lord Curzon opined that all might prefer a voluntary exchange, as between Greece and Bulgaria. But in the present situation, 'compulsion would very probably be found necessary for more reasons than one' (121). Should the conference decide on a 'voluntary exchange,' a term that lacked clarity given the chaotic refugee situation, 'months might pass before it was carried out.' Such a delay would exacerbate the refugee crisis in Greece and could prevent the planting of crops the following spring, particularly in Western Thrace. Camille Barrère of France and Venizelos likewise asserted the need for celerity in carrying out the exchange (119). No one raised other options, even the fig leaf of calling the exchange 'voluntary.' The commission agreed to the appointment of a sub-commission specifically charged with handling the exchange of populations.

In the sessions that followed, speaker after speaker denounced the very idea of a compulsory population exchange, yet (perhaps protesting too much) reluctantly admitted its absolute necessity as a matter beyond their control. On 13 December,

39 Article 1 of the Convention expressly forbade return to the country of origin without the express permission of the relevant government.

40 Territorial and Military Commission, 'Minutes of the Eighth Meeting, December 1, 1922, at 3:30 p.m., under the presidency of Lord Curzon', *Lausanne Conference*, 111–124.

İsmet lamented that 'constant wars,' first the Balkan Wars and then the First World War, 'placed many Turkish subjects in the position of aggressors against their own country, and led to their forcible repatriation by the invading army' (207).[41] The Conference of Lausanne had simply to concede that 'the idea of an exchange had forced itself on the attention of all,' and that this 'painful necessity' had become unavoidable. Seeing an opening, Venizelos made an argument he would repeat often: 'the idea of compulsory exchange of populations had not been put forward by the Greek delegation. On the contrary, such an exchange was repugnant to them' (210). Curzon also disowned any ownership of a compulsory exchange, or any British involvement in events leading to it. Curzon 'deeply regretted' a compulsory exchange, famously referring to it as 'a thoroughly bad and vicious solution, for which the world would pay a heavy penalty for a hundred years to come. He detested having anything to do with it' (212). Yet notwithstanding such rhetorical crocodile tears, neither he nor his colleagues considered any other solution.

The sub-commission on population exchange, chaired by Giulio Montagna of Italy, made its report on 8 January 1923.[42] This report clearly laid responsibility for the exchange at the feet of Nansen. The report recounted a rear-guard effort on the part of the Greeks to make the exchange 'voluntary,' but treated compulsory exchange as settled law, barring a decision otherwise on the part of the conference. The Montagna report put in writing the basis of a final agreement to mitigate the effects of the exchange by exempting the Christians in Constantinople and the Muslims in Western Thrace from the exchange.[43] These exceptions, as well as the vexed question of whether the Greek Orthodox Patriarchate ought to be allowed to remain in Constantinople, caused far more dispute when Montagna presented the report than the matter of compulsory exchange as such.[44]

---

41 'Territorial and Military Commission, 'Minutes of the Fourteenth Meeting, December 13, 1922, at 11 a.m., under the presidency of Lord Curzon', *Lausanne Conference*, 204–215.

42 'Report addressed to Lord Curzon, President of the First Commission, by M. Montagna. President of the Sub-Commission on the Exchange of Populations', 8 January 1923, *Lausanne Conference*, 328–337.

43 Much of the commercial elite of Constantinople was Christian (being mainly Greek), and the Muslims of Western Thrace comprised large numbers of Bulgarian- and Roma- speakers that Turkey wanted to protect, but not necessarily absorb. Stefanos Katsikas, 'The Muslims of Greece (1923–41)', *State-nationalisms in the Ottoman Empire: Greece and Turkey, Orthodox and Muslims, 1830–1945*, ed. Benjamin Fortna, 2013, 153–175, esp. 154–156.

44 Territorial and Military Commission, 'Minutes of the Twentieth Meeting, January 10, 1923, at 11 a.m., Lord Curzon in the Chair', *Lausanne Conference*, 313–320.

Politics Makes Law in Population Exchanges

As is commonly the case with the mass movement of peoples around the world in the twentieth century, uncontroversial numbers for either population exchange considered here remain difficult if not impossible to determine. Common estimates of some 300,000 persons affected by the Greek-Bulgarian exchange and some 1.6 million persons affected by the Greek-Turkish exchange raise as many questions as they answer. What is the proper context for thinking historically about the exchanges after the First World War, which after all constituted one episode in a long history of migration stretching well into the nineteenth century as the Ottoman Empire contracted? Population transfers of hundreds of thousands of people resulted from the Balkan Wars of 1912–1913. Even during the First World War, who should we count as persons exchanged? Excluding persons who fled as refugees and anyone who did not make a declaration to a Mixed Commission would seriously underestimate the demographic impact of population transfers, not to mention the human drama. Small wonder, then, that historians such as Theodora Dragostinova, Onur Yildirim, and Renée Hirschon have worked so hard to put 'people' back into the population exchanges. When did the exchanges even end? Cases as to just who was subject to the exchanges reached the Permanent Court of International Justice into the early 1930s. Legalism proved one way simply to make the exchanges comprehensible.

The focus here has revolved around situating the conventions authorizing the population exchanges in the history of international law, the history of state sovereignty, and peace-making in the aftermath of the First World War. To the extent that peace-making after the First World War was ever about building a liberal order under the banner of international law, the history of population exchanges charts the rapid decline and fall of that order. By the Conference of Lausanne, the original liberal Wilsonian trope of 'self-determination' had long morphed into 'national self-determination.' The 'self' entitled to self-determination was not the individual, but the ethno-national successor state to the multinational empires.

The Treaty of Neuilly with Bulgaria, the treaty made with the most marginal of the Central Powers, was the product of a deteriorating Paris Peace Conference. With the Americans gone, and the British, French, and Italians preoccupied with a host of other post-war issues, a modicum of liberalism coupled with distancing sufficed in the 'voluntary' exchange between Greece and Bulgaria. At least on paper, the convention prized the most treasured liberal value, individual choice. Greece was anxious to obtain international sanction for its territorial acquisitions in order to settle an influx of newly defined Greeks from Anatolia. Bulgaria, for its part, was anxious to end its exile from the international system. Both thus found these terms acceptable. Crucially, the Great Powers kept their signatures off the convention, and convinced themselves that signing the treaty did not ipso facto mean endorsing it. With these dubious origins, the convention entered the realm of international law.

The legalism of the Greek-Turkish population exchange had more overtly sinister implications, even in the short run. The Conference of Lausanne and its resulting treaty proceeded from a partial reversal of the outcome of the First World War through the war between Greece and Turkey. That war essentially severed the wartime alliance between Britain and France in the Middle East, and even challenged the coherence of the British Empire itself. The Great Powers needed to make an end to the war on the two sides of the Aegean. Greece and Turkey resembled the successor states of the former Habsburg and Romanov Empires in their self-image as ethno-national successor states. The Greek-Turkish convention established the state and state interests as the exclusive arbiters of ethnic identity. Christians became 'Greek' and Muslims 'Turkish' – full stop. None of the flood of crocodile tears shed at Lausanne changed an outcome now enshrined in international law. Between the wars, so renowned a liberal as the Franco-Greek jurist Nicolas Politis promoted the exchange as the foundation of a peace in the Aegean based on ethnic homogeneity and mutual interdependence.[45]

In the end, the Greek-Bulgarian and Greek-Turkish population exchanges as matters of international law contributed to a crucial precedent in the history of international relations. With time, the importance of the political precedent exceeded that of the legal precedent. From the first, the Great Powers sought distance from the exchanges and their human toll, a distance that increased between the two exchanges considered here. The international system could contribute to the drawing of internationally recognized borders. But after the system ratified these borders, successor states emerged as masters within them, save for circumscribed, humanitarian roles reserved for international organizations such as the League of Nations or the United Nations. 'The world', from the interwar period to the present, has largely stood aside as states regulated inclusion and exclusion by any means that they considered necessary. It proved a short step from international acceptance of 'population exchanges' to international acceptance of 'ethnic cleansing,' whether by the Red Army and national collaborators after 1945, Indians and Pakistanis after 1947, successor states to Yugoslavia after 1991,

45 See Marilena Papadaki, 'The "Government Intellectuals": Nicolas Politis – An Intellectual Portrait', *European Journal of International Law* 23/1, 2012, 221–231.

or Burma after 2017, or for that matter the Uyghurs of China today.[46] International theatrics have proved the variable; international acceptance the constant.

46 On the history of such population upheavals in Europe, see Ther, *The Dark Side of Nationalism*.

12

A Capitalist Peace? Money, Labour, and Refugee Resettlement in the Lausanne Accords

Laura Robson

The 1923 Treaty of Lausanne is justly famous – or, perhaps, justly infamous – for its sanctioning of ethnic cleansing in the guise of the 'population exchange' between Greece and Turkey, a fateful decision that enshrined the principles of ethnic homogeneity and segregation as a foundation of the post-WWI global political order. Its political and philosophical assumptions and underpinnings have been much discussed by historians, lawyers, and diplomats. But, of course, such a dramatic reimagining of populations involved practical and financial aspects as well, which are much less frequently discussed – indeed, often go totally unacknowledged. The well-known schemes of humanitarianism-cum-demographic engineering in the post-war Balkans and Eastern Mediterranean that followed on from the political decisions taken at Lausanne in fact involved the private financing of refugee resettlement and the creation of commercial enterprises deploying refugee labour.

In this way, the Lausanne Treaty was less novel than we sometimes imagine; it followed on from any number of schemes already underway at the nascent League of Nations, which had from its inception imagined itself as a kind of international operation to deploy refugee labour to buttress an emerging post-war economic order. The League's early approaches to Armenian refugees, whom it initially attempted to settle as workers in the Soviet Union as an economically stabilizing influence, served as a first attempt to make use of refugees to build a particular kind of economic order directed from various imperial centres. Following on from this regionalized approach, the League's High Commissioner for Refugees promoted another, more broadly conceived scheme for the use of refugee labour as needed to bolster the rebuilding of the global economic system: the Nansen Passport, which allowed participating countries to make use of refugee labour without incorporating refugees as citizens or even permanent residents. Informed by these experiences with Armenian and other refugees, the League was primed to view Lausanne's exchanged Anatolian Christian communities through a very particular lens: as a source of cheap, dependent labour in the development of industrial agriculture across rural areas of Greece. The years surrounding Lausanne thus produced a new conception of international refugee policy that envisioned active refugee resettlement in industrial employment as a valuable tool for the economic stabilization of a fragile new state – but also, more radically, as a potentially lucrative investment opportunity for private backers.

Post-war Economics and the Refugee Question

The League's architects were initially reluctant to engage with the questions of post-war economic reconstruction, assuming that the system would gradually but inevitably return to the pre-war norm of state absence from the economic sphere. But, as historian Patricia Clavin has noted, 'the ideology of non-intervention was profoundly changed by the context of peace.'[1] The Bolshevik overthrow of the Tsarist government in Russia, combined with extreme post-war economic precarity in the new states of Central and Eastern Europe, led the Allies – and especially the British, represented most notably by John Maynard Keynes – to call for a broader international effort to stabilize the system, both internationally and to satisfy domestic metropolitan populations increasingly demanding new kinds of social protections and economic guarantees. In February 1919, Britain, France, Belgium, Italy, and the United States banded together to create a 'Supreme Economic Council' intended to promote reconstruction in Western Europe on the wartime model of assistance from American banks.[2] A year later, under pressure from a number of prominent economists and bankers as well as humanitarians and diplomats, the new League spearheaded an 'International Financial Conference' to meet in Brussels in the autumn of 1920, to find 'a means of remedying [the

1 Patricia Clavin, *Securing the World Economy: The Reinvention of the League of Nations, 1920–1946*, 2013, 12.
2 Kathleen Burk, *Britain, America, and the Sinews of War*, 1985, 196ff.

financial crisis] and of mitigating the dangerous consequences arising from it.'[3] A new Economic and Financial Section (hereafter EFS) was formed as part of the League's Secretariat, under the leadership of the British civil servant Arthur Salter (formerly of the Allied Maritime Transport Council), to prepare for the meeting.

The League thus began to emerge as a primary venue for deciding the financial path forward from the ruin of the First World War. The issues at the conference ranged from the difficulties presented by the reparations agreements to the political threat posed by mass inflation and currency collapse across Central and Eastern Europe. Its main purpose, though, was not to settle the ongoing questions of financial responsibility among the war's winners and losers but to 'make the case to international financiers, notably in the USA, which had assumed the role of the world's banker, for financial aid to Central and Eastern Europe.'[4] In the run-up to the conference, the League asked member states to produce extensive documentation on their financial and economic circumstances: not only currency stability, trade practices and statistics but also domestic specifics like prices of goods and production of fossil fuels. Such an approach set up one of the central premises of post-war economic policy, one that would interact substantively with the League's other nation-building tasks: the new post-war order would be made up of identifiable nation-states with sealed borders, whose economic circumstances – like their ethnic, linguistic, and communal composition – could be known, compared, and altered with a view to more internationally desirable outcomes. From the inception of the League, therefore, its political vision for the new national order was deeply entangled with its attitude towards global finance: national ethnic homogeneity would stabilize not only states but markets, prices, and currencies.

Though the conference resulted in only one resolution – to maintain and further develop the League's newly-formed EFS, it established a new basis for international authority working in conjunction with powerful private interests. The next such meeting, which took place at Genoa in 1922, likewise defined international economic and financial interests well beyond the state. There, it was representatives from Europe's central and commercial banks who pressed the case that financial institutions should guarantee assistance to currencies experiencing dangerous levels of depreciation.[5] Through this mechanism of including private interests, particularly representatives of American investment capital, in political

3 World Peace Foundation, *Report on the Brussels Financial Conference,* 1920, 2.
4 Clavin, *Securing the World Economy,* 19.
5 Carole Fink, *The Genoa Conference: European Diplomacy, 1921–1922*, 1984.

decision-making about the post-war economic order, the League was becoming increasingly dependent on private financing – and therefore feeling the need to make the case that its endeavours could be not only humanitarian, stabilizing, and peace-guaranteeing but also profitable. This shift to private financing would shape and inform its approach to the refugee question that rapidly became one of the League's most important *raisons d'être.*

The League was not, initially, envisioned as having responsibility for the multiplicity of refugees displaced and denationalized by the war, but the entangled questions of refugee assistance, global employment and labour markets were already major topics of concern for the emerging international system. In the autumn of 1921, the Red Cross together with a number of private 'humanitarian' organizations (Save the Children, the League of Red Cross Societies, and a number of Russian relief organizations) approached the newly formed International Labour Organization (hereafter ILO) – one of the first agencies formed under the League of Nations and directed by French socialist Albert Thomas – with requests to assist with the practicalities of re-absorbing refugees into the global workforce. Their vision involved creating an emigration office to determine which countries might accept able-bodied refugees as workers, establishing a system of 'labour exchange' across Eastern Europe, and coordinating the work of private organizations seeking to place refugees in employment.[6] Such proposals were designed not only to deal with a destabilizing political problem but also to give the League an expanded political purview: as Red Cross president Gustave Ador put it, the League was 'the only supranational political authority capable of solving a problem which is beyond the power of exclusively humanitarian organizations.'[7] In September 1921, the Norwegian diplomat and former polar explorer Fridtjof Nansen accepted the new position of general commissioner to deal with the specific issue of 'White Russian' – that is, anti-Bolshevik – refugees dispersed throughout the European continent. His responsibilities included strategizing about refugee passports and identification papers; the coordination of private and state-level relief efforts; and, above all, finding permanent and gainful employment for the refugees now subsisting on (mostly private) relief funds all over Europe. From this beginning, then, the question of industrial capitalism and the potential role of displaced people within it, was situated at the very centre of the League's refugee relief efforts.

6 *Minutes of the 6th Session of the GB* [Governing Body] *of the ILO,* 1921, 51.

7 Cited in Atle Grahl-Madsen, 'The League of Nations and the Refugees,' in *The League of Nations in Retrospect*, 2010, 358.

At first, the League's definition of refugee applied solely to those displaced from Russia: 'any person of Russian origin who does not enjoy or who no longer enjoys the protection of the Government of the USSR, and who has not acquired another nationality.'[8] Denationalized Russians held particular symbolic value for the Allies as representative victims of socialist revolution. Their seamless incorporation into the global labour force (preferably far from Western Europe) was therefore of more than practical import; it would stand, League officials hoped, as a rebuke to the emerging Bolshevik government in the Soviet Union and a warning to workers' movements closer to home. But as it became clear that refugee resettlement in Europe was taking place on an informal, ad hoc, and often underground manner (by 1922 there were more than 300,000 Russian refugees in the city of Berlin alone), Western European and North American governments alike began to introduce new immigration restrictions and tighten their borders. In Britain, the Under-Secretary for Foreign Affairs declared that 'Cossacks, Kalmucks, priests, generals, judges and ladies' represented 'an intolerable burden.'[9] In the United States, Secretary of State Charles Evans Hughes declared that 'our restriction on immigration should be so rigid that it would be impossible for most of these people to enter the United States. Reference is especially made to Armenians, Jews, Persians, and Russians, all of which have been so driven hither and thither that they cannot be regarded as desirable populations for any country.'[10] Nansen's office had no funds to assist refugees directly; his only financial recourse, limited as it was, was to hire refugees for clerical positions in his own offices.[11] It seemed that other paths would have to be found.

Nansen harboured hopes that Armenians, if not 'White Russians,' could be repatriated to the Soviet Union to serve as workers in 'underpopulated' rural areas trying to recover from the devastation of the war. The Soviet Union's economic and political chaos stood as a threat to the fragile peace; refugees could help stabilize the situation in the moment, and perhaps would eventually help to construct a post-socialist rebuilding within Russia, with all the political baggage such a position carried. As Nansen put it in 1922, young refugees 'must be regarded as potential workers in the Russia of tomorrow, in other words, as soldiers in the economic army designed for the work of reconstruction which the Western States

8 John Hope Simpson, *The Refugee Problem: Report of a Survey,* 1939, 227.
9 Quoted in Peter Gatrell, *The Making of the Modern Refugee*, 2013, 56.
10 *New York Times*, 20 April 1920; cited in Benjamin Alexander, 'Armenian and American: The Changing Face of Ethnic Identity and Diasporic Nationalism, 1915–1955', PhD dissertation, CUNY, 2005, 111.
11 Gatrell, *Making of the Modern Refugee,* 56.

are now discussing.'[12] Such a plan, of course, required at least some degree of Russian cooperation. As the Czechoslovakian government told the League: 'In order that they may carry out this task they must first of all be fitted for these duties by receiving the required training and the necessary facilities for returning to Russia and entering upon their work in that country … Finally, safeguards must be obtained, on their behalf, from the Russian Government for the protection of their lives and liberty on their return to Russia, and for the grant of at least such civil rights as are indispensable for the economic development of any country.'[13]

Under considerable international pressure to reduce the refugee burden, the League now began cautiously to negotiate with the new Soviet regime over an Armenian 'return' to the Soviet republic – a process made easier after Lenin's death and Stalin's takeover, which paved the way for formal British and French recognition of the Bolshevik regime in 1924. The Soviet authorities themselves displayed mixed feelings over mass Armenian refugee resettlement. On the one hand, with the task of post-war rebuilding at hand, the problem of labour shortages was very real; refugees presented a possible solution and could help to construct a new Bolshevik state. Particularly in its very early years, the New Economic Policy was interested in promoting mass immigration for the purpose of increasing the number of industrial and agricultural workers.[14] On the other hand, widespread post-war privation and financial difficulties meant that it was an inopportune moment for the arrival of tens of thousands of destitute people who would certainly be, at least initially, heavily dependent on state assistance. Further, there was no certainty that the Armenians who would be admitted were loyal to the political precepts of Bolshevism. Still, the Soviet regime felt considerable pressure from the League – and indeed from the refugees themselves – to open the doors; the Red Army had after all included half a million Armenians, and there was significant Armenian communist organizing from Paris to Beirut.[15] Armenians themselves sometimes made the case for what they called 'repatriation' – not, in most cases, an accurate presentation of the phenomenon of refugee resettlement – through appeals that highlighted their capacity for useful labour.

12 League of Nations, *Minutes of the 12th Session of the GB of the ILO*, 1922, 80. This and subsequent references to ILO minutes are available at https://www.ilo.org/public/libdoc/ilo/P/09601/.

13 *Minutes of the 12th Session of the GB of the ILO*, 1922, 47.

14 Eric Lohr, *Russian Citizenship: From Empire to Soviet Union,* 2012, 158.

15 Peter Gatrell, 'Displacing and Re-placing Population in the Two World Wars: Armenia and Poland Compared,' *Contemporary European History* 16/44, 2007, 516, notes that 170,000 Armenians were killed during their service in the Red Army.

As one advocate put it, 'the nomadic life of the settlers, full of torments, has made them sturdy and capable workers' ready to serve the needs of the Soviet state as well as the Armenian project of nation-building.[16] In practice, then, to limit the numbers of resettlements and ensure ideological adherence to Bolshevism, Soviet officials created a system of security clearances that tested refugee applicants on their political affiliations, language skills, and local contacts. Those who did enter were subject to police surveillance for years to come. Still, some 300,000 Armenian refugees, most from camps in Turkey and Greece, were eventually resettled in Soviet Armenia, where they were explicitly tasked with working to stabilize and modernize the Soviet state.

Making Refugees Workers: the 'Nansen Passport'

Nevertheless, the accommodation with Soviet Armenia did not, as Nansen had hoped, signal the end of the refugee crisis, which still included large numbers of Russians, many other Armenians, and Assyrians, as well as assorted other displaced people throughout Europe, the Balkans, and the ex-Ottoman sphere. The question of refugee employment (and unemployment) was clearly now emerging as a fundamental dilemma for the nascent international system. On the one hand, the existence of so many dispossessed and homeless people constituted, in the minds of many, a clear and present political danger to the Allied countries, who feared them as potential sites of disruption, protest, and the dissemination of socialist ideas – a fate that large-scale refugee employment might help to avert. On the other hand, mass unemployment was a domestic political worry as well; and the Allies all feared that an influx of refugee labour into Western Europe or North America would have a negative impact on labour movements and workers' rights and create equally difficult metropolitan political instabilities.[17] The ILO's founding documents clearly expressed the League's worries: 'The well-being, physical, moral and intellectual, of industrial wage-earners is of supreme international importance.'[18] Without it, there could be no post-war stability, either economic or political.

One 'solution,' Thomas and his ILO colleagues thought, might be to place refugees in employment elsewhere, preferably in rural locations as far from Western Europe as possible, and they began to send commissions to promising locations

16 Cited in Gatrell, 'Displacing and Re-placing Population', 515.

17 *Minutes of the 39th Session of the GB of the ILO*, 1928, 342.

18 Article 427, *The Labour Provisons of the Peace Treaties*, 1920, 13.

to scout out the possibilities for mass refugee employment. Even this was not without its challenges; it raised the question, for instance, of whether labour safeguards in receiving countries would match labour law in Western Europe. 'If [the conference] now defeats this motion which asks for workers who emigrate the protection of reciprocity of rights in the legislation of countries they go to,' thundered the Italian representative to the International Labour Conference in 1919, 'it will then have confirmed the fact that this assembly recognizes the right of countries richly endowed in natural resources to maintain in a state of economic slavery those countries which are deficient in natural resources.'[19] With this issue unresolved (which, given both the resistance to international monitoring of national labour conditions and the basic premise of providing an ever-expandable secondary labour market outside Europe, was perhaps unresolvable), the ILO nevertheless began to approach a number of non-Western states about accepting refugee workers.

In promoting these schemes, the ILO sought to establish its own *bona fides* as a technocratic rather than political organization. 'The characteristic feature of these Commissions,' it declared, 'is that they are composed entirely of experts chosen for the single reason of their acknowledged competence. It is, of course, possible that some of these experts may be found either to belong to national administrative services or to have connection with employers' or workers' organizations. But such a circumstance could not in any way affect the purely technical nature of the advice for which they are asked.'[20] In 1921, the ILO – seeking to project just such an atmosphere of disinterested technical information – had put together a list of potential migrant-accepting countries that detailed the legal conditions under which migrant workers would operate in each, noting: 'The Conference recommended that the collective recruiting of workers in one country, with a view to their employment in another, should be permitted only by mutual agreement between the countries concerned and after consultation with employers and workers in each country in the industries concerned.'[21] Further, its 1921 'Emigration Commission' defended its balance among various stakeholders, public and private: 'The points of view of European and non-European emigrating and immigrating countries have been presented in an equitable manner despite the absence of certain delegates.' (Its representative added: 'It must finally be noted that big private organisations in the United States had sent representatives to Geneva and

19 League of Nations, *Record of Proceedings, International Labour Conference*, 1919, 154.
20 *Minutes of the 11th Session of the GB of the ILO,* 1922, 72.
21 *Proceedings, International Labour Conference*, 153.

that these were admitted by the Commission to attend its proceedings.'[22]) International resettlement policy was, the ILO coolly argued, not a question of political or civil rights but a neutral economic experiment in placing workers in contact with industrial employers across the globe.

Early attempts to realize this plan were haphazard at best. Following on failed wartime efforts to resettle Belgian refugees in Chile and South Africa, League and ILO representatives tried to forge contacts in China, Tunisia, Brazil, Argentina, and Peru (among others) for possible refugee employment. But the complications of travel, the reluctance of governments, and the resistance of refugees themselves all contributed to the general failure of such proposals. Instead, Nansen now decided, employment should be negotiated by the refugees themselves. In July 1922, he brought together sixteen governments to discuss the invention of a new legal document for Russian refugees: the identity card that came to be known as the 'Nansen Passport.' These papers, valid for just a year at a time, gave the bearer the ability – though not a guaranteed right – to move across international borders in search of work, and to reside (temporarily and on sufferance) in the countries acknowledging the validity of the document. In 1923 the passport system was extended to Greek refugees (one being Aristotle Onassis who in 1922, aged 16, fled from Smyrna to Greece with his family and who in the following year travelled alone on a Nansen Passport to Buenos Aires, Argentina, where he began his business career) and in the following year to Armenian refugees as well, and in 1926 it was amended to include the right to a return visa, allowing the holder to come back to the issuing state. In 1928 eligibility was further expanded to include 'any person of Assyrian or Assyro-Chaldean origin.'[23] Eventually, fifty-four states signed agreements to recognize Russian Nansen Passport holders and thirty-eight agreed to honour the passport system for Armenians (the number for Greeks being unknown).[24]

Historians and policymakers have often lauded the Nansen Passport as a valuable 'first step' towards the eventual construction of a more comprehensive

22 *Minutes of the 9th Session of the GB of the ILO*, October 1921, 358.

23 'Arrangement of 30 June 1928 Concerning the Extension to Other Categories of Refugees of Certain Measures taken in Favour of Russian and Armenian Refugees', United Nations Treaty Collection, *League of Nations Treaty Series* 89, 63 (https://treaties.un.org/doc/Publication/UNTS/LON/Volume 89/v89.pdf).

24 For a look at the evolution of the Nansen Passport, see Otto Hieronymi, 'The Nansen Passport: A Tool of Freedom of Movement and of Protection', *Refugee Survey Quarterly* 22/1, 2003, 36–47; Bruno Cabanes, *The Great War and the Origins of Humanitarianism, 1918–1924*, 2014, esp. Ch. 3.

international refugee policy.[25] And indeed, it did point the way to a later system of international refugee law: one that regarded refugees as workers above all, and encouraged states to imagine the stateless and displaced as a pool of mobile, temporary, lightly regulated labourers, with no political access in their host countries. As historian Keith Watenpaugh has written: 'As much as Nansen had hoped to restore dignity to refugees through the League's policies, the passports themselves bear witness to the moral and ethical vacuity (even uselessness) of the interwar refugee regime … It provided states with a reservoir of controllable workers deprived of any ability to claim political agency or civil rights.'[26] Under the Nansen system, refugees could help to rebuild the post-war global economy by offering their labour where it was needed, without challenging its ethno-national political framework by demanding residency or citizenship in the countries of their employment.

Refugee Loans: the Greek-Turkish Population Exchange and the Role of Private Capital

It was in this context of already-extant refugee policy, which increasingly imagined refugees as labourers in the service of a massive post-war rebuilding, that the Treaty of Lausanne was negotiated. By 1923, the Economic and Financial Organization (hereafter EFO), which had been formed following the unsatisfactory outcome of the Genoa Conference in the previous year, had become a permanent part of the League's structure and was engaged in large-scale data collection on both state finances and private commerce across the globe.[27] Its ties to industry went the other way as well, with its staff of fifty-six people receiving financing for their projects from private bodies like the Rockefeller Foundation – a private American philanthropic body funded with the Rockefeller family's Standard Oil money, interested in developing programmes in everything from global public health to industrial relations with a view to the long-term expansion of American economic markets around the world. When the World Economic Conference

25 As historian Claudena Skran wrote long ago, 'the beginning of international refugee law can properly be dated to the creation of the Nansen Passport system.' See Skran, *Refugees in Interwar Europe: The Emergence of a Regime*, 1995, 105.

26 Keith Watenpaugh, *Bread from Stones: The Middle East and the Making of Modern Humanitarianism*, 2015, 174.

27 Clavin notes that its publications ranged from statistical data on money and banking to information on foodstuffs, fossil fuels, and the chemical industry. See *Securing the World Economy*, 36.

– a follow-up to Brussels and Genoa – was convened in 1927 to convince states to move away from the protectionist policies that the EFO believed were hampering global economic recovery, it included not only representatives of state and banking interests but also a number of lobbyists for specific industries. The context was forming for a new financing of the League's 'humanitarian' work: it would look not just to states, charitable bodies that had represented the main locus for humanitarian relief efforts during the war, and private charitable donors, but to industry and finance. More novel still was the emerging promise that participation in such humanitarian ventures functioned not just to stabilize the world order and make Europe once again safe for investment but could be profitable in its own right.

Prior to the exchange, as we have seen, the post-war refugee issue had been dealt with mainly under the purview of the kinds of humanitarian and charitable organizations that had spearheaded so many relief efforts during the First World War – most prominently the American mission organization Near East Relief, but also the International Committee of the Red Cross and the YMCA's World's Committee, all members of the advisory committee Fridtjof Nansen had established as a corollary to his League appointment as High Commissioner for Refugees in 1921. Now, as Anatolian Christian refugees began to flee the Turkish army en masse during the Greek-Turkish war (particularly following the burning of Smyrna in 1922), the League had no money of its own to assist with the work of evacuation. Nansen raised separate donations, from both states and international organizations, to fund the evacuation of Greeks and Russians from Constantinople in 1922. Similarly, the ILO had no budget for the refugee-related work that it was undertaking by the early 1920s other than the general administrative budget for the Labour Office. In September 1922, Nansen appealed to the Assembly to allow him to use money earmarked for Russian refugee assistance to help the masses of people fleeing Anatolia into Greece – nearly 900,000 people by November. The refugees, in the main, could turn only to private charitable organizations for assistance: the International Red Cross (which bore sole responsibility for more than half a million refugees for six months at the height of the crisis), Near East Relief, Save the Children, and the All-British Appeal.[28] Further, the strain on the Greek state – and the political dangers posed by a large and desperate refugee population – was abundantly evident. As one early account recorded: 'the relief of distress was indeed as much a political necessity as a moral duty, for

28 Martin Hill, 'The League of Nations and the Work of Refugee Settlement and Financial Reconstruction in Greece', *Journal of Institutional and Theoretical Economics* 34, 1931, 267.

the danger of a starving population largely concentrated at a few strategic points was obvious.'[29] It was at this point that the League, together with the struggling Greek government, came to think that perhaps there was a way to make use of private investment funding for the dual projects of ethnically homogenizing the Balkans and stabilizing Europe for ongoing imperial economic expansion. 'It was evident,' wrote one observer not long after the exchange, 'that no piece-meal measure would suffice, but only some vast settlement scheme; and the Government was not slow to connect such a scheme with the secular problem of creating an ethnically homogenous Macedonia.'[30]

To support such a mass resettlement project – placing the (mainly urban) refugees on farmland in Macedonia as part of an enormous project of demographic engineering and agricultural development – Nansen began to press the League Council for practical support for an international loan, backed and to some degree guaranteed by the League, directly to the Greek government. Such a scheme would, Nansen thought, provide a new way of financing refugee settlement assistance to replace the many charitable bodies who were now beginning to withdraw from the scene. The first version of his plan came with a £750,000 loan from the Bank of England for refugee resettlement, on the condition that the use of the funds be supervised by an independent Refugee Settlement Commission that would ensure the proper use of the money, not for relief but solely for establishing the refugees in 'productive work' that would ultimately turn enough of a profit to repay the loan with interest. 'All assistance given,' the agreement read, 'shall be given on terms involving ultimate repayment.'[31]

The Refugee Settlement Commission became the central institution through which the process of refugee resettlement was financed. It maintained total control over all relevant funds, both the loan from the Bank of England and a matching fund from the Greek government, guaranteed by an International Financial Commission made up of British, French, and Italian representatives.[32] Furthermore, it was now the holder of more than 500,000 hectares of Macedonian land representing 'the large estates of the Turks in Macedonia in addition to such land as became

29 Ibid., 266.

30 Ibid., 267.

31 League of Nations, *Official Journal*, Vol. IV, 1923, 1509.

32 Hill notes that this Commission 'had been established at Athens by the Law of International Control of February 26th, 1898, after a series of defaults in the payment of the service of Greek foreign loans' – thus tying this scheme to a longer institutional history of Great Power financial intervention in Greece during the nineteenth century. See Hill, 'The League of Nations and the Work of Refugee Settlement', 270, fn.4.

available elsewhere through expropriation measures'[33], though it soon became clear that there would be considerable difficulty in legalizing and formalizing such expropriations, due both to legal challenges from the lands' former Muslim owners and to the fact that previous 'exchanges' had left some of this territory under the control of the earlier Greek-Bulgarian and Greek-Turkish population exchange commissions. In the face of these difficulties in establishing clear title to the land, the legal framework of this loan shifted to allow for physical possession without legal ownership. The Commission and the Bank of England agreed that it would accept the use of funds to settle people on land with a promise of eventual title, 'and that the Commission should be allowed a corresponding liberty to settle refugees on lands of which it was not *de jure* owner.'[34] In other words, the funding scheme was now – with the blessing and backing of the League – supporting the relocation of refugees on contested land, with the purpose not only of ethnically homogenizing Macedonia along the lines desired by the Greek government but also turning a profit for the investors funding the loan through the purchase of stock:

> The [Bank of England] loan was issued in December 1924 for a nominal amount of £12,300,000. Of this, £7,500,000 was offered for public subscription in London, £2,500,000 in Athens and the rest in New York. The loan was issued in England by Hambros Bank Ltd., in Greece by the National Bank of Greece, and in the United States by Speyer and Co. It was to bear nominal interest of 7% and the subscription price was fixed at 88%; the real interest for the subscriber was thus over 8% – approximately equivalent to the yield of the principal outstanding Greek foreign loans at that moment. The amount realized was just over £9,970,000, out of which the advances from the Bank of England, the National Bank of Greece and the Greek Government were repaid. The English block was offered for subscription first, and was very heavily over-subscribed in less than one hour. During the first five months of 1925 the price of the stock on the London market remained consistently above the issue price.[35]

Another, similar loan was floated in 1927 (following the 1926 overthrow of the Pangalos government and its replacement with the Kondylis regime), both as a

33 Ibid., 270.
34 Ibid., 272.
35 Ibid., 273.

mode of continuing the unfinished work of refugee resettlement and to stabilize the Greek economy in the face of this political instability. On this occasion, the money was explicitly tied to the stabilization of currency as well as refugee work: £3 million for ongoing refugee settlement, £3 million 'to provide liquid assets in the form of foreign exchange,' and another £3 million to pay off government debt.[36] The work that the Refugee Settlement Commission had done to connect investors with the project of remaking Macedonia as Greek was over quickly, as per the requirements of this post-war era. The commission dissolved itself in 1930, after having taken 'steps to secure the rights of the bondholders of the 1924 loan on the one hand, and of the refugees to the properties in their possession on the other', mainly through the signing of an agreement with the Greek government to complete some infrastructure schemes in the resettled areas and amortize the loan through additional annual payments.

This post-Lausanne scheme to fund refugee resettlement through appeals to private investors represented a centrally important model for future schemes of refugee resettlement. It tied all sorts of interests of the Allies – the stabilization of Eastern European currencies, the ethnic homogenization of the Balkan states, the settlement of large numbers of destitute refugees who might otherwise represent an entrée for Bolshevism – with the interests of private capital in Britain and the United States. It also began to indicate the shape of future humanitarian endeavours surrounding refugees, who were becoming a visible point of entry for transnational (and, often, neo-imperial) plans for developing and industrializing rural spaces in Central and Eastern Europe and the Middle East, to the commercial benefit of investors in North America and Western Europe. Lausanne thus set the stage for a new approach to displacement: one that, as one author has put it, was fully committed to 'treat[ing] refugees as labour migrants rather than subjects – or masses – of humanitarian need.'[37]

Refugees and the ILO

The Armenian resettlement schemes, the Nansen Passport system, and the private financing of the Greek refugee resettlement together signalled the advent of a firming League commitment that refugees were workers above all, whose resettlement could serve as a contribution to the remaking of the global economic system.

36 Hill, 'The League of Nations and the Work of Refugee Settlement', 281.

37 Evan Easton-Calabria, 'From Bottom-Up to Top-Down: The "Pre-History" of Refugee Livelihoods Assistance from 1919 to 1979', *Journal of Refugee Studies* 28/3, 2015, 419.

This approach took newly concrete form in the decision, taken in 1925, to place the League of Nations refugee-related operations under the authority of the ILO.

As we have seen, there was already significant cooperation and collaboration between the High Commissioner for Refugees and the ILO in the first years of their operation. After the first wave of Russian and Armenian refugees were dealt with in various ways, and the details of the Greek-Turkish population exchange appeared to be settled satisfactorily (at least to those pulling the levers in London, Paris, and Geneva), the relationship between refugee resettlement work and international labour policy was made still more explicit. In the spring of 1924, Nansen approached the League Council with a proposal that the ILO could formally take over some of the work of the Refugee Office, as a kind of preliminary step towards shutting down international refugee work entirely (an expression of faith in the stability of the emerging international system that would, of course, prove to be distinctly over-optimistic). Thomas, in his presentation to the ILO's Governing Body, explained the details (and the rationale) for this merging of agencies: 'The local agencies of the High Commissariat would be retained, and would still remain under its direction. The budget of the High Commissariat would form a special chapter entirely distinct from the rest of the budget of the International Labour Organisation.' He carefully added: 'The report at the same time gave the assurance that it was the intention of the Office to prevent the refugees from competing with the workers in the countries which they entered by accepting lower wages', to be accomplished by 'direct[ing] the refugees towards non-European countries.'[38] As the Italian representative to the ILO put it: 'the problem of the Russian refugees … had ceased to have a political character, and was now a technical problem of the finding of employment and emigration.'[39]

It was an assessment with which not everyone agreed. Humanitarian assistance of this kind, one opponent argued, did not fall under the purview of the ILO, whose chief purpose was 'to promote the conciliation of labour and capital.'[40] Another opponent, Louis Kershaw, declared that the League had 'merely entrusted the Office with work of an administrative character which could not be compared with the management of an employment exchange dealing with one and a half million refugees.'[41] The French representative, M. Jouhaux, agreed, but issued a caveat: the difficulties 'were not sufficient to justify an attitude of indifference towards the

38 *Minutes of the 23rd Session of the GB of the ILO*, 1924, 258, 259.
39 Ibid., 258–259.
40 Ibid., 259.
41 Ibid.

suffering people who were wandering throughout the world and might perhaps in the future become an element of danger to the development of social progress.'[42] When Nansen presented his case to a somewhat sceptical Governing Body at the ILO, he blended reassurance with threats of the chaos that a refusal to participate might bring. The ILO and the Refugee Office, he told the ILO's Governing Body, shared a vision of – and a stake in – the formation of a Geneva-regulated global labour market. 'It was essential that there should be some control of the placing of refugees … If the work of the High Commissariat came to an end, there would be disturbances of the labour market in various countries owing to clandestine emigration.'[43] Refugee assistance under the ILO's supervision could simply take the form of a labour exchange, aimed at preventing the flooding of the Western European labour market with low-wage migrant workers by directing refugee migration into colonial and semi-colonial regions for the purposes of agricultural development. This approach would simultaneously protect labour conditions and political stability in the metropole – thereby defusing the potential political threats posed by large displaced populations in Europe – and provide a useful source of cheap labour for (mostly Western-owned) commercial enterprises in colonial and semi-colonial settings overseas. Despite considerable dissent, and long and detailed arguments about the specifics of the financing, Nansen carried the day. In December 1924, the ILO officially took over responsibility for much of the League's refugee work, thus cementing the League's commitment to viewing the problem of refugeedom as essentially a problem of labour. It was a moment of update, crystallization, and formalization of the old imperial concept of refugee resettlement in the service of empire.

By 1928, the Office's *modus operandi* had been set: the High Commissioner (still Nansen, who had become increasingly invested in the question of Armenian settlement over the past few years) dealt with the 'political aspects' of the work, in particular negotiations with governments over the Nansen Passport, and assisted with the actual transport of refugees admitted to participating countries under these auspices. The Refugee Service of the ILO, by contrast, limited its purview to connecting Armenian and Russian (and, by the early 1930s, Assyrian) refugees with appropriate employment opportunities across the globe. Under the auspices of the ILO, the already-developed idea of exporting surplus refugee labour elsewhere (i.e., into colonial and semi-colonial regions far from Western Europe) was solidified into a grounding principle of refugee resettlement work. As

42 Ibid.

43 *Minutes of the 23rd Session of the GB of the ILO*, 1924, 261, 263.

the Governing Body of the ILO reported in its 1928 meeting: 'When the Service was transferred from the Secretariat of the League of Nations to the Office, it was believed that it was of a temporary character and that it would only have to finish the work which had been undertaken, obtaining the technical assistance of the Office for this purpose … [But] as a result of the uneasiness awakened by the preliminary symptoms of an economic crisis in France, it began to be thought that difficult as it was to transport the refugees to distant countries, it would be better to attempt to settle large numbers of refugees as permanent colonists, particularly in South America.'[44] After their resettlement, they could be stricken from the Refugee Sub-Committee's rolls: 'With a view to effecting a gradual reduction of the refugee problems, refugees once settled in permanent employment should, unless some special problem arises in regard to them, be regarded as having no further claim on the services of the Office.'[45]

In the later 1920s, this Lausanne-era model of profit-driven investment in refugee resettlement was extended still further, to the British and French mandate territories of the Arab Middle East. In French-run Syria, Armenian refugees were now made to invest in their own housing through government-provided loans subject to strict repayment plans. 'The tenant pays an agreed sum down,' one observer recorded, 'then after the first year pays 10s. a month. Damascus has a longer term for refunding than other parts of Syria owing to the poverty and bad economic conditions of Armenians in this city. In all other districts refugee tenants will have refunded their debt for their houses in five years.'[46] In Beirut, too, refugees participated in loan schemes to fund their housing: 'Each refugee gives roughly 15s. to purchase his plot of land. He is then left alone for one year, after which he is called upon to make returns according to the terms of his land purchase contract.'[47] In both Syria and Lebanon, Armenian refugees were enrolled as workers in French commercial enterprises and especially in schemes of agricultural development in rural areas, with a view to tightening French control over particular urban and rural landscapes and providing a justification for expropriating agricultural land from local Syrian Arab farmers and landowners.[48]

Britain, too, made use of the Lausanne model in its Middle Eastern territory.

44 *Minutes of the 38th Session of the GB of the ILO*, 1928, 173.

45 Annex A, 'Report of the Refugee Sub-Committee,' *Minutes of the 38th Session of the GB of the ILO*, 1928, 177.

46 George Gracey, 'Armenian Settlement in Syria', *Contemporary Review* 140, 1931, 87.

47 Ibid.

48 Ibid., 91; see also Laura Robson, *States of Separation: Transfer, Partition, and the Making of the Modern Middle East*, 2017, Ch. 3.

As they struggled to retain control over the new mandate of Iraq, British officials began to deploy Assyrian refugees (whom the British military had moved from Hakkari to the area around Baghdad in the late stages of the war) to develop and claim agricultural land in the oil-rich territory of Mosul, whose disposition between the new republic of Turkey and the new British mandate of Iraq was as yet uncertain. This scheme was eventually successful in its goal of formal international recognition – in the form of League of Nations approval – of Mosul's incorporation into mandatory Iraq under British control; and it left a large number of Assyrian refugees as a potential labour force not just for servicing, protecting, and supporting the British colonial occupation but also, crucially, for a rapidly developing oil extraction economy around Mosul and Kirkuk.[49]

*

Both before and after Lausanne, the new international system in the form of the League of Nations was constructing schemes for humanitarian and especially refugee relief with an eye to two related goals: the remaking of ethno-national landscapes under a modernized form of imperial rule, and the reconstruction of labour, capital, and agriculture to support the rebuilding of the post-war global economic order established by the Allies at the Paris Peace Conference. The League of Nations designed and implemented its refugee policy before, during, and after the Lausanne Treaty around these mutually reinforcing strategies and visions. This Lausanne-era 'humanitarianism', therefore, was being deployed across the territories of the old Russian, Habsburg, and Ottoman Empires within a specifically capitalist framework.

From the League's efforts to resettle Ottoman Armenians as rebuilders in the Soviet Union, to its efforts to make 'exchanged' Anatolian Christians into both financially productive workers and Greek nationals in the aftermath of the Greek-Turkish population exchange, and to the British and French use of Armenian and Assyrian refugees in Syria and Iraq as labour forces in the service of the colonial state, the post-war Balkans and the Middle East became sites for a new humanitarian finance system directed at the realization of an imperial-international political and economic order dominated by the Allies. The League's earliest refugee policies, for Russian, Greek and Armenian victims of war, sought above all to place displaced people in gainful employment within politically

49 For a detailed look at the demographics of oil labour, see Arbella Bet-Shlimon, *City of Black Gold: Oil, Ethnicity, and the Making of Modern Kirkuk*, 2019.

constrained circumstances: either as re-constructors of the shattered Soviet state, whose ongoing condition of chaos presented a serious concern for the Allies even as they eyed the emerging Bolshevik regime itself with suspicion and anxiety, or as mobile workers under the new 'Nansen Passport' system that could send them where the jobs were without allowing them political access to their host societies. When the moment of Lausanne arrived, then, the Allies already had an extant mode of thinking about refugees as workers whose labour could serve to buttress an emerging global order in which theoretically independent, sovereign ethnic nation-states nevertheless operated under the unstated political supervision and the more overt economic authority of the imperial powers. It was of no surprise, therefore, that the League decided to fund the resettlement of Anatolian Christians on Greek farms through a scheme of private investment and refugee repayment. The Treaty of Lausanne drew on the League's already-extant refugee policies to imagine 'exchanged' populations both as tools for the invention of ethnic nation-states and as active assistants in the task of producing viable, profitable, and industrializing economies that would financially benefit their backers in Western Europe and North America. It was a vision for an internationalist refugee policy that would, in the end, outlive the League itself.

13

At the Crossroads of History: Thanassis Aghnides, Ayrilios Spatharis and the Greek-Turkish Population Exchange

Haakon A. Ikonomou and Dimitris Kamouzis

Introduction

The Greek-Turkish Population Exchange, signed at Lausanne on 30 January 1923, was a major turning point for Greece and Turkey. Following the compulsory exchange, approximately 1,300,000 Greek Orthodox Christians were displaced from the Turkish coastline and inner Asia Minor and settled in Greece, while 350,000 Muslims primarily from Macedonia, Mytilene and Crete were forced to take the reverse direction, thus altering the two countries forever. This chapter revisits and reassesses the Greek-Turkish population exchange and its effects through the lives and actions of Thanassis Aghnides and Ayrilios Spatharis, two influential Ottoman Greek lawyers from Constantinople who played important roles in the formulation and implementation of the policies relating to those Greeks who were exchanged and became refugees in Greece and the ones who were exempted and remained as a minority in Turkey. The chapter argues that these two Constantinopolitan Greeks found themselves right at the intersection of communal, international, and transnational politics, which linked their personal trajectories with the post-1923 historical transformation of Greece and Turkey.

Aghnides would serve as the League of Nations Secretariat's most trusted intermediary, connecting the Secretariat with the Mixed Commission overseeing the population exchange, several refugee and humanitarian organisations, the League of Nations Council, and the Greek and Turkish Governments. As the Secretariat's legate, Aghnides was important in defining the presence of the League in the exchange policy. Moreover, as the only Greek national and local expert of the Secretariat, he became a trusted source of information to the Council. Thus, Aghnides serves as the perfect vehicle to explore the productive space between different agents and policy levels.

Spatharis, who had remained in Constantinople as an established member (*établis*) of the Greek Orthodox minority exempted from the population exchange, was the chief legal adviser of the Ecumenical Patriarchate of Constantinople on issues regarding the status of the Patriarchate and the minority, a position he retained even after he moved to Greece in 1934. His efforts to balance between Turkey's nation-building programme, Greece's transnational policies as the external protector of the minority and the League of Nations' interventions as the guarantor of the minority rights granted by the Lausanne Treaty (24 July 1923) to the Greeks of Constantinople offer an insight into the way the Patriarchate and the minority dealt with these different poles of authority during the post-Lausanne era.

Exploring Aghnides' and Spatharis' engagement with the forced population exchange, at the time and later in life, allows us, firstly, to usefully connect contemporary developments unfolding at different scales from 'the ground up' and from 'the top down.' Secondly, it permits us to appreciate the historical legacy of the exchange from an experiential and personal perspective. To this end the cultural and social influences on their growing up in late nineteenth / early twentieth century Constantinople are highlighted as a means to comprehend their later responses.[1] With this in mind, the chapter, combining material from Aghnides' personal papers held at the League of Nations Archives and Spatharis' Archive held at the Greek General State Archives with more traditional sources, connects the intergovernmental negotiations of the Great Powers, the League's role in overseeing the population exchange, and the religious, ethnic and national affiliations under negotiation on the ground.

---

1 For more substantial reflections on the biographical approach to writing about international organisations and historical events of global significance, see: Haakon A. Ikonomou, 'The biography as institutional can-opener: An investigation of core bureaucratic practices in the early years of the League of Nations Secretariat', *Organizing the 20th Century World: International Organizations and the Emergence of International Public Administration, 1920s-1960s,* eds. Karen Gram-Skjoldager, Haakon A. Ikonomou and Torsten Kahlert, 2020. For the concept of scales, see: Laura Almagor, Haakon A. Ikonomou and Gunvor Simonsen, 'Introduction', *Global Biographies. Lived History as Method,* eds. Laura Almagor, Haakon A. Ikonomou and Gunvor Simonsen, 2022.

A Phanariot Communalist in the Making

Ayrilios Spatharis was born in Constantinople on 5 July 1876[2] and was the scion of a prominent upper-class Constantinopolitan Greek family. His father Andreas Spatharis was a maths and physics professor at several Greek schools in the Ottoman capital including the esteemed Patriarchal Great School of the Nation (*Patriarchiki Megali tou Genous Scholi*), twice National Councillor of the Permanent National Mixed Council (hereafter PNMC)[3] in 1877 and 1894, musician, translator and renowned poet with roots from the Phanariot aristocracy of the Danubian principalities.[4] His mother Foteini Hourmouzi was the daughter of Miltiadis (or Michael) Hourmouzis, a Galata native who fought in the Greek Revolution of 1821 and served as deputy and vice-president of the Greek Parliament before gaining further reputation as a playwright, journalist and publisher of the Constantinopolitan Greek newspaper *Armonia*.[5] He grew up in the family mansion in the neighbourhood of Cibali, not far from the Phanar, seat of the Ecumenical Patriarchate of Constantinople.[6] Following the family tradition he graduated from the

---

2 General State Archives – Central Service (Γενικά Αρχεία του Κράτους – Κεντρική Υπηρεσία, hereafter *GSA – CS*), Ayrilios Spatharis Archive (Αρχείο Αυρηλίου Σπαθάρη, hereafter *ASA*), File 22: Spatharis to Metropolitan Haldias Kyrillos (15 May 1954).

3 Following the ratification of the 'National' (Εθνικοί) or 'General Ordinances' (Γενικοί Κανονισμοί) by the Porte in 1862 the affairs of the Greek Orthodox millet (*Rum milleti*) were administered by the Ecumenical Patriarch and two bodies, the Holy Synod consisting of twelve Metropolitans of the Ecumenical Throne and the 'Permanent National Mixed Council' (Διαρκές Εθνικό Μικτό Συμβούλιο) composed of four Metropolitans belonging to the Holy Synod and eight lay councillors. The PNMC was responsible for the supervision of schools, hospitals and public welfare institutions. It also had financial control over these communal institutions as well as over churches and monasteries attached to the Ecumenical Patriarchate. See: *Γενικοί Κανονισμοί περί Διευθετήσεως των Εκκλησιαστικών και Εθνικών Πραγμάτων των υπό τον Οικουμενικόν Θρόνον Διατελούντων Ορθοδόξων Χριστιανών, Υπηκόων της Α. Μεγαλειότητος του Σουλτάνου*, 1862.

4 Stavros Th. Anestidis, *Πατριαρχικής Μεγάλης του Γένους Σχολή Πάνθεον. Δεκαεπτά Προσωπογραφίες*, 2019, 119–129, 165–166; Eleftherios Th. Kasianis, *Ανδρέας Σπαθάρης. Ο Φαναριώτης Διδάσκαλος του Γένους και Ποιητής 1837–1901*, 1976, 15–16.

5 Konstantinos Papoulidis, 'Συμπληρωματικά στοιχεία για το Συνόδη και την Αιμιλία Παπαδημητρίου', *Makedonika* 18, 1978, 298–299; Kasianis, *Ανδρέας Σπαθάρης*, 17; 'Hourmouzi Foteini', Institute for Neohellenic Research, Modern Greek Visual Prosopography, Collection of Andreas Spatharis: http://pandektis.ekt.gr/pandektis/handle/10442/60124?locale=el (last accessed 15 March 2020); 'Χουρμούζης, Μιλτιάδης (ή Μιχαήλ)' in *Εκπαιδευτική Ελληνική Εγκυκλοπαίδεια – Παγκόσμιο Βιογραφικό Λεξικό*, Vol. 9B, 1991, 465; 'Αρμονία' in Stratis D. Tarinas, *Ο Ελληνικός Τύπος της Πόλης. Α' Μέρος – Εφημερίδες*, 2007, 44.

6 Kasianis, *Ανδρέας Σπαθάρης*, 16; M. Kesisoglou-Karystinou, 'Από το Τανζιμάτ στη Μικρασιατική Καταστροφή. Γεγονότα, Επιδράσεις και Επιπτώσεις στην Ενορία του Τζιμπαλί', *Η καθημερινή ζωή στην Κωνσταντινούπολη στο τέλος του 19ου και στις αρχές του 20ού αιώνα*, eds. Σύνδεσμος των εν Αθήναις Μεγαλοσχολιτών, 1999, 170.

Ayrilios Spatharis (1876–1957)

Thanassis Aghnides (1889–1984)

Patriarchiki Megali tou Genous Scholi in 1896[7] and went on to study law at the University of Athens and in France.[8] Upon his return to Constantinople he settled in the cosmopolitan quarter of Cihangir in Pera, established his own law office at Galata and began practising law.[9]

In a short period of time Spatharis built his reputation as a legal expert actively involved in Greek communal affairs. He was a distinguished member of the renowned Greek Literary Association of Constantinople (*Ellinikos Philologikos Syllogos Konstantinoupoleos*)[10] and after the Young Turk Revolution of July 1908 he joined the secret organisation, the Society of Constantinople (*Organosis Konstantinoupoleos*), which represented the Greek ethnocentric communal circles and organised the majority of the Greek deputies of the Ottoman parliament into a political body, the so-called 'Hellenic Party' (*Elliniki Omas*).[11] Furthermore in February 1910 he received an official licence to handle legal cases in front of the Greek Consular Court,[12] thus initiating a closer contact with the diplomatic authorities of Greece in Constantinople that would last until the late 1920s.

In the summer of that year the political clash between the Patriarchate and the Porte peaked. The main friction point became the Law regarding Churches, voted by the Ottoman Parliament on 14 June 1910 and ratified by Sultan Mehmed V on

7 His older brothers Kornilios and Romylos had also graduated from the same school in 1886. See Vasilis Kremmydas, *Οι Μεγαλοσχολίτες (1863–1974)*, 2007, 74, 89. For more information on Spatharis' brothers Ioulios, Kornilios and Romylos and their sister Aimilia see: Papoulidis, 'Συμπληρωματικά στοιχεία', 298–299; Anestidis, *Πατριαρχικής Μεγάλης του Γένους*, 165–166; Alfred Rizzo, ed., *1914 Annuaire Oriental – Oriental Directory. Commerce, Industrie, Administration, Magistrature*, 1921, 702; *Νέον Πνεύμα. Εβδομαδιαία Επιθεώρησις Εικονογραφημένη* [*Neon Pneyma. Evdomadiaia Epitheorisis Eikonografimeni*], 1/25, 12 April 1909, 420; Katerina Boura, 'Οι βουλευτικές εκλογές στην Οθωμανική Αυτοκρατορία: Οι Έλληνες βουλευτές 1908–1918', *Bulletin of the Centre for Asia Minor Studies* 4, 1983, 74.

8 *Orthodoxia*, Vol. ΛΒ, issue Δ, 1957, 415.

9 He stayed at 1 Soğancı Street and his office was at 13 Küçük Millet Han. See Rizzo, *1914 Annuaire Oriental*, 702; *GSA – CS, ASA*, File 22.

10 Spatharis joined in 1905 and served as the accountant and second vice-president of its board and as secretary of its educational committee. See: *Ο εν Κωνσταντινουπόλει Ελληνικός Φιλολογικός Σύλλογος. Σύγγραμμα Περιοδικόν. Τόμος ΛΒ'. Συλλογικά Έτη ΜΗ' και ΜΘ' 1908–1910*, 1911, ι', κγ', κδ'.

11 Dimitris Kamouzis, 'Elites and the formation of national identity. The case of the Greek Orthodox *millet* (mid-nineteenth century to 1922)', *State-Nationalisms in the Ottoman Empire, Greece and Turkey: Orthodox and Muslims, 1830–1945*, eds. Benjamin C. Fortna et al., 2013, 26–31; Athanasios Souliotis-Nikolaidis, *Οργάνωσις Κωνσταντινουπόλεως*, eds. Thanos Veremis and Katerina Boura, 1984, 228.

12 *GSA – CS, ASA*, File 23/1: Certification of the Royal General Consulate of Greece in Constantinople (16 May 1949).

21 June 1910, which curtailed the jurisdiction of the Phanar over the churches and schools in Macedonia in favour of the Bulgarian Exarchate.[13] Spatharis was amongst several lay representatives arrested by the police while trying to attend a National Assembly (*ethnosynelefsis*) called at the Phanar by the Ecumenical Patriarchate in order to discuss the recently passed legislation as well as the overall relations between the state and the Patriarchate. He refused to sign a document of abstention from the meeting and was interrogated before being eventually released on 6 September 1910.[14] His defiant attitude made a considerable impression in the local press – both Greek and Turkish – and earned him the public praise and the support of Patriarch Ioakim III and several important Constantinopolitan Greeks, thus solidifying his status as an advocate of the rights of the Patriarchate and the Greek Orthodox community.[15]

In October 1918 Spatharis was part of a small group of influential clerics and laymen who orchestrated the removal of Patriarch Germanos V[16] from the patriarchal throne on the grounds of his complacent attitude towards the physical and structural violence applied by the Committee of Union and Progress during World War I.[17] The overthrow of Germanos and the election of the archbishop of Bursa Dorotheos Mammelis as *locum tenens* of the patriarchal throne signalled the return of the ethnocentric elite to power. All the National Councillors of the new

13 *Proodos*, 14–16, 18–23 June 1910. On 14 August 1910 *Icho* (Ηχώ), a newspaper published by Spatharis, ran along with other Greek ethnocentric newspapers the protest memorandum submitted to the Porte by the Greek deputies. The memorandum had been written by the founder of the Society of Constantinople, Athanasios Souliotis-Nikolaidis, and was officially submitted on 12 August 1910. See: *Icho*, 14 August 1910; *Politiki Epitheorisis*, 15 August 1910; Souliotis-Nikolaidis, *Οργάνωσις Κωνσταντινουπόλεως*, 112–118. Spatharis edited *Icho* during the period 28 July–26 August 1910 and 6–9 February 1913. See: 'Ηχώ' in Tarinas, *O Ελληνικός Τύπος*, 71.

14 Spatharis was arrested on 1 September 1910. For an overall account of these events see: *Proodos*, 31 August, 3–7 September, 10–11 September 1910; *Politiki Epitheorisis*, 1 August, 5 September 1910; *Νέον Πνεύμα. Μηνιαίον Περιοδικόν Εικονογραφημένον* [*Neon Pneyma. Miniaion Periodikon Eikonografimeno*], 2/10–11, 1 September–1 October 1910, 481.

15 Ibid.

16 From the election of Metropolitan of Chalkedon Germanos Kavakopoulos as Patriarch in January 1913 and throughout World War I the *Rum milleti* was under the political control of the *antethnikoi* (anti-national)/anti-Ioakimist lay/clerical faction. See Kamouzis, 'Elites', 30–31.

17 The Hellenic Literary and Historical Archive, Eleftherios Venizelos Archive, 02/024: Metropolitan of Chalkedon Gregorios to Venizelos (2 November 1918); Dimitrios Mavropoulos, *Πατριαρχικαί σελίδες: Το Οικουμενικόν Πατριαρχείον από 1878–1949*, 1960, 64, 90–91; Dimitris Kamouzis, 'Out of Harm's Way? Structural Violence and the Greek Orthodox Community of Istanbul during World War I', *Journal of the Ottoman and Turkish Studies Association* 4/1, 2017, 189–211.

PNMC were supporters of the Greek irredentist policy of the *Megali Idea* (Great Idea), namely the ambition of creating a Greater Greece that would include the so-called 'Unredeemed Greeks' of Asia Minor (and thus Ottoman territories) into an expanded Greek nation. Spatharis was one of them, albeit a moderate one.[18]

On the one hand he participated in the seven-member committee appointed by Dorotheos[19] which compiled in June 1920 the official response of the Patriarchate refuting the claims of the memorandum that had been submitted by the Porte to the High Commissioners of the Great Powers earlier that year regarding the terms of the forthcoming peace treaty.[20] On the other hand he was quick to disassociate himself from the Venizelist hardliners who dominated communal affairs after November 1920, objecting to the disruption of relations with the Royalist government in Greece[21] and the election of the Venizelist Meletios Metaxakis as patriarch, a decision that he would later describe as 'an unacceptable challenge in every respect.'[22]

Spatharis was first and foremost a communalist. He had realised that the unilateral adoption of an overtly Greek nationalist policy by the Phanar combined with the severance of its traditional ties with Athens jeopardised the future of both the Patriarchate and the Constantinopolitan Greeks in case the Kemalist forces

18 Kamouzis, 'Elites', 32–33.

19 *GSA – CS, ASA*, File 1: Locum Tenens Dorotheos to Spatharis (1 June 1919); Dorotheos to Spatharis (15 June 1919). The other members of the committee were M. Ioannidis, M. Lygias, M. Theotokas, M. Karavokyros, K. Gkiokas and V. Mousouros-Gkikas.

20 The Patriarchate's response reiterated the accusations against the oppressive and violent policies of the Unionist regime and argued that the Ottoman Empire was still under the influence of the Committee of Union and Progress. Therefore, neither the Porte, nor the Turkish people who stood in solidarity with the CUP could invoke the principle of majority to claim contested territories. In addition, it challenged Ottoman statistics as inaccurate, while supporting the statistics of the Greek state and the Patriarchate in Constantinople and in areas claimed by Venizelos at the Paris Peace Conference, which showed that the Christians and, in some cases, specifically the Greeks formed the majority. See: *GSA – CS, ASA*, File 1: *Réponse du Patriarcat Œcuménique au Mémoire remis le 12 Février 1919 par la Sublime Porte aux Haut Commissaires des Grandes Puissances de l'Entente à Constantinople* (Constantinople: 7 June 1919); *Memorandum of the Sublime Porte communicated to American, British, French and Italian High Commissioners on 12th February 1919*, 1919.

21 Diplomatic and Historical Archives of the Hellenic Ministry of Foreign Affairs (hereafter *DHAMFA*), 1921, 2/4: Ministry of Foreign Affairs to Greek High Commission (1 November 1920); *DHAMFA*, 1921, 5/8: Pantazis to Ministry of Navy (1 December 1920); Mavropoulos, *Πατριαρχικαί σελίδες*, 132–133.

22 *GSA – CS, ASA*, File 23/4: Speech of Ayrilios Spatharis entitled 'Εξιστορήσεις από την ζωήν του Οικουμενικού Πατριαρχείου' and delivered at the Centre of Constantinopolitans in Athens on 11 January 1957. A revised version of the speech was published a month later in the political and financial review *Η Ετυμηγορία του Λαού* [*I Etymigoria tou Laou*], February 1957.

came out of the Greek-Turkish war victorious. His political insight along with his high sense of communal duty and his legal experience allowed him to remain in Constantinople when most of the leading figures of the community were fleeing to Greece during the mass exodus of September-December 1922.[23] The same attributes would make him indispensable with regards to the affairs of the Greek Orthodox minority of Constantinople after the signing of the Treaty of Lausanne in July 1923.

On the Way to Geneva: Religious Internationalism, Networks, Mobility and Recruitment[24]

Thanassis Aghnides was born in the town of Niğde in Cappadocia, in the Anatolian highlands of the Ottoman Empire in 1889, and received his early education at three different Christian institutions in the Ottoman Empire: one Greek Orthodox, one French Catholic and one American Protestant in the 1890s and early 1900s. It seems that he also attended the *Patriarchiki Megali tou Genous Scholi* at the Phanar – the elite institution for the local Phanariotes – in the late 1890s, but unlike Spatharis he did not graduate from the school.[25] He then enrolled in the French Catholic College of St. Joseph in Kadiköy on the Asiatic side of Constantinople in 1901.[26] The curriculum of the school emphasised French language, humanities, religion and the arts, and was taught mostly by monks, with some of the languages and arts classes being taught by hired professors.[27] Aghnides proved to be an excellent student, also taking a keen interest in music.[28] After

23 Kamouzis, 'Elites', 26–31; Alexis Alexandris, *The Greek Minority of Istanbul and Greek-Turkish Relations 1918–1974*, 1992 (originally published 1983), 82–83, 104.
24 This section partly builds on Haakon A. Ikonomou 'Wilsonian Moments: Thanassis Aghnides between Empire and Nation State', *Global Biographies*.
25 League of Nations Archives, Geneva (hereafter *LONA*), Private papers of Thanassis Aghnides, Folder 1 (hereafter *P1*), Document in Ottoman (translated by Firuzan Melike Sümertaş) on Thanassis Aghnides' attendance at the Grand Patriarchal School, by Michael Kleovoulos.
26 Archives of St. Joseph College (hereafter *ASTJC*), Institut des Frères des Écoles Chrétiennes. Collège Saint-Joseph A Kadi-Keuï. Distribution Solennelle des Prix présidée par Monsieur Bapst, Chargé d'affaires, Conseiller d'Ambassade, Officer de la Légion d'Honneur, 16 July 1902.
27 Frère Ange Michel, *Histoire de St-Joseph, 1870–1923*, 2003.
28 *ASTJC*, Distribution, 16 July 1902; *ASTJC*, Distribution Solennelle des Prix présidée par Son Excellence Monsieur Constans, Ambassadeur de France, prés la sublime porte, 8 July 1903; *ASTJC*, Distribution Solennelle des Prix présidée par Son Excellence Monsieur Constans, Ambassadeur de France, prés la sublime porte, 11 July 1904.

receiving his *baccalauréat* from St. Joseph, Aghnides changed scenery once again.[29]

Anatolia College, established by American Protestant missionaries in 1886 in the town of Merzifon in the Pontic Region near the Black Sea, proved a particularly influential experience for Aghnides.[30] The school attracted students from the Christian minorities, namely Armenians and Greeks, in the rural Pontic lands. Muslims, partly due to the strict law against proselytising, rarely enrolled. The college pursued the distinctly liberal mission of planting 'the seeds of a more progressive and fair civil society in which their pupils might pursue productive lives and determine their own destinies.'[31] Aghnides attended the 'secular' education of Anatolia College. English, spoken and written, was a key component of the education, thus adding a fourth language (following Greek, Turkish and French) to Aghnides' skillset – one that would become very handy when he returned to Constantinople. He graduated in 1908, again at the top of his class, and retained a lasting involvement with the college.[32] This completed a full decade at elite Orthodox, Catholic and Protestant educational institutions.

As the Ottoman Empire went through deep reforms giving more rights to religious groups while attempting to forge a new Ottoman identity (Tanzimat Reforms, 1839–1876)[33] and modernising its state administration and educational system,[34] and as its coastal cities were increasingly connected to global markets by imperial design and economic development, the Christian populations of Cappadocia, in the heart of the Anatolian plains, were pushed towards the Mediterranean shores.[35] Aghnides ended up living with extended family in Constantinople and, with excellent grades from his early education, qualified to study law.[36] Due to his particular language skills and the close ties between the foreign Christian schools and the diplomatic corps in Constantinople, he was also drawn into the French

29 Archives of Anatolia College (hereafter *AAC*), List of enrolments and graduations; *AAC*, List, Class of 1898 – Honorary Doctorate of Law, 1933.

30 John O. Iatrides, 'Introduction' in William McGrew, *Educating across cultures – Anatolia College in Turkey and Greece*, 2015.

31 Iatrides, 'Introduction', xv–xvi.

32 *LONA*, Personnel Files, Thanassis Aghnides, CV; *AAC*, List of enrolments and graduations; *AAC*, List, Class of 1898 – Honorary Doctorate of Law, 1933.

33 Niyazi Berkes, *The Development of Secularism in Turkey*, 1998.

34 Benjamin C. Fortna, *Imperial Classroom: Islam, the State, and Education in the Late Ottoman Empire*, 2002.

35 Aude Aylin De Tapia, 'Orthodox Christians and Muslims of Cappadocia: Intercommunal Relations in an Ottoman Rural Context (1839–1923)', PhD dissertation, 2016.

36 *LONA*, *P1*, Curriculum Vitae; *LONA*, Document in Ottoman (translated by Firuzan Melike Sümertaş) confirming completion of law degree, 1911–1912, to the highest level, 9 October 1912.

and British diplomatic community and started tutoring newly arrived diplomats in written and spoken Turkish and Greek.[37] One of his students was the British diplomat Harold Nicolson.[38]

Like so many Ottoman Greeks, however, Thanassis left the Ottoman Empire in the 1910s, probably in 1911. Coming from a relatively well-off and large Cappadocian family, he had the means and networks to facilitate a move westward. Together with his two brothers Elie and Nicolas, Thanassis moved to Belgium, where they lived with a distant family member for a while[39], before settling down in Paris. Here he retook his legal degree at the University of Paris but was increasingly drawn to the political work of the Ottoman Greeks of Paris.[40] During the latter half of the First World War, Aghnides wrote several music reviews on performances of Greek music. He used his reviews to convey an unmistakable preference for a new and enlarged Greece and a world order without Ottoman imperial tutelage. Aghnides spoke of peaceful coexistence between a brotherhood of well-defined nation states, with Greece thoroughly anchored in a 'Western' conception of modernity.[41]

His artistic work caught the eye of the liberal Greek statesman Eleftherios Venizelos, the main architect of the Greek entry into the First World War on the side of the Entente and the near realisation of the *Megali Idea*. According to Aghnides' own recollection, Venizelos, who was also in Paris at the time, called him in for a meeting sometime in 1915–1916 under the pretence that he wanted to discuss Aghnides' artistic publications.[42] This work, apparently, convinced Venizelos that Aghnides was of the right ideological persuasion, and Venizelos – in typical fashion – recruited the young Cappadocian to his personal diplomatic network.[43] Aghnides obliged and thus took a decisive step towards becoming a

37 *LONA*, *P1*, Thanassis Aghnides. Notice Biographique.

38 This was the beginning of a lasting and close friendship. In a letter dated 28 June 1938 – that is close to three decades later – Nicolson concludes affectionately to Aghnides 'What years it is since you pretended to teach me Turkish'. *LONA*, Personnel Files, My Dear Aghnides, From Harold Nicolson. 28 June 1938, London.

39 Recorded interview with Rika Aghnides. Conducted by Markos A. Bouketsidis-Skourtelis, 14 September 2019.

40 French National Archives (hereafter *FNA*), FACULTE DE DROIT – Fiches individuelles de scolarit. des étudiants n.s avant 1905, AJ/16/1806. AARNOUG – ALLEZAUD. An indication of this is his slipping grades.

41 Thanassis Aghnides, 'Vladimir Rosing and Greek Music', *The Musical Times*, 1 June 1918.

42 Thanassis Aghnides, 'Greek Art Itself Again', *The New World*, n.d.

43 Michael Llewellyn Smith, 'Venizelos' Diplomacy, 1910–23: From Balkan Alliance to Greek-Turkish Settlement', in *Eleftherios Venizelos. The Trials of Statesmanship,* ed. Paschalis M. Kitromilides, 2006, 137–138.

Greek national, though he would not gain his new citizenship until 1924.[44]

Towards the end of the First World War many Ottoman Greeks came to see the Greek state as a possible guarantor of their rights and security and became ardent supporters of the Venizelist conception of the *Megali Idea*.[45] After his recruitment, Aghnides was stationed to London as Director of Communications for the Greek Embassy during the last years of the First World War.[46] In particular, he reported on British and American views on Greece's territorial claims after a (potential) Allied victory. Aghnides thus played a part in Venizelos's plans to win Allied support for a 'Greater Greece of two continents and five seas.' Among other things, he wrote regularly for the periodical *La Méditerranée Orientale*, published by a group of Ottoman Greeks based in Paris and London. Here, he started to use terms such as 'national self-determination,' 'civilisational right' and 'minority protection', drew on and reviewed new scientific works on ethnicity, geography and the nation state, and formulated his analysis in explicitly Wilsonian language, placing Greece in a new international order of peaceful, liberal nations.[47]

By the end of the First World War, Aghnides had left the Foreign Service and returned to Paris and was looking for new work. Here he met his old student – the now well-established diplomat – Harold Nicolson, who worked for the British delegation at the Paris Peace Conference. Nicolson had recently been recruited to the Secretariat of the League of Nations by its first Secretary-General Sir Eric Drummond. Nicolson wrote to Drummond to recommend the 'young Greek' for a post in the League Secretariat. Given that Aghnides' candidacy was also supported by Venizelos and the Greek Foreign Minister Nikolaos Politis, the Secretary-General obliged.[48]

44 *LONA*, P273, 'Interview with Thanassis Aghnides', Geneva: Centre de Reserches sur les institutions internationales, 1966, 3; *LONA*, *P1*, Letter from Kaklamanos to Aghnides and Petridis, London 10 August 1918.

45 Mogens Pelt 'Bodosakis-Athanasiadis, a Greek Businessman from the East. A Case Study of an Ottoman Structure in Interwar Greece and the Interrelationship between State and Business', in *Middle East Studies in Denmark,* ed. L.E. Andersen, 1994, 65–81. For a detailed account of the support manifested by the Ottoman Greeks in Constantinople to Venizelos and the *Megali Idea* during the period 1918–1922 see Dimitris Kamouzis, *Greeks in Turkey: Elite Nationalism and Minority Politics in Late Ottoman and Early Republican Istanbul*, 2021, 43–124.

46 *LONA*, *P1*, Letter from Kaklamanos to Aghnides and Petridis, London 10 August 1918.

47 See Thanassis Aghnides, *La Méditerranée Orientale: revue bi-mensuelle politique, historique, scientifique*, 1917–1918.

48 *LONA*, Personnel Files S699–700, 'My Dear Drummond', From H. Nicolson, British Delegation, Paris, 4 July 1919; *LONA*, *P1*, Dear Politis (Mr. Minister), from Aghnides, 22 September 1919; *LONA*, *P1*, My dear Nicolson, from Eric Drummond, 23 July 1919.

Intersection Point: The Lausanne Treaty and Minority Rights

Whether Spatharis advised the Patriarchate concerning the rights of minorities being negotiated at the Lausanne Conference is hard to verify. But it cannot be excluded as a hypothesis. In his personal archive, one can find copies of Patriarch Meletios' correspondence with several important figures of the period including the head of the Greek delegation Eleftherios Venizelos and its members Dimitrios Kaklamanos and Michael Theotokas, as well as the representative of the Patriarchate at the conference, Metropolitan of Thyateira Germanos.[49] A comparison between Meletios' legal arguments and demands in his official responses and Spatharis' retrospective studies on these issues reveals an identity of interest not only in terms of context but also more importantly in the actual wording of the opinions expressed. These could be summed up as follows.

With regards to the Turkish request for the removal of the Patriarchate from Constantinople, Meletios argued that the office of the Ecumenical Patriarch as the Head of the Orthodox hierarchy worldwide was integrally connected with the Archiepiscopal Throne of Constantinople, just like the office of the Pope as the Head of the Catholic Church was connected with the Episcopal Throne of Rome. Therefore, it would be impossible to remove the Patriarchal Throne from Constantinople just as much as it would be impossible to remove the Holy See of the Catholic Church from Rome. He pointed out that such an attempt would irritate the Orthodox Christians around the world and would cause a serious backlash against Turkey creating new problems in the East.[50]

On the issue of the Greek Orthodox minority, Meletios speaking on behalf of the Holy Synod and the PNMC expressed his gratitude to Venizelos for exempting the Constantinopolitan Greeks from the imminent compulsory Greek-Turkish population exchange, but stressed the need for the establishment of rights with a reciprocal character safeguarding both the presence of the Greek Orthodox minority in Turkey and the presence of the remaining Muslims in Greece.[51] Meletios claimed that the Patriarchate would accept two different sets of rights, one ecclesiastical and one 'national,' which in this case meant lay. The former would allow the election of the Patriarch and the practice of his religious duties without the

49 See: *GSA – CS, ASA*, File 4.

50 *GSA – CS, ASA*, File 4: Patriarch Meletios to Venizelos (2 December 1922); Patriarch Meletios to Kaklamanos (7 December 1922); Ayrilios Spatharis, *Ο Ιδιαίτερος Προσωπικός Θεσμός του Ελληνορθοδόξου Τούρκου Υπηκόου (Άρθρον 42 Συνθήκης Λωζάννης) – Η Νομική Κατάστασις του Οικουμενικού Πατριαρχείου*, 1947, 48, 65; Ayrilios Spatharis, *Το Οικουμενικόν Πατριαρχείον. Αιωνόβιος Πανορθόδοξος Θεσμός*, 1958, 9–10, 12–13, 15, 23, 29.

51 *GSA – CS, ASA*, File 4: Patriarch Meletios to Venizelos (28 November 1922).

interference of the Turkish government and would guarantee the Patriarchate's jurisdiction over the churches and monasteries and their adjacent property as well as over ecclesiastical issues of a family or personal nature such as marriage and divorce. The other communal affairs would be administered by a lay council.[52]

On 30 January 1923, the Convention Concerning the Exchange of Greek and Turkish Populations was signed at Lausanne. The Turkish nationals of the Greek Orthodox religion established in Turkish territory and the Greek nationals of the Muslim religion established in Greek territory were considered as exchangeable (Article 1). The Greek Orthodox inhabitants of Constantinople and the Muslims of Western Thrace were excluded from the exchange (Article 2).[53] The rights of the exempted minorities were laid down in Articles 37–44 of the Treaty of Lausanne signed on 24 July 1923.[54] Regarding the Ecumenical Patriarchate, it was only verbally agreed that it could remain in Constantinople, but it would have to confine itself to strictly religious matters.[55]

However, adjusting to the new conditions proved to be a difficult task for the Patriarchate and the minority. In July 1924, exactly a year after the signing of the Treaty, Spatharis sent a detailed letter to the Constantinopolitan Greek doctor and deputy of Kavala in the Greek parliament Anastasios Misirloglou,[56] where he painted a grim picture of the situation in Constantinople.[57] The communal hospitals and schools were in a miserable financial state. In order to save funds, doctors were ordered to cut down on the range of medicines prescribed while the food provided to the patients was reduced to the bare minimum. Several schools

52 *GSA – CS, ASA*, File 4: Patriarch Meletios to Venizelos (2 December 1922); Patriarch Meletios to Metropolitan of Thyateira Germanos (9 December 1922); Spatharis, *Ο Ιδιαίτερος Προσωπικός*, 43–45, 64–65.

53 *Treaty Series No.16 (1923). Cmd. 1929. Treaty of Peace with Turkey and Other Instruments, Signed at Lausanne on July 24, 1923, together with Agreements between Greece and Turkey signed on January 30, 1923, and Subsidiary Documents forming part of the Turkish Peace Settlement*, 1923, 21, 175. According to Article 14 of the Treaty of Lausanne (24 July 1923), the Greek inhabitants of the islands of Imbros (*Gökçeada*) and Tenedos (*Bozcaada*) were later also exempted from the compulsory exchange.

54 Ibid., 29–33.

55 *Turkey No.1 (1923). Cmd. 1814. Lausanne Conference on Near Eastern Affairs, 1922–1923: Records of Proceedings and Draft Terms of Peace*, 1923, 326, 333; Dimitris Kamouzis, 'Incorporating the Ecumenical Patriarchate into Modern Turkey: The Legacy of the 1924 Patriarchal Election', *When Greeks and Turks Meet: Interdisciplinary Perspectives on the Relationship Since 1923*, ed. Vally Lytra, 2014, 228–229.

56 See 'Μισιρλόγλου, Αναστάσιος-Συμεών' in *Μεγάλη Ελληνική Εγκυκλοπαίδεια*, v. IZ, n.d., 262.

57 *GSA – CS, ASA*, File 22: Spatharis to Misirloglou (12 July 1924).

were forced to close due to the lack of resources and teaching personnel, the result of the dire economic situation of the country, anti-minority policies and the continuous voluntary exodus of the Constantinopolitan Greeks, which Spatharis described as a 'widely transmitted disease.'[58]

According to Spatharis, while this communal crisis was unfolding, the clergy at the Phanar ('callous and intellectually dead') were preoccupied with their hefty allowances and wasted a considerable amount of money on dubious and unnecessary employee recruitments. As he pointed out, the dissolution of the PNMC in October 1923[59] had facilitated the 'shameless manifestation of their predatory tendencies,' because among other things it had terminated any sort of control over the distribution of the subsidy provided by the Greek state to the Patriarchate, a matter Spatharis had officially dealt with as early as 1921.[60] He was especially critical of Patriarch Gregorios, whose election on 6 December 1923 had been approved by the Turkish authorities on the basis that he was trustworthy,[61] for living a lavish life despite the arduous circumstances.

Spatharis finally drew Misirloglou's attention to the minority's lack of preparation regarding the forthcoming application of the peace treaty terms and especially Article 42, which stipulated that the Turkish government would take the necessary measures in order to permit issues related to family law or personal status to be settled in accordance with the customs of these minorities. According to the Treaty, these measures would be elaborated upon by special commissions composed of representatives of the Turkish Government and of the minority in

58 Ibid. Spatharis argued that the best solution to deal with the financial problems related to communal education would be the merging of schools, a measure that was eventually applied in the summer of 1928. See Dimitris Kamouzis, 'A minority in a state of flux: Greek self-administration and education in post-Lausanne Istanbul, ca. 1923–1930', *State-Nationalisms*, eds. Fortna et al.,116–124.

59 For the dissolution of the PNMC by the Holy Synod see Kamouzis, 'Elites', 105–106.

60 On 26 January 1921 Dorotheos had appointed Spatharis as a member of a committee entrusted with the task to study 'the material obligations of the Greek government to the Ecumenical Patriarchate from a financial, legal and historical point of view.' Spatharis offered again his legal advice on the issue during the negotiations between the Patriarchate and the Greek Ministry of Foreign Affairs in 1923. *GSA – CS, ASA*, File 3: Locum Tenens Dorotheos to Spatharis (13 January 1921); PNMC to Alexandris (16 March 1923); Response draft to the document of the Greek government dispatched on 31 May 1923.

61 Gregorios Zervoudakis was elected Patriarch after Meletios' forced abdication on 15 October 1923. However, according to Spatharis, Gregorios' patriarchate was so mediocre to the point that 'he made Meletios' flaws seem like virtues.' Despite their own personal differences, Spatharis admitted that Meletios understood immediately the importance of the minority issues during the Lausanne negotiations. See Kamouzis, 'A minority', 108; *GSA – CS, ASA*, File 22: Spatharis to Misirloglou (12 July 1924).

equal number.[62] Spatharis asked rhetorically who would represent them and how would these representatives be selected, since the minority was ill-equipped and the Patriarchate was not allowed to assume this task. He argued that they should have already established a specific service for minority affairs and should have prepared the relevant files in advance, or else when the moment arrived to file their complaints, they would find themselves as always improvising at the last minute. His overall view on things demonstrated his frustration and apprehension:

> Unstable, without leaders, we gaze fatally to the next day. Communal life is dying, and our sick organism does not react at all. There is no consideration, no motivation, no effort to respond to the requirements of this new era.[63]

Nevertheless, Spatharis reassured Misirloglou that he continued to study and collect material in case his services were needed, and asked him to inform the Greek Foreign Minister Konstantinos Rentis about the current situation in Constantinople. His fears were soon confirmed.

On 16 November 1924, Gregorios passed away and on 17 December 1924 the Holy Synod elected the Archbishop of Derkoi Constantine Arapoglou as Patriarch Constantine VI, despite the unambiguous warnings of both the Turkish government and the Greek diplomatic authorities against his candidacy for the reason that he was considered exchangeable. As a result, on 30 January 1925 the Turkish authorities expelled Constantine to Greece. This action incensed Greek public opinion and forced Athens to appeal to the League of Nations. Although officially Ankara assumed an uncompromising attitude on the issue, the Turkish authorities tried to reach the following behind-the-scenes compromise with the Metropolitans of the Holy Synod and Georgios Exindaris, the head of the Greek delegation in the Mixed Commission for the Exchange of Populations: if the Holy Synod dismissed Constantine and elected a new non-exchangeable patriarch and if Greece withdrew its appeal to the League, Turkey would exempt all the exchangeable prelates from the exchange.[64]

In late February 1925 Spatharis wrote to Patriarch Constantine, who had settled temporarily in Thessaloniki, and to General Ioannis Metaxas, one of the central figures of the royalist / anti-Venizelist political elite in Greece, informing them

62 *Treaty Series No.16 (1923), Cmd. 1929*, 30–33.

63 *GSA – CS, ASA*, File 22: Spatharis to Misirloglou (12 July 1924).

64 Kamouzis, 'Incorporating', 231–238.

in detail about the negotiations that were taking place in Constantinople.[65] Spatharis expressed his devotion to Constantine[66] and claimed that the Constantinopolitan Greeks were furious with the 'despicable gang of the Phanar,' who were trying to 'Turkify' the Patriarchate.[67] Apparently a multifaceted effort to cancel the understanding between the government and the Holy Synod was under way[68] and according to one source at the time 'Spatharis had the prelates at the Phanar trembling.'[69] To this end, Spatharis sent a fiery article to Metaxas condemning the 'treacherous and selfish' stance of the Metropolitans and specific laymen, which was eventually published in the Athenian newspaper *Politeia*, unofficial organ of Metaxas' party the *Eleftherofrones*.[70]

Constantine responded to Spatharis that he would wait for the decision of the League of Nations on the Greek appeal, but he pointed out in a rather pessimistic tone that 'this is already known in advance.'[71] He was right. The Greek government did not even wait for the final decision of the Permanent Court of International Justice at The Hague. Realising that it had not received the international support it had anticipated from other European governments, Athens welcomed Ankara's proposals for a compromise. Thus, Patriarch Constantine was forced to resign on 22 May 1925, and a few days later the Turkish authorities confirmed that the exchangeable prelates could remain in Constantinople. Accordingly, Greece withdrew its appeal to the League of Nations, and on 13 July Vasilios Georgiadis, a candidate approved by the Turkish state, was elected as Patriarch Vasilios III.[72]

The Constantine affair allowed Turkey to represent the Patriarchate as a purely Turkish institution and undermine its international character, a claim that Spatharis

65 *GSA – CS*, Ioannis Metaxas Archive (hereafter *IMA*), File 44: Spiliotopoulou to Metaxas (3 March 1925); Spatharis to Metaxas (28 February 1925).
66 *GSA – CS*, *IMA*, File 44: Patriarch Constantine to Spatharis (3 March 1925).
67 *GSA – CS*, *IMA*, File 44: Spatharis to Metaxas (28 February 1925).
68 Ibid.
69 *GSA – CS*, *IMA*, File 44: Spiliotopoulou to Metaxas (3 March 1925).
70 *GSA – CS*, *IMA*, File 44: Spatharis to Metaxas (28 February 1925); *Politeia*, 10 March 1925. The article was entitled 'Υπό κοινού συμφέροντος κινούμενοι και …' and for reasons of safety it was supposedly sent from a special associate of the newspaper in Thessaloniki, who signed with the pen name 'Cato' (Κάτων). In June 1925, Spatharis published two more articles on the issue of the ban imposed by the Turkish government on these Constantinopolitan Greeks who had fled Constantinople in autumn 1922 and were not allowed to return despite the fact that they were considered non-exchangeable. Once again, he was presented as an associate from Thessaloniki and signed with the pen name 'Emigrant Phanariot' (Απόδημος Φαναριώτης). See *Politeia*, 5 and 7 June 1925; *GSA – CS*, *ASA*, File 6.
71 *GSA – CS*, *IMA*, File 44: Patriarch Constantine to Spatharis (3 March 1925).
72 Kamouzis, 'Incorporating', 238–239.

went into great lengths to refute in his later works.[73] He strongly disapproved of the compromise, arguing that Greece had wasted a unique opportunity to settle in an international court the exact status of the Patriarchate and in a way amend the failure to include relevant written terms in the Treaty of Lausanne.[74] In private, he would go even further and maintain that not only at Lausanne but also after the Balkan Wars as well as at Sèvres the Venizelist governments, rather than benefitting the Patriarchate, had actually caused more damage.[75]

Meanwhile in mid-1925, Ankara decided to adopt the Swiss Civil Code, which contradicted Article 42 of the Lausanne Treaty by clearly stipulating that issues related to family law or personal status would be settled in accordance with the customs of the minorities. In late May 1925 the government formed three mixed commissions composed of representatives of the state and of the Greek Orthodox, the Armenian and the Jewish minorities that would discuss the settlement of these issues. By October 1925, the government managed to extract from the Jewish and Armenian minorities an official renunciation of Article 42, thus increasing the pressure on the Greeks.[76]

As Spatharis had predicted, the Greek members of the Turkish-Greek commission were not elected by their fellow Greeks, but were state appointees, who the Turkish authorities expected to cooperate on the renunciation of Article 42. On 5 November 1925, these twenty-two Greek members issued an invitation to all the communities to elect representatives in order to discuss and come to a decision on the issue of family law and personal status.[77] Ayrilios Spatharis, who was elected representative of Stavrodromi,[78] publicly opposed the renunciation arguing that this would be a violation of the Treaty of Lausanne. As a result, on 24 November 1925 Spatharis and the rest of the elected members of Stavrodromi and Galata were apprehended by the police under the pretence that they wanted to organise a

73 Spatharis, *Ο Ιδιαίτερος Προσωπικός*, 61–75; Spatharis, *Το Οικουμενικόν Πατριαρχείον*.
74 Ibid., 73–74; Ibid., 21–23.
75 *GSA – CS, IMA*, File 44: Spatharis to Metaxas (28 February 1925).
76 Kamouzis, 'A minority', 109–110. With regards to the renunciations of the Jewish and Armenian minorities see: *GSA – CS, ASA*, File 7: Rapport de la Commission des Minorités Juives au Ministère de la Justice (10 September 1925); Rapport de l' Assemblée générale des Minorités Juives au Ministère de la Justice (15 September 1925); Rapport de la Commission des Minorités Arméniennes au Ministère de la Justice (17 October 1925); and Rapport de l' Assemblée générale des Minorités Arméniennes au Ministère de la Justice (17 October 1925).
77 Kamouzis, 'A minority', 109–111. For an official copy of the invitation see *GSA – CS, ASA*, File 7: Invitation to the Central Communal Boards and Church Boards of the Parishes of the *Rum* Minority within the prefecture of the Municipality of Constantinople and its suburbs (5 November 1925).
78 *GSA – CS, ASA*, File 7: Central Communal Board of Stavrodromi (20 November 1925).

meeting without the permission of the authorities. Three days later the communal assembly officially renounced Article 42. Spatharis, whose absence deprived the assembly of any serious legal opposition to the suggestions of the twenty-two-member committee, was released along with the rest of the arrested representatives after the end of the meeting.[79]

Spatharis argued that the assembly lacked any representative authority due to the systematic abstention of the Constantinopolitan Greeks from the communal elections, the violent exclusion of the representatives of Stavrodromi and Galata – the two most important communities – from the meeting and the fact that the twenty-two Greek members of the commission had not been selected by the minority. Furthermore, the renunciation was signed neither by the Patriarchate, nor by the excluded representatives.[80] From a legal point of view, he maintained that Article 42 was a term agreed in an international treaty and therefore could not be modified or even worse relinquished without the consent of all the signing members. As he pointed out, the Turkish Civil Code rendered Article 42 a dead letter contrary to the commitments undertaken by the Turkish delegation during the Lausanne negotiations.[81] However, as in the case of Constantine, the Greek state's official complaint to the League regarding the irregularities followed during the renunciation procedure produced no significant results.[82]

Spatharis' last meaningful involvement in communal affairs was in February 1927 when he participated in a special committee entrusted with the task to consider two possible plans for a new communal constitutional charter, one concise and one more elaborate. Spatharis, who was responsible for drafting the final version of the proposed constitution, maintained that they should take into account Ankara's post-Lausanne policy of engaging directly with the different institutions of the minorities. If this was still the case, he stated that he would support the proposal of a detailed plan. Referring to the draft submitted by the Jewish minority, Spatharis explained that the Turkish government had approved the administration of the communal schools and institutions by the Jewish lay leadership, but it had rejected the proposal for the establishment of a central executive body representing the minority to the authorities, which meant that they did not recognise the minority as a legal entity. If the government asked them to relinquish their

79 Kamouzis, 'A minority', 111.

80 Spatharis, *Ο Ιδιαίτερος Προσωπικός*, 32.

81 Spatharis, *Ο Ιδιαίτερος Προσωπικός*, 27–29, 34–35; Spatharis, *Το Οικουμενικόν Πατριαρχείον*, 29.

82 *DHAMFA*, 1925, B/37/11: Argyropoulos to Drummond (11 September 1926); Spatharis, *Ο Ιδιαίτερος Προσωπικός*, 36–38; Alexandris, *The Greek Minority*, 138–139.

minority rights in return for accepting some of their demands, Spatharis suggested to preserve the administration system as it was.[83]

In March 1927, a detailed draft of fourteen articles was prepared and submitted to Ankara for official approval. According to Article 2, the churches, the charitable institutions, the schools and the other educational institutions of the Rum minority (*Romaikis Meionotitos*) including their land, their property and their revenues would be administered by the lay authorities. The ones belonging to the parishes would be managed by the local communal boards and the ones belonging to the minority as a whole by its Administrative Council apart from the religious section of the churches. Article 8 made provision for the formation of an Administrative Council which would constitute the central representative body of the minority. It would consist of twelve councillors with a four-year term in office without pay.[84]

The submitted draft was the product of the collaboration between Spatharis and the Greek Consul-General in Constantinople, Konstantinos Sakellaropoulos. The latter had prompted Spatharis to promote the submission of a detailed charter of rights, arguing that the possible dismissal by Turkey of articles based on minority rights recognised by the Lausanne Treaty would allow Greece to expose these Turkish violations at the League of Nations. He also argued that if the charter of rights comprising the fourteen articles was not submitted beforehand, this would provide Turkey with the opportunity to claim that the Greek Orthodox Christians voluntarily renounced the articles of the treaty safeguarding their minority status.[85]

Spatharis was sceptical. He admitted that the draft was not perfect but was designed in such a way as not to make the situation worse and to help them endure the current challenging times. Nonetheless his long experience did not leave him much space for optimism: 'The Turks will never organise us, because they pursue our complete disintegration.'[86] In mid-August 1927, Sakellaropoulos reported that the groundwork for organising the minority yielded no results because the Constantinopolitan Greeks had not agreed to renounce their rights.[87] The lack of an administrative body similar to the abolished PNMC deprived the minority of a central authority that would supervise communal affairs and defend effectively their rights. By dealing directly with the boards of every parish the government avoided recognising the minority as one legal entity, thus limiting significantly the minority's opportunity to organise group representation on its behalf.

83 Kamouzis, 'A minority', 113–114.

84 Ibid., 114–115.

85 *DHAMFA*, 1927, 92/1: Sakellaropoulos to Michalakopoulos (27 February 1927).

86 *DHAMFA*, 1927, 92/1: Spatharis to Sakellaropoulos (29 March 1927).

87 *DHAMFA*, 1927, B/92/3: Sakellaropoulos to Michalakopoulos (16 August 1927).

Lausanne, the Population Exchange and its Impact on Greece[88]

Aghnides started out in the Minorities Section of the League Secretariat overseeing the Minorities Treaties signed by the new or re-established Central, Eastern and South-Eastern European states and Turkey, securing certain religious, educational and linguistic rights for national minorities. He was the only Greek in the section – otherwise dominated by Scandinavians – but had, apart from his legal and diplomatic background, very specific linguistic and religious competencies that made him a useful broker in what were often difficult negotiations and considerations.[89] He was then, after a short stint in the Disarmament Section, brought into the Political Section in 1922.[90] Drawing on his various skills, enhanced by his time with the Minorities Section, Aghnides was tasked with monitoring national and ethnic disputes in the Balkans and Asia Minor, starting with the Greek-Bulgarian population exchange.[91]

The League of Nations Secretariat initially played a relatively marginal role in the execution of both the Convention Concerning the Exchange of Greek and Turkish Populations (30 January 1923) and the Treaty of Lausanne (24 July 1923). Soon, however, the League would be involved in a number of ways that it did not anticipate. Firstly, it appointed the neutral members of the Mixed Commission overseeing the population exchange. Secondly, the Minorities Section monitored, negotiated and collected information on the many instances of violence and pressure against minorities.[92] Thirdly, in a more general way, the League Secretariat – and particularly the Political Section – became a nodal point for the governments, relief organisations, international commissions and other bodies that sought to influence the execution and outcome of the Treaty and the population exchange. With the Secretariat gaining this new role, Aghnides became one of

88 This section builds substantially on Ikonomou, 'The biography as institutional can-opener'.

89 Greece was very underrepresented in the 15 political and technical sections of the League Secretariat. Apart from seven temporary collaborators of the Information Section and one clerk in the Economic and Financial Section, there was only one other higher official from Greece: Solon George Xenakis, who worked as a Member of the Information Section from 1938 to 1940. *League of Nations Search Engine*, http://www.lonsea.de/pub/search_person?nat=128 (last accessed 31 August 2022).

90 *LONA*, S954, Monnet's Office, 3 August 1922.

91 *LONA*, S699, Memorandum, Eric Drummond, 22 November 1928. Due to the contested nature of the many similar disputes in Eastern Europe, these also fell to him, as he was of a 'neutral' nationality, without any evident vested interests.

92 Mads Drange, 'Supervisor, Facilitator and Arbitrator. A Study of the Minority Department in the League of Nations Involvement in the Forced Population Exchange between Greece and Turkey in 1923', 2017.

its intermediaries, connecting the Mixed Commission overseeing the exchange, various refugee and humanitarian organisations, the League Secretariat and Council, and the Greek and Turkish governments.

A particularly important role that Aghnides maintained during these years was that of personal contact point for Eleftherios Venizelos – who returned to Greek politics as chief negotiator at the Lausanne Conference – within the League Secretariat. Aghnides had a key part in keeping the dialogue going between the Greek statesman, League of Nations Secretary-General Eric Drummond, and the Director of the Political Section Paul Joseph Mantoux.[93] Here, he helped to 'interpret' Greek demands, concerns and politics within the League context and instructed the Greek government on how to best get their points across. Accordingly, he wrote to one of Venizelos's collaborators to explain that the political deals of the Council were made 'in advance and informally. In fact, the Council [simply] authorises the decisions that have been determined in private.' Aghnides therefore urged the member of the Greek delegation at Lausanne, Andreas Michalakopoulos, to make a trip to Geneva to discuss the matter of securing a loan from the Great Powers for the settlement and feeding of refugees in Greece before 'we will again appear unprepared before the League of Nations Council.'[94]

He was also decisive in keeping an informal backchannel between Fridtjof Nansen – High Commissioner for Refugees in the League of Nations and the chief architect of the forced population exchange agreement – and Venizelos before and during the Lausanne negotiations. Aghnides had been prompted by the Deputy High Commissioner for Refugees (on behalf of Nansen), and duly communicated to Venizelos, that he 'could achieve a lot through [...] direct correspondence with Nansen, as long as this is kept secret, otherwise the prestige of Mr. Nansen would be undermined to our loss.'[95] A few days before the opening of the conference, Aghnides would deliver a confidential message to Venizelos from Nansen arguing that the Turkish authorities depended on his (Nansen's) proposal for a voluntary exchange of populations 'upon all the Greeks' [*sic*]. 'Naturally', Nansen continued, 'I mean this exchange is [to be] mandatory.' The Turkish authorities, Nansen warned, were only insisting on a voluntary exchange because they knew he would not accept it. If the negotiations thus broke down:

93 This is based on an overview of the correspondence of Aghnides regarding this matter in *LONA*, *P1*, and the digital Eleftherios Venizelos Archives (hereafter, *VA*).

94 *VA*, Aghnides to Michalopoulos, League of Nations, Geneva, 23 January 1923. (Translation from Greek by Markos A. Bouketsidis-Skourtelis).

95 *VA*, Aghnides to Venizelos, League of Nations, Geneva, 18 October 1922. (Trans. Bouketsidis-Skourtelis).

> 'The Turks – after concluding peace – would turn to their usual methods, creating panic amongst Christians, who sadly abandon their property and assets [fleeing elsewhere]. In this way Turks seize all the property of the Christians. Possibly they may also resort to the arson of Pera [in Constantinople], as was the case in Smyrna.'[96]

Aghnides followed up by setting up a meeting between the two at Lausanne, with the message that Nansen wanted to settle the issue of population exchange at the conference.[97] These co-ordinations underpinned Venizelos' conclusion that a mandatory population exchange – despite the many regrettable consequences – was a necessary step to consolidate the Greek nation state and avoid further conflicts with, or a potential withdrawal from the negotiations of, the new Turkish state.[98]

Aghnides also worked with the population exchange in a more personal capacity. He helped ensure Greek official support for the relocation of Anatolia College, his alma mater, from Merzifon near the Black Sea in Turkey to Thessaloniki in Greece. President of Anatolia College George E. White stopped by Geneva to seek his direct assistance in the matter, and Aghnides happily obliged by putting White in contact with Venizelos and then asking Venizelos to write a letter endorsing his plan to relocate the school. Venizelos accepted, stating that if Aghnides knew 'the persons that undertook this matter to be serious people, then I am prepared to grant the required recommendation.'[99]

Likewise, Aghnides continued to hold a key position in following up on the repercussions of the population exchange. In 1924, Secretary-General Drummond sent Aghnides to report on the social, economic and political implications of the population exchange for Greece. To gain first-hand knowledge about the situation, Aghnides visited the refugee camps on the outskirts of Athens. He was struck by those who had lived comfortable lives in the Ottoman Empire and now had to 'resign themselves to live [...] four people in a room and work to earn their daily bread.' The Anatolian Greek Orthodox (upper) middle class, which he had

---

96 *VA*, Aghnides to Venizelos, League of Nations, Geneva, 17 November 1922. (Trans. Bouketsidis-Skourtelis).

97 Ibid.

98 Smith, 'Venizelos' Diplomacy'.

99 Aghnides forwarded his correspondence with Venizelos, including English translations, and that statesman's recommendation, to William McGrew, with explanatory notes, *AAC*, 29 September 1977 and 25 October 1977; McGrew, *Educating Across Cultures*, 190–191, 445. William McGrew has been so kind as to forward his correspondence with Aghnides to us. For this we are most grateful.

belonged to, uprooted in brutal fashion, had lost their former purpose and dignity. 'The fate of these people, especially those who belong to liberal professions, is really sad,' Aghnides maintained, as 'their capacities remain unused and as most of these refugees left their fortune in Asia Minor.' Nonetheless, Aghnides believed that the exchange would in the long run strengthen Greek-Turkish relations and mark a new dawn for Greece on its way to becoming a democratic state in a liberal world order based on Wilsonian principles. 'In this ferment of ideas,' Aghnides opined, 'refugees play a very important role.'[100]

At the time of his arrival, Greece was in a fragile state. Only three months earlier, Prime Minister Alexandros Papanastasiou had proclaimed Greece a republic, following the Royalist People's Party's disastrous extension of the military expeditions in Asia Minor. Papanastasiou, a close collaborator of Venizelos, was a left-leaning liberal, with lofty plans for a new republic built on liberal principles of the state. He helped establish the University of Thessaloniki, worked for a uniform Greek language, and pursued the same ideals of Hellenization through education as Venizelos had before him. Progressives or Liberals of the day were the zealots of a functioning, democratic, and – some would say – intrusive state, as a 'modern' answer to problems that in their opinion royalty and autocrats were unable to solve. Aghnides thought that Papanastasiou's policy of reconciliation – where he had given a general amnesty to officers and civil servants who had been dismissed for their political attitudes – had shifted the focus away from a struggle over polity, to a more fruitful struggle over politics. The policy of reconciliation was of great importance, the Foreign Minister told Aghnides, 'for the simple reason that the two champions, Venizelos (Republican) and Constantine (Monarch), had disappeared from the political scene.' 'My personal impression,' Aghnides wrote to Drummond, 'is that the people want to see at the head of matters a resolute man who will have the courage to rid Democratic Greece of the rubble of the monarchical Greece, rubble which clogs up the wheels of the State.'[101]

Aghnides' role in this was to see to it that this frail, new Republic – which he supported wholeheartedly – was moving in the right direction. He immediately found that almost all the Greek protagonists were positive towards the League. Nikolaos Politis, Greek Minister to Paris and Aghnides' chaperone for the duration of the visit, had intelligibly spread 'the idea of the League of Nations' in the Greek political milieu; Papanastasiou showed 'sincere curiosity' about the League; while

100 *LONA*, R1600, Voyage de M. Aghnides en Grèce, 25 June 1924.
101 Ibid.

Foreign Minister Georgios Roussos, having served as Greek Minister to Washington, was already 'imbued with Wilsonian principles' and even had the appearance of an American statesman. All assured Aghnides that the Greek Government was conducting their foreign policy in line with 'the spirit and the letter of the Covenant of the League of Nations.'[102] His first aim, then, to spread the gospel and connect Greece to the League, had all the political backing it needed to succeed and Aghnides went to the task with relentless energy.

Firstly, he arranged and took part in several conferences on specific themes of the League, one of which was attended by Papanastasiou. The Prime Minister gave a 'very impressive speech about the League of Nations,' Aghnides reported. 'One felt the idealism and sincerity of a man who could not conceal his emotion. His declaration of faith in the League of Nations made a great impression on the audience.'[103] Aghnides, upon the request of Papanastasiou, arranged for the speech to be published in a daily newspaper with a large circulation. Aghnides also met with the Hellenic League of Nations Association (hereafter HLNA), instructing them to be less formal in their published material, and to model their magazine on the English publication *Headway*. Furthermore, the contact between the Information Section of the League and Greece – going through the press bureau of the Ministry of Foreign Affairs – was enhanced, as Aghnides contacted the director of the bureau and asked him to collaborate closely with the HLNA. In accordance with instructions from Director Pierre Comert of the League Information Section, Aghnides promised to send them brochures and articles regularly for distribution in the Greek press.[104]

Lastly, he helped set up a Hellenic University Group for the League of Nations, and he hoped to get them well-established so as to be able to join the upcoming Assembly. The University Groups were meant to promote the process of 'moral disarmament' – producing and promoting teaching material for primary schools which was less militaristic, nationalistic or xenophobic, and which informed the children about the League, the Covenant and internationalism more generally. Aghnides gave the keynote address to the Group's first conference and could report back to Geneva that the Greek Foreign Minister had 'promised his full support' to the Hellenic University Group.[105]

His visit to Greece, in fact, constituted the starting point for a lasting

102 Ibid.
103 Ibid.
104 Ibid.
105 Ibid.

involvement in the question of resettling refugees in Greece, but also the broader mission of building a modern Greece, fully integrated in the new, liberal world order centred around the League of Nations. Indeed, while this falls outside the remit of this chapter, Aghnides was a close collaborator with Emmanuel Tsouderos, *the* key Greek politician and official in financial matters, in securing loans via the Financial Committee of the League of Nations to finance the resettlement of refugees.[106] Equally, Aghnides was the middleman between Greek (health) authorities, Director Ludwik Rajchman of the League of Nations Health Organization and the Rockefeller Foundation's International Health Division when Venizelos sought international assistance in reforming (or indeed establishing) the Greek public health sector in order to alleviate the massive health challenges of the refugee population.[107]

With his trajectory, from the Ottoman interior to Geneva, one can identify an attempt at aligning Christian ecumenical thinking with Wilsonian internationalism; League-centred multilateralism with Greek patriotism; and new technocratic visions of reform and modernity with the fate and well-being of the refugees that constituted his own past. In these efforts, and with his position, Aghnides embodied the challenges of the 'vertical' alignment of social, political, religious and ideological realities 'on the ground' and international(ist) designs for a new world order, in which Greece was but one piece of the puzzle.

End of the Road: Two Ottoman Greek Expatriates 'Return' to Constantinople

In 1934 Spatharis moved with his wife Smaro and his son Andreas to Athens,[108] where he continued to handle high-profile legal cases for the Ecumenical

106 Emmanuel Tsouderos Archives (GR IATE A3) (hereafter *ETA*), See in particular correspondence Aghnides – Tsouderos, 18 February 1926, 23 February 1926, 17 November 1926, 9 December 1926, 23 December 1926, 31 December 1926, 12 February 1927, 9 June 1927, 2 August 1927, 10 August 1927.

107 See particularly: *VA*, Geneva 29 October 1928; *LONA*, *P1*, Monsieur le Chargé d'affaires et Cher Ami (Monsieur D. Bikelas) – Geneva, 5 November 1928; *LONA*, *P1*, Aghnides to Doxiadès, Geneva, 23 February 1929; Karen Gram-Skjoldager and Haakon A. Ikonomou 'The League of Nations Secretariat – An Experiment in Liberal Internationalism?', *Monde(s) – Histoire, Espaces, Relations*, 19/1, 31–50. See also: Haakon A. Ikonomou 'A Catalyst of Public Health', *The Lausanne Project Blog*, 17 September 2021. https://thelausanneproject.com/2021/09/17/a-catalyst-of-public-health/ (last accessed 25 February 2022).

108 In 1934 Spatharis settled on Eptanisou Street and a year later moved to a house at the junction of Fylis and Ithakis Streets. See: *GSA – CS*, *ASA*, File 22.

Patriarchate, the Patriarchate of Alexandria, the Church of Crete and several upper-class Greeks still living in Constantinople.[109] At the same time he played an active role in the affairs of the expatriate Constantinopolitan Greek community in Greece. Once liberated from the suffocating ambiance of Constantinople and in the safety of Athens, Spatharis became quite vocal about the problems of the Patriarchate and the minority. In 1947 he composed a detailed memorandum for the Research Society 'Constantinople' (*Etaireia Meleton 'Konstantinoupolis'*), which enumerated all the Turkish violations of the terms of the Lausanne Treaty up till then.[110] His study focusing on Article 42 and the legal status of the Ecumenical Patriarchate published the same year was well received by several important religious and political figures both in Greece and Turkey.[111] In 1953 he was amongst the founders of the Centre of Constantinopolitans (*Kentro Konstantinoupoliton*, hereafter CoC) – possibly the most important post-war association of Greeks who had migrated from Constantinople, where he served as a member of the Committee of External Liaisons (*Epitropi Eksoterikon Epafon*).[112]

Despite his disappointment with the situation of the minority in Constantinople and the lack of interest demonstrated by the younger generations of expatriate Constantinopolitan Greeks towards the Phanar, Spatharis emphasised that they should never stop fighting.[113] He maintained this fighting spirit until the very end. In the aftermath of the 6–7 September 1955 pogrom in Constantinople, where organised mobs attacked the city's Greek Orthodox minority after false claims of a bomb going off in Atatürk's birthplace in Thessaloniki (at the time Turkey's consulate),[114] the General Secretary of the CoC Tatiana Stavrou delivered on 26

109 *GSA – CS, ASA*, Files 7, 9–11, 13–19.
110 *GSA – CS, ASA*, File 23/1: Research Society 'Constantinople' – Memorandum on the position of the Greek Orthodox Minority in Turkey, Athens, 1947.
111 Spatharis, *Ο Ιδιαίτερος Προσωπικός*. The Arch Secretary of the Holy Synod of the Ecumenical Patriarchate Archimandrite Iakovos Stefanidis, the Archbishop of Athens Spyridon, the Metropolitan of Sardeis Maximos, the Consul-General of Greece in Constantinople Michael K. Melas, the Vice Minister of Foreign Affairs Panagiotis Pipinelis, the former member of the MCEP Alexandros A. Pallis and the diplomats Andreas L. Kountouriotis and Michael Tsamados were some of the personalities who congratulated Spatharis for his book. See: *GSA – CS, ASA*, File 22.
112 *GSA – CS, ASA*, File 20/2: *Δελτίον Κέντρου Κωνσταντινουπολιτών*, 1958, 18, 21–23, 31–32, 44–47, 78–80, 82–86.
113 *GSA – CS, ASA*, File 22: Spatharis to Metropolitan Haldias Kyrillos (15 May 1954).
114 With regards to the violent events of 6–7 September 1955, see: Speros Vryonis Jr., *The Mechanism of Catastrophe: The Turkish Pogrom of September 6–7, 1955, and the Destruction of the Greek Community of Istanbul*, 2005; Dilek Güven, *6–7 Eylül Olayları: Cumhuriyet Dönemi Azınlık Politikaları ve Stratejileri Bağlamında*, 2005.

September 1957 a speech on behalf of Spatharis, who on that same day had suffered a heart attack.[115] Addressing the educators of the Greek schools of Constantinople, Spatharis offered words of encouragement. He maintained that the outgoing generations had suffered from time-to-time severe persecutions, which were much more intense compared to the most recent ones but did not lose their courage. On the contrary they remained 'unwavering guardians of the Motherland.' At the same time, he made a clear distinction between citizenship and nationality or national identity, a clear reiteration of the importance of their status as members of an exempted national minority officially recognised by the clauses of the Treaty of Lausanne:

> Citizenship is just an institutional connection, which does not imply the de-nationalisation of a person belonging to a different national group. Citizenship is one thing, but the unacceptable corruption and alteration of nationality is another.[116]

His final advice was a combination of emotional intensity and wisdom by someone who had lived through one of the most tumultuous and traumatic periods in the history of the Constantinopolitan Greeks:

> Rally together. Discipline brings more victories than courage, prudence prevails over violence. Take strength knowing that the most effective weapon of the weak is to retain his moral endurance high. The wounds of fate are admittedly deep. They are usually curable and only exceptionally do not heal.[117]

The following day, 27 September 1957, Spatharis passed away in Athens at the age of 81.[118] In his final work, published posthumously, Spatharis as a genuine Phanariot paid his respects for the last time to his beloved Patriarchate, lifting it above the smothering framework of Greek-Turkish relations:

> The Ecumenical Patriarchate as the Ultimate Head of Orthodoxy is not a Minority Religious Establishment, is not a Minority Religious Association,

115 *GSA – CS, ASA*, File 20/2: *Δελτίον Κέντρου Κωνσταντινουπολιτών*, 84.
116 Ibid., 85.
117 Ibid., 85–86
118 Ibid., 112–113.

> is not a Minority Religious Foundation, it has nothing in common with all the above, because it constitutes a Perennial Pan-Orthodox Institution. […] The Patriarchate of the Throne of Constantinople is Ecumenical, not Hellenic. […] The Ecumenical Patriarchate did not cease to act with religious reverence according to the terms imposed upon it at Lausanne. Therefore, our consciences are rightfully scandalised when we witness Mother Church, which symbolises the wholeness of Orthodoxy, suffering during the last years the impact of the fluctuations of the Greek-Turkish friendship, thus remaining a hostage in favour of the maintenance of that friendship between the two neighbouring states.[119]

In a similar vein, Aghnides published in 1964 *The Ecumenical Patriarchate of Constantinople in the light of the Treaty of Lausanne*, a detailed exposé of the dispute between Turkey and Greece about the attempted permanent expulsion of the Ecumenical Patriarchate from Constantinople. Varying between level-headed legal arguments and brief emotional escapades, the publication was a plea for a world governed by rules; a legal defence of the international status of the Patriarchate; an attack on violations of the Treaty of Lausanne by the Turkish state; and a demand that both the Greek and Turkish Governments seek peaceful resolution to their differences.

Aghnides finished the manuscript in 1961, only six years after the Constantinople pogrom, which had resulted in the mass departure of over 15,000 of the remaining 65,000 Greeks between 1955 and 1960. Aghnides was addressing a pressing political issue – and the strategic Turkification of his homeland. On the last page, he warned that if the Turkish state tried to expel the Orthodox seat, the Greek government could draw the attention of the General Assembly of the United Nations or that of the Security Council to any violation of the obligations assumed under the Lausanne Treaty. To keep tensions as low as possible, Aghnides recommended to avoid the Security Council and instead go through the General Assembly: 'We venture to make this recommendation bearing in mind the fate of the Greek population in Constantinople and the importance of maintaining friendly relations with our eastern neighbour in the very interest both of the Ecumenical Patriarchate and of the Greek minority in Turkey.'[120] This was also one

119 Spatharis, *Το Οικουμενικόν Πατριαρχείον*, 29–30; *GSA – CS*, *ASA*, File 20/2: *Δελτίον Κέντρου Κωνσταντινουπολιτών*, 117–122.

120 Thanassis Aghnides, *The Ecumenical Patriarchate of Constantinople in the Light of the Treaty of Lausanne*, 1964, 40.

of Aghnides' last actions before retirement, once again trying to align his belief in the international system with the struggles of his home of the past. He passed away in Geneva on 12 May 1984, at the age of 95.

Constantinople and the Patriarchate were foundational for Spatharis' committed and feisty communalism and Aghnides' broad and tolerant internationalism, which were expressed through their active involvement in the political developments following the Greek-Turkish exchange of populations and the Treaty of Lausanne. During the last stage of their lives, both Spatharis and Aghnides finally 'met' in Constantinople in spirit and 'conversed' on the basis of their common past – a childhood and adolescence filled with religion. Their long journey from the Ottoman capital to Athens and Geneva respectively had come to an end. They had returned home.

14

Framing Pasts and Futures at the Lausanne Conference

Hans-Lukas Kieser

The Conference of Lausanne consisted of several months of intense interactions. The plenipotentiaries emphasized the sublime task of achieving world peace, turning the page on the past and normalizing relations with Turkey after continuous war since 1914 and troubled diplomacy since 1911, when Italy had invaded Libya. On many levels, the form, content and decisions of the protracted negotiations in Lausanne set the course for a hundred years to come in the post-Ottoman world and for Western relations with that area. This chapter enters Lausanne's discursive universe with its defining historical arguments.[1]

Interlocution took place between the delegations and their various representatives, experts and associates, as well as with delegations that were not allowed to sit at the main table. To be added are sideshows, private conversations and soirées as well as several hundred journalists, lobbyists and figures of the private sector. Their reports, interviews, published statements or talks in the halls and corridors of grand hotels or backrooms and bars complete the picture of vibrant and expectant, at times cacophonic and often contradictory communications. The outcomes of this mega-event, however, were clear and incisive. They included historical visions, omissions or distortions that framed the process of decision-making. The Conference's historical arguments and frameworks defined historiography in

1 For a previous short article dealing with the subject, see Hans-Lukas Kieser, 'Macro et micro histoire autour de la Conférence sur le Proche-Orient tenue à Lausanne en 1922–23', *Mémoire vive. Pages d'histoire lausannoise* 13, 2004, 42–48.

Turkey and beyond. 'Lozan' (Turkish for 'Lausanne', but also for the Lausanne Conference and Treaty) was to take centre stage in the Kemalist writing of modern history.

Broadly speaking, my analysis approaches the Conference as a formative mega-event in which ageing Western European national-imperialists diplomatically compromised with 'anti-imperialist' ultranationalists of a hitherto Bolshevik-backed elite in Ankara. By 1922, they had won the day in Anatolia by military means. Almost all of them had been involved in the former national-imperial party-state of the Young Turks. The Conference's result – the Treaty of Lausanne – was not a compromise where no one lost out, but a pact that left wounds unhealed and made whole indigenous groups voiceless losers. Non-Turkish representatives did not sit at the Conference table, although Kurds and other non-Turkish ethnic groups lived within the borders of the so-called National Pact of 1920 (*Misak-i Milli*) that the Conference was supposed to endorse. There were a few token 'fig leaves' at the margins of the Turkish delegation in Lausanne, like Chief Rabbi Haim Nahum and ex-CUP Kurdish deputies.

This chapter pays particular attention to the Turkish delegation's use of history. Its main sources are the meetings in plenary, committee and sub-committee sessions,[2] to which it adds journalistic reports, diaries and memoirs. In its first general part, it introduces the context and conditions of the Conference, and the role played by historical arguments and registers. It then elaborates on how pasts and futures were concretely used and reframed, so that they gave room for a balance of interests at the negotiation table, i.e. primarily for a compromise of Ankara with the British and French mandatory powers. It finally considers the input of those excluded from the negotiations to the writing of history.

Revisiting Lausanne's Framing of History

For Turkey's president Mustafa Kemal (hereafter Atatürk), 'the questions brought forward at Lausanne's peace table did not exclusively concern the new regime, which was only three years old.' In the words of his programmatic speech in 1927

---

2 The Conference's published proceedings are accessible in French, the Conference's main language: *Conférence de Lausanne sur les affaires du Proche-Orient (1922–1923). Recueil des actes de la conférence*, 6 vols. Where possible, I quote from the abbreviated English version that covers only the first half of the Conference, i.e. November 1922 to February 1923: *Lausanne Conference on Near Eastern Affairs, 1922–1923: Records of Proceedings and Draft Terms of Peace*, 1923 (hereafter *Lausanne Conference*).

('Nutuk'), 'centuries-old accounts were settled.'[3] For him, Lausanne comprehensively engaged past and future. During the Conference, historical arguments, references, allegations, projections as well as promises for the future actually abounded. There were a number of speeches resembling historical dissertations.

By 1922–1923, the leadership in Ankara identified with what had begun as the Young Turk narrative of national-imperial salvation, its stations being the Young Turk Revolution (1908), the recovery of Edirne (1913) and the defence of Gallipoli (1915). However, national history now started for Ankara in 1919 and culminated in the victorious Anatolian wars. To this was soon added the diplomatic counter piece, the triumph at Lausanne, the international birth certificate of the Republic.[4] The Turkish delegation in Lausanne explicitly demarcated itself from empire, palace, dynasty and Young Turk rule, while at the same time insisting on, and claiming a nationally framed *Ottoman-Turkish* history. It asserted a post-1918 defence of self-determination over Anatolia, whilst accounts of the history of Ottoman victimhood at the hands of Europe were blazoned to an international audience: According to the Turkish delegation, the crucial and enduring plot of modern history consisted of Europe's age-old anti-Turk conspiracy aided by domestic agents who deserved punishment for treason. This narrative allowed the Turkish delegation to selectively reframe core claims in Lausanne: Ankara's sovereignty in Anatolia, weak minority rights and the rejection of any autonomy for non-Turkish ethnic groups, particularly the Armenians and the Kurds. For Atatürk himself, as he stated retrospectively, the Lausanne Treaty documented 'the collapse of a great murderous plot prepared against the Turkish nation for centuries and thought to have been completed by the Treaty of Sèvres. It is a political victory unprecedented in the history of the Ottoman era!'[5]

Based on a new national understanding of history that burgeoned since the early twentieth century,[6] Lozan thus not only contributed to rewriting modern and contemporary history. It also set, as we will see, 'Turanean ranging rods' for an endeavour leading to the racialist Turkish History Thesis of the 1930s, which made

3 Mustafa Kemal, *Nutuk*, 2015, 534. All translations by the author, if not otherwise indicated.
4 René Albrecht-Carrié, *France, Europe and the Two World Wars*, 1969, 135. See also Sara-Marie Demiriz, *Vom Osmanen zum Türken: Nationale und staatsbürgerliche Erziehung durch Feier- und Gedenktage in der Türkischen Republik 1923–1938,* 2018.
5 Kemal, *Nutuk*, 582.
6 Hans-Lukas Kieser, 'Die Herausbildung des türkisch-nationalen Geschichtsdiskurses (spätes 19.–Mitte 20. Jahrhundert)', in: *Vom Beruf zur Berufung. Geschichtswissenschaft und Nationsbildung in Ostmittel- und Südosteuropa im 19. und 20. Jahrhundert,* ed. Markus Krzoska and Christian Maner, 2005, 59–98.

the Turks 'proto-European' founders of human civilisation, and, as 'proto-Turks', the prehistoric indigenous people of Anatolia. Members of the Conference delegation, such as Rıza Nur (vice-chief delegate), Reşid Saffet Atabinen (secretary general), Yusuf Hikmet Bayur (counsellor) and Ahmet Esat Uras, probably also a counsellor, were already or later became prolific history writers. Less than ten years after the Conference, Atabinen, Bayur and Uras had joined the Turkish Historical Society under Atatürk's close supervision in Ankara.[7] From 1933 onwards Bayur took a leading role in the obligatory teaching of 'The History of Turkish Revolution', i.e. of contemporary history through Kemalist eyes.[8] The delegation's official translator Hüseyin Bey – a Sorbonne-trained historian and, from 1935, the Turkish vice-president of Robert College and the American College for Girls – led the Turkification of these formerly prestigious internationalist institutions.[9] Uras' 1950 book *The Armenians in History and the Armenian Question*, became the denialist 'bible' on the Armenian question. It includes a chapter on the Armenian question at the Lausanne Conference.[10]

After its defeat in World War I, the Ottoman Empire was lost, but ex-Young Turk forces reorganised in exile and in Ankara. They concentrated their attention on preserving their power and former gains, aiming at establishing unitary rule and a safe Turkish-Muslim haven in the whole of Asia Minor. The early 1920 National Pact codified this goal but left open precise borders except those with

---

7 First Committee (1930), then Association (1931) for the Study of Turkish History (*Türk Tarihi Tetkik Cemiyeti*), in 1935 renamed *Türk Tarih Kurumu*, Turkish Historical Society. Although there is no doubt about Uras' strong involvement in all historical issues regarding Armenians from Talât to Atatürk, the Swiss police records (Conférence de Lausanne 1922–23, S 112/95, Archives cantonales vaudoises, Lausanne) and those in Mustafa Özyürek ed., *Akşam Gazetesi Başyazarı Necmeddin Sadık (Sadak) Bey'in Lozan Mektupları,* 2019, 20–21, do not confirm Uras' presence in Lausanne. The civil servant Uras, who knew several languages including Armenian, had already been the CUP's expert for Armenian issues and Talât's close collaborator in the ministry of the interior. See Ali Çankaya, *Yeni Mülkiye Târihi ve Mülkiyeliler,* 1968–1969, Vol. 3, 1040–1041; and German journalist von Tyszka to the Undersecretary of State in the Foreign Office, Zimmermann, 1 October 1915, German Foreign Office Archive, DE/PA-AA/R14088.

8 See Y.H. Bayur, *Türk inkılâbı tarihi*, 1991.

9 John Freely, *A Bridge of Culture: Robert College – Boğaziçi University: How an American College in Istanbul Became A Turkish University*, 2012, 272–275. See also Erik Sjöberg, *Internationalism and the New Turkey: American Peace Education in the Kemalist Republic, 1923–1933,* 2022.

10 This chapter by Uras is largely the translation of the sources reproduced in the Armenian delegate Alexandre Khatissian's book on the question, see Alexandre Khatissian, *Éclosion et développement de la République arménienne*, 1989 (in Armenian 1930), 317–428. Esat Uras, *The Armenians in History and the Armenian Question*, 1988 (Turkish edition 1950).

Bolshevik Russia. Timely compromises in a common division of the South Caucasus ensured friendship with Moscow that in turn recognised the National Pact in the Treaties of Moscow and Kars of 1921. Two years later, the Treaty of Lausanne was tantamount to 'an international [Western] recognition of the demands formulated in the Turkish National Pact.'[11] Bolshevik support proved critical during Ankara's wars in Anatolia against the Treaty of Sèvres that had given room to non-Turkish – Armenian, Kurdish, and Greek – claims for self-determination in minor parts of Anatolia.

Military victory in Anatolia allowed defeated 'pariahs', as seen from the First World War victors – i.e. ex-Young Turks supported by Pan-Islamic networks and the Bolsheviks – to seize the momentum in Lausanne. Claiming anti-imperialist defence and national self-determination, the Turkish delegation consistently pointed a finger at defeated, war crime-committing Greek invaders – allegedly the only evil-doers in the room. By stressing the Greek-Turkish War of 1919–1922, it succeeded in blurring the roles of perpetrators and victims in the long decade of wars that the Conference was supposed to bring to a close. Plenipotentiary İsmet blamed others when lamenting that Anatolia was entirely destroyed – he ignored the fact that it was war and genocide by the Committee of Union and Progress (CUP) that had, by 1918, left Asia Minor in ruins. This primarily concerned Eastern Asia Minor, that is, territories beyond the Western Anatolian regions that the Greek army had advanced to.[12] By and large, the Conference turned a blind eye to Ankara's framing of history: the Ottoman Empire's policy of extermination and demographic engineering that in critical aspects went on until 1923 and beyond.

The Kemalist historical picture displayed Greeks and 'Europeans', not 'Asiatic despots', as standing on the wrong side of history and political ethics. This enabled the Kemalists to demand the revision of the former treaty, of its historical underpinning and its projection of Anatolia's futures. During the negotiations in Paris and in the resulting Treaty of Sèvres, the crimes committed during the war and the Young Turk dictatorship had stood at the forefront. In Lausanne, the Turkish delegation emphasised Ankara's recent successful war and Anatolia's imminent 'democratic', 'secular and modern' reconstruction under Kemalist leadership.[13] Thus, it succeeded in cementing a saga of anti-imperialist national-revolutionary

11 Bernard Lewis, *The Emergence of Modern Turkey,* 1961, 249.

12 *Lausanne Conference*, 342, 374, 390, 404, 573. See also (on Kirkuk and Greeks' destruction of 'whole Anatolia') Necmeddin Sadık's 'letters' of 22, 23 and 30 January and 4 February 1923: Özyürek ed., *Lozan Mektupları,* 232–242, 263, 286.

13 *Lausanne Conference*, 322, 333, 351. For the claim of democratic futures, see also 335 and 348.

liberation together with a narrative of modern European progress that its government would fully implement after its recognition in Lausanne. By accepting Ankara's main arguments and main claims, the Conference set the course for an enduring Western appeasement of Turkish ultranationalism. More generally, it introduced a diplomatic lexicon of compromise between post-Ottoman strongmen and Western democracies.

Ankara set a new paradigm in Lausanne. Turning relations upside down, it proved to the world how the Sèvres Treaty – the Near East-related pillar of the Paris-Geneva treaty system – could be cancelled and replaced by a treaty without a citation of the Covenant of Geneva's League of Nations in its first pass. Without any disguise, might now made right and wrote history. The reason for such success was simple: most Allied delegates, especially the French and Italian, were happy to end the status of war with Ankara without coming back to the First World War, except for economic and legal topics of own national interest.[14] Also, this vehement and violent Turkish-nationalist self-assertion was in line with the fundamental critique of the West by the Bolsheviks, which had struck fear into the hearts of many assembled in Lausanne. All delegates at the Conference table stressed world peace, cooperation, prosperity and shared interests. This striking rhetoric in the minutes was by no means surprising after the collapse of diplomacy which led to the First World War, whose end heralded the birth of the League of Nations and peace for all time. In keeping with the diplomatic language used by the League of Nations, most delegations refrained from using terms of culturalist or Orientalist belittlement and condescension, notably mention of 'Asiatic brutality' or 'Oriental despotism'. Before and outside the Conference, political language describing Turkey sounded different, especially in Britain.[15] Yet, the laudable abandonment of stereotypes – except Lord Curzon's at times blunt or condescending attitude – also sacrificed the clear language of facts with regards to mass murder or dispossession.

For the Allies, the forgetful, neglectful dealing with contemporary and ancient history served obvious interests: avoiding discussions, ending years of conflict and depletion; minimising the costs and risks of the mandates in the Levant; focusing on domestic problems in Europe, notably France on Germany and the payment of reparations. This situation mirrored the turbulent and tired state of

14 Jacques Thobie, *Intérêts et impérialisme français dans l'Empire ottoman, 1895–1914,* 1977; Andrea Gennai, *La Question d'Orient: La gestion multilatérale de la Dette Publique Ottomane*, 2015.

15 In his historical presentation on 12 December 1922, İsmet alluded with a few examples to its past omnipresence (*Lausanne Conference,* 201).

European democracies in the early 1920s and a penchant for a 'new realpolitik' with immediate results, without considering the future. The political project of the League, including the challenge of democracy, was shelved. Despite all the promises in Lausanne of reform and of the rule of law, the Republic of Turkey quickly evolved into a dictatorial party-state after the Conference. The massacre in Dersim in 1938, whose mostly Kurdish Alevi victims included Armenian survivors, was a poignant reminder of how the Conference had failed to face up to genocidal politics in Turkey and that it had accepted Ankara's restrictions of minority rights: only the remnants of non-Muslim populations in the country, that is Christians and Jews, but not Kurds or other non-Turkish groups, counted as minorities in the Lausanne Treaty.

For France and Italy in particular, starting already in 1921, ignoring crimes against minorities was the most rapid way to avoid further conflict with the Kemalists and to gain an advantage in competing European vested interests. Priority was the preservation of Italian ownership of the Dodecanese, the French Mandate in Syria and resuming business in Asia Minor resulting from pre-1914 investments. Lord Curzon, the British chief delegate and from November to February self-appointed Conference president, tried to insist on a peace that considered all the years from 1912 onwards. But he fought a losing battle on that front, although considering the pre-war years in conjunction with the conflicts thereafter would often have been historically pertinent. Britain, modern Europe's most exposed national-imperial power, was overstretched and had other (mainly imperial) priorities. In particular, it feared two spectres that favoured the Turkish nationalists: Bolshevism and – in mandatory Iraq and the crown colony India – Ankara-supporting Pan-Islamism. Nonetheless, Britain was the only actor in Lausanne who, besides Turkey, could at the end claim a triumphalist narrative of the Conference. Curzon managed to ensure three main goals: keeping open the Turkish Straits, Ankara's (partial) alienation from Moscow, and the perspective of an Iraqi, not Turkish, future for Mosul.[16] Yet, 'mired in its own imperial struggles', a moralising British Great Power had definitively become 'a less than legitimate voice of international justice.'[17]

The bold historical arguments, which the Turkish delegation proffered, obeyed

16 For a triumphalist British version of the Lausanne Conference, see for example Chapter XI, 'Lausanne: The Final Triumph', in Harold Nicolson, *Curzon: The Last Phase, 1919–1925: A Study in Post-War Diplomacy*, 1934, 314–350.

17 Michelle Tusan, '"Crimes against Humanity": Human Rights, the British Empire, and the Origins of the Response to the Armenian Genocide', *The American Historical Review* 119/1, 2014, 69.

the objective of full Turkish sovereignty over a maximum of national territory. Thanks to Lausanne, the National Pact resulted in a reorganised cartel of interest groups, internationally underpinned by the new treaty. In the emerging Republic, this pact took the place of an Anatolian constitutionality that would have had to be based on a democratic social contract. The organisers of a new power centre were ex-Young Turk cadres led by Atatürk. This leader renounced Islamic arguments as soon as he had won international credentials in Lausanne, and a few years later also his honorific title of a Muslim fighter against non-Muslims (*Gazi*).

In the final analysis, the Conference of Lausanne clearly failed to come to terms with the previous decade. In order to bring about compromise, the delegates forced a substantial reframing of history that alienated millions left out. As a result, the Treaty cut short all alternative futures imagined by various actors during the previous decade of wars, in particular any Armenian future in Anatolia, but also future self-determination which the Kurds, Rûm, Assyrians, and Arabs aspired to. Together with unresolved intrinsic conflicts and alternative historical understandings, important elements of projected (though frustrated) futures survived. Consequently, despite Kemalist triumph in 1923, a 'return of the repressed' (traumas, crimes, claims, aspirations) always loomed large and was feared by the Turkish Republic. This also included longings for an imperial Caliphate and a greater Turkey by (Pan-Turkish) nationalists or by Muslims who resented the Kemalists' assertive secularism after Lausanne. Labelled 'Sèvres Syndrome', this fear fuelled related conspiracy theories for the next century.[18]

Before Lausanne: Projecting Aftermaths of War During a Decade of War

During the long wartime (1912–1922), various visions of the aftermath of war had been voiced, but most of them were in the end frustrated. From 1912, and with singular intensity from August 1914 onwards, visions of 'new Turkey' ('yeni Türkiye') were produced in pamphlets, essays, novels, poems, discussions and speeches by mentors, writers and leaders of a novel Young Turk party-state, established and centred in Istanbul since 1913. Because of Russia's imperial collapse in the Caucasus in 1917, the imagination of new and grandiose futures of

18 On 'Sèvres Syndrome', see Baskın Oran, *Türkiye'de azınlıklar. kavramlar, teori. Lozan, iç mevzuat, içtihat, uygulama,* 2004, 160–162. See also Fatma M. Göçek, *The transformation of Turkey: redefining state and society from the Ottoman Empire to the modern era,* 2011, 98–184.

national-imperial Turkey proliferated toward the end of World War I. Allied with Wilhelmine Germany, wartime Turkey's rulers, ideologues and their sympathizers projected Pan-Turkish utopias that promised to restore and expand the Ottoman Empire, thus compensating for Muslim victimhood in modern history. Imagined by Ziya Gökalp and his circle of young acolytes who met in the headquarters of the ruling CUP in Istanbul, these visions were about a unitary modern Anatolian party-state of Turks combined with a Turkish-led bi- or tricontinental federative Sultanate-Caliphate.[19]

Persecuted Christian groups in the Ottoman Empire sought sheer survival during the First World War, while their representatives in exile lobbied for retributive justice and a collective renaissance. They spread the vision of Turkish misrule throughout history and imagined self-determined national futures in autonomous territories. Expecting support by a liberal West, their inflated demands were instead betrayed after the defeat of the Central Powers. 'We had created a dense atmosphere of illusion in our minds', as Hovhannes Katchznouni, a member of the Armenian Revolutionary Federation (*Tashnaktsutyun*) and leading figure in the Republic of Armenia from 1918 to 1920, wrote during the Lausanne Conference.[20] In contrast, Alexandre Khatissian opined in his more serene retrospective, written in the late 1920s, that the justice of the Armenians' main cause was not lost but deferred to a far future. He agreed that there had been number of illusions, miscalculations, mistakes and misplaced or inflated expectations. Khatissian had served in Kajaznuni's cabinet, but in contrast to the latter, he was also a member of the United Armenian Delegation (*Miatsyal Badviragutyun*) in Lausanne. This delegation was composed of representatives of the Republic of Armenia and the Paris-based diaspora leaders headed by Gabriel Noradungian. A former Ottoman diplomat and liberal-conservative foreign minister, Noradungian served as a successor of Boghos Noubar Pacha, the Armenian wartime leader in exile.[21]

From November 1914, Istanbul's foes, Britain chief amongst them, considered the Ottoman Empire under Young Turk party rule a nuisance. After Turkey's official entrance into war in October 1914, the Entente Powers planned to divide the Ottoman Empire (Sykes-Picot Agreement 1916) and exploit its geostrategic position and resources. They nurtured conflicting designs that ranged from

19 For a synthesis, see Hans-Lukas Kieser, 'Europe's Seminal Proto-Fascist? Historically Approaching Ziya Gökalp, Mentor of Turkish Nationalism', *Die Welt des Islams* 61, 2021, 431–438.

20 Hovhannes Katchznouni, *The Armenian Revolutionary Federation Has Nothing to Do Anymore. The Manifesto*, 1955 (written 1923), 6.

21 Khatissian, *Éclosion*, 317–428.

imperial realpolitik, including tricky promises in favour of their allies and Arab associates, to the declared will to punish Turkish regime members for crimes against humanity and to special commitments for Jewish and Armenian autonomies (Jewish 'national home' in Palestine, Armenian 'independence' including an eastern corner of Anatolia). The anti-colonialist rhetoric of the Bolshevik leaders and President Wilson, combined with the entrance of the United States into and Bolshevik retreat from the First World War, led to a revision of the Entente's plans in 1917 without annulling them. Numerous initiatives by third parties attempted to promote a general peace or separate peace treaties. They included initiatives by Pope Benedict XV, the Zimmerwald Socialist International and representatives of neutral countries, all of them seeking a speedy stop to bloodshed. Favouring compromise or (in the case of the Zimmerwald International) a world revolutionary socialist future, they never gained significant momentum. Istanbul's wartime leaders could not and did not want to contemplate the required compromises for peace before their ultimate defeat in the autumn of 1918. Imperial defeat led the CUP wartime cadres, Atatürk among them, to reconceive Turkey's future in post-imperial terms, settling for the Anatolian part of Gökalp's ideal. This was set forth in the National Pact.

Gökalp himself – the recognised spiritual father of Turkish nationalism – considerably adapted his ideology after 1918. During the Lausanne Conference, he published in Ankara his summa *Türkçülüğün Esasları* ('Principles of Turkism'). Its content partly conflicted with the nature of the state promised and the boundaries fixed at the conference. Although less explicitly Islamic and put more moderately and patiently than during the First World War, the main ideas in the book remained in line with Gökalp's Pan-Turkish thought: Asia Minor's Turkification – to be signed off in Lausanne – had to be followed by the Oghuz union ('Oğuz birliği'), that is, unification with the Turkmen (in the Caucasus, Iran, Turkistan and, implicitly, Iraq and Syria). The union of Turan was the third and last step; it would encompass all Turkic peoples – 'Turaneans' – as far as North-Western China.[22]

Lausanne's 'Diplomatic Fabric': Pasts, Politics, Futures – Powerfully Intertwined

Since 1923, the Treaty of Lausanne has been internationally regarded by diplomats and historians as a solid and constructive diplomatic milestone, i.e. as a

22 Ziya Gökalp, *Türkçülüğün esasları*, 2014, 28, 32.

compromise that made a clear break between before and after, war and peace, diplomatic collapse and repaired relations, old Ottoman and 'new (Kemalist) Turkey'. Special emphasis is often put on the fact that it was a 'negotiated peace' and not, like the rest of the treaties in the Paris system, a peace imposed by the victors.[23]

For many people on the ground in, or survivors from, Anatolia, however, it was entirely a victors', rulers' and perpetrators' 'peace'. Lasting frustration concerned not only the drastically side-lined and victimized groups like the Kurds, Armenians, Assyrians and the Greek-Orthodox native population of Anatolia (*Rûm/Romaioi*), but also many Turkish Sunni Muslims who were still used to an Ottoman imperial habitus, or at least to the rhetoric of the salvation of the sultanate-caliphate that Atatürk and his adherents had amply applied until 1922. The press sympathetic to Ankara went all out to win the trust of 'every Turk and Muslim' for the delegation's effort in Lausanne; it therefore applied an anti-European rhetoric the public was used to since 1911. 'If İsmet Pasha leaves Lausanne without signing a peace, every Turk and Muslim must know without any doubt that Europe, the merchant of money and self-interest, has still in no way offered to the Turkish nation a peace that does not sacrifice its future or sully its honour and betray the sanctified memory of the martyrs (*shahid*) that we gave during the last three years', the correspondent of the daily *Akşam* wrote in late December 1922 from Lausanne.[24]

Those Sunni Turks, who had identified with both Ankara's war for Anatolia and Istanbul's involvement in World War I, were distrustful of compromise and tended to reject territorial concessions. They notably claimed Mosul, Iskenderun and several islands as belonging to the Turkish motherland. Their Pan-Islamic solidarity, stressed by rulers since Sultan Abdulhamid II, was most strongly expressed in their loyalty to the Caliphate which had to be preserved. Their fear of the latter's weakening or abolition had been tangible since late 1922. Both from an imperial Islamic and a (Pan-)Turkish angle, therefore, these early post-Ottoman Turkish Muslims tended to perceive *Lozan* as a 'debacle' (*hezimet*) in the making. Such voices came to the fore during the Conference's break in March 1923 from members of the so-called Second Group in the National Assembly in Ankara when

23 For current works in this vein, see for example Roland Banken, *Die Verträge von Sèvres 1920 und Lausanne 1923: Eine völkerrechtliche Untersuchung zur Beendigung des Ersten Weltkrieges und zur Auflösung der sogenannten 'Orientalischen Frage'*, 2014; William Hale, *Turkish Foreign Policy since 1774*, 2013, 38–41; Zara Steiner, *The Lights that Failed. European International History 1919–1933*, 2007, 123–125.

24 'Letters' of 27–28 December 1922 by Necmeddin Sadık in *Lozan Mektupları,* 197–198.

they discussed the draft treaty of early February. The lament and accusation of this heterogenous group critical of Atatürk's emerging dictatorship included statements like 'They [Ankara's delegation] sell Mosul'; 'They [the Europeans] want to erase the caliphate and the caliphate's impact on the Islamic world'; 'With this document, [...] we lose the religious principles [...], we accept policies informed by the Christians [...] we put Turkey's future in danger and make it materially weak. [...] May God keep me off from permitting such an agreement;' 'Have we been cheated?'[25]

Many Muslims outside Turkey, who had been loyal to the Ottoman Sultan-Caliph until 1918, applauded and identified with Ankara's military victories and diplomatic re-empowerment, but felt alienated by Ankara's turn to Western civilisation in Lausanne. 'Al-ghazi's [Atatürk's] speeches left no doubt that Turkey initially revolted in order to defend Islam and the Caliphate, and to assert solidarity with the Muslims and hundreds of millions of Arabs', wrote the Lebanese notable Shafik Arslan, a prominent anti-colonialist and anti-Kemalist Arab voice in Swiss exile, who had been a loyal collaborator of the Young Turks in the 1910s. 'But as soon as the Lausanne Treaty was concluded', he continued, they regarded Islam as a 'detrimental principle that must be abolished, because [it is] inappropriate for a civilised nation.'[26]

The Turkish delegation's Vice-Chief Delegate Rıza Nur made a proud, yet unsatisfied retrospective assessment of the diplomatic success in 1923: 'However, this perfect treaty has a flaw. We gave freedom to the Bosphorus [instead of full Turkish control], we could not give autonomy to Western Thrace, we could not get reparations from the Greeks, we could not take the Turks of Iskenderun into our borders, Mosul was left to be settled later.'[27] Nur was a Turkist ultra still claimed as such by both Islamists and nationalists in contemporary Turkey. After the end of Kemalist single-party rule, these groups took Nur's and similar assessments as proof for their belief that Lausanne did not deliver the just reward for the Turkish victory and the blood shed by Turkish martyrs from 1911 to 1922. They continued

25 Taha Akyol and Sefa Kaplan eds., *Açık ve Gizli Oturumlarda Lozan Tartışmaları: TBMM'de Lozan Müzakereleri Tutanakları*, 2014, 576, 583, 586, 613. See also Nurullah Ardıç, 'Abolition of the Caliphate', in idem, *Islam and the Politics of Secularism: The Caliphate and Middle Eastern Modernization in the Early 20th Century*, 2012, 241–309.
26 Arabic journal *Al-Fath* 8/353 (1933), quoted in Mehdi Sajid, *Muslime im Zwischenkriegseuropa und die Dekonstruktion der Faszination vom Westen. Eine kritische Auseinandersetzung mit Šakīb ʾArslāns Artikeln in der ägyptischen Zeitschrift al-Fatḥ (1926–1935)*, 2015, 336.
27 Rıza Nur, *Hayat ve Hatıratım*, 1992, 447.

to resent the Lausanne-related end of the sultanate-caliphate and claimed that the Kemalists were duped by Europe. In particular, they blamed former Chief Rabbi Haim Nahum's alleged mentorship of İsmet and secret deals with Curzon for the abolition of the Caliphate. A book often referenced by proponents of this opinion – that in the 2010s and early 2020s include President Erdoğan's supporters – is Kadir Mısıroğlu's *Lozan: Zafer mi, hezimet mi?* (Lausanne – a victory or a debacle?). Mısıroğlu was an editor of Nur's memoirs that became accessible in the 1960s.[28]

The government of Ankara had abolished the Sultanate shortly before the Conference in order to prevent any representative of the still existing Sultanate-Caliphate with seat in Istanbul having a say in Lausanne. Though not on the Conference's official agenda, the abolition of the Caliphate was in line with the promise of the establishment of a modern, secular and law-bound republic presented by Ankara's delegation during negotiations. After the declaration of the Republic of Turkey on 29 October 1923, three months after the Treaty was concluded, Ankara consequently started to undertake incisive reforms in record speed, particularly adopting a Western civil law that abolished sharia. In Lausanne, Ankara's delegates had promised Western-style legal institutions, while de-emphasizing Islam and jihadism in their presentation of both the recent past and the future of Turkey. The ambitious timing and radical contents of Kemalist reforms after 1923, therefore, were substantially conditioned by the Conference's diplomatic-discursive matrix because the promised endorsement of Western standards, in return for which immediate League membership would be granted, helped appease the adversaries at the negotiation table. They helped to tone down international safeguards for minority rights and legal rights of foreigners. The Swiss Code of Obligations and Civil Code were introduced in 1926 and became the critical backbone of assertive secularism. The same prospect of European modernity served Ankara to compel the minorities to renounce in 1925 their autonomous civil law rights that the Lausanne Treaty had enshrined in international law.

Claiming the achievements of its millennia-old civilisation, Ankara's arguments on history went hand in hand with reform prospects as well as with efforts to hush up 'barbaric' elements of the past. Among the most sensitive items of the immediate past was the *jihad* until 1918; the extermination, dispossession and expulsion of Ottoman Christians; continued war in the name of Islam until the Conference; and last but not least, the manifest continuity of ex-CUP cadres in

28 Kadir Mısıroğlu, *Lozan: Zafer mi, hezimet mi?* 1992; for a recent example, see Vahit Özdemir, 'Lozan Barış Antlaşması revize edilmeli', *Independent Türkçe*, 25 July 2019.

Ankara. The most taboo subject in Lausanne was the 'Armenian Home'. Logically, Ankara's number one instruction (out of 14 points) to chief delegate İsmet read '1. The Eastern Border: an "Armenian Home" is out of the question, if it becomes an issue, the negotiations will be interrupted.'[29] The Conference's most ominous term and measure, disputed in its genesis and promotion, was compulsory population exchange. The term disguised and whitewashed what it historically completed: genocide and ethnic cleansing in Asia Minor during the decade before the Conference. This policy aimed to eliminate minorities and 'minority problems' and was directly related to the erasure of any Armenian autonomy in parts of Anatolia. International diplomacy and historiography after 1923 mistook Lausanne's 'population exchange' policy as a positive, 'brutal, but effective' (Bernard Lewis) tool for solving ethnoreligious conflicts.[30]

The late 1910s and early 1920s saw the writing and publication of several race-based histories authored by historian-politicians like Dr. Rıza Nur, Ahmed Ağaoğlu and Mehmet F. Köprülü. They prepared the way for a radical departure at the Conference:[31]the Turkish historical argumentation in Lausanne clearly preferred race over religion. Brotherhood with Kurds was now claimed in religious, historical *and* racial terms. Representatives of Kurdish descent in Lausanne – including Social Minister Fevzi Pirinççioğlu, Diyarbekir's bloodstained former CUP deputy[32] – served to make a display of undivided Kurdish support for the Kemalist negotiators, saying 'We Kurds are brothers with the Turks, we do not want to be separated, there is no difference between us.'[33] Repressing alterity no longer in religious terms as during the previous wars, but promoting Turkishness

29 Bilal Şimşir, ed. *Lozan Telgrafları I (1922–1923),* 1990, Vol. XIV, with reference to the Foreign Office Archives (Dışişleri Bakanlığı Arşivi, DBA, Ankara).

30 Lewis, *Emergence*, 250.

31 Mehmet Fuat Köprülü, *Türkiya Tarihi: Anadolu istilasina kadar Türkler*, 1923; Rıza Nur, *Türk Tarihi*, 1994, 14 Vols., originally published 1924–1926 by the Ministry of Education; Ahmed Agayef (alias Ağaoğlu), 'Türk medeniyeti tarihi', *Türk Yurdu*, 1999, Vol. 2, 303–307; idem, 'Mukaddime' [Preface] to *Pontus Meselesi*, 1922, quoted in Can Erimtan, 'Ottomans and Turks: Ağaoğlu Ahmed Bey and the Kemalist construction of Turkish nationhood in Anatolia', *Anatolian Studies* 58, 2008, 141–171.

32 See Hilmar Kaiser, *The extermination of Armenians in the Diarbekir region*, 2014, 337–339; Ü. Uğur 'Disastrous decade: Armenians and Kurds in the Young Turk Era, 1915–25', in eds. Joost Jongerden and Jelle Verheij, *Social relations in Ottoman Diyarbekir, 1870–1915*, 2012, 267–295.

33 Zinar Silopi, *Doza Kürdistan: Kürt Milletinin 60 Yıllık Esaretten Kurtuluş Savaşı Hatıraları*, ed. M. Bayrak, 1991, 62, quoted in the 2003 paper: M. Sami Denker, Erol Kurubaş, 'Jeo Politika ve Jeo Strateji Açısından Kürt Konusu, PKK ve Türkiye', https://dergipark.org.tr/en/download/article-file/55276, 2.

and Turanean kindredship, the delegation's historical argumentation prefigured the Turkish History Thesis with the latter's culturally Pan-Turkish references.

In political debates after the Great War, national claims, concepts and boundaries required an underpinning both in terms of civilisation and racial or ethnic history. The genre of history-writing by committed nationalists comprised premodern and ancient times. In the Turkish case, it emphasised great achievements by Turkish state-builders throughout millennia, whilst directly depreciating others, in particular Armenians and Kurds.[34] Politicised historical production at the eve of the Lausanne Conference regarded also the immediate past. No effort was spared to relativize, belittle or deny the extermination of Armenians. In the years before the Conference, Kara-Schemsi (alias Reşid Saffet Atabinen) had penned several books and leaflets in this vein. In his main arguments, he exonerated the state and 'the Turkish nation' for mass murder, put the blame on Kurds and others, and made a sweeping comparison of Armenian and Muslim suffering in modern history. He ridiculed the Armenian deaths, calling them 'jokes' compared to Turkish and Muslim victimhood.[35] A journalist, diplomat and member of Talât's and Ziya Gökalp's circle in the CUP headquarters, Atabinen had spread Gökalpian Pan-Turkism in the 1910s. A member of parliament after the Conference, Atabinen became a prolific member of the Turkish Historical Society in the 1930s, an admirer of Hitler, and an international advocate of the History Thesis until the 1950s.

Future-Shaping Arguments on History

Ankara's main goal in Lausanne was to achieve undivided and unrestricted sovereignty according to the National Pact on as much territory as possible, and to reject any claims by indigenous non-Turks regarding autonomy, dispossessions and crimes against humanity. The question was how the National Pact had to take concrete shape. At the negotiation table, a maximal territorial version of post-Ottoman Turkey was out of reach (i.e. inclusion of Western Thrace, Mosul, Aleppo and several Aegean islands close to the Anatolian coast). From this angle, Ankara's final diplomatic success in July 1923 was great but by no means

34 An extreme case of open racism is Rıza Nur. See his *Türk Tarihi* and his *Hayat ve Hatıratım* as well as his unpublished *Ermeni Tarihi* (Staatsbibliothek zu Berlin, Ms. Orient Quart 1394). In this vein also, an annexe to the December 1920 Treaty of Alexandropol, beside minimising Armenian population figures, denied an authentic Armenian culture, insisting that 'the Armenian music had Turkish origins' (quoted in Khatissian, *Éclosion*, 279).

35 Setting the tone: Kara-Schemsi (Atabinen), *L'extermination des Turcs*, 1919, 2.

absolute. However, it turned the vision of a fully Turkish Anatolian homeland (*Türk Yurdu*)[36] proposed by the new Turkist associations (*Türk Ocağı* and *Türk Yurdu,* with Gökalp as their star ideologue) and the CUP luminaries since 1912 into a reality.

Among the most remarkable Conference meetings regarding historical argumentation were those about population exchange on 1 December, about minorities in mid-December 1922 and about Mosul on 23 January 1923. The question on 23 January was whether Mosul should belong to Turkey or British-mandated Iraq. Bilateral Turkish-British conversations had taken place and memoranda exchanged in Lausanne since early December. Open debate started in the First Commission on 23 January 1923. That day with its two meetings, the first at 11am, the second at 6pm, turned out to be one of the most heated days of the Conference. Beside a few strong points, İsmet's argumentation revealed critical flaws, among them the racial definition of the Kurds as 'Turaneans' (thus as Turks for the matter in question). Whilst the British official position on Mosul 'smelt [of] oil', Curzon's priorities were considerations of empire and the mandate of Palestine.[37] In him İsmet faced a plenipotentiary whose knowledge of the region exceeded that of the others. This intellectual superiority led İsmet time and again to hyperbolic reactions and contentions. Champion of the Turkish nationalist antithesis to the Paris-Geneva post-WWI peace system, he insisted almost mechanically on full parity in every respect vis-à-vis the 'European imperialist' Curzon.

The competition for hegemony in historical argumentation went along with the claim to equivalence in matters of democracy. İsmet suggested that an exemplary democracy existed in Ankara where Kurds sat in the National Assembly. Any trouble for the government with the Kurds in recent history 'was due to incitement by certain consuls'. The Kurds had 'always enjoyed all the rights of citizens' and 'always collaborated with the Turkish Government'; there was 'not a single Kurd' who wanted the autonomy promised by Europe in exchange over unity with Turkey.[38] Throughout the 23 January discussions, İsmet remained stubborn in his contentions: the National Assembly 'was composed of the real and freely elected representatives of the Turkish people. All the inhabitants of Turkey, including both Turks and Kurds, were equally entitled to the franchise and enjoyed the same rights in the Grand Assembly, which thus afforded the world the most striking

36 H.-L. Kieser, *Türklüğe İhtida. 1870–1939 İsviçre'sinde Yeni Türkiye'nin öncüleri*, 2008.
37 Jonathan Conlin, 'An Oily Entente: France, Britain, and the Mosul Question, 1916–1925', *Diplomacy & Statecraft* 31/2, 2020, 246–249.
38 *Lausanne Conference*, 344–346.

example of a nation being directly administered by those best qualified to represent it.'[39] Curzon's response was sharp: 'Is there a single [Kurdish] one who was elected by a popular constituency? It is notorious that they are all nominated men [...].'[40] At the end of the evening meeting, İsmet again doubled down on his account. The handpicked Kurdish deputies, he insisted, 'had been elected under conditions of liberty and independence equal to those of all other countries.'[41]

Whilst reacting to a felt or real condescension from the British side, İsmet's pronouncements reflected the contemporary doctrine in Ankara rather than emotional reactions to the current situation. The Turkish claim to Mosul rested on the First Article of the National Pact:

> Inasmuch as it is necessary that the destinies of the portions of the Turkish Empire which are populated exclusively by an Arab majority, and which on the conclusion of the armistice of the 30th October 1918 were in the occupation of enemy forces, should be determined in accordance with the votes which shall be freely given by the inhabitants, the whole of those parts whether within or outside the said armistice line which are inhabited by an Ottoman Moslem majority, united in religion, in race and in aim, imbued with sentiments of mutual respect for each other and of sacrifice, and wholly respectful of each other's racial and social rights and surrounding conditions, form a whole which does not admit of division for any reason in truth or in ordinance.[42]

From Ankara's point of view, this statement made two strong arguments for a Turkish Mosul. First, the province of Mosul was not yet occupied by 30 October 1918. Second, it was preponderantly 'inhabited by an Ottoman Moslem majority, united in religion, in race and in aim.' The second argument was valid, if the Kurds were included in its definition of the Turkish nation, and if there was indeed a common Turkish-Kurdish desire for a Turkist future, an ideal modern Turkey, which Gökalp had defined in the early 1910s as one where religion, culture, and race are homogenous. Tantamount to 'Great Turkey', Gökalp's mythical and messianistic catchword 'Turan' had until 1918 been the main label for new Turkist visions of the past and future. Discredited after CUP war defeat, 'Turan' survived

39 *Lausanne Conference*, 396.
40 *Lausanne Conference*, 357.
41 *Lausanne Conference*, 404.
42 Translation by A.J. Toynbee in *Western Question in Greece and Turkey*, 1922, 207–210.

in the nationalist vocabulary, but moved from the centre to more discreet zones of articulation. İsmet declared Turks and Kurds to be from the same Turanean race and therefore to have been living in perfect harmony since the dawn of time. Ethnographically, according to him, Erbil and Kirkuk were to be recognized as entirely Turkish places. '[…] racial considerations suffice to prove that the Mosul Vilayet must return to Turkey', concluded the Turkish reply, dated 23 December 1922, to a British Memorandum regarding the Mosul Question. The reply added to the racial contention the argument of the general popular will. 'The Turks and Kurds, who constitute the great majority of the population of the Mosul Vilayet, are firmly determined to obtain the union of their countries to Turkey; no doubt is possible on this point.' İsmet insisted in his accompanying letter to the reply that the 'Turkish Government cannot for a moment consider abandoning its sovereign rights over Mosul, which forms an integral part of the Turkish mother country.'[43]

Thus, in the critical meetings of 23 January 1923, Ankara's plenipotentiary argued that 'the Kurdish people is Turanean', and 'as regards manners, usage and customs the Kurds do not differ in any respect from the Turks, and that these two peoples, while they speak different languages, form a single unit in respect of race, religion and manners.' Based on race and manners, he included the Yazidis in this definition.[44] Part derisive, part acerbic, Curzon's targeted, fine-grained response took one hour and a half. 'It was reserved for the Turkish delegation in one of their papers to discover for the first time in history that the Kurds were Turks. Nobody has ever found it out before. The origin of this people is somewhat obscure.' It was easy to tear down the Turanean argument and the pretence of a Turkish-Kurdish union by referring to recent facts, experience and recognized scholarship.[45] Undoubtedly Curzon's arguments were not made for the sake of historical truth or in defence of democracy, but to achieve success in the negotiations. This became clear in the discussions of a plebiscite that Ankara wanted, but Britain feared. There were good reasons to consider a referendum in the province of Mosul not viable and subject to Ankara's manipulation by way of bribes, bullying and (temporary) population transfers. It was again easy to expose Turkish inconsistence in wanting a referendum there but refusing it at any other place in Anatolia and Istanbul. In any case, nonetheless, Curzon's successful insistence against a plebiscite in the province of Mosul proved the loss of confidence in one

43 *Lausanne Conference*, 372 and 374–375.
44 *Lausanne Conference*, 342–343.
45 *Lausanne Conference*, 356. See also Harold Nicolson, *Curzon: The Last Phase, 1919–1925: A Study in Post-War Diplomacy*, 1934, 337.

of the League's most innovative instruments for fundamental decision-making. İsmet took this rejection as 'the most convincing proof of the weakness of the case brought forward against Turkey.'[46]

All Allied delegates prioritised the pursuit of economic, strategic and political designs over rights, democracy and historical truths that concerned millions of humans. When Curzon put the issue of minorities on the agenda of the First Commission, it resulted in three heated meetings from 12 to 14 December that brought the Conference to the brink of collapse. Once more, the Conference's agenda was set by the British delegation, which put the Turkish delegation at a disadvantage. İsmet wrote in his memoirs about the night before 12 December:

> After midnight, they informed us that the issue of the minorities was on the agenda of the next day. The clerk of the delegation did not wake me up because it was too late. In the morning, when I was going to get up calmly and start working because there was no session that day, they said we were going to the conference. No, there was nothing last night, I asked, since they hadn't told us about an agenda. Yes, they came after you went to bed, they said, but we didn't wake you up. They stated that the issue of minorities will be discussed. I scolded the clerk for not waking me up. At least, there was a historical study that we had prepared hastily on the issue of minorities in Ankara. I took it with me and went to the conference.[47]

Harold Nicolson, a member of the British delegation, admitted that the objective in putting the minorities on the agenda was to widen the breach between Moscow and Ankara and to make Ankara's representative take a stand regarding the League of Nations.[48] The latter objective was achieved as İsmet promised on 14 December to enter the League, as soon as the treaty was concluded; however this promise remained unfulfilled until 1932. Besides his Conference strategy, Curzon was able to appreciate the human scope and import of the minority question in his statements. Starting the meeting of 12 December, he implored the delegates 'to approach this vital question [of minorities] in a humane spirit.' He kept repeating that 'the eyes of the world are upon us', or 'the whole world had its eyes fixed on the conference room', i.e. Château d'Ouchy's dining-room. The

46 *Lausanne Conference*, 397.

47 İsmet İnönü, *İsmet İnönü'nün Hatıraları,* 1998, 113.

48 'It was an article of faith with the U.S.S.R. to forbid her satellites and associates to have any dealings with the "organised impotence of Geneva which serves only to further the designs of the capitalist imperialist Powers."' Nicolson, *Curzon: The Last Phase,* 315.

minorities problem, he insisted, excites more attention throughout the world than anything else, and 'according as it is settled in an equitable and reasonable spirit or the reverse, so shall we [the Allies] and they [Turks and Greeks] be judged.'

Minorities Used in Historical Arguments

İsmet's long speech on 12 December – his reading in French of the study prepared in Ankara – amounted to the government's diplomatically convenient historical argumentation on minorities.[49] To be added to this defining historical paper are İsmet's responses and statements of 13 and 14 December, his statements on the Armenian Question on 31 December 1922 and his speech on Mosul's history on 23 January 1923 as well as statements by Rıza Nur and other members of the Turkish delegation during or outside Conference meetings.

Much of İsmet's statements and speeches must have resulted from concerted efforts of the Turkish delegation, starting on the eve of the Conference, possibly edited by Atabinen. Other members particularly able to contribute were the Sorbonne-trained counsellor Yusuf Bayur, the legal counsellor Mehmed Münir (Talât's adviser during the conference of Brest-Litovsk), and Rıza Nur. There were others who had a say among the forty or so people belonging to the Turkish team in Lausanne, notably Baha Said Bey, Talât's and Ankara's expert for confessional groups, and experienced journalists like Hüseyin Çahit (Yalçın), Necmeddin Sadık (Sadak) and Nihat Reşat Belger.

Relevant national history regarding minorities began, according to the 12 December paper, with the heroic conquest of Constantinople in 1453 and a victorious Sultan's supreme tolerance vis-à-vis minorities. Ankara's delegates stressed two arguments against European insistence on minority rights in a 'new Turkey'. Firstly, European efforts in favour of late Ottoman minorities had amounted to making them treacherous agents of foreign, in particular Russian, powers. Secondly, Ottoman politics had displayed an exemplary treatment of minorities since Mehmed the Conqueror and thus anticipated the progress enshrined in the minority protection treaties established by the League of Nations. Ankara could therefore do without any European lessons and League oversight. Both arguments mirrored a mindset wide-spread amongst late Ottoman imperial elites. Labelled an 'objective examination', the assertions made in Lausanne claimed authority and established the main lines which Ankara for decades pronounced officially and publicly in history textbooks as well as diplomatic negotiations. Thus, on 12

49 Reproduced in *Lausanne Conference*, 190–204. See also *İnönü'nün Hatıraları*.

December, İsmet told his audience about the 'striking [Ottoman] tolerance' vis-à-vis minorities (i.e. non-Muslim *millet*) throughout history. Europe's post-WWI minority rights and protection were, he said, an old liberal Ottoman achievement, because '[…] the rights of minorities […] sought to be assured in the twentieth century under the guarantee of the League of Nations, were spontaneously accorded to the non-Mussulman elements of the Ottoman Empire'. Turkey had forever been a factor of high civilization and progress. 'Foreign instigations', foremost by Russia, caused 'mutual distrust and the unhappy events' in the harmonious 'great empire which the incessant attacks of malevolent neighbours had already appreciably weakened' by the late-eighteenth century. Blaming bygone Tsarist Russia was easy and avoided any self-critical introspection. As for the Armenians, 'up to the middle of the 19th Century' they 'had lived at peace and at full liberty in Turkey.' In the 'unhappy events', i.e. massacres, no fault whatsoever rested with 'the Turks' and their state. 'Turks have never failed to acknowledge the rights of the non-Moslem elements so long as the latter did not abuse the generosity of the country in which they lived in comfort for centuries.'[50]

Ankara's delegation also used the argument of loyal Turkish-speaking 'Orthodox Turks', as opposed to certain Rûm close to Greece. Yet, significantly, these Turkish Christians, too, were soon not offered any future in the Republic of Turkey, but transferred.[51] Much more than Orthodox Turks, the Jews served as a model minority. İsmet went regularly to play the 'Jewish trump card' along an imperial order of thought that had now to foster unitary nationalism. 'The example of the Jewish community, which [since four centuries] has not up to the present had to complain of any inhumane act on the part of the Turkish Government or people, would suffice to show that the blame for the distressing events in the case of the Greeks and the Armenians falls entirely upon themselves.'[52] Proffered at Lausanne's table, that was a convenient way of whitewashing history and a powerful blueprint for the blaming of the weak and the victim for being destroyed. Curzon made do with sarcastically asking whether the Armenian Ottoman community had killed itself.

Other European allies in the conference room, however, lacked a concerted counterargument against this kind of degrading argumentation. İsmet's display of continued good-will and tolerance toward Christian native populations, as long as they behaved the way the state expected of them, stood in total disconnect with

50 *Lausanne Conference*, 190–204.

51 See notably Halide Edip Adıvar, *Memoirs*, 1926, 372.

52 *Lausanne Conference*, 201.

what Ankara did and wanted. Again, the reaction was nothing more than a short sarcastic comment. 'Why were hundreds of thousands of Armenians now fugitives in every country in the world, when all they had to do was to return to the cordial embraces of the Turkish Government?'[53]

İsmet's historical argumentation adopted Atabinen's 1919 trope of the contemporary 'extermination of the Turks' by the West when he asserted on 12 December that 'the Turks of the Morea and Thessaly, are confronted with certain extermination' – so that quick compulsory population exchange was now required.[54] Countering Venizelos on Armenian suffering, he turned the table saying 'the last Government in the world which should dare to express in public its pity for the fate of the Armenians was the very Government which had been the direct cause of their misfortunes.' This meant that the Greek campaign had made Armenians suffer in the first place, not the previous CUP genocide and the defence of genocide gains by the CUP's successors.

Hyperbolic rhetoric completed İsmet's complacent, at times grotesque presentation of Turkish history on 12 December 1922. 'The pity, generosity and tolerance of the Turks always recoiled upon them to their disadvantage', İsmet lamented.[55] There was no fault on the Turkish side in this view of both pre-modern and contemporary history. Generalized guilt of defeated Greece served as an inflated, all-decisive criterion for the present. Ankara was now to count as a force of civilizational progress, whereas with Greece 'all the reactionary, mediaeval elements in the country were roused against the intellectual and enlightened classes' of the Turkish nation in 1919–1922.[56] Thus, Ankara's chief delegate kept on denying any continuity with the former CUP party-state to which members of the current government and of the delegation itself belonged. He asserted: 'the hands of the Turks now at work in their own country, which had been devastated and ruined by foreign invasion, were quite peculiarly clean. Those hands had never violated, invaded or devastated any foreign country [...].'[57]

Had they been given access to the Château d'Ouchy negotiations, Persian, Assyrian, Kurdish, Yazidi, Armenian and Arab representatives would have had totally different stories to tell about devastation of their land by invading Turkish forces. Curzon countered some of İsmet's most fantastic allegations. The French chief delegate Camille Barrère remained silent, but on 14 December complimented

53 *Lausanne Conference*, 208 and 211–212.
54 *Lausanne Conference*, 203.
55 *Lausanne Conference*, 189.
56 *Lausanne Conference*, 206.
57 *Lausanne Conference*, 219.

Ankara's delegation for a highly interesting discussion' that had 'arisen out of the minorities problem.' He was 'glad to see that very real progress towards conciliation had been made. [...] İsmet Pasha and the Turkish delegation had approached this question with true regard for equity and justice.'[58] From the beginning of the Conference, the French delegation sought, largely in vain, to preserve gains of a special relationship with Ankara based on the 1921 Accord of Ankara. Curzon was articulate, but short, about the historic meaning of compulsory population transfer. He knew the political constraints behind the euphemism of exchange. In the meeting of 13 December 1922, he 'deeply regretted that the solution now being worked out [for Anatolia's Rûm] should be the compulsory exchange of populations – a thoroughly bad and vicious solution, for which the world would pay a heavy penalty for a hundred years to come. He detested having anything to do with it.' Knowing the root cause and genesis of the transfer proposal, he added that 'to say it was a suggestion of the Greek Government was ridiculous', but indeed was nothing less than 'a solution enforced by the action of the Turkish Government in expelling these people from Turkish territory.'[59]

In retrospect however, Curzon's words during the December meeting look like smoke and mirrors – as after the Conference, London became a loyal adherent of Ankara's minority definition. By the end of January 1923, İsmet's delegation had succeeded in asserting its own, limited concept of minorities. The exclusion of minority rights for groups outside the traditional millet resulted from the work in Lausanne's Commission and Sub-commission meetings after 12 December. Fifteen years later, a desperate Alevi Kurdish representative reported on an impending genocide in Dersim. London's then Foreign Secretary found it opportune to inform Ankara that Britain did not give the least attention to this Kurdish voice. 'We feel that it would create a good impression if we could let the Turkish Government know, unofficially, that no notice has been taken of it [letter from Seyid Riza].' In Geneva, the League justified its inaction with the Kurds' exclusion from League minority protection at the Lausanne Conference.[60]

İsmet entrusted Rıza Nur with the negotiations on minority rights and population exchange in the Sub-commission formed on 14 December. On 6 January, the Allied delegates argued one last time in this sub-commission in favour of the

58 *Lausanne Conference*, 225.

59 *Lausanne Conference*, 212.

60 Letter of the British Embassy in Ankara to the Eastern Department of the Foreign Office, 5 October 1937, quoted in M. Kalman, 1995, 311; 'Political Situation in Turkey – Various correspondence', File R3640/1/12279/12279, League of Nations Archives, Geneva, https://archives.ungeneva.org/political-situation-in-turkey-various-correspondence.

resettlement of indigenous refugees, particularly for a modest 'Armenian home' for Armenian refugees under full Turkish sovereignty. This was a far cry from the independent Armenia originally projected by the League and the Sèvres Treaty. They received an Armenian, an Assyro-Chaldean and a Bulgarian delegation to hear their requests. Before listening to them, Rıza Nur furiously interrupted the meeting and left the room with his team that included Şükrü (Kaya). Kaya had been Talât's director in charge of the camps for surviving deportees in Northern Syria, where starvation and massacres completed the Armenian genocide. While still very agitated, Nur went to İsmet, told him about walking out of the Sub-committee meeting and proposed to go back to Ankara. But the latter responded, 'Well done, I congratulate you.' All in all, indeed, Nur had acted according to Ankara's instructions.[61]

Nur's Lozan-related private notes evidence an ultranationalist mindset. 'It is of vital interest and perfectly fair not to let any human of another race, of another language and another religion live in our homeland. For this reason, I have already been an extreme [şiddetli] Turkist Nationalist for many years'. For Nur, indigenous non-Turks and non-Muslims were 'a foreign element, a plague and microbes.' As for Kurdish Muslims, they were 'to be purified by a persistent assimilation program of their distinct language and race.'[62] In his 14 volume strongly racialist *Turkish History*, Minister Nur wrote that 'it is of utmost necessity that we annihilate all languages in Turkey and replace them with Turkish.' Hailing from a racial and racist understanding of history, the vice-chief delegate's idea of a purified state in Asia Minor came close to that of a discarding and mass-killing modern 'gardener state'.[63]

History at Lausanne's Sideshows

At and besides the Conference, İsmet repeatedly contrasted Turkey's Jews with allegedly disloyal Ottoman Christian subjects whom Europe had made its unfortunate agents. The age-old myth of Turkish-Jewish harmony served as an argument against any serious maltreatment of non-Turks in modern history, and in particular to deny the crimes against the Armenians.

---

61 *Conférence de Lausanne sur les affaires du Proche-Orient,* first series, 1923, Vol. 1, 541–549; *Lozan Telgrafları I*, Vol. XIV; *İnönü'nün Hatıraları,* 120; Khatissian, *Éclosion*, 353–355.

62 Nur, *Hayat ve Hatıratım*, 260.

63 As later framed by the sociologist Zygmunt Bauman: *Modernity and the Holocaust*, 1989; Nur, *Türk Tarihi*, 430 and 433.

Ankara's delegation thus showcased the Jews as a happy minority in harmony with a tolerant state since the late fifteenth century. The minority's representatives cooperated in this show that rested on the late nineteenth-century myth of Jews eager to win favours with the Ottoman state.[64] This was the case also during the 1910s when, against Armenian-related bad press in the West, Talât pushed for positive endorsements by the Jewish minority for his regime and cause. Subsequently, in early 1921, a newly established 'Permanent Bureau of the Turkish Congress in Lausanne' pushed the line of full embrace of Turkish rule by the Jews.[65] Related to this first 'Turkish Congress' in Lausanne, a Permanent Bureau in Lausanne was set up in May 1919 by diaspora nationalists in order to influence the peace negotiations that then took place in Paris. The argument of Turkish-Jewish harmony went strongly on with Ankara's delegation in 1922–1923. On 11 December 1922, a new Turkish-Sephardic Friendship Association organised a special soirée in Geneva. Besides journalists, the invitation included Swiss cantonal and federal representatives; İsmet, Nur and other members of the delegation, notably Chief Rabbi Haim Nahum, an acquaintance of Talât; members of the Turkish diaspora; and special Swiss friends like Pittard. At this occasion, the speech of the leader of Geneva's Jews perfectly attuned to Ankara's expectations, as the Turkish journalist Necmeddin Sadık (Sadak) reported with satisfaction.[66]

Another element of pro-Kemalist lobbying in Lausanne was the Swiss Society of Friends of Turkey, founded by Colonel Arthur Fonjallaz. A visit to Asia Minor during the Greek-Turkish War had made Fonjallaz a friend of the Kemalist cause, admirer of Atatürk's military genius and supporter of Ankara's vision of contemporary history. His new and short-lived (but effective) Swiss Society of Friends of Turkey met for the first time on 16 December 1922 during a soirée at the Lausanne Palace Hotel. Fonjallaz raised a toast and İsmet made a long speech, defending Turkish claims and flattering Swiss historic achievements. Lausanne University's Professor of Sociology, Maurice Millioud, in his speech expressed agreement with İsmet and emphasized Turkey's civilizational role for the Orient. Fonjallaz had

64 *Conférence de Lausanne sur les affaires du Proche-Orient,* first series, Vol. 1, 161, 163, 172. See Julia Phillips Cohen, 'A Model *Millet*? Ottoman Jewish Citizenship at the End of Empire', *Jews, Liberalism, Antisemitism: A Global History*, ed. Abigail Green and Simon Levis-Sullam, 2020, 209–231.

65 'What the Israelites think of the Turkish regime', *Turkey* 2, 1921, 7; Kieser, *Talaat*, 295–314.

66 Sadık's 'Letter' in the daily *Akşam*, 17 December 1922, 2, transcribed in *Lozan Mektupları,* 138–141. Sadık had worked during WWI as a journalist in the circle of Gökalp and Talât; he became Turkey's Foreign Minister in the late 1940s.

dozens of private meetings with İsmet, including in his private residence. A few years later, he became Switzerland's most notorious fascist and pro-Nazi.[67]

Pittard, Millioud's colleague from Geneva, participated at both soirées and lastingly made friends with İsmet. During and after the Conference, he gave succour to a new Kemalist historical consciousness, rhetorically blending Kemalist nation-building with Swiss understanding of democratic citizenship.[68] 'You will become the architect of an era, and its leader. The history of Turkey will, I am sure, inscribe your name on the pediment of the present period, next to that of your comrade and friend, Mustapha Kemal', Pittard wrote to İsmet on 28 October 1923, a day before the declaration of the Republic of Turkey. Already before the Conference, Pittard had had some exchanges on pre-modern and ancient Turkish topics with Atabinen. In the second half of the 1920s and in the 1930s, his role as a mentor of physical anthropology and ethnohistory for Atatürk's History Thesis proved seminal. Several times Atatürk's personal guest, he accepted to supervise the doctoral thesis of Ayşe Afetinan, the Turkish President's adoptive daughter. Based on craniology, this thesis laboured to prove that Anatolia was the 'homeland of the Turkish race'. Manifestly, as Pittard's notes suggest, the recognition provided by the Treaty of Lausanne lacked the historical credits that would have given the Turkish top leader peace of mind. He desired a confirmation that serious science could not offer him.[69]

Historical Wisdom Beyond Lausanne?

The outright rejection of Armenian claims in terms of territory, autonomy, reparation and justice was Ankara's number one priority in Lausanne. A *Türk Yurdu*

67 'A. Fonjallaz', Archives Cantonales Vaudoises; 'Conférence de Lausanne 1922–23', S 112/95, Archives cantonales vaudoises; Claude Cantini, *Le colonel fasciste suisse, Arthur Fonjallaz*, 1983.

68 In contrast to his Turkish friends, Pittard kept on paying lip service to the Armenian cause. In general, he also used the term 'race' only in quotation marks and disqualified it as entirely devoid of political meaning. Yet, this reservation got lost in his suggestive communications to Turkish audiences and to Atatürk himself in the late 1920s and in the 1930s. See H.-L. Kieser, 'Türkische Nationalrevolution, anthropologisch gekrönt. Kemal Atatürk und Eugène Pittard', *Historische Anthropologie* 14/1, 2006, 105–118.

69 Afet Inan (=Ayşe Afetinan), *L'Anatolie, le pays de la 'race' turque: recherches sur les caractères anthropologiques des populations de la Turquie, enquête sur 64.000 individus*, preface by Eugène Pittard, 1941. Bibliothèque Publique et Universitaire in Geneva (BPU), Pittard 2003/52. See also Caroline Montebello, *Eugène Pittard, un anthropologue genevois en Turquie nationaliste (1910–1950): idéologie d'exclusion, corruption intellectuelle et logiques sociales*, 2016.

in Ankara's National Pact meant the exclusion of Armenian autonomy and of reforms according to the regionalising and democratising standards of the February 1914 Agreement.[70] The ostentatious embrace of Kurds and Jews strengthened categorical 'otherisation' and depreciation of those domestic groups that posed a serious challenge at Lausanne's negotiation table to the concept of a unitary Turkish state in Anatolia.

In İsmet's words during the mid-December 1922 meetings, 'those Armenians who decide to remain in Turkey must already have recognised the unavoidable necessity of living as good citizens.' In condescending remarks a day later, he stated that 'the Armenians who desired to remain in Turkey would be able to live in brotherhood with their Turkish compatriots, who would be full of solicitude for them and would willingly forget the events of the past [i.e. Armenian misdeeds].'[71] Justice for the Armenians had been both a legal and emotional priority of the early League of Nations.[72] In Lausanne, the Allies achieved nothing positive for the homeless Armenian survivors. Once lip service had been paid to the destruction of a nation and the plight of surviving refugees, by early January 1923 no delegate was any longer willing to deal with the issue. The Armenian Question was shelved among 'questions remaining unsolved'.[73] Though the Armenian delegation dramatically failed in its goals, it had lent genocide survivors a public voice and born witness to unmet challenges of history. Through memoranda, public statements, personal letters, memoirs, and the pen of non-Armenian friends in Lausanne, it established the first rudiments of a fundamentally 'other history of Lausanne'.[74]

70 This Agreement had implemented Articles 60–61 of the 1878 Berlin Treaty by way of compromise with the Ottoman government. See H.-L. Kieser, Mehmet Polatel and Thomas Schmutz, 'Reform or cataclysm? The agreement of 8 February 1914 regarding the Ottoman eastern provinces', *Journal of Genocide Research* 17/3, 2015, 285–304. In this context, it is important to note that the historian Bayur starts his 'History of the Turkish Revolution' with the 1878 Ayastefanos [San Stefano] and Berlin Treaties: Bayur, *Türk inkılâbı tarihi,* Vol. 1.

71 *Lausanne Conference*, 203 and 208.

72 See Mark Toufayan, 'Empathy, humanity and the 'Armenian Question' in the internationalist legal imagination', *Revue québécoise de droit international* 24, 2011, 171–191. For a summary of Western promises to the Armenians, see the Memorandum on the Armenian Question, submitted to the Lausanne Peace Conference by the United Armenian Delegation, November 1922 (file, including a letter to the League's secretary-general on 9 December 1922: https://biblio-archive.unog.ch/Dateien/CouncilMSD/C-757-M-458–1922-VII_EN.pdf). See also 'Protection of Armenia – Mr. Hammarskjöld – Transmits memorandum […] for the protection and administration of Armenia', May 1920, League of Nations Archive, R566/11/3421/4539, https://lontad-project.unog.ch/idurl/1/3514.

73 Montagna report, 7 January 1923, *Lausanne Conference*, 305–308.

74 Archives including papers, correspondence, memoranda, etc., Noradungian Papers and Actes de la délégation nationale, Bibliothèque Nubar, Paris. A thoughtful insider memoir:

This 'other history' harbours the seeds for new understandings and a historically informed peace in Anatolia.

The Conference of Lausanne established a balance of interests among the imperial powers at a price that mortgaged the future. In exchange for the abolition of the Capitulations and weakened minority rights, Ankara promised to introduce a modern legal system upheld by an independent judiciary. Thus, in order to achieve full and immediate sovereignty at the Lausanne Conference, it promised a constitutional democracy that it was neither able nor really willing to implement in either the short or the long term. Non-Muslims, if 'grateful citizens', were tolerated, but not recognised as equal nationals; and they were put under pressure not to petition the League of Nations in Geneva. Kurds and other minorities did not count as minorities at all. It became clear that 'the minorities procedure adapted for the European States does not give the desired result when applied to Turkey', the League wrote in 1927.[75] As Kemalism turned totalitarian in the 1930s, democracy became an entirely distant utopia.

For five years from 1926, Ankara had to accept foreign legal advisers during transition to the new legal system promised in Lausanne. The then Justice Minister Mahmut Bozkurt put it this way: 'When we abolished the Capitulations in the Lausanne Peace Treaty, we took it upon ourselves at the same time to establish a whole new Turkish judicial organization with a new legal system, new laws and new courts.'[76] Well treated as guests, the advisers had very little say in a process that they were almost at any price to rubber-stamp for diplomatic convenience. They served to 'admit that the Turkish courts were working properly, as in all civilized countries, and that Turkish judges were competent in their duties', as İsmet stated in retrospect.[77] University of Geneva's Law Professor Georges Sauser-Hall emphasized the lack of roots and maturation of reforms that were primarily politically motivated. While publicly displaying the required optimism on 'progress',

---

Khatissian, *Éclosion*. A sharply self-critical manifesto: Katchznouni, *The ARF*. An important non-Armenian pen in Lausanne who enjoyed a direct connection to the Swiss Federal Councillor Motta: Antony Kraft-Bonnard, see Kraft-Bonnard, *L'Arménie à la Conférence de Lausanne*, 1923; idem, *Arménie, Suisse et Société des Nations*, 1924; idem, *Arménie, justice et réparation*, 1924; see also Sisvan Nigolian and Pascal Roman (eds.), *Sauver les enfants, sauver l'Arménie: la contribution du pasteur Antony Kraft-Bonnard (1919–1945)*, 2020.

75 Minority Commission Director Colban, 1 May 1927, to Secretary-General Drummond, quoted in Martin Scheuermann, *Minderheitenschutz contra Konfliktverhütung?* 2000, 367.

76 Mahmut Bozkurt, 'Türk Medenî Kanunu nasıl hazırlandı?' in: *Medenî kanunun XV. yıl dönümü için,* 1944, 8.

77 *İsmet İnönü'nün Hatıraları*, 54–55.

Ankara's adviser Sauser-Hall cautiously made clear in the 1930s that only in the future could a 'definitive judgment' be reached.[78]

In the final analysis, history and law in Lausanne served the affirmation of a new type of radical nationalism in interwar diplomacy. Tellingly, high diplomacy in Lausanne embraced both Benito Mussolini, Italy's new Fascist Prime Minister and Ankara's ultranationalists (both regimes being preoccupied with domestic consolidation). Sovereignty won at Lausanne was not that of Anatolia's people(s) or a 'sovereignty of law', to be proved by constitutionality and independent justice. It was about the will to unrestricted rule that late Ottoman national-imperial cadres successfully asserted vis-à-vis ageing European imperialists. Both sides pursued their interests on the back of those excluded from Lausanne's table. Turko-centric historical allegations together with bold, but unreliable promises of democratic modernisation, to be supervised by a putatively strong League of Nations, facilitated the pact struck between the powers. Consequently, Lausanne framed history with gaps, myths and taboos; and futures with unfulfilled prospects of constitutional rule. Admired by Europe's fascists, particularly the Nazis, the Lausanne Treaty established an anti-democratic notion of sovereignty and thus impeded modern democratic progress for decades to come.

78 Georges Sauser-Hall, *La réception des droits européens en Turquie*, 1938, 38. See also Hans-Lukas Kieser, Astrid Meier, Walter Stoffel eds., *Revolution islamischen Rechts: Das Schweizerische ZGB in der Türkei*, 2008.

15

Lausanne in Turkish Official and Popular Historiography: A 'War of Identities' in Turkey

Gökhan Çetinsaya

> 'They deceived us with a history that always lies'
> 'They tried to sell us Lausanne, as a victory'
>
> President Erdoğan (2016)[1]

In a 2018 survey by the Turkish polling company KONDA, forty-eight per cent of interviewees agreed that 'the Treaty of Lausanne will expire in 2023.'[2] In 2020, some thirty-eight per cent of the interviewees in another survey agreed with the statement that 'the Lausanne Treaty has secret clauses that will come into effect in 2023.'[3] In a third survey conducted in 2017, eighty-seven per cent agreed that 'European states want to divide Turkey today, just as they divided the Ottoman state in the past.' And seventy-three per cent concurred that 'the reforms requested by the European Union from Turkey are similar to those demanded from them in the Sèvres Treaty.'[4]

1 'Bizi hep yalan söyleyen tarihle aldattılar' (18 October 2016); 'Lozan'ı zafer diye yutturmaya çalıştılar' (29 September 2016). See Taha Akyol, 'İslamcıların popüler tarih söylemi,' *Karar*, 1 June 2021.

2 *Popülist Tutum, Negatif Kimliklenme ve Komploculuk* (KONDA, November 2018). For an earlier example, see *Nokta*, 3–9 October 1993.

3 https://turkiyeraporu.com/arastirma/hangi-komplo-teorilerine-inaniyoruz-1825/.

4 'Türkiye'de Kutuplaşmanın Boyutları' (İstanbul Bilgi Üniversitesi, November–December 2017).

These results testify to the major influence that popular historiography has in Turkey. In fact, historiography in Turkey is stuck between the grip of 'official' historiography and 'anti-official' historiography. The official historiography appears to reflect the mindset and discourse of the Kemalist establishment. The anti-official historiography aims to say the opposite of what official history declares, as part of its struggle against the Kemalist regime. The anti-official history field has been filled by popular historiography, with rightist and leftist versions.[5]

History in Turkey is perceived as a 'domain of faith' and a part of political-cultural identity. Historiography is perceived as one of the fields for conflicting identities to settle accounts with each other. Historical figures and events are 'ammunition' in this 'war of identities.' In this way, these identities attempt to prove the historical legitimacy of their existence and undermine that of their opponents. For about seventy years the Treaty of Lausanne has been one of the most controversial subjects in this regard.[6] For one side, the Treaty was a great victory, won without any concessions, a miraculous saga of diplomacy; for the other, a great defeat or rout, loss of empire or 'Great Turkey', even an international conspiracy.

This chapter seeks to explore the historical narrative on the Conference and the Treaty of Lausanne in official and popular historiography in Turkey. After presenting the basic arguments of the main sources of official history and historiography, it will show the alternative or opposite perceptions and defensive arguments in the field of popular history. The chapter will demonstrate what remains and what has changed since the 1920s in terms of the utilization of history in political discourses and politicized historical writing.

Official History and Historiography

The main sources of official history / historiography are the speeches and writings of Mustafa Kemal (hereafter Atatürk) and İsmet İnönü (hereafter İsmet). The most important source (and the first example) of official history / historiography on the Lausanne Conference and the Treaty is Atatürk's Speech (*Nutuk*). The *Nutuk* was

5 See Gökhan Çetinsaya, 'Abdülhamid'i Anlamak: 19. Yüzyıl Tarihçiliğine Bir Bakış', *Sosyal Bilimleri Yeniden Düşünmek: Toplum-Bilim ve Defter Dergileri Sempozyum Bildirileri*, 2001, 137–146. For popular historiography in Turkey in general see, Ahmet Özcan, *Türkiye'de Popüler Tarihçilik, 1908–1960*, 2011.

6 For an earlier discussion, see Fatma Müge Göçek, 'The Politics of History and Memory: A Multidimensional Analysis of the Lausanne Peace Conference (1922–23)', *Histories of the Modern Middle East: New Directions*, eds. H. Erdem et al., 2000, 207–228.

a long speech delivered by him in 1927, at the second congress of Cumhuriyet Halk Partisi (Republican People's Party). The text covered events from May 1919, when Atatürk became leader of the National Struggle, until the proclamation of the Republic of Turkey in October 1923. Although it was a personal account of events, it is regarded as a true and unquestionable historical account, and it has become the main basis of official republican history and the Kemalist popular historiography.[7]

In the *Nutuk*, four years after the signing of the treaty, Atatürk presented his view of Lausanne.[8] He evaluated the developments before, during, and after the conference. In Atatürk's words, it was a long and formidable process:[9]

> … because the questions brought forward on the agenda did not exclusively concern the new regime, which was only three or four years old. Centuries-old accounts were regulated. It was surely neither a simple nor a convenient task to find our way through such a mass of old and rubbishy accounts.

Atatürk's chronological account dwelt in particular on the conference interval (4 February 1923–23 April 1923) and the developments after İsmet's return.[10] Atatürk made a twelve-point comparison between the clauses of the Treaties of Sèvres and Lausanne and the other two peace proposals put forward by the Allies after the Armistice of Mudros, in March 1921 and March 1922.[11]

Atatürk's aim was to demonstrate the wide differences between the 'unbearable proposals' of the Allies and the advantageous outcome of Lausanne. He gave details of communications between Ankara and Lausanne and described points of disagreement between İsmet and Rauf Orbay, head of the government, as well as between the government and opposition in parliament (hereafter TBMM). Atatürk defended the actions of İsmet at length.[12] Finally, he concluded that:[13]

> The treaty of Lausanne is the document which reveals in a decisive manner

7 See Erik J. Zürcher, 'The Politician as Historian, Historians in Politics: On the *Nutuk* (Speech) of Mustafa Kemal Pasha', *The Young Turk Legacy and Nation Building: From the Ottoman Empire to Atatürk's Turkey*, 2010, 6–16.
8 *Nutuk*, 2015, 534ff; *A Speech delivered by Mustafa Kemal Atatürk (1927)* (hereafter *Speech*), 1963, 585ff.
9 *Nutuk*, 534–535; *Speech*, 585.
10 *Nutuk*, 550ff; *Speech*, 599ff.
11 *Nutuk*, 571ff; *Speech*, 620ff.
12 *Speech*, 634ff; *Nutuk*, 582ff.
13 *Speech*, 634; *Nutuk*, 582.

> the failure of a vast plot [*suikast*] which had been hatching for centuries against the Turkish nation, a plot which many believed they had carried to success through the Sèvres Treaty. It is a political victory which was not matched in the whole of Ottoman history.

Atatürk's use of the phrase 'plot' as he places Lausanne alongside the political achievements of the entire Ottoman history is noteworthy.[14]

The second important source of official history and Kemalist popular historiography is İsmet. Over fifty years, points of emphasis shifted in the accounts he gave of the negotiations, and they can be classified into several themes.[15] For İsmet the Lausanne Treaty represented independence, the establishment of a nation-state, the recognition of national existence, national rights, and international equality.[16] İsmet frequently mentions the issue of the Capitulations, primarily economic but especially judicial Capitulations. This was the major stumbling block to an independent nation-state, and the Treaty's hardest won victory.[17] One anecdote in particular served to indicate the extent of the challenges he faced. This was when Lord Curzon told him that:

> We are not satisfied. You do not accept any of our proposals, you reject them all. We put them all in our pockets. You have a devastated country, and you will have all kinds of needs. Tomorrow, you will come and kneel before us to rebuild a ruined country, and when you ask us for help, I will pull out whatever you rejected today and I will put them in front of you.[18]

İsmet proudly argues that after Lausanne, contrary to expectations, Ankara stood firm, and no concessions were made, and no gains were returned.[19] Another frequent emphasis is the peculiarity of the Treaty of Lausanne as the only surviving post-war settlement. As he put it:

---

14 Also see *Speech*, 620; *Nutuk*, 571: 'The second legislative period of the Grand National Assembly of Turkey coincided with a happy transition in the history of New Turkey. Our four years' fight for independence was crowned by a peace worthy of our national past.'

15 See İsmet İnönü, *Lozan Barış Konferansı: Konuşma, Demeç, Makale, Mesaj, Anı ve Söyleşileri* (hereafter *Lozan Barış Konferansı*), 2010.

16 İnönü, *Lozan Barış Konferansı*, 218–219 (20 March 1934); 229–231, 234 (24 July 1952); 243 (24 July 1959); 248 (24 July 1965); 274 (24 July 1973).

17 İnönü, *Lozan Barış Konferansı*, 229 (24 July 1952); 236 (24 July 1956); 248 (24 July 1965); 252 (24 July 1967).

18 For example, İnönü, *Lozan Barış Konferansı*, 248 (24 July 1965); 274 (24 July 1973).

19 İnönü, *Lozan Barış Konferansı*, 236 (24 July 1956).

> None of the treaties made after the First World War survived. Only the Lausanne Treaty is standing. After the Second World War, new treaties brought new issues and new conflicts to the world. The Treaty of Lausanne continues to carry its essential value for Turkey and the principles that will guide international relations.[20]

İsmet added that the Lausanne process set an example to the world, encouraging other nations to seize their destiny and become independent states.[21]

For İsmet, Lausanne was not only significant in terms of international law and politics, but also for internal policy:

> The Treaty of Lausanne (…) is the beginning of Turkey's civilizational move. The Lausanne Treaty has even been essential in preparing the international standard necessary for the establishment of a new Turkish society. The Turks, who have the notion of starting a great reform, will find that the conditions imposed by Lausanne are no obstacle to realizing their aspirations.[22]

In the 1960s and early 1970s, however, probably in response to criticisms made in popular historiography, İsmet began to admit some shortcomings in the treaty. He emphasized the 'many vital unfinished' issues, such as the Turkish Straits, foreign legal / judicial advisers, and cabotage. But, as he argued, the Treaty had evolved over time, and the incomplete items had been resolved in Turkey's favour.[23] In his final years, İsmet admitted his own shortcomings (especially his inexperience in diplomacy) as the chief delegate but argued that he had learned his lesson well and surmounted these obstacles.[24]

All in all, according to İsmet, Lausanne was a great success. When asked in 1971, almost half a century later, whether 'the results you achieved at the Lausanne Conference were in line with your hopes,' İsmet replied as follows:

> I have always been posed this question. I have posed this question myself. I

---

20 İnönü, *Lozan Barış Konferansı*, 274 (24 July 1973); Seha L. Meray, *Lozan Konferansı: Tutanaklar-Belgeler* (hereafter *Lozan Konferansı*), 1970, V-IX.

21 İnönü, *Lozan Barış Konferansı*, 236 (24 July 1956).

22 İnönü, *Lozan Barış Konferansı*, 235 (24 July 1953); 239, 241 (24 July 1957).

23 İnönü, *Lozan Barış Konferansı*, 248 (24 July 1965); 274 (24 July 1973); Meray, *Lozan Konferansı*, V-IX.

24 İnönü, *Lozan Barış Konferansı*, 264–269 (24 July 1971). Also see, 301: 'Because my experience and knowledge in political life is not that wide …'

> have always tried to consider whether there is a proportionality between what we wanted and what we have achieved … let me tell you the nature of the conference. A compromise is always essential in negotiating and bargaining between people. Man can never find what he hopes for but he must be satisfied with the result. It is necessary to identify the things that can and cannot be achieved …[25]

Like Atatürk, he also compared the Lausanne Treaty with the agreements made by the Ottomans:

> Among the many agreements made over hundreds of years Lausanne stands as an achievement to the benefit of the Turkish nation.[26]

The first example of such an official history in Turkey is *Tarih IV* [*History IV*].[27] This four-volume text was written for high school students by an official commission under the supervision of Atatürk himself. It was used as a textbook for a decade (1931–1941) and used afterwards as a basic text for official historiography, and Kemalist historiography (alongside with the *Nutuk*).

In volume four, discussion of the Lausanne Conference and Treaty greatly resembles the *Nutuk*, which it cites repeatedly. It is interesting to note that the role of Atatürk is regarded as crucial and unique. İsmet, on the other hand, is placed in a secondary position. Although İsmet was praised for his role in the Mudanya Armistice and Lausanne, it was carefully emphasized that his success was due to 'the Gazi's effective and accurate instructions.'[28] After explaining the clauses of the Lausanne Treaty, the authors came to the conclusion that:

> The Lausanne Peace Treaty is an international document and deed that affirms the full independence and sovereignty of the New Turkish State to the whole World. With the Treaty of Lausanne, the birth certificate of a national and independent Turkish state, the last of the nation-states born from the collapse of the Ottoman reign, was signed by all states.[29]

25 İnönü, *Lozan Barış Konferansı*, 264–268 (24 July 1971).
26 İnönü, *Lozan Barış Konferansı*, 248 (24 July 1965).
27 *Tarih IV: Kemalist Eğitimin Tarih Dersleri (1931–1941)* (hereafter *Tarih IV*), 2001, 125–131. Also see Türk Tarihinin Ana Hatları, 1930, 591.
28 *Tarih IV*, 125–127.
29 *Tarih IV*, 130.

The obvious attributes of the Treaty of Lausanne were the abolition of the Capitulations and the recognition of national sovereignty and independence in all areas. With the Treaty, a four-year struggle for independence under the guidance of the Great Gazi resulted in a peace worthy of the glory and honour of the nation. With it the New Turkish State came into existence, and there was no obstacle for the Turkish nation to develop freely.[30]

A comparison with the late Ottoman administration was also made:[31]

> Turkish power was reduced at Mudros and Sèvres at the hands of the sultans and courtiers. Turkish power was raised at Mudanya and Lausanne in the hands of Gazi and his friends. (…) Sèvres and the Sultan's government which accepted Sèvres destroyed the Turkish homeland and Turkish independence. Lausanne, on the other hand, ensured the integrity of the Turkish homeland and the independence of the Turkish State.

Tarih IV noted that some European writers called the War of Independence 'the Turkish miracle'. After explaining the hardships of the Ottoman Empire since 1911 and emphasizing the weak state of the Ottoman Empire (miserable condition of the army, finance, population) at the end of the First World War, and considering events in Anatolia between 1918 and 1922, it was obvious to the authors that 'miracle' was appropriate.[32] They concluded that 'in all these extremely adverse conditions':

> Mustafa Kemal alone, relying on his own genius, will and power; and the love, respect, and influence he gained in the Turkish nation with his victories in the General War, attempted to establish a new state and army. He gathered the Turkish nation around this purpose. He found money, soldiers, equipment, and supplies; everything had been found … and this attempt, which seemed impossible, that Mustafa Kemal began in Samsun in the spring of 1919, was realized with complete success in the autumn of 1922. This is the Turkish miracle.[33]

The emphasis on the role and person (even the sanctification) of Atatürk ('The greatest man raised by the Turkish nation') is striking:

30 *Tarih IV*, 130–131.
31 *Tarih IV*, 131.
32 *Tarih IV*, 131–132.
33 *Tarih IV*, 132.

> This miracle has two important factors: the Turkish nation and Mustafa Kemal (…) [who] embodies the great Turkish nation with his whole spiritual personality.[34]

Since 1923, each 24 July has been celebrated as 'Lausanne Day'. Various ceremonies were held at 'Lausanne anniversaries', and Atatürk and İsmet issued statements.[35] The emphasis on the prominence and sanctification of Atatürk continued during his lifetime.[36] After Atatürk, during the periods when İsmet dominated (1939–1950 and 1960–1965), the importance of Lausanne and the role of İsmet began to be emphasized. During the Democratic Party (*Demokrat Parti*, hereafter DP) period (1950–1960), emphasis on the role of Atatürk came to the fore again in the Lausanne Day celebrations, a result of antipathy for İsmet.[37] In general, the emphasis on the Treaty of Lausanne increased especially in the coup periods (1960–1965, 1980–1983).

During the establishment of a new nation-state, the construction of a new national history was also on the agenda. This included the construction of an official history. The basic narrative around the Conference and Treaty of Lausanne were prepared in this context. From the 1930s to the 1980s the official (and Kemalist popular) historiography on the Conference / Treaty of Lausanne shows differences over time, according to the stages of Turkish political and sociocultural turns.[38] While the basic narrative has not changed, its emphases and arguments have varied according to the issues of the day, especially under military regimes, when 'Atatürkism' was seen as a cure to all problems.

34 *Tarih IV*, 133.

35 See Gurbet Gökgöz, 'Belleklerden Silinmeye Yüz Tutan Bir Gün: Lozan Sulh Bayramı', *Çağdaş Türkiye Tarihi Araştırmaları Dergisi* 10/22, 2011, 95–114.

36 See Cemil Koçak, *İsmet İnönü ve Resmi Tarih*, 2020.

37 See Ahmet Gülen, 'Demokrat Parti Döneminde Lozan Algısı', *Atatürk Yolu Dergisi* 14/53, 2013, 77–100.

38 For official history, see, for example, Yavuz Abadan, 'Lozan'ın Hususiyetleri', *İ.Ü. Hukuk Fakültesi Dergisi* 4/15, 1938, 401–415; Afet İnan, *Türk İstiklali ve Lozan Muahedesi*, 1938; Nedim Ayzan, *Lozan*, 1940; Enver Ziya Karal, 'Lozan Zaferi ve Dersi (24 Temmuz [July] 1942)', *Ankara Üniversitesi Haftası*, 1944; Enver Behnan Şapolyo, *Türkiye Cumhuriyeti Tarihi (1918–1950)*, 1950; *Türkiye Dış Politikasında 50 Yıl: Lozan (1922–1923)*, 1973; *Lozan'ın 50. Yıl Armağanı*, 1978; *Atatürk İlkeleri ve İnkılap Tarihi*, I/1, 1990; *Lozan Barış Antlaşmasının 70. Yıldönümü (24 Temmuz* [July] *1993)*, 1993; *70. Yılında Lozan Barış Antlaşması (25–26 Ekim* [October] *1993)*, 1994; Şerafettin Yamaner, *Sevr ve Lozan*, 1999. For Kemalist popular history, see for example Burhan Cahit, *Mudanya-Lozan-Ankara*, 1933; Sabri Yılmaz, *Lozan Eri*, 1935; Ziya Altuna, *Lozan Sulhu'nun 42. Yıldönümü*, 1965; *Belgelerle Türk Tarihi Dergisi* 34, 1970.

There was no opposing account of Lausanne under the single-party regime (1923–1945). Starting from 1945 / 1946, with the start of the multi-party regime and transition to democracy, the first publications of anti-official historiography and the first examples of Lausanne criticism began to appear. This was intensified after İsmet left the presidency in 1950. Criticisms of the Single Party period practices (especially religious policies) and criticisms of the era of Atatürk and İsmet (1923–1945) were intertwined with criticisms of Lausanne.[39] In fact, the Treaty of Lausanne started to be seen as the basis of what the Kemalist regime accomplished. In this way, the Lausanne critique found its expression in popular historiography.

Popular Historiography

The perception of the Conference and the Treaty of Lausanne in popular historiography can be examined through the main identities found in Turkey: Kemalist, Nationalist, Islamist, Socialist.[40] Over the years, different coalitions of identities and different variations of popular history emerged. For example, beginning with the multi-party period after the Second World War, Nationalist-Conservatives appeared. In the 1990s, in the post-Cold War environment, the Neo-Kemalists and 'Sèvres Syndrome' emerged. Two competing perspectives or identities stand out in the Lausanne debate, which finds their expression in popular historiography: the Nationalist-Conservative/Islamist and the Neo-Kemalist.

Nationalist-Conservative/Islamist Popular Historiography

In the late 1940s and 1950s, in the new political and socio-cultural climate of Turkey, a new political-social group emerged under the broad name of 'nationalist-conservative' (*milliyetçi-muhafazakar*) or 'nationalist-sacredist' (*milliyetçi-mukaddesatçı*), composed of the new generation of Islamists and Turkists. The collaboration of the Turkists and Islamists under the broad name of 'nationalist-conservative/sacredist' continued well into the 1960s. Only in the second half of the 1960s was there a partial dissociation and differentiation between Turkists and Islamists.

39 In 1951, in the face of increasing criticism of Atatürk, the DP government enacted the law to protect Atatürk (Turkish Penal Code 5816), and İsmet (who was also the chief rival of the DP government) became the only focus of criticism.
40 See Hasan Kösebalaban, *Turkish Foreign Policy: Islam, Nationalism, and Globalization*, 2011; Jenny B. White, *Muslim Nationalism and the New Turks*, 2014.

The fiercest criticism against the Treaty of Lausanne came from this group of writers. They challenged the policies and discourses of Kemalism. One of the issues on their broad agenda (including religion, language, late Ottoman history, and the history of the National Struggle) was the Lausanne Treaty. At first a minor issue (in the late 1940s and early 1950s), it became a major issue, especially with the deterioration of relations with Greece over Cyprus from the mid-1950s onwards. Criticism strengthened in the 1960s and 1970s when almost all the Lausanne Treaty-related issues (such as the Patriarchate and the Dodecanese Islands) came onto the agenda of Turkish foreign and domestic policy.[41]

This group argued that the Lausanne Treaty was not a victory, but a defeat. They alleged that Atatürk and İsmet gave important concessions to the West at Lausanne, not only in terms of former Ottoman territories but also vital institutions of the Turkish-Islamic nation. The most important concession in this regard was the abolition of the Caliphate (and the following waves of 'secularization' in internal and foreign policy).

To support these claims these writers drew heavily on the arguments of the Second Group in the first TBMM as well as members of the First Group in the second TBMM.[42] They quoted the memoirs of Rıza Nur, İsmet's deputy at Lausanne, as well as those of Rauf Orbay and Kazım Karabekir.[43] All three names became opponents of the Kemalist regime from 1923–1924 onwards. The publication of Rıza Nur's controversial memoirs in 1967–1968 in particular appears to have fuelled criticisms of Lausanne.

Four names stand out in the Nationalist-Conservative/Islamist branch of popular historiography: Cevat Rıfat Atilhan, Necip Fazıl Kısakürek, Kadir Mısıroğlu and Mustafa Armağan. Cevat Rıfat Atilhan (1892–1967) was a leading anti-Semitic figure and a pioneering conspiracy theorist in Turkey. He had fought as an officer in the Balkan Wars, the First World War (including on the Palestinian front), and

41 When Islamist journals are examined, the relationship between criticism of Lausanne and the Cyprus issue (and other disputed issues regarding Lausanne) is clearly observed. Moreover, in the 1960s, the criticism of Lausanne was intertwined with the criticism of İsmet. See, for example, 'The bitter truth revealed by the conflict in the Aegean: Lausanne is a defeat', *Sebil* 30, 1976, https://katalog.idp.org.tr/pdf/6335/11335. For several examples along the same line, see https://katalog.idp.org.tr/arama?order_by=date&direction=asc&query=lozan&start_year=1961&end_year=1979.

42 See Ahmet Demirel, *Birinci Meclis'te Muhalefet: İkinci Grup*, 1994; Taha Akyol and Sefa Kaplan, *Açık ve Gizli Oturumlarda Lozan Tartışmaları*, 2013.

43 See Rıza Nur, *Hayat ve Hatıratım*, 1967–1968; Feridun Kandemir, *Hatıraları ve Söyleyemedikleri ile Rauf Orbay*, 1965; Kazım Karabekir, *Paşaların Hesaplaşması*, 1995; Mustafa Armağan, *Kızıl Pençe: Karabekir'in Gözüyle Kuruluş Yılları (1922–1933)*, 2016.

the Turkish War of Independence. He later became involved in business, publishing, and after 1945, politics. Atilhan supported Nazi Germany in the 1930s and 1940s and published anti-Semitic material. A prolific writer, he wrote over seventy books and thousands of articles.[44]

Necip Fazıl Kısakürek (1904–1983), a prominent poet and playwright who studied philosophy in Turkey and France, adopted a western lifestyle in his youth, and later during the 1930s embraced an Islamic worldview under the influence of a sheikh of the Naqshbandiyya-Khalidiyya tariqa. From then onwards, Kısakürek became a leading author and activist for the Islamist movement. Through his polemical and literary writings, and his journal *Büyük Doğu* (The Great East, 1943–1978), Kısakürek has influenced generations of nationalists, conservatives, and especially Islamists.[45] Atilhan and Kısakürek represent the first generation of Lausanne critics, who focused mainly on the Caliphate and claims of a Jewish conspiracy.

Kadir Mısıroğlu (1933–2019), who studied law, presented the most effective arguments in his three-volume book *Lausanne: victory or rout?*.[46] Mustafa Armağan (1961-), who studied history, represents the last generation; by making a synthesis of his predecessors' thoughts, he has become an influential figure thanks to his best-selling books and popular history magazine, *Derin Tarih*.[47] Mısıroğlu and Armağan's writings remain highly influential today, in digital form.

As the arguments and claims of these four are almost the same, I shall deal with them all together, classifying their arguments collectively instead of separately.[48]

---

44 See Aksel Erbahar, 'Atilhan, Cevat Rıfat', *Encyclopaedia of Jews in the Islamic World*, https://referenceworks.brillonline.com/entries/encyclopedia-of-jews-in-the-islamic-world/atilhan-cevat-rfat-SIM_000482; Rıfat N. Bali, 'Cevat Rıfat Atilhan', *Modern Türkiye'de Siyasi Düşünce: Muhafazakârlık*, 2009, 402–406; https://katalog.idp.org.tr/yazarlar/2384/cevat-rifat-atilhan.

45 See Şerif Mardin, 'Necip Fazıl Kısakürek', *The Oxford Encyclopaedia of the Modern Islamic World*, Vol. II, 1995, 436–437; Burhanettin Duran, 'Transformation of Islamist Political Thought in Turkey: From the Empire to the Early Republic (1908–1960): Necip Fazıl Kısakürek's Political Ideas', PhD dissertation, Bilkent University, 2001.

46 See http://kadirmisiroglu.com/.

47 See http://www.mustafaarmagan.com.tr/.

48 For Cevat Rıfat Atilhan, see *İslamı Saran Tehlike ve Siyonizm*, 1950, 173–176, and 1955, 310–314; 'Yanlış Yol, İflas Etmiş Siyaset', *Fedai* 9, 1964, 1 and 13.
For Kısakürek, see Dedektif X Bir, 'İşte', *Büyük Doğu* 5/2, 21 October 1949, 3–4; Dedektif X Bir, 'İfşa', *Büyük Doğu* 5/3, 28 October 1949, 3–4 and 16; Dedektif X Bir, 'İsmet İnönü ve Lozan'ın İç Yüzü', *Büyük Doğu* 6/29, 6 October 1950, 5 and 10–11.
For Kadir Mısıroğlu, see *Lozan: Zafer mi Hezimet mi?*, Vol. 1 (1965, 2nd revised edition: 1971), Vol. 2 (1973), Vol. 3 (1979).
For Mustafa Armağan, see *Efsaneler ve Gerçekler*, 2013; *Yakın Tarihin Kara Delikleri*, 2014;

For them, the Treaty of Lausanne was not a victory as presented by the Kemalist regime, but a rout (*hezimet*). The Turkish nation was victorious in the war but defeated at the negotiating table. Among them, only Armağan acknowledges that certain gains may have been made at Lausanne (especially economic, judicial, and political independence and equality), but for him they were not enough to represent victory. If there was a victor, then there had to be a loser. Who lost in Lausanne? Who stepped back? Who made important concessions? Britain, France, or Greece? It was the Turkish side! The victory was Britain's![49]

These writers did not view Sèvres as the standard by which to assess Lausanne. Despite the Kemalist slogan, 'Sèvres is Death, Lausanne is Life', for these authors Sèvres had been misrepresented. In any case, they argued, it was only a 'project' since it was never ratified. The main criterion for evaluating Lausanne should be the National Pact (*Misak-ı Milli*) of January 1920. Nor was the National Pact achieved at Lausanne; it represented the 'minimum homeland' (*asgari vatan*) deemed acceptable. A desire to cover up this inconvenient truth allegedly explained why the relevant article from the Pact did not appear in the version of that Pact presented in official history books.[50] If one compares it with the Sèvres Treaty, Lausanne may seem like a success, but if one compares it with the instructions given by the TBMM to İsmet, it must be seen as a failure. Armağan further argues that Sèvres and Lausanne were not that different: as many Articles of Sèvres were rolled over into Lausanne (for example, Articles on the minorities), some parts of Sèvres are still alive today.[51]

These writers have argued that at Lausanne the Turkish delegation made major errors leading to important losses and concessions. Firstly, they blame İsmet as an incompetent and unqualified negotiator, deficient in both hearing and understanding of foreign languages. Sending him to Lausanne had been a mistake. He and other members of the delegation (and in fact, all those in Ankara as well) were unprepared and allegedly suffered from an inferiority complex and planned to make peace as quickly as possible by granting every concession demanded. 'The wolf' Curzon by contrast, with the help of the British intelligence, directed the whole process like an orchestra conductor, so much so that he did not even participate in the second part of the conference. The real hero therefore was Curzon, not İsmet.

Cumhuriyet Efsaneleri, 2014; *Paşaların Hesaplaşması*, 2014; *Korku Duvarını Yıkmak*, 2014; *Öncesi ve Sonrasıyla Tek Parti Devri*, 2015; *Satılık İmparatorluk: Lozan ve Osmanlı'nın Reddedilen Mirası*, 2016.

49 Armağan, *Paşaların Hesaplaşması*, 219–220.

50 Cf. Mete Tunçay, 'Misak-ı Milli'nin 1. Maddesi', *Birikim* 18–19, 1976, 12–16.

51 Armağan, *Efsaneler ve Gerçekler*, 81–84.

Under these conditions, there was no prospect of achieving success at Lausanne. Hence there were serious losses, as judged against the National Pact. Mısıroğlu divides the losses of Lausanne into two, 'material' and 'spiritual' (*manevi*). The material losses were Mosul (and its oil), Western Thrace, Aleppo, Batumi, the Aegean and Dodecanese Islands, Cyprus, the Turkish Straits, war reparations from Greece, the Capitulations and some other concessions, as well as the Gallipoli cemeteries. The spiritual losses were the privileges given to the minorities, the Patriarchate issue, the Caliphate, and all the 'secret commitments to Westernization or secularization.' Mosul was the most prominent among the material losses, and the Caliphate was the most prominent among the spiritual losses.

All these writers believe that the greatest loss was the abolition of the Caliphate, supposedly granted in response to British pressure. At Lausanne, Atatürk and İsmet sacrificed this most valuable asset in return for the new republic's independence and survival. So began the elimination of religion and rise of secularism. The establishment of the Turkish Republic was, they claim, only granted after İsmet and Atatürk agreed to this condition. A Jewish and British conspiracy allegedly lay behind it all.[52] What was the hidden agenda of the British and the Jews? The British sought to control the Caliphate in order to control Muslims in their dominions. The Jews' purported goal was to establish a Jewish state in Palestine. The decision was taken at the First World Zionist Congress (1897) in Basel to create Palestine by breaking up the great Turkish (Ottoman) state. The British and Jews (supposedly a majority in the British cabinet) cooperated in the First World War to eliminate the danger of Islam, and to separate the Turks from the Islamic world, thus destroying Islamic unity. Turkish victory in the War of Independence (and Atatürk's emphasis on the Caliphate in this period) spoiled their plans. And so they used Lausanne to achieve their dastardly goal.

Our authors are in agreement that these and other evil forces such as the *Dönmes* (Jewish converts to Islam) and Freemasons employed an Ottoman Jew for this purpose: the former Chief Rabbi of the Ottoman Jewish community, Haim Nahum (or Hayim Naum but hereafter Nahum), who was an honorary adviser to the Turkish delegation.[53] 'A terrible Jewish genius', Nahum allegedly convinced

52 Conspiracy theories and anti-Semitism constitute the main components of their discourses. They explained everything in late Ottoman history as a Jewish conspiracy, from the Young Turk Revolution to the Lausanne Conference. See Doğan Gürpınar, *Conspiracy Theories in Turkey: Conspiracy Nation*, 2020, 26–43.

53 For Haim Nahum (1872–1960), see Aksel Erbahar, 'Nahoum (Nahum), Haim (Ḥayyim)', *Encyclopaedia of Jews in the Islamic World*, https://referenceworks.brillonline.com/entries/encyclopedia-of-jews-in-the-islamic-world/

İsmet (and Atatürk) to abolish the Caliphate in return for the recognition of Turkey's independence. Each author's version of this conspiracy differs in details. In Kısakürek's version, Nahum drew up a plan with the 'secret Jewish government' (*gizli yahudilik hükümeti*) in Turkey at the B'nai B'rith headquarters in Istanbul. Their plan was to make Atatürk 'dissolve the unity and consciousness of Islam' and 'to demolish the dominance and image of religion' in order to achieve their goal. Nahum met Lord Curzon in London, so the story goes, and assured him that he would convince the Turks to abolish the Caliphate and cut ties with the Muslim world, in exchange for the recognition of their independence.

In Atilhan's version of this fantasy Curzon and Nahum, in a secret meeting at London's Savoy Hotel, with the participation of Jewish ministers and advisers of the British government, set the following conditions for peace: the abolition of the Caliphate; the deportation of the Ottoman Dynasty and confiscation of all its properties; severing relations between Turkey and all other Muslim countries; and the revision of all *sharia* laws in accordance with secular principles.

As these authors see it, Nahum propagandized in favour of the Turks in America and Britain. He thus gained the trust of the national movement's leaders, joining the Turkish delegation at Lausanne and becoming İsmet's mentor. In one version, Nahum conveyed the conditions to İsmet who accepted the offer after consulting Ankara, and so the Treaty was signed. In another version, Atatürk called Nahum to Turkey and negotiated with him in Ankara or Izmir. According to a third version, the offer was made to İsmet before the breakdown in negotiations at Lausanne; when İsmet subsequently returned to Turkey, after some deliberation, he and Atatürk agreed to accept. Atatürk (and İsmet) then began to change their discourse and attitude towards the Caliphate and religion, which they formerly praised.

British attitudes in the negotiations' two phases are contrasted to bolster this mythical account. 'The crusader minded' Curzon's decision not to return to Lausanne after the hiatus allegedly proved that he had, thanks to the conspiracy, secured all he wanted. He is said to have told the House of Commons that: 'From now on the Turks will never find their old blessings and will never be able to hold their heads high again. This is because we extinguished their spiritual forces.' In inventing this version of events, the authors failed to notice that Curzon had not sat in the House of Commons since 1908. While he did defend the Treaty in the

nahoum-nahum-haim-hayyim-COM_0016340?lang=en; Esther Benbassa, *Haim Nahum: A Sephardic Chief Rabbi in Politics (1892–1923)*, 1995. Nahum was an anti-Zionist Jew, and he was not an official member of the Turkish delegation.

British parliament in 1924, he did so in the House of Lords, and in terms very different from those 'quoted' above.

Under the principle of *post hoc ergo propter hoc* Armağan and Mısıroğlu also claim that the British parliament waited for the abolition of the Caliphate before proceeding to ratify Lausanne. The Caliphate was abolished in March 1924, the Lausanne bill was placed before the House of Commons in April 1924, and the Treaty was ratified in August 1924. Armağan also cites King George V's January 1924 speech at the State Opening of Parliament: 'as soon as it [the Lausanne Treaty] has been passed, the Treaty will be ratified, and a new era of peaceful relations with Turkey will open.'[54] Armağan suggests that this 'new era' could be interpreted as a symbol for the abolition of the Caliphate, since the Muslim world without a Caliph certainly meant a new era for the British.

To summarize this version of events, only after the Caliphate question was solved was the Republic of Turkey internationally recognized. For Armağan, it comes as no surprise that steps for a new (Western) civil law were started just six days later.[55] Another concession, part of this fiendishly clever secret deal, set Turkey's new foreign policy: 'Peace at Home, Peace in the World.' That was allegedly Turkey delivering on its promise to cut off all relations with the Muslims who were under the occupation of the Western powers. In fact, this was Article 139 of Sèvres (and Lausanne's Articles 17–22).[56] For Armağan Lausanne was a Pyrrhic victory or even a Trojan horse![57] Lines Mısıroğlu added to the back cover of his book give the essence of the nationalist-conservative/Islamist critique of Lausanne: 'Lausanne was the table of loot from the vast imperial legacy. It was meant as vengeance against Islam in the person of the Turk and to leave the whole Islamic world without leadership!' At Lausanne, therefore, Turkey was turned into a small and strategically isolated country. Unless Turkey changes the Treaty of Lausanne it will never again become the 'Great Turkey.'

All other popular writers along the Nationalist-Conservative/Islamist line have repeated these four authors' claims with minor additions and modifications.[58]

54 'The King's Speech', 14 January 1924. *House of Lords Hansard Sessional Papers* 5th series, Vol. 56, 6–66.

55 Armağan, *Tek Parti Devri*, 31–37.

56 Armağan, *Cumhuriyet Efsaneleri*, 209–216; Armağan, *Tek Parti Devri*, 31–37.

57 Armağan, *Efsaneler ve Gerçekler*, 84; Armağan, *Cumhuriyet Efsaneleri*, 209–216.

58 See, for example, Abdurrahman Dilipak, *Cumhuriyete Giden Yol*, 2017, 314ff; Abdurrahman Dilipak, *İnönü Dönemi*, 1988, 85–91, 112–121 and 239–245; Ahmet Kabaklı, *Temellerin Duruşması*, 1990; Hasan Hüseyin Ceylan, *Büyük Oyun*, 1995; D. Mehmet Doğan, *Batılılaşma İhaneti*, 2015, 100–101; D. Mehmet Doğan, *Mağlubiyet İdeolojisinin Sonu*, 2007; *Gayrıresmi Yakın Tarih Ansiklopedisi*, Vol. II, 1993; *Tanzimat'tan Cumhuriyet'e Cumhuriyet'ten*

This alternative history has had significant influence on every segment of the Turkish right in general. Kısakürek and Mısıroğlu seem to have been particularly influential among various factions and generations of Islamists and Turkists.[59] This includes Necmettin Erbakan's 'National Outlook' (*Milli Görüş*) movement, and, obviously, the founders of the Justice and Development Party (AKP).[60] As a matter of fact, as a known devotee of Kısakürek (and Mısıroğlu), Erdoğan's critical statements in recent years regarding the Treaty of Lausanne should not surprise us.[61] The conservative-Islamist reading has become a counter-official narrative on Lausanne.

The Lausanne issue is also associated with the AKP's foreign policy moves in recent years, from policies towards Syria and Libya to the opening of Hagia Sofia and the planned Canal Istanbul project. Mustafa Armağan called for the AKP to settle accounts with Lausanne, for example.[62] He implied that the AKP's foreign policy is designed to remove the shackles Lausanne allegedly placed on Turkey's feet. He argues that Lausanne's provisions against Turkey's interests began to be torn down under AKP's rule. With the realization of the Canal Istanbul project, sovereignty over the Bosphorus will be restored to Turkey, for the first time since 13 November 1918, the day the Allies occupied Istanbul.[63]

The lines written by İbrahim Karagül, editor-in-chief of *Yeni Şafak*, who advocated a 'forward' or neo-Ottoman foreign policy for Turkey and the AKP, can be cited as yet another example. On the occasion of the 96th anniversary of the Treaty of Lausanne, Karagül argued that:

Günümüze Yakın Tarih Ansiklopedisi, Vol. II, n.d.

59 For example, Said Nursi quoted Kısakürek in one of his writings, and thus the Caliphate conspiracy claim has become a part of the teachings of *Nurculuk* movement. See Bediüzzaman Said Nursi, *Risale-i Nur Külliyatı*, Vol. II, 2002, 1820, 1825 and 1829.
For MHP and the *Ülkücü* movement, see Mustafa Çalık, *MHP Hareketinin Kaynakları ve Gelişimi, 1965–1980*, 1995, 123–124; Beşir Ayvazoğlu, 'Ah, O Eski Ülkücüler', *Türkiye Günlüğü* 50, 1998, 179–182.

60 See İhsan D. Dağı, *Kimlik, Söylem ve Siyaset: Doğu Batı Ayrımında Refah Partisi Geleneği*, 1998, 32–36.

61 For an example, https://www.hurriyetdailynews.com/row-over-lausanne-treaty-continues-to-roil-turkish-politics--104493. See also Sean R. Singer, 'Erdoğan's Muse: The School of Necip Fazil Kisakurek', *World Affairs* 176/4, 2013, 81–88; Kaya Genç, 'Reading Between the Lines: The slow reveal of Recep Tayyip Erdoğan's grandiose vision', *World Policy Journal* 35/2, 2018, 47–55; Svante E. Cornell, 'Erbakan, Kısakürek, and the Mainstreaming of Extremism in Turkey', *Current Trends in Islamist Ideology*, 2018, https://www.hudson.org/research/14375-erbakan-k-sak-rek-and-the-mainstreaming-of-extremism-in-turkey.

62 Armağan, *Efsaneler ve Gerçekler*, 81–84; Armağan, *Korku Duvarını Yıkmak*, 10.

63 Armağan, *Satılık İmparatorluk*, 168.

> Lausanne was not enough for us, so we never digested it. Because we never digested being imprisoned in Anatolia … we waited for the time, we hoped that global power shifts would open up a space for us. And that time has come … The West's centuries-old unilateral dominance came to an end, new powers took the stage, the global power map changed, and power gaps were formed … Just in this period; whatever forces were against us at the Sèvres table, they are the same forces and their representatives today … We are not trying to fight but to take our rightful place in the field of global power … Their game is over. We're just getting started![64]

Neo-Kemalist Popular Historiography

Neo-Kemalist popular historiography emerged in the 1990s. This Neo-Kemalist current reflects the challenges of the Özal and post-Cold War (and Globalisation) era in Turkish society. The effects of globalisation and socio-cultural transformation that prevailed in the late 1980s and early 1990s had opened up the Kemalist Pandora's box, out of which emerged multiple identities. Religious and ethnic identities, the two thorns in the side of Kemalism, reappeared in the 1990s.[65] A number of competing identities began to influence the Turkish political and socio-cultural scene. As a result, the questioning of existing structures, institutions, historical events, and taboos commenced. Media diversification, liberalisation, and the internet revolution intensified this process.

In the 2000s, the existing left-right divide in Turkey's political-social environment began to alter, and a new division emerged between 'globalists' and 'nationalists.'[66] While the latter believed that dynamics of globalisation would harm Turkey, the former believed that Turkey should integrate into globalisation for the common good. Both currents cross existing political / ideological and

---

64 İbrahim Karagül, 'Yüzyıllık Sabır', *Yeni Şafak*, 25 July 2019. Also see İbrahim Karagül, 'Musul ve Halep'in Kuzeyi Türkiye'ye Devredilmeli', *Yeni Şafak*, 24 October 2016, and İbrahim Karagül, 'Türkiye'yi Durdurmak Artık Mümkün Değildir', *Yeni Şafak*, 2 December 2016.

65 See, for example, Gökhan Çetinsaya, 'Rethinking nationalism and Islam: some preliminary notes on the roots of "Turkish-Islamic Synthesis" in modern Turkish political thought', *The Muslim World* 89/3–4, 1999, 350–376; Tanıl Bora, 'Nationalist Discourses in Turkey', *South Atlantic Quarterly* 102/2–3, 2003, 433–451.

66 See Ziya Öniş, 'Conservative Globalists versus Defensive Nationalists: Political Parties and Paradoxes of Europeanization in Turkey', *Journal of Southern Europe and the Balkans* 9, 2007, 247–261; Gökhan Çetinsaya, '2000'li Yılların Başlarında Türk Siyasi Hayatını Açıklayabilecek Bir Anahtar: Küreselleşme', *Türkiye Günlüğü* 97, 2009, 46–51.

social identities on a new axis. One of the most distinctive features of the anti-globalist coalition is 'Sèvres Syndrome.' It refers to a fear of national and territorial dismemberment by external powers (the West) and their internal collaborators (Kurdish nationalists / separatists and political Islamists). For these neo-nationalists or neo-Kemalists (*Ulusalcıs*), everything on the agenda of Turkish foreign and domestic policy invokes Sèvres, and therefore Lausanne: Kurds, Armenians, Cyprus, Greece, Northern Iraq, the IMF, the EU process, the United States and the [USA's] Greater Middle East Project.[67] A striking example of this trend is the tremendous success of a fictional story entitled *Metal Fırtına* (The Metal Storm). This 2004 depiction of a Turkish-American war mentions an 'Operation Sèvres' followed by partitioning of Anatolia by Greece, Armenia, and an independent Kurdistan. The book sold several hundred thousand copies in Turkey.[68]

Sèvres Syndrome has also found its expression in popular historiography, accompanied by anti-Semitic conspiracy theories, albeit this time with the contribution of a section of the Turkish left.[69] Popular history books of this genre have been published about Lausanne and Sèvres with special importance given to the anniversaries of Lausanne. For the leading figures of this mindset, the Treaty of Sèvres meant 'enslavement' or 'the death sentence of Turkishness'. For these, 'the West and their internal collaborators have not forgotten the Treaty of Sèvres in history's dust bin – they stored it in the deep freezer, but they have no more patience!' For them, 'what happens today is the revenge of Lausanne'; 'a Western plot to re-enact the Treaty of Sèvres.' 'What is currently being imposed on Turkey [by the EU] is today's Sèvres.' 'The Kurdish policy of the West is 'postmodern Sèvres'.' Lausanne, on the other hand, is 'the title deed of Turkey' and 'What

67 See Baskın Oran, *Türkiye'de Azınlıklar*, 2010, 160–162; Fatma Müge Göçek, 'Why Is There Still a Sèvres Syndrome? An Analysis of Turkey's Uneasy Association with the West', *The Transformation of Turkey: Redefining State and Society from the Ottoman Empire to the Modern Era*, 2011, 98–184; Dietrich Jung, 'The Sèvres Syndrome: Turkish Foreign Policy and its Historical Legacies', https://americandiplomacy.web.unc.edu/2003/08/the-sevres-syndrome/; M. Guida, 'The Sèvres Syndrome and "Komplo" Theories in the Islamist and Secular Press', *Turkish Studies*, 9, 2007, 37–52; Emre Erdoğan, 'The Sèvres Syndrome: A key to Understand Foreign Policy Attitudes of Turkish citizens', *Journal of Middle Eastern Politics and Policy*, 2021, 36–43.

68 See Kösebalaban, *Turkish Foreign Policy*, 167; Soli Özel, 'The Gathering Storm', *Foreign Policy* 149, 2005, 83–85; Lerna K. Yanık, '"Those Crazy Turks" That Got Caught in the "Metal Storm": Nationalism in Turkey's Best Seller Lists', *European University Institute Working Papers*, 2008, https://cadmus.eui.eu/handle/1814/8002.

69 See Gürpınar, *Conspiracy Theories in Turkey*, 44–60; Marc David Baer, 'An Enemy Old and New: The Dönme, Anti-Semitism, and Conspiracy Theories in the Ottoman Empire and Turkish Republic', *Jewish Quarterly Review* 103/4, 2013, 523–555.

happened today under AKP is the nullification of the title deed'; 'Opposition to Lausanne is opposition to the Republican regime'; 'Turkey's involvement in the EU process is an attempt to change the Treaty of Lausanne.'[70] In the mid-2010s, with the participation of the AKP, the anti-globalist coalition grew and became much stronger. Even if these new coalition partners cannot agree on the Lausanne issue, they agree on other issues such as Sèvres Syndrome and a mythical Jewish conspiracy.

The names of Turgut Özakman and Sinan Meydan stand out as the most widely read popular history authors of this group. They try to defend not only Lausanne but Atatürk and the 'history of Turkish Revolution' from Kısakürek, Mısıroğlu, and Armağan. Whereas the Lausanne arguments of classical Kemalism generally repeated what Atatürk and İsmet said and wrote, the neo-Kemalist writers reflect the concerns of Sèvres Syndrome, besides trying to answer accusations of Nationalist-Conservatives/Islamists, and some socialist and liberal (*İkinci Cumhuriyetçi*) authors.

Turgut Özakman (1930–2013), a well-known playwright in Turkey, studied law and theatre, and worked in the state radio-television (TRT) and the state theatre (DT) in different capacities.[71] His historical-novel of the Turkish War of Independence, *Şu Çılgın Türkler* (Those Crazy Turks), published in 2005, has sold around two million copies.[72] While Özakman is both the last example of Kemalist popular historiography and the first example of the neo-Kemalist genre, Sinan Meydan (born 1975), who studied history, represents the young generation of neo-Kemalist popular historians.[73] Both writers have some points in common: they accept that the Treaty of Lausanne has shortcomings, but point out that some of these (like the Turkish Straits and Hatay) were corrected later. Both critique an overreliance on the memoirs of Atatürk's opponents. They argue that the memoirs of Karabekir, Rıza Nur and Rauf Orbay are unreliable and have been deliberately misrepresented.

---

70 *Karanlıktan Aydınlığa Sevr ve Lozan: Seminer Notları*, 2010, 89–90, 177–180; *90. Yılında Lozan*, 2014; *80. Yılında Lozan Barış Antlaşması (24 Temmuz* [July] *2003)*, 2003. Also see Erol Manisalı, *Ahtapot Kollarındaki Dünya ve Türkiye*, 2003; Cahit Kayra, *Sevr Dosyası*, 2004; Hulki Cevizoğlu and Attila İlhan, *Bütün Kaleler Zaptedilmedi*, 2004; Cengiz Özakıncı, *Kalemin Namusu 1: Türk Savun Kendini*, 2019, 554–581.

71 https://tr.wikipedia.org/wiki/Turgut_Özakman.

72 By 2021 it reached a 463rd edition (https://www.bilgiyayinevi.com.tr/su-cilgin-turkler). Also see Alev Çınar and Hakkı Taş, 'Politics of Nationhood and the Displacement of the Founding Moment: Contending Histories of the Turkish Nation', *Comparative Studies in Society and History* 59/3, 2017, 657–689.

73 https://sinanmeydancom.tr.gg/.

The most detailed refutation of 'anti-Lausanne' writers was penned by Turgut Özakman.[74] In his 789-page book *Vahidettin, Mustafa Kemal and the National Struggle: Lies, Mistakes, Hype*, he settles accounts with all 'alternative historians', including liberals and socialists. He subjects their claims to logical critique, checks original sources and tries to correct them, using the historical literature on the Turkish Revolution. Özakman endeavours to reveal how these authors contradict themselves in their works, and how they modified or simply invented source material. Özakman targets Mısıroğlu and his 'three-volume fairy tale' for particular criticism. The latter's Lausanne claims are described as 'scenarios', the 'product of a vast and rich imagination.' All these fabrications and distortions are 'not history, they're simply neighbourhood coffee gossip' or a comedy, such as Shakespeare's *Much Ado About Nothing* (Hiç Üstüne Kuru Gürültü).[75]

The Caliphate / Nahum conspiracy theory comes in for detailed rebuttal in Özakman's work. He points out that there was no such speech by Curzon to the House of Commons; Nahum did not travel to Ankara or Izmir; the second phase of talks was not plain sailing; there was no change in Atatürk's attitude towards religion during the Izmir Economic Conference; there was no conspiracy about the Caliphate. Özakman argues that if one word of Mısıroğlu's claims were true about the secret deal, Britain would have been overly friendly to Turkey after Lausanne, but that was not the case.

As a spokesperson of Sèvres Syndrome, Sinan Meydan accuses the critics of the Lausanne Treaty of being Gülenists (*FETÖcü*), supporters of the [USA's] Greater Middle East Project and the pawns of imperialism. For Meydan, the real motivation of these critics is enmity towards the Republic and Atatürk.[76] In his book, *Panzehir* (Antidote), Meydan responds to Conservative-Islamist (and liberal and leftist) writers whom he describes as 'hitmen of imperialism.' In the section titled 'Lie 26: Lausanne is a Disgrace' (*Yalan 26: Lozan Hezimettir*),[77] Meydan complains that Lausanne is one of the most popular lies of the 'bigoted madmen' (*yobaz meczuplar*) and 'team of liberals' (*liboş takımı*). Moreover, he writes that the 'alternative history' propaganda of neo-Ottomanist writers has been successful, since it has come to be believed by tens of thousands of people: an example of mass ignorance in the information age.

74 Turgut Özakman, *Vahidettin, Mustafa Kemal ve Milli Mücadele: Yalanlar, Yanlışlar, Yutturmacalar*, 1997, 565–596.

75 Özakman, *Vahidettin,* 591.

76 See *90. Yılında Lozan*, 2014, 61.

77 Sinan Meydan, *Yalanlara, Çarpıtmalara, İftiralara Panzehir: Gerçeğe Çağrı*, 2015, 425ff. Cf. Sinan Meydan, *Hafıza*, 2019, 174ff, 339ff.

Meydan attempts to correct these 'mind-blowing lies' about Lausanne and emphasizes Turkey's achievements through official and academic history books, seeking to tell 'the truth about Lausanne.' Meydan particularly attempts to respond to the allegations of Mısıroğlu and Armağan. For him, Lausanne does not have secret clauses or protocols and 'Haim Nahum and the Caliphate conspiracy' is a raving (*deli saçması*) allegation or 'schizophrenic delirium of a madman with a fez' (*bir fesli delinin şizofrenik sayıklamaları*). He also challenges the claim that the Lausanne delegation was inadequate, defending İsmet's accomplishments at Lausanne: 'İsmet stood upright from the beginning, and did not assume a humble attitude'; 'He aged much during his extraordinary resistance in Lausanne.'

For Meydan, the claim that Turkey lost a lot of territories at Lausanne is a false or at very least a distorted claim, frequently voiced by 'enemies of the Republic'. He argues that Turkey did not lose any land in Lausanne (except for the island known in Turkey as Meis and in Greece as Kastellorizo). Western Thrace, the Aegean Islands, the Dodecanese Islands, Mosul, and Hatay were already under the occupation of the Allies. So, the founding fathers of the Republic cannot be criticized for losing them, but perhaps they can be critiqued for not getting them back.

To evaluate Lausanne Meydan argues it is necessary to compare the fourteen-item directive that Atatürk dictated to İsmet and the clauses of the Treaty. By comparing these with British demands, he attempts to give a 'scientific answer' to the question of whether 'Lausanne is a victory or a defeat.' After explaining the disadvantages Turkey faced at Lausanne, Meydan divides the issues into two categories. He argues that Turkey decided to resist 'without compromise' at all costs on Capitulations and an Armenian National Home. But on other issues Turkey followed a policy of 'obtaining the possible'. In this context, with the Treaty of Lausanne Turkey abolished the Capitulations and prevented the establishment of an Armenian state. Turkey was completely successful in achieving its *sine qua non* demands. As for those areas where 'obtaining the possible' was the guiding principle, after examining fifteen of those in detail, Meydan concludes that Turkey was partly successful in getting what she wanted. But he notes that desires and achievements are not equal. The abolition of the Capitulations, for example, is equivalent to several unachieved demands. If one evaluates Lausanne through the National Pact criteria, it was at least seventy per cent successful. Some results might have appeared as failures in 1923, but subsequently proved to be good for Turkey: Meydan gives the Patriarchate, Mosul, and Western Thrace issues as examples. In short, once the conditions of Turkey at that time, Turkey's demands, the expectations of the Allies, and the Articles of the Treaty are examined, Lausanne emerges as a 'definite success' for Turkey and a defeat for the West. That was why the Liberals criticised it in the British parliament.

Finally, Meydan attempts to respond to recently emerged 'urban legends' about Lausanne, such as that which claims Lausanne will expire after a century and that Ankara promised Britain and France that it would not develop Turkey's oilfields and mines. These 'irrational lies and fabrications of the enemies of Atatürk and the Republic' are frighteningly widespread.

> When you do a simple search on the internet, you will see how this Lausanne lie spread like an infectious disease. The surprising spread of this lie, especially among young people, shows that we are progressing rapidly towards becoming a society that never reads, never questions, and never thinks. Because in a society that reads even a little, questions a little, and thinks a little, it is impossible to find a person who would believe such a lie.

Manifestations of collective memory such as museums and literary genres, apart from popular history works, are surprisingly few. They all follow the official history narrative. There is only one museum devoted entirely to Lausanne, established by the University of Trakya in 2000 as the *Lozan Müzesi* (Lausanne Museum) in Karaağaç, and later (2015) re-named as *Milli Mücadele ve Lozan Müzesi* (Museum of the National Struggle and Lausanne).[78] The table on which the Treaty of Lausanne was signed, given to Turkey by the Swiss government in 2008, is exhibited in the First Turkish Grand National Assembly building in Ankara, now a museum.[79] A few theatre plays appeared about Lausanne, all reflecting the official history.[80]

Novels that mention Lausanne, on the other hand, focus not specifically on the Lausanne Conference but mainly on the exchange of the population between Greece and Turkey.[81] In the field of civil society, while the İnönü Foundation (*İnönü Vakfı*) stands out with its activities related to Lausanne, the Lausanne

78 See https://millimucvelozanmuzesi.trakya.edu.tr/ and https://edirne.ktb.gov.tr/TR-90112/milli-mucadele-ve-lozan-muzesi.html.

79 See Ozan Ozavci, 'The Lausanne Table: Symbol of Victory or Execution?' in https://thelausanneproject.com/2021/02/28/lausanne-table/ and Nissa Kashani et al, https://thelausanneproject.com/2021/12/31/returning-the-tables/.

80 For examples, see Erol Toy, 1992; Ataol Behramoğlu, 1993; Mehmet Baydur, 2001.

81 See Hercules Millas, 'The Exchange of Populations in Turkish Literature', *Crossing the Aegean: An Appraisal on the 1923 Compulsory Populations Exchange between Greece and Turkey*, ed. Renée Hirschon, 2003, 221–234.

Emigrants Foundation (*Lozan Mübadilleri Vakfı*) and its Association (*Lozan Mübadilleri Derneği*) tries to keep alive the memories of those who came from Greece to Anatolia. In 2010 they also established a museum (*Mübadele Müzesi,* Exchange Museum).[82]

In conclusion, in official and popular historiography in Turkey, the politics of identity govern perceptions and evaluations of Lausanne, as of all other historical questions. The details of this debate represent, on the one hand, a clash between different claims about the past and, on the other hand, manifestations of the framing of history. All these diverse interpretations show how the past is often presented as a mirror of what is supposedly really happening today. It also gives us clues to understand the complex interaction between politics, history, and identity in Turkey. Considering Turkey's current political and social crisis, it is clear that the 'war of identities' over historical events and people will continue.

82 http://www.lozanmubadilleri.org.tr/.

16

Diplomacy, Entertainment, Souvenir? *Guignol à Lausanne* (1923) and the Lausanne Conference in Caricature

Julia Secklehner

A group of men sit around a large round table, chaired by a jolly-looking man with bright cheeks and a pointy nose, his bold head framed by a crown of whimsical hair (Figure 1). He is Lord Curzon, British Secretary of State for Foreign Affairs and the initial coordinator of the Lausanne Conference. On his right, a large man with a protruding nose, fleeting chin and receding hairline, addresses him with one hand raised. He is Rıza Nur, second delegate of the Turkish delegation. The head of the delegation, İsmet İnönü (hereafter İsmet) sits next to him with his head resting on his arm, staring at the table. The other men sitting at the table are occupied with the study of colourful maps marked by little flags which read: Beau Séjour – Lausanne Palace – Savoy – Beau Rivage, hotels that hosted the delegations during the conference. Rather than marking the location of rival claims and contested borders, however, in the cartoon 'Plenary Session' the documents occupying the diplomats' attention appear to be a programme rather than a landscape, labelled with the balls, dances, and dinner menus that turned the Lausanne Conference into a social event for high-profile political figures.

Instead of leaving viewers to guess who's who, each man at the table is identified: next to the Turkish, British, French and Italian representatives, the cartoon includes the Greek representative Eleftherios Venizelos, the Japanese diplomat Baron Hayashi and his Soviet counterpart Vatslav Vorovsky, who would be assassinated at the Hotel Cecil not too long after the cartoon was produced. Light-hearted as it is, 'Plenary Session' nonetheless gives a comprehensive overview of the conference participants and their complex relations: the seating arrangements and the demeanour of the delegates indicate the complexities arising from the competing interests of the participating parties as well as the sheer exhaustion and desperation such diplomatic efforts induced. References to events such as the 'oriental evening' on the lower end of the table or 'American Bar' at the very top suggest the lengths organizers went to keep participants entertained. Leaving aside the social, political and economic consequences for millions of people in the Near East and beyond, the cartoon thus firmly locates the conference in Lausanne and, not without irony, depicts it as an event characterized by both serious debate and frivolous diversions: a crush of delegates, each distracted from and yet tormented by their own interest.

Drawn by Emery (also Imre or Emerich) Kelen (1896–1978), the cartoon is, in fact, not a one-off piece but was published as part of an album consisting of twenty-five lithographs compiled by Kelen and fellow cartoonist Alois (or Aloysius) Derso (1888–1964): *Guignol à Lausanne* (hereafter *GàL*). Printed in a numbered edition of three hundred copies and marketed as, in Kelen's words, 'a book that reasonable men can take home as a souvenir', the album was published in Lausanne during the conference to an appreciative audience.[1] It represents an exceptional record designed to speak first and foremost to the very participants it depicted. While countless newspapers and magazines covered the negotiations, none chronicled them in quite the way that Derso and Kelen did. Based on *GàL*'s extraordinary conference reporting, this chapter focuses on the album as a novel form of diplomatic cartooning. It explores how Derso and Kelen deployed a new style of pictorial journalism to cover high-profile diplomatic events, which originated in an unlikely meeting at Lausanne.

The Forgotten Chroniclers of the Lausanne Conference: Derso and Kelen

GàL's artists merit an introduction of their own: the artists' contributions to the history of caricature and cartooning have almost been forgotten today, even though Derso and Kelen's success at Lausanne paved the way for them to become the leading cartoonists for the League of Nations and, later, the United Nations.[2]

1 Emery Kelen, *Peace in their Time. Men Who Led Us In and Out of War, 1914–1945*, 1964, 117; Jean-Marie Bertin, 'Derso ile Kelen, Milletler Cemiyeti'nin unutulmaz kelle avcıları', *Şalom Dergi*, 2020, https://dergi.salom.com.tr/haber-318-derso_ile_kelen_milletler_cemiyetinin_unutulmaz_kelle_avcilari.html.

2 For an introduction see Stefan Slater and David Macfadyen, 'Hope, faith and reality. Visualising the League of Nations', *Illustration,* Winter 2020, 16–24.

As professional cartoonists and long-term migrants, records from the early lives of Derso and Kelen are difficult to trace. Works on paper, especially when produced for newspapers and periodicals, were often treated as ephemera in editorial offices, so that original drawings submitted were discarded, or simply taken home by staff members.[3] Wide circulation has left little by way of an archive of their work, exacerbated by its position somewhere between journalism ('picture journalists'), popular visual culture and fine art. Alongside this ephemeral status, the fact that the artists migrated across Europe and then to the United States further marginalized them in the history of cartoons and caricatures.[4] Though Derso and Kelen gained international recognition with their cartoons for the League of Nations in the 1920s and 1930s, including a well-received exhibition in London in 1934, they are overlooked in encyclopaedic studies of cartoon history and in biographical dictionaries of cartoonists.[5]

Today the artists' joint estate is hosted by Princeton University and includes several hundred drawings, manuscripts and personal documents.[6] Compiled predominantly by Kelen, these documents vouch for two extraordinarily prolific careers, a unique partnership spanning four decades of tireless engagement with global diplomacy.[7] Yet even though these documents emphasize just how extraordinary Derso's and Kelen's position was as 'pictorial journalists' in the service of the League of Nations and its successor, the United Nations, most of them date to the late 1920s or later. Their beginnings thus can only be partially reconstructed. *GàL* is of importance in this regard: just as it represents an unusual record of the Lausanne conference, it also marks Derso and Kelen's first collaborative work – one, which sealed their fate as an oxymoron: diplomatic cartoonists.

In 1922 Derso and Kelen arrived in Lausanne separately. They met at the press bar of the Lausanne Palace Hotel and began working together. At the point of their first meeting, Derso was already a seasoned political cartoonist, who had

3 This is described in Adolf Hoffmeister, 'Monteurdada John Heartfield', *Stále ješte ... výstava John Heartfield fotomontaže v upomínku na velkou mezinárodní výstavu karikatur v Mánesu v roce 1934*, ed. Adolf Hoffmeister, 1964, 10.

4 Derso and Kelen were both of Jewish origin and highly critical of National Socialism in their cartoons, which forced them to emigrate to the United States in 1939.

5 *The World Encyclopedia of Cartoons,* ed. Maurice Horn, 1998; Kees Kousemaker, *Lambiek Comiclopedia*, https://www.lambiek.net/comiclopedia.html.

6 The Derso and Kelen Collection, Seeley G. Mudd Manuscript Library, Princeton University https://findingaids.princeton.edu/catalog/MC205.

7 Details about their long careers are discussed in Stefan Slater and David Macfadyen, *Humour in Tragic Times: The Political Cartoons of Derso and Kelèn*, forthcoming.

covered post-WW1 treaty conferences in Versailles, Trianon, and Genoa.[8] His position was, in many ways, typical for a progressive Jewish artist of the pre-war generation, who challenged the conservatism of the Hungarian establishment after training abroad.[9]

Born as Alajos Dezső-Deutsch in Baja, southern Hungary (the Habsburg Empire until 1918), Derso studied painting in Paris and Berlin and began to contribute caricatures and cartoons to satirical newspapers in the 1910s. These included *Borsszem Jankó* (Johnny Peppercorn, 1868–1938), for example, one of Budapest's leading satirical magazines at the time. In addition to his work as a cartoonist, Derso was a book illustrator and graphic artist. He spent WW1 as a war artist for the Habsburg Imperial and Royal War Press Headquarters ('Das Kaiserliche und königliche Kriegspressequartier').[10] Following the coup of the reactionary regime of Miklós Horthy in Hungary in 1919, Derso, like many other progressive artists and Hungarians of Jewish origin, left the country. He travelled to Paris and, moving among Bohemian circles and Hungarian émigré groups meeting at Café du Dôme in Montparnasse, cultivated an image as a modern émigré artist from central Europe.[11]

Little else is known of his work in Paris, but it was at this point that he began to contribute caricature sketches to the French daily *Le Matin* (1884–1944), and it was in this capacity that he arrived in Lausanne.[12] Derso's work from this time, such as 'M. Lloyd George', featured prominently next to lengthy political analyses and reports. In the traditional mode of portrait caricature, these focused on exaggeration and abstraction of physical features. Lloyd George's features are transformed from those of a jolly old man to a twisted face between his arrival to and his departure from the Genoa conference, as the accompanying caption explains (Figure 2). On the same page, two further caricatures show Luigi Facta, the Italian head of the conference, and the American journalist Frank A. Vanderlip. The artist's abstracted portraits emulated the immediacy and quick reaction that one would expect of a daily newspaper.

8 Alois Derso, 'Derso draws and discusses "Homo Conferentiarum"!', *The Illustrated London News,* 22 February 1930, 282.
9 Mary Gluck, *Georg Lukács and his generation, 1900–1918*, 2011, 13–23.
10 AT-OeStA/KA FA AOK KPQ Akten 30 Kunstgruppe, KPQ-Mitglieder (Ansuchen um Aufnahme, diverse Personalunterlagen), Namen G, 1914–1918, Austrian State Archives, Vienna.
11 Biographies, Derso and Kelen Collection, MC205, Public Policy Papers, Department of Special Collections, Princeton University Library.
12 *Le Matin,* 139/13940, 20 May 1922, 1.

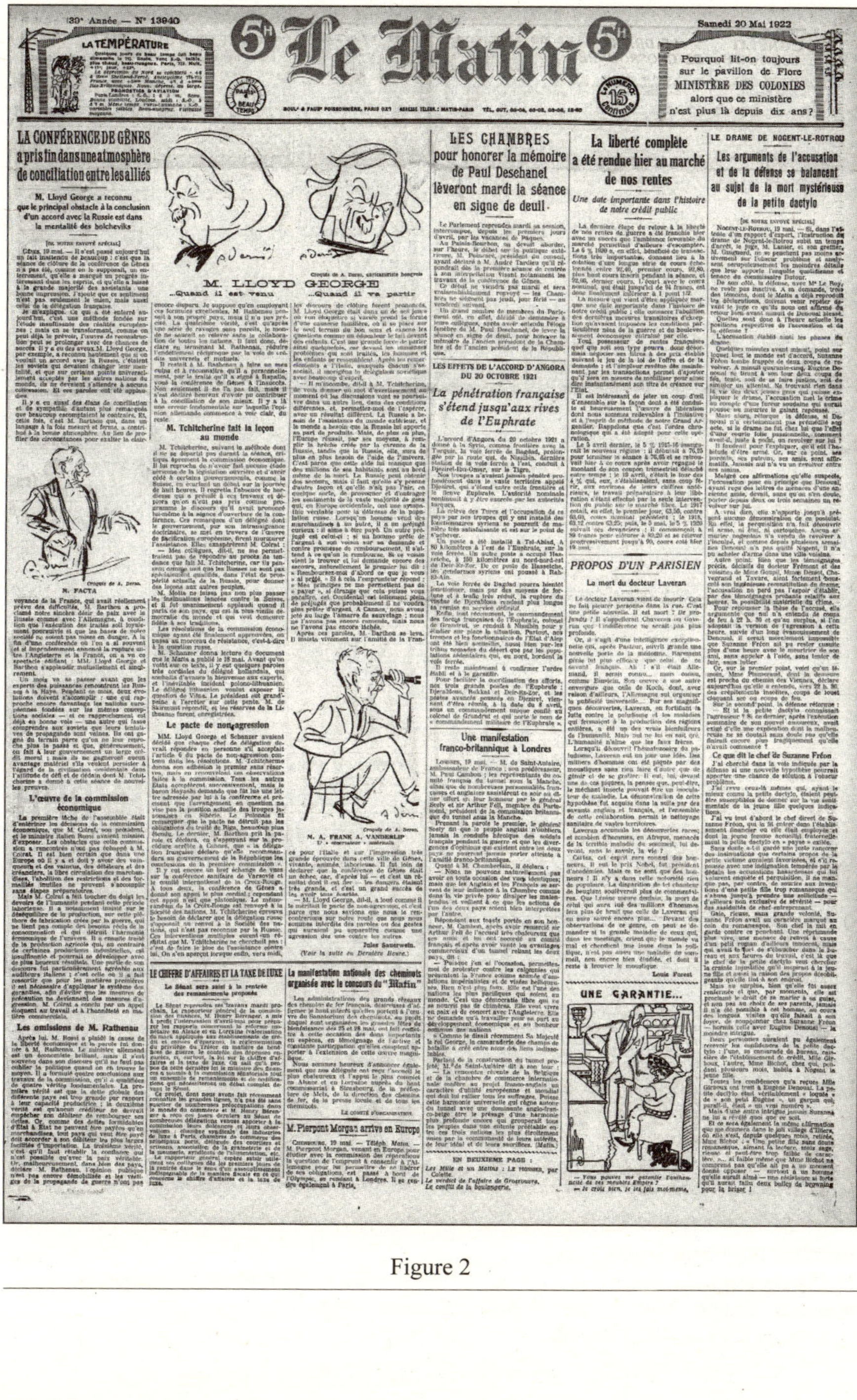

39e Année — N° 13840

Le Matin

Samedi 20 Mai 1922

Pourquoi lit-on toujours sur le pavillon de Flore MINISTÈRE DES COLONIES alors que ce ministère n'est plus là depuis dix ans?

LA CONFÉRENCE DE GÊNES a pris fin dans une atmosphère de conciliation entre les alliés

M. Lloyd George a reconnu que le principal obstacle à la conclusion d'un accord avec la Russie est dans la mentalité des bolcheviks

M. LLOYD GEORGE ...Quand il est venu ...Quand il va partir

M. Tchitcherine fait la leçon au monde

Le pacte de non-agression

L'œuvre de la commission économique

Les omissions de M. Rathenau

LES CHAMBRES pour honorer la mémoire de Paul Deschanel lèveront mardi la séance en signe de deuil

LES EFFETS DE L'ACCORD D'ANGORA DU 20 OCTOBRE 1921

La pénétration française s'étend jusqu'aux rives de l'Euphrate

Une manifestation franco-britannique à Londres

LE CHIFFRE D'AFFAIRES ET LA TAXE DE LUXE

La manifestation nationale des cheminots organisée avec le concours du "Matin"

M. Pierpont Morgan arrive en Europe

La liberté complète a été rendue hier au marché de nos rentes

Une date importante dans l'histoire de notre crédit public

PROPOS D'UN PARISIEN

La mort du docteur Laveran

UNE GARANTIE...

LE DRAME DE NOGENT-LE-ROTROU

Les arguments de l'accusation et de la défense se balancent au sujet de la mort mystérieuse de la petite dactylo

Ce que dit le chef de Suzanne Fréon

Figure 2

In fact, the spontaneity with which Derso seems to have committed such figures to paper was anything but: he always sketched from memory. As Kelen remembered, 'he ran around with a morgue of 10,000 faces in his head. He never forgot a face.'[13] Successful though he was as a cartoonist, Derso also continued other lines of work, such as book design. Even though Derso lived in French and Swiss exile for most of the interwar years, he continued to work and exhibit in Hungary.[14] In Lausanne, too, Derso supplemented his work for *Le Matin* with portrait postcards of the delegates, and his portrait caricatures for *West and East*, a travelogue written by the British sculptor and journalist Clare Sheridan (who also attended Lausanne) indicates that the artist also took on smaller commissions from colleagues who were also covering the conference.[15] The popularity of the postcards inspired *GàL*: seeing his compatriot deluged with orders for one-off souvenir albums of the postcards, Emery Kelen suggested a more ambitious project.[16]

Kelen was ten years Derso's junior, born to a Jewish family in Győr, Hungary (the Habsburg Empire until 1918). He was still a teenager when drafted into the Habsburg army, seeing action at the Isonzo front before suffering a nervous breakdown and being admitted to a psychiatric hospital, where he remained until the end of the war. In its immediate aftermath, Kelen made his first mark as a caricaturist in Hungary, contributing to *Borsszem Jankó* like Derso, as well as the leftist daily *Április* (April, 1918–1919). He participated in his first group exhibition in Győr in 1919, followed by another in 1922, although by that point he too had fled Horthy's Hungary.[17] Kelen then moved to Munich where he took painting classes with the painter Hans Hofmann (who later made a name as an Abstract Expressionist) and published cartoons in satirical magazines such as *Lustige Blätter* (Funny Papers, 1886–1944).

In 1922 Kelen found himself in Lausanne on a stopover after a brief career as a caricaturist for *Fußball* (Football, 1911–1944), an illustrated sports magazine founded by Adolf Müller, a prolific publisher for the National Socialist Party.[18]

13 'Aloysius Derso, Cartoonist, Dies; Drew Diplomats at Parleys Between World Wars', *New York Times,* 23 December 1964, 27.

14 *Magyar Grafika,* 11 February 1930, 5–6.

15 Clare Sheridan, *West and East,* New York, 1923. Caricatures by Derso also featured in other international newspapers, such as *Daily Mail,* 3 February 1923, 7, and *Yeni Mecmua,* 1 March 1923.

16 Kelen, *Peace in their Time,* 117; Imre Pérely, *Magyar rajzolóművészek,,* 1930; Géza Buzinkay, *Borsszem Jankó és társai. Élclapok és karikatúrák*, 1983.

17 *Dunántúli Hírlap*, 31 August 1919; *Dunántúli Hírlap,* 18 October 1922. I am grateful to Monika Bedő at the Győr library for sharing these newspaper clippings.

18 Kelen, *Peace in their Time,* 66.

He found his first commission as an international political cartoonist shortly after his arrival, when his caricature of the Italian Prime Minister Benito Mussolini, dashed off in the lobby of the Beau Rivage Hotel, was bought on the spot by Mahmud Azmi, Editor-in-Chief of the Egyptian satirical magazine *Al Kashkul* (The Begging Bowl, 1921–1934).[19] Azmi introduced Derso and Kelen to each other shortly after. This account of Kelen's beginnings in Lausanne, recounted in his humorous autobiography *Peace in their Time* (1964), emphasizes the important role chance played in the making of *GàL*.

It also sheds light on a different aspect of the Lausanne Conference – interaction between journalists – which would also play an important role in *GàL*. Kelen's memories of Lausanne outline the profile of international journalists at the conference. Indeed, the book's title may be a play on a title used by another famous artist covering Lausanne: Ernest Hemingway, whose 'In Our Time' and 'They All Made Peace – What Is Peace?', were both written in 1923.[20] While there seems to be no closer connection between Hemingway and our Hungarian cartoonists, these links nonetheless place *GàL* in a wider context of political cartooning in Lausanne at a time when both politics and cartooning were recalibrated.

Continuations of War and Empire: Cartooning the Lausanne Conference in the International Press

Political cartoons and caricature had been an important aspect of the media coverage of political events ever since the eighteenth century.[21] The popularity of satirical magazines as a dedicated form of pictorial journalism first peaked in the aftermath of the Napoleonic wars in France. In 1830, Charles Philipon founded *La Caricature* (1830–1843), and, two years later, *Le Charivari* (1832–1937). These magazines defended bourgeois, republican views, and helped one of their most prolific contributors, Honoré Daumier (1808–1879), to gain prominence as

19 Kelen, *Peace in their Time,* 91; Keren Zdafee, *Cartooning for a Modern Egypt*, 2019, 62–97; Al-Sayyid Marsot, 'Afāf Luṭfī. The Cartoon in Egypt', *Comparative Studies in Society and History* 13/1, 1971, 2–15; Gökçen Ertuğrul Apaydin, 'Modernity as Masquerade: Representations of Modernity and Identity in Turkish Humour Magazines', *Global Studies in Culture and Power* 12, 2005, 107–142; Ziad Fahmy, *Ordinary Egyptians*, 2020, 61–96.
20 J. Gifford ed., *'In Our Time' and 'They All Made Peace – What is Peace?' by Ernest Hemingway,* Victoria, 2015.
http://web.uvic.ca/~mvp1922/library/hemingway/time/Hemingway-In-Our-Time-1923.pdf.
21 David Kerr, *Caricature and French Political Culture 1830–1848. Charles Philipon and the Illustrated Press,* 2000, 117 and 145.

a political cartoonist.[22] The successes of *Le Charivari*'s biting political and social critique initiated a wave of satirical magazines dedicated to cartoons and caricatures across Europe's great empires. In Britain, Henry Mayhew and Ebenezer Landells established *Punch* (1841–2002), which was modelled on *Le Charivari* and bore the subtitle 'The London Charivari' as an homage to the Parisian original. *Punch* made artists such as John Tenniel (1820–1914) 'household names' within a few years of its first appearance in 1841.[23]

In the Ottoman Empire, Teodor Kassab published *Diyojen* (Diogenes, 1870–1873) and *Haylal* (Hello, 1873–1877), which he modelled on *Punch,* while *Şarivari* (1871) directly referenced *Le Charivari*.[24] These examples indicate that, despite their national focus, cartooning was part of a much wider international print culture. Emerging with the emancipation of the bourgeoisie and strengthened by the revolutions of 1848, concomitant with a slow relaxation of censorship laws, satirical magazines represented an important part of a rising mass culture, which offered critical and often hard-hitting views, and visualized the latest social and political events for its readers.[25]

The advent of the First World War initiated a fundamental change in the way cartoons and caricatures functioned and circulated. In her analysis of German, British, French and Russian satirical magazines in the period between 1914 and 1918, Lesley Milne has argued that 'laughter promotes social cohesion, raising the spirits and helping to maintain morale'.[26] *Punch* and *Le Rire* (The Laugh renamed *Le Rire Rouge* or The Red Laugh during the war), 'in a two-way communication with the trenches', provided a sense of continuity for readers through an established publishing format, a 'lifebelt' to readers in desperate times.[27] Magazines were used to uphold morale in the crises provoked by war, 'championing the national sense of self and mounting a patriotically defensive assertion of identity against the threat from outside'.[28] Additionally, individual artists published humorous albums to denigrate opponents in war. Works such as *The Rake's New*

22 Kerr, *Caricature and French Political Culture,* 4.
23 Richard Altick, *Punch: The Lively Youth of a British Institution, 1841–1851*, 1997, 17.
24 Elif Elmas, 'Teodor Kassab's Adaption of the Ottoman Shadow Theatre *Karagöz*', *Asian Punches: A Transcultural Affair*, eds. Hans Harder and Barbara Mittler, 2013, 250–252.
25 Frank Bösch, *Mediengeschichte. Vom asiatischen Buchdruck zum Fernsehen,* 2001, 107.
26 Lesley Milne, *Laughter and War. Humorous-Satirical Magazines in Britain, France, Germany and Russia*, 2017, 1; Libby Murphy, *The Art of Survival. France and the Great War Picaresque*, 2016; John Fraser, 'Propaganda on the Picture Postcard', *Oxford Art Journal* 3/2, 1980, 39–47.
27 Milne, *Laughter and War,* 9.
28 Milne, *Laughter and War,* 18.

Progress. Cartoons from 'Punch' Illustrating the Kaiser's Career, 1888–1914 indicate that cartoon albums, similar to *GàL,* circulated among soldiers during the war, albeit taking a distinctly less diplomatic approach to the topics discussed.[29]

In the direct aftermath of the war, caricatures and cartoons initially remained within specific national frameworks, and the central narrative of caricature and cartoons was shaped by considerations of the medium's aggressive potential, relating both to acts of resistance and attack. Their power, (art) historians and psychoanalysts became convinced, was rooted in their use of humour to simplify and crystallize specific situations for contemporary readers, even though their final effect was disputed between impressions of caricature as a weapon and caricature as a defusing agent.[30] In this vein, most popular responses to the Lausanne Conference followed the former – caricature as a weapon.

As a diplomatic event in which numerous countries and nations defended their own interests in the aftermath of a war on an unprecedented scale, the Lausanne Conference was frequently covered by cartoons and caricatures in newspapers and magazines published by all participating factions.[31] They drew upon a well-established imagery of friend and foe – with little consensus on who the 'good' and the 'evil' parties involved were. Cartoonists for the two leading Turkish satirical magazines *Karagöz* (Black Eye, 1908–1955) and *Akbaba* (Vulture, 1922–1977) often focused on the frail victory of the Kemalists, constantly threatened by the self-interest and patronizing attitudes of the Allied Powers. This included 'A Tale of Peace', for example, published in *Akbaba* on 12 July 1923 (Figure 3).[32] It shows a sequence of twenty small, simple drawings, in which a happy union between an allegory of Victory and Turkey, embodied by İsmet, is interrupted by the destructive efforts of the Allies. The relationship only succeeds after the Lausanne Conference's conclusion in July 1923 where, finally, the caption reveals, 'the lovers united with each other, and lived happily ever after'.[33] In line with *Akbaba*'s

29 *The Rake's New Progress. Cartoons from 'Punch' Illustrating the Kaiser's Career, 1888–1914,* ed. Punch Offices, London, 1915.

30 Eduard Fuchs, *Die Karikatur der europäischen Völker vom Jahre 1848 bis zur Gegenwart*, 1903; Sigmund Freud, *Wit and Its Relation to the Unconscious*, trans. Abraham Arden, 1916; Ernst Gombrich and Ernst Kris, 'The Principles of Caricature', *British Journal of Medical Psychology* 17, 1938, 319–342.

31 See Konstantinos Travlos, Doruk Akyüz, Ceren Mert-Travlos, 'Caricaturing the Enemy: Caricatures and the Greek-Turkish War 1919–1922', *The European Journal of Humour Research* 10/1, 2022, 57–81.

32 Discussed in detail by İlkim Büke Okyar, 'Black Eye and Vulture', *The Lausanne Project* (online), 2021, https://thelausanneproject.com/2021/07/12/black-eye-and-vulture/.

33 English Translation from Büke Okyar, 'Black Eye and Vulture'.

Figure 3

pro-national stance, the cartoon clearly visualized whom it supported – and whom it did not: İsmet's is a simple portrait caricature. By contrast, representatives of the Allied Powers feature as distorted national stereotypes, with grim facial expressions and threatening gestures. *Akbaba,* much like *Karagöz,* thus followed the well-established positioning of caricature as a political weapon, in which crude stereotypes were used to affirm the views of those the magazine sided with. While *Akbaba* also reserved a separate page to showcase cartoons from the international press – a fairly common practice for satirical magazines at the time – there was a clear editorial stance in favour of the Turkish national movement.[34]

Newspapers by the Allied Powers largely followed a similar formula. The British cartoonist Sidney Strube drew several cartoons about the conference for the tabloid *Daily Express* (1900–), in which Britain's political opponents in the Near East were often subjected to downright racist stereotyping. In a cartoon from 29 January 1923, for example, Prime Minister Bonar Law walks the streets as a police officer, while crude orientalist stereotypes wait to attack him in alleyways named after areas of British interest, including 'Mespot Lane', 'Palestine Entry' and 'Mosul Alley'.[35] Just as *Akbaba* presented İsmet as the hero in 'A Tale of Peace', the *Daily Express* showed the precise opposite: Bonar Law, the 'world's policeman' is threatened by the ill-meaning criminals of the Near East.

Even though a similar division between 'good' and 'evil' characters prevailed on both sides, the Western press resorted to an imaginary one in which national stereotypes were explicitly bound up with colonial hegemonies. The stereotype of the bloodthirsty Turk was widespread in the British and American press, for example, and found its most gruesome representations in cartoons about the Armenian Genocide. One example for this is 'Washing Blood with Oil', a cartoon from 1927, criticizing the double standards of US policy towards Turkey (Figure 4). Even though the cartoon's main criticism is directed at American opportunism, profiteering from oil deals with Turkey rather than standing up for human rights, this is visualized with the help of the stereotype of a bloodthirsty Turk.

Similar characterizations of an oriental, uncivilized Turkish opponent prevailed in reference to a much wider range of topics. Derso's and Kelen's contemporaries working for *Punch,* such as Leonard Raven-Hill, Bernard Partridge and Frank Reynolds, for example, would depict figures in the tradition of nineteenth-century French Orientalist painters such as Eugène Delacroix and Jean-Auguste-Dominique Ingres (Figure 5). Their romanticized visions of the Orient resurfaced

34 My thanks go to İlkim Büke Okyar who provided this information.

35 At the far back, 'Irish Mews' serves as a reminder of a different conflict in the background.

Mr. Coolidge to Moukhtar: (Dec. 5, 1927) "I am confident, the achievements and *ideals* of modern Turkey will become more widely understood."

Note.—The Kemalists murdered, since 1919, a million Christians, expelled two millions, and now hold in slavery over a hundred thousand Christian girls and children. Extermination or expulsion of the remaining 200,000 Christians is one of their avowed *ideals.*

Figure 4

PUNCH, OR THE LONDON CHARIVARI.—January 10, 1923.

THE ONE THING WANTING.

Mr. Lloyd George (*in Morocco*). "GLORIOUS! If ONLY THERE WERE A CONFERENCE HERE TO ROUND OFF A PERFECT DAY."

Figure 5

in *Punch* cartoons of the Lausanne Conference to evoke a world of 'exotic' difference for Western readers. Rather fittingly, Kelen described Lord Curzon's mindset entering the conference:

> It was his [Curzon's] belief that members of the British ruling class, like himself, had been especially entrusted by the Almighty with the task of bringing light to lesser folk, particularly those of the Near and Far East. He dedicated one of his books: *To those who believe that the British Empire is, under Providence, the greatest instrument for good that the world has ever seen.*[36]

The mentality at the core of Curzon's attitude, summarized as a 'happy marriage of idealism and imperialism' by Kelen, features in *Punch* caricatures of the conference with orientalised figures with hooked noses, large moustaches and turbans or fezes, and semi-clothed Moroccans with round, protruding eyes and large lips. Their Western opponents, jolly men in suit and tie, send out a clear message to readers; namely, that the negotiations were held under the auspices of Western hegemony. Confronted with challenges to British imperialism in the aftermath of the First World War, the British press thus assured readers that the old order still held sway.

In comparison to Turkish magazines such as *Akbaba,* this emphasis on superiority came with a notably old-fashioned visual language. While cartoons in *Akbaba* adopted single lines and flat surfaces to signal a modernization of visual language, the fine and detailed etchings in *Punch* reinforced the positioning of Britain as an old power – appearing rather outdated in the face of its modern competitors. The cartoons in *Punch* and *Akbaba* thus emphasized opposing standpoints in content as much as in style. Overall, their responses to the Lausanne Conference demonstrate that cartoons continued to play a central role as a combatant force in the popular press, prone to accentuate situations and debates. Derso's and Kelen's rendering of the conference in *GàL* could hardly have differed further from these approaches. Their work suggests that the debates about a new global political order also brought about a shift towards a different style of cartooning, which highlighted collaboration and diplomacy, rather than difference.

36 Kelen, *Peace in their Time,* 98.

The Overlooked Souvenir: *Guignol à Lausanne*

Like Derso's and Kelen's chance meeting, their collaboration emerged after some to-and-fro, spurred by the unpredictability of the conference, humorously described by Kelen:

> One day it looks as if the world is saved, the next as if it is ripe for fire and brimstone. One afternoon I entered Derso's boudoir with the news that the Turkish delegation was packing and threatened to go home to Ankara. 'All right,' he said. 'Let's publish this album'.[37]

GàL starts with a simple cover, which relates the album to traditions of popular satire and the international audiences that it is directed towards (Figure 6). A puppet theatre features centre-page, showing two bantering figures. The man to the left wears a top hat and smokes a pipe, his round stomach hanging over the barriers at the front: this is John Bull, representing the British side of the negotiations.[38] His opponent is dressed in a bright red cloak and fez, a moustache and large nose representing his most prominent facial features: he embodies the Turkish delegation. The tent above the men shows a small Swiss flag in reference to the conference location. The drawing summarizes the conference in a simple setting borrowed from popular puppet theatres, epitomized by characters such as Punch and Judy in English, Grand Guignol in French, and Karagöz and Hacivat in the Ottoman Empire.[39] The title above the drawing shows the French *Guignol à Lausanne* and, in Ottoman script, *Karagöz*.[40] The cover is deceptive in its simplicity: it includes all the central information for the album's content in one small drawing and title, yet the presentation of the Turk and John Bull somewhat misleadingly indicates that *GàL* simply illustrates the political bickering as it also featured in popular newspapers and magazines. In the twenty-five lithographs that follow, however, Derso's and Kelen's cartoons reveal a different approach. Indeed, the album challenges the established forms of visual radicalism and offers more nuanced solutions.

GàL by and large avoids taking clear political sides. Even though Kelen later displayed a clear dislike for the arrogance of the British delegation, and cautiously

---

37 Kelen, *Peace in their Time,* 118.

38 Tamara L. Hunt, *Defining John Bull. Political Caricature and National Identity in Late Georgian England*, 2003.

39 John McCormick and Bennie Pratasik, *Popular Puppet Theatre in Europe, 1800–1914*, 2004, 108–146.

40 Kelen, *Peace in their Time,* 118.

displayed sympathy for the Russians and the Turks, as well as sympathy for Mussolini's dramatic entrance, no nation in *GàL* comes off any worse than others, and the cartoonists even showed great flexibility in response to the sitters' reactions to their portraits. After the album's publication, some delegates requested to be redrawn if their caricature was not to their liking: Horace Rumbold, who took over negotiations for the British delegation after Curzon's departure, had a special sitting arranged with Kelen, feeling that İsmet's caricature was much better than his own.[41] The album's popularity and the delegates' interest in their own caricatures thus quickly helped Derso and Kelen to gain a reputation as Lausanne's cartoonists.

Their drawings, in turn, represented a historical as well as artistic record, which was constructed in agreement with the depicted parties. Kelen emphasized that the album's unusual take was due to the unusual circumstances of its time:

> Our paper airplane [*GàL*] was something new in the world, a sign of the radically changing times that President Wilson had brought about for our benefit. Not only did the people have a right to know what their diplomats were talking about, but diplomats also had a right to know what they were doing. It was good to have a couple of caricaturists to tell them.[42]

Written some forty years after the album's publication and after Kelen's successful career as a cartoonist for the League of Nations and, later, the United Nations as well as a television producer for the United Nations Information Office, this statement recalls *GàL*'s pertinence to its time – a period after a harrowing war, which formed a new world that, at least ideally, was to be based on national self-determination and democracy. The importance of precisely these elements can be detected in Kelen's comment; namely that debates now ought to take place in a more civil way, between diplomats, not soldiers. Leaving aside the events that were part and parcel of these diplomatic processes – mass migration and population exchanges – Derso and Kelen thereby also constructed a favourable view of great diplomatic conferences, focusing on individuals and local events, rather than their effects elsewhere.[43]

41 Kelen, *Peace in their Time,* 119.

42 Kelen, *Peace in their Time,* 119.

43 Sarah Shields, 'Forced Migration as Nation-Building: The League of Nations, Minority Protection, and the Greek-Turkish Population Exchange', *Journal of the History of International Law / Revue d'histoire du droit international* 18, 2016, 120–145. DOI: https://doi.org/10.1163/15718050–12340054.

That reference to 'a couple of caricaturists' implies, moreover, that Kelen saw his and Derso's position as cartoonists in a new light, too. In caricature's long tradition of providing an immediate response to contemporary events, it was important to find new ways of expression, which acknowledged the political changes taking place. Rather than positioning themselves as artists, at least in hindsight, Kelen positions *GàL* and succeeding projects as visual political commentary, produced in close collaboration with the parties depicted: while Derso and Kelen might not have been able to enter the room where discussions took place (in line with a strictly limited flow of information for the press), *GàL* indicates how the two artists slowly carved out a position for themselves, which enabled them to become part and parcel of the League of Nations' establishment.

This is not to say that the cartoons in the album disavowed stereotypes or sought to downplay friction and conflict. As is explored in more detail below, Derso's and Kelen's cartoons still employed certain stereotypes in terms of their treatment of gender and ethnic difference, stereotypes common at the time.[44] Yet rather than exaggerating conflict, *GàL* transcribed tense situations into leisurely settings of a predominantly non-violent nature. It focused almost exclusively on individuals rather than national stereotypes, shifting the cartoon's focus on to human interaction, rather than competing states. In doing so, the album deflected from the aggressive nature of political caricature through more nuanced registers of sharp humour without simplification of the cartoon's political content. The artists thus funnelled another of the cartoon's essential elements – its claim to truth – into the album, even considering the complex diplomatic relations they faced.

The Portraits

A significant part of the album consists of portrait caricatures. These adopted a simple format, portraying sitters in black and white pencil drawings in profile, their busts floating on the white page. The caricatures were neatly arranged by delegation and offered a comprehensive overview of the representatives of the participating countries – line after line, viewers encounter the elegantly dressed men who decided on the future of the Near East (Figure 7). They were all drawn by Kelen who remembered that 'I drew everybody, happy or miserable, I saw at

44 Ernst Gombrich, 'Magic, Myth and Metaphor: Reflections on Pictorial Satire', *The Essential Gombrich,* ed. Richard Woodfield, 1996, 336; Mikhail Bakhtin, *Rabelais and His World,* trans. Helene Iswolsky, 1984, 24.

the Lausanne Palace and the Beau Rivage'.[45] In comparison to the caricatures that Derso published in *Le Matin* at approximately the same time, the portraits are of a much gentler style. While this difference can be explained by the artists' initially rather different individual drawing and working practices (Kelen sketching from life, Derso from memory), the more nuanced and carefully drawn portraits in the album did not have the same purpose as a newspaper caricature. Produced with the sitters themselves as the prime audience, a different tone had to be struck.

Both examples emphasize their sitters' most prominent physical features in such a way that readers gain a glimpse into the sitters' inner life too. In the portraits of the delegations, this is even more remarkable than in the newspaper caricatures, given that all are shown in the same posture, in profile. The drawings underline and exaggerate the physical traits of each sitter, including receding hairlines and dishevelled comb-overs, fleeting chins, aristocratic demeanours, and a variety of protruding noses. They indicate the caricaturist's close observation of individual characters and point towards the artist's role beyond that of a distant spectator.[46] Kelen underlined his conviction of caricature's truth value in later years in one of his numerous ideas for books, articles and art drawing programmes, which aimed to define people's psychological characteristics, based on physiognomic markers he had observed over the years in his many prominent sitters.[47] In reference to Curzon, he would later note:

> My old on-the-spot drawings of Curzon reveal him to have been a far less formidable person than he looked. There is the proud pouter-pigeon chest, but it is shapeless, like that of a stuffed pouter pigeon, and his legs are spindly. I seemed to have the impression that his head was poorly sewn onto his body, and so I drew it, with a weak neck. The frontal bone is impressively moulded, precipitating deeply between the saturnine eyebrows toward a beak-like nose; but the upper lip is skimpy, and there are sunken areas in the upper jaw that caused his smile to spread loosely and formlessly from ear to ear. It is a bird face, but not that of an eagle; more of a young chicken hawk fallen out of its nest.[48]

45 Kelen, *Peace in their Time,* 118.

46 David Perkins, 'A Definition of Caricature and Caricature and Recognition', *Studies in Visual Communication* 2/1, 1975, 1–-24.

47 Emery Kelen, *Psychiatric Case Histories*, Book Suggestions; Derso and Kelen Collection, MC205, Public Policy Papers, Department of Special Collections, Princeton University Library.

48 Kelen, *Peace in their Time,* 107–108.

The accuracy with which the artist describes his own drawing shows how the exaggeration of physical features served as a comment on someone's character; in this instance referring to Curzon's departure after failing to reach agreement with İsmet.[49]

The comment also reveals Kelen's acute observational skills and the great level of detail with which he dissected those he portrayed, always attempting a psychological portrait as much as a physical likeness. That Kelen's portraits were sanctioned by their sitters is evident: they all added their stamp of approval in the form of a signature. Beyond the simplified impression of 'John Bull vs. the Turk' on the cover of *GàL*, the portrait galleries moved beyond national stereotypes and thus overcame one of the most dominant features in caricatures of international events at the time. The specificity with which each portrait was constructed allowed viewers to survey the different conference participants and for the portrayed to recognize themselves, striking a balance between individual caricatures and reporting on a large-scale international event.

Indeed, the conference delegations were not the only ones portrayed in *GàL*. Derso and Kelen also dedicated a separate portrait gallery to those who reported on the events, including the young American journalist Vincent Sheean, the editor of *Le Matin,* Jules Sauerwein, and Kelen's first Lausanne acquaintance, Azmi of *Al Kashkul* (Figure 8). Some of these caricatures were drawn by Derso, some by Kelen. While each artist still signed their work individually, each's style became adjusted to the other's by this point in time, indicating the first steps towards a joint body of work. At the centre of the portrait gallery, a cartoon by Derso further drew attention to the role of journalists at the conference. The image shows a Harlequin figure leaning against a bar, referred to as the popular Ottoman jester Karagöz. The gentleman in a top hat next to him remarks: 'entertaining the world isn't always a laugh, you know, my dear Karagöz'. Tongue-in-cheek, this reminds readers that caricature, too, is a serious business with regards to reporting on events with a global impact, such as the Lausanne Conference.

The portrait galleries of delegates and journalists overall amounted to seven pages of the album – almost a third of it in total. The significant space dedicated to them emphasizes the importance the caricaturists placed on individual figures or – as Kelen would later put it in the subtitle of his biography – 'the men who led us in and out of war'. Not least, the portraits serve as a kind of glossary or field guide, giving an overview of who was involved, and which delegation they

49 Behlül Ozkan, *From the Abode of Islam to the Turkish Vatan: The Making of a National Homeland in Turkey*, 2012, 97–98.

belonged to – a helpful feature in light of the more complex political cartoons on the remaining pages of the album.

The Hullabaloo of Conference Life

The most intriguing aspect of *GàL* is its political cartoons. Colourful, rich in detail and filled with a plethora of humorous references, Derso's and Kelen's elaborate drawings of the delegates in Lausanne showed the conference in quite a different light than the newspaper cartoons of their time. 'Plenary Session', introduced at the beginning of this essay, is one of these images, where the artists drew dozens of delegates in a busy setting to render the capriciousness of events at Lausanne. An even more experimental example of this is 'Masked Ball', signed by Kelen, which shows a lavish fancy dress ball at the Lausanne Palace Hotel during carnival season (Figure 9).

The cartoon is a wild constellation of delegates dressed up in colourful costumes, which Kelen employed as a commentary on the relationship between the different delegations. There are French toy soldiers – including the military commander Maxime Weygand – an Italian fairy in the figure of the Italian Ambassador to Turkey, Camillo Garroni, and an ancient Roman soldier, represented by the main Greek delegate Venizelos. Rather curiously, the French delegate Delacroix is a telephone pole in a play on his especially long neck, which is also pronounced in his caricature in the portrait gallery.

Aside from these harmless games of dress-up that these costumes might be filed under, however, Kelen also included some more problematic representations: the Japanese delegates, for example, resemble crude national stereotypes as geishas and martial arts aficionados (Hayashi Gonsuke climbing up the Delacroix telephone pole), as do the Romanians and Bulgarians at the bottom of the page. Even though the topic of the masquerade overall casts the scene as a light-hearted rendering of conference entertainment, the scene of the ball reveals that orientalist stereotypes nonetheless found their way even into the work of more nuanced cartoonists such as Derso and Kelen.

Curzon and İsmet happily dance hand in hand at the image's centre. They display the comical physical contrast between the large British Foreign Secretary and his small, wiry Turkish counterpart, which Kelen repeatedly exploits in caricature. The unlikely pair represented one of the artist's core interests at Lausanne:

> The two men collided head on: Curzon, a marquess who looked like a marquess; İsmet, a general who looked like a toy soldier. Curzon had the

> poised arrogance of a British aristocrat; İsmet, the humility of an Oriental bourgeois. Curzon, an artist of improvisation, spoke chiselled, nuanced English and was a skilful diplomatic craftsman. İsmet shone in Turkish, if he shone at all, and as a soldier, he might be called the antithesis of a diplomat.[50]

This sharp contrast between the two politicians emerges in the most humorous manner in 'Masked Ball'. Here, Curzon wears Turkish şalvar dress, while İsmet is dressed in Scottish attire with a kilt. Literally put into the other's shoes, the two appear to have left their differences behind, dancing the night away. Next to them, British-Turkish relations are taken to the next level in a marriage between Sir William Tyrrell and Mehmed Cavid. Diplomacy, the cartoon seems to imply, is at its most successful during moments of entertainment.

Where the portrait galleries offered a humorous close-up of various delegates, 'Masked Ball' also captured the tumultuous atmosphere at the conference and its social events. Most of the figures in the cartoon are identified by name and the focus lies on the interaction between them. Stereotypes and humorous juxtapositions help viewers to navigate the rich drawing. In terms of style, too, Kelen adopted a different manner of depiction compared to the portrait galleries, adding more colour and reducing shading and lines. Indeed, it is with scenes such as 'Masked Ball' where Derso's and Kelen's style of cartooning for the League of Nations first developed with a focus on strong black outlines, a carefully selected use of colour, and a characterization of figures between the individual and stereotypes, which speak to the portrayed and to a wider audience.

While the cartoons in *GàL* also include more conventional scenes of interaction, such as a polite meeting between Curzon and İsmet, where their diverging positions are manifested in their contrasting physical appearance, the album is most striking for its fantastic settings that would come to define Derso's and Kelen's cartoons in later years. These unusual settings helped to place the conference in a wider social and cultural context. The allusions to carnival season in 'Masked Ball' are a simple example of this, yet there are also instances in which the artists refer to more specific events.

'The Latest Discovery of Lord Carnarvon', for example, is composed like an Egyptian wall relief (Figure 10). It references the discovery of Tutankhamun's tomb in 1922, a world sensation, which gave ancient Egypt a regular presence in the satirical press – *Punch* cartoonists, for example, would repeatedly

50 Kelen, *Peace in their Time,* 102–103.

incorporate mummy figures and hieroglyph forms into their images.[51] Kelen's image, however, was rather more specific. It referred to an incident in Lausanne: on 11 January 1923, the former champion wrestler and Chairman of the Egyptian Committee of Oppressed Peoples in Lausanne, Abdul Hamid Said, attempted to strangle the chief of the Egyptian press bureau Mohammed Fanni at the Lausanne Palace Hotel after a disagreement over the so-called 'unmixing' of populations agreement.[52] Second to the left, among Said's faction in the cartoon is Azmi, Kelen's Egyptian acquaintance. The opposing parties, one in left, one in right profile, resemble hieroglyph characters, but they lift contemporary instruments such as brooms, sticks, and umbrellas to their defence. Said, six and a half feet tall and 250 pounds, towers above them like a giant in defence of the Committee of Oppressed Peoples.

Given Kelen's and Derso's own experience as migrants and Kelen's friendship with Azmi, the artists' sympathies seem clear in this case. This, however, did not keep Kelen from incorporating orientalising stereotypes, which are particularly obvious in the caricature of the black man below the wrestler. Kelen might have sided with the anti-imperialists, yet, again, he was not immune to their stereotypes. Indeed, in his biography, Kelen recounts a further incident featured in *GàL,* which merges a modest self-representation as 'penny-pinching caricaturist' with a candid flavour of orientalism:

> Each afternoon they would come to the surface and continue their sinister conspiracy to the tune of music at the *thé dansant* in the lobby of the Lausanne Palace Hotel. The British Empire stood solid only when a Parisian alley-ballerina, sparsely clad, appeared on the floor and performed calisthenics. Then all guttural plots ceased, and hundreds of Oriental eyes went pop.[53]

No matter how carefully *GàL* traced the Lausanne conference as a diplomatic event, nor how often Kelen would refer to his own 'otherness' as a Hungarian cartoonist, a Western-hegemonial undertone also prevailed in Derso's and Kelen's work.

In its references to a fight between a political representative and a journalist, moreover, 'The Latest Discovery of Lord Carnarvon' also shows the Lausanne

51 Rachel Mairs, 'Pith Helmets, Cross-dressing and Blackface: Fancy Dress in Colonial Egypt', *Everyday Orientalism*, 2021, https://everydayorientalism.wordpress.com/2021/08/02/pith-helmets-cross-dressing-and-blackface-fancy-dress-in-colonial-egypt/.
52 'Egyptians in a Fight in a Lausanne Hotel', *New York Times*, 11 January 1923, 18.
53 Kelen, *Peace in their Time,* 98–99.

Conference was not an occasion where the diplomats had the stage to themselves. The same topic is also picked up by Derso in 'Cercle de la Presse', which offers closer insight into the journalists' main place of congregation during the conference: the press bar (Figure 11). As the outcomes of the daily negotiations were communicated to journalists only via a press officer, the press bar was where time was spent until news arrived, and included prominent figures (such as Sauerwein) who brought their own typists, as well as their younger and less-known counterparts such as Kelen and Derso. 'Cercle de la Presse' captures both an impression of the long hours spent waiting, and the raunchy, drink-infused atmosphere that ensued in the process of killing time: while some pass the time drinking, flirting, chumming up to one another, others sit on the side-lines, as a small figure enters the scene from the right bringing news, to judge by the telegram in his raised hand.

With the cartoon of the press bar, *GàL* shows a world beside that of the delegates. While the two overlapped at dinners and parties – best illustrated by 'An Evening at Tchitcherin's', which shows the journalist Clare Sheridan dancing Kozachok with the Russian delegation – 'Cercle de la Presse' captures the extraordinary position of the journalists at the conference. Like the delegates, so too the journalists found a similarly balanced representation in *GàL*, with Derso and Kelen straddling both worlds. Sheridan's own account of evenings with the Russian delegation (drawn from the travelogue Derso illustrated) shows how different journalists' narratives intersected – not only in reference to the political decision-making, but also the mingling and socializing behind the scenes.[54]

By depicting the official business of the conference as well as the press bar, *GàL* showed the conference from different perspectives, and set it into a wider social context – levelling out the distinctions separating the elevated world of the decision-makers from the world of those who transmitted those decisions to the world at large.

Aside from the exceptional presence of Sheridan, however, there was a notable absence in this set-up: women, even though female delegates, journalists and partners were also part of the conference's wider social environment. The careful attention to social situations and individual characters in *GàL* predominantly extended to the male world of the conference; judging by the busty blondes in 'Cercle de la Presse', women appeared only as ready-made props rather than as individuals. Despite their variety, nuance and attention to character, therefore, Derso's and Kelen's cartoons highlight the lack of presence of women underlining that decision- and news-making remained in male hands, almost without exception.

54 Sheridan, *West and East,* 260–262.

Perfecting the Diplomatic Cartoon: *GàL* and the Peace Conference

On 24 July 1923 the Lausanne Treaty was signed, eight months after the opening of the conference. Derso and Kelen prepared the celebratory cartoon 'The Apotheosis of Peace' to mark the occasion (Figure 12). Even though it was finished later than the other works in the album, the cartoon was added as an appendix to *GàL* and represents a culmination of all the different aspects that made up the conference album. At the centre of the table the main delegates are shown signing the treaty document. Each also signed the cartoon, which Kelen recalled as 'a most delicate diplomatic endeavour, requiring tact, prudence, and psychology'.[55]

Set in heaven, the work shows a beatified Curzon chumming up to Mussolini and Poincaré under golden palm leaves and an enamoured pair of doves. To the top right, the image commemorates the Lausanne Palace Hotel and its manager, Colonel Steiner. Below them, members of the press watch the scene as angels. To the left, delegates and their associates watch the scene below the building of Lausanne University. There is clapping and cheering, dancing and fanfare, as well as music sounding from telegraph poles. As one may expect from a heavenly scene, all characters have a friendly or curious demeanour. At the image front, Derso and Kelen, one dressed like John Bull, the other like the Turk on the cover of *GàL,* add the finishing touches to a banner reading 'Peace. Lausanne, 24 July 1923'.

Peace is restored – albeit not at the hands of the delegates but the artists. 'The Apotheosis of Peace' thus concludes *GàL* as a tongue-in-cheek record of the Lausanne Conference, created primarily for those who had been involved in the negotiations. To the very end, Derso and Kelen tailored the album to a new style of cartooning which, in form as in content, showed their skills of commenting on complex political matters with a finely calibrated sense of humour. While popular newspaper cartoons of the conference tended to emphasize the conflicts between participating nations, Derso and Kelen captured the atmosphere of the conference in a much more nuanced manner.

Their cartoons and caricatures not only focused on the delegates, but also on their surrounding environment and networks in Lausanne. Each cartoon was finely attuned to convey the different voices present at the conference. While this approach did not save the artist's work from replicating orientalist and gender stereotypes, Derso and Kelen nonetheless succeeded in building an imagery which was considerably more balanced compared to international newspapers. Rather than inventing scenes, the cartoons can often be traced to specific events, be they

55 Kelen, *Peace in their Time,* 121.

local ones, as in 'Masked Ball', or international news, such as the discovery of Tutankhamun's tomb and the ensuing 'Egyptomania'.

At a time when caricature and cartoons were first and foremost understood as a political weapon, part of the propaganda machine of the First World War, Derso's and Kelen's subtle yet no less pointed approach offered a new way of recording political events, which built on collaboration and nuance, and which differed from the one-sided cartoons that chronicled the conference in the popular press. With an emphasis on light humour, Derso and Kelen developed a way of reporting on the conference in a diplomatic manner: they refrained from displaying preference for any one of the involved parties, represented individuals with kind humour rather than bitter attack, and paid limited attention to the political goals that were at stake, rather focusing on delineating the *atmosphere* of a conference set to negotiate peace after a long war.

List of Illustrations

Plates

Note

Where no source is given, the image is in the Public Domain.

Bibliography

INTRODUCTION

Primary Sources

Archives

Archives Ministère des Affaires étrangères et du Développement international, La Courneuve (AMAE)

Arxiv vneshnej politiki Rossijskoj imperii (Foreign Policy Archive of Imperial Russia), Moscow (AVPRI)

Başbakanlık Osmanlı Arşivi (Ottoman State Archives), Istanbul (BOA)

United States National Archives and Records Administration, College Park (NARA)

Published Documents

Documents on British Foreign Policy 1919–1939, First Series, 19 Vols., Medlicott, W.N., Dakin D. and Lambert, M.E., London.

Lausanne Conference on Near Eastern Affairs, 1922–1923: Records of Proceedings and Draft Terms of Peace, London, 1923.

Vneshnyaya politika Rossii XIX i nachala XX veka. Dokumenty rossijskogo Ministerstva inostrannyx del, Moscow, 1971.

Periodicals

Karagöz [Istanbul]

Vakit [Istanbul]

Secondary Sources

Akyol, T. and Kaplan, S. *Açık ve Gizli Oturumlarda Lozan Tartışmaları: TBMM'de Lozan Müzakereleri Tutanakları*, Istanbul, 2021.

Anscombe, F. F. *State, Faith, and Nation in Ottoman and Post-Ottoman Lands,* Cambridge (UK), 2014.

Aydın, C. 'Muslim Asia after Versailles,' in Zachmann, U.M. ed., *Asia After Versailles: Asian Perspectives on the Paris Peace Conference and the Interwar Order, 1919–1933,* Edinburgh, 2017, 55–76.

Aydın, C. *The Idea of the Muslim World: A Global Intellectual History,* Cambridge (USA), 2017.

Aydın, S. 'Resmi Tarihin Temeli: Ulusal Tarih Yazımı ve Resmi Tarihte Mitlerin Kaynağı', in F. Başkaya ed., *Resmi Tarih Tartışmaları* 1, Ankara, 2008, 43–83.

Ballian, A. *Relics of the Past: Treasures of the Greek Orthodox Church and the Population Exchange*, Milan, 2011.

Barlas, D. 'Friends or Foes? Diplomatic Relations Between Italy and Turkey, 1923–36', *International Journal of Middle Eastern Studies* 36, 2004, 231–252.

Beşikçi, M. *The Ottoman Mobilization of Manpower in the First World War*, Leiden, 2012.

Bethlen, I. *The Treaty of Trianon and European Peace*, London, New York, Toronto, 1934.

Blumi, I. *Ottoman Refugees, 1878–1939: Migration in a Post-Imperial World*, London, 2013, 30.

Bobrovnikov, V.O. 'Ruskii Kavkaz i Frantsuzkii Alzhir: sluchainoe skhodstvo ili obmen opytom kolonial'nogo stroitel'stva', *Imperial inter pares: rol'transferov v istorii Rossiiskoi imperii (1700–1917)*, Moscow, 2010, 182–209.

Borkov, A.V. and Loshkarev, A.V. 'Sovetskaya diplomatsiya i obcyzhdenie problem statusa chernomorskih prolivov na Lozanskoi Mezhdunarodnoi Konferenrsii, 1922–1923 gg.', *Mezhdunarodnye Otnosheniya*, 2003, 242–247.

Brown, L.C. ed. *Imperial Legacy: The Ottoman Imprint on the Balkans and Middle East*, New York, 1996.

Byers, A. *The Treaty of Versailles and the League of Nations*, New York, 2018.

Cassels, A. *Mussolini's Early Diplomacy,* Princeton, 1970.

Colley, L. *Britons: Forging the Nation, 1707–1837,* London, 1992.

Conlin, J. 'Debt, Diplomacy and Dreadnoughts: The National Bank of Turkey, 1909–1919', *Middle Eastern Studies* 52/3, 2016, 525–545.

Conlin, J. "Our Dear Resadiye': the Legend and the Loans behind Ottoman Naval Rearmament, 1908–14', *International History Review,* published online 22 June 2021.

Conlin, J. and Yazıcıoğlu, F. 'The Libyan War and Student Pan-Islamism: The Edinburgh Declaration of 1911', *International Journal of Middle East Studies* 54/2, 2022, 1–7.

Dalby, A. *Eleftherios Venizelos*, London, 2010.

Demirci, S. *Strategies and Struggles. British Rhetoric and Turkish Response: The Lausanne Peace Conference, 1922–1923*, Istanbul, 2005.

Demirci, S. *The Lausanne Conference: The evolution of Turkish and British diplomatic strategies, 1922–1923,* Ann Arbor, 2014.

DeNovo, J.A. *American Interests and Policies in the Middle East, 1900–1939*, Minneapolis, 1963.

Dockrill, M.L. and Goold, J.D. *Peace Without Promise: Britain and the Peace Conferences, 1919–23,* London, 1981.

Duclert, V. *La France Face au Génocide des Arméniens: Une nation impériale et le devoir d'humanité,* Paris, 2015.

Fieldhouse, D.K. *Western Imperialism in the Middle East, 1914–1958,* Oxford, 2006.

Fink, C. 'The Minorities Question at the Paris Peace Conference' in Boemeke, M.F. et al. eds., *The Treaty of Versailles: A Reassessment After 75 Years*, Cambridge (UK), 1998, 249–274.

Fink, C. *The Genoa Conference: European Diplomacy, 1921–1922,* Chapel Hill, 1984.

Fink, C., Frohn, A. and Heideking, J. eds. *Genoa, Rapallo, and European Reconstruction in 1922,* Cambridge (UK), 1991.

Frank, M. *Making Minorities History: Population Transfers in Twentieth Century Europe,* Oxford, 2017.

Fraser, T. G. *Contested Lands: A History of the Middle East since the First World War*, London, 2021.

Fromkin, D. *A Peace to End All Peace: The Fall of the Ottoman Empire and the Creation of the Modern Middle East,* London, 1989.

Genov, G.P. *Bulgaria and the Treaty of Neuilly,* Sofia, 1935.

Gerwarth, R. 'The Sky Beyond Versailles: The Paris Peace Treaties in Recent Historiography', *Journal of Modern History* 93/44, 2021.

Gerwarth, R. *The Vanquished: Why the First World War Failed to End*, London, 2016.

Giannakopoulos, G. 'A World Safe for Empires? A. J. Toynbee and the Internationalization of Self-Determination in the East (1912–1922)', *Global Intellectual History* 6/4, 2021, 484–505.

Gifford, J. ed. *'In Our Time' and 'They All Made Peace – What is Peace?' by Ernest Hemingway,* Victoria, 2015.

Gilmour, D. *Curzon: Imperial Statesman,* London, 1994.

Ginio, E. 'War, Civic Mobilization and the Ottoman Home-Front during the Balkan Wars', in Geppert, D. et al. eds., *The Wars Before the Great War: Conflict and International Politics before the Outbreak of the First World War*, Cambridge (UK), 2015, 92–113.

Göçek, F.M. 'The Politics of History and Memory: A Multidimensional Analysis of the Lausanne Peace Conference, 1922–1923', in Gershoni, I. et al. eds., *Histories of the Modern Middle East: New Directions*, London, 2002, 207–228.

Goldstein, E. *Winning the Peace: British Diplomatic Strategy, Peace Planning and the Paris Peace Conference, 1916–1920*, Oxford, 1991.

Grew, J. 'The Lausanne Peace Conference of 1922–1923', *Proceedings of the American Philosophical Society* 98/1, 1954, 1–10.

Güler, A. *Bin Yıllık Hesaplaşma: Lozan*, Istanbul, 2017.

Heper, M. *İsmet İnönü,* Leiden, 1998.

Hirschon, R. 'The Social Institutions of an Urban Locality of Refugee Origin in Piraeus', DPhil dissertation, University of Oxford, Oxford, 1976.

Hirschon, R. *Heirs of the Greek Catastrophe: The Social Life of Asia Minor Refugees in Piraeus*, Oxford, 1989.

Hirschon, R. *The Creation of Community: Well-being without Wealth in an Urban Greek Refugee Locality*, Washington D.C., 2000.

Hirschon, R. ed. *Crossing the Aegean: An Appraisal of the 1923 Compulsory Population Exchange between Greece and Turkey,* Oxford, 2003.

Hirschon, R. 'History's Long Shadow: the Lausanne Treaty and Contemporary Greco-Turkish Relations' in Anastasakis, O. et al. eds., *In the Long Shadow of Europe: Greeks and Turks in the Era of Postnationalism,* Leiden, 2009.

Holquist, P. 'To Count, to Extract, and to Exterminate: population, statistics and population politics in late imperial and Soviet Russia', in Martin, T. et al. eds., *A State of Nations: Empire and Nation-making in the Age of Lenin and Stalin*, New York, 2001.

İnönü, İ. *Defterler*, Istanbul, 2001.

İpekçi, A. ed. *İnönü Atatürk'ü Anlatıyor*, Istanbul, 1976.

Kedourie, E. *The Chatham House Version and other Middle Eastern Studies,* Chicago, 2004.

Kelen, E. *Peace in Their Time: Men Who Led Us In and Out of War, 1914–1945,* New York, 1963.

Kelly, S. 'How Far West?: Lord Curzon's Transcaucasian (Mis)Adventure and the Defense of British India, 1918–23', *International History Review* 35/2, 2013, 274–293.

Kieser, H.-L., Polatel, M. and Schmutz, T. 'Reform or Cataclysm? The Agreement of 8 February 1914 Regarding the Ottoman Eastern Provinces', *Journal of Genocide Research* 17/3, 2015, 285–304.

Koese, Y. 'Nestlé in the Ottoman Empire: Global Marketing with Local Flavor, 1870–1927', *Enterprise & Society* 9/4, 2008, 724–760.

Leonhard, J. *Der überforderte Frieden: Versailles und die Welt, 1918–1923,* Munich, 2018.

Lieberman, B. 'Ethnic Cleansing in the Greek-Turkish Conflicts from the Balkan Wars through the Treaty of Lausanne: Identifying and Defining Ethnic Cleansing', in Vardy, S.B. et al. eds., *Ethnic Cleansing in Twentieth-Century Europe*, Boulder, 2003.

Lieberman, B. *Terrible Fate: Ethnic Cleansing and the Making of Modern Europe,* Chicago, 2006.

Lieberman, B. 'Ethnic Cleansing versus Genocide?', in Bloxham, D. et al. eds., *Oxford Handbook of Genocide* Studies, Oxford, 2010, 43–60.

MacArthur-Seal, D. *Britain's Levantine Empire, 1914–1923,* Oxford, 2021.

Macartney, C.A. *Hungary and Her Successors: The Treaty of Trianon and Its Consequences, 1919–1937*, Oxford, 1968.

MacMillan, M. *Peacemakers: The Paris Conference of 1919 and Its Attempt to End the War,* London, 2001.

Manela, E. *The Wilsonian Moment, Self-Determination and the International Origins of Anticolonial Nationalism,* Oxford, 2007.

Mann, M. *The Dark Side of Democracy: Explaining Ethnic Cleansing,* Cambridge (UK), 2004.

Mansfield, P. *A History of the Middle East*, London, 2013.

Mathews, B. *The Clash of Colour: A Study in the Problem of Race,* London, 1924.

Mathews, B. *Young Islam on Trek: A Study of the Clash of Civilizations,* London, 1926.

McCarthy, J. *Death and Exile: the ethnic cleansing of Ottoman Muslims, 1821–1922,* Princeton, 1995.

Neiberg, M.S. *The Treaty of Versailles: A Concise History*, Oxford, 2017.

Nezhinskiy, L.N. and Ignatiev, A.V. eds. *Rossia I Chernomorskie prolivi (XVIII-XX stoletiya)*, Moscow, 1999.

Nicolson, H. 'Curzon', *Foreign Affairs,* January 1929, 9–10.

Nur, R. *Lozan Hatırları*, Istanbul, 1992.

Oğuz, Z. 'Matters of Conspiracy: oil prospects, geological knowledge, and temporality in Turkey', 2018 Conference of the Association of Social Anthropologists of the UK & Commonwealth.

Ozavci, O. 'Honour and Shame: The Diaries of a Unionist and the Armenian Question', in Kieser, H-L. et al. eds., *End of the Ottomans: The Genocide of 1915 and the Politics of Turkish Nationalism*, London, 2019, 193–220.

Ozavci, O. *Dangerous Gifts: Imperialism, Security, and Civil Wars in the Levant, 1798–1864*, Oxford, 2021.

Ozavci, O. 'A Priceless Grace? The Congress of Vienna of 1815, the Ottoman Empire and Historicizing the Eastern Question', *The English Historical Review*, 136/583, 2021, 1450–1476.

Özsu, U. *Formalizing Displacement: International Law and Population Transfers*, New York, 2015.

Philliou, C. *Biography of an Empire: Governing Ottomans in an Age of Revolution*, Berkeley, 2011.

Plumpe, W., Nützenadel, A., Schenk, C. *Deutsche Bank 1870–2020: The Global Hausbank,* London, 2020.

Provence, M. 'Ottoman Modernity, Colonialism, and Insurgency in the Interwar Arab East', *International Journal of Middle East Studies* 43/2, 2011, 205–225.

Provence, M. 'Stateless Revolutionaries and the Aftermath of the Great War', *Journal of Modern European History* 13/3, 2015, 401–418.

Provence, M. *The Last Ottoman Generation and the Making of the Modern Middle East,* Cambridge (UK), 2017.

Reimer, M. 'Converting the Missionaries' [review of Heather Sharkey, *Missionary Encounters*]', *Diplomatic History* 35/1, 2011, 47–50.

Robson, L. *States of Separation: Transfer, Partition, and the Making of the Modern Middle* East, Oakland, 2017.

Roessel, D. 'New Information on Hemingway's '3 very fine weeks' in Constantinople in 1922', *Resources for American Literary Study* 34, 2009, 107–128.

Said, E. *Culture and Imperialism*, New York, 1993.

Sharkey, H.J. *Missionary Encounters in an Age of Empire,* Princeton, 2008.

Sharp, A. *The Versailles Settlement: Peacemaking in Paris, 1919,* London, 1991.

Şimşir, B.N. *Lozan Telgrafları*, Ankara, 1990.

Smith, M.L. 'Venizelos' Diplomacy, 1910–23: From Balkan Alliance to Greek-Turkish Settlement', in Kitromilides, P.M. ed., *Eleftherios Venizelos: The Trials of Statesmanship*, Edinburgh, 2006.

Sonyel, R. *Turkish Diplomacy, 1918–1923: Mustafa Kemal and the Turkish National Movement,* London, 1975.

Steiner, Z. *The Lights That Failed: European International History, 1919–1933,* Oxford, 2005.

Stuart, J. 'Empire, Mission Ecumenism, and Human Rights: "Religious Liberty" in Egypt, 1919–1956', *Church History* 83/1, 2014, 110–134.

Suppan, A. *The Imperialism Peace Order in Central Europe: Saint-Germain and Trianon, 1919–1920*, Vienna, 2019.

Tachjian, V. *La France en Cilicie et en Haute-Mesopotamie: aux confins de la Turquie, de la Syrie et de l'Irak*, Paris, 2004.

Tağmat, Ç.D. *Lozan Konferansı'nda Yunan Diplomasisi, 1922–1923*, Istanbul, 2018.

Tooze, A. *The Deluge: The Great War and the Remaking of the Global Order, 1916–1931,* London, 2014.

Toynbee, A.J. *The Western Question in Greece and Turkey: a study in the contact of civilisations,* London, 1922.

Treanor, P.J. *Britain, Bulgaria and the Paris Peace Conference, 1918–1919: A Just and Lasting Peace?*, Lanham, 2020.

Uyani, N. *Dismantling the Ottoman Empire: Britain, America, and the Armenian Question,* London, 2016.

Venn, F. 'Oil, Anglo-American Relations and the Lausanne Conference', *Diplomacy and Statecraft* 20, 2009, 414–433.

Wasti, S.T. 'Mushir Kidwai and the Ottoman Cause', *Middle Eastern Studies* 30/2, 1994, 252–261.

Weitz, E.D. 'From the Vienna to the Paris System: International Politics and the Entangled Histories of Human Rights, Forced Deportations, and Civilizing Missions', *The American Historical Review* 113/5, 2008, 1313–1343.

White, S. *The Origins of Detente: The Genoa Conference and Soviet-Western Relations, 1921–1922,* Cambridge (UK), 1985.

White, W. ed. *Dateline: Toronto. Hemingway's Complete Dispatches for The Toronto Star, 1920–1924*, New York, 1985.

Wigen, E. 'Post-Ottoman studies: an area studies that never was', in Cstató, É.A. et al., *Building Bridges to Turkish: Essays in Honour of Bernt Brendemoen*, Wiesbaden, 2018, 313–324.

Winter, J. *The Day the First World War Ended, 24 July 1923: The Civilianization of War,* Oxford, 2022.

Yasamee, F.A.K. 'European Equilibrium or Asiatic Balance of Power? The Ottoman Search for Security in the Aftermath of the Congress of Berlin', in Yavuz, M.H. et al. eds., *War and Diplomacy: The Russo-Turkish War of 1877–78 and the Treaty of Berlin*, Salt Lake City, 2011.

Yavuz, M.H. and Sluglett, P. 'Introduction: Laying the Foundations for Future Instability,' in Yavuz, M.H. et al. eds., *War and Diplomacy: The Russo-Turkish War of 1877–1878 and the Treaty of Berlin*, Salt Lake City, 2011.

Yenen, A. 'Internationalism, Diplomacy and the Revolutionary Origins of the Middle East's 'Northern Tier'', *Contemporary European History*, 2021, 1–16.

Yılmaz, M. *British Opinion and the Lausanne Peace Conference and Treaty,* Istanbul, 1994.

Zarakol, A. 'States and Ontological Security: A Historical Rethinking', *Cooperation and Conflict* 52/1, 2017, 48–68.

Zürcher, E.J. ed. *Jihad and Islam in World War I*, Leiden, 2016.

CHAPTER 1

Ahmad, F. 'Ottoman Perceptions of the Capitulations, 1800–1914', *Journal of Islamic Studies* 11, 2000, 1–20.

Aksakal, M. 'Not 'by those old books of international law, but only by war': Ottoman Intellectuals on the Eve of the Great War', *Diplomacy & Statecraft* 15, 2004, 507–554.

Aksakal, M. *The Ottoman Road to War in 1914: The Ottoman Empire and the First World War*, Cambridge (UK), 2008.

Aksakal, M. and Genell, A.M. 'Salvation through War? The Ottoman Search for Sovereignty in 1914', in Brock, L. et al. eds., *The Justification of War and International Order: From the Past to the Present*, Oxford, 2021.

Aydın, C. *The Politics of Anti-Westernism in Asia: Visions of World Order in Pan-Islamic and Pan-Asian Thought*, New York, 2007.

Baykal, E.A.F. *The Ottoman Press, 1908–1923*, Leiden, 2019.

Bayur, Y.H. *Türk İnkilabı Tarihi*, Ankara, 1983.

Boogert, M. van den. *The Capitulations and the Ottoman Legal System: Qadis, Consuls and Beraths in the 18th Century*, Leiden, 2005.

Can, L. *Spiritual Subjects: Central Asian Pilgrims and the Ottoman Hajj at the End of Empire*, Stanford, 2020.

Can, L. and Genell, A.M. 'On Empire and Exception: Genealogies of Sovereignty in the Ottoman World', *Comparative Studies in South Asia, Africa and the Middle East* 40, 2020, 468–473.

Can, L. et al. eds. *The Subjects of Ottoman International Law*, Bloomington, 2020.

Cemal, A. *Memoirs of a Turkish Statesman, 1913–1919*, London, 1922.

Cemal, A. *Hâtırat: 1913–1919*, Istanbul, 1922.

Ceylan, A. *Osmanlı Taşra İdarî Tarzı Olarak Eyâlet-i Mümtâze ve Mısır Uygulaması*, Istanbul, 2014.

Çark, Y.G. *Türk Devlet Hizmetinde Ermeniler, 1453–1953*, Istanbul, 1953.

Çicek, T. *War and State Formation in Syria: Cemal Pasha's Governorate during World War I, 1914–1917*, London, 2016.

Der Matossian, B. *Shattered Dreams of Revolution: From Liberty to Violence in the Late Ottoman Empire*, Stanford, 2014.

Eldem, E. 'Capitulations and Western Trade: Western Trade in the Ottoman Empire', in Faroqhi, S.N. ed., *The Cambridge History of Turkey*, Vol. 3, Cambridge (UK), 2006.

Ekmekcioglu, L. 'Republic of Paradox: The League of Nations Minority Protection Regime and the New Turkey's Step-Citizens', *International Journal of Middle East Studies*, 2014, 675–679.

Eşrefoğlu, E. 'Mümtaze Kalemi ve Bulgaristan Belgeleri', *Güneydoğu Avrupa Araştırmaları Dergisi* 6–7, 1978, 189–203.

Findley, C. *Bureaucratic Reform in the Ottoman Empire: The Sublime Porte, 1789–1922*, Princeton, 1980.

Findley, C. *Ottoman Civil Officialdom: A Social History*, Princeton, 1989.

Fujinami, N. 'Between Sovereignty and Suzerainty: History of the Ottoman Privileged Provinces', in Okamoto, T. ed., *A World History of Suzerainty: A Modern History of East and West Asia and Translated Concepts*, Tokyo, 2019.

Genell, A.M. 'Ottoman Autonomous Provinces and the Problem of 'Semi-Sovereignty' in International Law', *Journal of Balkan and Near Eastern Studies* 18, 2016, 533–549.

Genell, A.M. 'The Well-defended Domains: Eurocentric International Law and the Making of the Ottoman Office of Legal Counsel', *Journal of Ottoman and Turkish Studies* 3, 2016, 255–275.

Genell, A.M. 'The End of Egypt's Occupation: Ottoman Sovereignty and the British Declaration of Protection', in Pergher, R. et al. eds., *Beyond Versailles: Sovereignty, Legitimacy, and the Formation of New Politics after the Great* War, Bloomington, 2019.

Hall, T.E. *The European Concert in the Eastern Question: A Collection of Treaties and Other Public Acts*, Oxford, 1885.

Hanley, W. 'When did Egyptians stop being Ottomans? An Imperial Citizenship Case Study', in Maas, W. ed., *Multilevel Citizenship*, Philadelphia, 2013.

Hanley, W. *Identifying with Nationality: Europeans, Ottomans, and Egyptians in Alexandria*, New York, 2017.

Hock, S. 'Waking us from this Endless Slumber: The Ottoman-Italian War and North Africa in the Ottoman Twentieth Century', *War in History* 26, 2017, 204–226.

İhsanoğlu, E. *Darülfünun: Osmanlı'da Kültürel Modernleşmenin Odağıi*, Istanbul, 2010.

Karakoç, E. 'Osmanlı Hariciyesinde Bir Ermeni Nazır: Gabriyel Noradunkyan Efendi', *Uluslararası İlişkiler Dergisi* 7, 2010, 157–177.

Kaşıyuğun, A. *Osmanlı Devleti'nin Birinci Dünya Savaşı'na Girişi*, Istanbul, 2015.

Kayalı, H. *Arabs and Young Turks: Ottomanism, Arabism, and Islamism in the Ottoman Empire, 1908–1918*, Berkeley, 1997.

Kayaoğlu, T. *Legal Imperialism: Sovereignty and Extraterritoriality in Japan, the Ottoman Empire, and China*, Cambridge (UK), 2010.

Kelen, E. *Peace in their Time: Men Who Led Us In and Out of War, 1914–1945*, New York, 1963.

Kelen, E, and Derso, A. *Guignol à Lausanne*, Lausanne, 1923.

Kieser, H-L. *Talaat Pasha: Father of Modern Turkey, Architect of Genocide*. Princeton, 2018.

Koloğlu, O. *Osmanlı'da son Tartışmalar: Mondros'tan Mudanya'ya*, Istanbul, 2008.

Lausanne Conference on Near Eastern Affairs, 1922–1923: Records of Proceedings and Draft Terms of Peace, London, 1923.

Low, M.C. 'Unfurling the Flag of Extraterritoriality: Autonomy, Foreign Muslims, and the Capitulations in the Ottoman Hijaz', *Journal of the Ottoman and Turkish Studies Association* 3, 2016, 299–323.

Low, M.C. *Imperial Mecca: Ottoman Arabia and the Indian Ocean Hajj*, New York, 2020.

Martens, F. *Traité de droit international*, Paris, 1883–1887.

Noradungian, G. *Recueil d'actes internationaux de l'empire ottoman*, Paris, 1897–1903.

Ozavci, O. *Dangerous Gifts: Imperialism, Security, and Civil Wars in the Levant, 1798–1864*, Oxford, 2021.

Ozavci, O. 'A Priceless Grace? The Congress of Vienna of 1815, the Ottoman Empire and Historicising the Eastern Question', *The English Historical Review* 136/583, 2021, 1450–1476.

Özsu, U. *Formalizing Displacement: International Law and Population Transfers*, Oxford, 2015.

Özsu, U. 'Ottoman Empire,' in Fassbender, B. et al. eds., *The Oxford Handbook of the History of International Law*, Oxford, 2012.

Özsu, U. and Skouteris, T. 'International Legal Histories of the Ottoman Empire: An Introduction to a Symposium', *Journal of the History of International Law / Revue d'histoire du droit international* 18, 2016, 1–4.

Palabıyık, M.S. 'The Emergence of the Idea of 'International Law' in the Ottoman Empire before the Treaty of Paris (1856)', *Middle Eastern Studies* 50, 2014, 233–251.

Palabıyık, M.S. 'International Law for Survival: Teaching International Law in the Late Ottoman Empire (1859–1922)', *Bulletin of the School of Oriental and African Languages* 78, 2015, 271–291.

Réchid, A. 'Les droits minoritaires en Turquie dans le passé et le présent,' *Revue générale de droit international public*, 1935, 293–341.

Réchid, A. 'L'Islam et le droit des gens', *Collected Courses of the Hague Academy of International Law/ Recueil des Cours* 60, 1937, 371–506.

Réchid, A. 'Kapitülasyonlar', *Dârülfünûn Hukuk Fakültesi ,cmuası* 6/37, 1928, 1–38.

Réchid, A. *Hukuku Umumiyei Düvel*, Istanbul, 1928.

Reynolds, M.A. *Shattering Empires: The Clash and Collapse of the Ottoman and Russian Empires 1908–1918*, Cambridge (UK), 2011.

Robson, L. 'Capitulation Redux: The Imperial Genealogy of the Post-WWI 'Minority' Regime', *The American Historical Review* 126/3, 2021, 978–1000.

Rodogno, D. *Against Massacre: Humanitarian Intervention in the Ottoman Empire 1815–1914*, Princeton, 2012.

Rubin, A. *Ottoman Nizamiye Courts: Law and Modernity*, London, 2011.

Rubin, A. 'Modernity as Code: The Ottoman Empire and the Global Movement of Codification', *Journal of Economic and Social History of the Orient* 59, 2016, 828–856.

Sluga, G. *The Invention of International Order: Remaking Europe after Napoleon,* Princeton, 2021.

Şeref, A. 'İmtiyazat-i Mezhebiye', *Sabah* 9, 1918.

Şimşir, B.N. *Lozan Telgrafları*, Ankara, 1990.

Temperley, H.W.V. *A History of the Peace Conference of Paris*, Vol. V, 'Economic Reconstruction and Protection of Minorities', London, 1920–1924.

Union interparlementaire. *Procès-verbaux de la Commission des détroits et des canaux maritimes*, The Hague, 1913.

CHAPTER 2

Primary Sources

Archives

CAB 23, Cabinet Minutes, Cabinet Papers, The National Archives, Kew, London.

CAB 27, Cabinet Committees, Cabinet Papers, The National Archives, Kew, London.

CAB 32, Imperial and Imperial War Conferences, Minutes and Memoranda, Cabinet Papers, The National Archives, Kew, London.

CAB 44, Committee of Imperial Defence, Historical Branch and Cabinet Office, Historical Section: War Histories, The National Archives, Kew, London.

FO 371, General Correspondence: Political, Foreign Officer Papers, The National Archives, Kew, London.

FO 608, Paris Peace Conference of 1919–1920: Correspondence, The National Archives, Kew, London.

FO 800, Private Collections, Earl of Balfour Papers, The National Archives, Kew, London.

PRO 30, Kitchener Papers, The National Archives, Kew, London.

L/P&S/, Departmental Papers, Political and Secret Separate Files, India Office Records, British Library.

Published Documents

Documents on British Foreign Policy, 1919–1939, 1st series, Vol. 13, Butler, R. and Bury, J.P.T. eds., London, 1962.

Foreign Relations of the United States: Paris Peace Conference, Vol. 5, Washington D.C., 1946.

H.H. Asquith: Letters to Venetia Stanley, Brock, M. and E. eds., Oxford, 1982.

Winston S. Churchill, Vol. 4, *Companion*, Part 2, Gilbert, M. ed., Boston, 1978.

Lloyd George: A diary, by Frances Stevenson, Taylor, A.J.P. ed., London, 1971.

Lloyd George Family Letters, 1885–1936, Morgan, K.O. ed., Cardiff, 1973.

Riddell, Lord. *Lord Riddell's Diary of the Peace Conference and After, 1918–1923*, London, 1933.

Periodicals

Punch [London]
The Times [London]

Private Papers

Admiral Mark Bristol Papers, Library of Congress, Washington D.C.
Marquess of Crewe Papers, University Library, Cambridge.
H.A.L. Fisher Papers, Bodleian Library, Oxford.
Joseph Grew Papers, Houghton Library, Harvard University.
P.R.C. Groves Papers, Liddell Hart Centre for Military Archives, King's College, London.
Hardinge of Penshurst Papers, University Library, Cambridge.
A.W.A. Leeper Papers, Churchill Archive Centre, Cambridge.
Richard Meinertzhagen Diary, Rhodes House Library, Oxford.
Sir Horace Rumbold Papers, Bodleian Library, Oxford.
Templewood (Sir Samuel Hoare) Papers, University Library, Cambridge.

Secondary Sources

Amery, L. *My Political Life*, London, 1953.
Andrew, C.M. and Kanya-Forstner, A.S. *France Overseas: The Great War and the Climax of French Imperial Expansion*, London, 1981.
Blunt, W.S. *The Future of Islam*, London, 1882.
Buzpinar, Ş.T. 'Opposition to the Ottoman Caliphate in the Early Years of Abdülhamid II: 1877–1882', *Die Welt des Islams* 36/1, 1996, 59–89.
Criss, N.B. *Istanbul under Allied Occupation 1918–1923*, Leiden, 1999.
Cromer, Earl of. *Germania Contra Mundum*, London, 1915.
Douglas, J.A. 'The Redemption of S. Sophia', *The Treasury*, 1919.
Elden, E. 'De quelle couleur était le cheval blanc de Franchet d'Espèrey? Petite enquête sur la vérité historique', in Schiltz, V. ed., *De Samarcande à Istanbul: étapes orientales. Hommages á Pierre Chuvin*, Paris, 2015, 285–301.
Gladstone, W. *Bulgarian Horrors and the Question of the East*, London, 1876.
Goldstein, E. 'British Peace Aims and the Eastern Question: The Political Intelligence Department and the Eastern Committee, 1918', *Middle Eastern Studies* 23/4, 1987, 419–436.

Goldstein, E. 'Great Britain and Greater Greece, 1917–1920', *Historical Journal* 32/3, 1989, 339–356.

Goldstein, E. 'Holy Wisdom and British Foreign Policy, 1918–1922: The St. Sophia Redemption Agitation', *Byzantine and Modern Greek Studies* 15, 1991, 36–64.

Goldstein, E. 'Redeeming Holy Wisdom: Britain and St. Sophia' in Hall, M. ed., *Towards World Heritage: International Origins of the Preservation Movement, 1870–1930*, London, 2011, 45–62.

Hirtzel, A. *The Church, The Empire, and The World*, London, 1919.

Huddleston, S. 'France and Turkey', *Eastern Europe* 5/2, 1921, 103–108.

Hyam, R. 'Churchill and the British Empire', in Blake, R. et al. eds., *Churchill*, New York, 1983.

Louis, W.R. *In the Name of God Go!: Leo Amery and the British Empire in the Age of Churchill*, New York, 1992.

Macfie, A.L. *The End of the Ottoman Empire, 1908–1923*, London, 1998.

Mackesy, P. *The War in the Mediterranean, 1803–1810*, Cambridge (USA), 1957.

Minault, G. *The Khilafat Movement: Religious Symbolism and Political Mobilization in India*, New York, 1982.

Poincaré, R. *Au Service de la France*, Vol. XI, À la récherche de la paix, Paris, 1974.

Prothero, G.W. *A Lasting Peace*, London, 1917.

Rossi, J.P., 'The Transformation of the British Liberal Party: A Study of the Tactics of the Liberal Opposition, 1874–1880', *Transactions of the American Philosophical Society* 68/8, 1978.

Sachar, H. *A History of Israel from the Rise of Zionism to Our Time*, New York, 1976.

Schneer, J. *The Balfour Declaration*, New York, 2010.

Seton-Watson, H. and C. *The Making of a New Europe: R.W. Seton-Watson and the Last Years of Austria-Hungary*, London, 1981.

Shannon, R. *Gladstone and the Bulgarian Agitation, 1876*, Hamden, 1975.

Townshend, C. *Desert Hell: The British Invasion of Mesopotamia*, Cambridge (USA), 2011.

Toynbee, A.J. *The Murderous Tyranny of the Turks*, London, 1917.

Yenen, A. 'Elusive Forces in Illusive Eyes: British Officialdom's Perceptions of the Anatolian Resistance Movement', *Middle Eastern Studies* 54/5, 2018, 788–810.

Zürcher, E.J. ed. *Jihad and Islam in World War I*, Leiden, 2016.

CHAPTER 3

Airapetov, O.R. *Vneshniaia politika Sovetskoi Rossii i SSSR v 1920–1939 godakh i istoki Vtoroi mirovoi voiny*, Moscow, 2020.

Anghie, A. *Imperialism, Sovereignty, and the Making of International Law*, Cambridge (UK), 2004.

Armianskii vopros na Lozannskoi konferentsii, Tbilisi, 1926.

Aydoğan, E. and Ortak, Ş. eds. *Dr. İbrahim Talî Bey'in (Öngören) Günlüğü*, Istanbul, 2000.

Baldry, J. 'Soviet Relations with Saudi Arabia and the Yemen, 1917–1938', *Middle Eastern Studies* 20/1, 1984, 53–80.

Bor'ian, B. *Armenia. Mezhdunarodnaia diplomatiia i SSSR,* Moscow, 1929.

Chernichenkina, N.I. ed. *Rus Arşivlerine Göre Moskova ve Kars Konferansları. Tutanaklar ve Belgeler*, Istanbul, 2014.

Cleveland, W. *Islam against the West: Shakib Arslan and the Campaign for Islamic Nationalism,* Austin, 1985.

Datskiv̄, I. *Ukraïns'ka diplomatiia (1917–1923 rr.) u konteksti svitovoï istoriï*, Ternopil, 2013.

Demirci, S. *Strategies and Struggles: British Rhetoric and Turkish Response: The Lausanne Conference, 1922–1923,* Istanbul, 2005.

Dullin, S., and Forestier-Peyrat, É. 'Flexible Sovereignties of the Revolutionary State: Soviet Republics Enter World Politics', *Journal of the History of International Law/Revue d'histoire du droit international* 19/2, 2017, 177–198.

Fink, C. *The Genoa Conference: European Diplomacy, 1921–1922*, Chapel Hill, 1984.

Fleury, A. and Imboden, G. eds. *Documents diplomatiques suisses*, Bern, 1988.

Forestier-Peyrat, É. 'Fighting Locusts Together: Pest Control and the Birth of Soviet Development Aid, 1920–1939', *Global Environment* 7/2, 2014, 536–571.

Forestier-Peyrat, É. 'Maisons étroitement surveillées. Consuls et maisons consulaires dans le Caucase soviétique de l'entre-deux-guerres" in Grenet, M. ed., *La maison consulaire. Espaces, fonctions et usagers XVIe-XXIe siècle*, Aix, 2021.

Getachew, A. *Worldmaking After Empire: The Rise and Fall of Self-Determination,* Princeton, 2019.

Gökay, B. *Soviet Eastern Policy and Turkey, 1920–1991: Soviet Foreign Policy, Turkey and Communism,* Abingdon, 2006.

Hirst, S.J. 'Transnational Anti-Imperialism and the National Forces: Soviet Diplomacy and Turkey, 1920–1923', *Comparative Studies of South Asia, Africa and the Middle East* 33/2, 2013, 214–226.

Hirst, S.J. and İşçi, O. 'Smokestacks and Pipelines: Russian-Turkish Relations and the Persistence of Economic Development', *Diplomatic History* 44/5, 2020, 834–859.

İnönü, İ. *Hatıralar,* Istanbul, 2009.

İşçi, O. *Turkey and the Soviet Union during World War II: Diplomacy, Discord, and International Relations,* London, 2019.

Jacobson, J. *When the Soviet Union entered World Politics,* Berkeley, 1994.

Kalandarishvili, L.N., Nefedova, T.I. and Tabakua, S.F. eds. *Bor'ba za pobedu sovetskoi vlasti v Adzharii. Dokumenty i materialy (1917–1921 gg.),* Batumi, 1961.

Kane, E., Kirasirova, M. and Litvin, M. eds. *Russian-Arab Worlds: A Documentary History*, Oxford, 2023.

Kheifets, A.N. *Sovetskaia diplomatiia i narody Vostoka, 1921–1927*, Moscow, 1968.

Khormach, I.A. *Vozvrashchenie v mirovoe soobshchestvo: bor'ba i sotrudnichestvo Sovetskogo gosudarstva s Ligoi natsii v 1919–1934 gg.*, Moscow, 2011.

Khormach, I.A. 'Sovetskaia Rossiia na Lozannskoi konferentsii po uregulirovaniiu polozheniia na Blizhnem Vostoke (1922–1923)', *Novaia i noveishaia istoriia* 2, 2019, 74–92.

Kirasirova, M. 'The 'East' as a Category of Bolshevik Ideology and Comintern Administration: The Arab Section of the Communist University of the Toilers of the East', *Kritika* 18/1, 2017, 7–34.

Korets'kyi, V.M. ed. *Ukraïns'ka RSR na mizhnarodnii areni. Zbirnyk dokumentiv (1917–1923 rr.),* Kyiv, 1966.

Kosach, G.G. *Kommunisty Blizhnego Vostoka v SSSR v 1920–1930-e gody*, Moscow, 2009.

Lehmann, M. *Eine sowjetische Nation. Nationale Sozialismusinterpretationen in Armenien seit 1945,* Frankfurt, 2012.

Liubimov, N.N. and Erlikh, A.N. *Genuezskaia konferentsiia. Vospominaniia uchastnikov*, Moscow, 1963.

Musatova, T.L. 'G.V. Chicherin i arabskii vostok', *Vestnik Ministerstva inostrannykh del* 21, 1990, 36–48.

Nejad, K.A. 'To break the feudal bonds: the Soviets, Reza Khan, and the Iranian left, 1921–1925', *Middle Eastern Studies* 57/5, 2021, 758–776.

Nezhinskii, L.N. and Ignat'ev, A.V. eds. *Rossiia i Chernomorskie prolivy (XVIII-XX stoletiia)*, Moscow, 1999.

Odgen, D. 'Britain and Soviet Georgia, 1921–22', *Journal of Contemporary History* 23/2, 1988, 245–258.

Qurbanova, J. and Piriyev, M. eds. *Azərbaycan-Türkiyə münasibətləri (1920–1922). Sənədlər və materiallar*, Baku, 2002.

Reynolds, M.A. 'Abdürrezzak Bedirhan: Ottoman Kurd and Russophile in the Twilight of Empire', *Kritika* 12/2, 2011, 411–450.

Smith, L.V. *Sovereignty at the Paris Peace Conference of 1919,* Oxford, 2018.

Sokol'skii, N. *Ocherki sovremennoi Turtsii*, Tbilisi, 1923.

Şimşir, B.N. *Lozan Telgrafları*, Ankara, 1990.

Ter Minassian, T. *Colporteurs du Komintern. L'Union soviétique et les minorités au Moyen-Orient*, Paris, 1997.

Volkov, D.V. *Russia's Turn to Persia: Orientalism in Diplomacy and Intelligence,* Cambridge (UK), 2018.

Volodarsky, M.I. *The Soviet Union and its Southern Neighbours: Iran and Afghanistan, 1917–1933*, Abingdon, 2013.

White, S. *The Origins of Détente: The Genoa Conference and Soviet-Western Relations, 1921–1922,* Cambridge (UK), 2005.

Yenen, A. 'The Other Jihad: Enver Pasha, Bolsheviks, and Politics of Anticolonial Muslim Nationalism during the Baku Congress' in Fraser, T.G. ed., *The First World War and its Aftermath: The Shaping of the Middle East*, London, 2015, 273–293.

Zherlitsyna, N.A. ''Zashchitnik ugnetennogo Marokko': Osveshchenie rifskoi voiny v Sovetskom Soiuze v 1920-x gg', *Vestnik Tomskogo gosudarstvennogo universiteta* 6, Moscow, 2016, 11–17.

CHAPTER 4

Adams, C. *Islam and Modernism in Egypt: A Study of the Modern Reform Movement Inaugurated by Mohammad Abduh*, Kuala Lumpur, 1933.

Aksakal, M. 'Not 'by those old books of international law, but only by war': Ottoman Intellectuals on the Eve of the Great War', *Diplomacy and Statecraft* 15/3, 2004.

Allen, H.E. *The Turkish Transformation: A Study in Social and Religious Development*, Chicago, 1935.

Ardıç, N. *Islam and the Politics of Secularism: The Caliphate and Middle Eastern Modernization in the Early 20th Century*, London, 2017.

Aydın, C. and Duran, B. 'Arnold Toynbee in Cold War Era Islamism: Sezai Karakoç's Civilizational Cosmopolitanism', *Comparative Studies of South Asia, Africa and the Middle East* 35/2, 2015.

Aydın, C. *The Politics of Anti-Westernism in Asia*, New York, 2007.

Azad, A.K. *'Khilafat and Jaziratul-Arab': Address delivered at the Bengal Provincial Khilafat Conference*, Bombay, 1920.

Berkes, N. *The Development of Secularism in Turkey*, London, 1998.

Bilsel, M.C. *Cemiyet-i Akvam*, Istanbul, 1924.

Bilsel, M.C. *Lozan*, Istanbul, 1933.

Conlin, J. and Yazıcıoğlu, F. 'The Libyan War and Student Pan-Islamism: The Edinburgh Declaration of 1911', *International Journal of Middle East Studies* 54/2, 2022.

Coudenhove-Kalergi, R. *An Idea Conquers the World*, New York, 1954.

Davison, R. *Reform in the Ottoman Empire, 1856–1876*, New York, 1973.

Demirhan, A. "We Can Defend Our Rights by Our Own Efforts': Turkish Women and the Global Muslim Question, 1870–1935', unpublished PhD dissertation, University of North Carolina at Chapel Hill, Chapel Hill, 2020.

Deringil, S. *The Well-Protected Domains: Ideology and the Legitimation of Powers in the Ottoman Empire 1876–1909*, London, 1998.

Esenbel, S. 'Friends in Opposite Camps or Enemies from Afar: Japanese and Ottoman Turkish Relations during the Great War' in Minohara, T. et al. eds., *The Decade of the Great War: Japan and the Wider World in the 1910s*, Leiden, 2014.

Foreign Relations of the United States, Paris Peace Conference. 'Stenographic Notes of a Meeting Held at President Wilson's House in the Place des État-Unis, Paris, on Saturday, May 17, 1919, at 4.30 pm.'

Formichi, C. 'Mustafa Kemal's Abrogation of the Ottoman Caliphate and Its Impact on the Indonesian National Movement' in al-Rasheed, M. et al. eds., *Demystifying the Caliphate: Historical Memory and Contemporary Contexts*, New York, 2013.

Froembgen, H. *Kemal Ataturk: A Biography*, New York, 1937.

Fukuyama, F. *The End of History and the Last Man*, London, 1992.

Gibb, H. et al. *Whither Islam: A Survey of Modern Movements in the Moslem World*, London, 1932.

Gusejnova, D. 'Europe to-morrow: the shifting frontiers of European civilization in the political thought of Richard Coudenhove-Kalergi', *Istanbul University Journal of Sociology* 38/2, 2019.

Gürel, P. *Wild Westernization: Figuring America in Twentieth Century Turkey*, New York, 2017.

Halit, H. *The Crescent Versus the Cross*, London, 1907.

Hasan, M. and Pernau, M. ed. *Regionalizing Pan-Islamism: Documents of the Khilafat Movement*, New Delhi, 2005.

Huntington, S. 'The Clash of Civilizations?', *Foreign Affairs* 72/3, 1993.

Hurewitz, J.C. 'The Europeanization of Ottoman Diplomacy: The Conversion from Unilateralism to Reciprocity in the Nineteenth Century', *Belleten* 25, 1961.

Jansen, M. *The Japanese and Sun Yat-sen*, Cambridge (USA), 1954.

Kara, İ. *Bir Düşünce Tarihi Metni Olarak İstiklâl Marşı*, Istanbul, 2021.

Kidwai, M.H. *The Future of the Muslim Empire: Turkey*, London, 1919.

Kidwai, M.H. *The Sword Against Islam; or, A Defence of Islam's Standard-Bearers*, London, 1919.

Kupchan, C. *No One's World: The West, the Rising Rest, and the Coming Global Turn*, New York, 2012.

Lerner, D. *The Passing of Traditional Society: Modernizing the Middle East*, New York, 1958.

Lewis, B. *The Emergence of Modern Turkey*, New York, 1961.

Liebisch-Gümüş, C. 'Defending Turkey on Global Stages: The Young Turk Reşit Saffet's Internationalist Strategy in 1919', *New Global Studies* 10/3, 2016.

Linke, L. *Allah Dethroned: A Journey Through Modern Turkey*, London, 1937.

Lowry, H. ed. *Clarence K. Streit's The Unknown Turks*, Istanbul, 2011.

Mahmud, S. *The Khilafat and England*, Patna, 1920.

Margulies, R. *The Terrible Turk: Batı'nın Gördüğü 'Türk'*, Istanbul, 2016.

Mathews, B. *Young Islam on Trek: A Study in the Clash of Civilizations*, New York, 1926.

McCarthy, J. *Death and Exile: The Ethnic Cleansing of Ottoman Muslims, 1821–1922,* Princeton, 1995.

McGhee, G.C. 'Turkey Joins the West', *Foreign Affairs* 32/4, 1954.

Mears, E.G. *Modern Turkey: A Politico-Economic Interpretation, 1908–1923*, New York, 1924.

Minawi, M. 'International law and the precarity of Ottoman sovereignty in Africa at the end of the nineteenth century', *The International History Review* 43/5, 2021.

Olmstead, A. T. E. 'The New Arab Kingdom and the Fate of the Muslim World', *University of Illinois Bulletin* XVI/17, 1918.

Özcan, A. *Pan-Islamism: Indian Muslims, the Ottomans and Britain, 1877–1924*, Leiden, 1997.

Price, C. *The Rebirth of Turkey*, New York, 1923.

Putnam, W.B.L. *The Conflict of Colour: Being a Detailed Examination of Racial Problems*, London, 1910.

Qureshi, M.N. *Ottoman Turkey, Atatürk and Muslim South Asia: Perspectives, Perceptions and Responses*, Oxford, 2014.

Qureshi, M.N. *Pan-Islam in British Indian Politics: The Politics of the Khilafat Movement, 1918–1924*, Karachi, 2009.

Rıza, A. *The Moral Bankruptcy of Western Policy Towards the East*, Ankara, 1988.

Rustow, D.A. 'Politics and Islam in Turkey 1920–1955' in Frye, R.N. ed., *Islam and the West*, The Hague, 1957.

Sadiq, M. *The Turkish Revolution and the Indian Freedom Movement*, Delhi, 1983.

Sherrill, C.H. *A Year's Embassy to Mustafa Kemal*, New York, 1934.

Shûmei, Ô. *Fukkô Ajia no Shomondai*, Tokyo, 1922.

Stoddard, L. *The New World of Islam*, New York, 1921.

Stoddard, L. *The Rising Tide of Color against White World-Supremacy. with an Introduction by Madison Grant*, New York, 1921.

Toynbee, A.J. *The Western Question in Greece and Turkey; A Study in the Contact of Civilisations*, London, 1923.

Trask, R. 'The 'Terrible Turk' and Turkish-American Relations in the Interwar Period', *The Historian* 33/1, 1970.

Trask, R. *The United States Response to Turkish Nationalism and Reform, 1914–1939*, Minneapolis, 1971.

VanderLippe, J.M. 'Racism and The Making of American Foreign Policy: the 'Terrible Turk' as Icon and Metaphor', *Research in Politics and Society* 6, 1999.

Ward, R.E. and Rustow, D.A. eds. *Political Modernization in Japan and Turkey*, Princeton, 1964.

Webster, D.E. *The Turkey of Ataturk: Social Process in the Turkish Reformation*, Philadelphia, 1939.

Williams, P. 'Wilson's 14 Points or War-Kemal Pasha', *Chicago Daily Tribune*, 4 May 1920.

Willis, J. 'Debating the Caliphate: Islam and Nation in the Work of Rashid Rida and Abul Kalam Azad', *The International History Review* 32/4, 2010.

Yasamee, F.A.K. *Ottoman Diplomacy: Abdülhamid II and the Great Powers, 1878–1888*, Istanbul, 1996.

Yenen, A. 'The Other Jihad. Enver Pasha, Bolsheviks, and Politics of Anticolonial Muslim Nationalism during the Baku Congress 1920' in Fraser, T.G. ed., *The First World War and its Aftermath: The Shaping of the Middle East*, London, 2015.

Yılmaz, H. *Kurtuluş Savaşımız ve Asya, Afrika'nın uyanışı: Hâkimiyeti Milliye yazılarıyla*, Istanbul, 2007.

Zaman, F. 'Pan-Islamism in Post-War Europe', unpublished paper presented at Cold War Islamism Symposium, Free University, Berlin, 2019.

Zwemer, S. *Across the World of Islam: Studies in Aspects of the Mohammedan Faith and in the Present Awakening of the Moslem Multitudes,* New York, 1925.

CHAPTER 5

'Lozan Konferansı – husûsî muhâbirlerimizin telgrafları, bizim de ellerimiz temizdir ve mukâyeseye hâzırız! 'Ismet Paşa Kurzon'a hakîkaten bir ders teşkîl eden bir cevâb vermiş ve hadîd re'îs çok yumuşamışdır!', *Hâkimiyet-i Milliye* 690, 19 December 1922.

'Lozan Konferansı müzâkerâtı hakkında Ra'ûf Bey'in nutkunun metni' *Vakit* 64, 19 December 1922.

'İcrâ Vekîlleri Re'îs Ra'ûf Bey Efendi'nin mühim beyânâtı', *Tanîn* 67, 19 December 1922.

'Amerikalıların ekalliyetleri himayeye hakkı var mı? Şarkdaki Hristiyanlardan evvel kendi memleketlerindeki zencileri, Katolik ve Musevileri kurtarsalar daha iyi olur!', *Tevhid-i Efkâr*, 28 December 1922.

'Swiss order Ahrens to leave', *New York Times*, 12 May 1923.

'Ismet Pasha's Safety', *The Manchester Guardian*, 12 May 1923.

'Swiss isolate Ismet, shadow Venizelos. Guard Conference delegates against Vorovsky's Fate – Turk leader no longer eats in public', *New York Times*, 21 May 1923.

'Ismet warned of murder plot; Swiss give him a Bodyguard', *New York Times*, 22 May 1923.

'Ismet in rage. Plot to assassinate. Lausanne Turks alarmed', *The Times of India*, taken from *The Times* (London), 23 May 1923.

Aharonian, A. 'Hay Bedutyun te *Home*?', *Saradarabadits Minchev Sevr yev Lozan*, Boston, 1943.

Akçam A. and Kurt, Ü. *Kanunların Ruhu: Emval-i Metruke Kanunlarında Soykırımın İzini Sürmek*, Istanbul, 2012.

Altuğ, S. 'From refugees to decent Syrian citizens: Armenians in Syria under the French Mandate (1921–1939)' in Dakessian, A. ed., *Armenians in Syria*, Beirut, 2018, 163–178.

Brubaker, R. 'Aftermaths of Empire and the Unmixing of Peoples: Historical and Comparative Perspectives', *Ethnic and Racial Studies* 18/2, 1995, 189–218.

Budak, M. *99 Soruda Lozan,* Istanbul, 2018.

Demirel, A. ed. *İsmet İnönü, Defterler 1919–1973*, Istanbul, 2001.

Ekmekcioglu, L. 'Kalanlar: Savaş Sonrasında ve Tek Parti Döneminde İstanbul Ermeni Cemmati' in Adanır, F. et al. eds., *1915: Siyaset, Tehcir, Soykırım*, Istanbul, 2015.

Ekmekcioglu, L. *Recovering Armenia: The Limits of Belonging in Post-Genocide Turkey*, Stanford, 2016.

Emin, A. 'Çivili sulh', *Vakit* 1804, 20 December 1922.

Hüseyin, C. 'Lozan Konferansı'nda Noel günleri kopan fırtına (Lozan Mektupları: 45)', *Tanîn* 79, 31 December 1922.

Khatissian, A. *Hayastani Hanrabedutyan Dzakumn u Zarkatsume*, Athens, 1930.

Khatissian, A. *Éclosion et Développement de la République Arménienne*, Athens, 1989.

Kieser, H-L. *When Democracy Died: The Middle East's Enduring Peace of Lausanne*, Cambridge (UK), 2023.

Kieser, H-L., Polatel, M., and Schmutz, T. 'Reform or Cataclysm? The Agreement of 8 February 1914 regarding the Ottoman Eastern Provinces', *Journal of Genocide Research* 14/ 3, 2015, 285–304.

Lausanne Conference on Near Eastern Affairs, 1922–1923: Records of Proceedings and Draft Terms of Peace, London, 1923.

Liebisch-Gümüş, C. 'Embedded Turkification: Nation Building and Violence within the Framework of the League of Nations 1919–1937', *International Journal of Middle East Studies* 52/ 2, 2020, 229–244.

Marashlian, L. 'The Armenian Question from Sèvres to Lausanne: Economics and Morality in American and British Politics, 1920–1923', PhD dissertation, UCLA, Los Angeles, 1992.

Marrus, M.R. *The Unwanted – European Refugees in the Twentieth Century*, Oxford, 1985.

Meray, S.L. ed. 'B. Azınlıklar Alt-Komisyonu', *Lozan Barış Konferansı: Tutanaklar Belgeler*, Ankara, 1970, 151–292.

Montgomery, G.R. 'The Massacres of Armenians in 1915', *Current History* (*New York Times* supplement) (1916–1940) 17/1, 1922, 25–28.

Nur, R. *Lozan Hatıraları*, Istanbul, 1992.

Papazian, V. *Im Hushere, Yerrort Hador*, Cairo, 1957.

Pashalian, L. 'Lozani khaghahgutyan khorkhrtazhoghove', *Aysor* 1/5, 1951.

Pashalian, L. *Lozani Khaghaghutyan Khorkhrtazhoghove*, Beirut, 1983.

Rıf'at. 'İstanbul Rumları, Ermeni Yurdu münâkaşası- Lord Kurzon ma'nâsız bir hiddet ve 'asabiyet İle müzâkerâtın inkıtâ'a uğrayacağı tehdîdinde bulunmuştur'. *Hakimiyet-i Milliye* 689, 18 December 1922.

Selek, S. ed. *İsmet İnönü Hatıralaları*, Istanbul, 2006.

Şimşir, B.N. ed. *Lozan Telgrafları I*, Ankara, 1990.

Şükrü, A. 'Ermenilerin konferans etrafındaki mesâ'isi', *Vakit* 1789, 5 December 1922.

Turan, Ş. *İsmet İnönü, Yaşamı, Dönemi ve Kişiliği*, Ankara, 2000.

Tusan, M. "Crimes against humanity': human rights, the British Empire, and the origins of the response to the Armenian Genocide', *The American Historical Review* 119/1, 2014, 47–77.

Tusan, M. *The British Empire and the Armenian Genocide: Humanitarianism and Imperial Politics from Gladstone to Churchill*, London, 2017.

Watenpaugh, K.D. *Bread from Stones: The Middle East and the Making of Modern Humanitarianism*, Oakland, 2015.

CHAPTER 6

Primary Sources

Archives

The National Archives, London:

FO 371/8019, Foreign Offices Files for China, 1919–1929.

FO 416/72, Persia, Further Correspondence Part XIV, January–June 1923, Confidential Print: Middle East.

FO 416/112, Annual Reports on Persia, 1922–1923, Confidential Print: Middle East.

FO 424/255, Turkey. Further Correspondence Part II, 1922, Confidential Print: Middle East.

FO 424/256, Turkey. Further Correspondence Part III, 1923, Confidential Print: Middle East.

British Library: India Office Records and Private Papers, London:

IOR/L/PS/18/C210.

IOR/L/PS/18/C211.

Archives du ministère de l'Europe et des Affaires Étrangères, La Courneuve:

P11838: Asie 1918–1940, Perse-Iran.

Periodicals

Chehreh Nama [Cairo]

Correspondance d'Orient: revue économique, politique & littéraire [Paris]

Habl ol-Matin [Calcutta]

Journal des débats politiques et littéraires [Paris]

Now Bahar [Tehran]

Setareh Iran [Tehran]

Shafagh-e Sorkh [Tehran]

Secondary Sources

Ahmadzadeh, H. & Stanfield, G. 'The Political, Cultural, and Military Re-Awakening of the Kurdish Nationalist Movement in Iran', *The Middle East Journal* 64/1, 2010, 11–27.

Aydın, C. *The Politics of Anti-Westernism in Asia*, New York, 2007.

Bast, O. 'Les 'buts de guerre' de la Perse neutre pendant la Première Guerre mondiale', *Relations internationales* 160/4, 2014, 95–110.

Bast, O. 'La mission persane à la Conférence de la Paix en 1919: Une nouvelle interprétation' in Bast, O. ed., *La Perse et la Grande Guerre*, Tehran, 2002, 375–425.

Bayāt, K. *Pāntorkism va Īrān*, Tehran, 1395 / 2015.

Bayāt, K. *Ravābet-e Īrān va Torkiyeh az soghūt-e dowlat-e o̱smānī tā bar āmadan-e nezām-e jomhūrī*, Tehran, 1394 / 2014.

Cameron Watt, D. 'The Saadabad Pact of 8 July 1937' in Dann, U. ed., *The Great Powers in the Middle East, 1919–1939*, 1988, 333–352.

Clayer, N., Giomi, F. & Szurek, E. 'Introduction' in Clayer, N. et al. eds., *Kemalism. Transnational Politics in Post-Ottoman World*, London, 2018, 1–37.

Cronin, S. *The Making of Modern Iran. State and Society under Riza Shah, 1921–1941*, London, 2003.

Dailami, P. 'Jangali Movement', in *Encyclopaedia Iranica*, Vol. XIV, 2008, 534–544, https://www.iranicaonline.org/articles/jangali-movement.

Debashi, A. ed. *Khāterāt-e perans Arfa'*, Tehran, 1378 / 1999.

Dehnavī, N. ed. *Asnādī az ravābet-e Irān va Torkiyeh*, Tehran, 1386 / 2007.

Dehnavī, N. ed. *Asnādi az ravabet-e siyāsī-e Torkiyeh va Erāq*, Tehran, 1386 / 2007.

Farahani, H. and Behbudi, H. ed. *Rūz-shomār-e tārikh-e moaser-e Iran*, Tehran, 1388 / 2010.

Gunter, M. 'Iran's Forgotten Kurds', *Journal of South Asian and Middle Eastern Studies* 43/2, 2020, 54–67.

Luizard, P-J. ed. *La vie de l'ayatollah Mahdî al-Khâlesî*, Paris, 2004.

Makī, H. *Tārīkh-e bīst sāleh-ye Īrān*, Tehran, 1359 / 1980.

Nejad, K. 'To break the feudal bonds: Reza Khan, the Soviets and the Iranian left, 1921–25', *Middle Eastern Studies* 57/5, 2021,758–776.

Toynbee, A.J. 'The New Status of Turkey', *Contemporary Review* 123, 1923.

Volodarsky, M. *The Soviet Union and Its Southern Neighbours*, London, 2016.

CHAPTER 7

Abisaab, R.J. and M. *The Shi`ites of Lebanon: Modernism, Communism and Hizbullah's Islamists*, Syracuse, 2014.

Andrew, C.M. and Kanya-Forstner, A.S. *The Climax of French Imperial Expansion, 1914–1924*, Stanford, 1981.

Anghie, A. *Imperialism, Sovereignty and the Making of International Law*, Cambridge (UK), 2004.

Batatu, H. *The Old Social Classes and the Revolutionary Movements of Iraq*, Princeton, 1978.

Collier, D. and Munck, G.L. 'Building blocks and methodological challenges: A framework for studying critical junctures', *Qualitative and Multi-Method Research* 15/1, 2017, 2–9.

Fromkin, D. *A Peace to End All Peace: The Fall of the Ottoman Empire and the Creation of the Modern Middle East*, New York, 2009 (originally published 1989).

Gelvin, J.L. *Divided Loyalties: Nationalism and Mass Politics in Syria at the Close of Empire*, Berkeley, 1998.

Al-Hakim, H. *al-Watha'iq al-tarikhiyya al-muta'alliqa bi al-qadiya al-Suriya*, Beirut, 1974.

Hourani, A. *Arabic Thought in the Liberal Age, 1798–1939*, London, 1962.

Husayn, F. *Muhaddirat `an mu'tamar Luzan wa Atharuh fi al-bilad al-`Arabiya*, Cairo, 1958.

Khoury, P.S. *Syria and the French Mandate: The Politics of Arab Nationalism, 1920–1945*, Princeton, 1987.

Lausanne Conference on Near Eastern Affairs, 1922–1923: Records of Proceedings and Draft Terms of Peace, London, 1923.

Manela, E. *The Wilsonian Moment: Self-Determination and the International Origins of Anticolonial Nationalism*, Oxford, 2007.

Mousa, S. 'A matter of principle: King Hussein of the Hijaz and the Arabs of Palestine', *International Journal of Middle East Studies* 9/2, 1978, 183–194.

Neep, D. *Occupying Syria under the French Mandate: Insurgency, Space and State Formation*, Cambridge (UK), 2012.

Paris, T.J. *Britain, the Hashemites and Arab Rule, 1920–1925*, London, 2003.

Pedersen, S. *The Guardians: The League of Nations and the Crisis of Empire*, Oxford, 2015.

Provence, M. *The Last Ottoman Generation and the Making of the Modern Middle East*, Cambridge (UK), 2017.

Shahrastan, M.A. *al-Mu`tamar al-Suri al`Amm 1919–1920*, Beirut, 2000.

Suyufi, Y. *Dhikra Istiqlal Suriya: 17 jumada al-thania 1338 al-muwafiq 8 maris sanat 1920*, Cairo, 1920.

Thomas, M. *Empires of Intelligence: Security Services and Colonial Disorder after 1914*, Berkeley, 2007.

Thompson, E.F. *How the West Stole Democracy from the Arabs: The Syrian Arab Congress of 1920 and the Destruction of Its Historic Islamic-Liberal Alliance*, New York, 2020.

Thompson, E.F. *Justice Interrupted: The Struggle for Constitutional Government in the Middle East*, Cambridge (USA), 2013.

Tooze, A. *The Deluge: The Great War, America and the Remaking of the Global Order, 1916–1931*, New York, 2014.

Wright, Q. *Mandates Under the League of Nations*, Chicago, 1930.

CHAPTER 8

Chester, C. 'Turkey Reinterpreted', *Current History* XVI/6, 1922, 939–946.

Child, R. *A Diplomat Looks at Europe*, New York, 1925.

Conlin, J. *Mr. Five Per Cent: The Many Lives of Calouste Gulbenkian, the World's Richest Man*, London, 2019.

Conlin, J. 'An Oily Entente: France, Britain, and the Mosul Question, 1916–1925', *Diplomacy & Statecraft* 31/2, 2020, 231–256.

Cooper, J. *Breaking the Heart of the World: Woodrow Wilson and the Fight for the League of Nations*, Cambridge (USA), 2001.

Cooper, J. 'A Friend in Power? Woodrow Wilson and Armenia' in Winter, J. ed., *America and the Armenian Genocide of 1915*, Cambridge (UK), 2003, 103–112.

Demirci, S. 'Turco-British Manoeuvres on the Mosul Question in the Lausanne Conference, 1922–1923', *British Journal of Middle Eastern Studies* 37/1, 2010, 57–71.

DeNovo, J. *American Interests and Policies in the Middle East, 1900–1939*, Minneapolis, 1963.

DeNovo, J. 'The Movement for an Aggressive Oil Policy Abroad, 1918–1920', *The American Historical Review* 61/4, 1956, 854–876.

Deringil, S. *The Well-Protected Domains: Ideology and the Legitimation of Power in the Ottoman Empire 1876–1909*, London, 1999.

Evans, L. *United States Policy and the Partition of Turkey, 1914–1924*, Baltimore, 1965.

Field, J. *America and the Mediterranean World 1776–1882*, Princeton, 1969.

Fortna, B.C. *Imperial Classroom: Islam, the State, and Education in the Late Ottoman Empire*, Oxford, 2002.

Fursenko, A. *The Battle for Oil: The Economics and Politics of International Corporate Conflict over Petroleum, 1860–1930*, trans. Freeze, G.L., London, 1990.

Gerretson, F. *History of the Royal Dutch*, Leiden, 1957.

Gibb, G. and Knowlton, E. *History of Standard Oil Company (New Jersey): The Resurgent Years 1911–1927*, New York, 1956.

Glad, B. *Charles Evans Hughes and the Illusions of Innocence: A Study in American Diplomacy*, Urbana, 1966.

Gordon, L. *American Relations with Turkey, 1830–1930: An Economic Interpretation*, Philadelphia, 1932.

Grabill, J. *Protestant Diplomacy in the Near East: Missionary Influence on American Policy, 1810–1927*, Minneapolis, 1971.

Grew, J. *Turbulent Era: A Diplomatic Record of Forty Years 1904–1945: Volume I*, New York, 1952.

Heinrichs, W. *American Ambassador: Joseph C. Grew and the Development of the United States Diplomatic Tradition*, Oxford, 1986.

Helmreich, P. *From Paris to Sèvres: The Partition of the Ottoman Empire at the Peace Conference of 1919–1920*, Columbus, 1974.

Hidy, R. and M. *Pioneering in Big Business 1882–1911*, New York, 1955.

Hogan, M. *Informal Entente: The Private Structure of Cooperation in Anglo-American Economic Diplomacy, 1918–1928*, Columbia, 1977.

Hollinger, D. *Protestants Abroad: How Missionaries Tried to Change the World but Changed America*, Princeton, 2017.

Johnson, R. *Remembered Yesterdays*, Boston, 1923.

Khalidi, R. *Resurrecting Empire: Western Footprints and America's Perilous Path in the Middle East*, Boston, 2004.

Laderman C. 'Sharing the Burden? The American Solution to the Armenian Question, 1918–1920', *Diplomatic History* 40/4, 2016, 664–694.

Laderman, C. *Sharing the Burden: The Armenian Question, Humanitarian Intervention, and Anglo-American Visions of Global Order*, Oxford, 2019.

Makdisi, U. *Faith Misplaced: The Broken Promise of U.S.-Arab Relations: 1820–2001*, New York, 2010.

Manela, E. *The Wilsonian Moment: Self-Determination and the International Origins of Anticolonial Nationalism*, New York, 2007.

Marashlian, L. 'The Armenian Question from Sèvres to Lausanne: Economics and Morality in American and British Policies, 1920–1923', PhD dissertation, UCLA, Los Angeles, 1992.

Nowell, G. *Mercantile States and the World Oil Cartel, 1900–1939*, Ithaca, 1994.

Oren, M. *Power, Faith, and Fantasy: America in the Middle East, 1776 to the Present,* New York, 2007.

Patrick A. *America's Forgotten Middle East Initiative: The King-Crane Commission of 1919*, London, 2015.

Patrick, A. 'Standard Oil in the Ottoman Lands, 1909–1927', working paper.

Patrick, A. 'Standard Oil and the Battle for the Ottoman Market, 1864–1914', *Diplomacy & Statecraft*, 2023 (forthcoming).

Patrick, A. "These People Know about Us': A Reconsideration of Attitudes towards the United States in World War I-Era Greater Syria', *Middle Eastern Studies* 50/3, 2014, 397–411.

Patrick, A. 'Woodrow Wilson, the Ottomans, and World War', *Diplomatic History* 42/5, 2018, 886–910.

Ritchie, D. 'Congress confronts the Armenian Genocide' in Winter, J. ed., *America and the Armenian Genocide of 1915*, Cambridge (UK), 2003, 276–293.

Russell, F. *The Shadow of Blooming Grove: Warren G. Harding in his Times*, New York, 1968.

Şahin, E. *Faithful Encounters: Authorities and American Missionaries in the Ottoman Empire*, Montreal, 2018.

Samuel, A.T. 'The Open Door and U.S. Policy in Iraq between the World Wars', *Diplomatic History* 38/5, 2014, 926–952.

Sonyel, S. *Turkish Diplomacy, 1918–1923: Mustafa Kemal and the Turkish National Movement*, London, 1975.

Stern, R. 'Oil Scarcity Ideology in US Foreign Policy, 1908–97', *Security Studies* 25/2, 2016, 214–257.

Stivers, W. *Supremacy and Oil: Iraq, Turkey, and the Anglo-American World Order, 1918–1930*, Ithaca, 1982.

Thompson, E.F. *How the West Stole Democracy from the Arabs: The Syrian Arab Congress of 1920 and the Destruction of its Historic Liberal-Islamic Alliance*, New York, 2020.

Tooze, A. *The Deluge: The Great War, America, and the Remaking of the Global Order, 1916–1931*, New York, 2014.

Toprani, A. 'An Anglo-American 'Petroleum Entente'?: The First Attempt to Reach an Anglo-American Oil Agreement, 1921', *Historian* 79/1, 2017, 56–79.

Trani, E. and Wilson, D. *The Presidency of Warren G. Harding*, Lawrence, 1977.

United States Department of State, *Register of the Department of State*, Washington D.C., 1872.

United States Department of State, *Register of the Department of State*, Washington D.C., 1911.

Vitalis, R. *Oilcraft: The Myths of Scarcity and Security that Haunt U.S Energy Policy*, Stanford, 2020.

Walther, K. *Sacred Interests: The United States and the Islamic World, 1821–1921*, Chapel Hill, 2015.

CHAPTER 9

Ali, O. 'The Career of Ozdemir: A Turkish Bid for Northern Iraq, 1921–1923', *Middle Eastern Studies* 53/6, 2017, 966–985.

Allen, L. *A History of False Hope: Investigative Commissions in Palestine*, Redwood City, 2020.

Arıkanlı, Z. 'British Legacy and Evolution of Kurdish Nationalism in Iraq (1918–1926)', *Alternatives: Turkish Journal of International Relations*, 2010, 29.

'Avalon Project – President Woodrow Wilson's Fourteen Points', http://avalon.law.yale.edu/20th_century/wilson14.asp.

Beck, P. "'A Tedious and Perilous Controversy': Britain and the Settlement of the Mosul Dispute, 1918–1926', *Middle Eastern Studies* 17/2, 1981, 256–276.

Brown, K. *A Biography of No Place: From Ethnic Borderland to Soviet Heartland*. Cambridge (USA), 2004.

Child, R. *A Diplomat Looks at Europe,* New York, 1925.

Conlin, J. 'An Oily Entente: France, Britain, and the Mosul Question, 1916–1925', *Diplomacy & Statecraft* 31/2, 2020, 231–256.

Coşar, N, and S. Demirci. 'The Mosul Question and the Turkish Republic: Before and After the Frontier Treaty, 1926', *Middle Eastern Studies* 42/1, 2006, 123–132.

Demirci, S. 'Turco-British Diplomatic Manoeuvres on the Mosul Question in the Lausanne Conference, 1922–1923', *British Journal of Middle Eastern Studies* 37/1, 2010, 57–71.

Hamelink, W. and Barış, H. 'Dengbêjs on Borderlands: Borders and the State as Seen through the Eyes of Kurdish Singer-Poets', *Kurdish Studies* 2/1, 2014, 34–60.

Lausanne Conference on Near Eastern Affairs, 1922–1923: Records of Proceedings and Draft Terms of Peace. London, 1923.

League of Nations. 'Question of the Frontier between Turkey and Iraq (Report by the Commission),' 20 August 1925. https://biblio-archive.unog.ch/Dateien/CouncilMSD/C-400-M-147–1925-VII_BI.pdf.

Lloyd, H. I. 'The Geography of the Mosul Boundary', *The Geographical Journal* 68/2, 1926, 104–113.

Makko, A. 'Arbitrator in a World of Wars: The League of Nations and The Mosul Dispute, 1924–1925', *Diplomacy & Statecraft* 21/4, 2010, 631–649.

Massicard, E. 'The Repression of the Koçgiri Rebellion, 1920–1921', *Online Encyclopaedia of Mass Violence*, n.d.

McDowall, D. *A Modern History of the Kurds*. London, 1996.

New York Times (Online); New York. 'Mosul Commission Starts Report Today', 25 April 1925. https://timesmachine.nytimes.com/timesmachine/1925/04/25/98824308.pdf?pdf_redirect=true&ip=0.

Olson, R. 'Kurds and Turks: Two Documents Concerning Kurdish Autonomy in 1922 and 1923', *Journal of South Asian and Middle Eastern Studies* 15/2, 1991.

Olson, R. *The Emergence of Kurdish Nationalism and the Sheikh Said Rebellion, 1880–1925*. Austin, 1989.

Ozavci, O. *Dangerous Gifts: Imperialism, Security, and Civil Wars in the Levant, 1798–1864*. Oxford, 2021.

Özoğlu, H. 'Exaggerating and Exploiting the Sheikh Said Rebellion of 1925 for Political Gains', *New Perspectives on Turkey* 41, 2009, 181–210.

'Reflections on the Mosul Problem', *Journal of The Royal Central Asian Society* 13/4, 1926, 350–364.

Rogers, J. 'The Foreign Policy of Small States: Sweden and the Mosul Crisis, 1924–1925', *Contemporary European History* 16/3, 2007, 349–369.

Scott, J. *The Art of Not Being Governed: An Anarchist History of Upland Southeast Asia*, New Haven, 2009.

Taha, M. 'Nation and Class Subjectivity in International Law and Its Institutions in the Middle East (1919–1939)', Law thesis, University of Toronto, Toronto, 2015.

Tejel, J. 'Making Borders from Below: The Emergence of the Turkish–Iraqi Frontier, 1918–1925', *Middle Eastern Studies* 54/5, 2018, 1–16.

The National Archives of the UK, Public Record Office, Foreign Office.

'Treaty of Peace with Turkey', Treaty Series No. 11, 1920. https://treaties.fcdo.gov.uk/awweb/pdfopener?md=1&did=63986.

Venn, F. 'Oleaginous Diplomacy: Oil, Anglo–American Relations and the Lausanne Conference, 1922–23', *Diplomacy & Statecraft* 20/3, 2009, 414–433.

Weitz, E. 'From the Vienna to the Paris System: International Politics and the Entangled Histories of Human Rights, Forced Deportations, and Civilizing Missions', *The American Historical Review* 113/5, 2008, 1313–1343.

Wright, Q. 'The Mosul Dispute', *The American Journal of International Law* 20/3, 1926, 453–464.

CHAPTER 10

'Affaire de la dette publique ottomane (Bulgarie, Irak, Palestine, Transjordanie, Grèce, Italie et Turquie), 18 avril 1925', *Recueil des Sentences Arbitrales*, Vol. I, New York, 2006, 529–614.

Alphand, H. *Le Partage de la Dette Ottomane et Son Règlement*, Paris, 1928.

Birdal, M. *The Political Economy of Ottoman Public Debt: Insolvency and European Financial Control in the Late Nineteenth Century*, London, 2010.

Blaisdell, D. *European Financial Control in the Ottoman Empire: A Study of the Establishment, Activities and Significance of the Administration of the Ottoman Public Debt*, New York, 1966 (originally published 1929).

Cahid, H. 'Siyasiyat: Düyun-ı umumiye müessesesinin namusuyla oynamamalı', *Tanin*, 4 December 1922.

Cavid, M. *Meşrutiyet Ruznâmesi*, Ankara, 2015.

Conférence de Lausanne sur les Affaires du Proche-Orient (1922–1923). Recueil des Actes de la Conférence. Deuxième Série, Tome I: Procès-Verbaux et Documents Relatifs à la Seconde Partie de la Conférence (23 Avril-24 Juillet 1923), Paris, 1923.

Eldem, V. *Harp ve Mütareke Yıllarında Osmanlı İmparatorluğu'nun Ekonimisi*, Ankara, 1994.

Feilchenfeld, E.H. *Public Debts and State Succession*, New York, 1931.

Hershlag, Z.Y. *Turkey: The Challenge of Growth*, Leiden, 1968.

Hoeflich, M.H. 'Through a Glass Darkly: Reflections upon the History of the International Law of Public Debt in Connection with State Succession', *University of Illinois Law Review* 1, 1982, 39–70.

İnönü, İ. *İsmet İnönü'nün Hatıraları: Büyük Zaferden Sonra Mudanya Mütarekesi ve Lozan Antlaşması*, Istanbul, 1998.

Jèze, G. *Le Partage des Dettes Publiques au Cas de Démembrement du Territoire*, Paris, 1921.

Kayalı, H. 'Elections and the electoral process in the Ottoman Empire, 1876–1919', *International Journal of Middle East Studies* 27/3, 1995, 265–286.

Landon-Lane, J. and Oosterlinck, K. 'Hope Springs Eternal… French Bondholders and the Soviet Repudiation', Working Paper CEB 05–013.RS, Université Libre de Bruxelles, Brussels, 2005.

'Lausanne and the Ottoman Debt', *The Economist*, 28 July 1923, 151.

Lausanne Conference on Near Eastern Affairs, 1922–1923: Records of Proceedings and Draft Terms of Peace, London, 1923.

'Lozan sulh konferansı muhabir-i mahsusumuzun işaratı: Pazar ertesi 27 teşrin-i sani: Maliye komisyonu', *İkdam*, 3 December 1922.

Medlicott, W.N., Dakin, D. and Lambert, M.E. eds. *Documents on British Foreign Policy 1919–1939. First Series, Vol. XVIII: Greece and Turkey, September 3, 1922 – July 24, 1923*, London, 1972.

Meray, S.L. ed. *Lozan Barış Konferansı: Tutanaklar Belgeler, Birinci Takım Cilt III*, Istanbul, 1993.

Moore, L. and Kaluzny, J. 'Regime change and debt default: the case of Russia, Austro-Hungary, and the Ottoman Empire following World War One', *Explorations in Economic History* 42, 2005, 237–258.

Nur, R. *Hayat ve Hatıratım*, Istanbul, 1967.

Oran, B. 'Lausanne Barış Antlaşması' in Oran, B. ed., *Türk Dış Politikası: Kurtuluş Savaşından Bugüne Olgular, Belgeler, Yorumlar. Cilt I: 1919–1980*, Istanbul, 2001, 215–238.

Öktem, E. 'Turkey: Successor or Continuing State of the Ottoman Empire?', *Leiden Journal of International Law* 24, 2011, 561–583.

Pamuk, Ş. 'The Ottoman Economy in World War I' in Broadberry, S. et al. eds., *The Economics of World War I*, Cambridge (UK), 2005.

Sack, A.N. *Les Effets des Transformations des États sur leurs Dettes Publiques*, Paris, 1927.

Saraçoğlu, Ş. 'Borçlar meselesinin halli', *Ülkü Halkevleri Mecmuası* 1/5, 1933, 337–344.

Sıtkı, İ. *La Répartition de la Dette Publique Ottomane par les Traités de Paix*, Paris, 1935.

Şimşir, B.N. ed. *Lozan Telgrafları I*, Ankara, 1990.

Şimşir, B.N. ed. *Lozan Telgrafları II*, Ankara, 1994.

T.B.M.M. Gizli Celse Zabıtları, Devre 1, Cilt 28, İctima Senesi 3, 3 March 1923.

T.B.M.M. Gizli Celse Zabıtları, Devre 1, Cilt 28, İctima Senesi 3, 4 March 1923.

T.B.M.M. Gizli Celse Zabıtları, Devre 1, Cilt 28, İctima Senesi 3, 6 March 1923.

T.B.M.M. Zabıt Ceridesi, Devre 1, Cilt 24, İctima Senesi 3, 3 November 1922.

T.B.M.M. Zabıt Ceridesi, Devre 2, Cilt 1, İctima Senesi 4, 22 August 1923.

T.B.M.M. Zabıt Ceridesi, Devre 2, Cilt 1, İctima Senesi 4, 23 August 1923.

Temiz, A. 'Velid Ebuzziya'nın Mektuplarına Göre Lozan', MA thesis, Marmara University, Istanbul, 2005.

'Turkey: Trade Agreements – Budget Balanced – Interest Rates', *The Economist*, 3 June 1933, 1191.
Türk Tarihi Tetkik Cemiyeti, *Tarih IV: Türkiye Cümhuriyeti*, Istanbul, 1931.
Wynne, W.H. *State Insolvency and Foreign Bondholders, Volume II: Selected Case Histories of Governmental Foreign Bond Defaults and Debt Readjustments*, New Haven, 1951.

CHAPTER 11

Primary Sources

Published Documents

'Convention Between Greece and Bulgaria Respecting Reciprocal Emigration, 27 November 1919', *American Journal of International Law* 14/4, 1920, Supplement: Official Documents, 356–360.

'Convention Concerning the Exchange of Greek and Turkish Populations, 30 January 1923', *American Journal of International Law* 18/2, 1924, Supplement: Official Documents, 84–90.

Department of State, *Papers Relating to the Foreign Relations of the United States, 1919: The Paris Peace Conference,* 13 Vols., Washington D.C., 1942–1947.

Lausanne Conference on Near Eastern Affairs, 1922–1923: Records of Proceedings and Draft Terms of Peace, London, 1923.

Ministère des Affaires Étrangers. *Conférence de Lausanne*, 2 Vols., Paris, 1923.

'Treaty of Peace Between the Allied Powers and Turkey, 10 August 1920', *American Journal of International Law* 15/3, 1921, Supplement, Official Documents, 179–295.

Secondary Sources

Busch, B.C. *Mudros to Lausanne: Britain's Frontier in West Asia, 1918–1923*, Albany, 1976.

Clark, B. *Twice a Stranger: The Mass Expulsions that Forged Modern Greece and Turkey*, Cambridge (USA), 2006.

Craig, G. and Gilbert, F. eds. *The Diplomats, 1919–1939*, Princeton, 1953.

Dragostinova, T. *Between Two Motherlands: Nationality and Emigration among the Greeks of Bulgaria, 1900–1949*, Ithaca, 2011.

Dragostinova, T. 'Navigating Nationality in the Emigration of Minorities between Bulgaria and Greece, 1919–1941', *East European Politics and Societies* 23/2, 2009, 185–212.

Dragostinova, T. 'Speaking National: Nationalizing the Greeks of Bulgaria', *Slavic Review* 67/1, 2008, 154–181.

Fortna, B.C. ed. *State-nationalisms in the Ottoman Empire: Greece and Turkey, Orthodox and Muslims, 1830–1945*, London, 2013.

Goldstein, E. and McKercher, B.J.C. eds. *Power and Stability: British Foreign Policy, 1865–1945*, London, 2003.

Güçlü, Y. 'The Struggle for Mastery in Cilicia: Turkey, France, and the Ankara Agreement of 1921', *International History Review* 23/3, 2001, 580–603.

Hirschon, R. ed. *Crossing the Aegean: An Appraisal of the 1923 Compulsory Population Exchange between Greece and Turkey*, New York, 2003.

Ladas, S.P. *The Exchange of Minorities: Bulgaria, Greece and Turkey*, New York, 1932.

McNair, Lord A. *The Law of Treaties*, Oxford, 1961 (originally published 1938).

Miller, D.H. ed. *My Diary at the Conference of Paris*, New York, 1924.

Meindersma, C. 'Population Exchanges: International Law and State Practice', *International Journal of Refugee Law* 9, 1997, Part I, 9/3, 335–363; Part II, 9/4, 613–653.

Özsu, U. *Formalizing Displacement: International Law and Population Transfers*, Oxford, 2015.

Pallis, A.A. 'Racial Migrations in the Balkans during the Years 1912–1924', *Geographical Journal* 66/4, 1925, 315–331.

Papadaki, M. 'The 'Government Intellectuals': Nicolas Politis – An Intellectual Portrait', *European Journal of International Law* 23/1, 2012, 221–231.

Payk, M. 'The History of International Law – or International Law in History? A Reply to Alexandra Kemmerer and Jochen von Bernstorff', https://www.ejiltalk.org/the-history-of-international-law-or-international-law-in-history-a-reply-to-alexandra-kemmerer-and-jochen-von-bernstorff/.

Payk, M. *Frieden durch Recht? Der Aufsteig des modernen Vökerrechts und der Friedensschluss nach dem Ersten Weltkrieg,* Berlin, 2018.

Payk, M. "What We Seek Is the Reign of Law': The Legalism of the Paris Peace Settlement after the Great War', *European Journal of International Law* 29/3, 2018, 809–824.

Prott, V. *The Politics of Self-Determination: Remaking Territories and National Identities in Europe, 1917–1923*, Oxford, 2016.

Smith, L.V. *Sovereignty at the Paris Peace Conference of 1919*, Oxford, 2018.

Ther, P. *The Dark Side of Nation States: Ethnic Cleansing in Modern Europe*, New York, 2014.

Ünlü, N. *The Legal Regime of the Turkish Straits*, Leiden, 2002.

Weitz, E. 'From the Vienna to the Paris System: International Politics, and the Entangled Histories of Human Rights, Forced Deportations, and Civilizing Missions', *The American Historical Review* 113/5, 2008, 1313–1343.

Yildirim, O. *Diplomacy and Displacement: Reconsidering the Turko-Greek Exchange of Populations, 1922–1934*, New York, 2006.

CHAPTER 12

Alexander, B. 'Armenian and American: The Changing Face of Ethnic Identity and Diasporic Nationalism, 1915–1955', PhD dissertation, CUNY, New York, 2005.

Bet-Shlimon, A. *City of Black Gold: Oil, Ethnicity, and the Making of Modern Kirkuk*, Stanford, 2019.

Burk, K. *Britain, America, and the Sinews of War*, Boston, 1985.

Cabanes, B. *The Great War and the Origins of Humanitarianism, 1918–1924*, New York, 2014.

Clavin, P. *Securing the World Economy: The Reinvention of the League of Nations, 1920–1946*, Oxford, 2013.

Easton-Calabria, E. 'From Bottom-Up to Top-Down: The 'Pre-History' of Refugee Livelihoods Assistance from 1919 to 1979', *Journal of Refugee Studies* 28/3, 2015, 412–436.

Fink, C. *The Genoa Conference: European Diplomacy, 1921–1922*, Chapel Hill, 1984.

Gatrell, P. 'Displacing and Re-placing Population in the Two World Wars: Armenia and Poland Compared', *Contemporary European History* 16/4, 2007, 511–527.

Gatrell, P. *The Making of the Modern Refugee*, Oxford, 2013.

Gracey, G. 'Armenian Settlement in Syria', *Contemporary Review* 140, 1931, 85–93.

Grahl-Madsen, A. 'The League of Nations and the Refugees' in Angenendt, A. ed., *The League of Nations in Retrospect,* Berlin, 2010.

Hieronymi, O. 'The Nansen Passport: A Tool of Freedom of Movement and of Protection', *Refugee Survey Quarterly* 22/1, 2003, 36–47.

Hill, M. 'The League of Nations and the Work of Refugee Settlement and Financial Reconstruction in Greece', *Journal of Institutional and Theoretical Economics* 34, 1931, 265–283.

International Labour Office. *The Labour Provisions of the Peace Treaties*, Geneva, 1920.

League of Nations. *Minutes of the Sessions of the GB of the ILO*, https://www.ilo.org/public/libdoc/ilo/P/09601/.

League of Nations. *Official Journal*, Vol. IV, Geneva, 1923.

League of Nations. *League of Nations Treaty Series*, Vol. 89, Geneva, 1929.

League of Nations. *Record of Proceedings, International Labour Conference*, Geneva, 1919.

Lohr, E. *Russian Citizenship: From Empire to Soviet Union*, Cambridge (USA), 2012.

Robson, L. *States of Separation: Transfer, Partition, and the Making of the Modern Middle East*, Oakland, 2017.

Simpson, J.H. *The Refugee Problem: Report of a Survey*, London, 1939.

Watenpaugh, K.D. *Bread from Stones: The Middle East and the Making of Modern Humanitarianism*, Oakland, 2015.

World Peace Foundation. *Report on the Brussels Financial Conference,* Boston, 1920.

CHAPTER 13

Primary Sources

Archives

Archives of Anatolia College, Thessaloniki.
Archives of St. Joseph College, Istanbul.
Diplomatic and Historical Archives of the Hellenic Ministry of Foreign Affairs, Athens.
Eleftherios Venizelos Archives, Chania.
Emmanuel Tsouderos Archives, Bank of Greece, Athens.
French National Archives, Pierrefitte sur Seine.
General State Archives – Central Service, Ayrilios Spatharis Archive, Athens.
Institute for Neohellenic Research, Modern Greek Visual Prosopography, Collection of Andreas Spatharis, Athens.
League of Nations Archives, Geneva.
The Hellenic Literary and Historical Archive, Athens.

Published Documents

Treaty Series No.16 (1923). Cmd. 1929. Treaty of Peace with Turkey and Other Instruments, Signed at Lausanne on July 24, 1923, together with Agreements between Greece and Turkey signed on January 30, 1923, and Subsidiary Documents forming part of the Turkish Peace Settlement, London, 1923.
Turkey No.1 (1923). Cmd. 1814. Lausanne Conference on Near Eastern Affairs, 1922–1923: Records of Proceedings and Draft Terms of Peace, London, 1923.

Periodicals

I Etymigoria tou Laou [Athens].
Icho [Constantinople].
La Méditerranée Orientale: revue bi-mensuelle politique, historique, scientifique [Paris].
Neon Pneyma [Constantinople].
Politeia [Athens].
Politiki Epitheorisis [Constantinople].
Proodos [Constantinople].

Interviews

Recorded interview with Rika Aghnides. Conducted by Markos A. Bouketsidis-Skourtelis, 14 September 2019.

Secondary Sources

Aghnides, Th. 'Vladimir Rosing and Greek Music', *The Musical Times*, 1 June 1918.

Aghnides, Th. 'Greek Art Itself Again', *The New World*, n.d.

Aghnides, Th. *The Ecumenical Patriarchate of Constantinople in the Light of the Treaty of Lausanne*, New York, 1964.

Alexandris, A. *The Greek Minority of Istanbul and Greek-Turkish Relations 1918–1974*, Athens, 1992 (originally published 1983).

Almagor, L. et al. eds. 'Introduction' in Almagor, L. et al. eds., *Global Biographies. Lived History as Method*, Manchester, 2022, 1–22.

Anestidis, S. Th. *Πατριαρχικής Μεγάλης του Γένους Σχολή Πάνθεον. Δεκαεπτά Προσωπογραφίες,* Athens, 2019.

Berkes, N. *The Development of Secularism in Turkey,* New York, 1998.

Boura, K. 'Οι βουλευτικές εκλογές στην Οθωμανική Αυτοκρατορία: Οι Έλληνες βουλευτές 1908–1918', *Bulletin of the Centre for Asia Minor Studies* 4, 1983, 69–85.

De Tapia, A.A. 'Orthodox Christians and Muslims of Cappadocia: Intercommunal Relations in an Ottoman Rural Context (1839–1923)', unpublished PhD dissertation, Istanbul, 2016.

Drange, M. 'Supervisor, Facilitator and Arbitrator. A Study of the Minority Department in the League of Nations Involvement in the Forced Population Exchange between Greece and Turkey in 1923', unpublished MA thesis, Oslo, 2017.

Εκπαιδευτική Ελληνική Εγκυκλοπαίδεια – Παγκόσμιο Βιογραφικό Λεξικό, Athens, 1991.

Fortna, B.C. *Imperial Classroom: Islam, the State, and Education in the Late Ottoman Empire*, Oxford, 2002.

Γενικοί Κανονισμοί περί Διευθετήσεως των Εκκλησιαστικών και Εθνικών Πραγμάτων των υπό τον Οικουμενικόν Θρόνον Διατελούντων Ορθοδόξων Χριστιανών, Υπηκόων της Α. Μεγαλειότητος του Σουλτάνου, Constantinople, 1862.

Gram-Skjoldager, K. and Ikonomou, H.A. 'The League of Nations Secretariat – An Experiment in Liberal Internationalism?', *Monde(s) – Histoire, Espaces, Relations*, 19/1, 2021, 31–50.

Güven, D. *6–7 Eylül Olayları: Cumhuriyet Dönemi Azınlık Politikaları ve Stratejileri Bağlamında*, Istanbul, 2005.

Iatrides, J.O. 'Introduction' in McGrew, W., *Educating across cultures – Anatolia College in Turkey and Greece*, London, 2015.

Ikonomou, H.A. 'The biography as institutional can-opener: An investigation of core bureaucratic practices in the early years of the League of Nations Secretariat' in Gram-Skjoldager, K. et al. eds., *Organizing the 20th Century World: International Organizations and the Emergence of International Public Administration, 1920s-1960s*, London, 2020, 33–48.

Ikonomou, H.A. 'Wilsonian Moments: Thanassis Aghnides between Empire and Nation State' in Almagor, L. et al. eds., *Global Biographies. Lived History as Method*, Manchester, 2022, 25–43.

Kamouzis, D. 'Elites and the formation of national identity. The case of the Greek Orthodox *millet* (mid-nineteenth century to 1922)' in Fortna, B.C. et al. eds., *State-Nationalisms in the Ottoman Empire, Greece and Turkey: Orthodox and Muslims, 1830–1945*, Oxford, 2013, 13–46.

Kamouzis, D. 'A minority in a state of flux: Greek self-administration and education in post-Lausanne Istanbul, ca. 1923–1930' in Fortna, B.C. et al. eds., *State-Nationalisms in the Ottoman Empire, Greece and Turkey: Orthodox and Muslims, 1830–1945*, Oxford, 2013, 101–131.

Kamouzis, D. 'Incorporating the Ecumenical Patriarchate into Modern Turkey: The Legacy of the 1924 Patriarchal Election' in Lytra, V. ed., *When Greeks and Turks Meet: Interdisciplinary Perspectives on the Relationship Since 1923,* London, 2014, 227–249.

Kamouzis, D. 'Out of Harm's Way? Structural Violence and the Greek Orthodox Community of Istanbul during World War I', *Journal of the Ottoman and Turkish Studies Association* 4/1, 2017, 189–211.

Kamouzis, D. *Greeks in Turkey: Elite Nationalism and Minority Politics in Late Ottoman and Early Republican Istanbul*, Oxford, 2021.

Kasianis, E. Th. *Ανδρέας Σπαθάρης. Ο Φαναριώτης Διδάσκαλος του Γένους και Ποιητής 1837–1901*, Athens, 1976.

Kesisoglou-Karystinou, M. 'Από το Τανζιμάτ στη Μικρασιατική Καταστροφή. Γεγονότα, Επιδράσεις και Επιπτώσεις στην Ενορία του Τζιμπαλί', *Η καθημερινή ζωή στην Κωνσταντινούπολη στο τέλος του 19ου και στις αρχές του 20ού αιώνα*, Athens, 1999, 159–178.

Kremmydas, V. *Οι Μεγαλοσχολίτες (1863–1974)*, Athens, 2007.

Mavropoulos, D. *Πατριαρχικαί σελίδες: Το Οικουμενικόν Πατριαρχείον από 1878–1949*, Athens, 1960.

Μεγάλη Ελληνική Εγκυκλοπαίδεια, Athens, n.d.

Michel, A. Frère. *Histoire de St. Joseph, 1870–1923*, Istanbul, 2003.

Ο εν Κωνσταντινουπόλει Ελληνικός Φιλολογικός Σύλλογος. Σύγγραμμα Περιοδικόν. Τόμος ΛΒ'. Συλλογικά Έτη ΜΗ' και ΜΘ' 1908–1910, Constantinople, 1911.

Papoulidis, K. 'Συμπληρωματικά στοιχεία για το Συνόδη και την Αιμιλία Παπαδημητρίου', *Makedonika* 18, 1978, 295–300.

Pelt, M. 'Bodosakis-Athanasiadis, a Greek Businessman from the East. A Case Study of an Ottoman Structure in Interwar Greece and the Interrelationship between State and Business' in Andersen, L.E. ed., *Middle East Studies in Denmark*, Odense, 1994, 65–81.

Rizzo, A. ed. *1914 Annuaire Oriental – Oriental Directory. Commerce, Industrie, Administration, Magistrature*, Constantinople, 1921.

Smith, M.L. 'Venizelos' Diplomacy, 1910–23: From Balkan Alliance to Greek-Turkish Settlement' in Kitromilides, P.M. ed., *Eleftherios Venizelos. The Trials of Statesmanship*, Edinburgh, 2006, 134–192.

Souliotis-Nikolaidis, A. *Οργάνωσις Κωνσταντινουπόλεως*, Athens, 1984.

Spatharis, A. *Ο Ιδιαίτερος Προσωπικός Θεσμός του Ελληνορθοδόξου Τούρκου Υπηκόου (Άρθρον 42 Συνθήκης Λωζάννης) – Η Νομική Κατάστασις του Οικουμενικού Πατριαρχείου*, Athens, 1947.

Spatharis, A. *Το Οικουμενικόν Πατριαρχείον. Αιωνόβιος Πανορθόδοξος Θεσμός*, Athens, 1958.

Tarinas S. D. *Ο Ελληνικός Τύπος της Πόλης. Α' Μέρος – Εφημερίδες*, Istanbul, 2007.

Vryonis, S. *The Mechanism of Catastrophe: The Turkish Pogrom of September 6–7, 1955, and the Destruction of the Greek Community of Istanbul*, New York, 2005.

CHAPTER 14

Adıvar, H.E. *Memoirs*, London, 1926.

Afetinan, A. *L'Anatolie, le pays de la 'race' turque: recherches sur les caractères anthropologiques des populations de la Turquie, enquête sur 64.000 individus*, Geneva, 1941.

Agayef (alias Ağaoğlu), A. 'Türk medeniyeti tarihi', *Türk Yurdu*, Ankara, 1999, 303–307.

Agayef (alias Ağaoğlu), A. *Pontus Meselesi*, Ankara, 1922.

Akyol, T. and Kaplan, S. eds. *Açık ve Gizli Oturumlarda Lozan Tartışmaları: TBMM'de Lozan Müzakereleri Tutanakları*, Istanbul, 2014.

Albrecht-Carrié, R. *France, Europe and the Two World Wars*, Geneva, 1969 (originally published 1960).

Ardıç, N. '*Islam and the Politics of Secularism: The Caliphate and Middle Eastern Modernization in the Early 20th Century*, London, 2012.

Banken, R. *Die Verträge von Sèvres 1920 und Lausanne 1923: Eine völkerrechtliche Untersuchung zur Beendigung des Ersten Weltkrieges und zur Auflösung der sogenannten 'Orientalischen Frage'*, Berlin, 2014.

Bauman, Z. *Modernity and the Holocaust,* Cambridge (UK), 1989.

Bayur, Y.H. *Türk inkılâbı tarihi*, Ankara, 1991 (originally published 1940).

Bozkurt, M. 'Türk Medenî Kanunu nasıl hazırlandı?', *Medenî kanunun XV. yıl dönümü için,* Istanbul, 1944, 7–20.

Çankaya, A. *Yeni Mülkiye Târihi ve Mülkiyeliler,* Ankara, 1968–1969.

Cohen, J.P. 'A Model *Millet*? Ottoman Jewish Citizenship at the End of Empire' in Green, A. et al. eds., *Jews, Liberalism, Antisemitism: A Global History*, London, 2020, 209–231.

Conférence de Lausanne sur les affaires du Proche-Orient (1922–1923). Recueil des actes de la conférence, Paris, 1923.

Conlin, J. 'An Oily Entente: France, Britain, and the Mosul Question, 1916–1925', *Diplomacy & Statecraft* 31/2, 2020, 231–256.

Demiriz, S. *Vom Osmanen zum Türken: Nationale und staatsbürgerliche Erziehung durch Feier- und Gedenktage in der Türkischen Republik 1923–1938,* Baden-Baden, 2018.

Freely, J. *A Bridge of Culture: Robert College – Boğaziçi University: How an American College in Istanbul Became A Turkish University*, Istanbul, 2012.

Gennai, A. *La Question d'Orient: La gestion multilatérale de la Dette Publique Ottomane*, MA thesis, University of Geneva, Geneva, 2015.

Göçek, F.M. *The transformation of Turkey: redefining state and society from the Ottoman Empire to the modern era,* London, 2011.

Gökalp, Z. *Türkçülüğün esasları*, Istanbul, 2014.

Hale, W. *Turkish Foreign Policy since 1774*, London, 2013.

İnönü, İ. *İsmet İnönü'nün Hatıraları,* Istanbul, 1998.

Kaiser, H. *The extermination of Armenians in the Diarbekir* region, Istanbul, 2014.

Kalman, M. *Belge ve Tanıklarıyla Dersim Direnişleri,* Istanbul, 1995.

Kara-Schemsi (alias Atabinen, R.S.). *L'extermination des Turcs*, Geneva, 1919.

Katchznouni, H., *The Armenian Revolutionary Federation Has Nothing to Do Anymore. The Manifesto*, New York, 1955.

Kemal, M. *Nutuk*, Istanbul, 2015.

Khatissian, A. *Éclosion et développement de la République arménienne*, Athens, 1989.

Kalman, M. *Belge ve Tanıklarıyla Dersim Direnişleri,* Istanbul, 1995.

Kieser, H.-L. 'Macro et micro histoire autour de la Conférence sur le Proche-Orient tenue à Lausanne en 1922–23', *Mémoire vive. Pages d'histoire lausannoise* 13, Lausanne, 2004, 42–48.

Kieser, H.-L. 'Die Herausbildung des türkisch-nationalen Geschichtsdiskurses (spätes 19.–Mitte 20. Jahrhundert)' in Krzoska, M. et al. eds., *Vom Beruf zur Berufung. Geschichtswissenschaft und Nationsbildung in Ostmittel- und Südosteuropa im 19. und 20. Jahrhundert*, Münster, 2005, 59–98.

Kieser, H.-L., Meier, A., Stoffel, W., eds. *Revolution islamischen Rechts: Das Schweizerische ZGB in der Türkei*, Zürich, 2008.

Kieser, H.-L. *Türklüğe İhtida. 1870–1939 İsviçre'sinde Yeni Türkiye'nin öncüleri*, Istanbul, 2008.

Kieser, H.-L., Polatel, M., Schmutz, T. 'Reform or cataclysm? The agreement of 8 February 1914 regarding the Ottoman eastern provinces', *Journal of Genocide Research* 17/3, 2015, 285–304.

Kieser, H.-L. 'Europe's Seminal Proto-Fascist? Historically Approaching Ziya Gökalp, Mentor of Turkish Nationalism', *Die Welt des Islams* 61, 2021, 411–447.

Köprülü, M.F. *Türkiya Tarihi: Anadolu istilasina kadar Türkler*, Istanbul, 1923.

Kraft-Bonnard, A. *L'Arménie à la Conférence de Lausanne*, Lausanne, 1923.

Kraft-Bonnard, A. *Arménie, Suisse et Société des Nations*, Geneva, 1924.

Kraft-Bonnard, A. *Arménie, justice et reparation*, Geneva, 1924.

Lewis, B. *The Emergence of Modern Turkey,* Oxford, 1961.

Lausanne Conference on Near Eastern Affairs 1922–1923: Records of Proceedings and Draft Terms of Peace, London, 1923.

Montebello, C. *Eugène Pittard, un anthropologue genevois en Turquie nationaliste (1910–1950): idéologie d'exclusion, corruption intellectuelle et logiques sociales*, Paris, 2016.

Mısıroğlu, K. *Lozan: Zafer mi, hezimet mi?*, Istanbul, 1992.

Nur, R. *Hayat ve Hatıratım*, Istanbul, 1992.

Nur, R. *Türk Tarihi*, Istanbul, 1994.

Nigolian, S., Roman, P. eds. *Sauver les enfants, sauver l'Arménie: la contribution du pasteur Antony Kraft-Bonnard (1919–1945)*, Lausanne, 2020.

Oran, B. *Türkiye'de azınlıklar. kavramlar, teori. Lozan, iç mevzuat, içtihat, uygulama*, Istanbul, 2004.

Özyürek, M. ed. *Akşam Gazetesi Başyazarı Necmeddin Sadık (Sadak) Bey'in Lozan Mektupları*, Ankara, 2019.

Sajid, M. *Muslime im Zwischenkriegseuropa und die Dekonstruktion der Faszination vom Westen. Eine kritische Auseinandersetzung mit Šakīb ʾArslāns Artikeln in der ägyptischen Zeitschrift al-Fatḥ (1926–1935)*, Berlin, 2015.

Sauser-Hall, G. *La réception des droits européens en Turquie*, Geneva, 1938.

Scheuermann, M. *Minderheitenschutz contra Konfliktverhütung?,* Marburg, 2000.

Silopi, Z. *Doza Kürdistan: Kürt Milletinin 60 Yıllık Esaretten Kurtuluş Savaşı Hatıraları*, Ankara, 1991.

Şimşir, B.N. ed. *Lozan Telgrafları I*, Ankara, 1990.

Steiner, Z. *The Lights that Failed. European International History 1919–1933*, Oxford, 2007.

Thobie, J. *Intérêts et impérialisme français dans l'Empire ottoman, 1895–1914,* Paris, 1977.

Toufayan, M. 'Empathy, humanity and the 'Armenian Question' in the internationalist legal imagination', *Revue québécoise de droit international* 24, 2011, 171–191.

Toynbee, A.J., *The Western Question in Greece and Turkey: A Study in the Contact of Civilisations,* London, 1922.

Tusan, M. 'Crimes against Humanity': Human Rights, the British Empire, and the Origins of the Response to the Armenian Genocide', *The American Historical Review* 119/1, 2014, 47–77.

Uğur Ü. 'Disastrous decade: Armenians and Kurds in the Young Turk Era, 1915–25' in Jongerden, J. et al. eds., *Social relations in Ottoman Diyarbekir, 1870–1915*, Leiden, 2012, 267–295.

Uras, E. *The Armenians in History and the Armenian Question*, Istanbul, 1988.

CHAPTER 15

70. Yılında Lozan Barış Antlaşması, 25–26 Ekim [October] *1993*, Ankara, 1994.

80. Yılında Lozan Barış Antlaşması, 24 Temmuz [July] *2003*, Istanbul, 2003.

90. Yılında Lozan, Istanbul, 2014.

A Speech delivered by Mustafa Kemal Atatürk (1927), Istanbul, 1963.

Akyol, T. and Kaplan, S. *Açık ve Gizli Oturumlarda Lozan Tartışmaları*, Istanbul, 2013.

Armağan, M. *Efsaneler ve Gerçekler*, Istanbul, 2013.

Armağan, M. *Yakın Tarihin Kara Delikleri*, Istanbul, 2014.

Armağan, M. *Cumhuriyet Efsaneleri*, Istanbul, 2014.

Armağan, M. *Paşaların Hesaplaşması*, Istanbul, 2014.

Armağan, M. *Korku Duvarını Yıkmak*, Istanbul, 2014.

Armağan, M. *Öncesi ve Sonrasıyla Tek Parti Devri*, Istanbul, 2015.

Armağan, M. *Satılık İmparatorluk: Lozan ve Osmanlının Reddedilen Mirası*, Istanbul, 2016.

Armağan, M. *Kızıl Pençe: Karabekir'in Gözüyle Kuruluş Yılları (1922–1933)*, Istanbul, 2016.

Atilhan, C.R. *İslamı Saran Tehlike ve Siyonizm*, Istanbul, 1950 and 1955.

Ayvazoğlu, B. 'Ah, O Eski Ülkücüler', *Türkiye Günlüğü* 50, 1998, 179–182.

Baer, M.D. 'An Enemy Old and New: The Dönme, Anti-Semitism, and Conspiracy Theories in the Ottoman Empire and Turkish Republic', *Jewish Quarterly Review* 103/4, 2013, 523–555.

Bali, R.N. 'Cevat Rıfat Atilhan', *Modern Türkiye'de Siyasi Düşünce: Muhafazakârlık*, Istanbul, 2009, 402–406.

Bediüzzaman, S.N. *Risale-i Nur Külliyatı*, Istanbul, 2002.

Benbassa, E. *Haim Nahum: A Sephardic Chief Rabbi in Politics (1892–1923)*, Tuscaloosa, 1995.

Bora, T. 'Nationalist Discourses in Turkey', *South Atlantic Quarterly* 102/2–3, 2003, 433–451.

Cevizoğlu, H. and İlhan, A. *Bütün Kaleler Zaptedilmedi*, Ankara, 2004.

Ceylan, H.H. *Büyük Oyun*, Ankara, 1995.

Cornell, S.E. 'Erbakan, Kısakürek, and the Mainstreaming of Extremism in Turkey', *Current Trends in Islamist Ideology*, Washington D.C., 2018.

Çalık, M. *MHP Hareketinin Kaynakları ve Gelişimi (1965–1980)*, Ankara, 1995.

Çetinsaya, G. 'Abdülhamid'i Anlamak: 19. Yüzyıl Tarihçiliğine Bir Bakış', *Sosyal Bilimleri Yeniden Düşünmek: Toplum-Bilim ve Defter Dergileri Sempozyum Bildirileri*, Istanbul, 2001, 137–146.

Çetinsaya, G. '2000'li Yılların Başlarında Türk Siyasi Hayatını Açıklayabilecek Bir Anahtar: Küreselleşme', *Türkiye Günlüğü* 97, 2009, 46–51.

Çınar, A. and Taş, H. 'Politics of Nationhood and the Displacement of the Founding Moment: Contending Histories of the Turkish Nation', *Comparative Studies in Society and History* 59/3, 2017, 657–689.

Dağı, İ.D. *Kimlik, Söylem ve Siyaset: Doğu Batı Ayrımında Refah Partisi Geleneği*, Ankara, 1998.

Demirel, A. *Birinci Meclis'te Muhalefet: İkinci Grup*, Istanbul, 1994.

Dilipak, A. *Cumhuriyete Giden Yol*, Istanbul, 2017.

Dilipak, A. *İnönü Dönemi*, Istanbul, 1988.

Doğan, M.D. *Batılılaşma İhaneti*, Ankara, 2015.

Doğan, M.D. *Mağlubiyet İdeolojisinin Sonu*, Ankara, 2007.

Duran, B. 'Transformation of Islamist Political Thought in Turkey: from the Empire to the Early Republic (1908–1960): Necip Fazıl Kısakürek's Political Ideas', PhD dissertation, Bilkent University, Ankara, 2001.

Erdoğan, E. 'The Sèvres Syndrome: A Key to Understand Foreign Policy Attitudes of Turkish Citizens', *Journal of Middle Eastern Politics and Policy*, 2021, 36–43.

Gayrıresmi Yakın Tarih Ansiklopedisi, Istanbul, 1993.

Genç, K. 'Reading Between the Lines: The Slow Reveal of Recep Tayyip Erdoğan's Grandiose Vision', *World Policy Journal* 35/2, 2018, 47–55.

Göçek, F.M. 'The Politics of History and Memory: A Multidimensional Analysis of the Lausanne Peace Conference (1922–23)' in Erdem, H. et al. eds., *Histories of the Modern Middle East: New Directions*, New York, 2000, 207–228.

Göçek, F.M. 'Why is there Still a Sèvres Syndrome? An analysis of Turkey's Uneasy Association with the West', *The Transformation of Turkey. Redefining State and Society from the Ottoman Empire to the Modern Era*, New York, 2011, 98–184.

Gökgöz, G. 'Belleklerden Silinmeye Yüz Tutan Bir Gün: Lozan Sulh Bayramı', *Çağdaş Türkiye Tarihi Araştırmaları Dergisi* 10/22, 2011, 95–114.

Guida, M. 'The Sèvres Syndrome and 'Komplo' Theories in the Islamist and Secular Press', *Turkish Studies* 9, 2007, 37–52.

Gülen, A. 'Demokrat Parti Döneminde Lozan Algısı', *Atatürk Yolu Dergisi* 14/53, 2013, 77–100.

Gürpınar, D. *Conspiracy Theories in Turkey: Conspiracy Nation*, New York, 2020.

İnan, A. *Türk İstiklali ve Lozan Muahedesi*, Istanbul, 1938.

İnönü, İ. *Lozan Barış Konferansı: Konuşma, Demeç, Makale, Mesaj, Anı ve Söyleşileri*, Ankara, 2010.
Jung, D. 'The Sèvres Syndrome: Turkish Foreign Policy and its Historical Legacies', https://americandiplomacy.web.unc.edu/2003/08/the-sevres-syndrome/.
Kabaklı, A. *Temellerin Duruşması*, Istanbul, 1990.
Kandemir, F. *Hatıraları ve Söyleyemedikleri ile Rauf Orbay*, Istanbul, 1965.
Karabekir, K. *Paşaların Hesaplaşması*, Istanbul, 1995.
Karanlıktan Aydınlığa Sevr ve Lozan: Seminer Notları, Istanbul, 2010.
Kayra, C. *Sevr Dosyası*, Istanbul, 2004.
Kemal, M. *Nutuk*, Istanbul, 2015.
Koçak, C. *İsmet İnönü ve Resmi Tarih*, Istanbul, 2020.
Kösebalaban, H. *Turkish Foreign Policy: Islam, Nationalism, and Globalization*, New York, 2011.
Lozan Barış Antlaşmasının 70. Yıldönümü, 24 Temmuz [July] *1993*, Ankara, 1993.
Lozan'ın 50. Yıl Armağanı, Istanbul, 1978.
Manisalı, E. *Ahtapot Kollarındaki Dünya ve Türkiye*, Istanbul, 2003.
Meray, S.L. ed. *Lozan Konferansı: Tutanaklar Belgeler*, Ankara, 1970.
Meydan, S. *Yalanlara, Çarpıtmalara, İftiralara Panzehir: Gerçeğe Çağrı*, Istanbul, 2015.
Meydan, S. *Hafiza*, Istanbul, 2019.
Mısıroğlu, K. *Lozan: Zafer mi Hezimet mi?*, Istanbul, 1965–1979.
Millas, H. 'The Exchange of Populations in Turkish Literature' in Hirschon, R. ed., *Crossing the Aegean: An Appraisal on the 1923 Compulsory Populations Exchange between Greece and Turkey*, New York, 2003, 221–234.
Nur, R. *Hayat ve Hatıratım*, Istanbul, 1967–1968.
Oran, B. *Türkiye'de Azınlıklar*, Istanbul, 2010.
Öniş, Z. 'Conservative globalists versus defensive nationalists: political parties and paradoxes of Europeanization in Turkey', *Journal of Southern Europe and the Balkans* 9, 2007, 247–261.
Özakıncı, C. *Kalemin Namusu 1: Türk Savun Kendini*, Istanbul, 2019.
Özakman, T. *Vahidettin, Mustafa Kemal ve Milli Mücadele: Yalanlar, Yanlışlar, Yutturmacalar*, Ankara, 1997, 565–596.
Özcan, A. *Türkiye'de Popüler Tarihçilik (1908–1960)*, Ankara, 2011.
Özel, S. 'The Gathering Storm', *Foreign Policy* 149, 2005, 83–85.
Singer, S.R. 'Erdoğan's Muse: The School of Necip Fazil Kisakurek', *World Affairs* 176/4, 2013, 81–88.

Tanzimat'tan Cumhuriyet'e Cumhuriyet'ten Günümüze Yakın Tarih Ansiklopedisi, Istanbul, n.d.

Tarih IV: Kemalist Eğitimin Tarih Dersleri (1931–1941), Istanbul, 2001.

Türk Tarihinin Ana Hatları, 1930.

Türkiye Dış Politikasında 50 Yıl: Lozan, 1922–1923, Ankara, 1973.

White, J.B. *Muslim Nationalism and the New Turks*, Princeton, 2014.

Yanık, L.K. "Those Crazy Turks' That Got Caught in the 'Metal Storm': Nationalism in Turkey's Best Seller Lists', *European University Institute Working Papers*, 2008, https://cadmus.eui.eu/handle/1814/8002.

Zürcher, E.J. 'The Politician as Historian, Historians in Politics: On the Nutuk (Speech) of Mustafa Kemal Pasha', *The Young Turk Legacy and Nation Building: From the Ottoman Empire to Atatürk's Turkey*, London, 2010, 6–16.

CHAPTER 16

'Aloysius Derso, Cartoonist, Dies; Drew Diplomats at Parleys Between World Wars', *New York Times,* 23 December 1964, 27.

'Egyptians in a Fight in a Lausanne Hotel', *New York Times,* 11 January 1923, 18.

Altick, R. *Punch: The Lively Youth of a British Institution, 1841–1851,* Columbus, 1997.

AT-OeStA/KA FA AOK KPQ Akten 30 Kunstgruppe, KPQ-Mitglieder (Ansuchen um Aufnahme, diverse Personalunterlagen), Namen G, 1914–1918, Austrian State Archives, Vienna.

Bakhtin, M. *Rabelais and His World,* trans. Iswolsky, H., Bloomington, 1984 (originally published 1965).

Bertin, J-M. 'Derso ile Kelen, Milletler Cemiyeti'nin unutulmaz kelle avcıları', *Şalom Dergi*, 1 May 2020, https://dergi.salom.com.tr/haber-318-derso_ile_kelen_milletler_cemiyetinin_unutulmaz_kelle_avcilari.html.

Bösch, F. *Mediengeschichte. Vom asiatischen Buchdruck zum Fernsehen,* Frankfurt, 2001.

Büke Okyar, İ. 'Black Eye and Vulture', *The Lausanne Project,* July 2021, https://thelausanneproject.com/2021/07/12/black-eye-and-vulture/.

Buzinkay, G. *Borsszem Jankó és társai. Élclapok és karikatúrák*, Budapest, 1983.

Derso, A. 'Derso draws and discusses "Homo Conferentiarum"!', *The Illustrated London News,* 22 February 1930, 282.

Dunántúli Hírlap, 31 August 1919.

Dunántúli Hírlap, 18 October 1922.

Elmas, E. 'Teodor Kassab's Adaption of the Ottoman Shadow Theatre *Karagöz*' in Harder, H. et al. eds., *Asian Punches: A Transcultural Affair*, Berlin, 2013, 245–270.

Ertuğrul Apaydin, G. 'Modernity as Masquerade: Representations of Modernity and Identity in Turkish Humour Magazines', *Global Studies in Culture and Power* 12, 2005, 107–142.

Fahmy, Z. *Ordinary Egyptians*, Redwood City, 2020.

Fraser, J. 'Propaganda on the Picture Postcard', *Oxford Art Journal* 3/2, 1980, 39–47.

Freud, S. *Wit and Its Relation to the Unconscious*, trans. Arden, A., London, 1916.

Fuchs, E. *Die Karikatur der europäischen Völker vom Jahre 1848 bis zur Gegenwart,* Berlin, 1903.

Gifford, J. ed. *'In Our Time' and 'They All Made Peace – What is Peace?' by Ernest Hemingway,* Victoria, 2015.

Gluck, M. *Georg Lukács and his generation, 1900–1918*, Cambridge (USA), 2011.

Gombrich, E. 'Magic, Myth and Metaphor: Reflections on Pictorial Satire' in Woodfield, R. ed., *The Essential Gombrich,* London, 1996, 331–352.

Gombrich, E. and Kris, E. 'The Principles of Caricature', *British Journal of Medical Psychology* 17, 1938, 319–342.

Hoffmeister, A. *Stále ještě... výstava John Heartfield fotomontaže v upomínku na velkou mezinárodní výstavu karikatur v Mánesu v roce 1934*, Prague, 1964.

Hunt, T. L. *Defining John Bull. Political Caricature and National Identity in Late Georgian England,* London, 2003.

Kelen, E. *Peace in their Time. Men Who Led Us In and Out of War, 1914–1945,* London, 1964.

Kelen, E. *Psychiatric Case Histories*, Book Suggestions; Derso and Kelen Collection, MC205, Public Policy Papers, Department of Special Collections, Princeton University Library, Princeton.

Kerr, D. *Caricature and French Political Culture 1830–1848. Charles Philipon and the Illustrated Press,* Oxford, 2000.

Kousemaker, K. *Lambiek Comiclopedia*, https://www.lambiek.net/comiclopedia.html.

Le Matin, 20 May 1922, 1.

Magyar Grafika, 11 February 1930, 5–6.

Mairs, M. 'Pith Helmets, Cross-dressing and Blackface: Fancy Dress in Colonial Egypt', *Everyday Orientalism,* 2021, https://everydayorientalism.wordpress.com/2021/08/02/pith-helmets-cross-dressing-and-blackface-fancy-dress-in-colonial-egypt/.

Marsot, A-S. 'Afāf Luṭfī. The Cartoon in Egypt', *Comparative Studies in Society and History* 13/1, 1971, 2–15.

McCormick, J. and Pratasik, B. *Popular Puppet Theatre in Europe, 1800–1914,* Cambridge (UK), 2004 (originally published 1998).

Milne, L. *Laughter and War. Humorous-Satirical Magazines in Britain, France, Germany and Russia,* Newcastle, 2017.

Murphy, L. *The Art of Survival. France and the Great War Picaresque*, Newhaven, 2016.

Ozkan, B. *From the Abode of Islam to the Turkish Vatan: The Making of a National Homeland in Turkey*, New Haven, 2012.

Pérely, I. *Magyar rajzolóművészek*, Budapest, 1930.

Perkins, D. 'A Definition of Caricature and Caricature and Recognition', *Studies in Visual Communication* 2/1 1975, 1–24.

Sheridan, C. *West and East,* New York, 1923.

Slater, S. and Macfadyen, D. 'Hope, faith and reality. Visualising the League of Nations,' *Illustration,* Winter 2020, 16–24.

Slater, S. and Macfayden, D. *Humour in Tragic Times: The Political Cartoons of Derso and Kelen*, forthcoming.

Travlos, K., Akyüz D., Mert-Travlos, C. 'Caricaturing the Enemy: Caricatures and the Greek-Turkish War 1919–1922', *The European Journal of Humour Research* 10/4, 2022.

Contributors

Mustafa Aksakal is Associate Professor of History and Nesuhi Ertegün Chair of Modern Turkish Studies at Georgetown University. He has written extensively on the Ottoman Empire in the nineteenth century and the history of the Ottomans in the First World War. He is the author of *The Ottoman Road to War in 1914* (2008).

Cemil Aydın is Professor of Global History at the University of North Carolina at Chapel Hill. His publications include *Politics of Anti-Westernism in Asia* (2007), *The Idea of the Muslim World: A Global Intellectual History* (2017), and 'Regions and Empires in Political History of the World, 1750–1924' in *An Emerging Modern World, 1750–1870*, edited by Jurgen Osterhammel and Sebastian Conrad (2018).

Gökhan Çetinsaya graduated from the Faculty of Political Science at Ankara University (1985) and received his PhD from the Department of Middle Eastern Studies at University of Manchester (1994). His doctoral dissertation won both the MESA and the BRISMES awards. He has taught at Hacettepe University (1986–2001), Istanbul Technical University (2002–2008), and Istanbul Şehir University (2009–2020), and he has held visiting scholarships at SOAS, Free University of Berlin and Woodrow Wilson International Center for Scholars. His publications include *The Ottoman Administration of Iraq, 1890–1908* (2006).

Jonathan Conlin is Professor of Modern History at the University of Southampton and co-founder with Ozan Ozavci of The Lausanne Project. A historian of Britain by training, he became interested in late Ottoman history while writing a biography of Calouste Gulbenkian, *Mr Five Per Cent* (2019), that won the BAC Wadsworth Prize for Business History and that has been translated into five languages. He has contributed articles on Ottoman Pan-Islamism, finance, naval rearmament and oil politics to *IJMES, Diplomacy & Statecraft, Middle East Studies* and *International History Review.*

Lerna Ekmekcioglu is the McMillan-Stewart Associate Professor of History at MIT. Her books include *Recovering Armenia: The Limits of Belonging in Post-Genocide Turkey* (2016). In 2006 she co-edited a volume in Turkish on the first five Ottoman Armenian feminists (*Bir Adalet Feryadı, Osmanlı'dan Türkiye'ye Beş Ermeni Feminist Yazar, 1862–1933*). She is currently collaborating with Dr. Melissa Bilal (UCLA) on a book and digital humanities project titled 'Feminism in Armenian: An Interpretive Anthology and Documentary Archive', the former to be published in 2024.

Étienne Forestier-Peyrat is Assistant Professor in Contemporary History at Sciences Po Lille, University of Lille. His publications include *Histoire du Caucase au XXe siècle* (2020). He has contributed articles to *Journal of Cold War Studies*, *Jahrbücher für Geschichte Osteuropas* and *Ab Imperio*.

Aimee M. Genell is Assistant Professor of History at the University of West Georgia. Her research focuses on the history of the late Ottoman Empire and its entanglements with Europe in the arena of international law. Her manuscript, *Empire by Law: The Ottoman Origins of the Mandate System in the Middle East* (under contract, Columbia University Press), traces the Ottoman roots of the post-imperial political order through an analysis of the inter-imperial contest over autonomous Egypt in the late nineteenth and early twentieth centuries. She has contributed articles to *Journal of Ottoman and Turkish Studies* and *Journal of Balkan and Near Eastern Studies*.

Erik Goldstein is Professor of History and International Relations at Boston University. His research interests include diplomacy, formulation of national diplomatic strategies, the origins and resolution of armed conflict, and negotiation. His books include *Winning the Peace: British Diplomatic Strategy, Peace Planning, and the Paris Peace Conference, 1916–1920* (1991), *The First World War's Peace Settlements: International Relations, 1918–1925* (2002), and *Aspects of British Policy and the Treaty of Versailles: Of War and Peace* (co-editor, 2020). He was founding editor of the journal *Diplomacy & Statecraft.*

Samuel J. Hirst is Assistant Professor in the Department of International Relations at Bilkent University. He is currently completing a book on Soviet-Turkish relations in the 1920s and 1930s. He has contributed articles to *Diplomatic History*, *Kritika*, and *Slavic Review*.

Haakon A. Ikonomou is Associate Professor at the Saxo Institute, University of Copenhagen (UCPH). He is currently a Gerda Henkel Fellow (2021–2023) with the project *European security in a changing world: general disarmament between international organization & state sovereignty, 1890s-1930s.* He is book review and online media editor of *Diplomatica*, director of the research group 'Europe and International Cooperation' at the Centre for Modern European Studies (CEMES, UCPH), and co-founder of the Global Biographies Working Group (GloBio). His latest publication (co-edited with Laura Almagor and Gunvor Simonsen) is *Global Biographies: Lived History as Method* (2022).

Dimitris Kamouzis is a Researcher at the Centre for Asia Minor Studies (Athens). He completed his PhD in History at the Department of Byzantine and Modern Greek Studies, King's College London. He has been a scholar of the Alexander S. Onassis Public Benefit Foundation, a Research Fellow of the John S. Latsis Public Benefit Foundation and the National & Kapodistrian University of Athens, and a Teaching Fellow at King's College London. His latest book is entitled *Greeks in Turkey: Elite Nationalism and Minority Politics in Late Ottoman and Early Republican Istanbul* (2021).

Hans-Lukas Kieser is Professor of Modern History at the University of Newcastle (New South Wales). His research focuses on the demise of the Ottoman Empire and emergence of Republican Turkey, analyzing the relationship between state formation, political violence and genocide. His books include a biography of Talât (2018), *Nearest East: American millennialism and mission to the Middle East* (2010) as well as several edited volumes, most recently *Remembering the Great War in the Middle East: From Turkey and Armenia to Australia and New Zealand (2022).* His new monograph *When Democracy Died: The Middle East's Enduring Peace of Lausanne* is forthcoming in May 2023.

Leila Koochakzadeh is a historian specializing in the history of nineteenth- and twentieth-century Iran, with a particular interest in the history of international relations, of institutions and of education. She holds a PhD in history from the Université de Montréal and has been teaching at the Institut Nationale des Langues et Civilisations Orientales (INALCO-Paris), as a lecturer since 2017.

Ozan Ozavci is Assistant Professor of History at Utrecht University and co-convenor of The Lausanne Project and the Security History Network. His publications include *Dangerous Gifts: Imperialism, Security, and Civil Wars in the*

Levant, 1798–1864 (2021), and *Intellectual Origins of the Republic: Ahmet Ağaoğlu and the Genealogy of Liberalism in Turkey* (2015). He is currently completing his third monograph on the two terms as ambassador to the Sublime Porte in Constantinople of the Scottish diplomat Sir Robert Liston, and co-editing a volume on the history of security in the nineteenth century.

Andrew Patrick is Associate Professor of History at Tennessee State University. He is the author of *America's Forgotten Middle East Initiative: The King-Crane Commission of 1919* (2015) and numerous articles about the relationship between the United States and the Middle East. He received his PhD in Middle Eastern Studies from the University of Manchester in 2011.

Laura Robson is the Oliver-McCourtney Professor of History at Penn State University. She is the author and editor of five books, most recently *The Politics of Mass Violence in the Middle East* (2020), a history of the relationship between violence and the state in the twentieth-century Eastern Mediterranean, and *Partitions: A Transnational History of 20th Century Territorial Separatism* (with Arie Dubnov, 2019), a comparative examination of the political 'solution' of ethnic partition in the world of twentieth-century empire and decolonization. With Jennifer Dueck, she is the co-founder and co-editor of the digital humanities project StatelessHistories.org.

Patrick Schilling is a doctoral candidate in late Ottoman history at Georgetown University. He holds an MA in History and Russian from the University of Glasgow and an MA in Ottoman history from Sabancı University. His doctoral dissertation examines the ways in which other imperial models shaped Ottoman governance during the Second Constitutional Period (1908–1920).

Julia Secklehner is an art historian and Research Fellow at the Art History Department of Masaryk University in Brno, Czech Republic. Her current research focuses on modernism beyond the metropolis in central Europe and is part of the ERC-funded collaborative project 'Continuity / Rupture: Art and Architecture in Central Europe, 1918–1939 (CRAACE)'. She also works on caricature, cartoons, and print culture, and co-ordinates the production of a graphic novel as part of The Lausanne Project.

Sarah Shields is Professor of History at the University of North Carolina at Chapel Hill, where she is currently researching the long-term impact of the

League of Nations on the Middle East. Her *Fezzes in the River: Identity Politics and European Diplomacy in the Middle East on the Eve of World War II* (2011) is a social and diplomatic history of the contest between France and Turkey over the Sanjak of Alexandretta (1936–1940). A previous book, *Mosul before Iraq* (2000), analyses the economy and society of nineteenth-century Mosul and the region surrounding it. She has also published articles on teaching, the Palestine mandate, and the Greek-Turkish population exchange.

Leonard V. Smith is Frederick B. Artz Professor of History at Oberlin College. He is the author of several books on France and the First World War and its aftermath, including *Sovereignty at the Paris Peace Conference of 1919* (2018). He has also published several articles on international law after the First World War. His most recent book is *French Colonialism from the Ancien Régime to the Present* (2023).

Elizabeth F. Thompson is Mohamed S. Farsi Chair of Islamic Peace at American University. She is author of *How the West Stole Democracy from the Arabs: The Syrian Congress of 1920 and the Destruction of its Historic Liberal-Islamic Alliance* (2020). Her previous book, *Justice Interrupted: The Struggle for Constitutional Government in the Middle East* (2013), examined how World War I altered Middle Eastern politics. Her first book, *Colonial Citizens: Republican Rights, Paternal Privilege, and Gender in French Syria and Lebanon* (2000), won two national prizes. Thompson is now completing a fourth book on World War I's impact, *The Debacle: A Memoir of Muslim-Christian Europe and Its Destruction, 1842–1962.*

Index

Note: Page numbers in *italic* are illustrations.